Lecture Notes in Computer Science   9842

Commenced Publication in 1973
Founding and Former Series Editors:
Gerhard Goos, Juris Hartmanis, and Jan van Leeuwen

More information about this series at http://www.springer.com/series/7409

Khalid Saeed · Władysław Homenda (Eds.)

Computer Information Systems and Industrial Management

15th IFIP TC8 International Conference, CISIM 2016
Vilnius, Lithuania, September 14–16, 2016
Proceedings

 Springer

Editors
Khalid Saeed
Bialystok University of Technology
Bialystok
Poland

Władysław Homenda (iD)
University of Bialystok
Vilnius
Lithuania

ISSN 0302-9743   ISSN 1611-3349   (electronic)
Lecture Notes in Computer Science
ISBN 978-3-319-45377-4   ISBN 978-3-319-45378-1   (eBook)
DOI 10.1007/978-3-319-45378-1

Library of Congress Control Number: 2016948607

LNCS Sublibrary: SL3 – Information Systems and Applications, incl. Internet/Web, and HCI

Preface

CISIM 2016 was the 15th of a series of conferences dedicated to computer information systems and industrial management applications. The conference was supported by IFIP TC8 Information Systems. This year it was held during September 14–16, 2016, in Vilnius, Lithuania, at The Faculty of Economics and Informatics in Vilnius, a Branch of the University of Bialystok, Poland.

About 90 papers were submitted to CISIM by researchers and scientists from universities around the world. Most of the papers were of high quality. Each paper was assigned to three referees initially, and the decision to accept was taken after receiving two positive reviews. In cases of conflicting decisions, another expert's review was sought for a number of papers. In total, about 218 reviews were collected from the referees for the submitted papers. Because of the strict restrictions of *Springer's Lecture Notes in Computer Science* series, the number of accepted papers was limited. Furthermore, a number of electronic discussions were held between the Program Committee (PC) chairs and members to decide about papers with conflicting reviews and to reach a consensus. After the discussions, the PC chairs decided to accept for publication in the proceedings book about 68 % of the papers submitted.

The main topics covered by the chapters in this book are biometrics, security systems, multimedia, classification and clustering with application, and industrial management. Besides these, the reader will find interesting papers on computer information systems as applied to wireless networks, computer graphics, and intelligent systems.

There were also three workshops and special sessions on Rough Set Methods for Big Data Analytics (organizer: Prof. Jaroslaw Stepaniuk), Scheduling in Manufacturing and Other Applications (organizers: Profs. Ewa Skubalska-Rafajłowicz and Wojciech Bożejko), and Intelligent Distributed Systems IDS (organizer: Prof. Jerzy Balicki).

We are grateful to the five esteemed speakers for their keynote addresses. The authors of the keynote talks were Profs. Miroslawa El Fray (West Pomeranian University of Technology, Poland), Jaap van den Herik (Leiden University, The Netherlands), Nobuyuki Nishiuchi (Tokyo Metropolitan University, Japan), Andrzej Skowron (Polish Academy of Sciences), and Qiang Wei (Tsinghua University in Beijing, China). Also Prof. Bohdan Macukow from Warsaw University submitted a very interesting invited paper. All the keynote and invited abstracts have been included in the proceedings.

We would like to thank all the members of the PC and the external reviewers for their dedicated efforts in the paper selection process. We also thank the honorary chairs of the conference, Profs. Ryszard Tadeusiewicz and Witold Pedrycz. Special thanks are extended to the members of the Organizing Committee, both the international and the local ones, and the Springer team for their great efforts to make the conference a success. We are also grateful to Andrei Voronkov, whose EasyChair system eased the submission and selection process and greatly supported the compilation of the proceedings. The proceedings editing was managed by Jiří Dvorský (Technical University of Ostrava, Czech Republic), to whom we are indeed very grateful.

We hope that the reader's expectations will be met and that the participants enjoyed their stay in the beautiful city of Vilnius.

September 2016   Khalid Saeed
                                                    Władysław Homenda

Organization

Program Committee

Waleed Abdulla	University of Auckland, New Zealand
Raid Al-Tahir	The University of the West Indies, St. Augustine, Trinidad & Tobago
Aditya Bagchi	Indian Statistical Institute, India
Anna Bartkowiak	Wrocław University, Poland
Rahma Boucetta	National Engineering School of Gabes, Tunisia
Lam Thu Bui	Le Quy Don Technical University, Vietnam
Nabendu Chaki	Calcutta University, India
Rituparna Chaki	West Bengal University of Technology, India
Agostino Cortesi	Ca' Foscari University of Venice, Italy
Pierpaolo Degano	University of Pisa, Italy
Jan Devos	Ghent University, Belgium
Andrzej Dobrucki	Wrocław University of Technology, Poland
Jiří Dvorský	VŠB-Technical University of Ostrava, Czech Republic
Pietro Ferrara	IBM T.J. Watson Research Center, USA
Riccardo Focardi	Ca' Foscari University of Venice, Italy
Marina Gavrilova	University of Calgary, Canada
Raju Halder	Ca' Foscari University of Venice, Italy
Christopher Harris	State University of New York, USA
Kauru Hirota	Tokyo Institute of Technology, Japan
Władysław Homenda	Warsaw University of Technology, Poland, *Co-chair*
Khalide Jbilou	Université du Littoral Côte d'Opale, France
Ryszard Kozera	The University of Western Australia, Australia
Flaminia Luccio	Ca' Foscari University of Venice, Italy
Jan Martinovič	VŠB-Technical University of Ostrava, Czech Republic
Pavel Moravec	VŠB-Technical University of Ostrava, Czech Republic
Romuald Mosdorf	Białystok University of Technology, Poland
Debajyoti Mukhopadhyay	Maharashtra Institute of Technology, India
Yuko Murayama	Iwate University, Japan
Hien Thanh Nguyen	Ton Duc Thang University, Vietnam
Nobuyuki Nishiuchi	Tokyo Metropolitan University, Japan
Andrzej Pacut	Warsaw University of Technology, Poland
Jerzy Pejaś	WPUT in Szczecin, Poland
Marco Pistoia	IBM T.J. Watson Research Center, USA
Jaroslav Pokorný	Charles University, Czech Republic
Piotr Porwik	University of Silesia, Poland
Jan Pries-Heje	The IT University of Copenhagen, Denmark

Tho Thanh Quan	Ho Chi Minh University of Technology, Vietnam
Isabel Ramos	University of Minho, Portugal
Khalid Saeed	Białystok University of Technology, Poland, *Co-chair*
Rafał Scherer	Częstochowa University of Technology, Poland
Ewa Skubalska-Rafajłowicz	Wrocław University of Technology, Poland
Kateřina Slaninová	VŠB-Technical University of Ostrava, Czech Republic
Václav Snášel	VŠB-Technical University of Ostrava, Czech Republic
Krzysztof Ślot	Lodz University of Technology, Poland
Zenon Sosnowski	Białystok University of Technology, Poland
Jarosław Stepaniuk	Białystok University of Technology, Poland
Marcin Szpyrka	AGH Kraków, Poland
Jacek Tabor	Jagiellonian University, Kraków, Poland
Andrea Torsello	Ca' Foscari University of Venice, Italy
Dao Trong Tran	Ton Duc Thang University, Vietnam
Nitin Upadhyay	BITS Pilani, India
Bay Dinh Vo	Ton Duc Thang University, Vietnam
Sławomir Wierzchoń	Polish Academy of Sciences, Warsaw, Poland
Michał Woźniak	Wrocław University of Technology, Poland
Sławomir Zadrożny	Polish Academy of Sciences, Warsaw, Poland

Additional Reviewers

Marcin Adamski	Białystok University of Technology, Poland
Piotr Artiemjew	University of Warmia and Mazury in Olsztyn, Poland
Fabrizio Baiardi	University of Pisa, Italy
Jerzy Balicki	Warsaw University of Technology, Poland
Stefan Brachmanski	Wrocław University of Technology, Poland
Stanislav Böhm	VŠB-Technical University of Ostrava, Czech Republic
Pavla Dráždilová	VŠB-Technical University of Ostrava, Czech Republic
Anna Gomolińska	University of Białystok, Poland
Ekaterina Grakova	VŠB-Technical University of Ostrava, Czech Republic
Agnieszka Jastrzebska	Warsaw University of Technology, Poland
Tomáš Karásek	VŠB-Technical University of Ostrava, Czech Republic
Andrei Karatkevich	University of Zielona Góra, Poland
Dong Hwa Kim	Hanbat National University, South Korea
Michal Krumnikl	VŠB-Technical University of Ostrava, Czech Republic
Miloš Kudělka	VŠB-Technical University of Ostrava, Czech Republic
Tomasz Łukaszuk	Białystok University of Technology, Poland
Krzysztof Marasek	Polish-Japanese Institute of Information Technology, Poland
Robert Milewski	Medical University of Białystok, Poland
Dang Nguyen	Ton Duc Thang University, Vietnam
Kiyoshi Nishikawa	Tokyo Metropolitan University, Japan
Eliška Ochodková	VŠB-Technical University of Ostrava, Czech Republic
Suhail Owais	Applied Science Private University, Jordan

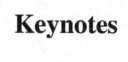

Keynotes

Nanotechnology for Medical Biosensing

Miroslawa El Fray

West Pomeranian University of Technology, Szczecin, Division of Biomaterials
and Microbiological Technologies, Nanotechnology Centre for Research
and Education, Al. Piastw 45, 71-311 Szczecin, Poland
mirfray@zut.edu.pl

Abstract. Nanotechnology is rapidly developing field with numerous potential
applications in health care. Recent developments in carbon-nanomaterials –
graphene in particular – offer a great deal of promise in achieving fast and
affordable platform for biosensing. Among dirrefent nanomaterials, graphene has
received worldwide attention due to high surface area, excellent electrical conductivity, strong mechanical strength, good thermal conductivity, high charge
carrier mobility, good optical transparency and ease of biological as well as
chemical functionalization. Such exceptional properties can be used in design of
fast, affordable, and simple devices for bioanalysis since appropriate biosensors
are required for early stage diagnosis of the disease as well as disease progression
monitoring.

Depending from the working principle, graphene-based biosensors can utilize their
electrical or electrochemical properties to selectively detect proteins, DNA, glucose or
cholesterol. Nanomaterial in such biosensor is used to construct a receptor capable to
interact with a target analyte. Next, the biological sensing element (bacteria, DNA)
connects to a transducer, which does the conversion from biological data to electrical
data. The transducer in turn connects to a measuring device translating the electrical
signal to a measurable quantity. The most common measurement techniques include
electrochemical impedance spectroscopy, field-effect transistors, cyclic voltammetry
(CV), and differential pulse voltammetry. Typically in bioelectrochemistry, the reaction
under investigation would either generate a measurable current (*amperometric*), a
measurable potential or charge accumulation (*potentiometric*) or measurably alter the
conductive properties of a medium (*conductometric*) between electrodes. Electrochemical sensing usually requires a *reference* electrode, a *counter* or auxiliary electrode
and a *working* electrode, with the graphene or graphene-polymer nanocomposites as
the most emerging materials for future bioelectronics devices. Such electrodes can be
printed via ultrasonic, non-contact printing for biological sensing (DNA or enzyme).

Graphene-based ink should enable the selectivelly detect the target biomolecules,
for example, attached DNA oligonucleotide probes for Group B *streptococcus* (GBS)
to the printed, graphene-platinum ink. The most important issue is to conjugate
biorecognition molecules to the ink in a way that they would remain functional, i.e. will
provide electrochemical signal.

References

1. Grieshaber, D., MacKenzie, R., Voros, J., Reimhult, E.: Sensors, **8**, 1400–1458 (2008)
2. Sobolewski, P., Piwowarczyk, M., El Fray, M.: Macromol. Biosci. (2016). DOI: 10.1002/mabi.201600081

Innovation and Big Data

H. Jaap van den Herik

Leiden Institute of Advanced Computer Science/Leiden Centre of Data Science
Leiden University, The Netherlands
jaapvandenherik@gmail.com

Abstract. In the World, we see that now and then well-known companies are in trouble since they do not innovate in time. They keep their well-established way of operating and adhere to their old fashioned business models. As a keynote speaker, I would like to advice the scientific community to pay more attention in their research to the possibilities of Big Data in relation to innovation.

This relation is rather delicate as can be seen from the following examples.

- The autonomously self driving car. The national and international car associations have to adapt their whole services can marketing system.
- TCrowdsourced online dispute resolution. Lawyers and Judges have to reconsider their system of comparing verdicts and law enforcement.
- Airbnb is changing the hotel-bed and breakfast commercial activities.
- Uber Taxi is changing the business model of Taxi companies.
- Blockchains with as application Bitcoin arc changing the position of the banking institutions.

The prevailing question is: What does Big Data add to this Development?

In the lecture we will emphasize the seven phases of data development, viz. Collecting Data, Cleaning Data, Interpreting Data, Analysing Data, Visualising Data, Narrative Science, Emergence of new Paradigms.

Moreover, emphasis will be placed on Obstacles: Public safety, Narrative Science, Commercial competition, and Privacy and ethics.

Finally, attention will be pointed to Sensitive data such as Racial or Ethnic Origin.

The general rule for companies is that the processing of sensitive data is prohibited without explicit consent (Directive 95/46/EC, article 8).

Usability Evaluation Method Using Biological Data

Nobuyuki Nishiuchi

Tokyo Metropolitan University, Japan
nnishiuc@sd.tmu.ac.jp

Abstract. Usability has been important factor on the design for the interface of product and system. The current evaluation methods used to assess the usability factors are interview and questionnaires. These are based on the subjective approach, therefore certain limitations are encountered. It is difficult to get the data on usability for a long duration, the quality of evaluation depends on the skill of the evaluator and these evaluation approaches are costly and time-consuming. Then, our research team has been studying the objective usability evaluation methods using biological data, some of which are eye movement and fingertip movement during the operations of the target interface. Based on the analysis of the captured data, the interface design can be sufficiently improved. In the keynote, basic idea and specific experiment of the proposed method will be presented.

Complex Adaptive Systems and Interactive Granular Computing

Andrzej Skowron

[1] Institute of Mathematics, Warsaw University, Banacha 2,
02-097 Warsaw, Poland
skowron@mimuw.edu.pl
[2] Systems Research Institute, Polish Academy of Sciences,
Newelska 6, 01-447 Warsaw, Poland

Abstract. Agent-based decision support in solving problems related to Complex Adaptive Systems (CAS) requires relevant computation models as well as methods for incorporating reasoning over computations performed by agents. To model, crucial for CAS, interactive computations performed by agents, we extend the existing Granular Computing (GrC) approach to Interactive Granular Computing (IGrC) by introducing complex granules (c-granules or granules, for short). Agents performing computations learn due to interaction with the environment how to perform actions and through interactions with the environment they discover relevant rules of behavior, not provided a priori. Many advanced CAS tasks may be classified as control tasks performed by agents aiming at achieving the high quality computational trajectories relative to the considered quality measures over the trajectories. Here, new challenges are to develop strategies to control and predict the behavior of the system. We propose to investigate these challenges using the IGrC framework. The reasoning, which aims at controlling computations, in order to achieve the required targets, is called an adaptive judgment. Adaptive judgment is more than a mixture of reasoning based on deduction, induction and abduction. IGrC is based on perception of situations in the physical world. Hence, the theory of judgment has a place not only in logic but also in psychology and phenomenology. This reasoning deals with granules and computations over them. Due to the uncertainty the agents generally cannot predict exactly the results of actions (or plans). Moreover, the approximations of the complex vague concepts, e.g., initiating actions (or plans) are drifting with time. Hence, adaptive strategies for evolving approximations of concepts are needed. In particular, the adaptive judgment is very much needed in the efficiency management of granular computations, carried out by agents, for risk assessment, risk treatment, and cost/benefit analysis. The discussed approach is developed in cooperation with many co-workers, in particular with Dr Andrzej Jankowski and is based on the work on different real-life projects.

Competitive Intelligence Analytics in the Big Data Context

Qiang Wei

Information Systems Group, Department of Management Science
and Engineering, School of Economics and Management, Tsinghua University,
Beijing 100084, China
weiq@sem.tsinghua.edu.cn

Abstract. Competitive intelligence is the action of defining, gathering, analyzing, and distributing intelligence about products, customers, competitors, and any aspect of the environment needed to support executives and managers making strategic decisions for an organization. Traditionally, competitive intelligence is detected and analyzed mainly by experts/managers based on the intra-organizational data/information. However, external big data (e.g. query log, social interaction, blog/twitter, online review, helpfulness votes, open media, etc.) becomes a more and more important source for conducting online competitive intelligence analysis, e.g., dynamic competitor identification and competitiveness degrees measuring with Google search query log, customer insights detection from online reviews, incremental competitive intelligence digests extraction with Internet news. Moreover, due to the 4V characteristics of the big data source, some intelligent and automatic methods should be developed to overcome the shortcomings of traditional methods conducted by human experts. In this talk, I will briefly introduce several related novel methods.

Contents

Optimization, Tuning

Scheduling in Manufacturing and Other Applications

Algorithms

Decisions

Intelligent Distributed Systems

Biometrics, Identification, Security

Miscellanous

Invited Paper

Neural Networks – State of Art, Brief History, Basic Models and Architecture

Bohdan Macukow[✉]

Faculty of Applied Mathematics and Information Science,
Warsaw University of Technology, Koszykowa 75, 00-662 Warsaw, Poland
B.Macukow@mini.pw.edu.pl

Abstract. The history of neural networks can be traced back to the work of trying to model the neuron. Today, neural networks discussions are occurring everywhere. Neural networks, with their remarkable ability to derive meaning from complicated or imprecise data, can be used to extract patterns and detect trends that are too complex to be noticed by either humans or other computer techniques. A brief history of the neural networks research is presented and some more popular models are briefly discussed. The major attention is on the feed-forward networks and specially to the topology of such the network and method of building the multi-layer perceptrons.

Keywords: Neural networks · History · Building feedforward net

1 What Is a Neural Network?

An Artificial Neural Network (ANN) is an information or signal processing system composed of a large number of simple processing elements which are interconnected by direct links and which cooperate to perform parallel distributed processing in order to solve a desired computational task. Neural networks process information in a similar way the human brain does. ANN is inspired by the way the biological nervous systems, such as the brain works - neural networks learn by example.

ANN takes a different approach to problem solving than that of conventional computing. Conventional computer systems use an algorithmic approach i.e. follow a set of instructions in order to solve a problem. That limits the problem solving capability to problems that we already understand and know how to solve. However, neural networks and conventional algorithmic computing are not in competition but complement each other. There are the tasks that are more suited to an algorithmic approach like arithmetic operations and the tasks that are more suited to neural networks approach.

2 History

The history of neural networks can be divided into several periods.

© IFIP International Federation for Information Processing 2016
Published by Springer International Publishing Switzerland 2016. All Rights Reserved
K. Saeed and W. Homenda (Eds.): CISIM 2016, LNCS 9842, pp. 3–14, 2016.
DOI: 10.1007/978-3-319-45378-1_1

2.1   First Attempts

The first step toward artificial neural networks came in 1943 when Warren McCulloch, a neurophysiologist and a young mathematician, Walter Pitts, developed the first models of neural networks. They wrote a paper *The Logical Calculus of the Ideas Immanent in Nervous Activity* on how neurons might work [1]. Their networks were based on simple elements which were considered to be binary devices with fixed thresholds. The results of their model were simple logic functions with "all-or-none" character of nervous activity.

In 1944 Joseph Erlanger together with Herbert Spencer Gasser identified several varieties of nerve fiber and established the relationship between action potential velocity and fiber diameter.

In 1949, Hebb a psychologist, wrote *The Organization of Behavior* [2], a work which pointed out the fact that neural pathways are strengthened each time they are used, a concept fundamentally essential to the ways humans learn.

2.2   Promising and Emerging Technology

In 1958, Rosenblatt a psychologist, conducted an early work on perceptrons [3]. The Perceptron was an electronic device that was constructed in accordance with biological principles and showed an ability to learn. He also wrote an early book on neuro-computing, *Principles of Neurodynamics* [4].

Another system was the ADALINE (ADAptive LInear Element) which was developed in 1960 by two electrical engineers Widrow and Hoff [5]. The method used for learning was different to that of the Perceptron, it employed the Least-Mean-Squares learning rule. In 1962, Widrow and Hoff developed a learning procedure that examines the value before the weight adjusts it.

2.3   Period of Frustration and Disgrace

Following an initial period of enthusiasm, the field survived a period of frustration and disgrace.

In 1969 Minsky and Papert wrote a *book Perceptrons: An Introduction to Computational Geometry* [6]. It was a part of a campaign to discredit neural network research showing a number of fundamental problems, and in which they generalized the limitations of single layer perceptron. Although the authors were well aware that powerful perceptrons have multiple layers and Rosenblatt's basic feed-forward perceptrons have three layers, they defined a perceptron as a two-layer machine that can handle only linearly separable problems and, for example, cannot solve the exclusive-OR problem.

Because the public interest and available funding becoming minimal, only several researchers continued working on the problems such as pattern recognition. But, during this period several paradigms were generated which modern work continues to enhance.

Klopf in 1972, developed a basis for learning in artificial neurons based on a biological principle [7]. Paul Werbos in 1974 developed the back-propagation learning method although its importance wasn't fully appreciated until a 1986.

Fukushima developed a stepwise trained multilayered neural network for the interpretation of handwritten characters. The original work *Cognitron: A self-organizing multilayered neural network* [8] was published in 1975.

In 1976 Grossberg in the paper *Adaptive pattern classification and universal recoding* [9] introduced the adaptive resonance as a theory of human cognitive information processing.

2.4 Innovation

In 1980s several events caused a renewed interest. Kohonen has made many contributions to the field of artificial neural networks. He introduced the artificial neural network sometimes called a Kohonen map or network [10].

Hopfield of Caltech in 1982 presented a paper *Neural Networks and Physical Systems with Emergent Collective Computational Abilities* [11]. Hopfield describe the recurrent artificial neural network serving as content-addressable memory system. His works persuaded hundreds of highly qualified scientists, mathematicians, and technologists to join the emerging field of neural networks.

The backpropagation algorithm, originally discovered by Werbos in 1974 was rediscovered in 1986 with the book *Learning Internal Representation by Error Propagation* by Rumelhart et al. [12]. Backpropagation is a form of a gradient descent algorithm used with artificial neural networks for error minimization.

By 1985 the American Institute of Physics began what has become an annual meeting - *Neural Networks for Computing*. In 1987, the first open conference on neural networks in modern times; the *IEEE International Conference on Neural Networks* was held in San Diego, and the *International Neural Network Society (INNS)* was formed. In 1988 the INNS journal *Neural Networks* was founded, followed by *Neural Computation* in 1989 and the *IEEE Transactions on Neural Networks* in 1990.

Carpenter and Grossberg in 1987 in *A massively parallel architecture for a self-organizing neural pattern recognition machine* [13] described the ART1 an unsupervised learning model specially designed for recognizing binary patterns.

2.5 Today

Significant progress has been made in the field of neural networks - enough to attract a great deal of attention and fund further research. Today, neural networks discussions are occurring everywhere. Advancement beyond the current commercial applications appears to be possible, and research is advancing the field on many fronts. Chips based on the neural theory are emerging and applications to complex problems developing. Clearly, today is a period of transition for neural network technology.

Between 2009 and 2012, the recurrent neural networks and deep feedforward neural networks were developed in the research group of Schmidhuber [14].

In 2014 the scientists from IBM introduced the processor (TrueNorth), with the architecture similar to that existing in the brain. IBM presented the integrated circuit the size of postage stamp able to simulate the work of the millions of neurons and 256 million of synapses in a real time. The system is able to execute from 46 to 400 billion synaptic operations per second.

3 Different Models of Neural Networks

A neural network can be thought of as a network of "neurons" organized in layers. The number of types of Artificial Neural Networks (ANNs) and their uses can potentially be very high. Since the first neural model by McCulloch and Pitts there have been developed hundreds of different models considered as ANNs. The differences in them might be the functions, the accepted values, the topology, the learning algorithms, etc. Also there are many hybrid models. Since the function of ANNs is to process information, they are used mainly in fields related to it. An ANN is formed from single units, (artificial neurons or processing elements - PE), connected with coefficients (weights), which constitute the neural structure and are organized in layers. The power of neural computations comes from connecting neurons in a network. Each PE has weighted inputs, transfer function and one output. The behavior of a neural network is determined by the transfer functions of its neurons, by the learning rule, and by the architecture itself. The weights are the adjustable parameters and, in that sense, a neural network is a parameterized system. The weighed sum of the inputs constitutes the activation of the neuron.

An ANN is typically defined by three types of parameters:

1. The interconnection pattern between the different layers of neurons.
2. The learning process for updating the weights of the weights.
3. The activation function that converts a neuron's weighted input to its output activation.

How should the neurons be connected together? If a network is to be of any use, there must be inputs and outputs. However, there also can be hidden neurons that play an internal role in the network. The input, hidden and output neurons need to be connected together. A simple network has a feedforward structure: signals flow from inputs, forwards through any hidden units, eventually reaching the output units. However, if the network is recurrent (contains connections back from later to earlier neurons) it can be unstable, and has a very complex dynamics. Recurrent networks are very interesting to researchers in neural networks, but so far it is the feedforward structures that have proved most useful in solving real problems.

3.1 Multilayer Perceptrons

This is perhaps the most popular network architecture in use today (Fig. 1). The units each perform a biased weighted sum of their inputs and pass this activation level through a transfer function to produce their output, and the units are arranged in a layered feedforward topology.

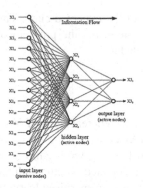

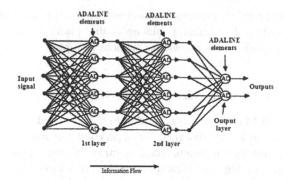

Fig. 1. The multilayer perceptron.   **Fig. 2.** An adaptive linear network (ADALINE).

3.2 ADALINE

Adaptive Linear Neuron or later Adaptive Linear Element (Fig. 2) is an early single-layer artificial neural network and the name of the physical device that implemented this network. It was developed by Bernard Widrow and Ted Hoff of Stanford University in 1960. It is based on the McCulloch–Pitts neuron. It consists of a weight, a bias and a summation function. The difference between Adaline and the standard (McCulloch–Pitts) perceptron is that in the learning phase the weights are adjusted according to the weighted sum of the inputs (the net). In the standard perceptron, the net is passed to the activation (transfer) function and the function's output is used for adjusting the weights. There also exists an extension known as Madaline.

3.3 ART

The primary intuition behind the ART model (Fig. 3) is that object identification and recognition generally occur as a result of the interaction of 'top-down' observer expectations with 'bottom-up' sensory information. The model postulates that 'top-down' expectations take the form of a memory template or prototype that is then compared with the actual features of an object as detected by the senses. This comparison gives rise to a measure of category belongingness. As long as this difference between sensation and expectation does not exceed a set threshold called the 'vigilance

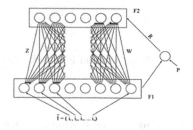

Fig. 3. The ART architecture

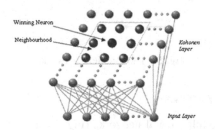

Fig. 4. Kohonen self-organising map.

parameter', the sensed object will be considered a member of the expected class. The system thus offers a solution to the 'plasticity/stability' problem, i.e. the problem of acquiring new knowledge without disrupting existing knowledge.

3.4 Self-organizing Feature Map

SOFM or Kohonen networks (Fig. 4) are used quite differently. Whereas most of other networks are designed for supervised learning tasks, SOFM networks are designed primarily for unsupervised learning. Whereas in supervised learning the training data set contains cases featuring input variables together with the associated outputs (and the network must infer a mapping from the inputs to the outputs), in unsupervised learning the training data set contains only input variables.

3.5 A Hopfield Network

A Hopfield network (Fig. 5) is a form of a recurrent artificial neural network popularized by John Hopfield in 1982. Hopfield nets serve as content-addressable memory systems with binary threshold nodes. They are guaranteed to converge to a local minimum, but convergence to a false pattern (wrong local minimum) rather than the stored pattern (expected local minimum) can occur. Hopfield networks also provide a model for understanding human memory.

3.6 The Simple Recurrent Network

SRN or Elman network (Fig. 6) it is really just a three-layer, feed-forward back propagation network. The only proviso is that one of the two parts of the input to the net work is the pattern of activation over the network's own hidden units at the previous time step.

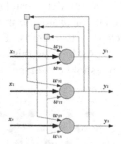

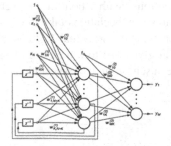

Fig. 5. The Hopfield network.   **Fig. 6.** Structure of an Elman network

3.7 CNN

Cellular neural networks (Fig. 7) are a parallel computing paradigm similar to neural networks, with the difference that communication is allowed between neighbouring units only. CNN main characteristic is the locality of the connections between the units. Each cell has one output, by which it communicates its state with both other cells and external devices.

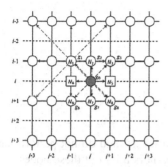

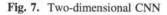

Fig. 7. Two-dimensional CNN

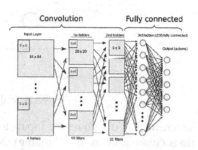

Fig. 8. Convolution neural network architecture.

3.8 Convolutional Neural Network

A convolutional neural network (Fig. 8) is a type of feed-forward artificial neural network whose individual neurons are arranged in such a way that they respond to overlapping regions tiling the visual field. Convolutional neural networks consist of multiple layers of small neuron collections which process portions of the input image. The outputs of these collections are then tiled so that their input regions overlap, to obtain a better representation of the original image; this is repeated for every such layer.

4 Topology, in Other Words – Network Architecture

In the Feed-Forward Artificial Neural Networks scheme, the data moves from the input to the output units in a strictly feed-forward manner. Data processing may spawn multiple layers, but no feedback connections are implemented. Examples of feed-forward ANN's would be a Perceptron (Rosenblatt) or an Adaline (Adaptive Linear Neuron) based net.

Recurrent ANN's. These types of ANN's incorporate feedback connections. Compared to feed-forward ANN's, the dynamic properties of the network are paramount. In some circumstances, the activation values of the units undergo a relaxation process so that the network evolves into a stable state where these activation values remain unchanged. Examples of recurrent ANN's would be a Kohonen (SOM) or a Hopfield based solution.

4.1 Inconsistency in Nomenclature

What is a layer? Some authors refer to the number of layers of variable weights but some authors describe the number of layers of nodes. Usually, the nodes in the first layer, the

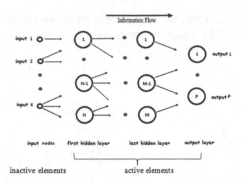

Fig. 9. A feedforward network.

input layer, merely distribute the inputs to subsequent layers, and do not perform any operations (summation or thresholding). NB.. some authors miss out these nodes.

A layer - it is the part of network structure which contains active elements performing some operation.

A multilayer network (Fig. 9) receives a number of inputs. These are distributed by a layer of input nodes that do not perform any operation – these inputs are then passed along the first layer of adaptive weights to a layer of perceptron-like units, which do sum and threshold their inputs. This layer is able to produce classification lines in pattern space. The output from the first hidden layer is passed to the second hidden layer. This layer is able to produce classification convex area etc.

5 How to Build a Feedforward Net?

The main problems faced building a feedforward network (without feedback loops) are:

- linear or nonlinear network?
- how many layers is necessary for the proper network's work?
- how many elements have to be in these layers?

A linear network it is a network where input signals are multiplied by the weights, added, and the result follows to the axon as the output signal of the neuron. Eventually some threshold can be used. Typical examples of a linear network are a simple perceptron and an Adeline network.

In a nonlinear network the output signal is calculated by a nonlinear function f(). The function f(?) is called neuron transfer function and its operations have to be similar to the operations of a biological neuron. Typical example of a nonlinear network is a sigmoidal network.

5.1 How Many Layers?

The simplest feedforward network has at least two layers – an input and an output (NB. such a networks are called single layer networks – active neurons are located only in an output layer). Usually between these layers there are multiple intermediate or hidden layers.

Hidden layers are very important they are considered to be categorizers or feature detectors. The output layer is considered a collector of the features detected and producer of the response.

5.1.1   The Input Layer

With respect to the number of neurons comprising this layer, this parameter is completely and uniquely determined once you know the shape of your training data. Specifically, the number of neurons comprising that layer is equal to the number of features (columns) in your data. Some neural networks configurations add one additional node for a bias term.

5.1.2   The Output Layer

Like the input layer, every neural network has exactly one output layer. Determining its size (number of neurons) is simple; it is completely determined by the chosen model configuration. The interesting solution is called "one out of N". Unfortunately, because of limited accuracy in network operation the non-zero signal can occur on each out elements. It is necessary to implement the special criteria for results post-processing and threshold of acceptance and rejection.

5.2   How to Build the Network

Too small network without hidden layer or too few neurons is unable to solve a problem and even the very long learning time will not help.

Too big network will cheat the teacher. Too many hidden layers or too many elements in the hidden layers yields to the simplification of task. The network will learn whole set of the learning patterns. It learns very a fast and precisely but is completely useless for solving any similar problem.

5.3   How Many Hidden Layers

Too many hidden layers yield to a significant deterioration of learning. There is a consensus as to the performance difference due to additional hidden layers: the situations in which performance improves with a second (or third, etc.) hidden layer are relatively infrequent. One hidden layer is sufficient for the large majority of problems. An additional layer yields the instability of gradient, and increases the number of false minima. Two hidden layer are necessary only if the learning refers the function with points of discontinuity. Too many neurons in the hidden layers may result in overfitting. Overfitting occurs when the neural network has so much information processing capacity that the limited amount of information contained in the training set is not enough to train all of the neurons in the hidden layers. Another problem can occur even when the training data is sufficient. An inordinately large number of neurons in the hidden layer may increase the time it takes to train the network and may lead to the increase of errors (Fig. 10). Using too few neurons in the hidden layers will, in turn, result in something called underfitting.

A rough prerequisite for the number of hidden neurons (for most of typical problems) is the rule of a geometric pyramid. The number of neurons in the consecutive layers has a shape of a pyramid and decrease from the direction of input to the output. The numbers of neurons in a consecutive layers are forming a geometric sequence.

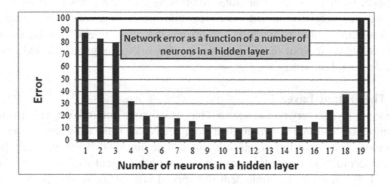

Fig. 10. Network error as a function of a number of neurons in a hidden layer.

For example, for the network with one hidden layer with n-neurons in the input layer and m-neurons in the output layer, the numbers of neurons in the hidden layer should be $NHN = \sqrt{n * m}$. For the network with two hidden layers $NHN1 = m * r2$ and $NHN2 = m * r$ where $r = \sqrt[3]{\frac{n}{m}}$.

The hidden neuron can influence the error in the nodes to which its output is connected. The stability of neural network is estimated by error. The minimal error denotes better stability, and higher error indicates worst stability. During the training, the network adapts in order to decrease the error emerging from the training patterns. Many researchers have fixed number of hidden neurons based on trial rule.

The estimation theory was proposed to find a number of hidden units in the higher order feedforward neural network. This theory is applied to the time series prediction. The determination of an optimal number of hidden neurons is obtained when the sufficient number of hidden neurons is assumed. According to the estimation theory, the sufficient number of hidden units in the second-order neural network and the first-order neural networks are 4 and 7 respectively.

6   Reviews of Methods How to Fix a Number of Hidden Neurons

To establish the optimal(?) number of hidden neurons, for the past 20 years more than 100 various criteria have been tested based on the statistical errors. The very good review was done by Gnana Sheela and Deepa in [15]. Below there is a short review of some endeavours:

- **1991:** Sartori and Antsaklis proposed a method to find the number of hidden neurons in multilayer neural network for an arbitrary training set with P training patterns.
- **1993:** Arai proposed two parallel hyperplane methods for finding the number of hidden neurons
- **1995:** Li et al. investigated the estimation theory to find the number of hidden units in the higher order feedforward neural network
- **1997:** Tamura and Tateishi developed a method to fix the number of hidden neuron. The number of hidden neurons in three layer neural network is $N - 1$ and four-layer neural network is $N/2 + 3$ where N is the input-target relation.
- **1998:** Fujita proposed a statistical estimation for the number of hidden neurons. The merits of this method are speed learning. The number of hidden neurons mainly depends on the output error.
- **2001:** Onoda presented a statistical approach to find the optimal number of hidden units in prediction applications. The minimal errors are obtained by the increase of number of hidden units. Md. Islam and Murase proposed a large number of hidden nodes in weight freezing of single hidden layer networks.
- **2003:** Zhang et al. implemented a set covering algorithm (SCA) in three-layer neural network. The SCA is based on unit sphere covering (USC) of hamming space. This methodology is based on the number of inputs.
- **2006:** Choi et al. developed a separate learning algorithm which includes a deterministic and heuristic approach. In this algorithm, hidden-to-output and input-to-hidden nodes are separately trained. It solved the local minima in two-layered feedforward network. The achievement here is the best convergence speed.
- **2008:** Jiang et al. presented the lower bound of the number of hidden neurons. The necessary numbers of hidden neurons approximated in hidden layer using multilayer perceptron (MLP) were found by Trenn. The key points are simplicity, scalability, and adaptivity. The number of hidden neurons is $N_h = n + n_0 - 0.5$ where n is the number of inputs and n_0 is the number of outputs. Xu and Chen developed a novel approach for determining the optimum number of hidden neurons in data mining. The best number of hidden neurons leads to minimum root means Squared Error.
- **2009:** Shibata and Ikeda investigated the effect of learning stability and hidden neurons in neural network. The simulation results show that the hidden output connection weight becomes small as number of hidden neurons increases.
- **2010:** Doukim et al. proposed a technique to find the number of hidden neurons in MLP network using coarse-to-fine search technique which is applied in skin detection. This technique includes binary search and sequential search. Yuan et al. proposed a method for estimation of hidden neuron based on information entropy. This method is based on decision tree algorithm. Wu and Hong proposed the learning algorithms for determination of the number of hidden neurons.
- **2011:** Panchal et al. proposed a methodology to analyse the behaviour of MLP. The number of hidden layers is inversely proportional to the minimal error.

References

1. McCulloch, W.S., Pitts, W.: A logical calculus of the ideas immanent in nervous activity. Bull. Math. Bioph. **5**, 115–133 (1943)
2. Hebb, D.: The Organization of Behavior. Wiley, New York (1949)
3. Rosenblatt, F.: The perceptron: a probabilistic model for information storage and organization in the brain. Psychol. Rev. **65**(6), 386–408 (1958)
4. Rosenblatt, F.: Principles of Neurodynamics. Spartan Books, Washington (1962)
5. Widrow, B., Hoff, M.: Adaptive switching circuits. Technical report 1553-1, Stanford Electron. Labs., Stanford, June 1960
6. Minsky, M.L., Papert, S.: Perceptrons: An Introduction to Computational Geometry. MIT Press, Cambridge (1969)
7. Klopf, A.H.: Brain function and adaptive systems - a heterostatic theory. Air Force Research Laboratories Technical Report, AFCRL-72-0164 (1972)
8. Fukushima, K.: Cognitron: a self-organizing multilayered neural network. Biol. Cyber. **20**, 121–136 (1975)
9. Grossberg, S.: Adaptive pattern classification and universal recoding. Biol. Cyber. **23**(3), 121–134 (1976)
10. Kohonen, T.: Self-organized formation of topologically correct feature maps. Biol. Cyber. **43**, 59–69 (1982)
11. Hopfield, J.J.: Neural networks and physical systems with emergent collective computational abilities. Proc. Natl. Acad. Sci. USA **79**, 2554–2558 (1982)
12. Rumelhart, D.E., Hinton, G.E., Williams, R.J.: Learning internal representations by error propagation. In: Parallel Distributed Processing: Explorations in the Microstructure of Cognition, vol. 1, pp. 318–362. MIT Press, Cambridge (1986)
13. Carpenter, G.A., Grossberg, S.: A massively parallel architecture for a self-organizing neural pattern recognition machine. Comp. Vis. Graph. Image Proc. **37**, 54–115 (1987)
14. Schmidhuber, J.: Deep learning in neural networks: an overview. Neural Netw. **61**, 85–117 (2014)
15. Gnana Sheela, K., Deepa, S.N.: Review on methods to fix number of hidden neurons in neural networks. Anna University, Regional Centre, Coimbatore 641047, India (2013)

Rough Set Methods for Big Data Analytics

Complex Adaptive Systems and Interactive Granular Computing

Andrzej Skowron[1,2](✉)

[1] Institute of Mathematics, Warsaw University, Banacha 2, 02-097 Warsaw, Poland
skowron@mimuw.edu.pl
[2] Systems Research Institute, Polish Academy of Sciences,
Newelska 6, 01-447 Warsaw, Poland

Extended Abstract. We discuss an approach to modeling of computations performed by Complex Adaptive Systems (CAS) based on Interactive Granular Computing (IGrC).

Complex adaptive systems (CAS) are made up of multiple interacting elements and have the capacity to change and learn from experience. The key problems of complex systems are difficulties with their formal modeling and simulation[1]. Some approaches to modeling CAS are based on agent-based models and/or complex network-based models (see, *e.g.*, [17,36]).

Decision support in solving problems related to CAS [6,33,36] requires relevant computation models for the agents as well as methods for incorporating reasoning over computations performed by agents. Agents are performing computations on complex objects (*e.g.*, behavioral patterns, classifiers, clusters, structural objects, sets of rules, aggregation operations, approximate reasoning schemes). In Granular Computing (GrC), all such constructed and/or induced objects are called granules.

To model, crucial for CAS, interactive computations [2] performed by agents, we extend the existing GrC approach to Interactive Granular Computing (IGrC) by introducing *complex granules* (*c-granules* or *granules*, for short).

Interactive granular computations (*computations in* IGrC, for short) were proposed as computational models for complex systems. Reasoning about the properties of computations in IGrC are based on *adaptive judgment*.

Computations in this model are performed on c-granules thanks to which it is possible to register, analyze, and synthesize the properties of interactions between physical objects perceived by agents.

We assume that the states of certain physical objects, occurring within a specific domain of activity of a given c-granule, are directly measurable. However, the states of other objects are perceived (approximated) indirectly using measurable states, obtained by interactions of physical objects from a particular domain of c-granule's activity. Each measurable state of a c-granule (at a given moment

---

[1] https://en.wikipedia.org/wiki/Complex_adaptive_system.

The original version of this chapter was revised: The acknowledgement section has been updated. The correction to this chapter is available at https://doi.org/10.1007/978-3-319-45378-1_65

K. Saeed and W. Homenda (Eds.): CISIM 2016, LNCS 9842, pp. 17–22, 2016.
DOI: 10.1007/978-3-319-45378-1_2

of the agent's time) corresponds to a concept. This concept is understood as a set of situations (configurations of physical objects), perceived within this very c-granule, and, thanks to interactions, leads to a specific state. In the proposed approach, the concept of a measurable state means that such states are represented by, *e.g.*, the values of a corresponding attribute or by the *satisfiability degrees* of corresponding to states concepts/formulas. Following the aggregation of c-granules, more complex c-granules, corresponding to structural objects, their properties, or relations over measurable states (*e.g.*, *preference relations*), can be represented by c-granules. C-granules are used by agents for perceiving current situations or states and undertaking, on this basis, of relevant actions.

The fundamental intuition behind the concept of a c-granule is the following: the control of an agent *ag* uses her/his c-granules for perceiving and/or accessing fragments of the surrounding physical world. Each c-granule consists of three architectural layers:

1. *Soft_suit, i.e.*, configurations of hunks which represent the properties of the *ag*'s environment of activity (including the properties of the present, past, and expected phenomena, as well as expected properties of interaction plans and/or the results of some interactions, potentially activated by a c-granule).
2. *Link_suit, i.e.*, communication channels (links) which transmit the results of interactions among accessible fragments of the agent's environment of activities and the results of interactions among different representations of properties in the soft_suit; according to the weight (significance) of the current *ag*'s needs, links may have assigned priorities, which reflect the results of judgment, performed by *ag*.
3. *Hard_suit, i.e.*, configurations of hunks accessible by links from the link_suit.

The hard_suits, link_suits, and soft_suits of more compound c-granules are defined using the relevant networks over already defined c-granules. The networks are satisfying some constraints which can be interpreted as definitions of types of networks. The link_suits of such more compound granules are responsible for transmission of interactions between the hard_suits and soft_suits represented by the corresponding networks. The results and/or properties of transmitted interactions are recorded in the soft_suits.

Any c-granule is making it possible to record in its soft_suit the perceived by it interactions in its hard_suit which are transmitted by the link_suit to the soft_suit. This is typical for sensory measurement. On the other hand, a c-granule may cause some interactions in its hard_suit by transmitting through its link_suit some interactions from the soft_suit. However, the c-granule may perceive the results (or properties) of such caused in the hard_suit interactions only by using the soft_suit. This is done on the basis of the transmitted results (or properties) of these caused interactions in the hard_suit by transmitting them back through the link_suit to the soft_suit. These results (or properties) may be different from the predicted ones which can be a priori stored in soft_suit. This is typical for performing of actions initiated by c-granules.

C-granules are generated by an agent *ag* depending on the specific configurations of spatio-temporal portions of physical matter (called hunks [5]) related to the *ag*. It should be underlined that any typical active c-granule is a dynamically changing entity. It means that all components of c-granules (*i.e.*, soft_suits, link_suits and hard_suits) are usually subject to continuous changes.

Many advanced tasks, concerning complex systems may be classified as control tasks performed by agents aiming at achieving the high quality computational trajectories of c-granules relative to the considered quality measures over the trajectories. Here, new challenges are to develop strategies to control, predict, and bound the behavior of the system. We propose to investigate these challenges using the IGrC framework.

The reasoning, which aims at controlling the computational schemes from time-to-time, in order to achieve the required targets, is called an *adaptive judgement*. Adaptive judgment plays a crucial role in the assessment of what is currently important, and what is less important. Therefore, it constitutes the basis for the evaluation and improvement of interaction plans that are being implemented. In a sense, judgment [3,4,13,14,35] may be treated as an elaboration of the concept of rational reasoning (especially about the properties of computations in IGrC) due to the necessity of taking into account not only mechanisms of logical reasoning, but also mechanisms that influence decisions, which are being made. These mechanisms pertain, *e.g.*, to perception, emotions, instinct, habits, intuition, fast thinking [13], and experience. Thus, adaptive judgment is not only limited to deduction, induction, and abduction. A deeper understanding of the concept of adaptive judgment should be supported by psychology and phenomenology [16]. This reasoning deals with granules and computations over them. Due to the uncertainty the agents generally cannot predict exactly the results of actions (or plans). Moreover, the approximations of the complex vague concepts initiating actions (or plans) are drifting with time. Hence, adaptive strategies for inducing changes in approximations of concepts are needed. In particular, the adaptive judgement is very much needed in the efficiency management of interactive granular computations, carried out by agents, for risk assessment, risk treatment, and cost/benefit analysis.

Thanks to c-granules, it is possible to register both the results of sensory measurements and their hierarchical aggregations, which are performed to discover new c-granules. The hierarchical c-granules discovered in this manner may ensure a deeper understanding of a perceived situation (see [1]). The statement above about the aggregation of c-granules (representing hierarchical aggregations of the results of sensory measures) refers to the main, according to Valiant[1], AI challenge, which is the characterization of "computational building blocks" [34] for perception.

The key role in the proposed approach is played by the techniques of adaptive and interactive discovery of c-granules (through interactions with the environment) and their further use. It turns out that in order to perform computations on c-granules, *ecorithms*, as understood by Valiant [33], should be used instead of classical algorithms. Apart from the analogy to Valiant's ecorithms, the IGrC-based proposed algorithms display a number of other features, which correspond to the motivations of scientific research in other domains (*e.g.*, learning systems,

---

[1] http://www.seas.harvard.edu/directory/valiant.

CAS, soft-computing, multi-agent systems, natural computations). The Wistech IGrC model is also related to the very foundations of AI, in particular, to the understanding of the essence of machine learning.

In particular, in Complex Systems Engineering (CSE) [7], the design and implementation of a complex project may be seen as the process of discovering, learning, processing (including communicating), and developing concepts (represented as c-granules), which are necessary to deal with a given project. The key to success in managing any complex project is a skillful approximation of complex vague concepts, represented by c-granules, and a skillful use of c-granules by those, who are in charge of a given project. Such approximations are responsible, *e.g.*, for initiation of actions performed by agents [7].

It is worth mentioning that the proposed model of interactive computations on c-granules differs from the Turing model.

The main ideas of IGrC have their roots in the research on rough sets, initiated by Pawlak [20–22,31]. At this point, we are particularly referring to Pawlak's approach to such concepts as: concept approximations, information systems, decision tables (as they are understood in a rough set theory) and Boolean reasoning about vague concepts.

The presented approach to the Wistech IGrC model is an extension of the joint research with Jankowski [8–12,19,26–28,30] The approach is a step towards realization of the Wisdom Technology (WisTech) program [7–10,29] in combination with IGrC, and is developed over years of experiences, based on the work on different real-life projects. The discussed model is called the Wistech IGrC model.

The results of the research presented in this paper may also be analyzed from the point of view of their potential contribution to advancements in dynamically developing scientific disciplines, such as CSE [18,25], granular computational models [23], interactive computational models [2], models of natural computing [24], models of learning systems [33], or models of computations performed by multi-agent systems [15,32].

Other issues such as communication language evolution and risk management in interactive computations will be discussed in more detail in our next papers (see also [7]).

Acknowledgements. This work was supported by the Polish National Science Centre (NCN) grant DEC- 2011/01/D /ST6/ 06981, and by the Polish National Centre for Research and Development (NCBiR) grant DZP/RID-I-44/8/NCBR/2016.

References

1. Bazan, J.: Hierarchical classifiers for complex spatio-temporal concepts. In: Peters, J.F., Skowron, A., Rybiński, H. (eds.) Transactions on Rough Sets IX. LNCS, vol. 5390, pp. 474–750. Springer, Heidelberg (2008)
2. Goldin, D., Smolka, S., Wegner, P. (eds.): Interactive Computation: The New Paradigm. Springer, Heidelberg (2006)

3. Grossi, D., Pigozzi, G.: Judgment Aggregation: A Primer, Synthesis Lectures on Artificial Intelligence and Machine Learning, vol. 27. Morgan & Claypool, Los Altos (2014)
4. Hager, P., Halliday, J.: Recovering Informal Learning Wisdom, Judgement and Community. Springer, Heidelberg (2006)
5. Heller, M.: The Ontology of Physical Objects. Four Dimensional Hunks of Matter. Cambridge Studies in Philosophy. Cambridge University Press, Cambridge (1990)
6. Holland, J.H.: Signals and Boundaries Building Blocks for Complex Adaptive Systems. The MIT Press, Cambridge (2014)
7. Jankowski, A.: Complex Systems Engineering: Wisdom for Saving Billions Based on Interactive Granular Computing. Springer, Heidelberg (2016, in preparation)
8. Jankowski, A., Skowron, A.: A wistech paradigm for intelligent systems. In: Peters, J.F., Skowron, A., Düntsch, I., Grzymała-Busse, J.W., Orłowska, E., Polkowski, L. (eds.) Transactions on Rough Sets VI. LNCS, vol. 4374, pp. 94–132. Springer, Heidelberg (2007)
9. Jankowski, A., Skowron, A.: Logic for artificial intelligence: Rasiowa - Pawlak school perspective. In: Ehrenfeucht, A., Marek, V.M., Srebrny, M. (eds.) Andrzej Mostowski and Foundational Studies, pp. 106–143. IOS Press, Amsterdam (2008)
10. Jankowski, A., Skowron, A.: Wisdom technology: a rough-granular approach. In: Marciniak, M., Mykowiecka, A. (eds.) Aspects of Natural Language Processing. LNCS, vol. 5070, pp. 3–41. Springer, Heidelberg (2009)
11. Jankowski, A., Skowron, A., Dutta, S.: Toward problem solving support based on big data and domain knowledge: interactive granular computing and adaptive judgement. In: Japkowicz, N., Stefanowski, J. (eds.) Big Data Analysis: New Algorithms for a New Society. Series in Big Data, vol. 16, pp. 49–90. Springer, Heidelberg (2016)
12. Jankowski, A., Skowron, A., Swiniarski, R.: Interactive complex granules. Fundamenta Informaticae 133(2–3), 181–196 (2014)
13. Kahneman, D.: Thinking, Fast and Slow. Farrar, Straus and Giroux, New York (2011)
14. Koehler, D.J., Harvey, N.: Blackwell Handbook of Judgment and Decision Making. Blackwell Publishing, Oxford (2004)
15. Liu, J.: Autonomous Agents and Multi-agent Systems: Explorations in Learning, Self-organization and Adaptive Computation. World Scientific Publishing, Singapore (2001)
16. Martin, W.M. (ed.): Theories of Judgment. Psychology, Logic, Phenomenology. Cambridge University Press, New York (2006)
17. Meia, S., Zarrabi, N., Lees, M., Sloot, P.M.: Complex agent networks: an emerging approach for modeling complex systems. Appl. Soft Comput. 37, 311–321 (2015)
18. National Aeronautics and Space Administration: NASA Systems Engineering Handbook. NASA Headquarters, Washington, D.C (2007)
19. Nguyen, H.S., Jankowski, A., Skowron, A., Stepaniuk, J., Szczuka, M.: Discovery of process models from data and domain knowledge: a rough-granular approach. In: Yao, J.T. (ed.) Novel Developments in Granular Computing: Applications for Advanced Human Reasoning and Soft Computation, pp. 16–47. IGI Global, Hershey (2010)
20. Pawlak, Z.: Rough sets. Int. J. Comput. Inf. Sci. 11, 341–356 (1982)
21. Pawlak, Z.: Systemy Informacyjne. Podstawy Teoretyczne (Information Systems. Theoretical Foundations). Wydawnictwa Naukowo-Techniczne (1983). http:// bcpw.bg.pw.edu.pl/dlibra/docmetadata?id=2327

22. Pawlak, Z.: Rough Sets: Theoretical Aspects of Reasoning About Data, System Theory, Knowledge Engineering and Problem Solving, vol. 9. Kluwer Academic Publishers, Dordrecht (1991)
23. Pedrycz, W., Skowron, S., Kreinovich, V. (eds.): Handbook of Granular Computing. Wiley, Hoboken (2008)
24. Rozenberg, G., Bäck, T., Kok, J. (eds.): Handbook of Natural Computing. Springer, Heidelberg (2012)
25. Sage, A., Rouse, W.: Handbook of Systems Engineering and Management. Wiley-Interscience, Hoboken (2014)
26. Skowron, A., Jankowski, A.: Interactive computations: toward risk management in interactive intelligent systems. Nat. Comput. doi:10.1007/s11047-015-9486-5
27. Skowron, A., Jankowski, A., Dutta, S.: Interactive granular computing. Granul. Comput. 1, 95–113 (2016)
28. Skowron, A., Jankowski, A., Swiniarski, R.: 30 years of rough sets and future perspectives. In: Ciucci, D., Inuiguchi, M., Yao, Y., Ślęzak, D., Wang, G. (eds.) RSFDGrC 2013. LNCS, vol. 8170, pp. 1–10. Springer, Heidelberg (2013)
29. Skowron, A., Jankowski, A., Wasilewski, P.: Risk management and interactive computational systems. J. Adv. Math. Appl. 1, 61–73 (2012)
30. Skowron, A., Stepaniuk, J., Jankowski, A., Bazan, J.G., Swiniarski, R.: Rough set based reasoning about changes. Fundamenta Informaticae 119(3–4), 421–437 (2012)
31. Skowron, A., Suraj, Z. (eds.): Rough Sets and Intelligent Systems. Professor Zdzislaw Pawlak in Memoriam. Series Intelligent Systems Reference Library, vol. 42-43. Springer, Heidelberg (2013)
32. Sun, R. (ed.): Cognition and Multi-Agent Interaction. From Cognitive Modeling to Social Simulation. Cambridge University Press, Cambridge (2006)
33. Valiant, L.: Probably Approximately Correct. Nature's Algorithms for Learning and Prospering in a Complex World. Basic Books, A Member of the Perseus Books Group, New York (2013)
34. Valiant, L.: Research interests. http://people.seas.harvard.edu/~valiant/researchinterests.htm
35. van Dalen, D. (ed.): Brouwer's Cambridge Lectures on Intuitionism (1951). Cambridge University Press, Cambridge (1981)
36. Yang, A., Shan, Y.: Intelligent Complex Adaptive Systems. IGI Global, Hershey (2008)

Innovation and Big Data

H. Jaap van den Herik$^{(\boxtimes)}$

Leiden Centre of Data Science, Leiden University, Leiden, The Netherlands
jaapvandenherik@gmail.com

Abstract. Innovation is an essential issue for companies and educational institutes. We have seen that well-known companies came into trouble since they did not innovate in time. They kept their well-established way of operating and adhered to their old-fashioned business models. The main topic of this contribution is to address the question: to what extent can the availability of Big Data support the innovation attempts of companies and educational institutes?

We start by mentioning five examples of innovation and relate them to data science and big data. We describe basic concepts and developments. We then formulate six possible classes of obstacles and take into account the use of sensitive data. Finally, we arrive at two conclusions and three recommendations.

Keywords: Big data · Obstacles · Sensitive data · Safeguards · Turn around management · Narrative science

1 Introduction

The current technological development is in a state of flux. New applications are followed by even newer ones. Many scientists see this concatenation of applications as a disruptive chain. For a proper understanding we mention five new developments (or applications of well-known concepts): (1) autonomous cars, (2) blockchains, (3) crowd sourced online dispute resolutions, (4) Airbnb, and (5) Uber Taxi. They can be seen as new paradigms that result from the combination of new and old technologies.

The question to what extent big data does support the innovation can be answered by investigating the string of activities that takes place in the study of data science. Data science is a new discipline in the academic world and in particular in the research world. It originates from computer science (informatics) and statistics. Big Data has mitigated the use of samples as is exploited by statisticians. This implies that for a proper handling of the available data no longer the well-known statistical sample techniques are sufficient, but that a new statistical approach has to be developed, i.e., reasoning in a Bayesian network.

In data science we nowadays distinguish seven phases of activities. They are: (1) collecting data, (2) cleaning data, (3) interpreting data, (4) analyzing data, (5) visualization of data, (6) narrative science, and (7) the emergence of new paradigms. The last phase has been instantiated by the five examples at the beginning of this section.

Below we will discuss the following topics and their obstacles: Real big data (Sect. 2); Definitions (Sect. 3); Small data (Sect. 4); Turn around management (Sect. 5); Criminal behavior (Sect. 6); Conclusions (Sect. 7), and Safeguards and recommendations (Sect. 8).

© IFIP International Federation for Information Processing 2016
Published by Springer International Publishing Switzerland 2016. All Rights Reserved
K. Saeed and W. Homenda (Eds.): CISIM 2016, LNCS 9842, pp. 23–30, 2016.
DOI: 10.1007/978-3-319-45378-1_3

2 Real Big Data

There are only two research areas where we face real big data, viz. particle physics (e.g., at Cern) and astrophysics (e.g., at Lofar). Two other areas where the storage of data is extremely large are DNA-research and Geo-research (in general). For social sciences we see enormous amounts of data stored in Wikileaks, on Dating sites, and in the Panama papers. Here we meet our first class of obstacles. They consist of transport problems, complexity problems, and reputation damage:

Obstacles (Class 1)	
Big data	Obstacles
CERN LOFAR	1. Transport problems (accessibility)
DNA GEO	2. Complexity problems (unrelated data)
Wikileaks Dating sites Panama papers	3. Reputation damage (side-effects/non anticipated)

3 Definitions

Big Data is a kind of container concept. Almost all disciplines have their own definition of Big Data. In this contribution we provide two definitions: a technical one and a business one. The technical definition is by White (2012).

Technical Definition: "Big Data is the term for a collection of data sets so large and complex that it becomes difficult to process using on-hand databases management tools or traditional data processing applications."

The challenges capture

1. curation,
2. storage,
3. search,
4. sharing,
5. transfer,
6. analysis,
7. visualization,
8. interpretation,
9. real-time (van Eijk 2013).

The second class of obstacles is defined by the characteristics of the collection of Big Data at hand. They are called the five V's:

Obstacles (Class 2)

The five V's are:

1. Volume
2. Velocity
3. Variety
4. Veracity
5. Value

The business definition of Big Data has been formulated by Phillips (2015).

Business Definition: "Big Data focuses on value creation, viz. to obtain operational benefits from data, and will then exploit the benefits for performance improvements." Two important capabilities are:

(1) Companies learn faster on their business trend,
(2) Companies can rely faster on the new trends than their competitors.

The third class of obstacles is defined by legal requirements and competitive behavior:

Obstacles (Class 3)

- The intention to make *infringements on the legal requirements* with reference to the commercial competition.

Examples come from the auto industry, among them Volkswagen.

4 Small Data

Next to big data there is small data. They constitute techniques which enables effective use of Big Data. A telling example is *cookies*. Originally, cookies were meant to bring relevant input to places where they are in a better environment, i.e., to be of better use in their "ecosystem".

Nowadays cookies are used for: personalization, profiling, advertisements, recording of behavior and for "selling purposes". The fourth class of obstacles is defined by privacy and security issues:

Obstacles (Class 4)

The main obstacles for small data are

- Privacy
- Security

5 Turn Around Management

Big data can be used for monitoring the life cycle of companies. We assume that the life cycle traverses through the following six stages: (1) Foundation of the company, (2) Establishing a healthy company, (3) Strategic crisis, (4) Earning crisis, (5) Liquidity crisis, and (6) Bankruptcy (cf. Adriaanse 2015). We will see the following development.

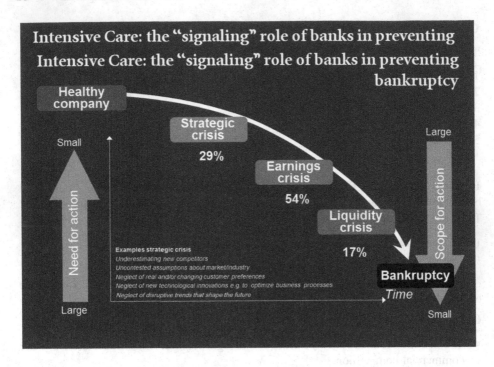

Intensive Care: the "signaling" role of banks in preventing bankruptcy

A proper recording of data within the company may serve as monitoring system and even as alert system for unexpected developments. The availability of big data will make the prediction very accurate.

The fifth class of obstacles is defined by privacy and ethical considerations as well as by commercial competition and legal opportunities:

Obstacles (Class 5)

The main obstacles for use of big data in Turn around management.

- Privacy
- Ethical considerations
- Commercial competition
- Legal opportunities

6 Criminal Behavior

An important case showing criminal behavior is the marathon bombing in Boston. We illustrate this marathon bombing by three pictures. In April 2014 an unexpected bomb exploded at the end of the Boston Marathon (see picture 1). There were sensor images and recorded pictures. The crowd was so big that no criminals involved in the attack could be identified. The police quarantined the city and attempted to find the criminals in their computer databases. They could not identify them. Finally, one brother was killed by police force (Dzjochar Tsjarnajev) in a gunfight and one day later Tamerlan Tsjarnajev was arrested albeit by a coincidence through a blood trace observed by an alert citizen.

If the bomb had been inspected accurately, it could have been established that its origin was Chechnya or a neighbor area, which would have refined the number of candidate criminals considerably. Once the criminals were caught, the recorded images afterwards produced evidence for what has happened and where the guilty persons stayed during the explosion.

To investigate such criminal behavior with modern technological means we see that a combination of Big Data, High Performance Computing, and Deep Learning is most effective. These three components form the basis of *narrative science*. It means that an intelligent program constructs the story and points to the criminals. This approach is also known under the name story telling. For lawyers it is called argumentation theory. The sixth class of obstacles is defined by privacy, public safety, technicalities of narrative science, and sensitive data:

Obstacles (Class 6)

- Privacy
- Public safety
- Narrative science
- Sensitive data

The investigations of criminal behavior have an important obstacle class 6 to take into account, viz. sensitive data (cf. Van Eijk 2015)

Sensitive Data

Obviously, some data are really personal, i.e., data revealing

(1) racial or ethnic origin,
(2) political opinions,
(3) religious or philosophical beliefs,
(4) trade-union membership, and
(5) the processing of data concerning health or sex life

The general rule for companies is that the processing of sensitive data is **prohibited** without explicit consent
(Directive 95/46/EC, article 8).

The "scientific" development of "disruptive" technology, the Road to Deep Learning, is:

The road to deep learning	
Artificial intelligence	1950–1990
Machine learning	1990–2000
Adaptivity	2000–2005
Dimension reduction	2005–2010
Deep learning	2010–2015
Big data and HPC	2012–2017
New statistics	2014–2019

7 Conclusions

From the above line of reasoning on the obstacles that occur when Big Data research is involved we may conclude the following:

Conclusion 1: For a legitimate commercial interest, a legal foundation is a necessary requirement. Such a requirement should constitute a careful balance between

- the legitimate commercial interest,
- the fundamental rights and liberties of the persons who possess the data (or to whom the data can be attributed). Keep here in mind the sensitive data.

Conclusion 2: For all who are working in the area of Technological Innovation and Social Innovation the Extrapolation as shown in below is relevant (cf. Van den Herik and Dimov 2011a, b).

8 Safeguards and Recommendations

To keep the delicate balance mentioned above, two safeguards are possible.

- To diminish attention and research efforts for Big Data and Deep Learning.
- To increase attention and research efforts for Big Data and Deep Learning.

From these two safeguards our preference goes to the second safeguard, provided that we are allowed to introduce three specific safeguards.

These are our *recommendations*.

- Increase research on AI systems for Big Data and Deep Learning with emphasis on moral constraints.
- Increase research on AI systems for Big Data and Deep Learning with emphasis on the prevention of AI systems to be hacked.
- Establish (a) a committee of Data Authorities and (b) an ethical committee.

Acknowledgements. This insight overview is the result of my cooperation with many colleagues. The following colleagues are singled out for their contribution to this article. I would like to thank Rob van Eijk, Daniel Dimov, Joost Kok, Aske Plaat, and Joke Hellemons. Moreover, I am grateful to Wladyslaw Homenda from Vilnius for the stimulating discussions we have had and for the invitation to communicate on Innovation.

References

Adriaanse, J.: Ethical challenges in turnaround management. Lecture at the Workshop Leadership Challenges with Big Data. Turning Data into Business, Erasmus University Rotterdam, 30 June 2015

Phillips, J.: Pass summit 2015 – Microsoft foundation session – Business Intelligence (2015)

Van den Herik, H.J., Dimov, D.: Towards crowdsourced online dispute resolution. In: Rohrmann, C.A., Sampaion Junior, R.B. (eds.) Revista da Faculdade de Direito Milton Campos, vol. 22, pp. 141–162. Del Rey, Belo Horizonte (2011a). ISSN 1415-0778

Van den Herik, H.J., Dimov, D.: Towards crowdsourced online dispute resolution. In: Kierkegaard, S.M., Kierkegaard, P. (eds.) Law Across Nations: Governance, Policy & Statutes, pp. 244–256. International Association of IT lawyers (IAITL), Denmark (2011b)

Van Eijk, R.: Towards a delicate balance in strategic innovations – update on privacy legislation. Lecture at the Workshop Leadership Challenges with Big Data. Turning Data into Business, Erasmus University Rotterdam, 30 June 2015

White, T.: Hadoop: The Definitive Guide. Storage and Analysis at Internet Scale, 3rd edn., p. 688. O'Reilly Media/Yahoo Press, Sebastopol (2012)

Van Eijk, R.: Social innovation & Big Data. [Presentation]. Amersfoort: IT Innovation Day (2013)

Imbalanced Data Classification: A Novel Re-sampling Approach Combining Versatile Improved SMOTE and Rough Sets

Katarzyna Borowska[✉] and Jarosław Stepaniuk

Faculty of Computer Science, Bialystok University of Technology,
Wiejska 45A, 15-351 Bialystok, Poland
{k.borowska,j.stepaniuk}@pb.edu.pl
http://www.wi.pb.edu.pl

Abstract. In recent years, the problem of learning from imbalanced data has emerged as important and challenging. The fact that one of the classes is underrepresented in the data set is not the only reason of difficulties. The complex distribution of data, especially small disjuncts, noise and class overlapping, contributes to the significant depletion of classifier's performance. Hence, the numerous solutions were proposed. They are categorized into three groups: data-level techniques, algorithm-level methods and cost-sensitive approaches. This paper presents a novel data-level method combining Versatile Improved SMOTE and rough sets. The algorithm was applied to the two-class problems, data sets were characterized by the nominal attributes. We evaluated the proposed technique in comparison with other preprocessing methods. The impact of the additional cleaning phase was specifically verified.

Keywords: Data preprocessing · Class imbalance · Rough sets · SMOTE · Oversampling · Undersampling

1 Introduction

Proper classification of imbalanced data is one of the most challenging problems in data mining. Since wide range of real-world domains suffers from this issue, it is crucial to find more and more effective techniques to deal with it. The fundamental reason of difficulties is the fact that one class (positive, minority) is underrepresented in the data set. Furthermore, the correct recognition of examples belonging to this particular class is a matter of major interest. Considering domains like medical diagnostic, anomaly detection, fault diagnosis, detection of oil spills, risk management and fraud detection [8,21] the misclassification cost of rare cases is obviously very high. The small subset of data describing disease cases is more meaningful than remaining majority of objects representing healthy population. Therefore, the dedicated algorithms should be applied to recognizing minority class instances in these areas.

© IFIP International Federation for Information Processing 2016
Published by Springer International Publishing Switzerland 2016. All Rights Reserved
K. Saeed and W. Homenda (Eds.): CISIM 2016, LNCS 9842, pp. 31–42, 2016.
DOI: 10.1007/978-3-319-45378-1_4

Over the last years the researchers' growing interest in imbalanced data contributed to considerable advancements in this field. Numerous methods were proposed to address this problem. They are grouped into three main categories [8, 21]:

- data-level techniques: adding the preliminary step of data processing - assumes mainly undersampling and oversampling,
- algorithm-level approaches: modifications of existing algorithms,
- cost-sensitive methods: combining data-level and algorithm-level techniques to set different misclassification costs.

In this paper we focus on data-level approaches: generating new minority class samples (oversampling) and introducing additional cleaning step (undersampling). Creating new examples of the minority class requires careful analysis of the data distribution. Random replication of the positive instances may lead to overfitting [8]. Furthermore, even applying methods like Synthetic Minority Oversampling Technique [5] (creation of new samples by interpolating several minority class examples that lie together) may not be sufficient for variety of real-life domains. Indeed, the main reason of difficulties in learning from imbalanced data is the complex distribution: existence of class overlapping, noise or small disjuncts [8, 11, 13, 15].

The VIS algorithm [4], incorporated into the proposed approach, addresses listed problems by applying dedicated mechanism for each specific group of minority class examples. Assigning objects into categories is based on their local characteristics. Although this solution considers additional difficulties, in case of eminently complex problems it may contribute to creation of noisy objects. Hence, the clearing mechanism is introduced as the second step of preprocessing. On the other hand, new preliminary step deals with uncertainty by relabeling ambiguous majority data. All negative (majority) instances belonging to the boundary region defined by the rough sets theory [16, 20] are relabeled to the positive class. Novel technique was developed to verify the impact of inconsistencies in data sets on the classifier performance. Only data sets described by nominal attributes were examined. However, discretization of attributes may allow applying proposed solutions to data including continuous values.

Although only the preprocessing techniques are discussed, we need to mention that there are numerous effective methods belonging to other categories, such as BRACID [14] (algorithm-level) or AdaC2 [21] (cost-sensitive).

2 Preprocessing Algorithms Overview

Since SMOTE algorithm [5] is based on the k-NN method, it is not deprived of some drawbacks related to the k-NN performance. Primarily, the k-NN technique is extremely sensitive to data complexity [9]. Especially class overlapping, noise or small disjuncts existing in imbalanced data negatively affects the performance of distance-based algorithms. Considering scenario of generating new minority examples by interpolating two minority instances that belong to different clusters (but were recognised as nearest neighbors), it is likely that new object will overlap with an example of majority class [19]. Hence, applying SMOTE to some domains may cause creating incorrect synthetic samples that fall into majority regions [2]. Methods like MSMOTE [12], Bordeline-SMOTE [10], VIS [4] were developed to address this problem. They assume that there are inconsistencies in data set and identify specific groups of minority class instances to select the most appropriate strategy of preprocessing.

On the other hand, there are numerous proposals of hybrid re-sampling methods. They combine oversampling with undersampling to ensure that improper newly-generated examples will be excluded before applying classifier. SMOTE-Tomek links and SMOTE-ENN [3] introduce the additional cleaning step to original SMOTE processing. The SMOTE-RSB$_*$ algorithm [17] eliminates overfitting by application of the rough sets theory and lower approximation of a subset. Defining the lower approximation of the minority class enables to remove generated synthetic samples that are presumably noise.

The rough set theory was also the inspiration for developing techniques discussed below. They are dedicated to data sets described by nominal attributes.

2.1   Rough Set Based Remove and Relabel Techniques

The method proposed in [18] considers applying the rough sets theory to obtain the inconsistencies in imbalanced data. The fundamental assumption of the rough set approach is that objects from a set U described by the same information are indiscernible. This main concept is source of the notion referred as indiscernibility relation $IND \subseteq U \times U$, defined on the set U. Let $[x]_{IND} = \{y \in U : (x,y) \in IND\}$ be an indiscernibility class, where $x \in U$. For any subset X of the set U it is possible to prepare the following characteristics [16]:

– the lower approximation of a set X: all examples that can be certainly classified as members of X with respect to IND;

$$\{x \in U : [x]_{IND} \subseteq X\}, \tag{1}$$

– the boundary region of a set X: all instances that are possibly members of X set with respect to IND;

$$\{x \in U : [x]_{IND} \cap X \neq \varnothing \,\&[x]_{IND} \nsubseteq X\}. \tag{2}$$

In described method two filtering techniques based on the presented rough set concepts were developed. Both of them require calculation of boundary region of minority class. Next step depends on the chosen method. The first one removes majority class examples belonging to the minority class boundary region that contains inconsistent objects. The second technique relabels all majority objects that belong to the minority class boundary region.

The Fig. 1 illustrates results of applying two described methods on artificial data. It also demonstrates the boundary region (with 16 objects) of minority class in the original data set (dashed line).

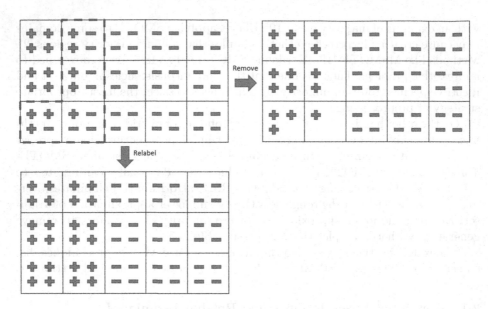

Fig. 1. Example of artificial data (60 objects, 15 indiscernibility classes, imbalance ratio $IR = 2.75$) described by two nominal attributes with three and five values. Data after filtering by the "Remove" technique ($IR = 2.25$). Data after applying "Relabel" technique ($IR = 1.5$).

2.2 Versatile Improved SMOTE and Rough Sets (VIS_RST)

The main idea of this new approach is to apply two preprocessing methods: oversampling and undersampling in order to generate minority class instances and ensure that no additional inconsistencies will be introduced to the original data set. This hybrid technique combines modified Versatile Improved SMOTE algorithm with the rough sets theory. Although the VIS method is considered as effective and flexible, introducing the step of removing noise from created minority examples may guarantee better results in classifying data with very complex distribution. The algorithm discussed in this paper is dedicated to data sets described by nominal attributes, however, it can be easily adjusted to the continuous data problems.

At the beginning of algorithm relabel technique is applied (described in Subsect. 2.1). It is based on rough set theory. Since numerous real-world data sets are imprecise (have nonempty boundary region), the relevancy of this process should be emphasized. Majority class samples belonging to the boundary region of minority class are transformed into minority class examples (their class attribute is modified). In other words, all examples that can be certainly classified neither as negative nor as positive samples are imposed to be considered as minority class members. Thus, the complexity of the problem becomes lower (by reducing inconsistencies) as well as the imbalance ratio is decreased.

Algorithm VIS_RST

INPUT: *DataSet*; Number of all instances S; Number of minority class samples M;
Number of nearest neighbors k

OUTPUT: *resultDataSet*: minority and majority class instances after preprocessing

1: Calculate the boundary region. Modify the class attribute of the majority samples belonging to the boundary region - relabel to minority class. Add the number of relabeled instances to the overall number of minority class examples M.

2: **for** $i \leftarrow 1$ **to** M **do**

3:     Calculate the distance between minority class objects and all other examples using kNN method.

4:     Calculate the number of nearest neighbors that belongs to the majority class and save this value in *majorityClassNeighbors* variable. Assign the positive instance i into one category (SAFE, DANGER or NOISE) considering the local characteristics (nearest neighbors):

5:     **if** $majorityClassNeighbors == k$ **then**

6:         $label[i] = NOISE$

7:     **else if** $majorityClassNeighbors < k/2$ **then**

8:         $label[i] = SAFE$

9:     **else if** $majorityClassNeighbors \geqslant k/2$ **then**

10:         $label[i] = DANGER$

11:     **end if**

12: **end for**

13: Calculate the total counts of objects belonging to each group and save these values in the following variables: *safe*, *danger*, *noise*. Based on these counts, choose the strategy (*mode*) of processing:

14: **if** $safe == 0$ **then**

15:     $mode := noSAFE$

16: **else if** $danger \geqslant 30\%M$ **then**

17:     $mode := HighComplexity$

18: **else**

19:     $mode := LowComplexity$

20: **end if**

21: Calculate the required number of minority class examples to create. The result save in N variable.

22: **for** $i \leftarrow 1$ **to** M **do**

23:     **if** $label \neq NOISE$ **then**

24:         Calculate the distance between minority class objects using kNN method, indexes of k nearest neighbors save in *nnarray* array.

25:         Create the synthetic examples following rules specified for the appropriate *mode*.

26:     **end if**

27: **end for**

28: **for** $i \leftarrow 1$ **to** N **do**

29:     Using calculations made at the beginning of algorithm, verify whether newly created synthetic object i belongs to the lower approximation of the minority class - if yes: add the example i to the *resultDataSet*. In the other case, remove generated sample i.

30: **end for**

In the next step minority data is categorized into three groups. To obtain the proper group for each sample the k-NN technique is applied. In order to consider both numeric and symbolic attributes the HVDM metric [23] was chosen to calculate distance between objects. The Heterogeneous Value Distance Metric is defined as:

$$HVDM(x, y) = \sqrt{\sum_{a=1}^{m} d_a(v, v')^2}$$

(3)

where x and y are the input vectors, m is the number of attributes, v and v' are the values of attribute a for object x and y respectively. The distance function for the attribute a is defined as:

$$d_a(v, v') = \begin{cases} 1, & \text{if } v \text{ or } v' \text{ is unknown} \\ normalized\_vdm_a(v, v'), & \text{if } a \text{ is nominal} \\ normalized\_diff_a(v, v'), & \text{if } a \text{ is linear} \end{cases}$$

(4)

The distance function consists of two other functions conformed to different kinds of attributes. Hence, the following function is defined for nominal features:

$$normalized\_vdm_a(v, v') = \sqrt{\sum_{c=1}^{C} \left| \frac{N_{v,c}}{N_v} - \frac{N_{v',c}}{N_{v'}} \right|^2}$$

(5)

where N_v is the number of instances in the training set that have value v for attribute a, $N_{v,c}$ is the number of instances that have value x for attribute a and output class c, C is the number of classes.

On the other hand, the function appropriate for linear attributes is defined as:

$$normalized\_diff_a(v, v') = \frac{|v - v'|}{4\sigma_a}$$

(6)

where σ_a is the standard deviation of values of attribute a.

Definition 1. *Depending on the class membership of the sample's k nearest neighbors, the following labels for the minority class are assigned:*

- *NOISE, when all of the k nearest neighbors represent the majority class,*
- *DANGER, if half or more than half of the k nearest neighbors belong to the majority class,*
- *SAFE, when more than half of the k nearest neighbors represent the same class as the example under consideration (namely the minority class).*

The mechanism of detecting within-class subconcepts enables to customize the oversampling strategy for each specific type of objects. Moreover, depending on the number of samples in mentioned groups two main modes of preprocessing minority data are proposed in modified VIS algorithm.

The first one, "HighComplexity", represents the case when the area surrounding class boundaries can be described as complex (at least 30 % of the minority class instances are the borderline ones – DANGER label) [15].

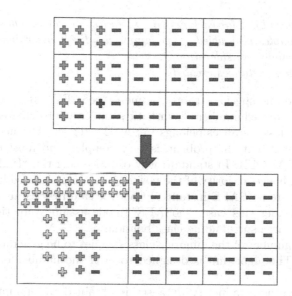

Fig. 2. Example of VIS_RSB preprocessing (relabel step is omitted): artificial data where minority objects are labeled as DANGER (orange), SAFE (green) and NOISE (red). The labels are assigned using $k = 3$ nearest neighbors and normalized_vdm metric. Grey objects are new minority class samples generated in respect of the assigned labels. (Color figure online)

Definition 2. *Since generating most of the minority synthetic samples in this region may lead to the overlapping effect, the following rules of creating new objects are applied for particular kinds of nominal data:*

- *DANGER: only one new sample is generated by replicating features of the minority instance under consideration,*
- *SAFE: as the SAFE objects are assumed to be the main representatives of the minority class, a plenty of new data is created in these homogeneous regions using majority vote of k nearest neighbors' features,*
- *NOISE: no new instances created (Fig. 2).*

The second mode, "LowComplexity", is appropriate for less complex problems.

Definition 3. *When the number of minority samples labeled as DANGER does not exceed 30 % of all minority class examples, the processing is performed according to the approach specified below:*

- *DANGER: many objects are created, because not sufficient number of minority class examples in this specific area may be dominated in the learning process by the majority class samples. Newly generated sample attributes' values are obtained by the majority vote of k nearest neighbors' features,*

- *SAFE: one new object for each existing instance is created. Therefore, number of SAFE examples is doubled. New sample has the same values of attributes as the object under consideration,*
- *NOISE: no new instances created.*

There is also one special strategy, namely "noSAFE". It was developed to ensure that the required number of synthetic samples will be created, even as any of the minority class instances belongs to SAFE category. Absence of the SAFE examples indicates that the problem is very complex and most of the objects are labeled as DANGER. In standard way of processing the "HighComplexity" mode is chosen, hence majority of the new objects are generated in safe regions. However, there are no SAFE instances, thus the safe regions are not specified. In order to consider this case, "noSAFE" mode assumes creation of all new examples in the area surrounding class boundaries.

The overall number of the minority class samples to be generated is obtained automatically. The algorithm is designed to even the number of objects from both classes.

The final synthetic minority data set is obtained by eliminating samples considered as noise. The algorithm inspired by rough set notions is applied to indicate which newly created examples are similar to the majority objects. Since only nominal attributes are considered in this analysis, the boundary region of the minority class is calculated. All synthetic samples that belong to the boundary region are removed. This additional cleaning step ensures that the generated data set is deprived of inconsistent objects. It is essential to select only these samples that are certainly members of the minority class.

3 Experiments

Six data sets were selected to perform experiments. All of them (except didactic) originally came from the UCI repository [22], but after conversions like adjusting them to the two-class problem they were published in Keel-dataset repository [1]. Only data sets described by the nominal attributes were chosen. They are presented in Table 1 (IR indicates the imbalance ratio).

Table 1. Characteristics of evaluated data sets

Dataset	Objects	Attributes	IR	Boundary region
dermatology-6	358	34	16.90	Empty
flare-F	1066	11	23.79	Nonempty
lymphography-normal-fibrosis	148	18	23.67	Empty
zoo-3	101	16	19.20	Empty
car_good	1728	6	24.04	Empty
didactic (see Fig. 1)	60	2	2.75	Nonempty

The aim of this experiment was to prepare comparison of four preprocessing methods. The classification without any re-sampling step was performed to establish a reference point for evaluation of algorithms. The following assumptions were made considering SMOTE and VIS_RST techniques:

- the number of nearest neighbors (k) was set to 5,
- the HVDM distance metric was applied,
- the imbalance ratio after generating new samples was 1.0.

The results of classification were evaluated by five measures:

- accuracy (Q) – the percentage of all correct predictions (both minority and majority class examples are considered),
- sensitivity (TP_{rate}) – the percentage of positive instances correctly classified,
- specificity (TN_{rate}) – the percentage of properly classified objects from the majority class.
- F-measure – the average of sensitivity and precision. Precision is the number of correctly identified positive samples divided by the number of all instances classified as positive (both properly and erroneously),

Table 2. Classification results for the selected UCI datasets: Q – accuracy, TP_{rate} – rate of true positives, TN_{rate} – rate of true negatives, F – F measure, AUC – area under the curve.

Method	Q	TP_{rate}	TN_{rate}	F	AUC	Q	TP_{rate}	TN_{rate}	F	AUC
	dermatology-6					flare-F				
noPRE	99.44	95.00	99.70	0.95	97.35	94.65	11.63	98.14	0.15	54.89
SMOTE	99.85	100.00	99.70	1.00	99.85	97.26	96.38	98.14	0.97	97.26
VIS_RST	99.70	99.70	99.70	1.00	99.70	98.48	99.16	97.80	0.98	98.48
Remove	99.44	95.00	99.70	0.95	97.35	96.08	37.21	98.74	0.45	67.98
Relabel	99.44	95.00	99.70	0.95	97.35	97.09	87.61	98.22	0.86	92.91
	lymphography-normal-fibrosis					zoo-3				
noPRE	97.97	50.00	100.00	0.67	75.00	94.06	40.00	96.88	0.40	68.44
SMOTE	98.94	97.89	100.00	0.99	98.94	97.40	96.88	97.92	0.97	97.40
VIS_RST	98.24	97.89	98.59	0.98	98.24	97.40	97.92	96.88	0.97	97.40
Remove	97.97	50.00	100.00	0.67	75.00	94.06	40.00	96.88	0.40	68.44
Relabel	97.97	50.00	100.00	0.67	75.00	94.06	40.00	96.88	0.40	68.44
	car_good					didactic				
noPRE	98.38	73.91	99.40	0.78	86.66	83.33	68.75	88.64	0.69	78.69
SMOTE	99.43	99.64	99.22	0.99	99.43	89.77	88.64	90.91	0.90	89.77
VIS_RST	99.16	99.52	98.79	0.99	99.16	100.00	100.00	100.00	1.00	100.00
Remove	98.38	73.91	99.40	0.78	86.66	100.00	100.00	100.00	1.00	100.00
Relabel	98.38	73.91	99.40	0.78	86.66	100.00	100.00	100.00	1.00	100.00

- AUC - area under the ROC curve. The Receiver Operating Characteristics (ROC) graphic depicts dependency between TP_{rate} and FP_{rate}. The FP_{rate} means the percentage of negative examples misclassified.

The AdaBoost.M1 algorithm [7] with decision trees C4.5 as weak learners was applied as the classifier. This technique represents the group of ensemble methods. The main purpose of combining decisions of multiple classifiers to obtain the aggregated prediction is improvement of generalization [21]. A five-folds cross validation was performed. The final experiments' results (presented in Table 2) are the average values of results from five iterations of processing.

Results of these experiments show that the higher complexity of analysed data set is, the better outcomes from applying proposed technique are. VIS_RST algorithm indicates that three real-world data sets are the most complex: flare-F, zoo-3 and car-good. One of these data sets, namely flare-F, has nonempty boundary region. Method proposed in this paper outperformed other techniques for this complex example. In all experiments both SMOTE and VIS_RST achieve higher values of AUC measure than the classification without preprocessing step. Remove and Relabel filters perform better only in case of nonempty boundary region. Relabel technique may be considered as more effective. It is worth noting that all minority samples generated by the VIS_RST method were in the lower approximation. Therefore, undersampling cleaning step was not needed.

4   Conclusions and Future Research

Firstly, the experiments revealed that the new VIS_RST method is comparable to the SMOTE algorithm when applied to data sets described only by the nominal features. The AUC measure of VIS_RST was higher for the flare-F data set. Proposed algorithm outperformed other techniques when evaluated data sets had nonempty boundary regions (flare-F and didactic). Secondly, the Relabel filtering technique performed better than the Remove approach for data set which has the nonempty boundary region (flare-F). In future research the performance of the proposed algorithm adjusted for the Big Data may be investigated. The application of the MapReduce paradigm [6] seems to be promising solution for large imbalance data problem.

Acknowledgements. The research is supported by the Polish National Science Centre under the grant 2012/07/B/ST6/01504.

References

1. Alcala-Fdez, J., Fernandez, A., Luengo, J., Derrac, J., Garca, S., Sanchez, L., Herrera, F.: KEEL data-mining software tool: data set repository, integration of algorithms and experimental analysis framework. J. Mult.-Valued Log. Soft Comput. **17**(2–3), 255–287 (2011)

2. Barua, S., Islam, M.M., Murase, K.: A novel synthetic minority oversampling technique for imbalanced data set learning. In: Lu, B.-L., Zhang, L., Kwok, J. (eds.) ICONIP 2011, Part II. LNCS, vol. 7063, pp. 735–744. Springer, Heidelberg (2011)
3. Batista, G.E.A.P.A., Prati, R.C., Monard, M.C.: A study of the behavior of several methods for balancing machine learning training data. SIGKDD Explor. Newsl. 6(1), 20–29 (2004)
4. Borowska, K., Topczewska, M.: New data level approach for imbalanced data classification improvement. In: Burduk, R., Jackowski, K., Kurzyński, M., Woźniak, M., Żołnierek, A. (eds.) Proceedings of the 9th International Conference on Computer Recognition Systems CORES 2015. Advances in Intelligent Systems and Computing, vol. 403, pp. 283–294. Springer, Switzerland (2016)
5. Chawla, N.V., Bowyer, K.W., Hall, L.O., Kegelmeyer, W.P.: SMOTE: synthetic minority over-sampling technique. J. Artif. Intell. Res. 16(1), 321–357 (2002)
6. Dean, J., Ghemawat, S.: MapReduce: simplified data processing on large clusters. Commun. ACM 51(1), 107–113 (2008)
7. Freund, Y., Schapire, R.E.: Experiments with a new boosting algorithm. In: Machine Learning: Proceedings of the Thirteenth International Conference, pp. 148–156 (1996)
8. Galar, M., Fernandez, A., Barrenechea, E., Bustince, H., Herrera, F.: A review on ensembles for the class imbalance problem: bagging-, boosting-, and hybrid-based approaches. IEEE Trans. Syst. Man Cybern. Part C (Appl. Rev.) 42(4), 463–484 (2012)
9. Garca, V., Mollineda, R.A., Snchez, J.S.: On the k-NN performance in a challenging scenario of imbalance and overlapping. Pattern Anal. Appl. 11(3–4), 269–280 (2008)
10. Han, H., Wang, W.-Y., Mao, B.-H.: Borderline-SMOTE: a new over-sampling method in imbalanced data sets learning. In: Huang, D.-S., Zhang, X.-P., Huang, G.-B. (eds.) ICIC 2005. LNCS, vol. 3644, pp. 878–887. Springer, Heidelberg (2005)
11. He, H., Garcia, E.A.: Learning from imbalanced data. IEEE Trans. Knowl. Data Eng. 21(9), 1263–1284 (2009)
12. Hu, S., Liang, Y., Ma, L., He, Y.: MSMOTE: improving classification performance when training data is imbalanced, computer science and engineering. In: Second International Workshop on WCSE 2009, Qingdao, pp. 13–17 (2009)
13. Jo, T., Japkowicz, N.: Class imbalances versus small disjuncts. SIGKDD Explor. Newsl. 6(1), 40–49 (2004)
14. Napierała, K., Stefanowski, J.: BRACID: a comprehensive approach to learning rules from imbalanced data. J. Intell. Inf. Syst. 39, 335–373 (2012)
15. Napierała, K., Stefanowski, J., Wilk, S.: Learning from imbalanced data in presence of noisy and borderline examples. In: Kryszkiewicz, M., Ramanna, S., Jensen, R., Hu, Q., Szczuka, M. (eds.) RSCTC 2010. LNCS, vol. 6086, pp. 158–167. Springer, Heidelberg (2010)
16. Pawlak, Z., Skowron, A.: Rudiments of rough sets. Inf. Sci. 177(1), 3–27 (2007)
17. Ramentol, E., Caballero, Y., Bello, R., Herrera, F.: SMOTE-RSB$_*$: a hybrid preprocessing approach based on oversampling and undersampling for high imbalanced data-sets using SMOTE and rough sets theory. Knowl. Inf. Syst. 33(2), 245–265 (2011). Springer
18. Stefanowski, J., Wilk, S.: Rough sets for handling imbalanced data: combining filtering and rule-based classifiers. Fundam. Inf. 72(1–3), 379–391 (2006)
19. Stefanowski, J., Wilk, S.: Selective pre-processing of imbalanced data for improving classification performance. In: Song, I.-Y., Eder, J., Nguyen, T.M. (eds.) DaWaK 2008. LNCS, vol. 5182, pp. 283–292. Springer, Heidelberg (2008)

20. Stepaniuk, J.: Rough-Granular Computing in Knowledge Discovery and Data Mining. Springer, Heidelberg (2008)
21. Sun, Y., Kamel, M.S., Wong, A.K.C., Wang, Y.: Cost-sensitive boosting for classification of imbalanced data. Pattern Recogn. **40**, 3358–3378 (2007)
22. UC Irvine Machine Learning Repository. http://archive.ics.uci.edu/ml/. Accessed 10 Apr 2016
23. Wilson, D.R., Martinez, T.R.: Improved heterogeneous distance functions. J. Artif. Intell. Res. **6**, 1–34 (1997)

Embedding the *V*-Detector Algorithm in FPGA

Maciej Brzozowski and Andrzej Chmielewski[✉]

Faculty of Computer Science, Białystok University of Technology,
ul. Wiejska 45a, 15-331 Białystok, Poland
{m.brzozowski,a.chmielewski}@pb.edu.pl

Abstract. The *b-v* model is a hybrid immune-based approach for detecting anomalies in high-dimensional datasets. It is based on a negative selection algorithm and utilizes both types of detectors to achieve better results in comparison to single detection models. Also, it is an interesting alternative to well known traditional, statistical approaches, because only positive (*self*) examples are required at the learning stage. As a result, it is able to detect even unnkown or never met anomalies and this fact is one of the most attractive features of this approach. However, especially in the case of on-line classification, not only high accuracy but also high efficiency is needed. Thus, we propose to embed some complex tasks in a reprogrammable FPGA to offload CPU and speed up the classification process. This paper presents a hardware implementation of the *V*-Detector algorithm, which is the most complex and time consuming part of *b-v* model.

Keywords: Artificial Immune System · Anomaly detection · FPGA

1   Introduction

An efficiency of *Natural Immune System* (NIS) is unsurpassed for all protection systems and verified over millions of years by living organisms. It is a very complex system focused on discrimination between own cells (called *self*) and pathogens (called *nonself*), which should be detected and eliminated. A nice feature of NISis that it does not need any example of *nonself* samples to detect them as only the information about its own cells is sufficient. Hence, every organism has a unique "protection system", capable of detecting even a new type of attack and tolerates only own cells which form its body.

This dedicated and highly efficient protection system against various types of pathogens was an inspiration for developing *Artificial Immune Systems* (AIS). Within this domain, many types of algorithms were proposed, mainly focused on computer system security solutions. However, the most popular is *Negative Selection Algorithm (NSA)* [7] with the ability of detecting novel, never met samples, a counterpart of pathogens. Based on deep investigations with various types of large and high-dimensional datasets, a solution called the *b-v* model [6] was proposed. It minimizes the problem of scalability, by involving both types of receptors: *b-* and *v*-detectors. This hybrid approach, presented by conducting

© IFIP International Federation for Information Processing 2016
Published by Springer International Publishing Switzerland 2016. All Rights Reserved
K. Saeed and W. Homenda (Eds.): CISIM 2016, LNCS 9842, pp. 43–54, 2016.
DOI: 10.1007/978-3-319-45378-1_5

numerous experiments, provides much better results in comparison to single detection models as well as traditional, statistical approaches, even though only positive (*self*) examples are required at the learning stage. It makes this approach an interesting alternative for well known classification algorithms, like SVM, k-nearest neighbours, etc. The b-v model is briefly described in Subsect. 2.3.

However, there are lots of domains where not only high accuracy is crucial. In some cases, very high efficiency is also required to examine all samples in a short time. On-line classification systems like firewalls, intruder detection and prevention systems, etc. are examples of applications which usually operate on huge amounts of data and over-lengthy delays, related with data processing, are unacceptable.

Thus, every way to increase the speed of detection process is highly desirable. One of them is embedding algorithms in a reprogrammable FPGA (Field Programmable Gate Array). Our preliminary results [3] conducted using b-detectors, have shown while generating them as well as during censoring samples, which are the most complex operations, can be parallelized and additionally computed without CPU utilization. As a result, censoring of millions samples took only a few ticks of the clock (a few nanoseconds).

In this paper we present our approach to embedding the V-Detector algorithm in FPGA as being a very important part of b-v model. All samples not recognized by very fast b-detectors are passed to V-Detector which is responsible for the final decision: censored sample is *self* or *nonself*. It operates on real-valued detectors (called v-detectors), in contrast to fast b-detectors represented as a binary string. Hence, this step is the most complex and time consuming in the whole process of detecting anomalies, especially in the case of high-dimensional datasets. Hardware implementation of this algorithm should significantly increase its efficiency.

2 Negative Selection

The NSA, proposed by Forrest *et al.* [8], is inspired by the process of thymocytes (i.e. young T-lymphocytes) maturation: only those lymphocytes survive which do not recognize any *self* molecules.

Formally, let $\mathcal{U}$ be a universe, i.e. the set of all possible molecules. The subset $\mathcal{S}$ of $\mathcal{U}$ represents the collection of all *self* molecules and its complement $\mathcal{N}$ in $\mathcal{U}$ represents all *nonself* molecules. Let $\mathfrak{D} \subset \mathcal{U}$ stand for a set of detectors and let $match(d, u)$ be a function (or a procedure) specifying if a detector $d \in \mathfrak{D}$ recognizes the molecule $u \in \mathcal{U}$. Usually, $match(d, u)$ is modelled by a distance metric or a similarity measure, i.e. we say that $match(d, u) = \texttt{true}$ only if $dist(d, u) \leq \delta$, where $dist$ is a distance and δ is a pre-specified threshold. Various matching function are discussed e.g. in [9,11].

The problem relies upon construction the set $\mathfrak{D}$ in such a way that

$$match(d, u) = \begin{cases} \texttt{false} & \text{if } u \in \mathcal{S} \\ \texttt{true} & \text{if } u \in \mathcal{N} \end{cases} \qquad (1)$$

for any detector $d \in \mathfrak{D}$.

A naive solution to this problem, implied by the biological mechanism of negative selection, consists of five steps:

(a) Initialize $\mathfrak{D}$ as empty set, $\mathfrak{D} = \emptyset$.
(b) Generate randomly a detector d.
(c) If $math(d, s) = \texttt{false}$ for all $s \in \mathcal{S}$, add d to the set $\mathfrak{D}$.
(d) Repeat steps (b) and (c) until the sufficient number of detectors will be generated.

A perfect *NSA* should cover whole $\mathcal{N}$ space by sets of detectors to detect all *nonself* samples. However, as shown by numerous experiments, scalability is a key issue here, regardless of the representation of samples used [6,12]. This problem is also discussed in this article.

2.1 Detectors and Algorithms

Generally, there are two type of receptors used:

- b-detectors - represented as binary string (Hamming space),
- v-detectors - represented as real-valued vectors.

For each of them, many algorithms with different matching rules were proposed. For binary representation, the most popular were presented in [2,7]. In the case of real-valued vectors, V-Detector algorithm [10] is the most known. Hardware implementation of this algorithm, described in details in Subsect. 2.2, is the main subject of this article.

Because, neither b- nor v-detectors were not capable to detect anomalies to a satisfactory degree, a b-v model here was proposed [6] (see Subsect. 2.3), which used both types of detectors to overcome the problem with scalability. As shown in the performed experiments, it provides much better results in comparison to single detection models as well as in comparison to traditional, statistical approaches, even though only positive self examples are required at the learning stage.

2.2 Real-Valued Representation

To overcome scaling problems inherent in Hamming space, Ji and Dasgupta proposed a real-valued *NSA*, termed *V-Detector* [10].

It operates on normalized vectors of real-valued attributes; each vector can be viewed as a point in the d-dimensional unit hypercube, $\mathcal{U} = [0, 1]^d$. Each *self* sample, $s_i \in \mathcal{S}$, is represented as a hypersphere $s_i = (c_i, r_s)$, $i = 1, \dots, l$, where l is the number of *self* samples, $c_i \in \mathcal{U}$ is the center of s_i and r_s is its radius. It is assumed that r_s is identical for all s_i's. Each point $u \in \mathcal{U}$ inside any *self* hypersphere s_i is considered as a *self* element.

The detectors d_j are represented as hyperspheres also: $d_j = (c_j, r_j)$, $j = 1, \dots, p$ where p is the number of detectors. In contrast to *self* elements, the radius r_j is not fixed but it is computed as the Euclidean distance from a randomly chosen center c_j to the nearest *self* element (this distance must be greater than r_s, otherwise the detector is not created). Formally, we define r_j as

$$r_j = \min_{1 \le i \le l} dist(c_j, c_i) - r_s. \tag{2}$$

The algorithm terminates if a predefined number p_{max} of detectors is generated or the space $\mathcal{U}\backslash\mathcal{S}$ is sufficiently well covered by these detectors; the degree of coverage is measured by the parameter co – see [10] for the algorithm and its parameters description.

In its original version, the V-Detector algorithm employs Euclidean distance to measure proximity between a pair of samples. Therefore, *self* samples and the detectors are hyperspheres (see Fig. 1(a)). Formally, Euclidean distance is a special case of Minkowski norm L_m, where $m \ge 1$, which is defined as:

$$L_m(\mathrm{x,y}) = \left(\sum_{i=1}^{d} |x_i - y_i|^m \right)^{\frac{1}{m}}, \tag{3}$$

where $\mathrm{x} = (x_1, x_2, \ldots, x_d)$ and $\mathrm{y} = (y_1, y_2, \ldots, y_d)$ are points in $\Re^d$.

Particularly, L_2-norm is Euclidean distance, L_1-norm is Manhattan distance, and L_∞ is Tchebyshev distance.

However, Aggarwal *et al.* [1] observed that L_m-norm loses its discrimination abilities when the dimension d and the values of m increase. Thus, for example, Euclidean distance has the best (among L_m-norms) metrics when $d \le 5$. For higher dimensions, the metrics with lower m (i.e. Manhattan distance) should be used.

Based on this observation, Aggarwal introduced *fractional distance metrics* with $0 < m < 1$, arguing that such a choice is more appropriate for high-dimensional spaces. Experiments, reported in [5], partially confirmed the efficiency of this proposition. For $0.5 < m < 1$, more samples were detected, in

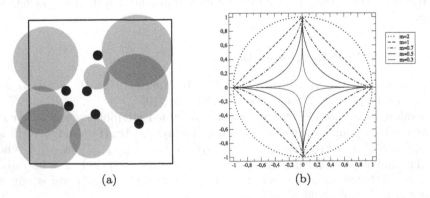

Fig. 1. (a) Example of performance V-Detector algorithm for 2-dimensional problem. Black and grey circles denotes *self* samples and *v*-detectors, respectively. (b) Unit spheres for selected L_m norms in 2D.

comparison to L_1 and L_2 norms. However, for $m < 0.5$ the efficiency rapidly decreased and for $m = 0.2$, none samples were detected. Moreover, these experiments also confirmed a trade-off between efficiency, time complexity and m. For fractional norms, the algorithm runs slower for lower m values; for $L_{0.5}$ the learning phase was even 2–3 times longer than for L_2.

Another consequence of applying fractional metrics for V-Detector algorithm is modification of the shape of detectors. Figure 1(b) presents the unit spheres for selected L_m-norms in 2D with $m = 2$ (outer most), $1, 0.7, 0.5, 0.3$ (inner most).

2.3   Brief Description of the b-v Model

The b-v model [6] is the only NSA, involving both types of detectors, namely b- and v-detectors. It was designed for anomaly detection in high-dimensional data, which are difficult to analyze due to the lack of appropriate similarity metrics which enable the covering of space $\mathcal{N}$ in sufficient degree and reasonable time. One of the important features of the b-v model is its ability to minimize the overlapping regions between sets of detectors. We do not expect that b-detectors cover the space $\mathcal{N}$ in sufficient degree, as it can consume too much time. On the other hand, fewer numbers of v-detectors should be generated because some part of space $\mathcal{N}$ is already covered by b-detectors. The main idea of this algorithm is depicted in Fig. 2.

Here, the b-detectors, as those providing fast detection, are used for preliminary filtering of samples. The samples which did not activate any of the b-detectors are censored by v-detectors next. As a result the overall duration of classification could be significantly reduced as fewer v-detectors were needed to cover space $\mathcal{N}$. Hence, this model is more efficient for on-line classification systems in comparison to standard negative selection approaches which are based only on one type of detectors.

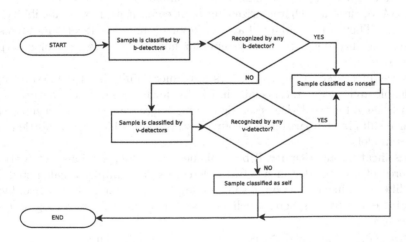

Fig. 2. Flow diagram of the classification process for b-v model.

Embedding the V-Detector algorithm in FPGA (see Sect. 3) should significantly affect the efficiency of the entire b-v model. This also opens the possibility of applying them in other domains, including devices used in the Internet of Things technology.

3 Hardware Approach to V-Detector Algorithm

As was already mentioned, classification with the V-Detector algorithm is a very complex and time consuming process because of its high complexity of performed calculations that need to be done on real-valued vectors. Time of classification of a single sample directly depends on its dimensionality ($\Re^d$) and number of detectors, because for each single sample, there is a need to calculate distance to generated detectors from set $\mathfrak{D}$. The described process, of course, might be divided into sub tasks to parallelize classification. As a result, the duration of this process should be significantly decreased. However, when calculations are performed on CPUs or GPUs processors, its efficiency is strictly restricted by number of processors and numbers of its cores.

One of the solutions, corresponding to the above restrictions, are programmable devices, especially Field Programmable Gate Array (FPGA) devices, providing a high performance, low power consumption and relatively low price in comparison to CPU/FPU solutions. FPGA is mainly designed to parallelize computational tasks. Therefore, it might be used in projects where the main indicator is performance. Designers equipped FPGA devices in specialized IP (Intellectual Property) blocks like multipliers, pre-adders and accumulators for increasing the number of computations per second and other more complicated blocks like embedded CPUs, DSP, Ethernet Physical Interfaces, PCI Express, DRAM controllers and many others. Moreover, some FPGA devices allow for the partial reconfiguration (reprogramming) during its operation - helping the system to adopt to rapidly a changing environment.

FPGA devices are characterized by high computing power, flexibility and scalability. They can be adapted as a base for on-line classification systems eg. firewalls and intruder detection systems for home use as well as for enterprise solutions.

As was presented in [3], b-detectors were successfully implemented in reprogrammable architectures, especially in FPGA devices. Hence, it is natural to try to do the same for the V-Detector algorithm, where we could expect more spectacular results in comparison to a software approach, which was a bottleneck in the b-v model.

Classification algorithm will be explained in further sections but firstly we must present how the distance between detectors and samples is calculated. The main difference, in comparison to software implementation, is the usage of hypercubes, instead of hyperspheres. Such a shape is more suitable for reprogrammable architecture.

Each *self* sample, $s_i \in \mathcal{S}$, is represented as a hypercube $s_i = (c_i, l_s)$, $i = 1, \ldots, l$, where l is the number of *self* samples, $c_i \in \mathcal{U}$ is the center of s_i and l_s

is half of the length of its side (edge). It is assumed, that l_s is identical for all *self* samples. Similar to software approach, each hypercube $u \in \mathcal{U}$ inside any *self* hypercube s_i is considered as a *self* element.

The detectors d_j are represented as hypercubes also: $d_j = (c_j, l_j), j = 1, \ldots, p$ where p is the number of detectors. In contrast to *self* elements, the half length of its side l_j is not fixed, but it is computed as the distance from a randomly chosen center c_j to the nearest *self* element (this distance must be greater than l_s, otherwise detector is not created).

Formally, we define l_j as:

$$l_j = \min_{1 \leq i \leq l} dist(c_j, c_i) - l_s, \tag{4}$$

where distance between two centers of hypercubes x and y is defined as:

$$dist(x, y) = \min_{1 \leq i \leq d} |x_i - y_i|. \tag{5}$$

Each hypercube is axis-aligned. It means, rotation of hypercube is not allowed. Two hypercubes are not overlapping when:

$$\min_{1 \leq i \leq d} |x_i - y_i| > l_x + l_y. \tag{6}$$

Figure 3 presents d-dimensional hypercubes. In Fig. 3(b) two detectors $d_1 = ([0], 1)$, $d_2 = ([5], 1)$ in one dimensional space are marked (grey colour). In Fig. 3(a) two detectors $d_1 = ([1, 3], 1)$ and $d_2 = ([3, 5], 1)$ are overlapping. In Fig. 3(c): $d_1 = ([1, 1, 1], 0)$, $d_2 = ([0, 6, 7], 0)$, $d_3 = ([5, 5, 0], 0)$ and

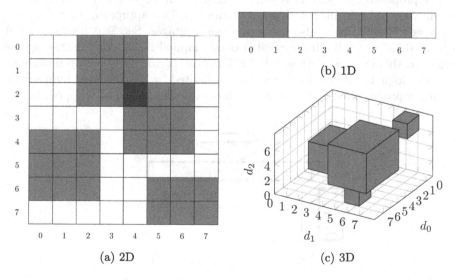

(a) 2D   (b) 1D   (c) 3D

Fig. 3. Example of axis-aligned v-detector hypercube in $\Re^d$.

$d_4 = ([5, 5, 5], 1)$ are examples in three dimensional space. In V-Detector classification process it is sufficient to state that sample overlap with one of the detectors. There is no need to state that detector includes the sample (sample overlaps a whole over the detector or overlaps its partially). In both cases, the sample should be rejected.

3.1 Emebedded V-Detector - The Fastest Approach

The first of the proposed solutions, denoted as V-Detector-$HFast$, for reprogrammable architectures holds the entire $\mathfrak{D}$ in target device resources. As a result, it should maximize the speed of classification process for V-Detector algorithm. The base concept allows the determination of distance between the single sample and the entire set of $\mathfrak{D}$ in one cycle of the designed system. Moreover, the classification process does not depend to such an extent on the number of dimensions as in the classical approach. Here, the universe set $\mathcal{U}$ is represented by bitmap with detectors modeled as hypercubes. The number of distinguish samples (represented as vectors) depends on the size of used internal memory.

Memory and other arithmetic operations are mapped into logic elements available on the reprogrammable device, in our case FPGA. For each dimension, a decoding vector responsible for choosing data from set $\mathfrak{D}$ is created, depending on the sample's coordinates. For each coordinate logical products are created of decoding vectors (for all dimensions) and its corresponding memory values. In the last step, the number of '1' in the logical product is counted. If this value is not equal to 0, it means, sample overlaps at least one detector. Figure 4 shows a simplified diagram of V-Detector (for one dimension) based on internal FPGA memory.

The proposed solutions for reprogrammable architectures is incredibly fast in classification of both single and group of samples. This approach, apart from the high-speed classification, also has some disadvantages. Set $\mathfrak{D}$ is held in FPGA internal RAM (very limited capacity) or is mapped in the logical area on the device. In this case, a synthesized classification algorithm is highly demanded for device logic resources. Therefore, we are limited by logic element numbers on the target programmable device, in which one, design has to be mapped. In this

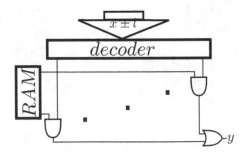

Fig. 4. V-Detector - the fastest approach for reprogrammable architectures.

case we have to choose a target device with appropriate logic elements overhead. The lack of adequate number of logical resources may lead to a decrease in the number of analyzed dimensions, or enforces the reduction of the resolution of the analyzed samples.

3.2 Embedded V-Detector - Approach Based on External Memory

The presented classification solution, denoted as V-Detector–$HRAM$, is based only on the resources provided by the target device, is characterized by constraints on the system resolution. One of the methods to increase the resolution of the system is to move the set of detectors from the internal device resources to external memory. In this case, part of the available resources has to be destined to calculate the read/write memory cell addresses. The designed component informs which memory lines are needed in the calcification process of each sample and chooses only the appropriate cells from them. The proposed solution is slowed down by time needed by external memory to perform write and read operations compared to the approach presented in Subsect. 3.1. When the system is properly scaled to expected samples (in numbers of dimensions and numbers of bits per dimension) i.e. $l_s = 0$ (is small as possible) classification process should need only one read operation from external memory.

For DE2-115 Development Board we were able to achieve a resolution of 2^{30} distinguishable samples.

4   Hardware V-Detector Approaches Evaluation

In the proposed solutions, the learning phase is simplified, in comparison to software implementation. The optimization process of $\mathfrak{D}$ set is not needed because its size does not affect the duration of classification of a single sample. Bitmap hypercube representation of $\mathcal{U}$ is constant and therefore the number of detectors has no impact on its size. Classification time is shorter because the designed components consider calculations only in the nearest surroundings of the sample. All the necessary calculations are performed at the level of the FPGA. Therefore, the designed component may process large amounts of data in a single period of time.

Both presented solutions were implemented and synthesized for Altera Cyclone IVE EP4CE115F29C7 device equipped on the DE2-115 Development and Education Board by using Quartus II 15.0. Figure 5(a) shows simplified diagrams of the actual designs. The core of the solution is Nios II processor with connected components via an Avalon bus. In the first stage, components were tested as operated independently. In the second stage, components were integrated into the system (Fig. 5(a)). In the future, both systems, V-Detector based on internal and on external RAM cells, will be equipped with two Ethernet interfaces 10/100/1000 and tested in a network environment (Fig. 5(b)). Another possibility of the further development is integrated design with PCI Express and use also of the desktop computer resources.

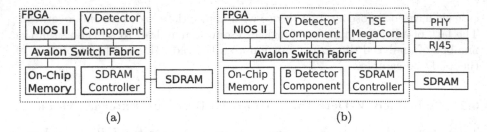

Fig. 5. System diagrams for FPGA device.

To measure performance (profiling) of the designed systems we used Altera Megacore Performance Counter Unit. The designed system was based on Nios II worked with 100 MHz frequency.

As was already mentioned in Subsect. 3.1, the dimensionality of samples which can be processed by V-Detector–$HFast$ algorithm is highly restricted by resources availability in target devices. In the case of Altera Cyclone IVE EP4CE115F29C7, which was used in our experiments, internal memory capacity is limited to 3888 kb. Such a restriction forced us to select a rather small dataset for testing. We chose the most popular dataset used for classification purposes, namely $Iris$, which consists of only 150 samples. Each of 4 attributes was represented by integer value from the range 0–3 (2 bits). Detectors were generated, assuming that one class of thew iris plant is regarded as set S during the learning stage. In all cases, samples were successfully classified. The main advantage of the hardware approaches was the duration of classification, and was presented in Table 1.

We can compare those values with the average time of classification achieved for software implementation executed on a PC equipped with Intel i7-3770 processor (8 cores) 3.4 GHz with 16 GB RAM. In this case, process censoring all samples took about 3 ms. It is about 20 times slower than V-Detector–$HFast$, and about 6 times slower than V-Detector–$HRAM$. Taking into consideration that the frequency of the CPU on the PC computer was 340 times higher, it can be easily computed how fast the hardware approach is.

Table 1. Comparison of average duration of classification process for V-Detector–$HFast$ and V-Detector–$HRAM$ algorithms for different number of bits per dimension (n) for $Iris$ dataset.

	$HFast$		$HRAM$			
	$n = 2$		$n = 2$		$n = 6$	
	time [ms]	time (clock)	time [ms]	time (clock)	time [ms]	time (clock)
Iris-setosa	0.18	17914	0.58	58181	0.58	58181
Iris-versicolor	0.18	17914	0.58	58061	0.58	58061
Iris-virginica	0.18	17914	0.58	58038	0.58	58038

Table 2. Comparison of average duration of classification process for software implementation and V-Detector–$HRAM$ algorithm applied to randomly selected subsets for KDD Cup 1999 dataset.

Software	$HRAM$	
time [ms]	time [ms]	time (clock)
106 000	45	4483698

Table 1 contains also the results of other classification experiments with the same dataset. Here, samples were represented as 4 dimension vectors with 6 bits per dimension. For V-Detector–$HFast$ this design was too big to map into available architecture. Thus experiments were conducted only for the V-Detector–$HRAM$ algorithm for which the classification process took 0.58 ms (the same time as in first experiment). Here, classification strictly depends on access time to external memory (read/write data operation). It is clear that all operations performed on internal resources are faster than on external memory. The increase in the number of dimensions does not significantly affect the time of classification. The most important is a properly scaled system (sample size).

However, the most spectacular results were obtained for some subsets of KDD Cup 1999 from UCI Machine Learning Repository. This database was too big for the current implementation of V-Detector–$HRAM$. Hence, only the samples of the ICMP protocol were used for tests with randomly selected 7 of 41 attributes (each coded on 4 bits). In this way, our test set contains 1074994 unique samples and an average of 683 detectors were used. During the tests we could observe, the duration of classification was more than 2000 times faster in the case of hardware implementation (see Table 2).

5   Conclusions

In this paper we present our approach to hardware implementation of the V-Detector algorithm, which is the most computationally complex part of b-v model. Our preliminary promising results with b-detectors was a first step for building a very fast classification system embedded in reprogrammable devices. To achieve this goal, we had to implement also the V-Detector algorithm, which operates on computationally complex real-valued vectors.

Here, we presented two different possible approaches, called V-Detector–$HFast$ and V-Detector–$HRAM$. Both of them have some disadvantages, which are mainly related with the limitation of used memory. However, V-Detector–$HRAM$ can be extended to be used with external memory, which can make this approach possible to be applied for much bigger datasets than those used in the experiments described in this paper.

The performed experiments confirmed that hardware implementations can significantly speed up the classification process, which usually is the most crucial in classification systems. Obtained preliminary results are a good starting point to build a hardware version of the b-v-model, dedicated for an on-line immune-based intrusion detection system.

Acknowledgment. This research was partially supported by the grants S/WI/3/13 and MB/WI/1/2014 of the Polish Ministry of Science and Higher Education.

References

1. Aggarwal, C.C., Hinneburg, A., Keim, D.A.: On the surprising behavior of distance metrics in high dimensional space. In: Van den Bussche, J., Vianu, V. (eds.) ICDT 2001. LNCS, vol. 1973, pp. 420–434. Springer, Heidelberg (2000)
2. Balthrop, J., Esponda, F., Forrest, S., Glickman, M.: Coverage and generalization in an artificial immune system. In: Proceedings of the Genetic and Evolutionary Computation Conference (GECCO 2002), New York, 9–13 July 2002, pp. 3–10 (2002)
3. Brzozowski, M., Chmielewski, A.: Hardware approach for generating b-detectors by immune-based algorithms. In: Saeed, K., Snášel, V. (eds.) CISIM 2014. LNCS, vol. 8838, pp. 615–623. Springer, Heidelberg (2014)
4. Chu, P.P.: RTL Hardware Design Using VHDL: Coding for Efficiency, Portability, and Scalability. Wiley-Interscience, New Jersey (2006)
5. Chmielewski, A., Wierzchoń, S.T.: On the distance norms for multidimensional dataset in the case of real-valued negative selection application. Zesz. Nauk. Politech. Białost. **2**, 39–50 (2007)
6. Chmielewski, A., Wierzchoń, S.T.: Hybrid negative selection approach for anomaly detection. In: Cortesi, A., Chaki, N., Saeed, K., Wierzchoń, S. (eds.) CISIM 2012. LNCS, vol. 7564, pp. 242–253. Springer, Heidelberg (2012)
7. Forrest, S., Hofmeyr, S.A., Somayaji, A., Longstaff, T.A.: A sense of self for unix processes. In: Proceedings of the 1996 IEEE Symposium on Research in Security and Privacy, pp. 120–128. IEEE Computer Society Press (1996)
8. Forrest, S., Perelson, A., Allen, L., Cherukuri, R.: Self-nonself discrimination in a computer. In: Proceedings of the IEEE Symposium on Research in Security and Privacy, Los Alamitos, pp. 202–212 (1994)
9. Harmer, P.K., Wiliams, P.D., Gunsch, G.H., Lamont, G.B.: Artificial immune system architecture for computer security applications. IEEE Trans. Evol. Comput. **6**, 252–280 (2002)
10. Ji, Z., Dasgupta, D.: Real-valued negative selection algorithm with variable-sized detectors. In: Deb, K., Tari, Z. (eds.) GECCO 2004. LNCS, vol. 3102, pp. 287–298. Springer, Heidelberg (2004)
11. Ji, Z., Dasgupta, D.: Revisiting negative selection algorithms. Evol. Comput. **15**(2), 223–251 (2007)
12. Stibor, T., Mohr, P.H., Timmis, J., Eckert, C.: Is negative selection appropriate for anomaly detection? In: GECCO 2005, pp. 321–328 (2005)
13. Vanderbauwhede, W., Benkrid, K.: High-Performance Computing Using FPGAs. Springer, New York (2013)

Attribute Reduction Based on MapReduce Model and Discernibility Measure

Michal Czolombitko$^{(\boxtimes)}$ and Jaroslaw Stepaniuk

Faculty of Computer Science, Bialystok University of Technology,
Wiejska 45A, 15-351 Bialystok, Poland
{m.czolombitko,j.stepaniuk}@pb.edu.pl
http://www.wi.pb.edu.pl

Abstract. This paper discusses two important problems of data reduction. The problems are related to computing reducts and core in rough sets. The authors use the fact that the necessary information about discernibility matrices can be computed directly from data tables, in the case of this paper so called counting tables are used. The discussed problems are of high computational complexity. Hence the authors propose to use the relevant heuristics, MRCR (**M**ap**R**educe **C**ore and **R**educt Generation) implemented using the MapReduce model.

Keywords: Rough sets · MapReduce · Reducts · Attribute reduction · Core

1 Introduction

Since the massive data could be stored in cloud platforms, data mining for the large datasets is hot topic. Parallel methods of computing are alternative for large datasets processing and knowledge discovery for large data. MapReduce is a distributed programming model, proposed by Google for processing large datasets, so called Big Data. Users specify the required functions Map and Reduce and optional function Combine. Every step of computation takes as input pairs $< key, values >$ and produces another output pairs $< key', values' >$. In the first step, the Map function reads the input as a set $< key, values >$ pairs and applies user defined function to each pair. The result is a second set of the intermediate pairs $< key', values' >$, sent to Combine or Reduce function. Combine function is a local Reduce, which can help to reduce final computation. It applies second user defined function to each intermediate key with all its associated values to merge and group data. Results are sorted, shuffled and sent to the Reduce function. Reduce function merges and groups all values to each key and produces zero or more outputs.

Rough set theory is mathematical tool for dealing with incomplete and uncertain information [6]. In the decision systems, not all of the attributes are needed in decision making process. Some of them can be removed without affecting the classification quality, in this sense they are superfluous. One of the advantage of

K. Saeed and W. Homenda (Eds.): CISIM 2016, LNCS 9842, pp. 55–66, 2016.
DOI: 10.1007/978-3-319-45378-1_6

rough set theory is an ability to compute the reductions of the set of conditional attributes, so called reducts.

In recent years, there has been some research works combining MapReduce and rough set theory. In [12] parallel method for computing rough set approximations was proposed. The authors continued their work and proposed in [13] three strategies based on MapReduce to compute approximations in incomplete information systems. In [11] method for computing core based on finding positive region was proposed. They also presented parallel algorithm of attribute reduction in [10]. However authors used model MapReduce only for splitting data set and parallelization computation using one of traditional reduction algorithm. In [4] is proposed a design of a Patient-customized Healthcare System based on the Hadoop with Text Mining for an efficient Disease Management and Prediction.

In this paper we propose a parallel method MRCR (MapReduce Core and Reduct Generation) for generating core and one reduct or superreduct based on distributed programming model MapReduce and rough set theory. In order to reduce the memory complexity, instead of discernibility matrix were used counting tables to compute discernibility measure of the datasets. The results of the experiments on real datasets show that the proposed method is effective for big data.

This paper is organized as follows. Section 1 includes background introduction to rough sets. Problem of attribute reduction and algorithm of generating core using counting tables are presented in Sect. 2. Parallel algorithm MRCR based on discernibility measure and MapReduce is proposed in Sect. 3. Results of experiments and analysis is presented in Sect. 4. Conclusions and future work are drawn in the last Section.

2   Reducing Number of Attributes

2.1   Reduct and Core Computation

Let $DT = (U, A \cup \{d\})$ be a decision table, where U is a set of objects, A is a set of conditional attributes and d is a decision attribute. Reduct is subset of conditional attributes $R \subseteq A$, sufficient to get information which we need from the decision table. Superreduct is not necessarily minimal set of those attributes. The core is a set of conditional attributes, which are cannot be removed from original data set without affecting the quality of the classification.

In order to compute the core and reduct we can use discernibility matrix introduced by Prof. Andrzej Skowron (see e.g. [6,8]). Discernibility Matrix is two dimensional table indexed by the objects. Cells of the discernibility matrix contains set with all of conditional attributes on which corresponding objects have different values. Number of not empty cells is discernibility measure of set A. The core is the set of all single element entries of the discernibility matrix. In some cases core can be an empty set.

However, memory complexity of creating discernibility matrix is equal to $(cardinality(U))^2 * cardinality(A)$. This makes impractical using this structure for large data sets, so called Big Data. Solution could be using counting tables to compute discernibility measure. In next subsection we present method for computing the core, which is base to finding one of the reducts.

2.2 Pseudocode for Generating Core Based on Discernibility Measure of a Set of Attributes

Generating core based on discernibility measure was discussed in [5]. Counting table CT is a two-dimensional array indexed by values of information vectors (vector of all values of an attribute set $B \subseteq A$) and decision values, where

$$CT(i,j) = cardinality(\{x \in U : \vec{x}_B = i \text{ and } d(x) = j\})$$

Pessimistic memory complexity of creating this type of matrix is equal to $cardinality(U) * cardinality(V_d)$, where V_d is a set of all decisions.

The discernibility measure $disc(B)$ of set of attributes $B \subseteq A$ can be calculated from the counting table as follows:

$$disc(B) = \frac{1}{2} \sum_{i,j} \sum_{k,l} CT(i,j) \cdot CT(k,l), \text{if } i \neq k \text{ and } j \neq l$$

The discernibility measure is the number of non empty cells in discernibility matrix.

Below is the pseudocode for this algorithm:

Input: decision table $DT = (U, A \cup \{d\})$
Output: $Core \subseteq A$
1: $Core \leftarrow \emptyset$ {Core is equal to empty set}
2: $CT \leftarrow 0$ {All values in counting table CT are equal to 0}
3: **for** $x \in U$ **do**
4:    $CT(\vec{x}_A, d(x)) \leftarrow CT(\vec{x}_A, d(x)) + 1$
5: **end for**
6: $disc(A) \leftarrow 0$
7: **for** $[x]_A \in U/IND(A)$ {$U/IND(A)$ is partition of U defined by A} **do**
8:    **for** $[y]_A \in U/IND(A)$ **do**
9:       **if** $\vec{x}_A \neq \vec{y}_A$ and $d(x) \neq d(y)$ **then**
10:          $disc(A) \leftarrow disc(A) + CT(\vec{x}_A, d(x)) \cdot CT(\vec{y}_A, d(y))$
11:       **end if**
12:    **end for**
13: **end for**
14: $CT \leftarrow 0$
15: **for** $a \in A$ **do**
16:    $B \leftarrow A - \{a\}$
17:    $disc(B) \leftarrow 0$
18:    **for** $x \in U$ **do**
19:       $CT(\vec{x}_B, d(x)) \leftarrow CT(\vec{x}_B, d(x)) + 1$
20:    **end for**
21:    **for** $[x]_B \in U/IND(A)$ **do**

22:     **for** $[y]_B \in U/IND(A)$ **do**
23:         **if** $\vec{x}_B \neq \vec{y}_B$ and $d(x) \neq d(y)$ **then**
24:             $disc(B) \leftarrow disc(B) + CT(\vec{x}_B, d(x)) \cdot CT(\vec{y}_B, d(y))$
25:         **end if**
26:     **end for**
27:   **end for**
28:   **if** $disc(B) < disc(A)$ **then**
29:       $C \leftarrow Core \cup \{a\}$
30:   **end if**
31: **end for**

Input to the algorithm is a decision table DT, and output is the core C of DT. In the beginning core C is initialized as empty set and all values in the counting table are set to zero. First loop in line 3 generate counting table for set of all conditional attributes. For each object in decision table, value in array is increased by one. Indexes of value are information vector of object and its value of decision. In the line 6 value of discernibility measure of set of all conditional attributes, $disc(A)$, is initialized as zero. Next two loops in lines 7 and 8 take subsequent equivalence classes to comparison. If information vectors of these classes are not equal, $disc(A)$ is increased by product of two values from the counting tables where indexes are values information vectors and different decisions. Next step is computing the discernibility measure of set of attributes after removing one of them. In line 14 all values in the counting table are set to zero. Loop in line 15 takes attribute a from set of all conditional attributes A. Set B is initialized as set of all conditional attributes after removing this attribute. Similarly as above, in lines 15–27 is calculated $disc(B)$. Finally, values of the discernibility measure of set of all attributes and after removing attribute a are compared in the line 28. In case of difference, this attribute is added to the core.

3   MapReduce Implementation - Proposed Method

The main concept of the proposed algorithm MRCR is parallel computation of counting tables and discernibility measure for each of conditional attributes and potential reducts. We extended the method proposed by us in [3] on parallel computing discernibility measure and adopt to computing the reduct.

Algorithm MRCR
Input: decision table $DT = (U, A \cup \{d\})$
Output: reduct R
 1: $Core \leftarrow ComputeCoreMR(DT)$ {See Step 1a & Step 1b }
 2: $B \leftarrow A - Core$
 3: $R \leftarrow Core$
 4: **while** $disc(A) > disc(R)$ **do**
 5:   **for** $a \in B$ **do**
 6:       $PR_a \leftarrow R \cup \{a\}$
 7:   **end for**

8:    $ComputeDiscMeasureMR(PR, DT)$ {See Step 2}
9:    $R \leftarrow max\_disc(PR_a))$ {function returns the set with the largest value of discernibility measure}
10:   $B \leftarrow B - R$
11: **end while**

The proposed algorithm consists of two main steps: compute core and one reduct. Both stages are composed of two operations Map and Reduce. After computing core, set B is initialized as a set of attributes that not in the core and reduct as a set attributes that are in core.

Table PR (potential reducts) is initialized in the line 6 as a collection containing sets that are unions of the reduct and the every attribute from set B. For each of these sets is parallel calculated the discernibility measure in the line 9. As a new reduct is chosen a set with the maximal discernibility measure and from set B is removed the attribute added to the reduct. Operations in lines 5–10 are repeated until the discernibility measures of the reduct and the set containing all conditional attributes aren't equal.

Step 1a. ComputeCoreMR - Counting Tables
Map
Input: key : subtable id, $value$: decision subtable $DT_i = (U_i, A \cup \{d\})$
Output: $< key', value' >$ pair where key' : $(\vec{x}_B, d(x))$ and $value'$ is id of the object x

1: **for** $x \in U_i$ **do**
2:    $key' \leftarrow (\vec{x}_A, d(x))$
3:    $value' \leftarrow$ id of the object x
4:    $emit(< key', value' >)$
5:    **for** $a \in A$ **do**
6:      $B \leftarrow A - \{a\}$
7:      $key' \leftarrow (\vec{x}_B, d(x))$
8:      $value' \leftarrow$ id of the object x
9:      $emit(< key', value' >)$
10:   **end for**
11: **end for**

Input to function Map are: key is a subtable id stored in HDFS, and $value$ is decision subtable $DT_i = (U_i, A \cup \{d\})$. First loop in line 1 takes an object from decision subtable DT_i and emits pair $< key', value' >$, where key' is information vector with respect to set of all conditional attributes and decision of the object x, and $value$ is id of the this object. Loop in line 5 takes attribute a from set of all conditional attributes A. Set B is initialized as set A after removing this attribute. Next step is emitting pair $< key', value' >$, where key' is information vector with respect to set B and decision of the object x, and $value'$ is id of this object.

Reduce
Input: $< key, value >$ where key : $(\vec{x}_B, d(x))$ and $value$ is the number of objects belonging to equivalence class $[x]_B$ with equal decision values from decision subtable DT_i.

Output: the files containing pairs $< key', value' >$ where $key : (\vec{x}_B, d(x))$ and
   $value'$ is the number of objects belonging to equivalence class $[x]_B$ with equal
   decision values from decision table DT.

1: $key' \leftarrow key$
2: $value' \leftarrow 0$
3: **for all** $value$ **do**
4:    $value' \leftarrow value' + value$
5: **end for**
6: $emit(< key', value' >)$

Input to function Reduce are $< key, value >$ pairs where $key : (\vec{x}_B, d(x))$ and
$value$ is the number of objects belonging to equivalence class $[x]_B$ with the same
decision from decision subtable DT_i. Function emits pairs $< key', value' >$,
where key' is $(\vec{x}_B, d(x))$ and $value'$ is a number of the objects associated with
this key from decision table DT. Each of these pair is emitting (See Fig. 1).

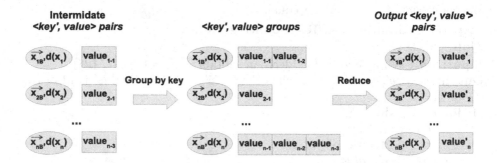

Fig. 1. The Reduce operation in the Step 1a

Step 1b. ComputeCoreMR - Discernibility Measure Map

Input: the files containing the pairs $< key, value >$ where $key : (\vec{x}_B, d(x))$ and
   $value$ is number of the objects belong to $[x]_B$ with the same decision value
   - $count(\vec{x}_B, d(x)))$

Output: $< key', value' >$ pair where key' is the removed attribute from the set
   of the conditional attributes and $value'$ contains $\vec{x}_B, d(x)$ and the number
   of objects belonging to equivalence class $[x]_B$ with equal decision values -
   $count(\vec{x}_B, d(x))$

1: **for all** $(\vec{x}_B, d(x))$ **do**
2:    $key' \leftarrow$ removed attribute
3:    $value' \leftarrow \vec{x}_B, d(x), count(\vec{x}_B, d(x))$
4:    $emit(< key', value' >)$
5: **end for**

Input to the Map operation is directory contains files with pairs $< key, value >$
where $key : (\vec{x}_B, d(x))$ and $value$ is number of the objects belong to $[x]_B$ with the
same decision value. Loop in the first line takes every pair $< key, value >$ and

emits $< key', value' >$ pair where key' is the removed attribute from the set of the conditional attributes and $value'$ contains $\vec{x}_B, d(x)$ and the number of objects belonging to equivalence class $[x]_B$ with equal decision values - $count(\vec{x}_B, d(x))$.

Reduce

Input: the pairs $< key, value >$ where key is the removed attribute a from the set of the conditional attributes A and $value : (\vec{x}_B, d(x), count(\vec{x}_B, d(x)))$

Output: $< key', value' >$ pair where key' is the removed attribute a from the set of the conditional attributes and $value'$ is the discernibility measure of set A after removing attribute a

1: $disc(A - \{a\}) \leftarrow 0$
2: **for all** $(\vec{x}_B, d(x), count(\vec{x}_B, d(x)))$ **do**
3:     **for all** $(\vec{y}_B, d(y), count(\vec{y}_B, d(y)))$ **do**
4:         **if** $\vec{x}_B \neq \vec{y}_B$ **and** $d(x) \neq d(y)$ **then**
5:             $disc(A - \{a\}) \leftarrow disc(A - \{a\}) + count(\vec{x}_B, d(x))) \cdot count(\vec{y}_B, d(y))$
6:         **end if**
7:     **end for**
8: **end for**
9: $key' \leftarrow a$
10: $value' \leftarrow disc(A - \{a\})$
11: $emit(< key', value' >)$

Input to the Reduce operation are pairs $< key, value >$ where key is the removed attribute a from the set A of conditional attributes and $value :$ $(\vec{x}_B, d(x), count(\vec{x}_B, d(x)))$. Two loops in lines 2 and 3 take subsequent lines from input to comparison. If these two pairs contains information about two different information vectors and decisions, $disc(A - \{a\})$ is increased by product of $count(\vec{x}_B, d(x))$ and $count(\vec{y}_B, d(y))$.

Computing the core consists of finding in the output files all attributes that cannot be removed from set A without decrease of the discernibility measure.

Step 2. ComputeDiscMeasureMR
Counting Tables - Map

Input: key : subtable id, $value$: decision subtable $DT_i = (U_i, A \cup \{d\})$, table PR - potential reducts

Output: $< key', value' >$ pair where $key' : (\vec{x}_B, d(x))$ and $value'$ is id of the object x

1: **for** $x \in U_i$ **do**
2:     **for** $PR_i \in PR$ **do**
3:         $key' \leftarrow (x\vec{P}R_i, d(x))$
4:         $value' \leftarrow$ id of the object x
5:         $emit(< key', value' >)$
6:     **end for**
7: **end for**

Input to function Map are: key is a subtable id stored in HDFS and $value$ is decision subtable $DT_i = (U_i, A \cup \{d\})$ and potential reducts.

Reduce operation is the same like in operation Reduce in the Step 1a. The discernibility measure is computing similarly like in the Step 1b so its description will be skipped.

The output of the second step are files containing subsets of the conditional attributes with their discernibility measure.

4   Experimental Results

The algorithm MRCR was running on the Hadoop MapReduce platform [1], where Hadoop MapReduce is a YARN-based system for parallel processing of big datasets. In the experiments, Hadoop 2.5.1 version was used. All the computation nodes have four 3.4 GHz cores processors and 16 GB of memory. All files were stored in HDFS. Each file was merged on blocks and each of those blocks was replicated tree times. A bound of the proposed method is available free disc space in distributed file system for files and temporary data.

In this paper, we present the results of the conducted experiments using data about children with insulin-dependent diabetes mellitus (type 1) and dataset KDDCup-99 from the machine learning data repository, University of California at Irvine [2].

Diabetes mellitus is a chronic disease of the body's metabolism characterized by an inability to produce enough insulin to process carbohydrates, fat, and protein efficiently. Treatment requires injections of insulin. Twelve conditional attributes, which include the results of physical and laboratory examinations and one decision attribute (microalbuminuria) describe the database used in our experiments. The data collection so far consists of 107 cases. The database is shown at the end of the paper [7]. A detailed analysis of the above data is in Chap. 6 of the book [8]. This database was used for generating bigger datasets consisting of $1 \cdot 10^6$ to $20 \cdot 10^6$ of objects. New datasets were created by randomly multiplying the rows of original dataset.

The data set KDDCup-99 consists of almost five million objects. Each object is described by forty one conditional attributes and one decision attribute. Informations gather in this dataset can be used to build a network intrusion detector. This database was used for generating smaller datasets consisting approximately of $0.25 \cdot 10^6$ to $5 \cdot 10^6$ of objects. New datasets were created by randomly splitting the rows of original dataset.

Numerical values in both datasets were discretized.

4.1   Speedup

In speedup tests, the dataset size is constant and the number of nodes grows in each step of experiment. To measure speedup, we used dataset diabetes contains $20 \cdot 10^6$ objects and whole KDDCup-99 dataset. The speedup given by the n-times larger system is measured as [9]:

$$Speedup(n) = \frac{t_n}{t_1}$$

where n is number of the nodes in cluster, t_1 is the computation time on one node, and t_n is the computation time on n nodes.

The ideal parallel system with n nodes provides n times speedup. The linear speedup is difficult to achieve because of the I/O operations data from HDFS and the communication cost between nodes of Hadoop cluster. Figure 2 shows that with the growth of the number of nodes, the speed performs better.

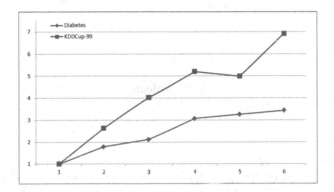

Fig. 2. Speedup

4.2   Scaleup

Scaleup analysis measures stability system when system and dataset size grow in each step of experiment. The scaleup coefficient is defined as follows [9]:

$$Scaleup(DT, n) = \frac{t_{DT_{1,1}}}{t_{DT_{n,n}}}$$

where $t_{DT_{1,1}}$ is the computational time for dataset DT on one node, and $t_{DT_{n,n}}$ is the computational time for n times larger dataset DT on n nodes.

Table 1 shows number of attributes in computed the core and the reduct for KDDCup-99 dataset.

Table 1. Size of the core and the reduct in scaleup experiment for KDDCup-99 dataset

Number of the nodes	1	2–3	4–5	6–17	18	19–20
Size of the core	4	18	26	30	31	32
Size of the reduct	8	20	26	30	31	32

Figure 3 shows the scalability of algorithm for KDDCup-99 dataset strictly depends on the size of the core and the reduct. For the diabetes dataset scalability of the proposed parallel algorithm stabilize when the number of the nodes is equal 15.

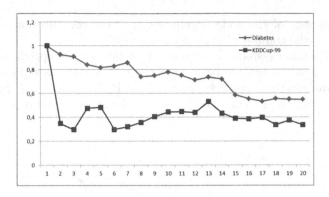

Fig. 3. Scaleup

4.3   Sizeup

In sizeup tests, the number of nodes is constant, and the dataset size grows in each step of experiment. Sizeup measures how much time is needed for calculations when the size of dataset is n times larger than the original dataset. Sizeup is defined as follows [9]:

$$Sizeup(DT) = \frac{t_{DT_n}}{t_{DT_1}}$$

where t_{DT_1} is execution time for a given dataset DT, and t_{DT_n} is execution time n times larger dataset than DT.

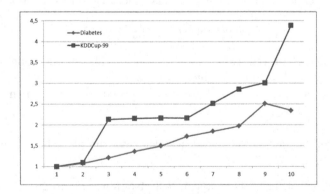

Fig. 4. Sizeup

Figure 4 shows the sizeup experiments results on twenty nodes. Results shows that the proposed algorithm copes well with the growing amount of data.

Conclusions and Future Research

In this paper, attribute reduction for large datasets based on rough set theory is studied. A parallel attribute reduction algorithm MRCR is proposed, which is based on the distributed programming model of MapReduce and the reduct computation algorithm using discernibility measure of a set of attributes. It is worth noting that a very interesting element of the paper is an usage of a counting table instead of a discernibility matrix. The results of the experiments show that the proposed method is efficient for large data, and it is a useful method for data mining and knowledge discovery for big datasets. Our future research work will focus on applications of distributed in-memory computing for attribute discretization.

Acknowledgements. This research was partially supported by the grant S/WI/3/2013 of the Polish Ministry of Science and Higher Education. The experiments were performed using resources co-financed with the European Union funds as a part of the "Centre for Modern Education of the Bialystok University of Technology" project (Operational Programme Development of Eastern Poland).

References

1. Hadoop MapReduce. http://hadoop.apache.org
2. UCI Repository of Machine Learning Databases, University of California, Department of Information and Computer Science, Irvine, CA. http://archive.ics.uci.edu/ml/datasets/KDD+Cup+1999+Data
3. Czolombitko, M., Stepaniuk, J.: Generating core based on discernibility measure and MapReduce. In: Kryszkiewicz, M., Bandyopadhyay, S., Rybinski, H., Pal, S.K. (eds.) PReMI 2015. LNCS, vol. 9124, pp. 367–376. Springer, Heidelberg (2015)
4. Lee, B.K., Jeong, E.H.: A design of a patient-customized healthcare system based on the hadoop with text mining (PHSHT) for an efficient disease management and prediction. Int. J. Soft. Eng. Appl. **8**(8), 131–150 (2014)
5. Nguyen, H.S.: Approximate Boolean reasoning: foundations and applications in data mining. In: Peters, J.F., Skowron, A. (eds.) Transactions on Rough Sets V. LNCS, vol. 4100, pp. 334–506. Springer, Heidelberg (2006)
6. Pawlak, Z., Skowron, A.: Rudiments of rough sets. Inf. Sci. **177**(1), 3–27 (2007)
7. Stepaniuk, J.: Knowledge discovery by application of rough set models. In: Polkowski, L., Tsumoto, S., Lin, T.Y. (eds.) Rough Set Methods and Applications. STUDFUZZ, vol. 56, pp. 137–233. Physica-Verlag, Heidelberg (2000)
8. Stepaniuk, J.: Rough-Granular Computing in Knowledge Discovery and Data Mining. SCI, vol. 152. Springer, Heidelberg (2008)
9. Xu, X., Jäger, J., Kriegel, H.P.: A fast parallel clustering algorithm for large spatial databases. Data Min. Knowl. Disc. **3**, 263–290 (1999)
10. Yang, Y., Chen, Z., Liang, Z., Wang, G.: Attribute reduction for massive data based on rough set theory and MapReduce. In: Yu, J., Greco, S., Lingras, P., Wang, G., Skowron, A. (eds.) RSKT 2010. LNCS, vol. 6401, pp. 672–678. Springer, Heidelberg (2010)

11. Yang, Y., Chen, Z.: Parallelized computing of attribute core based on rough set theory and MapReduce. In: Li, T., Nguyen, H.S., Wang, G., Grzymala-Busse, J., Janicki, R., Hassanien, A.E., Yu, H. (eds.) RSKT 2012. LNCS, vol. 7414, pp. 155–160. Springer, Heidelberg (2012)
12. Zhang, J., Li, T., Ruan, D., Gao, Z., Zhao, C.: A parallel method for computing rough set approximations. Inf. Sci. **194**, 209–223 (2012)
13. Zhang, J., Wong, J., Pan, Y., Li, T.: A parallel matrix-based method for computing approximations in incomplete information systems, systems. IEEE Trans. Knowl. Data Eng. **27**, 326–339 (2015)

Mapping Points Back from the Concept Space with Minimum Mean Squared Error

Wladyslaw Homenda[1,2] and Tomasz Penza[2(✉)]

[1] Faculty of Economics and Informatics in Vilnius,
University of Bialystok, Kalvariju g. 135, LT-08221 Vilnius, Lithuania
[2] Faculty of Mathematics and Information Science,
Warsaw University of Technology, ul. Koszykowa 75, 00-662 Warsaw, Poland
tomasz.penza@gmail.com

Abstract. In this article we present a method to map points from the concept space, associated with the fuzzy c–means algorithm, back to the feature space. We assume that we have a probability density function f defined on the feature space (e.g. a normalized density of a data set). For a given point w of concept space, we give explicitly a set of points in feature space that are mapped onto w and we give a formula for a reverse mapping to the feature space which results in minimum mean squared error, with respect to density f, of the operation of mapping a point of feature space into the concept space and back. We characterize the circumstances under which points can be mapped back into the feature space unambiguously and provide a formula for the inverse mapping.

1 Introduction

There is an effort among researchers today, to capture the mechanisms of human cognition that allow the mind to process abstract information. Their goal is to enable the machine to discern patterns, spot relations and make connections between objects and ideas, to reason and predict on the basis of knowledge and observation. To make this possible, computers must be able to form and process concepts. A cluster in a data set can be thought of as representing an abstract concept. We can thus use data clustering methods to extract concepts. With each clustering method, comes a way to measure to what degree a given data point belongs to a given cluster. If we regard these degrees of membership in different clusters as coordinates, we obtain a concept space of dimension equal to the number of clusters. We can then map numeric data from the feature space into the concept space and process it at the level of concepts. Many points of the feature space may end up being mapped onto the same point of concept space. Consequently, we run into a problem when we try to put the result of concept-level computations back into the feature space. In certain circumstances, if we want to have a reverse mapping from the concept space into the feature space, we have to accept that it will make errors, i.e. when we map an observation into the concept space, this reverse mapping will not map it back onto itself.

K. Saeed and W. Homenda (Eds.): CISIM 2016, LNCS 9842, pp. 67–78, 2016.
DOI: 10.1007/978-3-319-45378-1_7

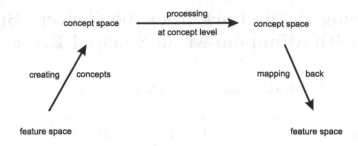

Fig. 1. Processing of data

In this text we work with a transformation from the feature space to the concept space associated with the fuzzy c–means algorithm which we denote with symbol $\mathcal{M}$. We will describe sets of points that $\mathcal{M}$ maps onto the same point of concept space. We will also determine under what conditions $\mathcal{M}$ is invertible and give a formula for its inverse. We will assume that there is a continuous probability density function defined on the feature space and we will present a formula for a reverse mapping G that allows minimum mean squared error (MSE), with respect to that probability density, of an operation of mapping an observation to the concept space via $\mathcal{M}$ and back via G. In practice such probability density might arise as a density of data points of some data set in the feature space. We propose an application of this reverse mapping as a defuzzification–like transformation of the results of concept–level processing, which is the last stage of the process outlined at Fig. 1. There is a long record of defuzzification methods and we refer to selected results in References without explicit discussion on them. Our approach is different in that we study a general reverse mapping and defuzzification discussed in this paper is a special case of such general transformation.

2 Preliminaries

2.1 Fuzzy c–means Algorithm

An analogue of k–means algorithm within fuzzy clustering is the fuzzy c–means algorithm (FCM) which lets us find c fuzzy clusters in a data set $\mathcal{D} = \{\boldsymbol{x}_1, \boldsymbol{x}_2, \ldots, \boldsymbol{x}_n\}$ – a subset of feature space $\mathbb{R}^h$. We denote the i–th cluster by C_i and its centroid as $\boldsymbol{\mu}_i$. For a given observation $\boldsymbol{x}_i$, its degree of membership in the cluster C_j is denoted by w_{ij} and given by the formula

$$w_{ij} = \frac{||\boldsymbol{x}_i - \boldsymbol{\mu}_j||^{-\frac{2}{m-1}}}{\sum\limits_{k=1}^{c} ||\boldsymbol{x}_i - \boldsymbol{\mu}_k||^{-\frac{2}{m-1}}} = \frac{1}{\sum\limits_{k=1}^{c} \left(\frac{||\boldsymbol{x}_i-\boldsymbol{\mu}_j||}{||\boldsymbol{x}_i-\boldsymbol{\mu}_k||} \right)^{\frac{2}{m-1}}}$$

where $m > 1$ is a parameter called the fuzzifier. For every data point, its membership in different clusters sums up to 1. Each fuzzy cluster is represented by its weighted mean $\boldsymbol{\mu}_i = \sum_{j=1}^{n} w_{ji} \boldsymbol{x}_j / \sum_{j=1}^{n} w_{ji}$. These two formulas are mutually referential. At each step of the algorithm only one of them will be satisfied, but the clustering that the algorithm will output will approximately satisfy them both.

The fuzzifier m controls how fuzzy the resulting clustering will be. The higher the fuzzifier, the less distinct the values of membership and thus the fuzzier the clustering. When m converges to 1, for each observation one of its cluster memberships converges to 1 and the rest converge to 0, so in the limit the clustering becomes hard.

Before running the algorithm, we must choose the number c of clusters that we want to form, the fuzzifier m and the threshold ε. The threshold will let us terminate the algorithm when upon iteration all the memberships w_{ij} changed by less than ε. The algorithm is as follows.

1. Randomly initialize all the degrees of membership w_{ij} with numbers from the unit interval.
2. Compute all the weighted means $\boldsymbol{\mu}_i$ using current values w_{ij}.
3. Compute all the membership degrees w_{ij} using current values $\boldsymbol{\mu}_i$.
4. If any of values w_{ij} changed by more than ε, go to step 2.

FCM endeavors to minimize the loss function $\sum_{i=1}^{n} \sum_{j=1}^{c} w_{ij} \|\boldsymbol{x}_i - \boldsymbol{\mu}_j\|^2$ which never increases after an iteration of the loop. Thanks to the threshold ε the algorithm always converges. The final clustering depends on the initial values w_{ij}, which are assigned randomly, thus the clusters will vary each time we run FCM. It is advised to run the algorithm several times and choose the best result. We can evaluate clusterings using cluster validity indices. They can also help us pick an optimal number of clusters c.

2.2   Mapping $\mathcal{M}$

Suppose that in the feature space $\mathbb{R}^h$, we used FCM with fuzzifier set to m to find c fuzzy clusters and we obtained the set of centroids $\mathcal{C} = \{\boldsymbol{\mu}_1, \boldsymbol{\mu}_2, \dots \boldsymbol{\mu}_c\}$. Mapping $\mathcal{M_C} : \mathbb{R}^h \longrightarrow [0,1]^c$, assigns to $\boldsymbol{x} \in \mathbb{R}^h$ a vector of its degrees of membership in the respective clusters, which is a point of the concept space $[0,1]^c$. For $\boldsymbol{x} \in \mathbb{R}^h \backslash \mathcal{C}$, we have

$$\mathcal{M_C}(\boldsymbol{x}) = \left(\frac{1}{\sum\limits_{k=1}^{c} \left(\frac{\|\boldsymbol{x} - \boldsymbol{\mu}_i\|}{\|\boldsymbol{x} - \boldsymbol{\mu}_k\|} \right)^{\frac{2}{m-1}}} \right)_{i=1,\ 2,\ \dots,\ c}$$

We extend $\mathcal{M_C}$ continuously onto $\mathbb{R}^h$ by defining $\mathcal{M_C}(\boldsymbol{\mu}_i)$ to be a vector whose i–th coordinate is 1 and all its other coordinates are 0. For now we will write simply $\mathcal{M}$, but we will invoke the subscript in Sect. 3.3, when we will need to refer to mapping $\mathcal{M}_{\widehat{\mathcal{C}}}$ for a subset $\widehat{\mathcal{C}}$ of the set of centroids $\mathcal{C}$. $\mathcal{M}$ is continuously differentiable on $\mathbb{R}^h \backslash \mathcal{C}$. We will invert $\mathcal{M}$ in circumstances when it is possible and otherwise we will provide a formula for the most accurate reverse mapping to the feature space.

If we exclude the trivial case of just one centroid, the values of $\mathcal{M}$ on set $\mathbb{R}^h \backslash \mathcal{C}$ are all contained in the subset $W = \{(w_1, w_2, ..., w_c) \in (0,1)^c \mid \sum_{i=1}^{c} w_i = 1\}$ of concept space. For $c = 3$ this subset would be an interior of a triangle inside the cube $[0,1]^3$ with vertices $(1,0,0)$, $(0,1,0)$ and $(0,0,1)$, i.e. points of the concept space corresponding to the centroids. Even though elements of W have c coordinates, they have only $c - 1$ degrees of freedom, because the last coordinate is given by the first $c - 1$ coordinates: $w_c = 1 - \sum_{i=1}^{c-1} w_i$. Let P denote the projection onto the first $c - 1$ coordinates, i.e. $P(\boldsymbol{w}) = P(w_1, w_2, ..., w_c) = (w_1, w_2, ..., w_{c-1})$. For any $\boldsymbol{w} \in W$ and $X \subset W$, we will denote their images $P(\boldsymbol{w})$ and $P(X)$ under P by $\underline{\boldsymbol{w}}$ and $\underline{X}$ respectively. Set $\underline{W} = \{(w_1, w_2, ..., w_{c-1}) \in (0,1)^{c-1} \mid \sum_{i=1}^{c-1} w_i < 1\}$ is an open subset of $\mathbb{R}^{c-1}$. For any point $\underline{\boldsymbol{w}}$ in $\underline{W}$, w_c can be reconstructed using the equation above, so P is a bijection. Identity $\boldsymbol{w} = (\underline{\boldsymbol{w}}, w_c)$ relates the elements of these two sets and whenever symbols $\boldsymbol{w}$ and $\underline{\boldsymbol{w}}$ appear in the same context, they are always bound by this identity. P is actually a homeomorphism between $\underline{W}$ and W which makes W a $(c-1)$–dimensional manifold.

3 Sets Mapped onto the Same Point of Concept Space

3.1 Preimage of a Point of Concept Space

Preimages of points of W under $\mathcal{M}$, when they are nonempty, are spheres of some dimension embedded in $\mathbb{R}^h$, except for a special case when the preimage is a linear manifold. We define $\mathbb{R}^0$ to be a space containing only a zero 1×1 vector and $\mathcal{B}^0(0, R)$ and $\mathcal{S}^{-1}(0,0)$ to be equal to $\mathbb{R}^0$.

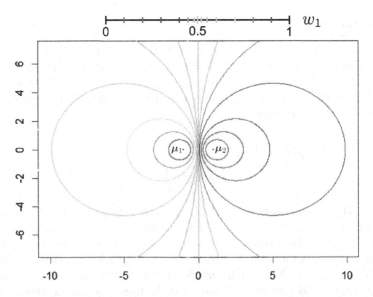

Fig. 2. Preimages of points $(w_1, 1 - w_1)$ for $h = 2$ and $c = 2$.

For a set containing at least two elements, $\mathcal{C} = \{\mu_1, \mu_2, \ldots, \mu_c\} \subset \mathbb{R}^h$, a point in W, $w = (w_1, w_2, \ldots, w_c)$ and $m > 1$, we define the following values

1. M is a $(c-1) \times h$ matrix whose i-th row is $(\mu_i - \mu_c)^T$
2. u is a column vector of length $c-1$ such that $u_i = \frac{1}{2}\|\mu_i - \mu_c\|^2$
3. v is a column vector of length $c-1$ such that $v_i = -\frac{1}{2}(w_i^{1-m} - w_c^{1-m})$
4. M^+ is the Moore–Penrose pseudoinverse of M
5. $Q = I - MM^+$
6. $a = M^+u$, $\quad b = M^+v$
7. $r = \mathrm{rank}M$, $d = h - r$
8. If $d > 0$, U is a $h \times d$ matrix whose columns form an orthonormal basis of the linear subspace $\{(I - M^+M)x \mid x \in \mathbb{R}^h\}$ of $\mathbb{R}^h$ of dimension d. If $d = 0$, U is a zero vector of $\mathbb{R}^h$
9. If $Qu = 0$, matrix H is $\left[\, U \,\middle|\, \frac{b}{\|b\|} \right]$ for $d > 0$ and $\frac{b}{\|b\|}$ for $d = 0$. If $Qu \neq 0$, it is U.

Matrix U can be obtained by selecting a maximal set of linearly independent columns of matrix $I - M^+M$, orthogonalizing it, normalizing each vector and taking the resulting set of vectors as columns of U. Values of M, u, a, Q, d and U depend only on $\mathcal{C}$, while values of v, b and H depend on both $\mathcal{C}$ and w. We will treat v, b and H as functions of variable $\underline{w} = (w_1, w_2, \ldots, w_{c-1}) \in \underline{W}$. These functions are continuous.

We need above definitions to provide a description of the preimage $\mathcal{M}^{-1}(w)$ of $w \in W$, which is split into two cases depending on if the set of centroids lies on a sphere or not. In each case if the conditions are not met, then the preimage is empty (no point of $\mathbb{R}^h$ is mapped onto w). We define $w_{eq} = (\frac{1}{c}, \frac{1}{c}, \ldots, \frac{1}{c})$. Symbol $\mathcal{S}^n$ stands for the unit n-sphere $\mathcal{S}^n = \{y \in \mathbb{R}^{n+1} \mid \|y\| = 1\}$ which is a subset of $\mathbb{R}^{n+1}$.

Set of Centroids Lies on a Sphere (Equivalent to $Qu = 0$)

If $Qv = 0$ and $w_c^{1-m} \geq 2(a \cdot b + \|a\|\|b\|)$, then the preimage is nonempty. For $w \neq w_{eq}$, it is a d–sphere of radius R embedded in $\mathbb{R}^h$ centered at point p

$$\mathcal{M}^{-1}(w) = \left\{ p + RHy \,\middle|\, y \in \mathcal{S}^d \right\}$$

with

$$R = \frac{\sqrt{(2a \cdot b - w_c^{1-m})^2 - 4\|a\|^2\|b\|^2}}{2\|b\|}$$
$$p = \mu_c + a + \frac{w_c^{1-m} - 2a \cdot b}{2\|b\|^2}b$$

For $w = w_{eq}$ the preimage is a linear manifold of dimension d

$$\mathcal{M}^{-1}(w_{eq}) = \left\{ \mu_c + a + Uy \,\middle|\, y \in \mathbb{R}^d \right\}$$

Set of Centroids Does not lie on a Sphere (Equivalent to $Qu \neq 0$)

If $Qv \neq 0$, $Qu \cdot Qv = -||Qu||||Qv||$ and
$$||b||^2||Qu||^2 + (2a \cdot b - w_c^{1-m})||Qu||||Qv|| + ||a||^2||Qv||^2 \leq 0$$
$$(||b||^2||Qu||^2 + (2a \cdot b - w_c^{1-m})||Qu||||Qv|| + ||a||^2||Qv||^2 = 0, \text{ when } d = 0)$$
then the preimage is nonempty. It is a $(d-1)$–sphere of radius R embedded in $\mathbb{R}^h$ centered at point p. If $d > 0$
$$\mathcal{M}^{-1}(w) = \left\{ p + RUy \mid y \in \mathcal{S}^{d-1} \right\}$$
and if $d = 0$
$$\mathcal{M}^{-1}(w) = \{p\}$$
with
$$R = \sqrt{-||b||^2 \left(\frac{||Qu||}{||Qv||} \right)^2 - (2a \cdot b - w_c^{1-m})\frac{||Qu||}{||Qv||} - ||a||^2}$$
$$p = \mu_c + a + \frac{||Qu||}{||Qv||}b$$

Let n represent a dimension of the spherical preimages for a given $\mathcal{C}$. If preimage of $w \neq w_{eq}$ is nonempty, then it is given by $\mathcal{M}^{-1}(w) = \{p + RHy \mid y \in \mathcal{S}^n\}$. Columns of $h \times (n+1)$ matrix H form an orthonormal set of vectors which entails that a linear transformation defined by this matrix is distance–preserving. It maps objects from $\mathbb{R}^{n+1}$ into $\mathbb{R}^h$ without distortion, so the formula for a preimage describes embedding of $\mathcal{S}^n$ into $\mathbb{R}^h$, scaling it to have radius R and the translating it so that it is centered at poin p.

Functions p and R are defined on set $W\backslash\{w_{eq}\}$. They are continuous which together with continuity of H implies that a slight change in $\underline{w}$ results in only a slight change of position, radius and spatial orientation of sphere $\mathcal{M}^{-1}(w)$. If $d > 0$, then the set of centroids lies on some linear manifold of dimension smaller than h. Mapping $\mathcal{M}$ is not invertible if and only if $Qu = 0$ or $d > 0$, in other words if and only if the set of centroids lies on a sphere or on a linear manifold of dimension smaller than h. Thus, if there are at least $h+1$ centroids, then $\mathcal{M}$ is typically invertible (unless they are unfortunately positioned) and we can map points from the concept space back into the feature space precisely. On the other hand, if there are at most h centroids, then they always lie on some sphere, so $\mathcal{M}$ is not invertible. If $\mathcal{M}$ is invertible, then $\mathcal{M}^{-1}(w) = p(\underline{w})$.

3.2   Derivatives of b, p and R

Functions b and p are continuously differentiable everywhere on $W\backslash w_{eq}$ and R on its subset where it is nonzero. We introduce symbols for three $(c-1) \times 1$ vectors $1 = [1, 1, \ldots, 1]^T$, $v_I = (1-m)[w_1^{-m}, w_2^{-m}, \ldots, w_{c-1}^{-m}]^T$ and $v_c = (1-m)[w_c^{-m}, w_c^{-m}, \ldots, w_c^{-m}]^T$. We let $\text{diag}(x)$ denote a diagonal matrix with coordinates of vector x on its diagonal and we put $s = \frac{R^2+||a||^2}{||b||^2}$. We can now write the differentials
$$Dv = -\tfrac{1}{2}[v_c 1^T + \text{diag}(v_I)]$$
$$Db = M^+ Dv$$

In case of $Qu = 0$ we have

$$\nabla R = \frac{1}{R}\left[Db^T\left(\sqrt{s}a - sb\right) + \frac{\sqrt{s}}{2}v_c\right]$$
$$Dp = \frac{1}{||b||^2}b\left[Db^T\left(2\sqrt{s}b - a\right) - \frac{1}{2}v_c\right]^T - \sqrt{s}Db$$

In case of $Qu \neq 0$ we define $t_0 = \frac{||Qu||}{||Qv||}$ and we have

$$\nabla R = \frac{t_0}{2R}\left[\frac{1}{||Qv||^2}\left(2t_0||b||^2 + 2a\cdot b - w_c^{1-m}\right)Dv^TQ^TQv - 2Db^T\left(a + t_0b\right) - v_c\right]$$
$$Dp = t_0 M^+\left[I - \frac{1}{||Qv||^2}vv^TQ^TQ\right]Dv$$

3.3 Reduced Set of Centroids

In this section, we will specify a $\widehat{c}$ element subset $\widehat{\mathcal{C}}$ of the set of centroids $\mathcal{C}$, such that for every $w \in W$, preimage $\mathcal{M}^{-1}(w)$ under $\mathcal{M}$ is the same as preimage of some $\widehat{w} \in \widehat{W}$ under mapping $\mathcal{M}_{\widehat{\mathcal{C}}} : \mathbb{R}^h \longrightarrow [0,1]^{\widehat{c}}$, which corresponds to the set of centroids $\widehat{\mathcal{C}}$. We will use the hat symbol to indicate that a given object corresponds to this reduced set of centroids, e.g. $\widehat{b}$ is b computed for the set of centroids $\widehat{\mathcal{C}}$.

The i–th row of M is of the form $(\mu_i - \mu_c)^T$, so let's say that i–th row of M and centroid μ_i correspond to each other. Let S be a set containing μ_c and all the centroids that correspond to some set of r linearly independent rows of M. If $Qu = 0$, then we set $\widehat{\mathcal{C}} = S$. This set lies on a sphere. If $Qu \neq 0$, we take another centroid μ_k such that $S \cup \{\mu_k\}$ does not lie on a sphere and we set $\widehat{\mathcal{C}} = S \cup \{\mu_k\}$. We can find μ_k by checking for each centroid if amending S with it results in $\widehat{Q}\widehat{u} \neq 0$.

Let $k_1, k_2, \ldots, k_{\widehat{c}}$ be the indices of centroids that we put into $\widehat{\mathcal{C}}$. We define transformation $T : W \longrightarrow \widehat{W}$ with formula

$$T(w) = \frac{1}{\sum_{i=1}^{\widehat{c}} w_{k_i}}\left(w_{k_1}, w_{k_2}, \ldots, w_{k_{\widehat{c}}}\right)$$

For any $w \in W$, $\mathcal{M}^{-1}(w) = \mathcal{M}_{\widehat{\mathcal{C}}}^{-1}(T(w))$. T is invertible and continuous on W. We let $\widehat{w}$ denote $T(w)$ and we let $\underline{\widehat{w}}$ denote $\widehat{P}(T(w))$. Elements of sets $\widehat{W}$ and $\underline{\widehat{W}}$ are in one-to-one correspondence with elements of set W (and with each other), so we will use symbols $\widehat{w}$ and $\underline{\widehat{w}}$ respectively to denote elements of these sets. Thus we have for $w \in W$, $\mathcal{M}^{-1}(w) = \mathcal{M}_{\widehat{\mathcal{C}}}^{-1}(\widehat{w})$. For every $w \in W$, we have $\widehat{R}(\underline{\widehat{w}}) = R(\underline{w})$, $\widehat{p}(\underline{\widehat{w}}) = p(\underline{w})$, $\widehat{U} = U$, $\widehat{b}(\underline{\widehat{w}}) = b(\underline{w})$ and $\widehat{H}(\underline{\widehat{w}}) = H(\underline{w})$. Though unless $\widehat{\mathcal{C}} = \mathcal{C}$, $D\widehat{b}(\underline{\widehat{w}})$ is not equal to $Db(\underline{w})$, because these matrices have different number of columns. The same is true for $D\widehat{p}$ and $\nabla\widehat{R}$.

4   Reverse Mapping with Minimal MSE

Let's assume that there is a continuous probability distribution, with a continuous probability density function f, defined on the feature space $\mathbb{R}^h$. Function f can be interpreted as density of points of some data set $\mathcal{D} \subset \mathbb{R}^h$. For a real data set, such density can be approximated using statistical density estimation methods. Figure 2 shows an example of a simple probability density function derived from a data set. In this chapter, we will look for a reverse mapping G from the concept space to the feature space which allows minimum mean squared error (MSE), with respect to f, of an operation of mapping points of feature space to concept space via $\mathcal{M}$ and then back to feature space via G, cf. Fig. 3. Let $\boldsymbol{X}$ be a random vector distributed according to density f. MSE of this operation is given by expression $\mathbb{E}\big|\big|\boldsymbol{X} - G(\mathcal{M}(\boldsymbol{X}))\big|\big|^2$, so the function that minimizes it is equal to conditional expectation $G(\boldsymbol{w}) = \mathbb{E}\big(\boldsymbol{X}\big|\mathcal{M}(\boldsymbol{X}) = \boldsymbol{w}\big)$ almost everywhere (Fig. 4).

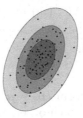

Fig. 3. Contour plot of a simple probability density derived from a data set in a two–dimensional feature space.

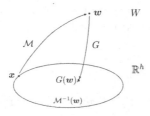

Fig. 4. Point $\boldsymbol{x}$ of $\mathbb{R}^h$ is mapped by $\mathcal{M}$ onto a point $\boldsymbol{w}$ of W which in turn is mapped back into $\mathbb{R}^h$ by G.

4.1   Parameterization of Feature Space

For $n > 0$, we parametrize almost all of the unit sphere $\mathcal{S}^n \subset \mathbb{R}^{n+1}$ by n angular coordinates $\boldsymbol{\theta} = (\theta_1, \theta_2, ..., \theta_n)$ that range over set $\Theta = (0, \pi)^{n-1} \times (0, 2\pi) \subset \mathbb{R}^n$.

$$
y(\theta) = \begin{bmatrix} \cos(\theta_1) \\ \sin(\theta_1)\cos(\theta_2) \\ \sin(\theta_1)\sin(\theta_2)\cos(\theta_3) \\ \vdots \\ \sin(\theta_1)\cdots\sin(\theta_{n-1})\cos(\theta_n) \\ \sin(\theta_1)\cdots\sin(\theta_{n-1})\sin(\theta_n) \end{bmatrix}
\quad
y^{-1}(x) = \begin{bmatrix} \arccos\dfrac{x_1}{\sqrt{x_{n+1}^2+x_n^2+\cdots+x_1^2}} \\ \arccos\dfrac{x_2}{\sqrt{x_{n+1}^2+x_n^2+\cdots+x_2^2}} \\ \vdots \\ \arccos\dfrac{x_{n-1}}{\sqrt{x_{n+1}^2+x_n^2+x_{n-1}^2}} \\ 2\operatorname{arccot}\dfrac{x_n+\sqrt{x_{n+1}^2+x_n^2}}{x_{n+1}} \end{bmatrix}
$$

Vector y has length $n+1$ and y^{-1} length n. The (i,j)–th element of $(n+1)\times n$ matrix Dy is

$$
\frac{\partial y_i}{\partial \theta_j} = \begin{cases} 0 & \text{if } i < j \\ -\sin(\theta_1)\ldots\sin(\theta_{i-1})\sin(\theta_i) & \text{if } i = j \\ \sin(\theta_1)\ldots\sin(\theta_{j-1})\cos(\theta_j)\sin(\theta_{j+1})\ldots\sin(\theta_{i-1})\cos(\theta_i) & \text{if } j < i \le n \\ \sin(\theta_1)\ldots\sin(\theta_{j-1})\cos(\theta_j)\sin(\theta_{j+1})\ldots\sin(\theta_n) & \text{if } i = n+1 \end{cases}
$$

For $n = 0$, we set $\Theta = \{-1,1\}$ and we parametrize $\mathcal{S}^0$ with an identity $y : \Theta \longrightarrow \{-1,1\}$. Let $\mathcal{I}_s$ be a subset of W such that preimages of its points are nondegenerate spheres. We define transformation $\psi : \widehat{\mathcal{I}_s} \times \Theta \longrightarrow \mathbb{R}^h$ as follows

$$
\psi(\widehat{w},\theta) = \psi_w(\theta) = p(w) + R(w)H(w)y(\theta)
$$

For a fixed $\widehat{w}$, it is a bijection between Θ and $\mathcal{M}^{-1}(w)$. Mapping ψ is a bijection onto $\mathcal{M}^{-1}(\mathcal{I}_s)$ whose complement in $\mathbb{R}^h$ is of measure zero if $\mathcal{M}$ is not invertible. ψ is continuously differentiable. (if $n = 0$, it is continuously differentiable for a fixed θ). If $Qu = 0$, then

$$
D_{\widehat{w}}\psi = D\widehat{p} + Hy\nabla\widehat{R}^T + \frac{Ry_{n+1}}{||b||}\left(I - \frac{1}{||b||^2}bb^T\right)D\widehat{b}
$$

and if $Qu \neq 0$, then

$$
D_{\widehat{w}}\psi = D\widehat{p} + Uy\nabla\widehat{R}^T
$$

If $n > 0$, then also

$$
D_\theta\psi = RHDy
$$

For $n > 0$, we define $\mathcal{J}(w,\theta)$ as the Jacobian of ψ, $\mathcal{J}(w,\theta) = \big|\det[D_w\psi \mid D_\theta\psi]\big|$ and for $n = 0$, as $\mathcal{J}(w,\theta) = \big|\det D_w\psi\big|$.

4.2   Reverse Mapping

We define a subset of W, $\mathcal{I}_f = \{w \in W \mid \exists x \in \mathcal{M}^{-1}(w)\ f(x) > 0\}$. The following mapping $G : \mathcal{I}_f \longrightarrow \mathbb{R}^h$, allows the minimum MSE of the operation we discussed above. For $w \in \mathcal{I}_f \cap \mathcal{I}_s$,

$$
G(w) = \frac{\int_\Theta \psi_w(\theta)f(\psi_w(\theta))\mathcal{J}(\widehat{w},\theta)\mathrm{d}\lambda^n}{\int_\Theta f(\psi_w(\theta))\mathcal{J}(\widehat{w},\theta)\mathrm{d}\lambda^n}
$$

and for all other $w \neq w_{eq}$ in its domain $G(w) = p(\underline{w})$. Symbol λ^n stands for Lebesgue measure on $\mathbb{R}^n$. Value of an integral of a vector–valued function is a vector of integrals of its component functions. For $w \in \mathcal{I}_f \cap \mathcal{I}_s$, we can rewrite the above formula as

$$G(w) = p(\underline{w}) + \left(\int_\Theta f(\psi_w(\theta)) \mathcal{J}(\widehat{w}, \theta) \mathrm{d}\lambda^n \right)^{-1} R(\underline{w}) H(\underline{w}) \int_\Theta y(\theta) f(\psi_w(\theta)) \mathcal{J}(\widehat{w}, \theta) \mathrm{d}\lambda^n$$

If $w_{eq} \in \mathcal{I}_f$, then $G(w_{eq})$ can be arbitrary as this single value has no bearing on the value of MSE. G is continuous on $\mathcal{I}_f \backslash \{w_{eq}\}$.

For $w \in \mathcal{I}_f \cap \mathcal{I}_s$, $\theta \in \Theta$ and $x \in \mathcal{M}^{-1}(\mathcal{I}_s)$, we define

$$\phi(w, \theta) = \sqrt{\det \left(D_{\widehat{w}} \psi(\widehat{w}, \theta)^T D_{\widehat{w}} \psi(\widehat{w}, \theta) \right)}$$

$$\Phi_w(x) = \phi\left(w, \psi_w^{-1}(x)\right) = \phi\left(w, y^{-1}\left(\tfrac{1}{R} U^T (x - p)\right)\right)$$

Integrals below are over the embedded n–sphere that is the preimage of w and is an n–dimensional manifold. If $Qu \neq 0$ and $n > 0$, then for $w \in \mathcal{I}_f \cap \mathcal{I}_s$,

$$G(w) = \frac{\int\limits_{\mathcal{M}^{-1}(w)} x f(x) \Phi_w(x) \mathrm{d}S^n}{\int\limits_{\mathcal{M}^{-1}(w)} f(x) \Phi_w(x) \mathrm{d}S^n}$$

This alternative form enables approximation of this value by summing over sets of points spaced regularly and finely on the n–sphere $\mathcal{M}^{-1}(w)$ embedded in $\mathbb{R}^h$.

4.3 Algorithm

Based on this work we may consider the following algorithm for mapping a point from the concept space to the feature space. We are given set $\mathcal{C} \subset \mathbb{R}^h$ of centroids of c clusters and a probability density function f defined on $\mathbb{R}^h$ or a data set $\mathcal{D} \subset \mathbb{R}^h$. If we are given a data set, we will find values of f with density estimation methods. We compute M, M^+, Q, u, a, r, d and U. Based on Qu we ascertain which case we are dealing with and we compute H and n. We determine a reduced set of clusters $\widehat{\mathcal{C}}$.

The input of the algorithm is $w \in [0, 1]^c$ and the output is $x \in \mathbb{R}^h$. When value of x is set, the algorithm stops. Let μ be a centroid of the cluster in which w has the highest membership.

1. Project w onto W orthogonally/in the direction of the origin.
2. Compute v, b and Qv.
3. If conditions for $\mathcal{M}^{-1}(w)$ to be nonempty are not met, set $x = \mu$.
4. If $w \neq w_{eq}$, compute p and R.
5. If $d = 0$ and $Qu \neq 0$ or if $R = 0$, set $x = p$.
6. Check if f is positive on any point of $\mathcal{M}^{-1}(w)$. If not, set $x = p$.
7. Compute an approximation of $G(w)$ and set x to its value.

Table 1. Comparison of MSE

h	c	p	$G(\boldsymbol{w})$
3	3	22.58	15.35
4	4	25.37	19.19
7	7	8.21	6.75
4	3	48.65	25.95
5	4	23.72	20.22
6	5	25.71	23.23

We tested above algorithm against assigning to $\boldsymbol{w} \in W$ a mean of $\mathcal{M}^{-1}(\boldsymbol{w})$ (which in case of FCM is $\boldsymbol{p}$). Each data set consisted of c clouds of points generated using multivariate normal probability distributions of different means and covariance matrices. Results are in Table 1.

4.4 Application

The reverse mapping from the concept space to the feature space that we derived, is best fitted – in terms of MSE – to a given probability density function defined on the feature space which can be a density of some data set in the feature space. We will discuss an application of this mapping to the problem of defuzzification of results of computation on fuzzy data. Suppose we have a training set T whose each element consists of k input points $\boldsymbol{x}_1^i$, $\boldsymbol{x}_2^i$, ..., $\boldsymbol{x}_k^i$ of feature space $\mathbb{R}^h$ and one output point $\boldsymbol{x}_0^i$ of feature space. All the feature space points from T put together, constitute a data set $\mathcal{D}$ on which we use FCM to find c fuzzy clusters and a set of their centroids $\mathcal{C}$. We transform every $\boldsymbol{x}_j^i$ into $\mathcal{M}(\boldsymbol{x}_j^i)$, to obtain a concept-level training set T_c. Using some machine learning method, we train on T_c an operation F_c, working on the level of concept space, that returns a point of concept space based on k input points of concept space. Let G be a minimum MSE reverse mapping associated with $\mathcal{C}$, found for f – a density of data set $\mathcal{D}_{\text{out}} \subset \mathcal{D}$ consisting only of output points. G has minimum MSE when defuzzifying output points of the training set T_c, so we may expect it to defuzzify other outputs well.

Furthermore, for all sets of input points from T_c, F_c is fitted to return a point close to a correct output point $\mathcal{M}(\boldsymbol{x}_0^i)$ and G is fitted to map to a point of feature space close to $\boldsymbol{x}_0^i$. Thus, the composition $F = G \circ F_c \circ \mathcal{M}$ may be a good fit for training set T as an operation that returns a point of feature space based on k input points of feature space. This approach may be useful in case of data which is easier modeled at the concept level than at the numeric level.

5   Conclusion

We presented a reverse mapping from concept space to feature space, best fitted – in terms of MSE – to a given probability density function defined on feature space or a given data set in feature space. Similar reverse mappings could be obtained for different transformations into the concept space. Maybe transformation that allows more precise reverse mapping could be constructed. Many aspects of this work leave room for further research. In the described application the concept-level operation may return points that do not lie in set W. Effectiveness of various approaches to amend this situation can be investigated, such as orthogonal projection onto W or projection onto W in the direction of the origin. Also there may be better ways to treat the points of W that drop out at steps 3 and 6 of the algorithm. For a point of W that has a nonempty preimage, but density f is zero on all its points, it might be a good treatment to map it onto the point of its preimage that is closest to the mean of $\mathcal{D}$ weighted by f. The second important direction of research is approximation of f in a situation when we do not have access to any data set in the feature space.

References

1. Bezdek, J.C., Ehrlich, R., Full, W.: FCM: the fuzzy c-means clustering algorithm. Comput. Geosci. **10**(2–3), 191–203 (1984)
2. Broekhoven, E.V., Baets, B.D.: Fast and accurate center of gravity defuzzification of fuzzy system outputs defined on trapezoidal fuzzy partitions. Fuzzy Sets Syst. **157**(3), 904–918 (2006)
3. Dave, R.N., Bhaswan, K.: Adaptive fuzzy c-shells clustering and detection of ellipses. IEEE Trans. Neural Netw. **3**(5), 643–662 (1992)
4. van Leekwijck, W., Kerre, E.E.: Defuzzification: criteria and classification. Fuzzy Sets Syst. **108**(2), 159–178 (1999)
5. Liu, X.: Parameterized defuzzification with maximum entropy weighting function - another view of the weighting function expectation method. Math. Comput. Model. **45**(1–2), 177–188 (2007)
6. Madau, D.P., Feldkamp, L.A.: Influence value defuzzification method. Fuzzy Syst. **3**, 1819–1824 (1996)
7. Roventa, E., Spircu, T.: Averaging procedures in defuzzification processes. Fuzzy Sets Syst. **136**(3), 375–385 (2003)

Representatives of Rough Regions
for Generating Classification Rules

Piotr Hońko(✉)

Faculty of Computer Science, Bialystok University of Technology,
Wiejska 45A, 15-351 Białystok, Poland
p.honko@pb.edu.pl

Abstract. Rough set theory provides a useful tool for describing uncertain concepts. The description of a given concept constructed based on rough regions can be used to improve the quality of classification. Processing large data using rough set methods requires efficient implementations as well as alternative approaches to speed up computations. This paper proposes a representative-based approach for rough region-based classification. Positive, boundary, and negative regions are replaced with their representatives sets that preserve information needed for generating classification rules. For data divisible into a relatively low number of equivalence classes representatives sets are considerably smaller than the whole regions. Using a small representation of regions significantly speeds up the process of rule generation.

Keywords: Rough sets · Classification rules · Representative-based approach

1 Introduction

Rough set theory [5] has found a wide application in processing uncertain data. It enables to describe a concept represented by a subset of the universe in an alternative way. Such a description identifies objects that certainly (lower approximation) and possibly (upper approximation) belong to the concept. The thus created rough set (i.e. the pair of lower and upper approximations) can further be used to improve classification of uncertain data. For example, based on the lower (upper) approximation one can construct classification rules that assign objects to the concept certainly (possibly) correctly.

Processing large data using rough set methods may be a challenging task. Some methods require a more efficient implementation to make them applicable to processing huge amount of data. For example, a direct implementation of the definition of rough sets requires polynomial time to find approximations of a given concept. These computations can be speeded up e.g. by adapting sort algorithm that needs linear-logarithmic time [4].

P. Hońko—The project was funded by the National Science Center awarded on the basis of the decision number DEC-2012/07/B/ST6/01504.

Published by Springer International Publishing Switzerland 2016. All Rights Reserved
K. Saeed and W. Homenda (Eds.): CISIM 2016, LNCS 9842, pp. 79–90, 2016.
DOI: 10.1007/978-3-319-45378-1_8

Even though using efficient implementations, processing the whole data may still be time or space consuming. Another solution for shortening the run-time and saving memory is to apply a representative-based approach. Instead of the whole data, only its previously found representatives are processed. The crucial step in this approach is to find representatives that preserve information essential for the goal of data processing.

Several representative-based approaches were applied in rough set theory. In [2] the set of representatives is defined as a minimal universe subset whose objects possess all properties under consideration. A similarity relation-based rough set approach was used in [3] to find representative cases in the problem of case-based reasoning. In [1] an object for which there is only one minimal universe subset (each subset belongs to a given covering of the universe) the object belongs to is understood as the representative of this subset. A minimal set of representatives in tolerance rough sets is identified in [6] by a prime implicant of the Boolean function over the variables corresponding to objects. Representatives used in [7] for the classification task are constructed based on maximal neighborhoods of objects in the positive region (i.e. lower approximation).

The goal of this paper is to propose a representatives sets of rough regions for classification rule generation. Positive, boundary, and negative regions (that can be constructed based on lower and upper approximations) are replaced with their representatives sets. A representative is defined as a pair of information vector corresponding to an object (limited to the attributes under consideration) and the cardinality of the equivalence class represented by the vector. The representatives sets of the three regions are constructed simultaneously using sort-based algorithm. Classification rules are generated from the representatives sets using an adaptation of sequential covering algorithm.

Unlike the above-described approaches, a representative proposed in this study includes not only an object of the universe but also information on its equivalence class that is essential for generating classification rules. Benefits of the approach are clearly visible for data that is divisible into relatively low number of equivalence classes. For such data representatives sets of regions are considerably smaller than the whole regions, thereby the generation of classification rules can significantly be accelerated.

The rest of the paper is organized as follows. Section 2 restates basic notion from rough set theory and proposes a representative-based approach for rough region-based classification rule generation. Section 3 develops algorithms using the proposed approach. Experimental research is reported in Sect. 4. Concluding remarks are provided in Sect. 5.

2   Rough Regions and Their Representatives for Generating Classification Rules

This section restates basic notions from rough set theory. It also proposes representatives sets of rough regions and shows how to use them in generation of classification rules.

2.1   Rough Regions

To store data to be processed, an information system is used.

Definition 1. *[5] (information system) An information system is a pair $IS = (U, A)$, where U is a non-empty finite set of objects, called the universe, and A is a non-empty finite set of attributes.*

Each attribute $a \in A$ is treated as a function $a : U \rightarrow V_a$, where V_a is the value set of a.

An object $x \in U$ can be represented by an information vector $\mathbf{x} = (a(x) : a \in A)$. Let $\mathbf{x}_B = (a(x) : a \in B)$, where $B \subseteq A$, be a B-information vector.

Essential information about data is expressed by an indiscernibility relation.

Definition 2. *[5] (indiscernibility relation) An indiscernibility relation $IND(B)$ generated by $B \subseteq A$ on U is defined by $IND(B) = \{(x, y) \in U \times U : \forall_{a \in B} a(x) = a(y)\}$.*

Any indiscernibility relation partitions the universe into equivalence classes. Let $\mathcal{E} = U/IND(B)$ be the family of equivalence classes of $IND(B)$ on U.

A concept that is not definable (i.e. it is not a union of some equivalence classes) can alternatively be described using approximations.

Definition 3. *[5] (rough approximations) Let $AS_B = (U, IND(B))$ be an approximation space. The lower and upper approximations of a subset $X \subseteq U$ in AS are defined, respectively, by*

1. $LOW(AS_B, X) = \bigcup \{E \in \mathcal{E} : E \subseteq X\}$,
2. $UPP(AS_B, X) = \bigcup \{E \in \mathcal{E} : E \cap X \neq \emptyset\}$.

Using approximations one can partition the universe into three regions.

Definition 4. *[5] (rough regions) The positive, boundary, and negative regions of a subset $X \subseteq U$ in $AS_B = (U, IND(B))$ are defined, respectively, by*

1. $POS(AS_B, X) = LOW(AS_B, X) = \bigcup \{E \in \mathcal{E} : E \subseteq X\}$,
2. $BND(AS_B, X) = UPP(AS_B, X) \setminus LOW(AS_B, X) = \bigcup \{E \in \mathcal{E} : E \cap X \neq \emptyset \wedge E \nsubseteq X\}$,
3. $NEG(AS_B, X) = U \setminus UPP(AS_B, X) = \bigcup \{E \in \mathcal{E} : E \cap X = \emptyset\}$.

The positive (negative) region includes objects that certainly belong (not belong) to the concept. The boundary region includes, in turn, uncertain objects.

2.2   Representatives of Rough Regions

The following representatives of equivalence classes and regions are proposed.

Let $\widehat{E}_B = (\mathbf{x}_B, c)$ be a representative of an equivalence class E, where $B \subseteq A, x \in E$ and $c = |E|$.

Definition 5. *(representatives sets of rough regions) The representatives sets of positive, boundary, and negative regions of a subset* $X \subseteq U$ *in* $AS_B = (U, IND(B))$ *are defined, respectively, by*

1. $\widehat{POS}(AS_B, X) = \{\widehat{E}_B : E \subseteq X\}$,
2. $\widehat{BND}(AS_B, X) = \{\widehat{E}_B : E \cap X \neq \emptyset \wedge E \nsubseteq X\}$,
3. $\widehat{NEG}(AS_B, X) = \{\widehat{E}_B : E \cap X = \emptyset\}$.

If the concept to be approximated is known before computing the equivalence classes, its rough regions can be defined using the equivalence classes computed separately for the concept and its complement.

Let $\mathcal{E}_X = X/IND(B)$, where $X \subseteq U$. Let also $\widehat{E}_B \simeq \widehat{E'}_B \Leftrightarrow \mathbf{x}_B = \mathbf{y}_B$, where $\widehat{E}_B = (\mathbf{x}_B, c)$ and $\widehat{E'}_B = (\mathbf{y}_B, c')$.

The following alternative definition of rough regions is proposed.

Proposition 1. *For any* $X \subseteq U$ *in* $AS_B = (U, IND(B))$ *the following hold.*

1. $POS(AS_B, X) = \bigcup\{E \in \mathcal{E}_X : \forall_{E' \in \mathcal{E}_{X^c}} \widehat{E}_B \not\simeq \widehat{E'}_B\}$;
2. $BND(AS_B, X) = \bigcup\{E \cup E' : E \in \mathcal{E}_X, E' \in \mathcal{E}_{X^c} : \widehat{E}_B \simeq \widehat{E'}_B\}$.
3. $NEG(AS_B, X) = \bigcup\{E \in \mathcal{E}_{X^c} : \forall_{E' \in \mathcal{E}_X} \widehat{E}_B \not\simeq \widehat{E'}_B\}$.

Proof. 1. Let $L = POS(AS_B, X)$ and $R = \bigcup\{E \in \mathcal{E}_X : \forall_{E' \in \mathcal{E}_{X^c}} \widehat{E}_B \not\simeq \widehat{E'}_B\}$.

The case "$\Rightarrow$". We have $E \subseteq X \Rightarrow X^c \subseteq U \setminus E$ (a), $\mathcal{E}_X = \{E \cap X : E \in \mathcal{E}\}$(b). We obtain $E \subseteq L \Leftrightarrow E \in \mathcal{E} \wedge E \subseteq X \Leftrightarrow \forall_{(x,y) \in E \times U \setminus E}(x,y) \notin IND(B) \wedge E \cap X = E \Rightarrow \forall_{(x,y) \in E \times X^c}(x,y) \notin IND(B) \wedge E \in \mathcal{E}_X$ by (a) and (b). Hence, we obtain $E \in \mathcal{E}_X \wedge \forall_{E' \in \mathcal{E}_{X^c}} \widehat{E}_B \not\simeq \widehat{E'}_B \Leftrightarrow E \subseteq R$.

The case "$\Leftarrow$". We have $E \in \mathcal{E}_X \Rightarrow E \subseteq X$(c), $E \in \mathcal{E}_X \Leftrightarrow \forall_{(x,y) \in E \times X \setminus E}(x,y) \notin IND(B)$(d).

We obtain $E \subseteq R \Leftrightarrow E \in \mathcal{E}_X \wedge \forall_{E' \in \mathcal{E}_{X^c}} \widehat{E}_B \not\simeq \widehat{E'}_B \Rightarrow E \subseteq X \wedge \forall_{(x,y) \in E \times X \setminus E}(x,y) \notin IND(B) \wedge \forall_{(x,y) \in E \times X^c}(x,y) \notin IND(B) \Leftrightarrow E \subseteq X \wedge \forall_{(x,y) \in E \times U \setminus E}(x,y) \notin IND(B) \Leftrightarrow E \subseteq X \wedge E \in \mathcal{E} \Leftrightarrow E \in L$ by (c) and (d).

2–3. These can be shown analogously to the first point.

The representatives sets of rough regions can also be constructed using the families of equivalence classes of the concept and its complement.

Let $\widehat{E}_B \oplus \widehat{E'}_B = (\mathbf{x}_B, c+c') = (\mathbf{y}_B, c+c')$ for $\widehat{E}_B = (\mathbf{x}_B, c)$ and $\widehat{E'}_B = (\mathbf{y}_B, c')$ such that $\widehat{E}_B \simeq \widehat{E'}_B$.

Proposition 2. *For any* $X \subseteq U$ *in* $AS_B = (U, IND(B))$ *the following hold.*

1. $\widehat{POS}(AS_B, X) = \{\widehat{E}_B \in \mathcal{E}_X : \forall_{E' \in \mathcal{E}_{X^c}} \widehat{E}_B \not\simeq \widehat{E'}_B\}$;
2. $\widehat{BND}(AS_B, X) = \{\widehat{E}_B \oplus \widehat{E'}_B : E \in \mathcal{E}_X, E' \in \mathcal{E}_{X^c}, \widehat{E}_B \simeq \widehat{E'}_B\}$;
3. $\widehat{NEG}(AS_B, X) = \{\widehat{E}_B \in \mathcal{E}_{X^c} : \forall_{E' \in \mathcal{E}_X} \widehat{E}_B \not\simeq \widehat{E'}_B\}$.

Proof. 1. We obtain $\{\widehat{E}_B \in \mathcal{E}_X : \forall_{E' \in \mathcal{E}_{X^c}} \widehat{E}_B \not\simeq \widehat{E'}_B\} = \{\widehat{E}_B : E \subseteq \bigcup\{E \in \mathcal{E}_X : \forall_{E' \in \mathcal{E}_{X^c}} \widehat{E}_B \not\simeq \widehat{E'}_B\}\} = \{\widehat{E}_B : E \subseteq POS(AS_B, X)\} = \widehat{POS}(AS_B, X)$ by Definition 5 and Proposition 1.

2. **Lemma 1.** *For any $E \in \mathcal{E}_X$ and $E' \in \mathcal{E}_{X^c}$ the following holds $\widehat{E}_B \oplus \widehat{E'}_B = (\widehat{E \cup E'})_B$.*

   The lemma can easily be proven by the definition of the $\oplus$ operation.
   We obtain $\{\widehat{E}_B \oplus \widehat{E'}_B : E \in \mathcal{E}_X, E' \in \mathcal{E}_{X^c}, \widehat{E}_B \simeq \widehat{E'}_B\} = \{\widehat{E}_B \oplus \widehat{E'}_B : E \cup E' \subseteq \bigcup\{E \cup E' : E \in \mathcal{E}_X, E' \in \mathcal{E}_{X^c} : \widehat{E'}_B \simeq \widehat{E'}_B\} = \{(\widehat{E \cup E'})_B : E \cup E' \subseteq BND(AS_R, X)\} = \widehat{BND}(AS_B, X))$ by the lemma, Definition 5 and Proposition 1.

3. This can be shown analogously to the first point.

2.3 Classification Rules Generated from Representatives Sets

In rough set theory classification rules are usually generated based on one of the lower or upper approximations.

Definition 6. *(rough approximation rule) A rough approximation rule in $AS_B = (U, IND(B))$ is an expression of the form $\alpha \rightarrow \beta$, where $\alpha = \bigwedge_{i=1}^k (a_i, v_i), \beta = (app, v), a_i \in A$ $(v_i \in V_{a_i})$ are condition attributes and app $(app \in \{lower, upper\}, V_{app} = \{0, 1\})$ is the decision attribute such that $d(x) = 1 \Leftrightarrow x \in APP(AS_B, X)$ for any $x \in U$ and a given $X \subseteq U$.*

Let $match_X(r)$ be the matching of a rule r over $X \subseteq U$, i.e. the set of objects from X that satisfy the rule premise. Let also $\widehat{X}_B = \{\widehat{E}_B : E \in \mathcal{E}_X\}$ be the representatives set of $X \subseteq U$.

Definition 7. *(matching of rule over representatives set) The matching of a rule r over a representatives set $\widehat{X}_B$, denoted by $match_{\widehat{X}_B}(r)$, is defined as follows $(\mathbf{x}_B, c) \in match_{\widehat{X}_B}(r) \Leftrightarrow x \in match_X(r)$.*

Proposition 3. *For any rough approximation rule r the following holds*

$$match_{\widehat{X}_B}(r) = (\widehat{match_X(r)})_B.$$

Proof. We obtain $(\mathbf{x}_B, c) \in (\widehat{match_X(r)}) \Leftrightarrow (\mathbf{x}_B, c) \in \{\widehat{E}_B : E \in \mathcal{E}_{match_X(r)}\} \Leftrightarrow x \in \bigcup\{E : E \in \mathcal{E}_{match_X(r)}\} \Leftrightarrow x \in match_X(r) \Leftrightarrow (\mathbf{x}_B, c) \in match_{\widehat{X}_B}(r)$ by Definition 7.

Let $card_{\widehat{X}_B}(match_{\widehat{X}_B}(r)) = \sum_{(\mathbf{x}_B, c) \in match_{\widehat{X}_B}(r)} c$.

Proposition 4. *For any rough approximation rule r the following holds*

$$card_{\widehat{X}_B}(match_{\widehat{X}_B}(r)) = |match_X(r)|.$$

Proof. Let $\{x_1, \ldots, x_n\} \subseteq X$ be the set of objects from X matching a given rule r. We have $match_X(r) = \{x_1, \ldots, x_n\} = \{x_1^1, \ldots, x_{n_1}^1, x_1^2, \ldots, x_{n_2}^2, \ldots, x_1^k, \ldots, x_{n_k}^k\} = \bigcup_{i=1}^k E^i$, where $E^i = \{x_1^i, \ldots, x_{n_i}^i\}$ is an equivalence class. Hence, $|match_X(r)| = \sum_{i=1}^k |E^i|$. We also have $card_{\widehat{X}_B}(match_{\widehat{X}_B}(r)) = \sum_{(\mathbf{x}_B, c) \in match_{\widehat{X}_B}(r)} c = \sum_{E \in \mathcal{E}_{match_X(r)}} |E| = \sum_{i=1}^k |E^i|$.

The below example illustrates the notions introduced in this section.

Example 1. Given a data table of patients who are suspected to be sick with flu.

$U \setminus A$	Temperature	Headache	Weakness	Nausea	Flu
1	Very high	Yes	Yes	No	Yes
2	Normal	No	No	No	No
3	High	No	No	No	No
4	Normal	No	Yes	No	Yes
5	Normal	No	Yes	No	No
6	High	Yes	No	Yes	Yes
7	Very high	No	No	No	No
8	Normal	Yes	Yes	Yes	Yes

Consider the approximation space $AS_B = (U, IND(B))$, where $B = \{headache, weakness\}$, and the concept of patients sick with flu represented by the set $X = \{1, 4, 6, 8\}$.

We obtain $U/IND(B) = \{\{1,8\}, \{2,3,7\}, \{4,5\}, \{6\}\}, POS(AS_B, X) = \{1,6,8\}, BND(AS_B, X) = \{4,5\}$ and $NEG(AS_B, X) = \{2,3,7\}$.

Let $\mathbf{x}_B^1 = (yes, yes), \mathbf{x}_B^2 = (no, yes), \mathbf{x}_B^3 = (yes, no), \mathbf{y}_B^1 = (no, no), \mathbf{y}_B^2 = (no, yes)$. We obtain $\widehat{X}_B = \{(\mathbf{x}_B^1, 2), (\mathbf{x}_B^2, 1), (\mathbf{x}_B^3, 1)\}, \widehat{X^c}_B = \{(\mathbf{y}_B^1, 3), (\mathbf{y}_B^2, 1)\}, \widehat{POS}(AS_B, X) = \{(\mathbf{x}_B^1, 2), (\mathbf{x}_B^3, 1)\}, \widehat{BND}(AS_B, X) = \{(\mathbf{x}_B^2, 1) \oplus (\mathbf{y}_B^2, 1)\}$ and $\widehat{NEG}(AS_B, X)) = \{(\mathbf{y}_B^2, 1)\}$.

Consider the rule $r : (weakness, yes) \to (lower, 1)$. Let $P = POS(AS_B, X)$ and $N = BND(AS_B, X) \cup NEG(AS_B, X)$. We obtain $|match_P(r)| = |\{1,8\}| = 2$ and $|match_N(r)| = |\{4,5\}| = 2$.

We obtain $card_{\widehat{P}_B}(match_{\widehat{P}_B}(r)) = card_{\widehat{P}_B}(\{(\mathbf{x}_B^1, 2)\}) = 2, card_{\widehat{N}_B}(match_{\widehat{N}_B}(r)) = card_{\widehat{N}_B}(\{(\mathbf{x}_B', 2)\}) = 2$, where $(\mathbf{x}_B', 2) = (\mathbf{x}_B^2, 1) \oplus (\mathbf{y}_B^2, 1)$.

3 Algorithms for Computing Representatives of Rough Regions and Generating Classification Rules

This section proposes a sort-based algorithm for computing representatives sets of rough regions. It also adapts a sequential covering algorithm to generate classification rules from representatives sets.

Firstly, a sort-based algorithm for computing lower and upper approximations will be recalled [4]. It can be outlined as follows.

1. Given an information system $IS = (U, A)$, a subset $B \subseteq A$ and a concept $X \subseteq U$.
2. Sort objects from U (represented by B-information vectors) in the lexicographical order.
3. Form the equivalence classes based on objects that are equal according to the order.
4. Form approximations: If an equivalence class is included in X, then add the class to the lower approximation; If an equivalence class and X have at least one common element, then add the class to the upper approximation.

The algorithm needs $O(|B||U|log|U|)$ time to sort objects, and $O(|U|)$ time to form approximations, assuming that the information on the membership to the concept is associated with each object of the universe.

The algorithm called $ComputeRegionRep$ for computing representatives sets of rough regions is proposed.

Let $(\mathbf{x}_B, c) \preceq (\mathbf{y}_B, c') \Leftrightarrow \forall_{a \in B} a(x) \leq a(y)$ and $(\mathbf{x}_B, c) \prec (\mathbf{y}_B, c') \Leftrightarrow (\mathbf{x}_B, c) \preceq (\mathbf{y}_B, c') \wedge \exists_{a \in B} a(x) < a(y)$.

Algorithm 1: $ComputeRegionRep$

Data: $AS_B = (X \cup X^c, IND(B))$ – an approximation space with the specified concept X to be approximated;

Result: $(repPOS, repBND, repNEG)$ – a triple of the representatives sets of the positive, boundary, and negative regions;

begin
    $repPOS := \emptyset; repBND := \emptyset; repNEG := \emptyset;$
    $Y := mergeSortUnique(X, B); Y' := mergeSortUnique(X^c, B);$
    $i := 1; j := 1;$
    while $i < |Y|$ **or** $j < |Y'|$ **do**
        if $j > |Y'|$ **then**
         | $repPOS := repPOS \cup \{Y[i], \ldots, Y[|Y|]\}; i = |Y|;$
        end
        else if $i > |Y|$ **then**
         | $repNEG := repNEG \cup \{Y'[j], \ldots, Y'[|Y'|]\}; j = |Y'|;$
        end
        else if $Y[i] \prec Y'[j]$ **then**
         | $repPOS := repPOS \cup \{Y[i]\}; i := i + 1;$
        end
        else if $Y[i] \simeq Y'[j]$ **then**
         | $repBND := repBND \cup \{Y[i] \oplus Y'[j]\}; i := i + 1; j := j + 1;$
        end
        else
         | $repNEG := repNEG \cup \{Y'[j]\}; j := j + 1;$
        end
    end
end

Algorithm 1 needs not more than $O(|B||X|log|X|) + O(|B||X^c|log|X^c|)$ time to compute representatives of equivalence classes for sets X and X^c. The equality holds when each object is indiscernible with itself only. The cost of joining the representatives is $O(|U|)$. We have $O(|B||X|log|X|) + O(|B||X^c|log|X^c|) + O(|U|) \geq O(|B||U|log|U|)$. The equality holds for $|X| = |X^c|$.

The $mergeSortUnique(X)$ function is defined as follows.

1. Form the initial representative of X, i.e. $\widehat{X}_B = \{(\mathbf{x}_B, 1) : x \in X\}$.
2. Order $\widehat{X}_B$ using the merge sort algorithm that applies the following comparison function

$$compare((\mathbf{x}_B, c), (\mathbf{x}'_B, c')) = \begin{cases} (\mathbf{x}_B, c), & (\mathbf{x}_B, c) \prec (\mathbf{x}'_B, c'); \\ (\mathbf{x}'_B, c'), & (\mathbf{x}'_B, c') \prec (\mathbf{x}_B, c); \\ (\mathbf{x}_B, c) \oplus (\mathbf{x}'_B, c'), & (\mathbf{x}_B, c) \simeq (\mathbf{x}'_B, c'). \end{cases}$$

The algorithm called $GenerateRuleSet$ adapts sequential covering one to generate classification rules from representatives sets.

Algorithm 2: $GenerateRuleSet$

Data: $repPOS, repBND, repNEG$ – the representatives sets of the three
            regions; app – the type of approximation;
Result: RS – a rule set generated over APP;
begin
    $RS := \emptyset$; $\beta := (app, 1)$;
    $P := repPOS$; $N := repNEG$;
    if $app = lower$ **then** $N := N \cup repBND$;;
    else $P := P \cup repBND$;
    ;
    while $P \neq \emptyset$ **do**
        $\alpha := \emptyset$; $N' := N$;
        while $N' \neq \emptyset$ **do**
            $c := findBestCandidate(P, N')$;
            $\alpha := \alpha \wedge c$; $N' := match_{N'}(\alpha \rightarrow \beta)$;
        end
        $P := P \setminus match_P(\alpha \rightarrow \beta)$;
    end
    $RS := RS \cup \{\alpha \rightarrow \beta\}$;
end

The $findBestCandidate$ function uses any measure that calculates the rule quality based on its matching.

4   Experiments

This section describes experimental research that concerns computation of rough regions and their representatives sets, as well as generation of classification rules based on them.

Six datasets (Table 1) taken from the UCI Repository (archive.ics.uci.edu/ml) were used in the experimental research. The approach was implemented in C++ and tested using a laptop with Intel Core i5, 2.3 GHz, 4 GB RAM, Windows 7.

Function 3: $findBestCandidate$

Data: P, N – the representatives sets of the approximation and its complement;
  $\alpha \rightarrow \beta$ – the current rule; $q\_measure$ – quality measure;
Result: c – the best candidate to add to the rule;
begin

  $p := card_P(match_P(\alpha \rightarrow \beta))$; $n := card_N(match_N(\alpha \rightarrow \beta))$;
  $q := q\_measure(p, q)$; $C := generateCandidates(\alpha \rightarrow \beta)$;
  foreach $c' \in C$ **do**

    $p' := card_P(match_P(\alpha \wedge c' \rightarrow \beta))$; $n' := card_N(match_N(\alpha \wedge c' \rightarrow \beta))$;
    $q' := q\_measure(p', q')$;
    if $q' > q$ **then**
      | $c := c'$; $q := q'$;
    end

  end

end

Table 1. Characteristics of datasets.

Symbol	Dataset	No. attributes	No. objects
D1	Bank marketing	17	45K
D2	Connect-4	43	67K
D3	Skin segmentation	4	245K
D4	KDD cup 1999 Data (10%)	42	494K
D5	Record linkage comparison patterns (10%)	10	574K
D6	Poker hand (testing data)	11	1000K

To compute rough regions a slight modification of the algorithm described in the beginning of Sect. 3 was used. Equivalence classes are generated in the same way, but instead of approximations, regions are computed. Before generation of regions, each object is assigned the label informing whether the object belongs to the concept. Thanks to this, it is enough to scan the universe once to check what region a given equivalence class belongs to. Representatives set of rough regions were generated using Algorithm 1.

Table 2 shows the run-time (given in seconds) for generating regions (standard approach, denoted by std.) and their representatives (representative-based approach, denoted by rep.). For both the approaches the same distribution of data was used (the concept and its complement are equinumerous, denoted by 1-1). Since for the proposed approach a change in data distribution may influences the run-time (see the time complexity analysis in Sect. 3), additional two distributions of data were used (in the first (second) distribution the concept is three times smaller (bigger) than its complement, denoted by 1-3 (3-1)). The table includes also the size of each representatives set given in percentage (the ratio between the number of representatives and the cardinality of the universe multiplied by 100). Independent of the data distribution the regions and their representatives do not change. That is why the size of representatives sets is given once. For each dataset four tests were carried out: the subset of the attribute set included 25 %, 50 %, 75 %, 100 % of its attributes (Attributes were taken in the order they appear in the datasets).

Table 2. Computation of regions and their representatives sets

		25	50	75	100		25	50	75	100
std. 1-1	D1	0.39	0.41	0.41	0.42	D2	0.73	0.89	0.95	0.95
rep. 1-1		**0.34**[a]	0.53	0.53	0.53		**0.48**	**0.72**	1.42	1.63
rep. 1-3		0.35	0.54	0.54	0.54		0.48	0.72	1.48	1.76
rep. 3-1		0.35	0.53	0.53	0.55		0.47	0.73	1.47	1.72
rep. (size)		8.04	90.79	100	100		0.98	19.35	78.62	100
std. 1-1	D3	1.50	1.59	1.65	1.67	D4	5.20	6.13	8.60	9.92
rep. 1-1		**1.27**	**1.39**	**1.47**	**1.48**		**3.09**	**3.35**	**6.60**	**7.85**
rep. 1-3		1.27	1.41	1.50	1.52		3.19	3.41	6.78	8.12
rep. 3-1		1.26	1.411	1.50	1.51		3.18	3.47	6.72	8.02
rep. (size)		0.10	8.50	20.99	20.99		11.58	11.62	20.30	29.47
std. 1-1	D5	4.24	5.40	6.08	6.80	D6	7.75	9.08	9.89	9.97
rep. 1-1		**2.96**	**3.99**	**4.52**	**4.70**		**5.84**	**8.91**	13.14	13.18
rep. 1-3		3.0	4.06	4.51	4.83		5.92	9.35	13.67	13.84
rep. 3-1		2.98	4.07	4.564	4.88		5.93	9.26	13.64	13.80
rep. (size)		0.04	0.57	01.16	01.54		<0.01	01.06	92.72	99.79

[a]A run-time obtained by the proposed approach that is shorter than that for the standard one is written in bold.

The results show that if a representatives set is decidedly smaller than the universe, then the run-time is shorter. When the size is close to that of the universe, especially when they are equal, the run-time may be longer. That reason is that Algorithm 1 needs additional operations compared with the standard approach, namely it joins representatives if they are constructed based on the same information vector.

A small size of a representatives set does not always imply a considerably shorter run-time (see e.g. $D1$-25). According to sort-based algorithm we need $log|U|$ steps to sort $|U|$ objects. In the proposed approach, the number of representatives to sort is fewer than or equal to $|U|$. The run-time may depend on how fast (i.e. in which steps) representatives are joined. For example, if most representatives are joined in the last step, then the run-time is inconsiderably shorter.

The run-times obtained for data distributions 1-3 and 3-1 are slightly longer than those for 1-1. Namely, on average we have respectively 3.25 % and 2.73 % longer run-times. In theory, based on the analysis of the time complexity, we should obtain the same results for data distributions 1-3 and 3-1 (about 3.34 %

longer run-time than for 1-1[1]). In practice, the run-time depends, in a sense, on data distribution since equivalence classes are computed separately for the concept and its complement. Therefore, a change in the concept may cause a change in its equivalence classes. Thus, the run-time of computing representatives sets for different concepts may vary.

To generate classification rules from the whole regions, sequential covering algorithm was used. The general mechanism of rule generation is the same as in Algorithm 2 that is used for generating rules from representatives sets. In both cases, the coverage measure was used to evaluate the quality of rules. Rules were generated from the upper approximation of a concept (the union of positive and boundary regions) since it is always different form an empty set.

Table 3 presents results of rule generation for data distribution 1-1 as well as the size of rule sets, denoted by $|RS|$. Since the algorithms for rule generation are not so efficient as those for region computation, then some experiments that were time-consuming (i.e., experiments needing over 30 min to finish computations – denoted by *) were interrupted.

Table 3. Ruleset generation

		25	50	75	100		25	50	75	100
std. 1-1	D1	13.88	*	*	*	D2	1.42	49.62	169.07	347.03
rep. 1-1		**3.09**	*	*	*		**0.07**	**7.52**	**123.83**	**344.12**
$|RS|$		1180	?	?	?		85	157	288	419
std. 1-1	D3	61.78	*	*	*	D4	*	*	*	*
rep. 1-1		**0.16**	**1321.86**	*	*		*	*	*	*
$|RS|$		256	13323	?	?		?	?	?	?
std. 1-1	D5	5.67	162.63	285.76	430.72	D6	3.81	5.74	*	*
rep. 1-1		**0.02**	**9.27**	**26.55**	**52.87**		**<0.001**	**0.46**	*	*
$|RS|$		150	1663	2206	2671		4	4	?	?

The results clearly show that rule generation from representative sets is decidedly less time-consuming. On average, the proposed approach is 2.7 times faster. If the size of a representatives set is close to that of the universe (see $D2$-75 and $D2$-100), the run-time is also closer to that obtained for the whole universe. However, unlike for region computation, the algorithm for generating rules from representatives sets does not perform additional operations. Thanks to this, the time needed for computing rules from a representatives set of the size equal to that of the universe should not be longer than in the standard case (see $D2$-100).

A relatively small representatives set does not guarantee a short run-time. For example, it is needed over 22 min to accomplish computations for $D3$-50. The

---

[1] The value is computed according to the formula $(a|U|log(a|U|) + (1 - a)|U|log((1 - a)|U|))/(2 * 0.5|U|log(0.5|U|))$, where $a \in (0, 1)$ defines the data distribution.

reason is a relatively big number of rules (13323). Namely, one rule is generated for each object of the set to be described by rules.

5   Conclusion

This paper has proposed an alternative approach to computation of rough regions for generating classification rules. Representative sets that replace positive, boundary, and negative regions include essential information needed during rule generation.

The approach enables to speed up computations of rough regions for data divisible into a relatively low number of equivalence classes. Compared with the standard approach the run-time of rule generation is significantly shorter if a representatives set is small. For representatives sets close to the whole universe in terms of size results are slightly better.

Thanks to employing an efficient sort algorithm for computing representatives set of rough regions the approach can find application in processing large datasets, especially those considered in the field of Big Data. An ease of adaptation of sequential covering algorithm to generating rules from representatives of rough regions shows that the approach can be combined with any rule generation algorithm that uses the matching measure.

References

1. Bonikowski, Z.: Algebraic structures of rough sets in representative approximation spaces. Electr. Notes Theor. Comput. Sci. **82**(4), 52–63 (2003)
2. Demri, S., Orłowska, E.: Logical analysis of indiscernibility. In: Orłowska, E. (ed.) Incomplete Information: Rough Set Analysis. STUDFUZZ, vol. 13, pp. 347–380. Physica, Heidelberg (1998)
3. Geng, L., Chan, C.W.: An algorithm for automatic generation of a case base from a database using similarity-based rough approximation. In: Abraham, A., Koppen, M. (eds.) HIS. Advances in Soft Computing, vol. 14, pp. 571–582. Physica, Heidelberg (2001)
4. Nguyen, S.H., Nguyen, H.S.: Some efficient algorithms for rough set methods. In: IPMU 1996, vol. 3, pp. 1451–1456. Physica (2001)
5. Pawlak, Z.: Rough Sets: Theoretical Aspects of Reasoning about Data. Kluwer Academic, Dordrecht (1991)
6. Stepaniuk, J.: Rough-Granular Computing in Knowledge Discovery and Data Mini. SCI, vol. 152. Springer, Heidelberg (2008)
7. Zhang, B., Min, F., Ciucci, D.: Representative-based classification through covering-based neighborhood rough sets. Appl. Intell. **43**(4), 840–854 (2015)

Hardware Supported Rough Sets Based Rules Generation for Big Datasets

Maciej Kopczynski$^{(\boxtimes)}$, Tomasz Grzes, and Jaroslaw Stepaniuk

Faculty of Computer Science, Bialystok University of Technology,
Wiejska 45A, 15-351 Bialystok, Poland
{m.kopczynski,t.grzes,j.stepaniuk}@pb.edu.pl
http://www.wi.pb.edu.pl

Abstract. In this paper we propose a combination of capabilities of the Field Programmable Gate Arrays based device and PC computer for rough sets based data processing resulting in generation of decision rules. Solution is focused on big datasets. Presented architecture has been tested in programmable unit on real datasets. Obtained results confirm the significant acceleration of the computation time using hardware supporting rough set operations in comparison to software implementation.

Keywords: Rough sets · FPGA · Hardware · Rules

1 Introduction

The rough sets' theory was developed in the eighties of the twentieth century by Prof. Z. Pawlak and is an useful tool for data analysis. A lot of rough sets algorithms were implemented in scientific and commercial tools for data processing. Data processing efficiency problem is arising with increase of the amount of data. Software limitations leads to the search for new possibilities.

Field Programmable Gate Arrays (FPGAs) are the digital integrated circuits which function is not determined during the manufacturing process, but can be programmed by engineer any time. One of the main features of FPGAs is the possibility of evaluating any boolean function. That's why they can be used for supporting rough sets calculations.

At the moment there are some hardware implementation of specific rough set methods. The idea of sample processor generating decision rules from decision tables was described in [11]. In [8] authors presented architecture of rough set processor based on cellular networks described in [10]. In [3] a concept of hardware device capable of minimizing the large logic functions created on the basis of discernibility matrix was developed. More detailed summary of the existing ideas and hardware implementations of rough set methods can be found in [4].

None of the above solutions is complete, i.e. creates a system making it possible to solve each problem from wider class of basic problems related to rough sets. Our aim is to create such a system. Authors are working on fully operational System-on-Chip (SoC) including central processing unit based on Altera NIOS II

© IFIP International Federation for Information Processing 2016
Published by Springer International Publishing Switzerland 2016. All Rights Reserved
K. Saeed and W. Homenda (Eds.): CISIM 2016, LNCS 9842, pp. 91–102, 2016.
DOI: 10.1007/978-3-319-45378-1_9

core implemented in Stratix III FPGA and co-processor for rough sets calculations. More details on previous authors' work can be found in [1, 5–7, 14].

2   Introductory Information

2.1   Notions

Let $DT = (U, A \cup \{d\})$ be a decision table, where U is a set of objects, A is a set of condition attributes and d is a decision attribute.

Notions and definitions used in pseudocode shown in next section are presented below for the clarity of understanding:

- t - pair (a, v), where a is a condition attribute and v is a value for this attribute,
- $[t]$ - set of objects fulfilling single condition $t = (a, v)$, i.e. $[(a, v)] = \{x \in U : a(x) = v\}$
- $[T]$ - set of objects fulfilling every condition $t \in T$, i.e. $[T] = \bigcap_{t \in T}[t]$

2.2   Algorithm for Hardware Supported Rule Generation

This section describes pseudocode for an algorithm of rule generation based on LEM2 (**L**earning from **E**xamples **M**odule - version **2**) solution presented by Grzymala-Busse in [2]. We called this algorithm HRG2-LEM2 (**H**ardware **R**ules **G**eneration version **2** – **LEM2**). There are two main differences between HRG2-LEM2 algorithm and one described by Grzymala Busse. First is that HRG2-LEM2 is using hardware supported units for operations related to counting the elements as well as creating and checking sets of objects fulfilling a given condition. Second important difference is introduction of input dataset decomposition that allows for processing data by fixed size hardware modules. Further details on hardware part are presented in Sect. 3. Algorithm parts supported by hardware are prefixed with [$H1$] or [$H2$] in pseudocode. [$H1$] is module for calulating objects classes (unit *dtComparator*), while [$H2$] is module for calculating number of objects fulfilling condition $t = (a, v)$ (unit *avCounter*). Further details are included in Sect. 3.2. For clarity of understanding, algorithm pseudocode is kept as close as possible to the original one. Authors avoided diving into hardware details, because pseudocode would become hardly understandable. Results generated by hardware blocks and their design is presented in Sect. 3.2.

HRG2-LEM2 Algorithm (Hardware Rules Generation version 2 – LEM2)

INPUT: decision table $DT = (U, A \cup \{d\})$, precomputed lower approximations set LA
OUTPUT: global rules set GR
1: $GR \leftarrow \emptyset$
2: **for** $vd \in$ every value of d **do**
3:     $lowerApprox \leftarrow LA(vd)$

4:     $G \leftarrow lowerApprox$
5:     $LR \leftarrow \emptyset$
6:     **while** $G \neq \emptyset$ **do**
7:         $T \leftarrow \emptyset$
8:         $T_G \leftarrow \{t : [t] \cap G \neq \emptyset\}$
9:         **while** $T = \emptyset$ **or** [H1] $[T] \not\subseteq lowerApprox$ **do**
10:            [H2] $t \leftarrow$ choose $t \in T_G$ with maximum value of $|[t] \cap G|$. If more such
               t exist, then choose first t with minimum value of $|[t]|$
11:            $T \leftarrow T \cup \{t\}$
12:            [H1] $G \leftarrow [t] \cap G$
13:            $T_G \leftarrow \{t : [t] \cap G \neq \emptyset\} \setminus T$
14:        **end while**
15:        **for** $t \in T$ **do**
16:            **if** [H1] $[T \setminus \{t\}] \subseteq lowerApprox$ **then**
17:                $T \leftarrow T \setminus \{t\}$
18:            **end if**
19:        **end for**
20:        $LR \leftarrow LR \cup \{T\}$
21:        [H1] $G \leftarrow lowerApprox \setminus \bigcup_{T \in LR}[T]$
22:     **end while**
23:     **for** $T \in LR$ **do**
24:        **if** [H1] $\bigcup_{T' \in LR \setminus \{T\}}[T'] = lowerApprox$ **then**
25:            $LR \leftarrow LR \setminus \{T\}$
26:        **end if**
27:     **end for**
28:     $GR \leftarrow GR \cup LR$
29: **end for**

Input of the algorithm is decision table DT and precomputed lower approximations set LA for every decision class related to value of decision attribute d. Output is global rule set GR. Main algorithm loop in line 2 runs for every value vd of attribute d because lower approximations were precomputed for every decision class related to values of d attribute. Given lower approximation is loaded into set $lowerApprox$ in line 3. Then $lowerApprox$ is copied to the temporary set G in line 4. This set is recomputed during rule creation process performed by loop in lines 9 to 14. Local rules set LR (initialized as empty in line 5) stores rules generated for the given lower approximation (loop in lines 6 to 22). Set T that can be interpreted as single created consists of conditional parts (pairs (a, v)). All possible combinations of conditional parts based on objects in set G, are created in line 8 and are stored in set T_G. This is introductory step that leads to definition of all available condition parts of rule created by loop in lines 9 to 14. Every iteration of loop leads to adding new conditional part to the rule. In line 10 best part t of the rule is chosen according to presented constraint. Line 11 adds part t to the constructed rule T. Sets G and T_G are recalculated respectively in lines 12 and 13. Purpose of recalculation is removing objects covered by current rule and limit amount of possible conditional parts for future iterations of loop. Loop in lines 15 to 19 is for cutting the created rule. Cutting means removing redundant condition parts of created rule. Loop iterates over every part of temporary rule T. If rule T without its one part t is still subset of lower approximation *lowerApprox* (line 16), then part t is removed from rule T (line 17). New rule T is added to the local rules set LR in line 20. Set G is recalculated in line 21 by using all rules from LR set. Loop in lines 23 to 27 is used for cutting local rule set LR. Purpose of this operation is removing redundant rules covering objects that are covered by other rules. Loop iterates over every rule T stored in LR. If local rule set LR without its one part T is still subset of lower approximation *lowerApprox* (line 24), then part T is removed from rule set LR (line 25). Finally, local rule set LR is added to the global rule set GR.

Example of the execution of LEM2 algorithm can be found in [2]. Description of subsequent dataset processing performed by hardware units is shown in Sect. 2.3.

2.3   Hardware Dataset Processing in Proposed Algorithm

As it was mentioned, every line in pseudocode shown in Sect. 2.2 prefixed by [H1] or [H2] is processed by respective hardware unit. Input dataset is divided by control software into fixed-size parts which are subsequently processed by responsible for given operation hardware unit. General pseudocode for such processing is shown below:

HRG2-LEM2 Algorithm Dataset Processing

INPUT: decision table $DT = (U, A \cup \{d\})$, additional data dependant on type of operation
OUTPUT: operation result structure O
1: initialize O structure
2: **for** $cnt \leftarrow 0$ **to** $m - 1$ **do**
3:     $RAM_{set} \leftarrow \{x \in U : x_{cnt \cdot n}$ **to** $x_{(cnt+1) \cdot n - 1}\}$
4:     $O_{part} \leftarrow$ result of calculations performed on RAM_{set} objects set
5:     $O \leftarrow$ combine O and O_{part} structures
6: **end for**

Input of the hardware control algorithm is decision table DT and, required by type of performed operation, additional data. Output is general operation result structure O. Loop in lines 2 to 6 is responsible for choosing parts of input decision table DT. Decision table is divided into m parts, where each of them have the fixed size of n objects. Selected part denoted as RAM_{set}, is loaded into internal FPGA's RAM memory (more details in Sect. 3.1) in line 3. Line 4 is responsible for storing partial results of given operation in general result structure O_{part}. Obtained results are combined together with previous ones using general structure O.

Brief descriptions of two hardware units as well as operation result structures O and O_{part} are given below:

- [H1] - hardware block for calulating objects classes (unit *dtComparator*). Result structure is set represented by binary values, where 1 means that given object is in output set, while 0 means that given object is not in output set. Objects and attributes are processed in parallel by checking given attribute-value pairs. One or more pairs are passed to the module, which then performs comparisons using parts of decomposed input dataset and creates binary sets as a result.
- [H2] - hardware block for calculating number of objects fulfilling conditions $t = (a, v)$ (unit *avCounter*). Result structure is one-dimensional array containing number of objects equal and not equal for defined conditions t. Size of array corresponds to number of condition attributes. Similar to previous module, operations on objects and attributes are performed in parallel. Multiple pairs $t = (a, v)$ are passed to the module and returned results are number of objects that are equal and not equal to given pair.

2.4 Data to Conduct Experimental Research

In this paper, we present the results of the conducted experiments using two datasets: Poker Hand Dataset (created by Robert Cattral and Franz Oppacher) and data about children with insulin-dependent diabetes mellitus type 1 (created by Jarosław Stepaniuk).

First dataset was obtained from UCI Machine Learning Repository [9]. Each of 1 000 000 records is an example of a hand consisting of five playing cards drawn from a standard deck of 52. Each card is described using two attributes (suit and rank), for a total of 10 predictive attributes. There is one decision attribute that describes the "Poker Hand". Decision attribute describes 10 possible combinations of cards in descending probability in the dataset: nothing in hand, one pair, two pairs, three of a kind, straight, flush, full house, four of a kind, straight flush, royal flush.

Diabetes mellitus is a chronic disease of the body's metabolism characterized by an inability to produce enough insulin to process carbohydrates, fat, and protein efficiently. Twelve conditional (physical examination results) and one decision attribute (microalbuminuria) describe the database. The database consisting of 107 objects is shown at the end of the paper [12]. An analysis can be found in Chap. 6 of the book [13].

The Poker Hand database was used for creating smaller datasets consisting of 1 000 to 1 000 000 of objects by selecting given number of first rows of original dataset. Diabetes database was used for generating bigger datasets consisting of 1 000 to 1 000 000 of objects. New datasets were created by multiplying the rows of original dataset. Numerical values were discretized and each attributes value was encoded using four bits for both datasets. Every single object was described on 44 bits for Poker Hand and 52 bits for Diabetes. To fit to memory boundaries in both cases, objects descriptions had to be extended to 64 bits words by filling unused attributes with 0's. Thus prepared hardware units doesn't have to be reconfigured for different datasets until these datasets fit into configured and compiled unit.

3 System Architecture and Hardware Realization

Startix III FPGA contains processor control unit implemented as NIOS II embedded core. Softcore processor supports hardware block responsible for rules generation. Hardware calculation blocks are synthesized together with NIOS II inside the FPGA chip. Development board provides other necessary for SoC elements like memories for storing data and programs or communication interfaces to exchange data and transmit calculation results.

3.1 Softcore Control Unit

Hardware modules are controlled by software execeuted in softcore processor. Main goal of this implementation is:

- read and write data to hardware modules,
- prepare input dataset,
- perform operations on sets,
- control overall operation.

Initially preprocessed on PC dataset is stored on Secure Digital card in binary version. Preprocessing includes discretization and calculation of lower approximations. In the first step of operation, dataset is copied from SD card to external DDR2 RAM module. Results of subsequent operations are stored in FPGA built-in RAM memories (MLAB, M9k and M144k).

MLAB blocks are synchronous, dual-port memories with configurable organization 32×20 or 64×10. Dual-port memories can be read and written simultaneously what makes operations faster. M9k and M144k are also synchronous, dual-port memory blocks with many possible configurable organizations. These blocks give a wide possibility of preparing memories capable of storing almost every type of the objects (words) – from small ones to big ones.

3.2 Hardware Implementation

Hardware implementation, created after analysis of the algorithm HRG2-LEM2 described in Sect. 2.2, was focused on accelerating the operations of calculating number of objects fulfilling attribute-value pairs (a, v) stored in decision table. Another primary important operation was generating sets of objects fulfilling conditions given as (a, v) pairs. Hardware blocks were implemented as combinational units, what means that all calculations are performed in one clock cycle. Nature of performed operation gives possibility of using them for parallel computing systems.

Two hardware modules were prepared. First of them is *avCounter* used for parallel counting number of objects occurrences. Second one is *dtComparator*, which in parallel generates sets of objects fulfilling given conditions. Below are the descriptions of prepared modules.

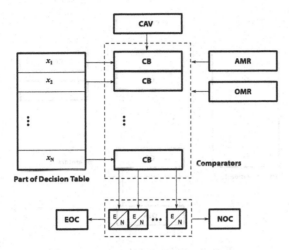

Fig. 1. *avCounter* module, where N is a number of objects in part of decision table

Diagram of *avCounter* module is shown on Fig. 1. Inputs of this module are:

- DATR - decision table containing data for processing,
- CAV - set of conditional attributes' values represented by (a, v),
- AMR - attributes mask register for disabling attributes which are not taken into consideration,
- OMR - object mask register for choosing objects which are processed.

Outputs of the module return the number of objects' occurrences fulfilling each of (a, v) pair. Returned result represents both values (EOC and NOC) which are calculated in line 10 in algorithm HRG2-LEM2 described in Sect. 2.2.

Comparator block (CB) shown on Fig. 2 is used to compare the values from CAV register and values of given objects' attributes.

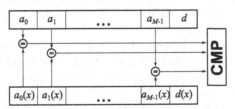

Fig. 2. *avCounter* primary building block, where M is a number of condition attributes

Diagram of *dtComparator* module is shown on Fig. 3. Inputs of this module are:

- DATR - decision table containing data for processing,
- CPDR - defines if conditional part of the rule (or pair (a, v)) is defined on input,

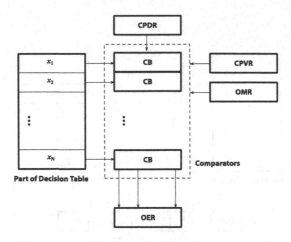

Fig. 3. *dtComparator* module

- CPVR - contains conditional parts of the rule,
- OMR - object mask register for choosing objects which are processed.

Output of the module (OER) returns the set of objects which fulfills each conditional part of the rule.

Single comparator block for *dtComparator* module is similar in principles to the one used by *avCounter*. This block is used to compare the values from CPVR register with objects from decision table.

avCounter and *dtComparator* are designed as a combinational circuits and thus do not need a clock signal for proper work. Amount of time needed to obtain correct results depends only on propagation time of logic blocks inside the FPGA. This property allows to significantly increase the speed of calculations because the time of propagation in contemporary FPGAs usually do not exceed 10 ns. However, for the proper cooperation with external control blocks, as well as to perform other parts of the HRG2-LEM2 algorithm, both hardware modules must be controlled by the clock.

Main design principle of presented solution assumes, that each of described modules process fixed in size part of dataset. Results of calculations are stored using software implemented inside NIOSII softcore processor. Biggest impact on time of calculation is due to the parallel processing of many objects and all attributes in single clock cycle. Both modules are configured to process 64 objects described by maximum 16 attributes (condition and decision). Extending possibilities of these modules needs simple reconfiguration in VHDL source code and recompilation of hardware units. The same applies to control software.

4   Experimental Results

Software implementation on PC was prepared in C language and the source code was compiled using the GNU GCC 4.8.1 compiler. Results were obtained using a PC equipped with an 8 GB RAM and 4-core Intel Core i7 3632QM with maximum 3.2 GHz in Turbo mode clock speed running Windows 7 Professional operational system. Software for NIOS II softcore processor was implemented in C language using NIOS II Software Build Tools for Eclipse IDE.

Quartus II 13.1 was used for design and implementation of the hardware using VHDL language. Synthesized hardware blocks were tested on TeraSIC DE-3 development board equipped with Stratix III EP3SL150F1152C2N FPGA chip. FPGA clock running at 50 MHz for the sequential parts of the project was derived from development board oscillator.

Timing results were obtained using LeCroy waveSurfer 104MXs-B (1 GHz bandwidth, 10 GS/s) oscilloscope for small datasets. Hardware time counter was introduced for bigger datasets.

It should be noticed, that PCs clock is $\frac{clk_{PC}}{clk_{FPGA}} = 64$ times faster than development boards clock source.

Algorithm HRG2-LEM2 described in Sect. 2.2 was used for hardware implementation. Software implementation used HRG-LEM2 algorithm (described in paper that is reviewed), which differs from above in lack of dividing data into parts - all data is stored in PC memory. In current version of hardware implementation, authors used data which was preprocessed on PC in terms of discretization and calculation of lower approximations. Time needed for these operations was not taken into consideration in tests related to both types of implementation. Presented results show the times for generating global rule set using pure software implementation (t_S) and hardware supported rule generation (t_H). Results are shown in Table 1 for Diabetes and Poker Hand datasets. Last two columns in table describe the speed-up factor without (C) and with (C_{clk}) taking clock speed difference between PC and FPGA into consideration. k denotes thousands and M stands for millions.

In this case, one size of hardware execution unit was used, which consumed 15 679 of 113 600 Logical Elements (LEs) total available. This number includes also resources used by NIOS II softcore processor.

Figure 4 presents a graph showing the relationship between the number of objects and execution time for hardware and software solution for both datasets. Both axes use logarithmic scale.

Presented results show big increase in the speed of data processing. Hardware module execution time compared to the software implementation is 5 to more than 7 500 times faster. If we take clock speed difference between PC and FPGA under consideration, these results are much better - speed-up factor is up to 485 000 for Poker Hand and Diabetes datasets.

Hardware modules speed-up factors for both datasets are similar. It is worth to notice, that it doesn't matter what is the width in bits of single object from dataset, unless it fits in assumed memory boundary. Hardware processing unit takes the same time to finish the calculation for every object size, because it always performs the same type of operation. Differences between hardware solutions comes from the nature of data and number of loops iterations.

Table 1. Comparison of execution time between hardware and software implementation for Diabetes and Poker Hand datasets using HRG2-LEM2 algorithm

Objects	Software - t_S	Hardware - t_H	$C = \frac{t_S}{t_H}$	$C_{clk} = 64\frac{t_S}{t_H}$
—	$[s]$	$[s]$	—	—
Diabetes dataset				
1k	4.057	0.798	5.084	325.373
2k	18.304	1.385	13.216	845.817
5k	187.784	3.308	56.767	3 633.064
10k	1 265.410	6.537	193.577	12 388.900
20k	8 101.699	12.886	628.721	40 238.145
50k	62 002.117	37.008	1 675.371	107 223.721
100k	264 164.271	89.297	2 958.261	189 328.678
200k	1 712 942.929	339.162	5 050.520	323 233.298
500k	6 935 214.679	1 065.438	6 509.260	416 592.618
1M	27 908 410.629	3 679.876	7 584.063	485 380.044
Poker Hand dataset				
1k	0.361	0.069	5.244	335.646
2k	1.635	0.124	13.148	841.452
5k	16.620	0.277	60.051	3 843.241
10k	111.835	0.571	195.866	12 535.449
20k	722.089	1.148	629.042	40 258.669
50k	5 186.988	3.261	1 590.498	101 791.898
100k	23 220.455	7.469	3 109.115	198 983.372
200k	145 131.541	29.408	4 935.072	315 844.590
500k	572 771.477	96.699	5 923.252	379 088.126
1M	2 352 553.246	325.329	7 231.314	462 804.119

For software execution time comparison of Poker Hand and Diabetes datasets shows, that number of attributes and characteristic of the dataset have big impact on computation time. For hardware implementation characteristic of the dataset has biggest impact.

Let comparison of attributes' values between two objects or iterating over dynamic list of elements be an elementary operation. k denotes number of conditional attributes and n is the number of objects in decision table. Computational complexity of software implementation of the rules generation is $\Theta(kn^4)$ according to algorithm HRG2-LEM2 shown in Sect. 2.2. Using hardware implementation, complexity of rules generation is $\Theta(n^4)$. The k is missing, because our solution performs comparison between all attributes in $\Theta(1)$ - all attributes' values between two objects are compared in single clock cycle. Additionally, rule generation module performs comparisons between many objects at time.

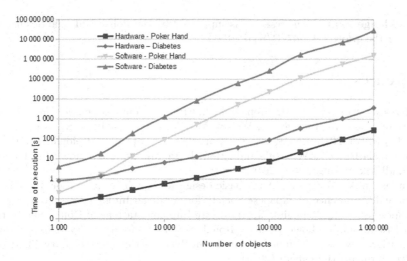

Fig. 4. Relation between number of objects and calculation time for hardware and software implementation using HRG2-LEM2 algorithm for both datasets

Many real datasets are built of tens or hundreds of attributes, so it is impossible to create a single hardware structure capacious enough to process all attributes at once. In such case decomposition must be done in terms of attributes, thus the computational complexity of software and hardware implementation will be almost the same, but in terms of time needed for data processing, hardware implementation will be still much faster than software implementation. The reason for this is that most comparison and counting operations are performed by the hardware block in parallel in terms of objects and attributes.

Conclusions

The hardware implementation is the main direction of using scalable rough sets methods in real time solutions. As it was presented, performing rule generation using hardware implementations gives us a big acceleration in comparison to software solution, especially in case of bigger datasets. It can be noticed, that speed-up factor is increasing with growing datasets.

Hardware supported rule generation calculation unit was not optimized for performance in this paper. Processing time can be substantially reduced by increasing FPGA clock frequency, modifying control unit and introducing triggering on both edges of clock signal.

Future research will be focused on optimization of presented solution: different sizes of hardware rule generation unit will be checked, as well as results related to performing the calculations in parallel by multiplying hardware modules. Using FPGA-based solutions it is relatively easy, because multiplication of execution modules needs only few changes in VHDL source code. Most time-consuming part will be design and implementation of parallel execution control unit.

Acknowledgements. The research is supported by the Polish National Science Centre under the grant 2012/07/B/ST6/01504.

References

1. Grześ, T., Kopczyński, M., Stepaniuk, J.: FPGA in rough set based core and reduct computation. In: Lingras, P., Wolski, M., Cornelis, C., Mitra, S., Wasilewski, P. (eds.) RSKT 2013. LNCS, vol. 8171, pp. 263–270. Springer, Heidelberg (2013)
2. Grzymala-Busse, J.W.: Rule Induction, Data Mining and Knowledge Discovery Handbook. Springer, US (2010)
3. Kanasugi, A., Yokoyama, A.: A basic design for rough set processor. In: The 15th Annual Conference of Japanese Society for Artificial Intelligence (2001)
4. Kopczyński, M., Stepaniuk, J.: Hardware Implementations of Rough Set Methods in Programmable Logic Devices, Rough Sets and Intelligent Systems - Professor Zdzisław Pawlak in Memoriam, Intelligent Systems Reference Library 43, pp. 309–321. Springer, Heidelberg (2013)
5. Kopczyński, M., Grześ, T., J. Stepaniuk: FPGA in rough-granular computing: reduct generation. In: The 2014 IEEE/WCI/ACM International Joint Conferences on Web Intelligence, WI 2014, vol. 2, pp. 364–370. IEEE Computer Society, Warsaw (2014)
6. Kopczynski, M., Grzes, T., Stepaniuk, J.: Generating core in rough set theory: design and implementation on FPGA. In: Kryszkiewicz, M., Cornelis, C., Ciucci, D., Medina-Moreno, J., Motoda, H., Raś, Z.W. (eds.) RSEISP 2014. LNCS, vol. 8537, pp. 209–216. Springer, Heidelberg (2014)
7. Kopczyński, M., Grześ, T., Stepaniuk, J.: Core for large datasets: rough sets on FPGA, concurrency, specification & programming. In: 24th International Workshop: CS&P 2015, vol. 1, pp. 235–246. University of Rzeszow, Rzeszow (2015)
8. Lewis, T., Perkowski, M., Jozwiak, L.: Learning in hardware: architecture and implementation of an FPGA-based rough set machine. In: 25th Euromicro Conference (EUROMICRO 1999), vol. 1, p. 1326 (1999)
9. Lichman, M.: UCI Machine Learning Repository http://archive.ics.uci.edu/ml. School of Information and Computer Science, University of California, Irvine (2013)
10. Muraszkiewicz, M., Rybiński, H.: Towards a parallel rough sets computer. In: Ziarko, W.P. (ed.) Rough Sets, Fuzzy Sets and Knowledge Discovery, pp. 434–443. Springer, London (1994)
11. Pawlak, Z.: Elementary rough set granules: toward a rough set processor. In: Pal, S.K., Polkowski, L., Skowron, A. (eds.) Rough-Neurocomputing: Techniques for Computing with Words, Cognitive Technologies, pp. 5–14. Springer, Berlin (2004)
12. Stepaniuk, J.: Knowledge discovery by application of rough set models. In: Rough Set Methods and Applications. New Developments in Knowledge Discovery in Information Systems. Physica-Verlag, Heidelberg, pp. 137–233 (2000)
13. Stepaniuk, J.: Rough-Granular Computing in Knowledge Discovery and Data Mining. Springer, Heidelberg (2008)
14. Stepaniuk, J., Kopczyński, M., Grześ, T.: The first step toward processor for rough set methods. Fundamenta informaticae **127**, 429–443 (2013)

Images, Visualization, Classification

Information Density Based Image Binarization for Text Document Containing Graphics

Soma Datta[✉], Nabendu Chaki, and Sankhayan Choudhury

Department of Computer Science and Engineering, University of Calcutta,
JD2 Block, Sector III, Saltlake, Kolkata, India
soma21dec@yahoo.co.in, nabendu@ieee.org, sankhayan@gmail.com

Abstract. In this work, a new clustering based binarization technique has been proposed. Clustering is done depending on the information density of the input image. Here input image is considered as a set of text, images as foreground and some random noises, marks of ink, spots of oil, etc. in the background. It is often quite difficult to separate the foreground from the background based on existing binarization technique. The existing methods offer good result if the input image contains only text. Experimental results indicate that this method is particularly good for degraded text document containing graphic images as well. USC-SIPI database is used for testing phase. It is compared with iterative partitioning, Otsu's method for seven different metrics.

Keywords: Iterative partitioning · NTSC color format · Wiener filter · Binarization · Entropy

1 Introduction

It is very important to maintain the documents and the legacy of the document. To fulfill these purpose document image processing takes a vital role. Document image binarization is usually performed in optical character recognition (OCR) [1, 2] and image searching. This involves handwriting recognition, extracting logos and pictures from a graphical image. The main purpose of document image processing [3] is reduction of paper usage, easy access to the documents with lowest storage cost. At this point the most challenging task is to segment the region of interest (ROI) for further analysis. The simplest method for image segmentation [4] is thresholding based binarization which is also an essential technique in enhancement and biomedical image analysis. The output of this process is a binary image [5]. Though researchers work upon document image binarization for several years, the thresholding of compound document images still remains a challenging task due to its sensitivity to noise, illumination, variable intensity and sometimes insufficient contrast. It has been observed that some of the existing methods [6–10] offer very good result for text document. However, the performance degrades when a degraded text document contains some graphical images in it. We refer this type of document as compound document in the

© IFIP International Federation for Information Processing 2016
Published by Springer International Publishing Switzerland 2016. All Rights Reserved
K. Saeed and W. Homenda (Eds.): CISIM 2016, LNCS 9842, pp. 105–115, 2016.
DOI: 10.1007/978-3-319-45378-1_10

rest of this paper. In this research work, we aim to devise a new segmentation methodology that would be good for the compound documents. We separate the entire image into three regions as the background, only text region and the graphical image. Our proposed method keeps a good balance both for text and graphics in the degraded compound documents. The proposed binarization method is based on cluster density information. It consists of six phases. These are noise removal with image normalization, entropy calculation, fuzzy c_mean clustering, segmenting of each region based on the clustering output, applying local threshold based binarization and finally integrating the segmented region. Each of these phases is described detail in the design methodology section.

2   Survey on Existing Techniques

Document image binarization has drawn lot of attention in the machine vision research community. Some of the highly cited methods are discussed in this section in a nutshell. Parker et al. proposed a method based on Shen-Castan edge detector to identify object pixels [7]. This method creates a surface using moving least squares method used to threshold images. Chen et al. proposed enhanced speed entropic threshold selection algorithm [8]. This method works upon the selection of global threshold value using maximin optimization procedure. O'Gorman proposed a global approach based on the measurement of information on local connectivity. The threshold values are incorporated at intensity level. Thus this method has advantages of local as well as global adaptive approaches. Liu et al. proposed a method based on grey scale and run length histogram. This method carefully handles noisy and complex background problems. Chang et al. worked upon stroke connectivity preservation issues for graphical images [11]. Their proposed algorithm is able to eliminate the background noise and enhancement of grey levels of texts. This method is used to extract the strokes from low level density as well as darker background. Shaikh et al. [12] proposed iterative partitioning method. In this method, entire input image is divided into four equal sub images if the number of peaks is greater than two in the input image. This process will continue until the sub image contains less than two histogram peaks. This binarization method is offering good result for very old, faded, stained documented images but fails for medical image segmentation. In Otsu's [13] method, the thresholding is based on the class variance criterion and the histogram of the input image. This method segments the image into two classes, so that the total variance of different classes is maximized. Otsu's binarization technique produces good result for graphical images; however it can't properly binaries the old spotted document.

3   Design of New Information Density Based Binarization Technique

3.1   Image Acquisition and Enhancement

The design methodology follows a pipelined approach starting with image acquisition and ending with binarization. Histogram based Otsu's method may provide satisfactory result when documented images are clear. However in reality the old and multiple times photocopied documents are not so good. Hence these documents are often not binarized properly using Otsu's method.

Otsu's method is a histogram based generalized binarization. Information density based segmentation is not done here. The algorithm assumes that the input image contains foreground and background pixels and it then calculates the optimal threshold that separates the two regions. USC-SIPI database [14] is used for testing phase. The quality and size of the original image is not changed. Instead of this database we have also tested our proposed method with some sample documented scanned images that consists of text and graphical images (Fig. 1).

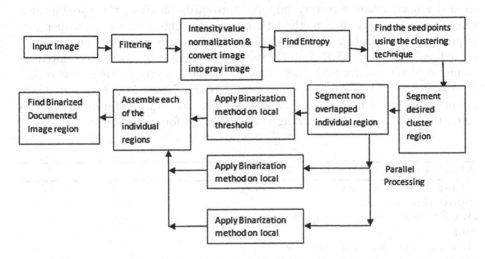

Fig. 1. Block diagram of proposed method

Image enhancement improves the visual quality of the input image for further processing techniques. The qualities of some images are not so good. Most of the image contains speckle noise, salt and pepper noises and some random noises. Here Wiener tilter is used to remove that kind of mixture noises. This filter is a linear filter to remove additive noise and blurring of the images. It offers good result to reduce the mean square error rate. These filters are often applied in the frequency domain. The corresponding output image is $W(f_1, f_2)$ as follows:

$$W(f_1, f_2) = \frac{H^*(f_1, f_2) S_x(f_1, f_2)}{|H(f_1, f_2)|^2 * S_x(f_1, f_2) + S_y(f_1, f_2)} \tag{1}$$

Here, $S_x(f_1, f_2)$ and $S_y(f_1, f_2)$ represent the power spectrum of the original image and the noisy image respectively and $H(f_1, f_2)$ means the blurred filter. The Wiener filter performs deconvolution during minimization of least square error as follows,

$$e_2 = E\{(f - \widehat{f})^2\} \tag{2}$$

Here E is the mean value and f is the un-degraded image.

3.2 Convert Input Color Image into Gray Scale Image

Color of a pixel is represented as the combination of chrominance and luminance. Chrominance is the color components of the input image and luminance is the intensity. This intensity is calculated as the weighted means of red, green and blue (RGB) component. Now image is in three dimensional that requires a massive computational time. Hence RGB images are converted into gray scale image using NTSC color format [2].

3.3 Intensity Value Normalization

Intensity normalization is very important towards handling the variable light intensity. Basically it is a method that maps the intensity values as per prerequisite. Normalization transforms an n dimensional grayscale image represented as, $Img = \{X \subseteq R^n\} \rightarrow \{Min, Max\}$. Image Img consist the intensity values in between Min and Max. This image is converted into a new image, $Img = \{X \subseteq R^n\} \rightarrow \{new\_Min, ..., new\_Max\}$. New image Img consist the intensity values in between new_Min and new_Max. Normalization is done by using the histogram. The following steps are made for normalization.

Algorithm 1. Intensity Value Normalization

Assumptions: Input image should be in gray scale.
Input: Gray scale image.
Output: Scaled intensity image.
Step
1: Read input image and find its size.
2: Find the cumulative distribution function as $Q(x) = \sum_{i=1}^{x} h(i)$ where x is the gray scale value and h is the image histogram.
3: Calculate new gray scale values using

$$h(i) = round(\frac{Q(1) - Q_{min}}{X * Y - Q_{min}} * (L - 1)) \qquad (3)$$

where Qmin is the shortest value of the cumulative distribution function. X, Y represents the number of columns and rows of the input image and L is the number of gray levels that are used.
4: New image is created by replacing original gray values by the newly calculated gray values and compare this with the original.
5: Stop

3.4 Find the Most Informative Regions

Input images may contain the actual information along with some distortion due to oil ink etc. Hence, it is very much important to segment the actual informative region. In order to find the most informative region, texture based information have been used. Among many texture properties, entropy is used to do the needful. Entropy [15,16] refers to the disorder, uncertainty or randomness of the given dataset. The following algorithm is used to find the most informative regions. The covariance or probability of randomness is higher in the text area but it is less in non text area.

Algorithm 2. ROI segmentation

Assumptions: Input image should be in gray scale.
Input: Gray scale image.
Output: Only most wanted region.
Step
  1: Find the sub image ($row1 - n/2$ to $row2 + n/2$ and $col1 - n/2$ to $col1 + n/2$) where row1 and col1 is two variable and n denotes the row, column of the sub-window.
  2: Repeat step1 for all row1 is in between $row1 - n/2$ to $row1 + n/2$ and for all col1 is in between $col1 - n/2$ to $col1 + n/2$.
  3: Repeat step 4 to 6 for all sub images and store the entropy value in row1 and col1.
  4: Calculate histogram of n*n sub image and store the result in a vector hist.
  5: Normalized histogram is stored at hist_normalized $hist\_normalized = hist/(n*n)$
  6: Find all the points at hist_normalized where value is 0 and replace that value by1.
  7: Calculate entropy element and store them into cee vector
     $cee(i) = hist\_normalized(i) * \log_2 normalized(i)$, i is used to denote index.
  8: Add all entries from cee(i) and multiply the result by (-1)
  9: Stop

3.5   Segment Individual Non-overlapped Regions

The next step is to segment the individual non-overlapped regions. Clustering method [17,18] has been applied to find out different cluster seed points that are shown in Fig. 2a. Here three cluster points have been found. Now our target is to segment each individual clustering region as shown in Fig. 2b, c and d. The next step is to segment each of the regions.

$$Single\_Region\_Set = \{P : P \; is \; a \; subset \; of \; Region\_point\_Set\}$$

Elements of set P form a vector containing row and column number of a pixel. P contains the coordinates of all pixels of a single region. There is no common element between any two elements of $Single\_Region\_Set$.

$P_1 \cup P_2 \cup P_3 \cup P_n = Region\_point\_set$ Where $P_1, P_2,, P_n$ are all elements of $Single\_Region\_Set$, n is the total no of elements in $Single\_Region\_Set$. $P_i \cap P_j = \phi$ where P_i, P_j are any two elements of $Single\_Region\_Set$ and value of i, j may be 1, 2, 3..n but $i \neq j$. Each component of $Single\_Region\_Set$ contains the coordinates of a single contour, and they are found by applying procedure segment each region.

Algorithm 3. Clustering Segmentation

Assumptions: Let $E = \{e1, e2, e3..., en\}$ is the set of entropy values in entropy matrix. $C = \{C1, C2, C3\}$ is the set of initial cluster centers.

Input: Gray scale image.

Output: Based on entropy calculation the image is segmented into three groups.

Step

1: Initial cluster centers are $\{C1, C2, C2\}$ i.e. c = 3 where, C1 is the average entropy value of most informative region in the document. C2 is the average entropy value of less informative region. C3 is the average entropy value of in between region.

2: Calculate the fuzzy membership 'F_{ij}' using

$$F_{ij} = \frac{1}{\sum_{k=1}^{e=3}(\frac{D_{ij}}{D_{ik}})^{(2/m-l)}} \tag{4}$$

Where, F_{ij} are the elements of F_M matrix (fuzzy membership matrix), D_{ij} is the Euclidean distance between i^{th} object and j^{th} cluster centre. D_{ik} is the Euclidean distance between i^{th} object and j^{th} cluster center, m is a constant.

3: New fuzzy centers New_F_j is calculated using,

$$New\_F_j = (\frac{(\sum_{i=1}^{n}(F_{ij})^m X_i)}{(\sum_{i=1}^{n}(F_{ij})^m)})\forall j = 1, 2, ...c \tag{5}$$

4: Repeat Step 2 and 3 until $\|F\_M(k+1)F\_M(k)\| < \beta$ Where, 'k', 'β' are the iteration step and termination criterion between [0, 1] respectively. $F\_M(k) = (F_{ij})n * c$ is a fuzzy membership matrix after k_{th} iteration and $F\_M\_(k+1)$ is used to denote after $(k+1)^{th}$ iteration. j is the objective function.

5: Find all the points which belong to the most informative region cluster. This cluster has C1 center and contains the pixel position of the image of most informative region.

6: Stop

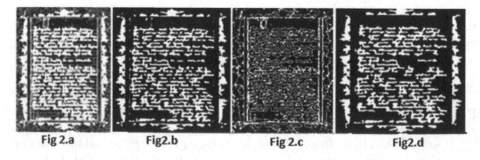

Fig 2.a   Fig2.b   Fig 2.c   Fig2.d

Fig. 2. (a) After applying clustering technique. (b) First most informative region whose cluster centre is 74.1604. (c) Second most informative region whose cluster centre is 167.7177. (d) Third most informative region whose cluster centre is 225.7846

Algorithm 4. Segment region

Input: The binary matrix that does not contain any false contours.
Output: The coordinates of each contour.
Step
  1: Find any coordinate from input binary matrix (*region_matrix*), containing value 1 and this point is called seed point.
  2: Find all other coordinates of the binary matrix that belongs to the same contour with the seed point. It is implemented using the stack, 8-connectivity and 4 connectivity properties.
  3: The points obtained from step2 are the points that represent a single contour. These points are sent to the next phase for further processing.
  4: Repeat step2 to step3 using a newly found seed value that belongs to a separate region. This iterative process will continue until all disjoint regions are extracted.
  5: Stop

After applying segment each region algorithm, the wanted regions are segmented. Now apply global binarization technique on the segmented regions. Threshold value for binarization is calculated as follows [19].

Algorithm 5. Binarization

Input: Gray scale image.
Output: binary image.
Step
  1: Initial threshold value $T = (min\_intensity + max\_intensity)/2$
  2: Partition the image into two regions, R1 consists of value (pixels)$< T$ and R2 consists of value(pixels) $> T$.
  3: For each region, calculate the average intensity value I1 and I2.
  4: Preserve the old threshold value and update the threshold value with the new threshold value that is obtained from step3.
  5: Continue this iterative process from step2 to step4 until the absolute difference between preserved value and new threshold value is less than tolerance parameter.
  6: Stop
---

4 Performance Analysis

For performance analysis some degraded document images are used that are collected from multiple sites. Our method is tested on the USC-SIPI database arbitrarily for experimental verification purpose. The results are shown in Fig. 3.

In this work, we have compared seven different metrics in between Otsu's method, iterative partitioning and our proposed method. The seven metrics are recall, precision, F_measure, PERR or pixel error rate, MSE or mean squared error, SNR or signal to noise ratio and peak signal to noise (PSNR) [12,20]. Theoretically recall is the probability of a relevant document is retrieved during

Input image   After Otsu's Method   Iterative Partitioning Our Method

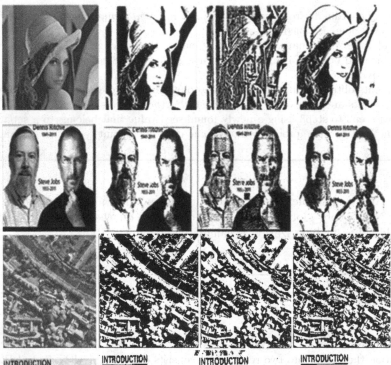

Fig. 3. Comparative study

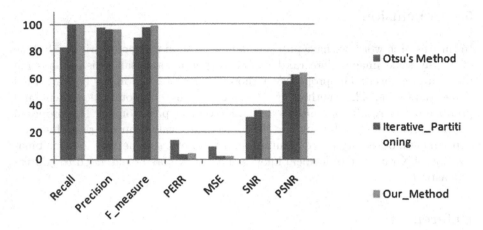

Fig. 4. Average performance graph on 7 matrices for the said methods

search and precision is the probability of whether a retrieved document is relevant or not. However in both of these methods, some text region has been lost. In our method, none of the text region has lost and only the black shirt comes as white due to no change of entropy of that region. Iterative partitioning offers poor result in both the cases as it partitions the image into four sub block based on the histogram. The Table 1 shows the average performance analysis between Otsu's method, iterative partitioning and our proposed method.

Performance analysis table shows that the probability of retrieval of relevant document is 99.5 % and the precision is 96.45 % which are quite good. On the other hand misclassification rate is also less than Otsu's method and iterative partitioning. Our method performs much better than the other two methods in the presence of Gaussian and random noises. It makes obvious that the information density based binarization technique is more noise resistive than other two binarization techniques.

Table 1. Performance analysis

Performance measurement matrices	Otsu binarization technique	Iterative partitioning	Our proposed method
Recall	82.96	99.44	99.50
Precision	97.87	95.88	96.45
F_measure	89.82	97.62	98.89
PERR	14.17	3.69	3.91
MSE	9.32	2.39	2.10
SNR	31.12	36.08	35.55
PSNR	57.20	62.13	63.67

5   Conclusion

In this research work, we have proposed a new method using clustering technique of a gray scale image. Here random noises, pepper and salt noises, Gaussian noises are removed. The proposed method has been tested on the benchmarked image data-base. This method easily separates the compound document and produce better result than Otsu's method, iterative partitioning. The proposed method also offers good result for the above said evaluation metrics. However, experimental observation finds limitation of the proposed method towards binarization of X-ray type of medical images. The work may be extended to address this aspect.

References

1. Thillou, C., Gosselin, B.: Segmentation-based binarization for color degraded images. In: Wojciechowski, K., Smolka, B., Palus, H., Kozera, R.S., Skarbek, W., Noakes, L. (eds.) Computer Vision and Graphics, pp. 808–813. Springer, Heidelberg (2006)
2. Gonzalez, R.C., Woods, R.E.: Digital Image Processing. Pearson Education India, New Delhi (2009)
3. Namboodiri, A.M., et al.: Document structure and layout analysis. In: Chaudhuri, B.B. (ed.) Digital Document Processing. Springer, London (2007)
4. Dinan, R.F., Dubil, J.F., Malin, J.R., Rodite, R.R., Rohe, C.F., Rohrer, G.D.: Document image processing system. US Patent 4,888,812, 19 December 1989
5. Jaimes, A., Mintzer, F.C., Rao, A.R., Thompson, G.: Segmentation and automatic descreening of scanned documents. In: Electronic Imaging 1999, International Society for Optics and Photonics, pp. 517–528 (1998)
6. Ghosh, P., Bhattacharjee, D., Nasipuri, M.: Blood smear analyzer for white blood cell counting: a hybrid microscopic image analyzing technique. Appl. Soft Comput. 46, 629–638 (2016)
7. Parker, J.R., Jennings, C., Salkauskas, A.G.: Thresholding using an illumination model. In: Proceedings of the Second International Conference on Document Analysis and Recognition, 1993, pp. 270–273. IEEE (1993)
8. Chen, W.T., Wen, C.H., Yang, C.W.: A fast two-dimensional entropic thresholding algorithm. Pattern Recogn. 27(7), 885–893 (1994)
9. Yanowitz, S.D., Bruckstein, A.M.: A new method for image segmentation. In: 9th International Conference on Pattern Recognition, 1988, pp. 270–275. IEEE (1988)
10. Ghosh, P., Bhattacharjee, D., Nasipuri, M., Basu, D.K.: Medical aid for automatic detection of malaria. In: Chaki, N., Cortesi, A. (eds.) CISIM 2011. CCIS, vol. 245, pp. 170–178. Springer, Heidelberg (2011)
11. Yang, J.D., Chen, Y.S., Hsu, W.H.: Adaptive thresholding algorithm and its hardware implementation. Pattern Recogn. Lett. 15(2), 141–150 (1994)
12. Shaikh, S.H., Maiti, A.K., Chaki, N.: A new image binarization method using iterative partitioning. Mach. Vis. Appl. 24(2), 337–350 (2013)
13. Otsu, N.: A threshold selection method from gray-level histograms. Automatica 11(285–296), 23–27 (1975)
14. California, S.: USC-SIPI image database, University of Southern California. http://sipi.usc.edu/database/

15. Jain, A.K.: Fundamentals of Digital Image Processing. Prentice-Hall Inc., Upper Saddle River (1989)
16. Abutaleb, A.S.: Automatic thresholding of gray-level pictures using two-dimensional entropy. Comput. Vis. Graph. Image Process. **47**(1), 22–32 (1989)
17. Datta, S., Chaki, N.: Person identification technique using RGB based dental images. In: Saeed, K., Homenda, W. (eds.) CISIM 2015. LNCS, vol. 9339, pp. 169–180. Springer, Heidelberg (2015)
18. Han, Y., Shi, P.: An improved ant colony algorithm for fuzzy clustering in image segmentation. Neurocomputing **70**(4), 665–671 (2007)
19. Chaki, N., Shaikh, S.H., Saeed, K.: Exploring Image Binarization Techniques. SCI, vol. 560. Springer, New Delhi (2014)
20. Su, B., Lu, S., Tan, C.L.: Binarization of historical document images using the local maximum and minimum. In: Proceedings of the 9th IAPR International Workshop on Document Analysis Systems, pp. 159–166. ACM (2010)

MRI Texture-Based Classification of Dystrophic Muscles. A Search for the Most Discriminative Tissue Descriptors

Dorota Duda[1]([✉]), Marek Kretowski[1], Noura Azzabou[2,3],
and Jacques D. de Certaines[2,3]

[1] Faculty of Computer Science, Bialystok University of Technology,
Wiejska 45a, 15-351 Bialystok, Poland
{d.duda,m.kretowski}@pb.edu.pl
[2] Institute of Myology, Nuclear Magnetic Resonance Laboratory, Paris, France
[3] CEA, I2BM, MIRCen, NMR Laboratory, Paris, France

Abstract. The study assesses the usefulness of various texture-based tissue descriptors in the classification of canine hindlimb muscles. Experiments are performed on T2-weighted Magnetic Resonance Images (MRI) acquired from healthy and Golden Retriever Muscular Dystrophy (GRMD) dogs over a period of 14 months. Three phases of canine growth and/or dystrophy progression are considered. In total, 39 features provided by 8 texture analysis methods are tested. Features are ranked according to their frequency of selection in a modified Monte Carlo procedure. The top-ranked features are used in differentiation (i) between GRMD and healthy dogs at each phase of canine growth, and (ii) between three phases of dystrophy progression in GRMD dogs. Three classifiers are applied: Adaptive Boosting, Neural Networks, and Support Vector Machines. Small sets of selected features (up to 10) are found to ensure highly satisfactory classification accuracies.

Keywords: Golden Retriever Muscular Dystrophy (GRMD) · Duchenne Muscular Dystrophy (DMD) · Texture analysis · Feature selection · Classification · MRI T2

1 Introduction

Duchenne Muscular Dystrophy (DMD) is a genetic disorder affecting approximately 1 in 3,600 boys worldwide [1]. It is caused by the absence of dystrophin, a protein that plays an essential role in supporting fiber strength, mainly in the skeletal and cardiac muscles. In affected individuals dystrophin is not synthesized normally, which results in progressive muscle degeneration. This leads to permanent progressive disability (decreased mobility, deformities, cardiomyopathy, and respiratory failure) and premature death [2]. No treatment can reverse the fatal muscle destruction and there is still no effective cure for DMD.

© IFIP International Federation for Information Processing 2016
Published by Springer International Publishing Switzerland 2016. All Rights Reserved
K. Saeed and W. Homenda (Eds.): CISIM 2016, LNCS 9842, pp. 116–128, 2016.
DOI: 10.1007/978-3-319-45378-1_11

The Golden Retriever Muscular Dystrophy (GRMD) canine model is the most widely used in research on potential treatment of DMD in humans. It mimics the human DMD model in many aspects [3]. Important information about the progression of the disease and/or its response to therapy can be obtained, in an atraumatic manner, using Magnetic Resonance Imaging (MRI). However, the interpretation of image content is not a trivial task. Great hope is placed in computer-aided image recognition methods, especially those based on texture analysis (TA) [4,5]. The use of appropriately selected textural features in the tissue differentiation process could reduce the need for invasive diagnostic methods, such as those involving needle biopsies, which can considerably weaken already degenerated muscles.

Many different TA methods have been successfully employed for tissue characterization in the classification process [6–8]. Research has shown that not all of these methods provide equally useful features. The study [4] presents the theoretical basis for the suitability of various MRI-TA methods for muscular tissue characterization in healthy and GRMD dogs. The authors noted that muscle properties are not the only important factors in choosing the most appropriate TA method. The shape and size of the image regions analyzed (*Regions of Interest*, ROIs) are also critical. Many ROIs may be narrow and very small, which disqualifies some TA methods, particularly those that analyze pairs of pixels in which a long distance separates the two pixels in the pair. This problem was also observed in another study [9], which investigated the potential of different MRI-TA techniques for characterization of canine hindlimb muscles (GRMD and healthy). The study also showed that the use of all possible textural features does not always ensure the best classification results.

The aim of the present study is to find the most suitable tissue descriptors in the muscle differentiation process based on the T2-weighted MRI. Images are derived from GRMD and healthy dogs and correspond to three phases of canine growth and/or dystrophy progression [4]. Muscular tissue is characterized using features provided by eight TA methods. First, a modified Monte Carlo (MC) feature selection [10] is used to assess the relative importance of each feature in the tissue recognition process. Then the features are ranked. Finally, the top-ranked features are used to describe tissues in various classification tasks.

The next section gives a short overview of related work. Section 3 describes methods making it possible to find the most discriminative features. Next, the experimental setup is detailed. In Sect. 5 the results are presented and discussed. Conclusions and perspectives are outlined in the final section.

2   Related Work

There have been few studies on texture-based characterization of dystrophic muscles in GRMD (and healthy) dogs. However, some recent research has shown that texture analysis has great potential for characterization of dystrophy progression or differentiation between affected and healthy canine muscles. In the work [11], different MRI biomarkers derived from T2-weighted images were used to quantify longitudinal disease progression and to differentiate between GRMD and healthy dogs at different phases of canine growth and/or dystrophy development. Three phases were considered: at 3, 6, and 9–12 months of age. Non-textural (MRI-based) and textural features were used to characterize seven types of muscles of the proximal pelvic limbs. The textural features were based on the gray-level histogram (GLH) and run length matrices (RLM) [12]. According to statistical tests, all the textural features were significantly different in the two classes of dogs (GRMD and healthy). This was observed at each phase of life. Moreover, classification experiments, run with Linear Discriminant Analysis (LDA), produced better results when textural features were used.

Yang *et al.* [13] attempted to follow texture changes in GRMD and healthy dogs, imaged over a period of 14 months. They focused on moment-based TA methods, applying Legendre and Zernike moments. Their feature vectors were analyzed by Principal Component Analysis (PCA) and classified by the SVM classifier [14]. Here too, three typical phases of canine growth were considered. The moment-based texture descriptors provided important discriminatory information for distinguishing between two dog classes at each phase.

The same database of images was analyzed in our previous work [9], as both studies are part of the European COST Action BM1304 project ("MYO-MRI") aimed at exploring strategies for muscle imaging texture analysis. We differentiated between GRMD and healthy dogs at each of three phases of canine growth. Textural features were extracted using statistical, model-based, and filter-based TA methods. Eight sets of features, each derived from a different method, were considered separately. The set of all features derived from all methods was also tested. Experiments involving five classifiers showed that highly satisfactory classification results can be obtained with certain (relatively small) sets of features, especially those based on RLM and co-occurrence matrices (COM) [15]. The work did not perform any feature selection nor attempt to differentiate between tissues in different phases of dystrophy development.

3   Evaluation of the Usefulness of Features

All the evaluations are performed on a *training set*. This set is created by characterizing each ROI with the same set of features (in our case textural). ROIs are labeled by assigning information to them about their "class". This information can be related to the presence or absence of disease or to the phase of disease progression. The relative importance of each textural feature in the tissue identification process is assessed in the study using Monte Carlo feature selection, initially proposed by Draminski *et al.* [10]. This procedure was chosen due to its proven effectiveness and reliability, and because it does not require any initial assumptions. It returns a ranking of features according to their importance. Further classification experiments allow us to identify the subsets of features that ensure the most satisfactory differentiation between ROI classes.

3.1   Modified Monte Carlo Feature Selection

The method initially described by Draminski *et al.* was slightly modified and adapted to our needs. Our proposal is schematized in Fig. 1. The number of objects in the initial data set and the number of tissue descriptors (features) for each observation are denoted by p and d, respectively. First, q observations are randomly chosen from the initial training set ($q < p$) and characterized by a small number (m) of randomly chosen features, $m \ll d$. This is followed by a single execution of the selection procedure, based on this truncated data set. These two steps are repeated many times (denoted by r), each time with a different subset of observations and a different subset of features. Next, the "incidence frequency rate" is calculated for each feature. This is the ratio between the number of cases in which the feature is selected and the number of times it occurs in the subsets of randomly chosen features describing the truncated data sets (subjected to selection). Finally, the features are ranked according to their incidence frequency rate, from the highest to the lowest rate. The top-ranked features are considered to be potentially the most important in the tissue recognition process.

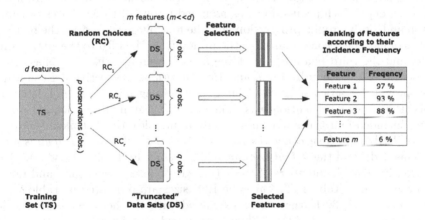

Fig. 1. Assessing the relative importance of each feature in the tissue identification process. The course of a modified Monte Carlo feature selection method

Reducing the number of features before proceeding to each repetition of the selection procedure is not only aimed at shortening the computation time. Guyon and Elisseeff [16] pointed out that some features may not prove informative separately, but only when combined with other features. By performing multiple repetitions of the selection procedure, each time with a different small subset of randomly chosen features at input, we can identify features which prove useful independently of the combination in which they are initially found.

3.2   Texture-Based Classification

Once the ranking of features (according to their incidence frequency rates) is completed, we can determine how many top-ranked features would be sufficient to ensure very good differentiation between tissue classes. At this stage, d experiments are conducted. In the ith experiment ($i = 1, \ldots, d$), i top features from the ranking are used as tissue descriptors. In each of d experiments the usefulness of the considered subset of features is assessed by the quality of the classification it can provide. Classification accuracies are estimated by the standard 10-fold cross-validation procedure, repeated 10 times.

4   Experimental Setup

The images were gathered at the Nuclear Magnetic Resonance Laboratory of the Institute of Myology, Paris (France). Acquisitions were performed over a period of 14 months, using a 3T Siemens Magnetom Trio TIM imager/spectrometer. A precise description of all acquisition protocols was provided in [17]. Information concerning image pre-processing, completed prior to tissue characterization, can be found in our previous work [9]. Only T2-weighted spin echo sequences were chosen for our investigations. Images were collected from 10 dogs: 5 with GRMD and 5 healthy dogs. In total, 38 acquisitions were available (from 3 to 5 for each dog). Each acquisition was assigned to one of three phases of canine growth and/or dystrophy progression [4]. The first phase comprised the first four months of life, the second phase was the period from the fifth to the sixth month of life, and the third phase began at the age of seven months. The phases were represented in the study by 14, 9, and 15 acquisitions, respectively. Each acquisition provided a series of 12 to 14 images. The images had a size of 240×320 pixels, the in-plane resolution was $0.56\,\text{mm} \times 0.56\,\text{mm}$. ROIs defined on the images included four types of canine hindlimb muscles: the *Extensor Digitorum Longus* (EDL), the *Gastrocnemius Lateralis* (GasLat), the *Gastrocnemius Medialis* (GasMed), and the *Tibial Cranialis* (TC). Only ROIs of at least 100 pixels were considered. The numbers of ROIs (for each phase, tissue class, and muscle type) are given in Table 1. The average ROI sizes are presented in Table 2.

For each ROI, 39 features were extracted with the homemade application *Medical Image Processing* [18]. They were based on: the gray-level histogram (GLH), gradient matrices (GM) [19], co-occurrence matrices (COM), run-length matrices (RLM), gray level difference matrices (GLDM) [20], Laws' texture energy measures (LTE) [21], the fractional Brownian motion model (FB) [22],

Table 1. Numbers of suitable ROIs (for each phase, tissue class, and muscle type)

	Phase 1		Phase 2		Phase 3	
	GRMD	Healthy	GRMD	Healthy	GRMD	Healthy
EDL	45	52	56	48	73	136
GasLat	43	30	34	24	31	85
GasMed	64	60	43	37	60	113
TC	53	73	87	64	81	157

Table 2. Average ROI sizes in pixels (for each phase, tissue class, and muscle type)

	Phase 1		Phase 2		Phase 3	
	GRMD	Healthy	GRMD	Healthy	GRMD	Healthy
EDL	156	202	189	239	160	279
GasLat	189	161	220	184	199	220
GasMed	293	290	379	395	328	426
TC	165	205	250	255	236	316

Table 3. Textural features considered (and their abbreviations)

Method	Features
GLH	average (Avg), variance (Var), skewness ($Skew$), kurtosis ($Kurt$)
GM	average ($GraAvg$), variance ($GraVar$), skewness ($GraSkew$), kurtosis ($GraKurt$)
COM	angular second moment ($AngSecMo$), entropy ($Entr$), inverse difference moment ($InvDiffMo$), correlation ($Corr$), sum average ($SumAvg$), difference average ($DiffAvg$), sum variance ($SumVar$), difference variance ($DiffVar$), sum entropy ($SumEntr$), difference entropy ($DiffEntr$), contrast ($Contrast$)
RLM	short run emphasis ($ShortEm$), long run emphasis ($LongEm$), gray level non-uniformity ($GlNonUni$), run length non-uniformity ($RlNonUni$), fraction of image in runs ($Fraction$), low gray level runs emphasis ($LowGlrEm$), high gray level runs emphasis ($HighGlrEm$), run length entropy ($RlEntr$)
GLDM	average ($gAvg$), entropy ($gEntr$), contrast ($gContrast$), angular second moment ($gAngSecMo$), inverse difference moment ($gInvDiffMo$)
LTE	entropy of a ROI filtered with Laws' masks ($E_3L_3, S_3L_3, S_3E_3, E_3E_3, S_3S_3$)
FB	fractal dimension ($FractalDim$)
AC	autocorrelation ($Autocorr$)

and the autocorrelation model (AC) [23]. Full feature names and their abbreviations are given in Table 3.

We used some preliminary classification experiments to determine the best settings for each TA method. As a result, the number of image gray levels was reduced from 256 (initially) to 64 for the COM, RLM, and GLDM methods. Four standard directions of pixel arrangement (0°, 45°, 90°, and 135°) were considered in applying the COM, GLDM, RLM, and AC methods. Only the smallest distances between pixels in pairs (1 and 2) were considered for the COM, GLDM, FB, and AC methods. Features calculated for different directions (and different distances between pixels) were averaged. The LTE method used only

3×3 zero-sum convolution kernels. Images obtained with kernel pairs consisting of a mask and its transposition were added.

Feature selection was performed with the Weka tool [24]. A single selection procedure was repeated $r = 200,000$ times. Each time, two-thirds of the available observations ($q = 2/3p$) were randomly chosen from the original data set. The proportions between observations representing each class in the truncated data set were the same as in the original data set. Observations were characterized each time by a randomly chosen set of 8 features, which was about 20 % of all the features initially calculated ($m = 0.2d$). For each selection procedure, the usefulness of each candidate subset of features was estimated by a wrapper (supervised) method *WrapperSubsetEval* combined with a C4.5 Decision Tree [25] classifier (called *J48* in Weka). This classifier was used because of its simplicity, good performance, and very short induction time. This last property is important when a single selection procedure must be repeated hundreds of thousands of times. Classification accuracies were assessed by a 10-fold cross-validation. The space of subsets of features was searched using the *BestFirst* strategy with the *Forward* searching direction.

Classification experiments were also conducted with the Weka tool. Three classifiers were utilized: Adaptive Boosting (AdaBoost) [26], back-propagation Neural Network (NN) [27], and nonlinear Support Vector Machines (SVM). The AdaBoost classifier was trained for 100 iterations and used the C4.5 tree as the underlying algorithm. The Neural Network used a sigmoidal activating function and had one hidden layer in which the number of neurons was equal to the average number of considered features and the number of tissue classes. Support Vector Machines used Platt's Sequential Minimal Optimization (SMO) algorithm [28] and a second-degree polynomial kernel.

Two problems were considered during the classification experiments. The first was to differentiate between GRMD and healthy dogs at each of the three phases of canine growth and/or dystrophy progression. The second was to differentiate between tissues at three phases of dystrophy progression in GRMD dogs.

5   Results and Discussion

The experiments were run separately for each type of muscle (EDL, GasLat, GasMed, and TC), and were repeated using three classifiers. Firstly, a modified MC feature selection was performed and the most frequently selected features were detected. Secondly, the number of features sufficient to ensure satisfactory differentiation between tissue classes was assessed by testing different subsets of top-selected features. Finally, the differences between classification qualities obtained with selected features and all possible features were examined.

5.1   The Most Frequently Selected Features

The most frequently selected features are listed in Table 4, separately for each of four muscle types and each classification problem (defined at the end of the the previous section). Based on Table 4 a detailed comparison of the most appropriate textural features for each case could be performed.

Table 4. The 5 most frequently selected features for each classification task and each muscle type. The first three rows concern differentiation between GRMD and healthy dogs at different phases of canine growth. The last row concerns differentiation between tissues at three phases of dystrophy progression in GRMD dogs. Feature names are preceded by their incidence frequency rates [%] in the modified MC feature selection.

	EDL	GasLat	GasMed	TC
Phase 1	(87.4) $InvDiffMo$	(59.4) $Entr$	(87.8) $FractalDim$	(71.6) $GlNonUni$
	(86.1) $gInvDiffMo$	(49.9) S_3L_3	(65.2) $GraAvg$	(68.7) $GraAvg$
	(65.2) $AngSecMo$	(39.0) $GraAvg$	(39.3) $gInvDiffMo$	(66.2) $gInvDiffMo$
	(39.8) $gAngSecMo$	(37.7) $gAngSecMo$	(39.1) $InvDiffMo$	(65.7) $InvDiffMo$
	(39.4) $gAvg$	(34.8) $SumEntr$	(29.4) $HighGlrEm$	(65.6) $LongEm$
Phase 2	(71.6) Avg	(77.6) $SumAvg$	(73.0) $SumAvg$	(81.3) $LowGlrEm$
	(69.0) $SumAvg$	(75.8) Avg	(72.7) Avg	(65.8) Avg
	(68.8) $LowGlrEm$	(71.5) $HighGlrEm$	(72.3) $HighGlrEm$	(65.4) $SumAvg$
	(66.9) $HighGlrEm$	(71.3) $LowGlrEm$	(66.0) $LowGlrEm$	(51.7) $HighGlrEm$
	(65.0) $GraVar$	(51.4) $RlEntr$	(25.5) $Entr$	(50.5) $gAvg$
Phase 3	(94.7) $GlNonUni$	(77.2) $LowGlrEm$	(80.5) $S3S3$	(96.4) $GlNonUni$
	(86.3) $RlNonUni$	(76.1) $HighGlrEm$	(79.9) $HighGlrEm$	(88.8) $GraAvg$
	(85.9) $LowGlrEm$	(66.4) Avg	(78.0) $LowGlrEm$	(88.7) $RlNonUni$
	(83.2) $HighGlrEm$	(62.7) $SumAvg$	(76.1) Avg	(85.8) $FractalDim$
	(77.2) S_3S_3	(49.8) Var	(73.1) $SumAvg$	(83.0) $LowGlrEm$
GRMD	(83.6) $LowGlrEm$	(60.8) $gEntr$	(79.3) $RlNonUni$	(83.5) $GraAvg$
	(78.1) $HighGlrEm$	(60.2) $DiffEntr$	(73.1) $Entr$	(78.9) $LowGlrEm$
	(75.9) $SumAvg$	(53.2) $gContrast$	(63.4) $GlNonUni$	(73.4) $Entr$
	(72.7) E_3E_3	(52.4) $Contrast$	(61.1) $GraAvg$	(71.3) $SumAvg$
	(71.1) $GraVar$	(48.5) $LongEm$	(51.6) $AngSecMo$	(69.2) Avg

First we will compare the results for the differentiation between healthy and GRMD dogs at each phase of canine growth. The sets of most frequently selected features can be seen to be different for each classification task. However, some TA methods proved more useful than others for each phase. At the beginning of canine growth (the first phase), when dogs are still very small and thus ROIs occupy small areas in the images, the COM and GLDM methods seem to be the most suitable. Note that in our experiments these methods take into account only small distances between pixels in pairs. Features selected fairly often, irrespective of muscle types, are $InvDiffMo$ (COM-based) and $gInvDiffMo$ (GLDM-based). These features are numerical descriptors of local image homogeneity and are inversely related to the contrast measure. Two other features encountered,

AngSecMo and *gAngSecMo* (COM- and GLDM-based, respectively), are also measures of local homogeneity.

In the second phase, the RLM method proves more accurate. Two RLM-based features, *LowGlrEm* and *HighGlrEm*, are top-ranked for each muscle type. The usefulness of such features could be explained by changes occurring in the muscles as dystrophy progresses. In healthy dogs, muscles display regular fibers, which may result in fairly regular pixel runs in the image. In GRMD dogs, necrotic fibers are abundant and fibers may even appear in clusters. These changes may result in frequent small darker and lighter regions in the image. In fact, the *LowGlrEm* and *HighGlrEm* features reflect the distribution of low and high gray level values, respectively. These distributions differ between the two dog classes. Two other frequently selected features, *Avg* (GLH), and *SumAvg* (COM), are also related to pixel gray-level distributions.

In the third phase, almost exclusively RLM-based features are at the top of all four rankings. In addition to the still common *LowGlrEm* and *HighGlrEm* features, *GlNonUni* and *RlNonUni* are encountered as well. The *Avg* and *SumAvg* features are also selected, but not so often as in the second phase.

Differentiation between the three phases of dystrophy progression in GRMD dogs requires the use of features derived from several TA methods. In this case identification of the best method is more difficult. At least one RLM- and one COM-based feature prove to be good tissue descriptor for each muscle type. The usefulness of RLM-based features could be explained again by already described changes in affected muscles. Continuous development of the dystrophy entails the disappearance of regular muscle structures (visible on MRI as homogeneous texture primitives and quite regular pixel runs). The same reasons determine the suitability of COM- and GM-based features, selected as well. Features obtained from above methods are various measures of the presence, frequency and size of different texture elements, changing over the dystrophy progression.

5.2   Estimation of a Sufficient Number of Selected Features

The plots in Fig. 2 show how the classification quality changes when consecutive features from the feature incidence frequency rankings are added to the set of tissue descriptors. We will present only the results obtained by the AdaBoost classifier for the TC muscle. Similar plots were observed for other classifiers and other muscle types.

Analysis of the plots in Fig. 2 reveals that high classification accuracies can be obtained with a small subset of the set of features originally considered. Moreover, adding the top-ranked features to the set of tissue descriptors results in fairly rapid improvement of classification accuracy. However, this improvement is not strictly proportional to the number of features. Beyond a certain number of features the quality of classification does not increase significantly, and may even decrease. This threshold usually does not exceed 10 features.

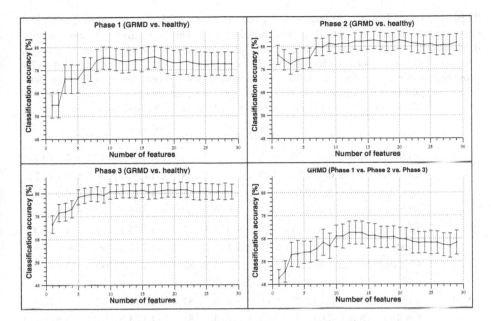

Fig. 2. Classification accuracy achieved with different numbers of the most frequently selected features. The results were obtained using the AdaBoost classifier, for the TC muscle. The first three plots concern differentiation between GRMD and healthy dogs at different phases of canine growth. The last plot concerns differentiation between tissues at three phases of dystrophy progression in GRMD dogs.

5.3 Classification Improvements Due to Feature Selection

Table 5 presents the best classification results obtained with sets of selected features. Results are given separately for each of four differentiation problems and for each of four muscle types. Each result is followed by the percentage by which the classification quality has been improved as compared to the quality obtained in the same differentiation task but considering all the available 39 features. It can be seen that using the best set of selected features always improves the classification accuracy in comparison with the case where all the possible textural features are applied as tissue descriptors. Sometimes the improvement is not significant, and feature selection mainly reduces the time and memory requirements for feature extraction and for training of classifiers. In many cases the improvement is considerable, even exceeding 10 %. The best classification results (more than 99 %) were observed in the first phase, when the presence or absence of disease was recognized in the EDL muscle (using the NN and SVM classifiers). Lower classification accuracies were achieved during differentiation between the three phases of dystrophy progression in GRMD dogs. This task seems to be the most difficult, as the best result was about 71.3 % correctly recognized cases.

126   D. Duda et al.

Table 5. Classification accuracies [%] (and standard deviations) achieved with the best sets of selected features (for each muscle type). The first three columns concern differentiation between GRMD and healthy dogs at different phases of canine growth. The last column concerns differentiation between tissues at three phases of dystrophy progression in GRMD dogs. Results are followed by the percentage by which the classification quality was improved in comparison to the case where all possible features were used. The results were obtained with the AdaBoost, NN, and SVM classifiers.

Classifier	Muscle	Phase 1	Phase 2	Phase 3	GRMD
AdaBoost	EDL	$97.9 \pm 2.5\,(1.7)$	$93.5 \pm 3.9\,(1.3)$	$88.1 \pm 3.4\,(0.7)$	$66.7 \pm 5.2\,(0.7)$
	GasLat	$81.7 \pm 6.3\,(12.6)$	$91.5 \pm 5.6\,(3.8)$	$89.7 \pm 4.0\,(3.2)$	$56.6 \pm 7.7\,(4.3)$
	GasMed	$84.7 \pm 5.2\,(2.0)$	$93.4 \pm 5.0\,(5.1)$	$88.6 \pm 3.7\,(2.2)$	$61.1 \pm 6.1\,(4.4)$
	TC	$83.7 \pm 4.7\,(4.3)$	$90.7 \pm 3.8\,(2.9)$	$89.5 \pm 3.4\,(1.3)$	$70.6 \pm 5.2\,(4.9)$
NN	EDL	$99.9 \pm 0.5\,(0.7)$	$93.6 \pm 3.9\,(1.8)$	$87.2 \pm 3.3\,(3.1)$	$63.7 \pm 4.9\,(3.3)$
	GasLat	$83.5 \pm 6.6\,(11.9)$	$97.9 \pm 3.1\,(2.5)$	$90.8 \pm 3.7\,(5.6)$	$56.5 \pm 6.7\,(9.8)$
	GasMed	$80.0 \pm 5.9\,(2.5)$	$96.3 \pm 3.1\,(4.4)$	$89.5 \pm 3.7\,(2.7)$	$60.2 \pm 5.7\,(1.9)$
	TC	$79.9 \pm 5.6\,(2.2)$	$91.7 \pm 3.6\,(3.8)$	$88.5 \pm 3.5\,(1.9)$	$70.0 \pm 5.1\,(5.7)$
SVM	EDL	$99.8 \pm 0.7\,(0.2)$	$95.0 \pm 3.3\,(5.0)$	$87.5 \pm 3.1\,(0.1)$	$70.3 \pm 5.1\,(3.9)$
	GasLat	$78.5 \pm 5.6\,(6.9)$	$98.1 \pm 2.7\,(3.1)$	$88.7 \pm 4.1\,(4.9)$	$58.4 \pm 5.8\,(10.2)$
	GasMed	$83.8 \pm 5.8\,(3.5)$	$96.3 \pm 3.1\,(4.8)$	$88.6 \pm 4.2\,(2.0)$	$62.0 \pm 5.1\,(7.9)$
	TC	$82.6 \pm 5.1\,(1.9)$	$92.7 \pm 3.3\,(1.5)$	$88.9 \pm 3.3\,(1.0)$	$71.3 \pm 5.2\,(3.8)$

6   Conclusion and Future Work

The aim of the study was to find the best texture-based tissue descriptors for four types of canine hindlimb muscles (EDL, GasLat, GasMed, and TC) at each of three identified phases of canine growth and/or dystrophy progression. A total of 39 textural features, derived from 8 TA methods, were analyzed. Classification experiments were conducted separately for each muscle type. They involved differentiation either between healthy and GRMD dogs at different phases, or between tissues at different phases in GRMD dogs only. The experiments enabled us to conclude the following. (i) The best discrimination (or nearly the best, and not significantly different from the best) can be obtained with a small set of selected features (up to 10). (ii) The best TA methods can be different for each phase of canine growth. The COM- and GLDM-based features can be the most useful in the first phase, the RLM-based features together with some of the GLH- and COM-based features in the second, and the RLM features in the third. (iii) Classification accuracy can be significantly improved when only a few selected features are used as tissue descriptors.

Differentiation between three phases of disease progression in GRMD dogs proved to be the most difficult task. However, it is important to find a satisfactory solution to this problem if texture analysis is to be applied to assessment of the canine response to treatment. In the future, experiments should be conducted on a larger database. Other TA methods could also be considered. It would be interesting to analyze tissue descriptors derived from different muscle types at a time. Other image modalities could also be considered. Finally, it would be useful to describe how textural features change over the dystrophy progression.

Acknowledgments. This work was performed under the auspices of the European COST Action BM1304, MYO-MRI. It was also performed in the framework of the grant S/WI/2/2013 (Bialystok University of Technology), founded by the Polish Ministry of Science and Higher Education.

References

1. Haldeman-Englert, C.: Duchenne Muscular Dystrophy: MedlinePlus Medical Encyclopedia. Medline Plus. U.S. National Library of Medicine (2014). https://www.nlm.nih.gov/medlineplus/ency/article/000705.htm
2. Sarnat, H.B.: Muscular dystrophies. In: Kliegman, R.M., Stanton, B.F., Geme, J.W., Schor, N.F., Behrman, R.E. (eds.) Nelson Textbook of Pediatrics, 19th edn. Saunders Elsevier, Philadelphia (2011)
3. Kornegay, J.N., Bogan, J.R., Bogan, D.J., Childers, M.K., Li, J., et al.: Canine models of Duchenne muscular dystrophy and their use in therapeutic strategies. Mamm. Genome 23(1–2), 85–108 (2012)
4. De Certaines, J.D., Larcher, T., Duda, D., Azzabou, N., Eliat, P.A., et al.: Application of texture analysis to muscle MRI: 1-What kind of information should be expected from texture analysis? EPJ Nonlinear Biomed. Phys. 3(3), 1–14 (2015)
5. Lerski, R.A., de Certaines, J.D., Duda, D., Klonowski, W., Yang, G., et al.: Application of texture analysis to muscle MRI: 2-Technical recommendations. EPJ Nonlinear Biomed. Phys. 3(2), 1–20 (2015)
6. Castellano, G., Bonilha, L., Li, L.M., Cendes, F.: Texture analysis of medical images. Clin. Radiol. 59(12), 1061–1069 (2004)
7. Hajek, M., Dezortova, M., Materka, A., Lerski, R.A. (eds.): Texture Analysis for Magnetic Resonance Imaging. Med4Publishing, Prague (2006)
8. Nailon, W.H.: Texture analysis methods for medical image characterisation. In: Mao, Y. (ed.) Biomedical Imaging, pp. 75–100. InTech Open (2010)
9. Duda, D., Kretowski, M., Azzabou, N., de Certaines, J.D.: MRI texture analysis for differentiation between healthy and golden retriever muscular dystrophy dogs at different phases of disease evolution. In: Saeed, K., Homenda, W. (eds.) CISIM 2015. LNCS, vol. 9339, pp. 255–266. Springer, Heidelberg (2015)
10. Draminski, M., Rada-Iglesias, A., Enroth, S., Wadelius, C., Koronacki, J., Komorowski, J.: Monte Carlo feature selection for supervised classification. Bioinformatics 24(1), 110–117 (2008)
11. Fan, Z., Wang, J., Ahn, M., Shiloh-Malawsky, Y., Chahin, N., et al.: Characteristics of magnetic resonance imaging biomarkers in a natural history study of golden retriever muscular dystrophy. Neuromuscul. Disord. 24(2), 178–191 (2014)
12. Galloway, M.M.: Texture analysis using gray level run lengths. Comput. Graph. Image Process. 4(2), 172–179 (1975)
13. Yang, G., Lalande, V., Chen, L., Azzabou, N., Larcher, T., et al.: MRI texture analysis of GRMD dogs using orthogonal moments: a preliminary study. IRBM 36(4), 213–219 (2015)
14. Vapnik, V.N.: The Nature of Statistical Learning Theory, 2nd edn. Springer, New York (2000)

15. Haralick, R.M., Shanmugam, K., Dinstein, I.: Textural features for image classification. IEEE Trans. Syst. Man Cybern. Syst. **SMC–3**(6), 610–621 (1973)
16. Guyon, I., Elisseeff, A.: An introduction to variable and feature selection. J. Mach. Learn. Res. **3**, 1157–1182 (2003)
17. Thibaud, J.L., Azzabou, N., Barthelemy, I., Fleury, S., Cabrol, L., et al.: Comprehensive longitudinal characterization of canine muscular dystrophy by serial NMR imaging of GRMD dogs. Neuromuscul. Disord. **22**(Suppl. 2), S85–S99 (2012)
18. Duda, D.: Medical image classification based on texture analysis. Ph.D. thesis, University of Rennes 1, Rennes, France (2009)
19. Lerski, R., Straughan, K., Shad, L., Boyce, D., Bluml, S., Zuna, I.: MR image texture analysis - an approach to tissue characterization. Magn. Reson. Imaging **11**(6), 873–887 (1993)
20. Weszka, J.S., Dyer, C.R., Rosenfeld, A.: A comparative study of texture measures for terrain classification. IEEE Trans. Syst. Man Cybern. **6**(4), 269–285 (1976)
21. Laws, K.I.: Textured image segmentation. Ph.D. thesis, University of Southern California, Los Angeles, CA, USA (1980)
22. Chen, E.L., Chung, P.C., Chen, C.L., Tsai, H.M., Chang, C.I.: An automatic diagnostic system for CT liver image classification. IEEE Trans. Biomed. Eng. **45**(6), 783–794 (1998)
23. Gonzalez, R.C., Woods, R.E.: Digital Image Processing, 2nd edn. Addison-Wesley, Reading (2002)
24. Hall, M., Frank, E., Holmes, G., Pfahringer, B., Reutemann, P., Witten, I.H.: The WEKA data mining software: an update. SIGKDD Explor. **11**(1), 10–18 (2009)
25. Quinlan, J.: C4.5: Programs for Machine Learning. Morgan Kaufmann, San Francisco (1993)
26. Freund, Y., Shapire, R.: A decision-theoretic generalization of online learning and an application to boosting. J. Comput. Syst. Sci. **55**(1), 119–139 (1997)
27. Rojas, R.: Neural Networks. A Systematic Introduction. Springer, Berlin (1996)
28. Platt, J.C.: Fast training of support vector machines using sequential minimal optimization. In: Scholkopf, B., Burges, C.J.C., Smola, A.J. (eds.) Advances in Kernel Methods - Support Vector Learning, pp. 185–208. MIT Press, Cambridge (1998)

Detection of Orbital Floor Fractures
by Principal Component Analysis

Daniel Krpelik[1], Milan Jaros[1], Marta Jarosova[1], Petr Strakos[1],
Tereza Buresova[2], Alena Vasatova[1], and Tomas Karasek[1(✉)]

[1] IT4Innovations National Supercomputing Center,
VSB-Technical University of Ostrava, Ostrava, Czech Republic
tomas.karasek@vsb.cz
[2] The University Hospital in Ostrava, Ostrava, Czech Republic

Abstract. Principal component analysis (PCA) is a statistical method
based on orthogonal transformation, which is used to convert possibly
correlated datasets into linearly uncorrelated variables called principal
components. PCA is one of the simplest methods based on the eigenvector analysis. This method is widely used in many fields, such as signal
processing, quality control or mechanical engineering. In this paper, we
present the use of PCA in area of medical image processing. In the medical image processing with subsequent reconstruction of 3D models, data
from sources such as Computed Tomography (CT) or Magnetic Resonance Imagining (MRI) are used. Series of images representing axial slices
of human body are stored in Digital Imaging and Communications in
Medicine (DICOM) format. Physical properties of different body tissues
are characterized by different shades of grey of each pixel correlated to the
tissue density. Properties of each pixel are then used in image segmentation and subsequent creation of 3D model of human organs. Image segmentation splits digital image into regions with similar properties which
are later used to create 3D model. In many cases accurate detections of
edges of such objects are necessary. This could be for example the case
of a tumour or orbital fracture identification. In this paper, identification
of the orbital fracture using PCA method is presented as an example of
application of the method in the area of medical image processing.

1 Introduction

Despite CT and MRI are widely used by medical doctors for diagnostic purposes
their potential is still not fully utilized. Those modalities provide 2D images of
3D objects and although medical doctors learn how to read and interpret them,
they provide only partial information. Extraction of additional information such
as size, area or volume of desired object has to be done manually and it is
labour-intensive. Information about volume is crucial for example for surgeons,
who are planning liver resections where remaining volume of liver is matter of life

© IFIP International Federation for Information Processing 2016
Published by Springer International Publishing Switzerland 2016. All Rights Reserved
K. Saeed and W. Homenda (Eds.): CISIM 2016, LNCS 9842, pp. 129–138, 2016.
DOI: 10.1007/978-3-319-45378-1_12

or death. Volume of upper respiratory tract serves in diagnoses of sleep apnea. Size of orbital floor fracture is important when doctors are making decision whether patient should undergo surgery or conservative treatment. Those are just examples of additional information requested by doctors which cannot be obtained automatically from CT or MRI images.

Image processing could be an option how to reduce labour intensity, shorten the time of diagnostic processes and increase fidelity of the results. Above mentioned quantities are measured on 3D models which are created usually in several following steps. First, image noise is reduced by image filtering. Than image segmentation consisting of localization of objects and its boundaries is performed. Last step is 3D surface reconstruction.

If the 3D model is created by the mentioned steps, further detection of significant features like edges can be highly important. These features can localize major changes in overall shape of the model. While working with medical data, localization of such changes can lead, e.g., to direct detection of fractures in bones or tumours in soft tissues.

PCA method is used here to detect the points on the edge of the fracture. The edges are identified by calculating eigenvalues and eigenvectors of covariance matrix and establishing ratios between the calculated eigenvalues. In this paper PCA method is applied for detection of orbital floor fracture.

This paper is organized as follows. In Sect. 2 we describe example of identification of orbital floor fracture. In Sect. 3 PCA method is described followed by Sect. 4 where object identification is explained. In Sect. 5 details about fracture area reconstruction can be found. Section 6 concludes whole paper.

2   Model Example

In this paper PCA is used for identification of orbital floor fracture from 3D virtual model of the human orbit. There is a very thin bone on the bottom side of the human eye orbit. Since this bone is the most fragile part of the orbit it is predisposed to fractures (see Figs. 1 and 2). Fracture of this bone can be determined from CT scans, but to determine the extension of the fracture, only rough approximate methods have been used so far. These methods rely on manual determination of most distant points on fracture boundary. The fracture size can then be assessed by calculating the ratio of distance between two points of fracture boundary, to the distance between another two points, representing orbital floor boundary. All point are selected in one CT image where the fracture diameter is maximal [Ploder02]. Another way is to select points denoting fracture boundary in two perpendicular planes and approximate the fracture by geometrical primitives (e.g. ellipse). Area of such primitives can be determined from known equations [Goggin15]. In this approach CT image with maximal fracture diameter is also used. Although both above mentioned methods were shown to be inaccurate, they are widely used as they require little human expert intervention and less time compared to purely manual segmentation. Manual segmentation requires manual selection of all points denoting the fracture on

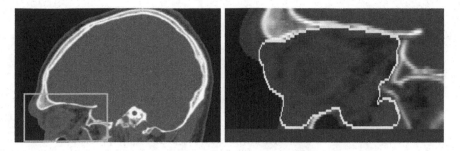

Fig. 1. Model example: Left image depicts eye area denoted by yellow rectangle on CT scan image of a skull. Right image shows boundary (pink colour) of inner eye region identified by segmentation algorithm. (Color figure online)

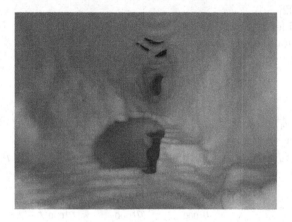

Fig. 2. 3D reconstruction of orbital floor. Hole on the bottom side represents sought fracture.

each individual CT image followed by area calculation from selected voxels. Our implemented method is based on semi-automatic segmentation and keeps the human expert intervention minimal.

3   Covariance Matrix and Principal Component Analysis

First, let us introduce the basic terms which will be used later in this paper. To distinguish, whether particular object is 1D, 2D or 3D we need to know the relationship between points representing this object. Let $P \subset \mathbb{R}^3$ be the set of all data points. For each point $p \in P$ set of neighbouring nodes could be found as

$$N_p = \left\{ q \mid p, q \in P, \ |pq| = \sqrt{(p_x - q_x)^2 + (p_y - q_y)^2 + (p_z - q_z)^2} < d_{3D} \right\}.$$

$$(1)$$

The example of set of points for which covariance matrix will be created is depicted on Fig. 3.

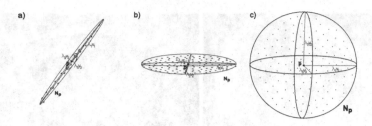

Fig. 3. Point distribution: (a) linear, (b) planar, (c) spherical

Recognition of geometric patterns in an image by the invariant moment was first introduced by 1962 Hu [Hu62]. In this work two-dimensional moment was used. Later, the invariant moment was extended to the third dimension by [Maas99, Gross02].

Let us consider the set N_p to be solid in such a way that $B \subset \mathbb{R}^3$. Then $(i+j+k)$-th moment is defined by the equation

$$m_{ijk} = \iiint\limits_B x^i y^j z^k \ f(x,y,z) \ dxdydz, \tag{2}$$

where $i, j, k \in \mathbb{Z}_0^+$ and $f(x,y,z)$ is the mass density function of solid B. Let $f(x,y,z) = 1$ for $\forall p \in P$.

If we set $(i+j+k) \le 2$, coordinates of the centre of gravity $\bar{p}$ of the solid B could be defined as

$$\bar{p} = \left(\bar{x} = \frac{m_{100}}{m_{000}}, \ \bar{y} = \frac{m_{010}}{m_{000}}, \ \bar{z} = \frac{m_{001}}{m_{000}} \right), \tag{3}$$

where m_{000} is the mass of the solid B and $m_{100}, m_{010}, m_{001}$ are the static moments with respect to the coordinate planes yz, xz, xy.

The $(i+j+k)$-th centralized moment of the solid B is defined by

$$\mu_{ijk} = \iiint\limits_B (x - \bar{x})^i (y - \bar{y})^j (z - \bar{z})^k \ f(x,y,z) \ dxdydz. \tag{4}$$

To obtain central moment invariant to its size we have to normalize it

$$\widehat{\mu_{ijk}} = \frac{\mu_{ijk}}{\mu_{000}} = \frac{\iiint\limits_B (x - \bar{x})^i (y - \bar{y})^j (z - \bar{z})^k \ f(x,y,z) \ dxdydz}{\iiint\limits_B (x - \bar{x})^0 (y - \bar{y})^0 (z - \bar{z})^0 \ f(x,y,z) \ dxdydz}. \tag{5}$$

After the numerical approximation of the normalized centralized moment we get

$$\widehat{\mu_{ijk}} = \frac{\sum\limits_{n=1}^{|N_p|} (x_n - \bar{x})^i (y_n - \bar{y})^j (z_n - \bar{z})^k}{\sum\limits_{n=1}^{|N_p|} (x_n - \bar{x})^0 (y_n - \bar{y})^0 (z_n - \bar{z})^0}, \tag{6}$$

$$\widehat{\mu_{ijk}} = \frac{1}{|N_p|} \sum_{n=1}^{|N_p|} (x_n - \bar{x})^i (y_n - \bar{y})^j (z_n - \bar{z})^k. \tag{7}$$

Finally, covariance matrix for each point $p \in P$ and its neighbours could be assembled as

$$C_p = \begin{pmatrix} \widehat{\mu_{200}} & \widehat{\mu_{110}} & \widehat{\mu_{101}} \\ \widehat{\mu_{110}} & \widehat{\mu_{020}} & \widehat{\mu_{011}} \\ \widehat{\mu_{101}} & \widehat{\mu_{011}} & \widehat{\mu_{002}} \end{pmatrix}. \tag{8}$$

The matrix C_p could be simplified by substituting the moments

$$C_p = \frac{1}{|N_p|} \sum_{n=1}^{|N_p|} \begin{pmatrix} (x_n - \bar{x})^2 & (x_n - \bar{x})(y_n - \bar{y}) & (x_n - \bar{x})(z_n - \bar{z}) \\ (x_n - \bar{x})(y_n - \bar{y}) & (y_n - \bar{y})^2 & (y_n - \bar{y})(z_n - \bar{z}) \\ (x_n - \bar{x})(z_n - \bar{z}) & (y_n - \bar{y})(z_n - \bar{z}) & (z_n - \bar{z})^2 \end{pmatrix}, \tag{9}$$

$$C_p = \frac{1}{|N_p|} \sum_{n=1}^{|N_p|} \left(\begin{bmatrix} x_n - \bar{x} \\ y_n - \bar{y} \\ z_n - \bar{z} \end{bmatrix} [x_n - \bar{x} \; y_n - \bar{y} \; z_n - \bar{z}] \right), \tag{10}$$

$$C_p = \frac{1}{|N_p|} \sum_{n=1}^{|N_p|} (q_n - \bar{p})^T (q_n - \bar{p}), \tag{11}$$

where $q \in N_p$ and $\bar{p}$ is the center of gravity of the set N_p.

For purpose of implementation, Eq. (11) could be rewritten to the form of matrix multiplication

$$Q_p = \begin{bmatrix} x_1 & y_1 & z_1 \\ x_2 & y_2 & z_2 \\ x_3 & y_3 & z_3 \\ \vdots & \vdots & \vdots \\ x_{|N_p|} & y_{|N_p|} & z_{|N_p|} \end{bmatrix}, \quad J = \begin{bmatrix} 1 & 1 & \cdots & 1 \\ 1 & 1 & \cdots & 1 \\ 1 & 1 & \cdots & 1 \\ \vdots & \vdots & & \vdots \\ 1 & 1 & \cdots & 1 \end{bmatrix}, \tag{12}$$

$$S_p = Q_p - J^T Q_p \frac{1}{|N_p|}, \tag{13}$$

$$C_p = S_p^T S_p, \tag{14}$$

where Q_p is the matrix composed of coordinates of a set N_p, matrix J is square matrix of all ones and the matrix multiplication $J^T Q_p \frac{1}{|N_p|}$ represents the center of the gravity of the set N_p.

The covariance matrix C_p contains only real numbers, it is symmetric positive semi-definite and its dimension is $n = 3$. It means that all its eigenvalues are real with a complete set of the orthonormal eigenvectors. If this is a case we could say that there exists an orthogonal matrix Q and a diagonal matrix D such that

$$C_p = QDQ^T. \tag{15}$$

The diagonal elements of the matrix D are the eigenvalues $\lambda_1 \geq \lambda_2 \geq \lambda_3$ and columns of the matrix Q are the orthonormal eigenvectors v_1, v_2, v_3 of the matrix C_p

$$C_p = \begin{pmatrix} v_1^T & v_2^T & v_3^T \end{pmatrix} \begin{pmatrix} \lambda_1 & 0 & 0 \\ 0 & \lambda_2 & 0 \\ 0 & 0 & \lambda_3 \end{pmatrix} \begin{pmatrix} v_1 \\ v_2 \\ v_3 \end{pmatrix}. \tag{16}$$

4   Object Recognition

An auxiliary 3D model is acquired by prior segmentation of CT images. Surface of this model is then converted into cloud of points. Following task is to select points which lie on the fracture boundary. This is solved by the classification of neighbourhood of each single point in the cloud. Auxiliary model surface is a 2D object in 3D space. Points of the fracture boundary are determined based on violation of planarity in their neighbourhoods.

Object recognition, respectively classification whether object is 1D, 2D or 3D is based on properties of eigenvalues $\lambda_1 \geq \lambda_2 \geq \lambda_3$. Eigenvalues are obtained by spectral decomposition of matrix C_p in Eq. (14) and they will represent the shape of the set N_p by the ellipsoid [Gross02, Demantke11]. Ellipsoid representing linear, planar or spheric behaviour of neighbours is depicted in Fig. 3. If $\lambda_1 >> \lambda_2, \lambda_3 \cong 0$, the point p is marked as linear. If $\lambda_1, \lambda_2 >> \lambda_3 \cong 0$, the point p is assigned to the planar group. If $\lambda_1 \cong \lambda_2 \cong \lambda_3$, the point p belongs to spheric group.

For the detection of a fracture we divide the points into two groups, P_{planar} and $P_{boundary}$ using the criteria

$$a_{planar} = \frac{\lambda_3}{\sum\limits_{d} \lambda_d}, \tag{17}$$

$$P_{planar} = \{p | p \in P : a_{planar} \leq \epsilon\}, \tag{18}$$

$$P_{boundary} = \{p | p \in P : a_{planar} > \epsilon\}, \tag{19}$$

where $\sum\limits_{d} \lambda_d$ is the normalization coefficient and ϵ is the tolerance parameter. If $a_{planar} > \epsilon$, the point is on the edge and it is assigned to the group $P_{boundary}$. Otherwise the point is on the plane and it is assigned to the group P_{planar}.

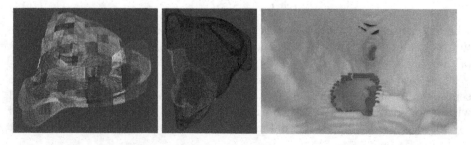

Fig. 4. Conversion of voxels to point cloud (left) selection of cloud subset highlighted in green color (middle) and result of automatic boundary points extraction (right) (Color figure online)

Points on the fracture boundary are not the only ones, which are differentiated by the feature calculated in Eq. (17). A subset of model surface is chosen prior to the segmentation. Resulting segmented points are shown on Fig. 4.

5 Reconstruction of Fracture Area

Fracture is in fact the absence of bone and as such it cannot be localized based solely on pixel/voxel intensity values but rather on its relative position to the other parts of human body. The course of work involves prior segmentation and reconstruction of either undamaged bone area or eye orbit interior as sought fracture boundary lies on the intersection of their surfaces. The eye orbit interior is composed of soft tissue and in many cases leaks through the fracture into air cavity bellow, creating a droplet-like structure. The fracture boundary itself is then searched as a distinctive subsection of selected auxiliary object surface, mainly determined by relatively extreme curvature in its neighbourhood.

This curvature is then exploited in two ways. Firstly, in case of both manual and automated point selection, this curvature is used for reconstruction of fracture boundary. Working hypothesis is that the shortest Jordan curve on the object surface passing through selected points is a good approximation of fracture boundary. Secondly, since the curvature is a distinctive feature, it may be used to extract boundary points via automated segmentation of auxiliary model vertices.

In applied method, we are reconstructing the fracture boundary. Fracture interior itself is impossible to determine, because we cannot evaluate, which specific surface shape is the correct one. Fracture interior is reconstructed heuristically as a piecewise planar surface bounded by found fracture boundary. Alternative methods could prefer smooth surfaces and reconstruct fracture interior for example via solving Laplace problem with Dirichlet boundary.

Proposed method for Jordan curve localization assume that selected points are vertices of auxiliary object mesh and are distributed sparsely around sought boundary. The points in the case of manual point selection are selected on the CT scan images and might not correspond with any vertex in the auxiliary object mesh. This is solved simply by selecting the closest vertex in the mesh for each manually selected point. In case of automated point selection we usually acquire a dense cloud of points, which denies requirement on sparsity. This might be solved automatically by, e.g., the k-means clustering, in which case we select output k-means centroids positions and treat those as a compression of initially dense cloud of points.

The following boundary reconstruction consists of two steps. First we construct a rough approximation of boundary consisting only of selected points and edges, and directly connecting them across Euclidean space. In terms of creating boundary, these points have to be properly ordered. This is a special case of travelling salesman problem for Euclidean metric space, which is generally NP-hard. Although a good polynomial approximation is known, we, for the sake of simplicity, use a greedy algorithm.

Our greedy algorithm starts with arbitrary triangle (a cycle with 3 vertices) and iteratively lengthens the cycle by inserting new point in between a pair of consecutive points from previous iteration. The pair is selected in such a way that the resulting new cycle is the shortest one among those considered (length being measured as a sum of distances between all consecutive points in the cycle). This algorithm is polynomial and given our assumptions, it yields good approximation of sought shortest cycle.

As a next step we refine found boundary by replacing edges in between consecutive points by the shortest paths between them on the auxiliary object mesh. This can be done effectively via Dijkstra algorithm [Dijkstra59] or some of

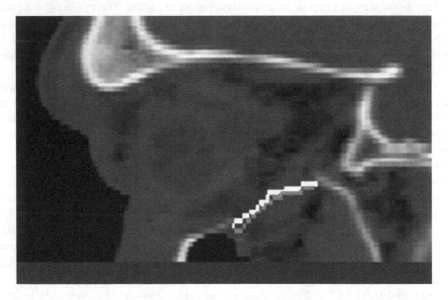

Fig. 5. Fracture extraction - backward projection: manual point selection (pink), automatic point selection (yellow) (Color figure online)

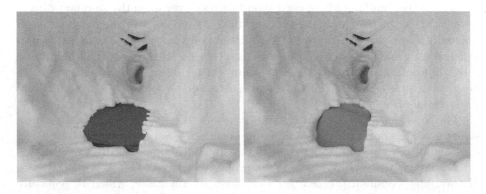

Fig. 6. 3D visualization of fracture extraction: manual point selection (pink), automatic point selection (yellow) (Color figure online)

its approximating variants. To ensure properties of Jordan curve a simple post-processing consisting of removing the inner cycles, which may occur because of independent runs of Dijkstra algorithms, is carried out.

Resulting reconstructed fracture area is visualized on Figs. 5 and 6.

6   Conclusion

A method for edge recognition applied to detect orbital floor fracture was examined in this paper. The method is based on utilization of auxiliary 3D models obtained by segmentation of CT scan images. The problem of fracture reconstruction was converted to a problem of segmentation of auxiliary model mesh vertices and edges.

Proposed method requires selection of specific vertices on auxiliary model mesh. This selection was carried out both manually and automatically, via discriminating features based on PCA, and the results have been compared visually. Once the points were selected, algorithm chose appropriate subset of edges from auxiliary model mesh to reconstruct fracture boundary. These edges were selected so that they correspond with the shortest paths between selected points. This was carried out by Dijkstra algorithm.

Although the throughout validation of the size of orbital floor fracture based on semi-automatic segmentation is still pending, preliminary results based on expert based validation of fracture areas projected backward into CT images show promising results. PCA based point selection provides satisfactory results and thus it deserves further development. For example, the used discriminative feature, the relative magnitude of the smallest eigenvalue, is unable to fully capture all the parts of the fracture boundary. Finding better discriminative feature which could overcome this problem will be our future work.

Acknowledgement. This work was supported by The Ministry of Education, Youth and Sports from the National Programme of Sustainability (NPU II) project "IT4Innovations excellence in science - LQ1602" and from the Large Infrastructures for Research, Experimental Development and Innovations project "IT4Innovations National Supercomputing Center - LM2015070". All CT images used in this paper were provided by The University Hospital in Ostrava.

References

[Hu62]   Ming-Kuei, H.: Visual pattern recognition by moment invariants. IRE Trans. Inf. Theor. **8**(2), 179–187 (1962)

[Maas99]   Maas, H.-G., Vosselman, G.: Two algorithms for extracting building models from raw laser altimetry data. ISPRS J. Photogramm. Remote Sens. **54**, 153–163 (1999)

[Gross02]   Gross, H., Thoennessen, U.: Extraction of lines from laser point clouds. In: ISPRS Commission III Photogrammetric Computer Vision PCV (2006)

[Demantke11] Demantke, J., Mallet, C., David, N., Vallet, B.: Dimensionality based scale selection in 3D lidar point clouds. Int. Arch. Photogramm. Remote Sens. Spatial Inf. Sci. **XXXVIII–5/W12**, 97–102 (2011). doi:10.5194/isprsarchives-XXXVIII-5-W12-97-2011

[Goggin15] Goggin, J., Jupiter, D.C., Czerwinski, M.: Simple computed tomography-based calculations of orbital floor fracture defect size are not sufficiently accurate for clinical use. J. Oral Maxillofac. Surg. **73**(1), 112–116 (2015). ISSN 0278-2391

[Ploder02] Ploder, O., Klug, C., Voracek, M., Burggasser, G., Czerny, C.: Evaluation of computer-based area and volume measurement from coronal computed tomography scans in isolated blowout fractures of the orbital floor. J. Oral Maxillofac. Surg. **60**(11), 1267–1272 (2002). ISSN 0278-2391

[Dijkstra59] Dijkstra, E.W.: A note on two problems in connexion with graphs. Numer. Math. **1**, 269–271 (1959)

An Approach to Cell Nuclei Counting in Histological Image Analysis

Maryna Lukashevich and Valery Starovoitov$^{(\boxtimes)}$

Faculty of Economics and Informatics in Vilnius,
University of Bialystok, Vilnius, Lithuania
Lukashevich@bsuir.by, valerystar@mail.ru

Abstract. The paper describes a technique for automated cell nuclei counting. In this study, the primary goal is to provide simple and effective automated scheme of cell nuclei counting. The experiments on public data set of histology images have demonstrated acceptable level of calculation results.

Keywords: Histological analysis · Machine analysis · Cell nuclei counting

1 Introduction and Motivation

The most important and rapidly developing areas in the field of visualization and control of microscopic objects is development of automated computer vision systems. Computer analysis of microscopy cell images has many real-life applications in a wide range of areas including diagnosis of a disease, morphological cell analysis and statistics [1]. It plays an important role in biomedical research and bioinformatics. Microscopic analysis approach is particularly important in solving the following problems: malignant transformation of normal cells and cancer cell detection, morphological changes in cells, dynamic changes in the cells during therapeutic procedures [2].

For that reason, automatic counting of cell nuclei is a key block in systems for microscopic analysis of cell images. Since 1970s automated methods of histological analysis have been developed [1,2]. Detection of cellular structures and cell counting are common tasks for many investigations.

Some researchers have applied thresholding for cell counting in the investigated images. It is a simple way for separating objects of interest from the background. Another approach is to segment images using different edge detection (LoG filter, Laplacian filtering, etc.). However, detection and segmentation of cell nuclei is a challenging task, since the cells have a complex and a nonuniform structure. Another feature of histological image is non-uniform illumination, which also applies limitations on the use of standard approaches.

In recent years many methods have been proposed for cell nuclei segmentation, separation and classification in histological analysis. More sophisticated

K. Saeed and W. Homenda (Eds.): CISIM 2016, LNCS 9842, pp. 139–147, 2016.
DOI: 10.1007/978-3-319-45378-1_13

approaches consist of several image processing stages. These methods are based on traditional image processing algorithms like adaptive contour model, watershed, morphological operations, k-means, Support vector machine, etc. [3–12].

Recent works suggest combining different approaches for increasing performance. Several excellent reviews about methods for nuclei detection, segmentation and classification can be found in [1, 2].

The main methods for cell nuclei segmentation, separation and classification are presented in Table 1.

Table 1. Short summary of state-of-the-art cell nuclei segmentation, separation and classification

Solvable task	Methods
Segmentation	Adaptive contour model, adaptive thresholding, morphological operations, watershed, k-means, H-maxima transform, region growing, Gaussian mixture model
Separation	Distance transform, watershed transform, concavity detection, edge path selection
Classification	Texture, morphology, texture and morphology, texture/morphology/intensity with Support vector machine, texture/morphology/topology with Bayesian, intensity with k-means clustering, intensity & texture with Adaboost

In our research we study the problem of automatically counting of cell nuclei in histological images of their size and shape.

Depending on the quality of prepared medication and used optical equipment, microscopy image can be both grayscale and color. The large number of different objects in histological images is a serious disadvantage for analysis of this class of images. Unfortunately, cell nuclei analysis is challenging task because of the complexity of the natural objects (noisy images, background heterogeneity, variations in object characteristics). Most of the cell nuclei are part of histological structures with complex and irregular visual features [13]. Samples of microscopy images and their intensity histograms are presented in Fig. 1. Shape of histograms shows that the problem of automatic nuclei detection and segmentation in histological images is difficult by thresholding.

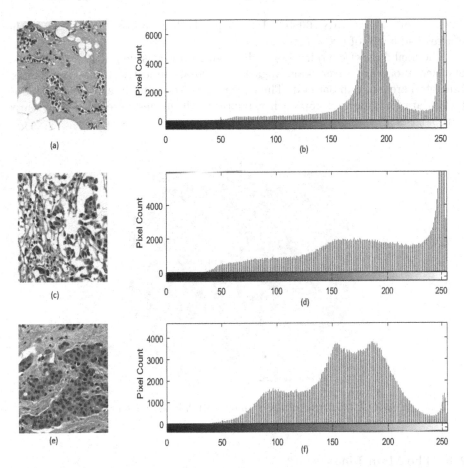

Fig. 1. H&E image samples (a), (c), (e) and their intensity histogram (b), (d), (f) respectively.

2 Methods and Materials

The investigated images are digital microscopy images stained with H&E (Hematoxylin & Eosin) from a publicly available data set [14,15]. Authors [14,15] used whole slide and tissue microarrays derived from tissue samples available through routine diagnostic. The histological slides were using the Zeiss Mirax Scan side scanner. The slide scanner was equipped with Zeiss Plan-Apochromat 20x (numerical aperture = 0.8) and an AVT Marlin F-146C Firewire $1/2''$ CCD camera with $4.65\,\mu m \times 4.65\,\mu m$ pixel size. Combine with the 20x objective and 1x C-mount adapter the resulting image resolution is $0.23\,\mu m \times 0.23\,\mu m$. All slides were scanned at 20x and performed at full resolution. The resulting images were converted to the Virtual Slide Format with actual image data encapsulated and saved as JPEG image files with 85 % JPEG quality. The image sizes vary from

33280×29184 pixels to 70080×159000 pixels, but the analyzed field of the images had a size of 600×600 pixels.

The final dataset contains 7931 cells from 36 color tissue images. The images of different organs (breast, kidney, gastric mucosa, connective tissue, small intestine, etc.) are found in data set. The nuclei center coordinates are used as ground truth data for proposed approach validation. All images were labeled by three pathologists, Fig. 2.

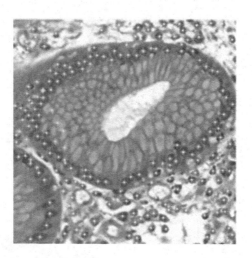

Fig. 2. An example of H&E image with labeled nuclei centers.

2.1   The Main Idea

The proposed approach for cell nuclei counting in histological image analysis consists of the following stages: 1. RGB color space regularization; 2. image intensity adjusting; 3. guided filtering; 4. thresholding; 5. morphological processing.

The preprocessing stage includes several steps. Original images contain a limited number of primary colors such as pink, purple and shades of blue. It is proposed to reduce the number of colors in the original image palette using Minimum Variance Quantization. Minimum variance quantization cuts the RGB color cube into smaller boxes (not necessarily cubical shape) of different sizes, depending on how the colors are distributed in the image. If the input image actually uses fewer colors than the number specified, the output colormap is also smaller, Fig. 3.

For the tested data set this procedure is almost visible to the human eye because of the limited number of colors in the difference between original images and same images after regularization is hardly visible (Fig. 3), but it is crucial for further image analysis stages.

After that we try to increases the contrast of the images by a contrast enhancement procedure.

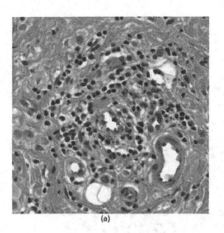
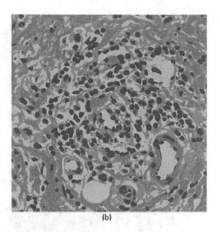

(a)   (b)

Fig. 3. (a) An input image, (b) the image after requantization. (Color figure online)

The next step is using guided filter. The filter performs edge-preserving smoothing of images, using content of a second image, called a guidance image, to influence the filtering. The guidance image can be the original image itself, a another version of the original image, or a completely different image. Guided image filtering is a neighborhood operation, like other filtering operations, but takes into account pixel statistics in the corresponding spatial neighborhood of the guidance image when calculating the value of the output pixel [16].

Then we apply binarization by Sauvola local image thresholding [17–19] for separation nuclei and background, see Fig. 4.

We clean the obtained binary images by opening and closing with a small structure element. After that we count automatically the number of black blobs corresponding to the cell nuclei.

Opening and closing to the binary images we apply analysis help us to clean the binary images. They are both derived from the fundamental operations of erosion and dilation. Like those operators they are normally applied to binary images, although there are also gray level versions. The basic effect of an opening is somewhat like erosion in that it tends to remove some of the foreground (bright) pixels from the edges of regions of foreground pixels.

2.2   Nuclei Counting and Method Validation

We have tested implementations (in Matlab) of the proposed approach in 36 images from the data set described above.

The typical parameter values used in our experiments are shown in Table 2.

Example of analysis results on H&E images is shown in Fig. 5.

The performance of calculation was calculated using TP (true positive), FN (false negative) and FP (false positive) events. The performance parameters precision and recall calculating using (1)–(2).

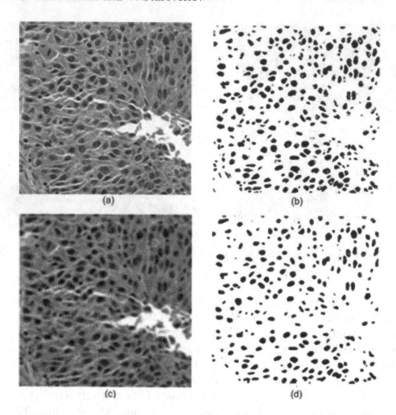

Fig. 4. Improvement in binarization by guided filtering: (a) input grayscale image, (b) thresholding without guided filtering; (c) input grayscale image after guided filtering; (d) thresholding after guided filtering.

Table 2. Typical parameters values

Processing stage	Parameters	Different values
Minimum variance quantization	Amount of color space	4
Guided filtering	Mask size balance between data matching and smoothing	33 0.5
Sauvola local image thresholding	Local thresholding with M-by-N neighbourhood threshold	45 × 45 0.35
Morphology	Radius of structuring elements shape of structuring elements	1 disk

$$Precision = \frac{TP}{TP + FP} \tag{1}$$

$$Recall = \frac{TP}{TP + FN} \tag{2}$$

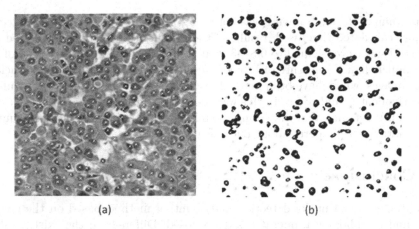

(a)   (b)

Fig. 5. (a) An example of the original image and (b) its binary variant with the centers of cell nuclei labeled by experts.

A measure that combines precision and recall is the harmonic mean of precision and recall, the traditional F-measure or balanced F-score (3):

$$F = 2 \cdot \frac{Precision \cdot Recall}{Precision + Recall} \qquad (3)$$

We compared the results with recent advances in this area [7,9,10], Table 3.

Table 3. Detection results of the proposed approach, Wienert's, Al-Kofahi's methods in precision and recall values

	Proposed	Wienert	Al-Kofahi
Precision	0.833 ± 0.01	0.908 ± 0.04	0.707 ± 0.13
Recall	0.920 ± 0.01	0.859 ± 0.04	0.916 ± 0.04
F-measure	0.8743	0.8828	0.7980

3   Discusion

Table 2 shows the best parameters for the tested image database. Developed approach can be adapted to different nuclei counting task. Its main advantage is automatically approach for cell nuclei counting. In future, it is necessary to automatization the process of the initial parametrs settings depending on images. Cell nuclei with small area were lost because we used the guided filter and mathematical morphology. But it allows us to get more accurate results for other cells. This is due to the fact that the improved thresholding results (disappear small areas that are not true cell nuclei). Future work will be focused on improving the segmentation stage and enlargement of the tested image data set. In contrast to the known algorithms, the proposed approach does not segment all of the nuclei in images.

The aim of the experiments was not to improve metrics Precision and Recall. We just calculated them with results of the similar research. In our method the value of F-measure is equal to 0.8743. It is bigger than F- measure of Al-Kofahi, but smaller than F- measure of Wienert results. There are a lot of small nucleus in the images, which have been marked by the experts. These nucleus difficult to correctly identify and count. In this way, we obtain decrease Precession accuracy. More subtle settings allow detecting the missing small nucleus, but this requires coordination with experts about nuclei features.

4   Conclusions

An automated cell nuclei detection and counting method based on the guided filter and morphological operations is proposed. Different to the existing algorithms, the proposed approach does not segment nuclei in images. It only detects the cell nuclei in a histological image and estimate the number of the detected nuclei. It avoids complicated algorithmic computations and provides good accuracy in the cell nuclei counting. The software prototype developed in our study may be considered as an automatic tool for a cell nuclei analysis.

References

1. Irshad, H., Veillard, A., Roux, L., Racoceanu, D.: Methods for nuclei detection, segmentation, and classification in digital histopathology: a review current status and future potential. IEEE Rev. Biomed. Eng. **7**, 97–114 (2014)
2. Chen, S., Zhao, M., Wu, G., Yao, C., Zhang, J.: Recent advances in morphological cell image analysis. Comput. Math. Methods Med. **2012**, 10 (2012). Hindawi Publishing Corporation
3. Jung, C., Kim, C.: Impact of the accuracy of automatic segmentation of cell nuclei clusters on classification of cell nuclei clusters on classification of thyroid follicular lesions. Cytometry Part A **85A**, 709–719 (2014)
4. Saharma, H., Zerbe, N., Heim, D., Wiener, S., Behrens, H., Hellwich, O., Hufnagl, P.: A multi-resolution approach for combining visual information using nuclei segmentation and classification in histopathological images. In: Proceedings of the 10th International Conference on Computer Vision, Theory and Applications (VISAPP 2015), pp. 37–46 (2015)
5. Alilou, M., Kovalev, V., Taimouri, V.: Segmentation of cell nuclei in heterogeneous microscopy images: a reshapable temlates approach. Comput. Med. Imaging Graph. **37**, 488–499 (2013)
6. Kowal, M., Filipczuk, P.: Nuclei segmentation for computer-aded diagmosis of breast cancer. Int. J. Appl. Math. Comput. Sci. **24**(1), 19–31 (2014)
7. Wienert, S., Helm, D., Saeger, K., Stenziger, A., Beil, M., Hufnagl, P., et al.: Detection and segmentation of cell nuclei in virtual microscopy images: a minimum-model approach. Nat. Sci. Rep. **2**, 503 (2012)
8. Zang, C., Xiao, X., Li, X., Chen, Y.-J., Zhen, W., Chang, J., Zheng, C., Liu, Z.: White blood cell segmentation by color-space-based k-means clustering. Sensors **14**, 16128–16147 (2014). doi:10.3390/s140916128

9. Song, Y., Cai, W., Huang, H., YueWang, D.D., Feng, M.C.: Region-based progressive localization of cell nuclei in microscopic images with data adaptive modeling. BMC Bioinf. **14**, 173 (2013)
10. Coelho, L.P., Shariff, A., Robert, F.: Murphy nuclear segmentation in microscope cell images: a hand-segmented dataset and comparison of algorithms. In: Proceedings of IEEE International Symposium Biomedical Imaging, pp. 518–521 (2009)
11. Signolle, N., Revenu, M., Plancoulaine, B., Herlin, P.: Wavelet-based multiscale texture segmentation in application to stromal compartment characterization on virtual slides. Sig. Process. **90**(8), 2412–2422 (2010)
12. Lezoray, O., Elmoataz, A., Cardot, H., Gougeon, G., Lecluse, M., Elie, H., Revenu, M.: Segmentation of cytological image using color and mathematical morphology. Acta Stereologica **18**, 1–14 (1999)
13. Loukas, C.G., Wilson, G.D., Vojnovic, B., Linney, A.: An image analysis-based approach for automated counting of cancer cell nuclei. Tissue Sect. Cytomettry Part A **55A**, 30–42 (2003)
14. Al-Kofahi, Y., Lassoued, W., Lee, W., Roysam, B.: Improved automatic detection and segmentation of cell nuclei in histopathology images. IEEE Trans. Biomed. Eng. **57**(4), 841–852 (2010)
15. Al-Kofahi, Y., Lassoued, W., Grama, K., Nath, S.K., Zhu, J., Oueslati, R., et al.: Cell-based quantification of molecular biomarkers in histopathology specimens. Histopathology **59**(1), 40–54 (2011)
16. Xu, L., Lu, C., Xu, Y., Jia, J.: Image smoothing via L0 gradient minimization. ACM Trans. Graph. 30(6), article 174, December 2011
17. Sauvola, J., Pietikainen, M.: Adaptive document image binarization. Pattern Recognit. **33**, 225–236 (2000)
18. Shafait, F., Keysers, D., Breuel, T.M., Efficient implementation of local adaptive thresholding techniques using integral images. In: Document Recognition and Retrieval XV (2008)
19. Stathis, P., Kavallieratou, E., Papamarkos, N.: An evaluation technique for binarization algorithms. J. Univ. Comput. Sci. **14**(18), 3011–3030 (2008)

Automatic Segmentation Framework for Fluorescence in Situ Hybridization Cancer Diagnosis

Marcin Stachowiak and Łukasz Jeleń(✉)

Department of Compuer Engineering,
Wrocław University of Science and Technology,
Wybrzeże Wyspiańskiego 27, 50-370, Wrocław, Poland
lukasz.jelen@pwr.edu.pl

Abstract. In this paper we address a problem of HER2 and CEN-17 reactions detection in fluorescence in situ hybridization images. These images are very often used in situation where typical biopsy examination is not able to provide enough information to decide on the type of treatment the patient should undergo. Here the main focus is placed on the automatization of the procedure. Using an unsupervised neural network and principal component analysis, we present a segmentation framework that is able to keep the high segmentation accuracy. For comparison purposes we test the neural network approach against an automatic threshold method.

Keywords: FISH · Pattern recognition · Image processing · Computer aided diagnosis · Breast cancer · Nuclei segmentation · HER2 · Dot counting · SOM · PCA

1 Introduction

According to the data provided by the National Cancer Registry, breast cancer is one of the most often diagnosed cancers among middle–age women [1]. Just in Poland, before 2016, there were 17144 diagnosed cases of breast cancer. This number is increasing year after year. For instance, between 2009 to 2012 there was an increase of 1280 diagnosed cases. The same records show that out of 17144 cancer cases there were 5651 deaths in 2012 which is 341 more than in 2009. Most of these cases could have been fully recovered if the diagnosis would be made in the early stage of the disease, because cancers in their early stages are vulnerable to treatment.

To reduce the number of deaths it is crucial to perform a reliable and fast diagnosis that will allow for the determination of an appropriate treatment. For this purpose when a suspicious growth is found during the screening mammography tests a fine needle aspiration biopsy (FNA) or a core biopsy (CB) is taken. During these examinations a small sample from the questionable breast tissue is extracted and a prognostic factor is evaluated according to the so called Bloom–Richardson

© IFIP International Federation for Information Processing 2016
Published by Springer International Publishing Switzerland 2016. All Rights Reserved
K. Saeed and W. Homenda (Eds.): CISIM 2016, LNCS 9842, pp. 148–159, 2016.
DOI: 10.1007/978-3-319-45378-1_14

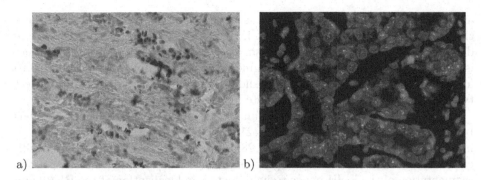

Fig. 1. HER2 slides. (a) ImmunoHistoChemistry staining image, (b) FISH test image. (Color figure online)

scheme [3]. This procedure, called a malignancy grading, allows the pathologist to describe the type of cancer in detail and estimate its behavior with or without undertaking treatment. Sometimes, when a difficult case is under diagnosis, the above techniques might require additional tests. This is why, for a more accurate diagnosis, a set of different examinations are performed. They will test for the presence of a HER2 gene and HER2 receptors that stimulate the growth of cancer cells. HER2 expression plays an important role in breast cancer diagnosis and the appropriate treatment is chosen accordingly to its status [11].

To determine the status of breast cancer biomarker such as human epidermal growth factor receptor 2 (HER2) a routine ImmunoHistoChemistry (IHC) or Fluorescence in situ hybridization (FISH) tests are performed.

- **ImmunoHistoChemistry** – is a staining process that shows if HER2 receptors and hormone receptors are present on the surface of the cancer cells (see Fig. 1a). This test helps in identification of the antigens in cells. This is possible due to binding of antibodies to the proteins. The final diagnosis is based on the estimation of different markers that may appear within and around the tumor cells [31].
- **Fluorescence in Situ Hybridization** – is a test that allows for a visualization of genes, in this case HER2 gene [15] (see Fig. 1b). In breast cancer diagnosis it is used to determine if the cancer cells have additional copies of that gene. The rule here is that the more genes one can distinguish, the more HER2 receptors the cells have.

  According to the American Society of Clinical Oncologists (ASCO) and College of American Pathologists (CAP) [13,25], also known as ASCO/CAP, the complete FISH examination also requires estimation of chromosome 17 centromere enumeration probe (CEP17 or CEN-17) [27]. The final diagnosis is based on the HER2 to CEN-17 ratio [8].

According to Hicks and Kulkarni [10], both of the above tests are equivalent for the evaluation of the breast cancer HER2 status. In this study we are focusing on the FISH examination. As reported in literature [2,23,26], the problem of distinguishing the HER2 and CEN-17 reaction within the FISH slides is not an easy task. The main problem here is a segmentation of the reactions, where the HER2 reactions are visible in the image as red dots while the CEN-17 are detectable as green dots. Due to a small size of the regions of interest there is a need to find the best possible segmentation algorithm that will be able to localize both kinds of dots within the slide. Here, we took an opportunity to test two techniques that will be appropriate for this challenging task.

Automatic cancer nuclei detection and segmentation from medical images has been widely studied in the literature [4,21]. One can find various reports on applying different imaging techniques [6,22,28], segmentation methods [17] or classification approaches [7] to solve this problem. In this study we are concerned on the segmentation of the FISH image to help doctors in localization of the HER2 and CEN-17 reactions. For this purpose, a thresholding based segmentation was investigated and its results were compared with segmentation based on the unsupervised neural network. Application of neural networks for segmentation was widely studied in literature [5,20]. Substantial portion of the reports deals with segmentations based on self–organized maps (SOMs). Yao et al. [30] have successfully applied SOMs to segment sonar images where each pixel of the input image is classified with the proposed neural network. Gorjizadeh et al. [9] used a similar idea for segmentation of noisy medical images.

In 2001, Lerner et al. [2] described a neural network approach for detection of fluorescence in situ hybridization images. Their method is based on classification between a pair of in– and out–of–focus images. They use the in–focus images for further estimation of the FISH reactions. Results presented by the authors show an accuracy of 83–87 %. Another approach, reported by Kiszler et al. [15], describes a semi–automated procedure applied to fluorescence in situ hybridization images. This procedure is based on the adaptive thresholding and the final counting is based on the selected areas of the image.

It can be easily noticed that Machine Learning is a popular tool for developing support software for supporting a diagnosis process of specialists. This is why as a main contribution of this paper we propose a fully automatic procedure for segmentation of HER2 and CEN-17 reactions that can be further counted to estimate the final FISH diagnosis. The final decision is based on the ASCO/CAP recommendations [13] that give a full route for HER2 testing in breast cancer.

2   Dataset

For the purpose of this study we have collected a database of 80 fluorescence in situ hybridization images with a size of 1376×1032 pixels recorded with a resolution of 200 pixels per inch. Example of the images in the database is shown in Fig. 2. Based on these examples it is easy to notice how difficult the automated segmentation of such images is.

Images were recorder with an Olympus BX61 fluorescence microscope with X-Cite series 120Q EXFO fluorescent system. The microscope was equipped with a CCD Olympus XC10 camera working with a Cell-F visualization software. To capture the image it was required to use fluorescent filter such as 30-151332G-Ov2C146747 filter made by Abbott with a magnification of 60x and 100x.

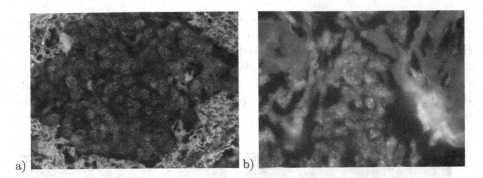

a)   b)

Fig. 2. Example of images in the database.

The database is a courtesy of dr. Anna Lis–Nawara and prof. Michał Jeleń, the head of the Department of Pathology and Oncological Cytology at the Wroclaw Medical University, Wrocław, Poland.

3   HER2 and Cen-17 Segmentation

In computer vision, segmentation is a very crucial step that influences all subsequent phases of the classification systems. In medical image processing, the segmentation stage is always a very difficult task and that makes it a very active field of research [12,18,19]. In this research, we investigated two segmentation methods that will allow for the proposition of the automated segmentation framework for fluorescence in situ hybridization images. The first method is a simple thresholding were the threshold is automatically selected. The second method is an unsupervised neural network method where we made use of the self–organizing maps for segmentation of the receptors.

3.1   Simple Thresholding

To provide automatization of the segmentation procedure we decided to investigate one of the simplest automatic thresholding techniques proposed by Ridler and Calvard [24]. This method is based on a bimodal histogram of image gray levels. A threshold T is sought on the histogram curve according to Eq. 1.

$$T = \frac{\mu_1 + \mu_2}{2}, \tag{1}$$

where μ_1 and μ_2 are the means of the components separated by T. These means are calculated iteratively starting form the initial threshold that is typically set to an average gray level of the image.

As mentioned before, HER2 reactions are visible as red dots and CEN-17 reactions are detectable as green dots. If we convert an RGB image to grayscale we would loose that information and therefore we need to apply the above mentioned segmentation to a color image. This means dividing the image into three separate planes (R, G and B). Each plane will represent the main color in the RGB color space. Looking at the nature of the images we can notice that the HER2 reactions are emphasized in a red channel and the CEN-17 reactions are affirmed in the green plane (see Fig. 3). We can take that information into consideration and apply Ridler and Calvard method to red and green image channels. Results of the application of this simple automatic thresholding method are presented in Sect. 4.1.

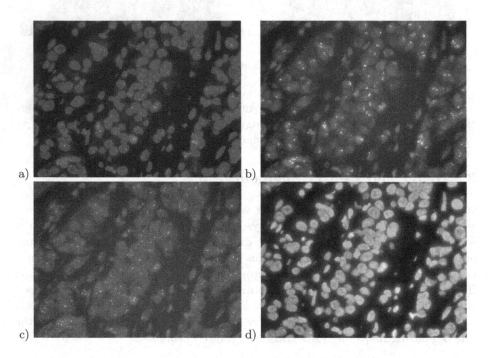

Fig. 3. FISH image RGB channels. (a) Original image, (b) Red channel, (c) Green channel, (d) Blue channel. (Color figure online)

3.2   Segmentation with Self Organizing Maps

As mentioned in Sect. 1 self–organized maps (SOMs) can be successfully applied for a segmentation task. They reduce the input space into representative features according to a self–organizing process and are trained in an unsupervised manner [16]. These networks consist of only one layer with a linear transfer function for its neurons. It uses a comprehensive learning algorithm for weights estimation that updates the weight of only one, winning neuron for each input pattern. According to Kohonen [16] the introduction of an additional weight change of the neighboring neurons with smaller step size results in better correspondence to the features of the input data.

To train the SOM network we start with initialization of weights (w) with small random values and for each input data a winning neuron $(\overrightarrow{i}(x))$ is found according to Eq. 2. Neighboring weights $(w_j(n+1))$ are then calculated according to Eq. 3.

$$\overrightarrow{i}(x) = \arg\min_j \| \overrightarrow{x}(n) - w_j \|, \tag{2}$$

where $\overrightarrow{x}(n)$ is an input vector.

$$w_j(n+1) = w_j(n) + \eta(n)[x(n) - w_j(n)] \tag{3}$$

where $\eta(n)$ is a neighboring function.

According to Kohonen, the neighborhood taken into consideration should be Gaussian and he suggests the neighborhood description according to Eq. 4.

$$\Lambda_{j,j^o}(n) = \exp\left(-\frac{|r_j - r_{j^o}|^2}{2\sigma^2(n)}\right) \tag{4}$$

where j^o is the winning neuron and $|r_j - r_{j^o}|$ is a distance between the winning node and the $j - th$ node, and σ^2 is a Gaussian variance.

From this we can notice that this is an adaptive procedure, because the neighborhood and learning rate depend on the current iteration. Due to this fact our neighborhood should be as large as the output space at the start and should be decreasing during the iterations according to the Eq. 5. We can take the same reasoning for the step size, which should be big at the beginning and progressively decrease according to Eq. 6 until it reaches zero.

$$\sigma(n) = \frac{1}{c_\sigma + d_\sigma n} \tag{5}$$

$$\eta(n) = \frac{1}{a_\eta + b_\eta n} \tag{6}$$

where a_η, b_η, c_σ and d_σ are constants.

Here we have adopted the SOM methodology to solve a segmentation problem for detection of HER2 and CEN-17 reactions in fluorescence in situ hybridization images. This task is divided into several stages. At first, we extract the red and green components from the RGB image, because these two channels provided the best localization of the reactions. Then we have applied a morphological reconstruction on both channels to extract the candidates of the red and green dots that represent HER2 and CEN-17 reactions respectively. These are actually the image maxima. Determination of these maxima can provide many misleading results such as multiple one–pixel dots. Some of these would also include background noise and for that reason there is a need to flatten them with reconstruction.

This method is actually a morphological erosion and dilation followed by the reconstruction procedure according to the description of Vincent [29].

According to Vincent, for an image I, called a mask, a reconstructed image (I_r) for a given marker M is calculated as a union of the connected components if the image which contain at least one mask pixel (see Eq. 7).

$$I_r = \bigcup_{M \cap I_k \neq 0} I_k \tag{7}$$

To localize candidates for HER2 and CEN-17 indicators we first apply erosion and dilation to appropriate image channels and then we apply a reconstruction algorithm described above. A dilated image was used as a marker and eroded image was treated as a mask (see Fig. 5). As a result a flatten maxima area is obtained.

Knowing the exact location of each of the maxima we have to check if the area it represents is actually red. For this purpose, an color image is divided into areas equivalent to a bounding boxes of the image containing the maxima. All of these areas serve as a feature vector presented as an input to the neural network. If we take an area of 5×5 px the obtained feature vector will contain 75 input weights. Such a large number of features suggests a high correlation between the features and therefore a dimension reduction is justified.

To remove redundancy and to reduce a feature vector length, all data was analyzed with principal component analysis (PCA) [14] that used the singular value decomposition to determine the coefficients. Application of the PCA allowed for the reduction of the feature vector down to 3 independent components that characterize the variance changes in 97 %.

Such a feature vector is then presented as an input to the neural network which finds the areas concentrated around these tree groups. Analysis of obtained clusters determines the appropriate dots. Results of SOM segmentation are presented in Sect. 4.1.

4   Experimental Investigations

As mentioned in the previous section, to propose an automatic segmentation framework we need to concentrate on counting the visible HER2 and CEN-17 reactions. We propose to convert a color image into three components (red, green, blue) and search for the maxima on the red and green images. By applying the simple thresholding method to these channels we were able to obtain most of the reactions with a threshold value automatically selected for each image. Unfortunately, this might lead to some problems in situations where some colors can contain higher values of red component that the red color itself. For that reason we split the procedure into two phases. In the first phase the algorithm looks for a red image maxima which serve as red dot indicators. In the next step we classify these indicators with a SOM network to determine which of them represent red dots. We can apply the same procedure for localizing green dots.

When all reactions are detected it possible to calculate the a so called FISH coefficient that will be used for further diagnosis. Such a calculation is based on the ASCO/CAP [13] recommendation where a HER2 to CEN-17 ratio is calculated. Using this value we can further decide if the diagnosed case is FISH positive or negative. The main aim of this experimental work was to check the effectiveness of the SOM based segmentation approach applied to the database of the fluorescence in situ hybridization images in order to propose an automatic diagnosis system.

4.1 Results and Discussion

In this section, results of the automatic segmentation techniques described in Sect. 3 are presented. In Fig. 4 we present an example of the segmentation obtained with simple automatic thresholding. From the example we can see that most of the reactions were localized and could be used for further FISH diagnosis calculations. It is easy to notice that after all, it will lead to some inaccuracies, especially in the red channel. The reason for that is that some of the nuclei assume some shades of red which will be misinterpreted with such a simple thresholding calculation. This will basically mean that the modes of the red channel histogram are not well separated. This scenario is better visualized in Fig. 7a.

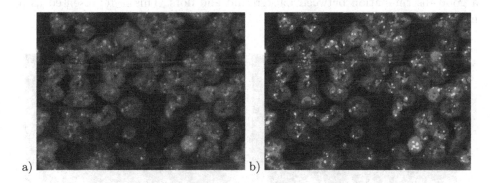

Fig. 4. Results of simple thresholding (Color figure online).

Taking the above into consideration we noted that application of the global thresholding will lead to misinterpretations due the fact that there are diverse intensity values in different parts of the image. This is why we decided to flatten the image maxima. This will allow us to use larger maxima areas instead of single peaks. For this purpose we decided to apply erosion and dylation operation followed by reconstruction according to the description in Sect. 3.2. Results of the reconstruction are presented in Fig. 5.

From the results we can notice the detection of multiple one–pixel dots can provide many misleading results. This is because some of them will also include background noise, what could be noticed in case of simple thresholding.

Having the maxima determined and localized we can now check if the areas that are around the maxima contain red or green dot. As already described

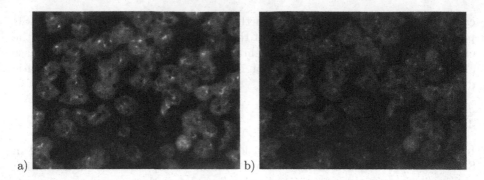

Fig. 5. Results of morphological reconstruction. (a) Red channel, (b) Green channel. (Color figure online)

we proceed with division of the color image into sub–images that contain the maxima and treat it as a feature vector for SOM network. After dimension reduction we classify each of the extracted areas as a background or a red/green dot. A result of this operation is presented in Fig. 6. On the figure we can notice a good discrimination between background and dots. This is represented as a marker of a localization result.

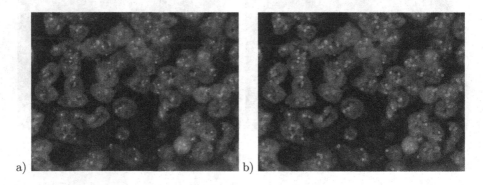

Fig. 6. Results of SOM segmentation. (a) Original image, (b) Segmented dots (Color figure online).

The presented segmentation results show that the SOM neural networks were able to properly distinguish HER2 and CEN-17 receptors. The main problem of this method occurs in a situation shown on Fig. 7b. Here a localization of green dots can be problematic but, in comparison with simple thresholding, we can still notice much better localization, especially in a red component.

To complete the full automatic diagnosis, a number of red and green dots was calculated and HER2 to CEN-17 ratio was calculated. Based on the calculated ratio and according to ACSO regulations a FISH score was evaluated. For the

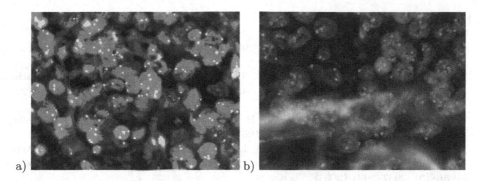

Fig. 7. Examples of incorrect segmentations. (a) Simple thresholding, (b) SOM segmentation (Color figure online).

simple thresholding 44 out of 80 images provided similar results as an expert pathologist diagnosis. The other method provided better results were 61 images had similar responds.

5   Conclusions and Future Work

In this study a problem of automatic segmentation of HER2 and CEN-17 reactions from Fluorescence in Situ Hybridization images was addressed. We have proposed a fully automatic segmentation framework that is able to detect dots representing reactions of human epidermal growth factor receptor 2 and chromosome 17 centromere enumeration probe with high precision. Form the results we can draw a conclusion that neural network based method is able to segment these reactions more accurate than the described simple thresholding method. As already mentioned this is caused by multiple one–pixel dots which eliminates a possibility of application of a global thresholding methods. It was shown that utilization of a reconstruction methodology along with morphological erosion and dylation allows for a better localization of the reactions.

Although the results presented here are optimistic there are a few problems that can impair the overall diagnosis. The main issue is a localization of the dots in areas where they are not visible, as shown in Fig. 7. Another problem that can be distinguished here is segmentation of large number of dots as one large single dot. This can lead to incorrect interpretation of the result as several dots are counted as one.

One of the possibilities to improve the accuracy of the diagnosis would be an application of deep and convolutional neural networks which are showing to be very effective in cancer diagnosis. The main problem with these methods is necessity of a large number of training samples. This might be difficult to achieve as not all of the cases are stored digitally. This and other issues that are addressed here will be further researched as a future work.

References

1. National Cancer Registry, December 2013. http://85.128.14.124/krn/. Accessed 18 Apr 2016
2. Lerner, B., Clocksin, W.F., Dhanjal, S., Hultén, M.A., Bishop, C.M.: Automatic signal classification in fluorescence in situ hybridization images. Cytometry **43**(2), 87–93 (2001)
3. Bloom, H.J.G., Richardson, W.W.: Histological grading and prognosis in breast cancer. Br. J. Cancer **11**, 359–377 (1957)
4. Cheng, H.D., Cai, X., Chen, X., Hu, L., Lou, X.: Computer-aided detection and classification of microcalcifications in mammograms: a survey. Pattern Recogn. **36**(12), 2967–2991 (2003)
5. Duraisamy, M., Jane, F.M.M.: Cellular neural network based medical image segmentation using artificial bee colony algorithm. In: 2014 International Conference on Green Computing Communication and Electrical Engineering (ICGCCEE), pp. 1–6, March 2014
6. Filipczuk, P., Fevens, T., Krzyżak, A., Monczak, R.: Computer-aided breast cancer diagnosis based on the analysis of cytological images of fine needle biopsies. IEEE Trans. Med. Imaging **32**(12), 2169–2178 (2013)
7. Filipczuk, P., Krawczyk, B., Woźniak, M.: Classifier ensemble for an effective cytological image analysis. Pattern Recogn. Lett. **34**(14), 1748–1757 (2013)
8. García-Caballero, T., Grabau, D., Green, A.R., Gregory, J., Schad, A., Kohlwes, E., Ellis, I., Watts, S., Mollerup, J.: Determination of HER2 amplification in primary breast cancer using dual-colour chromogenic in situ hybridization is comparable to fluorescence in situ hybridization: a European multicentre study involving 168 specimens. Histopathology **56**(4), 472–480 (2010)
9. Gorjizadeh, S., Pasban, S., Alipour, S.: Noisy image segmentation using a self-organized map network. Adv. Sci. Technol. Res. J. **9**(26), 118–123 (2015)
10. Hicks, D.G., Kulkarni, S.: HER2+ breast cancer: review of biologic relevance and optimal use of diagnostic tools. Am. J. Clin. Pathol. **129**, 263–273 (2008)
11. Hicks, D.G., Schiffhaue, L.: Standardized assessment of the HER2 status in breast cancer by immunohistochemistry. Lab Med. **42**(8), 459–467 (2011)
12. Jeleń, Ł., Krzyżak, A., Fevens, T., Jeleń, M.: Influence of pattern recognition techniques on breast cytology grading. Sci. Bull. Wroc. Sch. Appl. Inform. **2**, 16–23 (2012)
13. Ji, Y., Sheng, L., Du, X., Qiu, G., Chen, B., Wang, X.: Clinicopathological variables predicting HER-2 gene status in immunohistochemistry-equivocal (2+) invasive breast cancer. J. Thorac. Dis. **6**(7), 896–904 (2014)
14. Jolliffe, I.T.: Principal Component Analysis, 2nd edn. Springer, Berlin (2002)
15. Kiszler, G., Krecsák, L., Csizmadia, A., Micsik, T., Szabó, D., Jónás, V., Prémusz, V., Krenács, T., Molnár, B.: Semi-automatic fish quantification on digital slides. Diagn. Pathol. **8**(1), 1–4 (2013)
16. Kohonen, T.: The self-organizing map. Proc. IEEE **78**, 1464–1480 (1990)
17. Kowal, M., Filipczuk, P.: Nuclei segmentation for computer-aided diagnosis of breast cancer. Appl. Math. Comput. Sci. **24**(1), 19–31 (2014)
18. Kowal, M., Filipczuk, P., Obuchowicz, A., Korbicz, J., Monczak, R.: Computer-aided diagnosis of breast cancer based on fine needle biopsy microscopic images. Comput. Biol. Med. **43**(10), 1563–1572 (2013)
19. Lezoray, O., Elmoataz, A., Cardot, H., Gougeon, G., Lecluse, M., Revenu, M.: Segmentation of cytological images using color and mathematical morphology. In: European Conference on Stereology, Amsterdam, Netherlands, p. 52 (1998)

20. Long, J., Shelhamer, E., Darrell, T.: Fully convolutional networks for semantic segmentation. CoRR, abs/1411.4038 (2014)
21. Moghbel, M., Mashohor, M.: A review of computer assisted detection/diagnosis (CAD) in breast thermography for breast cancer detection. Artif. Intell. Rev. **39**(4), 305–313 (2013)
22. Nagarajan, M.B., Huber, M.B., Schlossbauer, T., Leinsinger, G., Krol, A., Wismüller, A.: Classification of small lesions on dynamic breast MRI: integrating dimension reduction and out-of-sample extension into CADx methodology. Artif. Intell. Med. **60**(1), 65–77 (2014)
23. Netten, H., van Vliet, L.J., Vrolijk, H., Sloos, W.C.R., Tanke, H.J., Young, I.T.: Fluorescent dot counting in interphase cell nuclei. Bioimaging **4**(2), 93–106 (1996)
24. Ridler, T.W., Calvard, S.: Picture thresholding using an iterative selection. IEEE Trans. Syst. Man Cybern. **8**, 630–632 (1978)
25. Slamon, D.J., Leyland-Jones, B., Shak, S., Fuchs, H., Paton, V., Bajamonde, A., Fleming, T., Eiermann, W., Wolter, J., Pegram, M., Baselga, J., Norton, L.: Use of chemotherapy plus a monoclonal antibody against HER2 for metastatic breast cancer that overexpresses HER2. N. Engl. J. Med. **344**(11), 783–792 (2001)
26. Tanke, H.J., Florijn, R.J., Wiegant, J., Raap, A.K., Vrolijk, J.: CCD microscopy and image analysis of cells and chromosomes stained by fluorescence in situ hybridization. Histochem. J. **27**(1), 4–14 (1995)
27. Tibau, A., López-Vilaró, L., Pérez-Olabarria, M., Vázquez, T., Pons, C., Gich, I., Alonso, C., Ojeda, B., y Cajal, T.R., Lerma, E., Barnadas, A., Escuin, D.: Chromosome 17 centromere duplication and responsiveness to anthracycline-based neoadjuvant chemotherapy in breast cancer. Neoplasia **16**(10), 861–867 (2014)
28. Velikova, M., Lucas, P.J.F., Samulski, M., Karssemeijer, N.: On the interplay of machine learning, background knowledge in image interpretation by Bayesian networks. Artif. Intell. Med. **57**(1), 73–86 (2013)
29. Vincent, L.: Morphological grayscale reconstruction in image analysis: applications and efficient algorithms. IEEE Trans. Image Process. **2**, 176–201 (1993)
30. Yao, K.C., Mignotte, M., Collet, C., Galerne, P., Burel, G.: Unsupervised segmentation using a self-organizing map and a noise model estimation in sonar imagery. Pattern Recogn. **33**, 1575–1584 (2000)
31. Zaha, D.C.: Significance of immunohistochemistry in breast cancer. World J. Clin. Oncol. **5**(3), 382–392 (2014)

Neural Network Classification of SDR Signal Modulation

Jakub Stebel[1], Michal Krumnikl[1,2(✉)], Pavel Moravec[1,2], Petr Olivka[1], and David Seidl[1]

[1] Department of Computer Science, FEECS VŠB – Technical University of Ostrava,
17. listopadu 15, 708 33 Ostrava-Poruba, Czech Republic
{jakub.stebel.st,michal.krumnikl,pavel.moravec,
petr.olivka,david.seidl}@vsb.cz
[2] IT4Innovations National Supercomputing Center,
VŠB – Technical University of Ostrava,
17. listopadu 15, 708 33 Ostrava-Poruba, Czech Republic

Abstract. With the rising popularity of Software Defined Radios (SDR), there is a strong demand for automatic detection of the modulation type and signal parameters. Automatic modulation classification is an approach to identify the modulation type and its parameters such as the carrier frequency or symbol rate. In electronic warfare, it enables real-time signal interception and processing. In civil applications, it can be used, e.g., by the amateur radio operators to automatically set the transceiver to the appropriate modulation and communication protocol. This paper presents a modulation classification driven by a neural network. A set of signal features are provided as an input of the neural network. The paper discusses the relevance of different signal features and its impact on the success rate of the neural network classification. The proposed approach is tested on both artificial and real samples captured by the SDR.

Keywords: Software defined radio · Neural networks · Signal processing · Modulation · Classification · Signal features

1 Introduction

With the rising popularity of software defined radios (SDR), there is a strong demand for automatic detection of the modulation type and the signal parameters. SDR is a radio communication system where the traditional radio components (e.g. amplifiers, mixers, filters, demodulators, etc.) were replaced by means of software. Such a design produces a system which can receive and transmit different radio modulations based solely on the software's specification. Nowadays, SDR is becoming the dominant technology in radio communications.

This work was supported by The Ministry of Education, Youth and Sports from the National Programme of Sustainability (NPU II) project "IT4Innovations excellence in science - LQ1602" and by the Grant of SGS No. SP2016/58, VŠB - Technical University of Ostrava, Czech Republic.

© IFIP International Federation for Information Processing 2016
Published by Springer International Publishing Switzerland 2016. All Rights Reserved
K. Saeed and W. Homenda (Eds.): CISIM 2016, LNCS 9842, pp. 160–171, 2016.
DOI: 10.1007/978-3-319-45378-1_15

The concept of the software defined radio has been extensively studied since the late nineties. From the beginning there has been a strong demand from the military for software defined radios capable of intercepting and decoding various radio transmissions. The ability to automatically detect the modulation type is crucial for monitoring wireless communication but also for effective signal jamming.

Automatic Modulation Classification (AMC) is an approach to identify the modulation type and its parameters such as the carrier frequency or symbol rate. AMC systems were introduced in military and in a short time appeared in commercial applications. In military applications, involving electronic warfare, it enables real-time signal interception and processing. In civil applications it can be used, e.g., by the amateur radio operators to automatically set the transceiver to the appropriate modulation and communication protocol.

The automatic modulation detection algorithms are crucial parts of adaptive modulation techniques which are nowadays used in almost all wireless mobile cellular systems. Assuming the transmitter has the capability to choose the modulation (based on the changing environment and detected interference) it can significantly influence the quality of ongoing transmission. In such cases, the receiver must be able to detect the dynamically changing modulation [15, 16].

2   State of the Art

The AMC approaches can be divided into three main classes: statistical methods, decision theoretic methods and feature based methods. First AMC techniques were based on calculating the time domain parameters like amplitude, instantaneous frequency or phase shift of the signal [5,8]. The subsequent signal classification can be based on an automatic histogram separation method [8]. The histogram is calculated using the instantaneous phase estimation. Other techniques rely on a time domain analysis, calculating envelope characteristics of the signal [2].

The majority of the decision theoretic methods are based on the assumption that the Likelihood functional of the observed waveform provides all necessary information for signal detection and estimation of transmission parameters and modulation. In these approaches, the classification problem is formulated as a multiple-hypothesis problem, where modulation is selected from a candidate list based on maximizing the likelihood radio [6].

The statistical signal approaches exploits various properties of the signal to gain information about the analysed signal. More advanced techniques employ higher order correlation, cumulant based methods or higher order statistics [4]. One of the biggest disadvantages of the statistic approaches is their lower resistance to noise [1].

Neural networks approaches involve experiments with different configurations, learning techniques and selection of optimal input parameters. The popular approach is to involve a multi-layer perceptron network [10,14], however there is a possibility that the training procedure will get stuck due to a local optimum of the cost function. This can be avoided by using a radial basis function network [9].

A more detailed description of algorithms can be found in [11,16] and a recent survey of AMC approaches was published in [13].

The herein proposed algorithm combines the statistical driven approaches with neural networks. We will explore two neural networks mentioned in this section, specifically radial basis function network and feed forward network.

3 Signal Model

Suppose the incoming waveform $r(t)$ containing signal $s(t)$ with an additive white Gaussian noise $n(t)$

$$r(t) = s(t) + n(t). \tag{1}$$

The modulation changes a sine wave $s(t)$ to encode information. The equation representing the sine way can be written as:

$$s(t) = \sqrt{2Sa(t)} \cos(\omega t + \theta(t) + \Phi_K), \tag{2}$$

where S is the power of the signal, $a(t)$ is its amplitude, ω denotes the carrier frequency, $\theta(t)$ carrier phase and Φ_K is the modulation phase. For phase-shift keying (PSK) modulation, Φ_K is a value from the set of complex phases $\{\Phi_1, \Phi_2, \Phi_3, \ldots\}$, denoted as the constellation of the modulation. The aim of the automatic modulation classifier is to extract features such as carrier frequency, phase offsets, I/Q origin offset in the constellation plane, etc., to classify the type and order of modulation in signals from noisy environments.

4 Selection of Statistic Features

The selection of the proper statistic features plays the key role in the success of the proposed automatic modulation classification algorithm. We need to select those statistical features that are most selective for different aspects of the processed signal. It is also necessary to maintain the diversity of the selected features in order to be able to capture all possible variations in modulations.

The first discussed feature γ_{max} depends on the variation of the amplitude. It is defined as a maximum value of the spectral power density of the normalized and centered instantaneous amplitude:

$$\gamma_{max} = \frac{max|DFT(A_{cn})|^2}{N}, \qquad A_{cn}[n] = \frac{A[n]}{\mu_A} - 1,$$

where A is the vector of the instantaneous amplitude and μ_A is the arithmetic mean of the instantaneous amplitude [16].

The maximum value of the spectral power density γ_{max} provides a significant differentiation characteristic between two groups of radio transmissions - the one that uses an amplitude to encode the data and the second that uses a

different means (e.g. frequency changes). For the first group (AM and ASK) this
parameter gives significantly higher values than for the other. On the borderline
of these two groups we can find the QAM modulations which combine both ASK
and PSK features. For the modulations based on the frequency changes the value
of γ_{max} is almost zero.

The standard deviation of the absolute value of the normalized and centered
instantaneous amplitude (σ_{aa}) should provide a similar discrimination as γ_{max}.
The value of σ_{aa} is given by

$$\sigma_{aa} = \sqrt{\frac{1}{N}\left(\sum_{n=1}^{N} A_{cn}^2[n]\right) - \left(\frac{1}{N}\sum_{n=1}^{N} |A_{cn}[n]|\right)^2}, \tag{3}$$

where N is the number of complex samples and $A_{cn}[n]$ is a vector of normalized
centered instantaneous amplitude [3, 11, 16].

The ability to differentiate between the amplitude and frequency modulations
is almost the same as γ_{max}. As our model does not detect the number of states
in the digital communication, σ_{aa} may be considered redundant. Because both
features are amplitude dependent it is possible that the neural network might
have a problems to discriminate AM and ASK, or possibly ASK, PSK and QAM.

The standard deviation of the absolute value of the non-linear component of
the instantaneous phase can be used to detect phase changes. It separates the
hypothetical modulation space into two groups, one represented by FM, FSK,
PSK, QAM and second by AM, ASK, BPSK modulations. Feature σ_{ap} should
separate QAM modulations, but our experiments showed that it classifies BPSK
modulations in the same way. The standard deviation of the absolute value of
the non-linear component is defined as

$$\sigma_{ap} = \sqrt{\frac{1}{N_c}\left(\sum_{A_n[n]>A_t} \phi_{NL}^2[n]\right) - \left(\frac{1}{N_c}\sum_{A_n[n]>A_t} |\phi_{NL}[n]|\right)^2}, \tag{4}$$

where N_c is the number of complex samples above the noise level and $\phi_{NL}[n]$ is
a vector of non-linear component of instantaneous phase [3, 11].

The variance of the phase deviation σ_{dp} helps to distinguish BPSK from
other modulations not employing the phase changes. It gives additional information to σ_{ap}. The standard deviation of the non-linear component of the direct
instantaneous phase is calculated as

$$\sigma_{dp} = \sqrt{\frac{1}{N_c}\left(\sum_{A_n[n]>A_t} \phi_{NL}^2[n]\right) - \left(\frac{1}{N_c}\sum_{A_n[n]>A_t} \phi_{NL}[n]\right)^2}. \tag{5}$$

Both characteristics σ_{ap} and σ_{dp} are suitable for separating digital modulations
with phase changes from the analogous frequency modulations including analog
phase modulation.

The standard deviation of the absolute value of the normalized and centered instantaneous frequency σ_{af} is sensitive to frequency changes and is primary used to differentiate between the binary and multi-state phase modulations. The formula for calculating σ_{af} is as follows

$$\sigma_{af} = \sqrt{\frac{1}{N_c}\left(\sum_{A_n[n]>A_t} f_N^2[n]\right) - \left(\frac{1}{N_c}\sum_{A_n[n]>A_t}|f_N[n]|\right)^2} \qquad (6)$$

$$f_N[n] = \frac{f_m[n]}{f_s}, \qquad f_m[n] = f[n] - \mu_f,$$

where N_c is the number of complex samples above the noise level, $f[m]$ is the vector of instantaneous frequency and μ_f is the arithmetic average of instantaneous frequency [3,11,16]. Experiments showed that this feature can be also useful for recognizing PSK and QAM, however it is not suitable for classifying analog frequency modulations and phase modulations.

The final feature we have used as an input to the neural network is the spectrum symmetry around the carrier frequency. The symmetry is calculated according the formulas

$$P = \frac{P_L - P_U}{P_L + P_U}, \qquad f_{cn} = \frac{f_{cn}N}{f_s} - 1,$$

$$P_L = \sum_{n=1}^{f_{cn}}|X_c[n]|^2, \qquad P_U = \sum_{n=1}^{f_{cn}}|X_c[n + f_{cn} + 1]|^2$$

where f_s is the sampling rate, f_c is the carrier frequency and $(f_{cn} + 1)$ is the sample position corresponding to carrier frequency.

For symmetric modulations as ASK, AM or QAM this value is close to zero, however for asymmetric FM or PM modulations it shows how the energy is shifted in frequency spectrum based on the transmitted information.

5   Neural Network Classification

The classification process is based on the neural network implemented in Encog library [7]. The input vector is composed of a set of characteristic features as introduced in the previous section. In the proposed detector we use two types of neural networks. The first one is the most commonly used type, Feed Forward Network (FFN). In this network information moves in only one direction, from the input nodes, through the hidden nodes to the output nodes, without loops or cycles. The second type is more sophisticated Radial Basis Function Network (RBN). The output of this network is a linear combination of radial basis functions of the inputs and neuron parameters. In our application, the RBN network should be able to handle the noisy signal better than the simpler Feed Forward Network [12].

For both models we have used supervised learning method based on a back-propagation. The training was performed on fully artificial data set for a given noise to signal ratio. The goal was to learn neural network to distinguish between seven types of different modulation (AM, FM, PM and ASK, FSK, PSK, QAM). Each modulation is represented by one class of output layer. The training set was composed of approximate 10 000 input vectors for each modulation. Samples with different modulations were created in the GRC framework. The total size of the set is more than 11.5 GB of binary data.

The essential parameter of the input vector is the window size, determining the number of complex samples used for the features calculation. The longer the time period is (by increasing the window size), the more reliable information we obtain from the statistical evaluation. For our experiments we have used the window size set to 16384 complex samples. The input samples were normalized before the training phase.

The Encog library provides the option for a cross-validation of the trained model. For this step we have divided our generated data set into two parts, 70 % were used for the training phase and 30 % for the validation step. The number of repetition was set to 5. The cross-validation should assess how the results of a statistical analysis will generalize to an independent data set. For the RBN network we have obtained the validation error equal to 9.79 %, while the Feed Forward Network had the validation error equal to 21.75 %.

6 Implementation Details

The implementation of the proposed algorithm was done in C# and comprised highly optimized signal processing algorithms from the GNU Radio Companion (GRC) libraries. The flow chart of the algorithm is depicted in Fig. 1.

The application loads into the memory the deserialized model of the neural network and the content of the input file containing the I/Q data. If the filtering is enabled, the signal is passed through the band pass filter. Data are loaded into the processing window and the DFT is calculated. The DFT is used to detect the signal presence and obtain basic signal features. The calculation of the characteristic signal features (as described in Sect. 4) is performed in parallel and the results are passed into the neural network (see Sect. 5). Classification results are printed on the console and saved into the file for later analysis.

7 Learning Phase and Validation

During the first phase we have evaluated the success rate of the proposed classification algorithm on the artificial data set. The signals used for the evaluation were different from the one used during the learning phase. The main parameters and carrier frequencies varied across the samples. The tests were performed on signals with different signal-to-noise ratio (SNR). The SNR ratio varied from the complete absence of the noise to the level of 15 dB. The noise was added to the originally generated noiseless samples. To simplify the evaluation, we have

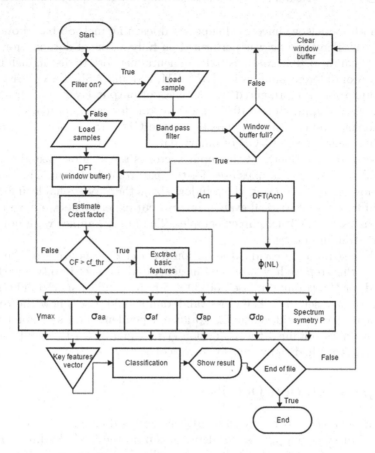

Fig. 1. Flow chart of the proposed algorithm

divided the testing data into three groups with different SNR ratio ranging from 15 dB to 45 dB with 10 dB step. The last tested group (the fourth) contains the samples without the added noise.

The tests in the second phase were performed on the real samples received by SDR. The SNR values of the received signal was determined by GRC module Frequency Xlating FIR Filter and low pass filter coefficients.

8   Experimental Results

Theoretically, the success rate of the classification performed by FFN and RBN on the synthetic data set can be estimated by the cross-error estimation implemented in the Encog library. According to these estimations we may expect better performance of the RBN, since it had more than 90 % success rate during the learning phase. In the following sections we will evaluate the success rate of both neural networks on the artificial data set and the real world data set composed of signals received by the SDR receiver.

8.1 Synthetic Data Set

The results of the RBN classification of the synthetic noise free signals is summarised in Table 1. From the first glance, we can see that the neural network tends to classify most signals as the ASK modulation. If we look closer, we can see that this trend is characteristic for related modulations – mainly AM, but also QAM and PSK, which is understandable. The detection of frequency modulations is however less accurate. FM and PM modulations are well detected; nevertheless the FSK modulation was not detected at all. It seems that the proposed RBN network is unable to classify this type of modulation.

Much better results were obtained from the FFN classification. Table 2 presents the results of FFN on the same data set. We can see (in contrast to the RBN) that the FFN is able to correctly classify frequency and amplitude modulations. This model provides better classification results for FSK and PSK. The errors of misclassification PSK and QAM modulations are expected, for the same reason as already mentioned.

Table 3 shows the behaviour of the RBN classification performed on signals with added white noise. The success rate of the detection of amplitude modulations increased, but for remaining modulations the performance decreased.

Table 1. RBN classification accuracy (%) of pure signals without noise

Signal mod.	Recognized modulation						
	AM	FM	PM	ASK	FSK	PSK	QAM
AM	**10.34**	0.00	0.00	89.66	0.00	0.00	0.00
FM	0.31	**48.45**	22.62	19.22	0.00	5.27	4.13
PM	0.93	51.44	**40.41**	4.12	0.00	1.86	1.24
ASK	1.10	0.00	0.00	**98.90**	0.00	0.00	0.00
FSK	20.76	7.98	16.27	44.71	**0.00**	4.39	5.89
PSK	0.66	17.61	16.76	61.86	0.00	**0.00**	3.11
QAM	17.09	32.04	0.00	43.79	0.00	0.19	**6.89**

Table 2. FFN classification accuracy (%) of pure signals without noise

Signal mod.	Recognized modulation						
	AM	FM	PM	ASK	FSK	PSK	QAM
AM	**85.32**	0.00	0.00	0.41	0.00	14.27	0.00
FM	0.00	**86.57**	12.09	0.00	1.03	0.00	0.31
PM	0.10	33.55	**51.93**	0.00	0.00	13.81	0.62
ASK	4.61	0.00	0.00	**67.41**	0.00	0.00	27.98
FSK	0.20	32.54	19.26	0.00	**31.83**	7.09	9.08
PSK	0.66	0.00	0.00	16.01	0.00	**50.28**	33.05
QAM	0.68	0.00	6.12	0.29	16.41	33.88	**42.62**

Table 3. RBN classification accuracy (%) of signal with noise (SNR 35–45 dB)

Signal mod.	Recognized modulation						
	AM	FM	PM	ASK	FSK	PSK	QAM
AM	**28.62**	1.45	0.00	69.32	0.00	0.31	0.30
FM	1.11	**26.54**	71.11	0.37	0.00	0.49	0.38
PM	12.62	57.04	**15.54**	8.45	0.00	4.59	1.76
ASK	1.03	0.00	0.00	**98.97**	0.00	0.00	0.00
FSK	0.00	53.32	22.52	2.84	**0.00**	12.43	8.89
PSK	0.57	34.31	0.00	65.03	0.00	**0.09**	0.00
QAM	0.58	0.00	0.00	91.45	0.00	0.39	**7.58**

Table 4. FFN classification accuracy (%) of signal with noise (SNR 35–45 dB)

Signal mod.	Recognized modulation						
	AM	FM	PM	ASK	FSK	PSK	QAM
AM	**86.45**	1.76	3.93	0.00	0.10	0.00	7.76
FM	0.62	**30.74**	60.12	0.00	0.12	3.21	5.19
PM	0.63	37.96	**42.75**	0.00	11.46	0.00	7.20
ASK	31.97	0.00	0.00	**0.00**	0.00	0.00	68.03
FSK	0.00	74.72	0.00	0.00	**25.19**	0.09	0.00
PSK	0.66	0.09	0.00	0.00	0.00	**34.59**	64.66
QAM	0.78	0.10	0.00	0.00	0.00	22.15	**76.97**

Small improvements are visible in the classification of FFN in Table 4. Added noise slightly improved the performance since it helped generalize inputs. The misclassification errors remained with the related modulations.

With increasing noise level we can see further degradation of RBN classifications. Table 5 illustrates this observation. The success rate for the majority of modulations fell to around 10 % and misclassifications are appearing even between non-related modulations. Such results indicate that RBN network will not be suitable for real world samples as they would contain a significant amount of noise.

In contrast, FFN retained good classification performance even in the presence of noise. Table 6 summarize the classification accuracy of the signals with SNR values of 15–25 dB. The model can still reliable detect the main classes of the modulations and in most cases correctly classifies the exact modulation type. Additionally, the misclassification happens only between the related modulations.

Based on the results on the synthetic data set, we have decided to perform the experiments on the real world signals only with the FFN model.

Table 5. RBN classification accuracy (%) of signal with noise (SNR 15–25 dB)

Signal mod.	Recognized modulation						
	AM	FM	PM	ASK	FSK	PSK	QAM
AM	**10.66**	9.63	2.28	75.16	0.00	1.04	1.23
FM	0.49	**11.98**	86.79	0.74	0.00	0.00	0.00
PM	13.89	50.68	**14.63**	15.47	0.00	2.92	2.41
ASK	0.40	0.00	0.00	**99.60**	0.00	0.00	0.00
FSK	0.00	10.61	72.99	0.43	**0.00**	13.46	2.51
PSK	0.19	51.75	0.00	33.08	0.00	**8.29**	6.69
QAM	0.19	31.10	0.00	63.17	0.00	1.46	**4.08**

Table 6. FFN classification accuracy (%) of signal with noise (SNR 15–25 dB)

Signal mod.	Recognized modulation						
	AM	FM	PM	ASK	FSK	PSK	QAM
AM	**74.95**	4.76	6.42	0.10	0.93	0.00	12.84
FM	0.25	**25.80**	66.42	0.00	0.00	0.74	6.79
PM	0.52	35.84	**50.05**	0.00	11.70	0.00	1.89
ASK	1.62	0.00	0.00	**35.73**	0.00	0.00	62.65
FSK	0.09	31.58	43.05	0.00	**25.20**	0.00	0.08
PSK	0.47	0.28	10.18	0.00	0.00	**34.50**	54.57
QAM	0.58	0.19	0.00	0.00	0.00	16.04	**83.19**

8.2   Real World Data Set

The real world signals were captured by SDB522RT. It is a small USB DVB-T receiver compatible with RTL-SDR library. Similar DVB-T dongles based on the Realtek RTL2832U can be used as a cheap SDR and are becoming extremely popular among electronic enthusiast. The highest theoretically possible sample-rate is 3.2 MS/s in frequency range 52–2200 MHz with a gap from 1100 MHz to 1250 MHz. As a source of FM modulated signals we have used local radio stations operating in the radio band from 88 to 108 MHz. The ASK and PSK modulations were found in signals transmitted in range from 300 MHz to 320 MHz. QAM and QPSK modulations are used in digital transmission of private security and public safety agencies around 391 MHz. The FSK modulation was not found in any received signals. The AM modulation was captured from local radio stations operating in longwave and medium wave bands. Since the SDR is unable to receive signals below 52 MHz, an RF upconverter (Ham It Up v1.3 with 125 MHz oscillator) was used to shift signal into the receiving range of SDR. Table 7 presents the results of classification of these signals.

Table 7. FFN classification accuracy (%) of samples captured by SDR receiver

Signal mod.	Recognized modulation					
	AM	FM	ASK	FSK	PSK	QAM
AM	**1.00**	0.00	88.00	0.00	0.00	11.00
FM	0.07	**0.00**	0.75	99.11	0.07	0.00
ASK	70.44	0.00	**29.59**	0.00	0.00	0.00
PSK	0.00	0.00	0.00	31.07	**68.93**	0.00
QAM	0.00	0.00	46.23	0.00	53.77	**0.00**

The AM radio transmissions were classified correctly only in 1 %, however related ASK and QAM modulations were detected in 88 % and 11 %. If we consider ASK as a special type of AM modulation with a finite number of possible amplitude values, this error is understandable. FM modulation was similarly misclassified as FSK (which is related to the FM in similar way, by using only a finite number of frequency changes). ASK was misclassified as AM mainly due to low SNR, as this classification is sensitive to noise. PSK modulation was classified in 69 % occurrences correctly. QAM modulation was classified in 46 % occurrences as ASK and 54 % PSK. This is natural as QAM is the combination of ASK and PSK and the general detection is hard.

Generally we can see that the success rate is lower than the values obtained from the synthetic data set. We have analysed the reasons and found that some parameters had significantly different values than the values obtained from the synthetic data sets. This was true especially of γ_{max}, where the real world FM modulated signals generated values ten times lower than the one used during the learning phase. The similar behaviour was observed with σ_{aa}. We suspect that these two significant differences degraded the classification abilities of the used neural network.

9   Conclusion

In this paper we have presented an automatic modulation classification based on the neural network. The proposed approach is based on calculating specific statistic features of the input signal that are used as an input to the neural network. The selection of the proper statistic features was discussed in more detail. Two types of neural networks were evaluated, the Radial Basis Function Network and Feed Forward Network. Both networks were learned using a synthetic data set and then evaluated on both synthetic and real world samples.

The experiments showed that the Feed Forward Network outperformed Radial Basis Function Network, especially in cases, where signal contained higher level of noise. For real world samples the classification success rate was lower, mainly due to the different characteristics of signals. Several modulations captured by SDR receiver had significantly different key characteristics than the signals we have artificially created for the learning phase.

What we see as a next logical step is to create a learning dataset based on the real world samples captured by the SDR. This task will be laborious but is necessary as there is a lack of large generally available data set of this kind. By doing this we can provide a better set for learning neural network. In addition to this, we should reconsider the selection of statistic features as some features did not provide enough information for unambiguous classification.

References

1. Ahn, W.H.: Automatic modulation classification of digital modulation signals based on Gaussian mixture model. In: UBICOMM 2014: The Eighth International Conference on Mobile Ubiquitous Computing, Systems, Services and Technologies, pp. 275–280 (2014)
2. Azzouz, E., Nandi, A.: Automatic Modulation Recognition of Communication Signals. Springer, New York (2013)
3. Bagga, J., Tripathi, N.: Automatic modulation classification using statistical features in fading environment. Int. J. Adv. Res. Electr. Electron. Instrum. Eng. 2(8), 3701–3708 (2013)
4. Beidas, B.F., Weber, C.L.: Asynchronous classification of MFSK signals using the higher order correlation domain. IEEE Trans. Commun. 46(4), 480–493 (1998)
5. Chan, Y.T., Gadbois, L.G.: Identification of the modulation type of a signal. Sig. Process. 16(2), 149–154 (1989)
6. Huan, C.Y., Polydoros, A.: Likelihood methods for MPSK modulation classification. IEEE Trans. Commun. 43(2/3/4), 1493–1504 (1995)
7. Heaton, J.: Encog: library of interchangeable machine learning models for Java and C#. J. Mach. Learn. Res. 16, 1243–1247 (2015)
8. Jondral, F.: Automatic classification of high frequency signals. Sig. Process. 9(3), 177–190 (1985)
9. Khurshid, A.A., Gokhale, A.P.: Classification system for digital signal types using neuro fuzzy system and PSO. In: Nature & Biologically Inspired Computing, NaBIC, pp. 373–378 (2009)
10. Liu, A.S., Qi, Z.II.U.: Automatic modulation classification based on the combination of clustering and neural network. J. China Univ. Posts Telecommun. 18(4), 13–38 (2011)
11. Popoola, J.J., Olst, R.: Automatic recognition of analog modulated signals using artificial neural networks. Comput. Technol. Appl. 2, 29–35 (2011)
12. Santos, R., Rupp, M., Bonzi, S., Fileti, A.M.: Comparison between multilayer feedforward neural networks and a radial basis function network to detect and locate leaks in pipelines transporting gas. Chem. Eng. Trans. 32, 1375–1380 (2013)
13. Thakur, P.S., Madan, S., Madan, M.: Trends in automatic modulation classification for advanced data communication networks. Int. J. Adv. Res. Comput. Eng. Technol. 4(2), 496–507 (2015)
14. Wang, H.K., Zhang, B., Wu, J.P., Han, Y.Z., Wu, X.W., Jia, R.S.: A research on automatic modulation recognition with the combination of the rough sets and neural network. In: Pervasive Computing Signal Processing and Applications (PCSPA), pp. 807–810 (2010)
15. Zhu, Z.: Automatic classification of digital communication signal modulations. Ph.D. thesis, Brunel University (2014)
16. Zhu, Z., Nandi, A.K.: Automatic Modulation Classification: Principles, Algorithms and Applications, pp. 66–69. Wiley, Hoboken (2015)

Skull Stripping for MRI Images Using Morphological Operators

Joanna Swiebocka-Wiek(✉)

Faculty of Physics and Applied Computer Science,
AGH University of Science and Technology, 30-059 Cracow, Poland
jsw@agh.edu.pl

Abstract. One of the most common MRI (Magnetic Resonance Imaging) use is a brain visualisation. Brain anatomy is highly complicated therefore it might be difficult to extract only these structures which have diagnostic value. In a consequence it is so necessary to develop and apply most efficient brain's segmentation algorithms. One of the first steps in case of neurological MRI analysis is skull stripping. It involves removing extra-meningeal tissue from the head image, therefore it is essential to find the best method to determine the brain and skull boundaries. In T1-weighted images, cerebrospinal fluid (CSF) space and skull are dark, that is why the edges between the brain and the skull are well-marked but even strong edges might be unsettled because of finite resolution during MRI acquisition or the presence of other anatomical partial structures within the brain (connections between the brain and optic nerves or brainstem). There are many ways to perform this operation, none of them is not so great as to constitute a standard proceedings. In many cases, there are limitations associated with the development environment, license and images input that hinder skull stripping without specialised software. Proposed method is free of these constraints. It is based on application of morphological operations and image filtration to enhance the result of the edge detection and to provide better tissues separation. The efficiency was compared with other methods, common in commercial use, and the results of this comparison was presented in this paper.

Keywords: Skull stripping · Brain extraction · Morphological operators · Image segmentation · MRI

1 Introduction

Skull stripping is a process of the brain tissue segmentation (cortex and cerebellum) from surrounding region (skull and nonbrain area). It is also a very important pre-processing step which precedes further analysis in case of many MRI neurological images (such as image registration or tissue classification) [7]. In clinical practice, this method is widely used in developing automated methods for progress evaluation of neurodegenerative diseases such as: Alzheimer's disease, multiple sclerosis and other neurological disorders like brain aging or even some mental illness.

In search of the most effective skull stripping techniques there were proposed many innovative automatic and semiautomatic brain segmentation techniques

© IFIP International Federation for Information Processing 2016
Published by Springer International Publishing Switzerland 2016. All Rights Reserved
K. Saeed and W. Homenda (Eds.): CISIM 2016, LNCS 9842, pp. 172–182, 2016.
DOI: 10.1007/978-3-319-45378-1_16

[1–3,6], particularly in the filed of MR image processing. However, published studies comparing common used algorithms [5] demonstrate that each of methodologies has significant number of advantages and disadvantages as well, so it's very difficult to find one approach which could be consider as the ideal solution.

These factors result in increasing need for the further development and examination of new effective skull stripping methods. In this paper one of approaches will be introduced.

2   Proposed Method

All images used and processed in this paper are the private property of the Author. They were registered in the John Paul II Hospital in Cracow. The images were registered with the following acquisition parameters: magnetic field: 3T, Spin Echo sequence, T1-weighted, slice thickness: 3 mm and contrast application). During selection of images for algorithms evaluation, the key criteria was to ensure their representativeness (to choose the most common type of images, which are also most often processed and compared in scientific dissertations). Algorithm was tested on images in all 3 projections, all scans were acquired in the middle of the T1-weighted session so that the area of the brain was possibly the greatest in in any case.

Skull stripping techniques can be divided into 3 main categories [7]:

- **Intensity-Based methods.** They are based on the threshold classification. The main disadvantage of this approach is its significant sensitivity for intensity fluctuations (in case of MRI caused for example by magnetic field inhomogeneity, registered noise or even device's properties)
- **Morphology-based Methods.** The basic idea is to combine the use of morphological operations, thresholding and edge detection techniques, in order to separate the area of the brain from the surrounding tissue in the most precisely way.
- **Deformable Model-based Methods** which applied the active contour deformation and fitting to localise brain area and its identification by using image characteristic.

The algorithm presented in this paper belongs to morphology-based methods' group. It was implemented using JAVA and MATLAB environment [9–11]. The proposed method has 5 steps.

1. image thresholding (segmentation),
2. filling the gaps in extracted objects using morphological operators,
3. edge detection and improving the edges if it's needed
4. selection of the largest area in the image and creating a binary mask
5. combining the binary mask and the input image as an output image.

The simplicity of this method which is clear, is one of its more significant advantages rather than flaws. In comparison with the methods used commonly and commercially (AFNI, FSL, Robex algorithm), the proposed algorithm due to its simplicity has a lower computational complexity, process .jpg and DICOM files (usually in these formats medical data are available for patients), enables work on other operating platforms than UNIX, does not require a specialized knowledge about program's structure (the only requirement is to install the MCR Installer on computers without Matlab environment). At the same time, despite its simplicity, the algorithm gives good visual results. Furthermore its proper working was confirmed by combining the input image and the image with brain extraction mask borders. Mask borders and brain borders in anatomical image are nearly the same! The obtained results of algorithms application and comparison with other methods were shown in further parts of this paper.

2.1   Image Thresholding

Image thresholding is essential for best algorithm's effectiveness. It allows to separate the background noise and foreground brain tissues [8]. In this paper 3 techniques were tested [9]:

- **Global Thresholding.** It relies on selection of the arbitrary threshold (usually it is gray scale image mean or median intensity) and its comparing with each pixel value. If the value is greater than or equal to the threshold the pixel is converted to white (for values smaller than threshold pixel became black).
- **Local Thresholding.** In this method separate threshold is determined for a particular part of the image or each pixel individually. Frequently the threshold is calculated as mean or median intensity value in pixel's surrounding with defined radius.
- **Mixed Thresholding** which is the same as the local thresholding with only one difference: if the mean or median local to a given pixel differs, by more than a predetermined value from the global threshold, global thresholding is applied.

The best results were obtained for mixed thresholding method. Local thresholding leaves too many details in the image, which made it unclear with specific structures poorly separated. In case of global thresholding part of the important (from the diagnostic point of view) edges were removed from the image, what disqualifies this method for further application. In Figs. 1, 2, 3 the results for each technique and each imaging plane were presented.

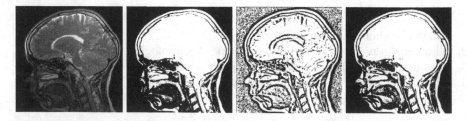

Fig. 1. Different thresholding method comparison (sagittal plane). From left to right: input image, global threshold, local threshold, mixed threshold

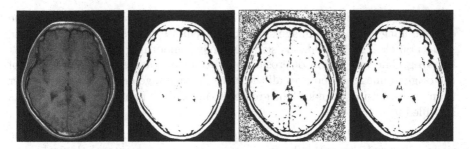

Fig. 2. Different thresholding method comparison (horizontal plane). From left to right: input image, global threshold, local threshold, mixed threshold

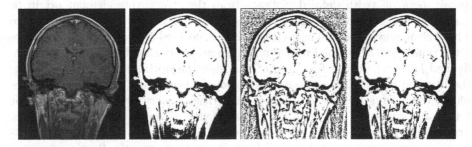

Fig. 3. Different thresholding method comparison (coronal plane). From left to right: input image, global threshold, local threshold, mixed threshold

2.2 Designing a Mask for the Brain Extraction

The next step was to create a mask which multiplied by the input image would allow to extract only the brain tissue region. Mask was designed using morphological operations, which are based on the application of so called (*structural element*). It is a set of pixels which may have different shapes and sizes and contain any combination of 0 and 1 values. If pixel's value is not significant it could be marked in structural element as z. Following morphological operators were applied in proposed method:

- **Dilatation** (thickening). The structural element is compared with each pixel of the image. If at least one pixel the neighborhood has a value equal to "1", the focal point also receives it (in another case is assigned the value "0"). Types of structural element strongly affects the output image.
- **Erosion** (thinning). This operation applies rotated structural element for each pixel in the image. If even one pixel in the neighborhood has a value equal to "0", the focal point also receives this value. Otherwise, its value does not change. This is an operation which is the inverse of dilatation. Erosion is significantly influenced by the choice of the structural element

- **Opening**. Imposition of dilatation operation on the result of the erosion of the original image. It causes image smoothing (removal of details, the greater the structural element is used, the stronger image smoothing can be observed).
- **Closing**. The imposition of erosion operations on the result of dilatation of the original image. It removes all the holes in the image and the concave lower than the structural element (the greater structural element, the more elements are filled in).

During creating the mask, the main goal was to examine the influence of the various structural elements (shape, size) and the sequence morphological operations selection, for the output mask image. Matlab packages allows to analyze up to nine types of structural elements with different shapes and sizes: diamond (with defined radius), disk (with defined radius), line (with defined length and angle), octagon (with defined distance from the structuring element origin to the octagon's size, along to the vertical and horizontal axis), pair (the structure with 2 elements), periodicline, rectangle (with specified 2-piece vector defining its size), square (with specified width) and even arbitrary structural element (shape defined by user). In the first step of choosing the optimal structural element, the line and periodicline options were rejected. Assuming that in each imaging plane, the brain structure is nearly symmetrical, structural element should not favor any processing direction. In a consequence it cannot take the angle as a procedure input parameter. In the next step, the square and rectangular structural elements were rejected as well form the further analysis. It was examined that increasing their size of even one pixel can cause unwanted sharpening of the brain edges. The mask constructing procedure should guarantee keeping the edges unchanged in their course and shape, because of their diagnostic value. On the other hand, rectangular structural element was used as very effective in later algorithm's stages for removing single black pixel (or small group of pixels) within a created mask. Disk, square, diamond and octagon structural elements were tested. It was assumed that due to the edge course, the structural element size can not be too high. Disk with radius equal to 3 has 25 elements (5×5 matrix) and square element with width equal to 5 and give same unsatisfactory results. Diamond with the same radius 3 and octagon in the smallest possible size has 49 elements (7×7 matrix). That is why the maximum acceptable radius of structural element was assigned as 2. For this size disk and diamond look identical. Finally, the disk element with radius equal to 2 was chosen as providing the best visual results. Unfortunately even then it was not possible to avoid leaving some small unwanted clusters of black pixels. In some cases these clusters caused additional signal areas extractions inside the mask area. Therefore in this step all the gaps in the image were removed by using morphological operators once again (square structural element as it was mentioned before). In Figs. 4, 5, 6 the received masks for each imaging plane were shown.

2.3   Edge Detection

Edge detection allows to verify if there is a correlation between the edges of the mask (applied for the brain extraction) and the anatomical edges of the input

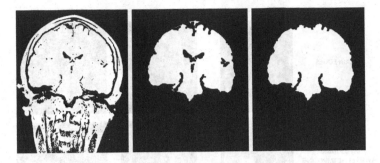

Fig. 4. The following steps of creating mask for brain region extraction (coronal plane). From left to right: image after mixed thresholding, mask received after image erosion, mask revised by removing small areas from the image

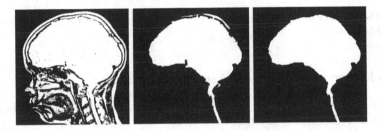

Fig. 5. The following steps of creating mask for brain region extraction (sagittal plane). From left to right: image after mixed thresholding, mask received after image erosion, mask revised by removing small areas from the image

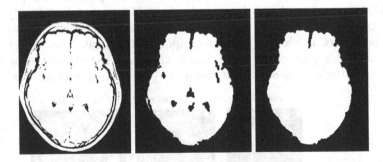

Fig. 6. The following steps of creating mask for brain region extraction (horizontal plane). From left to right: image after mixed thresholding, mask received after image erosion, mask revised by removing small areas from the image

image. Overlap of the brain's boundaries in the input image with the boundaries set by the proposed skull stripping method would prove that algorithm is correct. For each imaging plane the Canny edge detection filter was applied. Next, image presenting the edges was combined with corresponding input image. In each case correlation was confirmed which means that mask corresponds to the brain area and that it can be applied for the brain extraction.

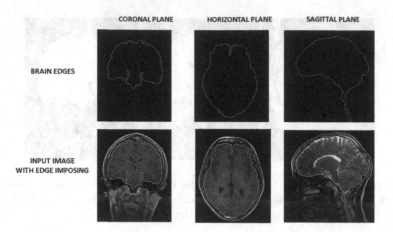

Fig. 7. The effect of imposing the edge of the brain extraction mask on the input image (in all planes)

2.4   Selection of the Largest Area in the Image

The main purpose of next step is to find the largest area in the image of connected white pixels representing the brain tissue.

The goal was achieved by assigning labels to each object in the image and counting the number of pixels with a given tag. This operation was performed using built-in Matlab functions. Based on the results a mask representing the brain area was created. With the received mask it was possible to separate the brain tissue (represented by white pixels) from the area diagnostically irrelevant(background represented by black pixels). The last algorithm step was combining the binary mask image and an input MRI image. The output image consists only this part of the input image that corresponds to the brain tissue. In Fig. 8 the results of skull stripping for each imaging plane was shown.

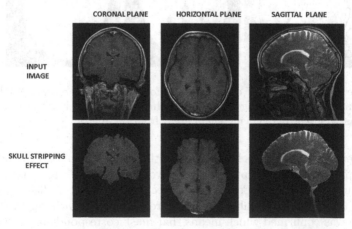

Fig. 8. Skull stripping result after algorithm implementation in all planes

The method gave the satisfactory and promising results, although after more careful analysis it can be seen that some part of the information is missing. It is particularly visible on the edges of the isolated brain (white matter area). In addition, the edges are slightly sharpened, and in a consequence the shape of the brain is not recreated in an ideal way.

2.5   Comparison with Other Methods

To be able to fully evaluate the algorithm's capabilities it is necessary to compare it with other commonly used brain extraction methods.

The most popular are AFNI (3DSkullStrip module) [13] and FSL (BET algorithm) [14]. AFNI approach is automated process based on three steps: preprocessing (removing artifacts and brain positioning), expanding a spherical surface (until it envelopes the brain) and finally creating all sets of masks and surfaces for brain modeling. FSL is a set of libraries of analysis tools for fMRI (Functional Magnetic Resonance Imaging), MRI and DTI (Diffusion Tensor Weighting) brain imaging data. Unfortunately, it was found that both programs have certain limitations, critical for the comparing them with proposed algorithm. The main difficulty is related to the type of supported files: both programs process only files with the .nii extension (Neuroimaging Informatics Technology Initiative, NIfTI), optionally .dcm files (Digital Imaging and Communications in Medicine, DICOM) after their conversion to .nii. During preparing this article Author did not have access to this kind of files and conversion was obligatory. The second limitation is that program dependant on operating system: both programs run under Unix and MacOS (none of them runs directly under Windows environment). What is more AFNI approach requires at leat 16 MRI scans (only 3D brain extraction is possible), what ultimately made it impossible to compare developed algorithm with AFNI results. Taking it into consideration, it is crucial to highlight the advantages of the Authors method and its suitability for processing .jpg files, specially under the Windows operating system. Short comparison of the developed algorithm and methods AFNI and FSL was shown in the Table 1.

Obtained images were compared with FSL-BET results and some alternative method, also based on using morphological operators. In case of alternative approach first step was image global thresholding with the threshold equals to After that small noise speckles were removed by using *bwareaopen* function(the

Table 1. Comparison of the author's method with FSL and AFNI approach.

Criteria	Author's method	FSL	AFNI
Supported files	DICOM, JPG, BMP, PNG, TIFF	NIFTI, DICOM	NIFTI, DICOM
Operating system	WINDOWS	Unix, Mac OS	Unix, Mac OS
Difficulties	—	—	At least 16 scans required

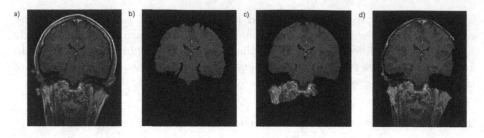

Fig. 9. Comparison of the proposed method (b), FSL-BET result (c) and the alternative Matlab approach (d). Horizontal plane. Methods description was presented in the text

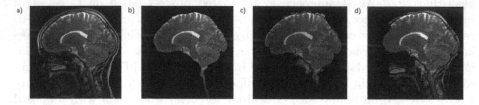

Fig. 10. Comparison of the proposed method (b), FSL-BET result (c) and the alternative Matlab approach (d). Sagittal plane. Methods description was presented in the text

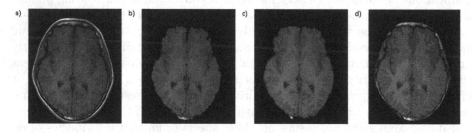

Fig. 11. Comparison of the proposed method (b), FSL-BET result (c) and the alternative Matlab approach (d). Coronal plane. Methods description was presented in the text

concept of speckles means all connected components that have fewer than 10 pixels). In next step the holes in binary image were removed by applying *imfill* function. In a final step single erosion with disk structural element (radius 15) was made. The results of all method comparison were shown in Figs. 9, 10, 11. As it can be seen only in case of horizontal plane all methods gave similar results. In case of sagittal and coronal plane, proposed in this paper method not only makes it possible to eliminate the skull structure but also extract only the brain tissue. This was possible thanks to an implementation in the algorithm the part which is responsible for the selection of the largest area in the image. Based on this area, filtration mask was built. It can also be noted that in the alternative method filtration leads to the removal some of the brain tissue sections which is unacceptable in case of diagnostic applications. In addition FSL methods in coronal plane leaves some redundant tissue.

Another approach to verify the algorithm's effectiveness is to evaluate its performance in the boundary conditions. In this case, it is the analysis of images in which the share of the signal from the skull and the brain tissue is comparable. It turns out that the algorithm may encounter some difficulties at the stage of segmentation (thresholding). The main cause is the lack of the cerebrospinal fluid signal which low intensity (dark, similar to black color) would precisely separate two light areas: the skull and brain tissue. As a result, even in the case of mixed thresholding, automatically predetermined threshold is too low and the tissues are not separated properly. The implementation of further steps of the algorithm was considered unreliable. That is why algorithm's application in the boundary conditions will be a subject of further development and research. The obtained results was presented in Fig. 12.

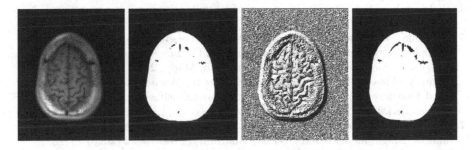

Fig. 12. Different thresholding method comparison (horizontal plane). From left to right: input image, global threshold, local threshold, mixed threshold

3   Summary and Conclusions

In this paper a skull stripping method for T1-weighted MRI images based on using morphological operators was proposed. The algorithm gives satisfactory and promising results. However despite the fact the area of the skull was removed from the image completely, closer image analysis shows cerebrospinal fluid (CSF) space the was partially preserved, while it should be removed as well. This will be the subject of further work and algorithm improvement. Another challenge is to correct edge detection of the brain area i.e. by using morphological gradients. In the present algorithm's version, the edges are sharpened, what is related to the partial loss of information on the borders of the area. Proposed method was compared with the commonly used solutions which have certain limitations associated with programming environment (AFNI, FSL). The algorithm assured comparable and is some cases even better results. High efficiency of the algorithm is associated with the use of the thresholding as one of the basic processing steps which allows for precise separation of the structures. It is planned to perform the algorithm's evaluation on a large database of images to confirm its effectiveness for images with a higher degree of complexity. The algorithm has a preliminary study status, therefore it is also planned in a future to compare its efficiency with other common used skull stripping methods and taking into consideration gray-scale morphology.

References

1. Somasundaram, K., Shankar, R.S.: Skull stripping of MRI using clustering and resonance method. Int. J. Knowl. Manag. e-Learn. **3**, 19–23 (2011)
2. Somasundaram, K., Shankar, R.S.: Automated skull stripping method using clustering and histogram analysis for MRI human head scans. Int. J. Adv. Res. Comput. Sci. Technol. **2**, 117–122 (2014)
3. Carass, A., Wheeler, M.B.: A joint registration, segmentation approach to skull stripping. In: Biomedical Imaging: From Nano to Macro IVth IEEE Symposium, pp. 656–659 (2007)
4. Sadananthan, S.A., Zheng, W., Chee, M.: Skull stripping using graph cuts. NeuroImage **49**, 225–239 (2010)
5. Fennema-Notestine, C., Ozyurt, I.B.: Quantitative evaluation of automated skull-stripping method applied to contemporary and legacy images, effects of diagnosis, bias correction, and slice location. Hum. Brain Mapp. **27**(2), 99–113 (2006)
6. Grau, V., Mewes, A.U.J., Alcaniz, M., Kikinis, R., Warfield, S.K.: Improved watershed transform for medical image segmentation using prior information. IEEE Trans. Med. Imaging **23**(4), 447–458 (2004)
7. Zhuang, A.H., Valentino, D., Toga, A.: Skull-stripping magnetic resonance brain images using a model-based level set. NeuroImage **32**, 79–92 (2006)
8. Tadeusiewicz, R., Mietanski J.: Pozyskiwanie obrazw medycznych oraz ich przetwarzanie, analiza, automatyczne rozpoznawanie i diagnostyczna interpretacja. Student Scientific Society Publishing (2011). (in Polish)
9. Landini, L., Positano, V., Santarelli, M.F.: Advanced Image Processing in Magnetic Resonance Imaging. Taylor Francis Group, Boca Raton (2005)
10. Gonzalez, R., Woods, R., Eddins, S.: Digital Image Processing Using Matlab. Prentice Hall Inc., Upper Saddle River (2009)
11. http://www.mathworks.com
12. http://www.mathworks.com/matlabcentral/answers/172701-how-to-perform-skull-stripping-using-matlab
13. AFNI homeage. https://afni.nimh.nih.gov/
14. FSL homepage. http://fsl.fmrib.ox.ac.uk/fsl/fslwiki/BET

Empirical Assessment of Performance Measures for Preprocessing Moments in Imbalanced Data Classification Problem

Paweł Szeszko$^{(\boxtimes)}$ and Magdalena Topczewska

Faculty of Computer Science, Bialystok University of Technology, Bialystok, Poland
p.szeszko@gmail.com, m.topczewska@pb.edu.pl

Abstract. The article concerns the problem of imbalanced data classification, when classes, into which elements belong, are not equally represented. In the classification model building process cross-validation technique is one of the most popular to assess the efficacy of a classifier. While over-sampling methods are used to create new objects to obtain the balance between the number of objects in classes, inappropriate usage of the preprocessing moment has a direct impact on the achieved results. In most cases they are overestimated. To present and assess this phenomenon in this paper three preprocessing techniques (SMOTE, Safe-level SMOTE, SPIDER) and their modifications are used to make new elements of data sets to balance cardinalities of classes, and two classification methods (SVM, C4.5) are compared. k-folds cross-validation technique ($k = 10$) considering two moments of preprocessing approaches is performed. The measures as precision, recall, F-measure and area under the ROC curve (AUC) are calculated and compared.

1 Introduction

The problem of imbalanced classes in datasets is deemed to be one out of ten the most important data exploration tasks nowadays. Therefore more and more scientists focus on developing methods that can provide the improvement of model performance for such difficult data. Many techniques to deal with the problem have been proposed [4,8].

The issue appears when the cardinality of at least one class is lower than the cardinality of remaining classes. In the two classes task the *imbalance ratio* describes the proportion of the majority (*negative*) class objects to the minority (*positive*) class and can vary depending on a dataset.

Classification models created on the basis of such data have to cope with misclassification errors of the minority class. This is the consequence of the fact that many classifiers consider the misclassification errors equally for all objects, regardless of the class to which they belong. However, in such cases the costs of incorrectness vary markedly. Considering for instance cancer diseases, the number of ill patients can be significantly smaller than the healthy or the

© IFIP International Federation for Information Processing 2016
Published by Springer International Publishing Switzerland 2016. All Rights Reserved
K. Saeed and W. Homenda (Eds.): CISIM 2016, LNCS 9842, pp. 183–194, 2016.
DOI: 10.1007/978-3-319-45378-1_17

sick for other reasons. Another well-known example is fraud detection, when a fraud occurs relatively infrequently. In mentioned situations the great emphasis is placed on the correct classification of minority class objects, definitely greater than in the majority class elements.

To reduce the impact of imbalance between the number of objects in particular classes, three groups of approaches have been proposed: data level, algorithm level and cost-sensitive level.

The algorithms belonging to the first category – data-level approach – operate on data objects solely and they are independent from the classification models. In undersampling methods superfluous objects are removed, thus the subset of original dataset is created to be used in model building process. In oversampling methods existing objects, from positive class in particular, can be replicated or new objects can be created. The third approach is constituted by hybrid methods – superfluous objects are removed and new necessary elements are created. The second group describes algorithm-level approaches in which instead of data, existing model-building algorithms are adjusted to classify objects regardless of the disparity between cardinalities of classes.

Finally, the last category considers unequal misclassification costs, because false negative and false positive costs are not the same as in cancer patients example. An important issue here is to determine the cost ratio or the cost matrix. The aim of cost-sensitive level methods is to build models with minimum misclassification costs.

By creating new objects, replicating or removing existing ones, the number of objects as well as the distributions of classes in a dataset are changed. Then to proceed the classification process and assess the efficacy of classification methods, one has to be cautious. In certain articles, the authors do not apply data preprocessing in appropriate moment while using cross-validation techniques, and they test the performance of the model on the artificial examples as well. It can lead to the overestimated results of the classification.

The aim of this paper is to compare the results obtained for two different moments of imbalanced datasets preprocessing and their influence on the classification performance measures as well as to assess empirically the overestimation level. Three data-level approaches using k-nearest neighbour technique [5] are considered: SMOTE [3], Safe-level SMOTE [2] and SPIDER [10] and two classifiers are used: C4.5 and SVM using John Platt's sequential minimal optimization algorithm for training a support vector classifier.

2   Data Preprocessing

In this paper three approaches to the construction of classifiers from imbalanced data sets are compared: SMOTE, Safe-level SMOTE and SPIDER.

2.1   SMOTE

The SMOTE (Synthetic Minority Over-sampling Technique) [3] is the most versatile method and enables to create new objects of the minority class. For each

p positive object, among its k nearest neighbours also belonging to the positive class, N/100 objects are sampled randomly with replacement, where N is a number of objects to generate. To compute the position of a new element, the difference between feature vector values of the considered object and a chosen neighbour should be calculated and multiplied by a *gap* – a random number between 0 and 1. The new object is then generated by adding that result to the feature vector of an examined p object.

2.2   Safe-Level SMOTE

Safe-level SMOTE [2] is a modification of the original SMOTE algorithm. It draws particular attention to the classes of objects that encircle examined positive objects. For each examined positive p element the safe-level indicator (sl_p) is defined and calculated as the number of positive instances among its k nearest neighbours. Additionally, one randomly selected neighbour is chosen (n), and for this element safe-level indicator (sl_n) is also computed. In the next step *safe level ratio* $(sl_{ratio} = \frac{sl_p}{sl_n})$ is calculated and one of five cases is chosen:

– if $sl_{ratio} = \infty$ and $sl_p = 0$, no new object is generated, because p and n are treated as noisy, i.e. elements situated in the negative class area;
– if $sl_{ratio} = \infty$ and $sl_p \neq 0$, n is noisy; p object is replicated; so *gap* $= 0$;
– if $sl_p = sl_n$, then $sl_{ratio} = 1$ and *gap* is a random number between 0 and 1; new object will be situated between p and n;
– if $sl_{ratio} > 1$, p object is safer than n object, because in its surroundings there are more safer positive objects, hence *gap* is a random number between 0 and $\frac{1}{sl_{ratio}}$ to situate a new object closer to p;
– if $sl_{ratio} < 1$, n object is safer than p object, hence *gap* is a random number between $1 - sl_{ratio}$ and 1 to situate a new object closer to n.

The number of iterations is matched to balance the cardinalities of classes.

2.3   SPIDER

The selective preprocessing algorithm SPIDER [10] combines local over-sampling of the minority class with filtering difficult objects from the negative class. The method assigns to each object one of two labels: safe – if its classification result using k-nearest neighbour rule $(k = 3)$ is correct, or noisy otherwise. The special D set is created and all noisy majority class objects are transferred into it to remove them from a dataset at the end of the algorithm. Three techniques of a dataset modification can be mentioned.

Weak amplification method increases the importance of the minority class objects labelled as noisy by their replications. The number of replications depends on the number of safe objects among three neighbours of each examined element. Additionally, all noisy majority class elements are removed from a dataset.

Weak amplification and relabelling adds an adjective step to the previous method. For elective noisy positive object, some among its three negative noisy neighbours are relabelled as positive elements. Modified negative elements are removed from the D set.

The third method is called *strong amplification* and is focused on all positive class objects. The importance of each safe element is increased by its replication – the number of copied objects equals the number of negative objects among its nearest neighbours. The modification of noisy positive elements depends on the k-nearest neighbours classification results when $k = 5$. In the correct result case, the number of replications is the same as for safe objects, otherwise instead of three, five nearest neighbours for each examined element are taken into considerations.

3   Classification Model Performance

Predictive model creating is one of the main goals of machine learning process. Models built using existing elements from a dataset should give an answer which class a new unclassified object should be assigned to. To compare model building algorithms we need methods that can predict performance of a model for objects that were unused in a training process, because the model is fitted to the data on which it was constructed. Therefore training and test sets should be independent and it is very necessary issue if we try to assess performance of the classification models in real situations.

3.1   Estimating the Predictive Model Performance

For the purpose described in a previous paragraph a cross-validation method was proposed. It divides the input set into independent training and test sets.

If the input dataset is large, it can be just randomly divided into two parts: training and test sets, for example in proportion 2:1. It is called a *hold-out method*. The main advantage of this approach is low cost of computing resources. A big disadvantage is uncertainty that the class distributions are represented in both parts properly, hence received results may not present a real efficacy of a model. This problem can be solved with repeated random division of the input dataset, but still there is no certitude that appropriate elements have been chosen to the test sets.

An approach that should provide proper representation of objects in a test set is k-fold cross-validation technique [7]. This method divides the input set into k parts. In each of k iterations k-th part is used as a test set and other objects are used for a model training. In advance of a division the order of the objects should be changed randomly. Additionally, the stratification process can be performed to preserve the distributions of classes in training and test tests.

In this paper 10-folds cross-validation process has been chosen for calculations.

In the class imbalance problem, when data need preprocessing, there is another issue to reflect – the moment of preprocessing. It might seem to be correct to prepare datasets first and then initiate classification process, as presented in the Fig. 1. However, it is not appropriate mode of an action, since new

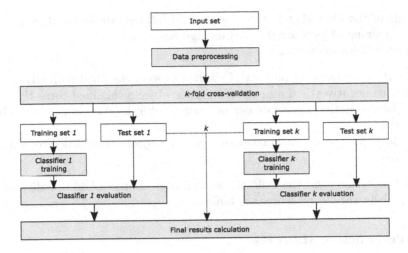

Fig. 1. Incorrect cross-validation process

artificial objects will take part in testing process, and the results will be affected directly [11]. Due to that fact the appropriate approach is to run preprocessing algorithms for each training set internally during cross-validation process to not include synthetic elements into test sets, as shown in the Fig. 2.

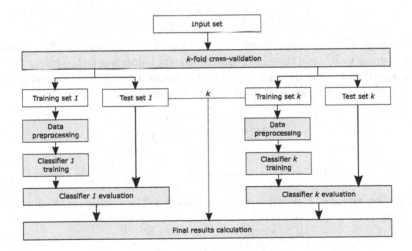

Fig. 2. Correct cross-validation process

3.2 Classification Quality Assessment Methods

Comparison methods of various classification techniques constitute an important element of the machine learning process. In the case of two classes problem, the

elements of the class that is the object of an interest are denoted as *positive*, while remaining objects are denoted as *negative*.
We use the following notation:

- TP (true positives) – a number of *positive* objects classified correctly
- TN (true negatives) – a number of *negative* objects classified correctly
- FN (false negatives) – a number of *positive* objects classified incorrectly as *negative*
- FP (false positives) – a number of *negative* objects classified incorrectly as *positive*

These four terms form the cells of the confusion matrix. Additionally, on the basis of them various measures are built.

3.3   Performance Measures

The most popular and well-known measures describing the performance of a classifier are the *accuracy* Q (1) computed as the proportion of the objects classified correctly:

$$Q = \frac{TP + TN}{TP + FP + TN + FN}, \tag{1}$$

and the *error rate* Err_{rate} (2) respectively, as the proportion of misclassified objects:

$$Err_{rate} = \frac{FP + FN}{TP + FP + TN + FN}. \tag{2}$$

These measures are not appropriate for the case of the imbalanced class problem, when the error weights of the misclassified objects belonging to the minority class are not equal as for the majority class or the remaining classes. To comprehend of such a problem *precision* (3) and *recall* (4) have been introduced:

$$Precision = \frac{TP}{TP + FP}, \tag{3}$$

$$Recall = Sensitivity = TP_{rate} = \frac{TP}{TP + FN}. \tag{4}$$

Furthermore, there is *F-measure* that is defined as the harmonic mean of precision and recall

$$F = \frac{(1 + \beta^2) \cdot Precision \cdot Recall}{\beta^2 \cdot Precision + Recall}, \tag{5}$$

and AUC is the the area under the ROC curve [9]

$$AUC = \frac{1 + TP_{rate} - FP_{rate}}{2}, \tag{6}$$

where $FP_{rate} = \frac{FP}{FP + TN}$.

4   Experiment

The experiment concerning the influence of the data preprocessing moment on the final results of the classification methods has been performed. 25 datasets from KEEL [1] repository were selected and their characteristics is presented in the Table 1. These datasets were created on the basis of 10 datasets from UCI repository [12].

Table 1. Characteristics of the datasets

Dataset	#objects	#attributes	#minority	IR
ecoli-0vs1	220	7	77	1.86
ecoli1	336	7	77	3.36
ecoli2	336	7	52	5.46
ecoli3	336	7	35	8.60
ecoli4	336	7	20	15.80
glass*	214	9	51	3.20
glass0	214	9	70	2.06
glass1	214	9	76	1.82
glass2	214	9	17	11.59
glass4	214	9	13	15.46
glass5	214	9	9	22.78
glass 6	214	9	29	6.38
haberman	306	3	81	2.78
iris0	150	4	50	2.00
new-thyroid1	215	5	35	5.14
new-thyroid2	215	5	35	5.14
pima	768	8	268	1.87
vehicle0	846	18	199	3.25
vehicle1	846	18	217	2.90
vehicle2	846	18	218	2.88
vehicle3	846	18	212	2.99
vowel0	988	13	90	9.98
wisconsin	683	9	239	1.86
yeast1	1484	8	429	2.46
yeast3	1484	8	163	8.10

Calculations have been performed using classes as parts of the Weka data mining software [6] and own application. Precision, recall, F-measure and AUC have been calculated for two moments of preprocessing and for two classification algorithms and ten preprocessing variants. To reduce the randomness of the results each 10-folds cross-validation process was repeated 10 times with different random number generator seed. Next, the differences between two points were calculated and examined. As modification of SMOTE algorithm also the number of synthetic objects was verified.

The numbers in the SMOTE $100, 200, \ldots, 500$ versions denote % of the minority class elements that were generated. The SMOTEAuto indicates that after preprocessing process the number of objects in the classes was balanced. For the SVM method $C = 100$ and linear kernel have been chosen to be presented in the paper.

To compare the differences between appropriate and inappropriate preprocessing moments during model evaluation, the t-test for dependent observations or the Wilcoxon signed-rank test were applied according to the normal or non-normal distributions of samples. The significance level was set at the level of 0.05. To unify the results, median values and the range as adequate statistics for all cases are presented in the Table 2.

For the whole range of datasets and methods, the average value of the precision difference between appropriate and inappropriate moment of preprocessing is at the level of 0.1792 ± 0.1259 (median 0.1691). The average value of the recall difference equals 0.0711 ± 0.0976 (median 0.0478); the average value of the F-measure difference: 0.1373 ± 0.1099 (median 0.1244) and the average value of the AUC difference: 0.0421 ± 0.0507 (median 0.0274).

For the C4.5 algorithm these results are as follows: precision: 0.1814 ± 0.1261 (median 0.1719); recall: 0.1154 ± 0.1011 (median 0.0920); F-measure: 0.1546 ± 0.1141 (median 0.1420) and AUC: 0.0659 ± 0.0546 (median 0.0532). For the SVM algorithm adequately: precision: 0.1768 ± 0.1259 (median 0.1667); recall: 0.0267 ± 0.0701 (median 0.0178); F-measure: 0.1200 ± 0.1028 (median 0.1063) and AUC: 0.0183 ± 0.0320 (median 0.0111). All these results are statistically significantly different than zero.

Apart from statistics, p-values for particular methods and algorithms are presented in the Table 2. In almost all cases there is a statistically significant difference between average results in two moments of preprocessing. Only for spider-type methods in few cases there is no statistical difference for SVM algorithm. The linear decision function not proper for the structure of data in classes may be the reason. Additionally two figures present the variability of F-measure differences (Fig. 3) and AUC differences (Fig. 4) for particular datasets and methods. Horizontal lines on the graphs show median value for each method.

The largest differences between mean values and two moments of preprocessing have been noticed for glass2 (precision: 0.42; recall: 0.26; F-measure: 0.36; AUC: 0.12), glass4 (precision: 0.30; recall: 0.21; F-measure: 0.27; AUC: 0.11) and haberman (precision: 0.33; F-measure: 0.23; AUC: 0.07). The quantities of the difference are astounding and further investigation will be performed. Inappropriate moment of data preprocessing while using cross-validation techniques, regardless of the classification method, may have large impact on the results giving too optimistic result of the classification process.

Table 2. Results for precision, recall, F measure and AUC using three preprocessing methods and their modifications for two classification algorithms

	Precision					
	C4.5			SVM		
method	*Me*	*Range*	p	*Me*	*Range*	p
slsmote	0.1826	0.0000; 0.6311	<0.0001	0.2439	0.0000; 0.5825	<0.0001
smote100	0.0685	0.0065; 0.1986	<0.0001	0.1050	0.0000; 0.2023	<0.0001
smote200	0.1637	0.0000; 0.3183	<0.0001	0.1826	0.0000; 0.3125	<0.0001
smote300	0.1866	0.0000; 0.3880	<0.0001	0.2345	0.0000; 0.3671	<0.0001
smote400	0.2184	0.0000; 0.4446	<0.0001	0.2631	0.0000; 0.4154	<0.0001
smote500	0.2297	0.0000; 0.4527	<0.0001	0.2796	0.0000; 0.4747	<0.0001
smoteAuto	0.2043	0.0000; 0.5665	<0.0001	0.2092	0.0000; 0.5835	<0.0001
spider-strong	0.1866	-0.0011; 0.5403	<0.0001	0.1367	0.0000 ;0.4031	<0.0001
spider-weak	0.1290	0.0000; 0.4388	<0.0001	0.1268	-0.0135; 0.3277	<0.0001
spider-weak-rel	0.1169	0.0000; 0.4445	<0.0001	0.1263	-0.0135; 0.3078	<0.0001
	Recall					
method	*Me*	*Range*	p	*Me*	*Range*	p
slsmote	0.1271	0.0128; 0.6533	<0.0001	0.0452	0.0000; 0.2945	<0.0001
smote100	0.0709	-0.0277; 0.2647	<0.0001	0.0097	-0.0296; 0.0944	0.0001
smote200	0.0843	0.0064; 0.2294	<0.0001	0.0318	-0.0036; 0.2153	<0.0001
smote300	0.0858	0.0000; 0.2955	<0.0001	0.0293	0.0000; 0.2307	<0.0001
smote400	0.1000	-0.0022; 0.3458	<0.0001	0.0242	-0.0007; 0.2138	<0.0001
smote500	0.0971	0.0111; 0.3117	<0.0001	0.0273	0.0000; 0.1910	<0.0001
smoteAuto	0.0896	-0.0020; 0.4203	<0.0001	0.0236	-0.0050; 0.1330	<0.0001
spider-strong	0.1222	0.0009; 0.5724	<0.0001	0.0010	-0.2037; 0.2171	0.587
spider-weak	0.1002	0.0000; 0.5204	<0.0001	0.0108	-0.1910; 0.2185	0.129
spider-weak-rel	0.0932	0.0000; 0.4998	<0.0001	-0.0229	-0.1802; 0.1800	0.048
	F Measure					
method	*Me*	*Range*	p	*Me*	*Range*	p
slsmote	0.1618	0.0066; 0.6437	<0.0001	0.1561	0.0000; 0.5205	<0.0001
smote100	0.0852	0.0066; 0.2576	<0.0001	0.0761	0.0000; 0.1472	<0.0001
smote200	0.1254	0.0088; 0.2703	<0.0001	0.1070	0.0000; 0.2714	<0.0001
smote300	0.1496	0.0094; 0.3492	<0.0001	0.1508	0.0000; 0.2951	<0.0001
smote400	0.1641	0.0097; 0.4080	<0.0001	0.1773	0.0000; 0.3658	<0.0001
smote500	0.1654	0.0104; 0.3937	<0.0001	0.1907	0.0000; 0.3934	<0.0001
smoteAuto	0.1440	0.0059; 0.5113	<0.0001	0.1422	0.0000; 0.4893	<0.0001
spider-strong	0.1495	0.0004; 0.5578	<0.0001	0.1022	-0.0657; 0.2886	<0.0001
spider-weak	0.1169	0.0004; 0.4786	<0.0001	0.0587	-0.0455; 0.2317	0.0004
spider-weak-rel	0.1181	0.0004; 0.4731	<0.0001	0.0841	-0.0261; 0.2125	<0.0001
	AUC					
method	*Me*	*Range*	p	*Me*	*Range*	p
slsmote	0.0684	0.0065; 0.1986	<0.0001	0.0215	0.0000; 0.1475	<0.0001
smote100	0.0341	0.0003; 0.0993	<0.0001	0.0053	-0.0081; 0.0462	<0.0001
smote200	0.0451	0.0006; 0.1152	<0.0001	0.0164	0.0000; 0.1054	<0.0001
smote300	0.0516	-0.0006; 0.1418	<0.0001	0.0126	0.0000; 0.1089	<0.0001
smote400	0.0516	-0.0001; 0.1461	<0.0001	0.0112	-0.0010; 0.1069	<0.0001
smote500	0.0457	0.0018; 0.1542	<0.0001	0.0109	-0.0004; 0.0972	<0.0001
smoteAuto	0.0450	-0.0011; 0.1994	<0.0001	0.0111	-0.0017; 0.0779	<0.0001
spider-strong	0.0757	0.0004; 0.2834	<0.0001	0.0076	-0.0921; 0.1122	0.063
spider-weak	0.0639	0.0004; 0.2552	<0.0001	0.0051	-0.0866; 0.1122	0.440
spider-weak-rel	0.0621	0.0004; 0.2613	<0.0001	0.0068	-0.0818; 0.0937	0.303

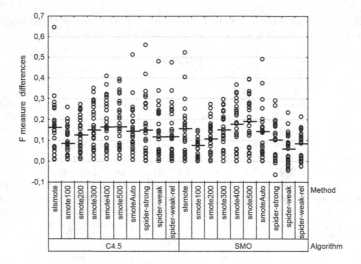

Fig. 3. Variability of F measures differences

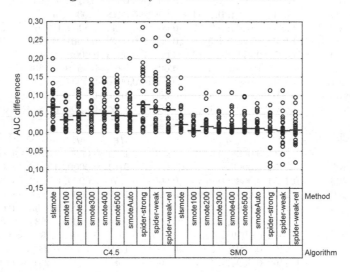

Fig. 4. Variability of differences between AUC values

5   Conclusions

Class imbalance datasets is nowadays a common occurrence, mainly due to the possibility of collecting large amounts of information. This phenomenon may have a direct impact on the performance of classification methods, because most classifiers are designed to maximize the accuracy or minimize the error rate. Assuming the equality of misclassification errors, the classifiers are usually overwhelmed by negative class objects, which leads to degradation of the performance of the classifier. Data preprocessing can be a good approach overcoming the disparity between classes cardinalities. However, the calculations should be performed in an attentive matter to not obtain excessively positive results. Even if the results are overestimated for about a few percent, each incorrect decision should be avoided.

There is a significant influence of the moment choice when preprocessing is performed. Results differences vary depending on a chosen classification algorithm and specific dataset. In most cases rates are inflated if preprocessing is performed before cross-validation. There are two reasons of this issue. Firstly, synthetic objects that are put into test sets are closely related to their prototypes in training sets, causing overfitting of a model. Secondly, proportions of classes in test sets in this method are not the same as real proportions that were given in the input sets and it affects the values of calculated rates.

The results occurred astounding and further investigation for various classification methods and datasets will be performed.

Acknowledgements. This work was performed in the framework of the grant S/WI/2/2013 (Bialystok University of Technology), founded by the Polish Ministry of Science and Higher Education.

References

1. Alcalá-Fdez, J., Fernández, A., Luengo, J., Derrac, J., García, S.: Keel data-mining software tool: data set repository, integration of algorithms and experimental analysis framework. Mult.-Valued Log. Soft Comput. **17**(2–3), 255–287 (2011)
2. Bunkhumpornpat, C., Sinapiromsaran, K., Lursinsap, C.: Safe-level-SMOTE: safe-level-synthetic minority over-sampling technique for handling the class imbalanced problem. In: Theeramunkong, T., Kijsirikul, B., Cercone, N., Ho, T.-B. (eds.) PAKDD 2009. LNCS, vol. 5476, pp. 475–482. Springer, Heidelberg (2009)
3. Chawla, N.V., Bowyer, K.W., Hall, L.O., Kegelmeyer, W.P.: SMOTE: synthetic minority over-sampling technique. J. Artif. Intell. Res. **16**, 321–357 (2002)
4. Chawla, N.V., Japkowicz, N., Kotcz, A.: Editorial: special issue on learning from imbalanced data sets. SIGKDD Explor. **6**(1), 1–6 (2004)
5. Cover, T., Hart, P.: Nearest neighbor pattern classification. IEEE Trans. Inf. Theor. **13**(1), 21–27 (1967)
6. Hall, M., Frank, E., Holmes, G., Pfahringer, B., Reutemann, P., Witten, I.H.: The weka data mining software: an update. SIGKDD Explor. Newsl. **11**(1), 10–18 (2009)
7. Hastie, T., Tibshirani, R., Friedman, J.: The Elements of Statistical Learning: Data Mining Inference and Prediction. Springer, Berlin (2009)
8. He, H., Garcia, E.A.: Learning from imbalanced data. IEEE Trans. Knowl. Data Eng. **21**(9), 1263–1284 (2009)
9. Krzanowski, W.J., Hand, D.J.: ROC Curves for Continuous Data. Chapman & Hall/CRC, London (2009)
10. Stefanowski, J., Wilk, S.: Selective pre-processing of imbalanced data for improving classification performance. In: Song, I.-Y., Eder, J., Nguyen, T.M. (eds.) DaWaK 2008. LNCS, vol. 5182, pp. 283–292. Springer, Heidelberg (2008)

11. Altini M.: Dealing with imbalanced data: undersampling, oversampling and proper cross-validation. http://www.marcoaltini.com/blog/dealing-with-imbalanced-data-undersampling-oversampling-and-proper-cross-validation. Accessed 4 Apr 2016
12. UC Irvine Machine Learning Repository. http://archive.ics.uci.edu/ml/. Accessed 15 Feb 2016

Optimization, Tuning

Optimization of Chosen Transport Task by Using Generic Algorithms

Anna Burduk$^{(\boxtimes)}$ and Kamil Musiał

Mechanical Department, Wrocław University of Technology, Wrocław, Poland
anna.burduk@pwr.wroc.pl,
kamil.musial@student.pwr.wroc.pl

Abstract. The paper presents genetic algorithms, their properties and capabilities in solving computational problems. Using a genetic algorithm an optimization task of transportation - production regard to the transport and processing of milk will be investigated. For the network of collection centers and processing plants (factories) the cost-optimal transportation plan regarding to raw materials to the relevant factories will be established. It is assumed that the functions defining the costs of processing are polynomials of the second degree. To solve the problem the program that uses genetic algorithms written in MATLAB will be used.

Keywords: Optimization of production systems · Generic algorithms

1 Introduction

The main purpose of transportation in a company is the system organization and synchronization of physical flow of materials from manufacturers or wholesalers to consumers through all phases of the process, in accordance with the principles of logistics management [1, 5, 6, 10].

Expenditure on transport a large part of total costs, which make the difference between the cost of goods producing and price paid by the consumer. In addition, some of the goods should be transported as quickly as possible due to the limited period of validity. These reasons tend to pay attention to the problem of transport optimizing [9]. At the same time the continuous technological and information advances guarantees the emergence of new methods that can be successfully used in solving transport problem. Transport issues are most often used to [5, 8]:

- optimal products transport planning, taking into account the minimization of costs, or time of execution
- optimization of production factors distribution in order to maximize production value, profit or income.

Genetic algorithms belong to group of stochastic algorithms. The basic principle of their functioning is based on the imitation of biological processes, namely the processes of natural selection and heredity. Genetic algorithms are gaining more and more areas of applications in the scientific, engineering and even in business circles, as an effective tool for efficient searching [1, 4]. The reason for this is obvious: genetic algorithms are

© IFIP International Federation for Information Processing 2016
Published by Springer International Publishing Switzerland 2016. All Rights Reserved
K. Saeed and W. Homenda (Eds.): CISIM 2016, LNCS 9842, pp. 197–205, 2016.
DOI: 10.1007/978-3-319-45378-1_18

a simple and at the same time powerful tool to search for better solutions. In addition, they are free from the essential constraints imposed by the strong assumptions about the search space, i.e. continuity, existence of derivatives, modality of the objective function, etc. A typical problem solved by genetic algorithm consists of [2, 3, 5, 7]:

- optimization problem - finding the best solution of all allowable,
- a set of allowable solutions - the set of all possible solutions to the task (not only the optimal),
- the evaluation function (adjustment) - the function that determines the quality of each possible solution. It establishes an ordinal relationship on the set of feasible solutions. In other words, because this function, one can sort all the solutions from best to worst solution of the problem,
- coding method - a function that represents each acceptable solution in the form of string code, which is in the form of a chromosome. Basically, more interesting should be the inverse function. This is a function that, on the basis of chromosome, creates a new feasible solution. In fact, to solve the task the only basic function is required, analogous to nature. Nature has complicated 'knowledge' on how to create an adult from an embryo. I would be enough that each of the individuals will be stored in the memory of genotype, on the basis of which he was created.

2   The Mathematical Model of Transport – Production Task

In the following example optimization of transport - production tasks for the processing of milk will be considered. For network of collection points and processing plants, according to its algorithm, the cost-optimal distribution of transport tasks has been determined. It is assumed that the functions defining the costs of conversion are polynomials of the second degree. To solve the problem a program written in MATLAB based on the genetic algorithm, equalizing marginal costs is used.

Enterprise processing a uniform material has m collection points and n plants processing this material. Additional information should be known:

- unit cost of transportation from any collection point to individual processing plants,
- amount of material collected at each point of supply,
- functions defining the cost of the material processing at each plant, depending on the size of the processing.

Features defining the costs of conversion are convex and square functions. They take into account only the variable costs, which depend on the size of production. The entire acquired material must be transported to the plant and converted there. It is assumed that plants are able to process the supplied amount of material (the possibility of processing by plants are known). This increases the production capacity of plants, but also results in an increase in the unit cost of production. Rising costs of conversion are a natural limitation of the size of production of each establishment.

It is needed to establish a plan of material supplies to individual plants and processing of raw materials in these plants, so the total costs of transport and processing were minimal. The following designations have been adopted:

i - the number of the collection (supplier number),
j - number of the processing plant (recipient number),
x_{ij} - the amount of raw material transferred from the i-th supplier to the j-th recipient,
x_j - the amount of raw material processed by the j-th recipient,
a_i - the amount of raw material, which must be send by i-th supplier,
c_{ij} - the unit cost of transport from the i-th supplier to the j-th recipient,
$f_j(x_j)$ - the cost of processing x_j units of raw material in the j-th plant (at j-th recipient).

Furthermore assumed that the convex cost function f_i is a second degree polynomial of the form:

$$f_j(x_j) = c_j x_j + e_j x_j^2, c_j, e_j > 0 \tag{1}$$

where:

c_j - describes the minimum unit cost of processing,
e_j - determines the growth rate of unit cost.

The first derivative of this function is determined by the marginal cost of processing:

$$F'_J(X_J) = C_J + 2E_J X_J \tag{2}$$

while the second derivative - the rate of increase in the marginal cost:

$$F''_J(X_J) = 2E_J \tag{3}$$

The average cost of processing the j-th plant is determined by the formula:

$$K^P_J(X_J) = C_J + E_J X_J \tag{4}$$

The problem of determining the optimal supply plan of raw material and its processing can be presented in the form of a non-linear decision task.
Variables x_{ij} and x_j are sought that:

$$\sum_{i=1}^{m} \sum_{j=1}^{n} c_{ij} x_{ij} + \sum_{j=1}^{n} f_j(x_j) \to min. \tag{5}$$

By the conditions:

$$\sum_{j=1}^{n} x_{ij} = a_i; (i = 1, \ldots, m), \tag{6}$$

$$\sum_{i=1}^{m} x_{ij} = x_j; (j = 1, \ldots, n) \tag{7}$$

$$x_{ij}, x_j \geq 0; (i = 1, \ldots, n) \tag{8}$$

The objective function (5) minimizes the total cost of transport and processing. Condition (6) provides that each supplier will send all owned raw material. Condition (7) forces the processing in the j-th plant of all the raw material to which it is delivered. Task (5–7) is the task of quadratic programming with a special - transport structure. It can be solved by using an algorithm equalizing the marginal cost, which is based on genetic algorithm.

Marginal cost, the cost of which the manufacturer incurs due to the increased size of production of the good by one unit. It is the increase in total costs associated with producing an additional unit of a good. If the plant increases its production by one unit, then the total cost of production will increase. The difference in the size of the costs manufacturer incur earlier and costs incurred after the increase in production is a marginal cost. It is, therefore, the cost of producing an additional unit of a good.

The concept of marginal cost can also be formulated in relation to the consumer and is then taken as the cost of acquiring an additional unit of a good. The marginal cost is an important micro-economic category. It was observed that for typical business processes marginal costs initially decrease with the increase in production until the technological minimum is reached. Further increase of production over a minimum of technology, however, increases the unit cost of further increases in production and thus rising marginal costs. This observation is important in microeconomic analysis of the behavior of the manufacturer and determining the optimal level of production. According to economic theory, marginal cost cannot be negative. This means that the increase in production may entail reducing the total cost.

Method of equalizing the marginal cost based on genetic algorithm consists of:

- determination of the best possible, an acceptable solution output,
- improvement of new solutions X^1, X^2, …, by offset equalizing marginal costs.

A string of new obtained solutions X^1, X^2, …, X^r,…., does not need to be finished. It is therefore interrupted at some point of calculations. It is important, however, that the final solution does not deviate too far away (in terms of objective function value) from the optimum solution. JCC algorithm comes down to the following steps:

1. Determine the initial solution:
   (a) for the i-th supplier ($i = 1$, …, m) the route with minimal marginal cost is set,
   (b) on the selected route an entire supply of i-th supplier is located,
   (c) update the marginal costs in the column of the selected route.
   Then move on to the next vendor, and repeating steps (a)–(c) until the supply is disposed for all suppliers.
2. Make sure the current solution Xr meets the criterion of optimality. If so, the final solution is optimal. If not- return to step 3.
3. Make sure the solution Xr is ε - accurate. If so, finish the calculations. If not, go to step 4.
4. Improving the solution by shifting equalizing marginal costs and return to step 2.

Having designated solution Xr and the matrix of marginal costs Kr for each supplier, lets settle the differences between the maximum realized cost and the minimal cost.

3   Solving the Problem of Transport and Production Using a Genetic Algorithm

The study involved the delivery of milk (about 2 000 m^3/month). The task was formulated as follows:

Six suppliers (in 6 cities): *D1, D2, D3, D4, D5, D6* supplies milk to two factories: *S1, S2*, with restrictions:
S1: can accept and process 700 or 1000 m^3 of milk,
S2: can accept and process 1 500 m^3 of milk.

Data are summarized in Table 1 below and include:

unit transportation costs (in PLN per km),
offered monthly deliveries Ai (m^3),
monthly demand of factories Bj (m^3).

The task is solved with the help of developed in MATLAB genetic algorithm equipped with a graphic interface GUI. The aim of the task is to determine the optimal marginal cost of "material processed" transport from any supplies, to one of two factories, taking into account its processing capacity.

Table 1. Unit transportation costs, supply and demand

Suppliers		Factories			
	Supply A_j [m^3]	Variant v1		Variant v2	
		S1	*S2*	*S1*	*S2*
D1	400	5	60	5	60
D2	70	40	60	40	60
D3	100	70	15	70	15
D4	300	70	5	70	5
D5	420	100	50	100	50
D6	200	100	80	80	100
Demand B_j [m^3]		700	1500	1000	1500

3.1   Solving the Transport- Production Problem of in the General Scheme of Genetic Algorithm

Population. The first step is to number all suppliers. Created chromosome has a length such as the number of suppliers. In the following genes another supplier is saved. For example, if the gene number 1 "represents" city X and gen number 2 city Y it means that the provider moves from town X to Y. In this way, genes in the chromosome are arranged exactly as the city cycle. For a sample of six cities connected with road, a sample chromosome mapping cycle may look like this:

$$[1\,4\,6\,2\,3\,5]$$

The Evaluation Function (Cost). The function of evaluation is the total minimum cost of transport and processing.

Selection. Simulation using the roulette wheel assigns the probability of choosing each individual directly on the basis of a single evaluation function. The sum of the probabilities assigned to each chromosome is equal to 1, which means that if the area of a circle is the sum of the values of the objective function of population individuals, then each of them is associated with a circle section. In the current example, it six fields exist.

Crossover. One-point crossover. Individuals are combined sequentially in pairs:

5.39	5.8
5.8	6.51

Parent 1: [3 4 6 2 1 5]
Parent 2: [4 1 5 3 2 6]
Among the offspring duplicates of existing individuals may appear. Duplicates do not bring anything to the database all the genes are subjected to forced mutation.

Mutation. After giving birth to offspring, approx. 50 % of generation mutates.

3.2   Solution to the Problem in MATLAB

After entering all necessary data, information about the correct solution of the problem is obtained (Fig. 1). On the y-axis the accuracy of the solution (in %), and on the x-axis the number of iterations (max = 5) is given.

If the solution is optimal- accurate results in a table showing the following information:

- amount of processing at the individual plants,
- the total cost of the transportation and processing of milk,
- the cost of transport,
- the cost of processing,
- average costs,
- marginal costs,
- way of the deployment of milk.

The calculations examined several variants, the supply of milk did not change but both demand (processing capacity), and processing costs (description of function) were variable. For example, variant v1 adopted by Table 1 the following demand: for factory $S1$ - 700 m^3/month, and for the factory $S2$ - 1500 m^3/month.

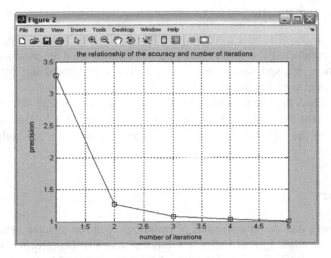

Fig. 1. The dialog box of the program - the relationship of the accuracy and the number of iterations

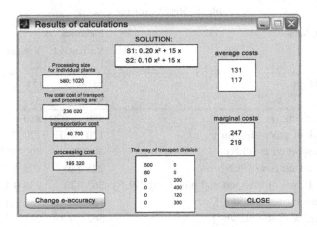

Fig. 2. Terms of the calculation in the program for variant v1

Also, based on studies carried out it was assumed that the processing functions have the following form:

$$f_1(x_1) = 15x_1 + 0.2x_1^2 \text{ and } f_2(x_2) = 15x_2 + 0.1x_1^2$$

In the case of variant V2 (data according to Table 1) adopted the demand: for factory *S1* - *1* 000 m³/month and for the factory *S2* - 1500 m³/month. Processing functions have the form:

$$f_1(x_1) = 10x_1 + 0.2x_1^2 \text{ and } f_2(x_2) = 10x_2 + 0.1x_1^2$$

3.3   Summary of Results

Collective summary of results is shown in Table 2. There is placed sample of simulation results conducted for several variants, which are varied in parameters of processing function, transportation costs, the possibility of processing by individual factory. Statement contains the best results.

The chart shows that the total cost of the task for variant v1 is 267 420 PLN and it is more than 40 000 PLN higher than the costs of the variant v2. This difference is primarily due to the fact that for small factories processing costs are higher than for larger ones.

4   Summary

The study shows that the effective use of resources spent on process management is only possible through system logistics solutions that will be effective in terms of technical information and simultaneously optimized in terms of financial outlay.

Table 2. Results for the task

Suppliers	Factories			
	Variant v1		Variant v2	
Solution	S1: $0.2x^2 + 15x$			
	S2 $0.1x^2 + 15x$			
Processing [m^3]	580	1 020	880	720
Stock of processing [m^3]	120	480	120	780
Transport costs [PLN]	40 700		40 700	
Processing costs [PLN]	226 720		195 320	
Total costs of transport and processing [PLN]	267 420		236 020	
Average costs [PLN/m^3]	186	82	131	117
Marginal costs [PLN/m^3]	362	362	247	219
The way of transport divisions				
D1	500	0	500	0
D2	80	0	80	0
D3	0	200	0	200
D4	0	400	0	400
D5	0	120	0	120
D6	0	300	300	0

The proposed work approach using solving the problem of production and transport costs with convex function should facilitate decision-making processes of transport and production management. Genetic algorithms fully confirmed its effectiveness for the problem, minimizing total costs of transport and processing.

Unlikely the classic optimizing methods that give determined outcome, the Genetic Algorithms do not guarantee finding the best solution. An efficient GA using is complex because of mutation- random component. Executing the same algorithm for the same task a few times may obtain various results.

The relationship of the accuracy and the number of iterations (Fig. 1) has been obtained and showed to find out how many iterations should be performed to achieve adequate (not random) results. Task become more complex when computing time is also significant and it is necessary to guarantee find the optimum between result accuracy and computing time or when it is required to clearly determinate if obtained solution is the best one.

References

1. Ayough, A., Zandieh, M., Farsijani, H.: GA and ICA approaches to job rotation scheduling problem: considering employee's boredom. Int. J. Adv. Manuf. Technol. **60**, 651–666 (2012)
2. Burduk, A.: Artificial neural networks as tools for controlling production systems and ensuring their stability. In: Saeed, K., Chaki, R., Cortesi, A., Wierzchoń, S. (eds.) CISIM 2013. LNCS, vol. 8104, pp. 487–498. Springer, Heidelberg (2013)
3. Govindan, K., Jha, P.C., Garg, K.: Product recovery optimization in closed-loop supply chain to improve sustainability in manufacturing. Int. J. Prod. Res. **54**(5), 1463–1486 (2016)
4. Guvenir, H.A., Erel, E.: Multicriteria inventory classification using a genetic algorithm. Eur. J. Oper. Res. **105**(1), 29–37 (1998)
5. Jachimowski, R., Kłodawski, M.: Simulated annealing algorithm for the multi-level vehicle routing problem. Logistyka **4**, 195–204 (2013)
6. Krenczyk, D., Kalinowski, K., Grabowik, C.: Integration production planning and scheduling systems for determination of transitional phases in repetitive production. In: Corchado, E., Snášel, V., Abraham, A., Woźniak, M., Graña, M., Cho, S.-B. (eds.) HAIS 2012, Part II. LNCS, vol. 7209, pp. 274–283. Springer, Heidelberg (2012)
7. Nissen V.: Evolutionary algorithms in management science. An overview and list of references. Papers on Economics & Evolution, Report No. 9303, European Study Group for Evolutionary Economics (1993)
8. Sahu, A., Tapadar, R.: Solving the assignment problem using genetic algorithm and simulated annealing. Int. J. Appl. Math. **36**(1) (2007)
9. Yusoff, M., Ariffin, J., Mohamed, A.: Solving vehicle assignment problem using evolutionary computation. In: Tan, Y., Shi, Y., Tan, K.C. (eds.) ICSI 2010, Part I. LNCS, vol. 6145, pp. 523–532. Springer, Heidelberg (2010)
10. Zegordi, S.H., Beheshti Nia, M.A.: A multi-population genetic algorithm for transportation scheduling. Transp. Res. Part E: Logist. Transp. Rev. **45**(6), 946–959 (2009)

Fast Branch and Bound Algorithm
for the Travelling Salesman Problem

Radosław Grymin$^{(\boxtimes)}$ and Szymon Jagiełło

Department of Control Systems and Mechatronics, Faculty of Electronics,
Wrocław University of Science and Technology, Wrocław, Poland
radoslaw.grymin@pwr.edu.pl

Abstract. New strategies are proposed for implementing algorithms based on *Branch and Bound* scheme. Those include two *minimal spanning tree* lower bound modifications, a design based on the fact that edges in the optimal tour can never cross in the euclidean TSP and parallelization of Branch and Bound scheme. Proposed approaches are compared with primary algorithms.

Keywords: Branch-and-Bound · Dynamic programming · Parallel algorithm

1 Introduction

Branch and Bound (Branch and Bound, BnB, branch & bound) is an approach advised for designing exact algorithms solving $\mathcal{NP}$-hard combinatorial optimization and discrete problems. Branch and Bound was introduced by Land and Doig in 1960 [10]. Until the late 1970s, it was the state-of-the-art method for almost all big and complex problems that could not be solved by other techniques known at that time. And it is still used everywhere, where small improvement of solution leads to big rise in profits. Branch and Bound uses a tree search strategy to implicitly enumerate all possible solutions to a given problem, applying pruning rules to eliminate regions of the search space that cannot lead to a better solution [11].

In this article we are considering a minimization problem and the whole used terminology relates to it. In order to optimally solve the problem, Branch and Bound algorithm divides the whole set of solutions $\mathcal{X}$ into mutually exclusive and exhaustive subsets $\mathcal{X}_j$, where $j \in \mathcal{S} = \{1, 2, 3, \ldots, s\}$. In every moment of its work, algorithm stores the best found solution so far x_{ub} and its value called *upper bound* and the set of subsets not yet analysed. Branch and Bound does not search these subsets to which it is assured that they do not contain optimal solution x^*, so it is much more effective than an exhaustive search. Decision, if some subset should be analysed or not, is based on its bound and objective function value counted for currently best found solution $K(x_{\mathrm{ub}})$. For minimization problem, such bound is called *lower bound* and it is lower or equal to all objective function values evaluated for every element of related subset. It is marked as LB. If for a certain subset, the lower bound is equal or greater than the value of the best solution found so

© IFIP International Federation for Information Processing 2016
Published by Springer International Publishing Switzerland 2016. All Rights Reserved
K. Saeed and W. Homenda (Eds.): CISIM 2016, LNCS 9842, pp. 206–217, 2016.
DOI: 10.1007/978-3-319-45378-1_19

far, such subset is removed from the set of subsets not yet analysed and will be no more considered. A good lower bound is a basic requirement for an efficient Branch and Bound minimization procedure [12].

The idea of Travelling Salesman Problem, TSP for short, relies in visiting every city by the sale representative from the given set of n cities exactly once [9], starting from and returning to the home city. In this article we are considering a symmetric TSP, where the distance between two cities is the same in each opposite direction. We also assume that there is a direct connection from each node to every other one. Formally, this problem is described as a search for the shortest Hamiltonian cycle [7] in the complete and symmetric graph $\mathcal{K}_n = (\mathcal{V}_n, \mathcal{E}_n)$ containing $n = |\mathcal{V}_n|$ nodes and $m = |\mathcal{E}_n| = \binom{n}{2}$ edges. Nodes are numbered from 1 to n. We assume without loss of generality that the home city is the node with index number 1. Edge e, which connects nodes i and j, is marked as $\{i, j\}$ or $\{j, i\}$ and their distances are stored in the distance matrix D_n.

Branch and Bound algorithm for TSP constructs solutions by visiting cities. On each step there may be more than one remaining city to visit. The process of constructing solutions can be presented as a decision tree. Each node in such tree refers to a subset of the solution set and a lower bound can be established for it. Branch and Bound algorithm creates solutions by exploring such tree. It will not visit these nodes of the decision tree, for which it has certainty that it will not lead to the optimal solution.

The role of parallel algorithms in solving NP-hard problems significantly increased in the last decade. Bożejko proposed an improvement for speeding up the process of solving a single machine scheduling problem with total tardiness cost function by parallelization of generation of paths [2], a parallel genetic algorithm for the flow shop scheduling problem [4] and a method for solving permutational routing problems by population-based metaheuristics [5]. The same author designed new parallel objective function determination methods for the job shop scheduling [3] and flow shop [1] problems. Jagiełło and Żelazny proposed a parallel cost function approach for the Distance Constrained Vehicle Routing Problem which was designed to work on Graphics Processing Units (GPUs) [8]. In this paper we propose a parallel Branch and Bound design for the TSP problem.

2   Lower Bounds

The *lower bound* $LB(\mathcal{X}_j)$ for a given node in the decision tree (that reflects to a certain set of solutions $\mathcal{X}_j$) is evaluated as a sum of the travelled distance $MIL(\mathcal{X}_j)$ and the lower estimation of the remaining distance $LE(\mathcal{X}_j)$,

$$LB(\mathcal{X}_j) = MIL(\mathcal{X}_j) + LE(\mathcal{X}_j). \tag{1}$$

It should be noted, when the travelling salesman visited k cities, the remaining way is a Hamiltonian path starting from the last visited city, that visits every city not visited so far and returning to the home city. It is showed in Fig. 1.

The *lower estimation* estimates from the bottom an overall length of such shortest Hamiltonian path. This path is described by the following properties:

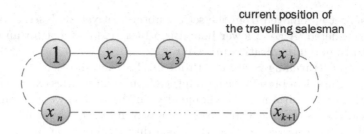

Fig. 1. Searched Hamiltonian cycle. The tour that has to be passed is marked by the dashed line.

(a) it does not visit already visited k nodes,
(b) each node of the considered graph is visited only once,
(c) there exists a subpath linking every two nodes of the considered graph,
(d) it assumes beginning and ending node,
(e) if the number of not visited cities is greater than one and travelling salesman is not currently in the home city, he cannot directly pass the way from the current city to some not visited city and immediately return to the home city,
(f) it is built from $n - k + 1$ edges,
(g) the first and the last city of the Hamiltonian path are connected with only one city.

By the relaxation of above constraints, we get *lower estimation* of the remaining distance $LE(\mathcal{X}_j)$. The weaker relaxation, the greater value of the lower estimation and it leads to better *lower estimation* (that rejects more solutions).

The Total Length of the Shortest Feasible Connections. The weakest and the most simple *lower estimation LE* of the remaining distance is obtained by counting the total length of the shortest not visited edges. It satisfies the constraints (a) and (b). Relaxation of constraints involves removal of constraints (b), (c), (d), (e), (f) and (g).

In order to evaluate the *lower estimation*, the distances associated with the inaccessible connections are removed from the weight matrix. Firstly, zeros from the main diagonal are removed. If the travelling salesman comes out from the city i, the numbers in the row with index i should be removed from the weight matrix. Afterwards, if travelling salesman enters the city with index j and it is not a home city, then from the weight matrix, values from the column j are removed. Moreover, if city with index j is not a second last one (such city, after which travelling salesman returns to the home city), value d_{j1} must be removed from the weight matrix. We determine the number of the remaining connections r that have to be passed as

$$r = n - k + 1, \tag{2}$$

where n is the number of all cities and k is the number of visited cities.

Values that were not removed from the weight matrix are sorted in the non-decreasing order and form a finite sequence (a_n). The sum of the first r values is the *lower estimation* of the remaining distance. Then, the *lower bound* can be computed from (1).

The Weight of the Minimum Spanning Tree. In this case, the *lower estimation* of the remaining distance LE and the *lower bound* is equal to the weight of the minimum spanning tree for the complete sub-graph that consists of the city where actually the travelling salesman is located x_k, not having visited cities so far $\{x_{k+1}, x_{k+2}, x_{k+3}, \ldots, x_n\}$ and the home city $x_1 = 1$. It satisfies the constraints (a), (c) and (f). Relaxation involves removal of the constraints (b), (d), (e) and (g). In order to evaluate the minimum spanning tree weight, Prim's algorithm is used. When the weight of the minimum spanning tree is computed (and it is also a value of the *lower estimation LE*), (1) will be used to determine the *lower bound.*

The Weight of the Minimum Spanning Tree – 1st Modification. Algorithm was proposed by Mariusz Makuchowski from Department of Control Systems and Mechatronics of Wrocław University of Science and Technology (personal communication, November 3, 2014). The *lower estimation* of the remaining distance is evaluated as a sum of minimum spanning tree weight for graph consisting of the cities not having been visited so far $\{x_{k+1}, x_{k+2}, x_{k+3}, \ldots, x_n\}$ and the home city $x_1 = 1$ and the sum of weights of two shortest edges connecting the home city with nearest not visited edge and the current city with nearest not visited edge. If travelling salesman is currently in the home city, *lower estimation* is counted as a sum of the weight of minimal spanning tree in the graph containing not visited cities and doubled distance from the home city to the nearest not visited node. It satisfies the constraints (a), (c), (f) and (g). Relaxation involves removal of the constraints (b), (d) and (e).

The Weight of the Minimum Spanning Tree – 2nd Modification. It is the improved version of the previous algorithm. The *lower estimation* of the remaining distance is evaluated as a sum of minimum spanning tree weight for graph consisting of not visited cities $\{x_{k+1}, x_{k+2}, x_{k+3}, \ldots, x_n\}$ and the sum of two weights of edges connecting the home city and the current city with not visited cities (and these cities must be different). If the travelling salesman is currently in the home city, the *lower estimation* is a sum of weight of the minimum spanning tree in graph containing not visited cities and the sum of two weights of shortest edges connecting home city with different not visited cities so far. It satisfies constraints (a), (c), (e), (f) and (g). Relaxation involves removal of constraints (b) and (d).

3 Priority of Analysed Sets

The order in which the algorithm searches the decision tree is very important. The size of the priority queue will grow fast if leaves are rarely visited and new upper bounds will not be found. The algorithm must have a tendency to search the graph towards leaves. By assigning a priority to sets stored in the priority queue we control the way the algorithm will search the decision tree.

We chose the following way of counting priority that promotes subsets with the lowest increase of lower bound

$$P = \frac{1}{AI}, \tag{3}$$

$$AI = \frac{LB}{k}. \tag{4}$$

where P, AI, LB and k denote the subsets priority in the queue, the mean increase of the lower bound, the lower bound and the number of visited cities accordingly.

4   Parallel Branch and Bound Algorithm

In the parallel algorithm we use a pool approach with arbitrary fixed number of processes. It means that program executes in several processes and one of them will be called *supervisory process* and the rest will be called *worker processes* (see Fig. 2). In the initialization phase, *supervisory process* reads the instance data from the TSPLIB file, generates the weight matrix and distributes it to all *worker processes*. It also establishes the best solution found so far and the upper bound by running 2-opt algorithm on the result of the nearest neighbour algorithm. It stores the priority queue of solution sets not analysed so far and the best solution so far.

During computation phase, if some *worker process* notifies the *supervisory process* about its idle state via WORKER_FINISHED_TASK message and if there are still some solutions sets to be analysed in the priority queue, the supervisory process pops the first solution set with the highest priority and sends it to the *worker process* via PERFORM_TASK_REQ message and stores the information that the process is performing task. Algorithm stops when there are no more sets in the priority queue to analyse and if all worker processes informed *supervisory process* that they finished analysing task by sending WORKER_FINISHED_TASK.

Each *worker process* stores the upper bound value. If some *worker process* found a solution with the objective function value smaller than the upper bound, it sends this solution with upper bound update proposal to the *supervisory process* in UPPER_BOUND message. The *supervisory process* checks if the proposed upper bound value is better than the currently stored one. If it is true, the new best solution so far and the new upper bound value are stored in the *supervisory process*, the new upper bound value is distributed to all *worker processes* in the UPPER_BOUND message except one which found it and all subsets with the lower bound greater than the new upper bound are removed from the priority queue. Otherwise, the new proposed upper bound value is discarded. Such check is important in a situation when two workers find better solutions (with different objective function values) than the best solution found so far and simultaneously send proposal to the *supervisory process* for changing the best solution found so far and the upper bound. If the *supervisory process* obtains upper bound with smaller value first, it will update upper bound and when it obtains one with greater value, second upper bound value change proposal will be discarded after the check.

Worker processes divide set obtained in the PERFORM_TASK_REQ message into subsets. If the subset has only one element it means that the worker found a solution. Otherwise, if obtained subsets contains more than one element, it calculates lower bounds for them. On the basis of the lower bound and the upper bound it is established if the optimal solution can belong to the obtained subset. If it is true, the subset is send back to the *supervisory process* via TASK_PUSH_REQ.

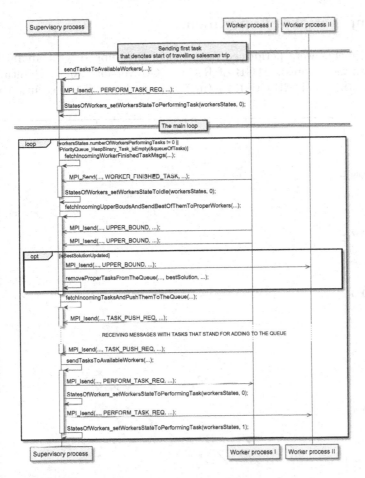

Fig. 2. Sequence diagram that describes solving TSP by the Parallel Branch and Bound algorithm. The initialization part of algorithm was omitted.

5   Intersections in Euclidean TSP

The edges in an optimal tour can never cross in an euclidean TSP. If edges $\{i, k\}$ and $\{j, l\}$ did cross, they would constitute the diagonals of a quadrilateral $\{i, j, k, l\}$ and could profitably be replaced by a pair of opposite sides [6]. Instances for which all points are located on the same line are the only exceptions. Based on that fact two algorithms were proposed. The first one is a modification of the *Brute force* method the second is an adjustment of the *Branch and Bound (Branch and Cut)* approach. Before adding an edge to the current sub-tour it is probed for crossings with any of the edges of the current sub-tour. If an intersection occurs, the edge will not be added, thus the whole branch will be omitted.

6   Computational Experiments

The experiments were performed on a machine equipped with an Intel X980 CPU (6 physical cores), 24 GB of RAM, GCC version 4.6.3 (Ubuntu/Linaro 4.6.3-1ubuntu5) and MPICH 1.4.1 (mpic++, mpirun). The execution time of

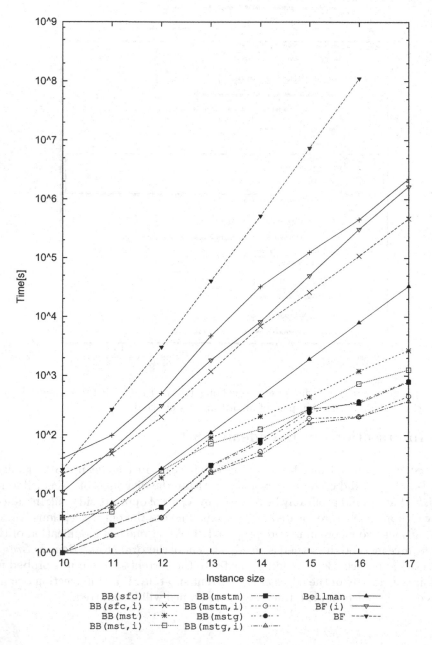

Fig. 3. Execution time for random data (log_{10} scale)

the specified approaches was measured. The sequential algorithms put under test were:

- *Branch and Bound* (*Branch and Cut*) with four different lower bound approaches and without and with intersection checking:
  - the shortest feasible connections (BB(sfc), BB(sfc,i)),
  - the minimum spanning tree (BB(mst), BB(mst,i)),
  - the minimum spanning tree – 1st modification (BB(mstm), BB(mstm,i)),
  - the minimum spanning tree – 2nd modification (BB(mstg), BB(mstg,i)).
- Bellman-Held-Karp dynamic algorithm (Bellman),
- Brute force without and with intersections checking (BF, BF(i)).

For the reason that the algorithms were compared with Brute force method only small problem instances were used. TSPLIB contained only two benchmarks, which fulfilled this requirement: *burma14* and *ulysses16*. The results obtained from working with those data sets are presented in Table 1.

Table 1. Execution time for selected benchmarks

Instance	Time[s]			
	BB(sfc)	BB(sfc,i)	BB(mst)	BB(mst,i)
burma14	21.5	5.4	0.8	0.4
ulysses16	125930.3	4703.4	375.9	54.2

Instance	Time[s]			
	BB(mstm)	BB(mstm,i)	BB(mstg)	BB(mstg,i)
burma14	0.3	0.2	0.3	0.2
ulysses16	138.8	26.9	117.2	23.3

Instance	Time[s]		
	Bellman	BF	BF(i)
burma14	0.5	500.6	18.6
ulysses16	7.9	109855.2	423.3

It is quite interesting that the dynamic programming design performed so well as it performed best out of all algorithms for the *ulysses16* data set. A single case is unfortunately not enough for accurate conclusions. Due to the small number of available benchmarks 7 random instances of sizes from 10 to 17 were generated. Function *rand* (stdlib) initialized with the seed 734834 was used to obtain x,y values from the range from 0 to 100. The results were presented in Table 2 and in Fig. 3.

The BF method was not tested against the *rand17* instance for the reason that the experiment would take too long (estimated 22 days). The results clearly indicate that the BF and BB algorithms benefit from checking intersections. The modified BB method was vastly faster than its basic version for each

Table 2. Execution time for random data

	Time[s]			
Instance	BB(sfc)	BB(sfc,i)	BB(mst)	BB(mst,i)
rand10	40	22	4	4
rand11	98	48	6	5
rand12	502	200	19	25
rand13	4730	1181	90	72
rand14	32429	6933	206	126
rand15	123877	25805	438	272
rand16	450761	107754	1197	734
rand17	2224033	467889	2693	1266

	Time[s]			
Instance	BB(mstm)	BB(mstm,i)	BB(mstg)	BB(mstg,i)
rand10	1	1	1	1
rand11	3	2	3	2
rand12	6	4	6	4
rand13	31	24	30	23
rand14	82	53	74	46
rand15	272	191	238	159
rand16	348	206	371	202
rand17	791	454	814	374

	Time[s]		
Instance	Bellman	BF	BF(i)
rand10	2	26	11
rand11	7	270	55
rand12	27	3050	313
rand13	109	40627	1840
rand14	456	516886	8200
rand15	1895	7363261	49481
rand16	7912	111510649	308037
rand17	33052	————	1642004

lower estimation. Even the BF(i) method has been proved to be working faster than the BB(sfc) algorithm. Both *mst* lower bound adjustments (1-Makuchowski, 2-Grymin) proved to be superior compared to the standard approach. As expected the dynamic programming technique operated faster than BB(sfc), BB(sfc,i), BF and BB(i) but slower than *mst* based BB designs (*rand10* is the only exception). The BB(mstg,i) method turned out to be the leading solution resulting in shortest execution times for each test instance. Instance size dependent speedup obtained in comparison to the BF, Bellman and BB(mst) algorithms is presented in Fig. 4.

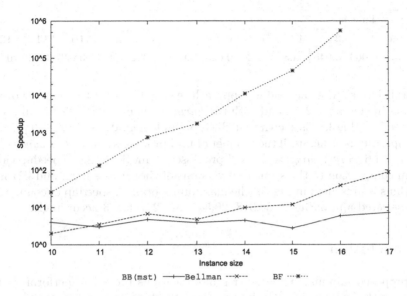

Fig. 4. BB(mstg,i) speedup compared to selected algorithms for the burma14 benchmark (log_{10} scale)

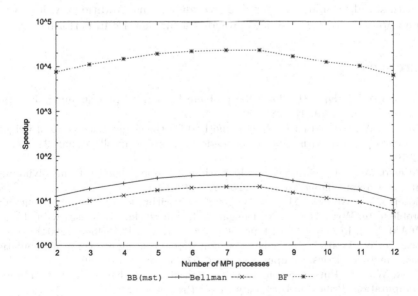

Fig. 5. BB(mstg,i) speedup compared to selected algorithms (log_{10} scale)

Table 3. Parallel $BB(mstg,i)$

	Time[s]										
Instance	2	3	4	5	6	7	8	9	10	11	12
burma14	0.066	0.045	0.034	0.026	0.023	0.022	0.022	0.030	0.040	0.049	0.079

Parallel version of the leading approach was tested with the number of mpi processes in the range 2–12 and with the *burma14* benchmark. The results were presented in Table 3. It is shown that the mpi implementation utilizes all physical cores. Speedup is rising until the number of mpi processes equals 7 (1 *supervisory process* and 6 *worker processes*). MPI processes count dependent speedup calculated in comparison to the sequential versions of the BF, Bellman and BB(mst) algorithms is presented in Fig. 5. The maximum obtained speedup in comparison to the selected approaches is 38.318, 20.545 and 22755.273 accordingly.

7 Conclusion

Both proposed minimal spanning tree modifications proved to perform greatly faster than the base version. The intersections checking approach was successfully combined with Branch And Bound and Brute force designs and provided additional improvements. The Branch and Bound used with 2nd minimum spanning tree modification as lower estimation algorithm and combined with intersections checking mechanism turned out to be the best solution and achieved a massive speedup when compared to the Brute force, Bellman, and Branch and Bound used with standard minimal spanning tree algorithms. Additionally, its parallel version appeared to scale well and provided a further rise in performance.

References

1. Bożejko, W.: Solving the flow shop problem by parallel programming. J. Parallel Distrib. Comput. **69**, 470–481 (2009)
2. Bożejko, W.: Parallel path relinking method for the single machine total weighted tardiness problem with sequence-dependent setups. J. Intell. Manuf. **21**, 777–785 (2010)
3. Bożejko, W.: On single-walk parallelization of the job shop problem solving algorithms. Comput. Oper. Res. **39**, 2258–2264 (2012)
4. Bożejko, W., Wodecki, M.: Parallel genetic algorithm for the flow shop scheduling problem. In: Wyrzykowski, R., Dongarra, J., Paprzycki, M., Waśniewski, J. (eds.) PPAM 2004. LNCS, vol. 3019, pp. 566–571. Springer, Heidelberg (2004)
5. Bożejko, W., Wodecki, M.: Solving permutational routing problems by population-based metaheuristics. Comput. Ind. Eng. **57**(1), 269–276 (2009)
6. Cook, W.J.: In Pursuit of the Traveling Salesman: Mathematics at the Limits of Computation. Princeton University Press, Princeton (2012)
7. Feiring, B.: An efficient procedure for obtaining feasible solutions to the n-city traveling salesman problem. Math. Comput. Modell. **13**(3), 67–71 (1990)

8. Jagiełło, S., Żelazny, D.: Solving multi-criteria vehicle routing problem by parallel tabu search on GPU. Procedia Comput. Sci. **18**, 2529–2532 (2013)
9. Jünger, M., Rinaldi, G., Reinelt, G.: The traveling salesman problem. Handbooks Oper. Res. Manage. Sci. **7**, 225–330 (1995)
10. Land, A.H., Doig, A.G.: An automatic method of solving discrete programming problems. Econometrica: J. Econometric Soc. **28**, 497–520 (1960)
11. Morrison, D.R., Jacobson, S.H., Sauppe, J.J., Sewell, E.C.: Branch-and-Bound algorithms: a survey of recent advances in searching, branching, and pruning. Discrete Optim. **19**, 79–102 (2016)
12. Toffolo, T.A.M., Wauters, T., Malderen, S.V., Berghe, G.V.: Branch-and-Bound with decomposition-based lower bounds for the Traveling Umpire Problem. Eur. J. Oper. Res. **250**(3), 737–744 (2016)

Simulations for Tuning a Laser Power Control System of the Cladding Process

Piotr Jurewicz[1], Wojciech Rafajłowicz[2], Jacek Reiner[1],
and Ewaryst Rafajłowicz[2(✉)]

[1] Faculty of Mechanical Engineering,
Wrocław University of Science and Technology, Wrocław, Poland
jacek.reiner@pwr.edu.pl
[2] Faculty of Electronics, Wrocław University of Science and Technology,
Wrocław, Poland
ewaryst.rafajlowicz@pwr.edu.pl

Abstract. Our aim is present the methodology of simulations for repetitive processes and tuning control systems for them in the presence of noise. This methodology is applied for tuning a laser power control system of the cladding process. Even the simplest model of this process is nonlinear, making analytical tuning rather difficult. The proposed approach allows us to select quickly the structure of the control system and to optimize its parameters. Preliminary comparisons with experimental results on a robot-based laser cladding systems are also reported. These comparisons are based on the temperature measurements, observations by a camera and IR camera.

Keywords: Control system · Simulations · IR camera · Laser cladding

1 Introduction

Additive manufacturing for building (or printing) 3D structures, e.g., laser cladding process is apparently one of the most promising cost and time intensive technologies. A laser power control is a crucial factor for the high quality of the cladding process (see [13]). Other factors that influence building a 3D body from a melted powder include the powder supply rate and the velocity of the laser head movements. The process is so complicated that several models of it have been proposed (see, e.g., [6,8]), but even the simplest of them – adopted from [13] also in this paper – is described by a nonlinear differential equation, which has to be extended by adding differential equations of a controller and a filter. Thus, the proper selection of the control system structure and tuning of its parameters requires extensive simulations, because direct experiments on a real systems are forbidden as being dangerous – the laser power is about 1 kW. The construction of the robot that performs movements of the laser head is shown in Fig. 1 (left panel), while the right panel shows the laser head with a camera that looks at the cladding process along the laser beam. Notice that in [1] an

© IFIP International Federation for Information Processing 2016
Published by Springer International Publishing Switzerland 2016. All Rights Reserved
K. Saeed and W. Homenda (Eds.): CISIM 2016, LNCS 9842, pp. 218–229, 2016.
DOI: 10.1007/978-3-319-45378-1_20

original, alternative construction that is specifically designed station, which is based on a three-axis CNC machine equipped with the laser head. The results presented in this paper are expected to be useful also for this new construction.

Our aim in this paper is to propose a methodology for running such simulations. The needs for an extension of control systems simulations methodology stems from the following features of the laser cladding:

- the process is a repetitive one, i.e., the laser heating head moves back and forth when developing a 3D object (see [12] for a review of repetitive processes and their applications),
- radiation/optical sensors (e.g. camera, pyrometer) or thermovision – infra-red camera can be used for the process monitoring,
- the repetitive process is time-varying between the passes of the laser head (see the right panel in Fig. 2, where the temperature of a hot, melted metal lake is gradually growing from pass to pass).

Notice that similar features are present in 3D printers and in other additive, powder based technologies, which can make the methodology proposed here more universal.

From the view-point of the designing a control system our in this paper goals are the following:

1. to tune parameters of the PI controller so as to minimize a control quality criterion that is specific for the laser power control task, namely, we penalize too large jumps of the laser power,
2. to decide whether a filter that makes the control signal smoother should be used or not.

The reason for considering the second goal is in extremely large variations in measurements of the lake temperature. This fact can be seen in Fig. 2 (right panel), in which one can observe spikes that differ by ±50–100 degrees from the mean temperature of the surroundings, while typical errors are at the levels ±20. These errors are caused either by image processing, since it is very difficult to locate the hottest place of the lake (see Fig. 2 – left panel) or by a pyrometer that averages the lake temperature, but at the turning points it averages partly the lake temperature and partly the temperature of the surrounding (see [3] for extensive investigations of cladding profess by IR camera). One can expect that such a filter will act also as an anti-wind up module (see, e.g., [7] for practical explanations of wind-up phenomenon in control systems with PI controllers). The paper is organized as follows. In the next section we describe the models of:

- the dependence of the lake temperature on the laser power,
- proportional-integral (PI) controller,
- control signal smoothing module

and the methodology of simulations is presented. Then, we use this methodology to reach the two goals mentioned above. Finally, we present an excerpt of the results obtained from experimental implementation of the proposed control system.

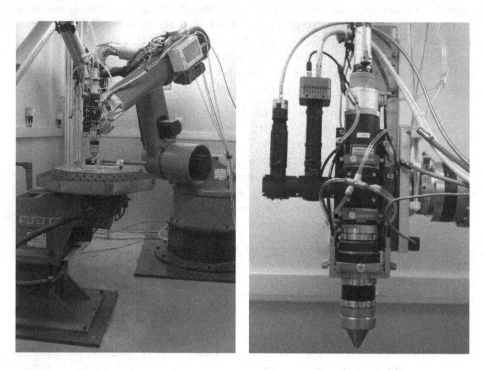

Fig. 1. Cladding robot (left panel) and the laser head with a camera (right panel)

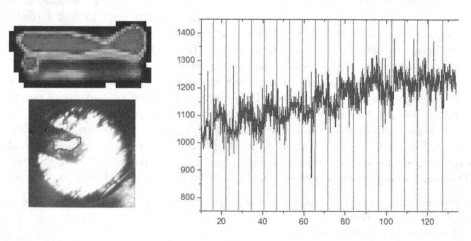

Fig. 2. Left panel – image of the first cladding pass with the lake marked (lower left panel) and IR image of the lake (upper left panel). Temperatures of the lake – several cladding passes (right panel)

2   Laser Power Control – Model and Simulation Methodology

A mathematical model for one laser pass of the dependence between the laser power $Q(t)$ and the lake temperature $y(t)$ has been adapted from the paper of Tang and Landers Part I [13] (later abbreviated as TL). It has the following form:

$$\tau y'(t) + y(t) = K\,(Q(t))^\beta, \quad y(0) = y_0 \tag{1}$$

where y_0 - given initial temperature. The constants in (1) are defined as follows (compare [13]):

- $\beta = 6.25\,10^{-2}$ is an experimentally selected constant,
- $\tau = 2.96\,10^{-2}$ – in sec. is the system time constant.

Overall system gain K (amplification) is defined by

$$K = K_1\,(V^\alpha)\,(M^\gamma) = 1413.58, \tag{2}$$

where:

- $K_1 = 0.5\,10^\beta\,1.42\,10^3$ is empirically established system amplification,
- $V = 3.4$ in mm/sec is the laser traverse speed,
- $M = 4.0$ in g/min – the powder supply rate,
- $\alpha = -7.1\,10^{-3}$ and $\gamma = 3.0*10^{-3}$ experimentally selected constants.

In [5] a more exact nonlinear model for the lake temperature is derived that takes into account also the laser head position. One can incorporate this model in our simulation methodology, replacing (1) by the model from [5]. However, model (1) occurred to be sufficiently exact for a constant speed of the laser head, since then t simultaneously specifies the head position.

For a multi-pass cladding process we have to extend model (1) by including the heat exchange between passes. We propose the simplest model that can incorporate the influence of the temperature at k-th pass $y_k(t)$ on the temperature at $(k + 1)$ pass, i.e., $y_{k+1}(t)$ of the following form: for passes $k = 0, 1 \ldots$

$$\tau\,y'_{k+1}(t) + y_{k+1}(t) = K\,(W_{k+1}(t))^\beta + \xi\,y_k(t), \quad y_{k+1}(0) = Y_k(0), \ t \in (0, T), \tag{3}$$

where $T > 0$ is the pass length (the time that the laser head needs to travel along a 3D object under construction), $W_k(t)$ is the laser power at k-th pass at time t, while ξ is the coefficient that governs the influence of the temperature at k-th pass, denoted as $Y_k(t)$, on the lake temperature at the next pass. Due to forth and back movements of the laser head, for $t \in [0, T]$ $Y_k(t)$ is defined as follows:

$$Y_k(t) = \begin{cases} y_k(t) & \text{if} & k \text{ odd}, \\ y_k(T - t) & \text{if} & k \text{ even} \end{cases} \tag{4}$$

In order to run (3) we need also the initial condition along the pass, which is assumed to be $Y_0(t) = Y_0 = const, t \in [0, T]$, where Y_0 is the temperature of the base.

temp.

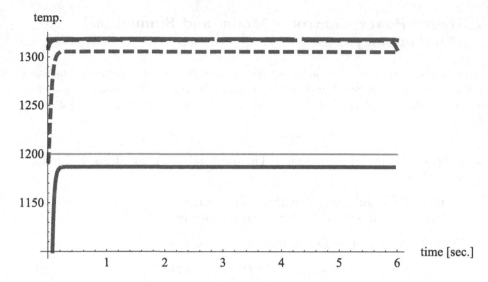

Fig. 3. The results of pass-to-pass simulations – the lake temperature growth from pass 1 (solid curve) through pass 2 (the shortest dashed line) to pass 4 (the longest dashed line). The solid straight line – the desired temperature of the lake

To check model (3), it was run with a constant laser power $W = 0.2\,\mathrm{kW}$. The results are shown in Fig. 3. Comparing it to Fig. 2 (right panel) one can observe similar qualitative behavior, i.e., the lake temperature grows from pass to pass, and then it stabilizes at the level of about 1250–1300 °C. Notice that in Fig. 3 the temperatures from subsequent passes are tilled, while in Fig. 2 they are joined serially.

The analysis of Fig. 2 reveals why a control system for the lake temperature stabilization is necessary. Namely, at the points where the laser head turns back one can observe the essential growth of the lake temperature, since at a short time the laser operates twice at the same regions, near the end points. In [7] the proportional-integral (PI) controller is proposed, together by an anti-wind-up by the feedback from the saturation block to the input of PI controller. The control system scheme that is proposed in this paper is depicted in Fig. 4. It consists of PI-controller followed by a control signal smoothing module. The PI-controller that is usually described as follows:

$$q(t) = K \left(e(t) + \frac{1}{T_i} \int_0^t e(\tau)\,d\tau \right), \tag{5}$$

where $K > 0$ is the amplification, $T_i > 0$ is the time of doubling of the error signal $e(t)$, while $q(t)$ is the controller output. For the purposes of our simulations it is convenient to rewrite (5) as follows:

$$q_k(t) = K_P e_k(t) + K_I \int_0^t e_k(\tau)\,d\tau, \tag{6}$$

where $K_P > 0$ is the amplification of P-that, $K_I > 0$ is the amplification of I-path, $e_k(t) = y_{ref}(t) - y_k(t)$ is the tracking error at k-th pass and $y_{ref}(t)$ is the reference signal, which is assumed to be constant[1] in this paper. The integral term in (6) reduces the tracking error and reduces the laser power variability. However, due to large measurement errors, this reduction is not sufficient. For this reason, the control smoothing exponentially weighted moving average (CSEWMA) filter is added in the control loop (see Fig. 4). In fact, CSEWMA is a low pass filter with a specific parametrization that allows its intuitive tuning (see [10]). Being the low-pass filter, CSEWMA acts also as an anti-wind-up device by reducing large changes of the laser power. For our purposes the CSEWMA filter is described as follows:

$$W_k'(t) = -h\, W_k(t) + h\, q_k(t), \quad W_k(0) = W_k^0, \qquad (7)$$

where W_k^0 is defined as

$$W_k^0 = \begin{cases} W_{k-1}(0) & \text{if} \quad k \text{ odd}, \\ W_{k-1}(T) & \text{if} \quad k \text{ even}. \end{cases} \qquad (8)$$

while $0 < h < 1$ is a smoothing parameter. Its role is easy to interpret when a finite difference approximation is considered:

$$W_k(t + \Delta t) = (1 - h\, \Delta t)\, W_k(t) + h\, \Delta t\, q_k(t). \qquad (9)$$

Hence, the output of the filter at $t + \Delta t$ is a weighted combination of its older output $W_k(t)$ and its input $q_k(t)$. Smaller values of h force more smoothing.

Algorithm 1 – Algorithm for Simulating a Repetitive Control System

Step (0) Select $K_P > 0$, $K_I > 0$, $0 < h < 1$, $y_{ref}(t)$ and the number of passes $kmax$. Set pass counter $k = 1$ and $Y_0(t) = Y_0$, $t \in [0\,T]$.

Step (1) Solve the following system of coupled differential and integral equations for $t \in (0, T)$

$$\tau\, y_k'(t) + y_k(t) = K\, (W_{k+1}(t))^\beta + \xi\, Y_{k-1}(t), \quad y_{k+1}(0) = Y_k(0), \qquad (10)$$

$$q_k(t) = K_P\, (y_{ref}(t) - y_k(t)) + K_I \int_0^t (y_{ref}(\tau) - y_k(\tau))\, d\tau, \qquad (11)$$

$$W_k'(t) = -h\, W_k(t) + h\, q_k(t), \quad W_k(0) = W_k^0. \qquad (12)$$

Step (2) Update $Y_k(t)$ and W_k^0 according to, (4) and (8), respectively. If $k < kmax$, set $k := k + 1$ and go to Step 1), otherwise, STOP.

---

[1] It is reasonable to consider also time-varying $y_{ref}(t)$ so as to compensate a shape of 3D body at the laser turning points, but the discussion on this is outside the scope of our paper.

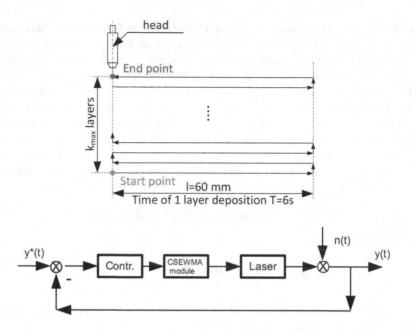

Fig. 4. Upper panel – the scheme of laser cladding as a repetitive process. Lower panel – a closed loop system with a controller combined with the CSEWMA module – control along the pass

Several remarks are in order concerning the above algorithm.

1. The pass index k is used for $y_k(t)$, $W_k(t)$ and $q_k(t)$ for readability. However, in the implementation it suffices to store only four lists that contain the sampled versions of current $W_k(t)$ and $q_k(t)$ as well as sampled versions of $y_{new}(t)$ and $y_{old}(t)$ to store the sampled versions of $y_k(t)$ and $y_{k-1}(t)$, respectively, and then to change the contents of $y_{old}(t)$ by $y_{new}(t)$ at Step 2.
2. The algorithm has been extensively tested by the authors. The excerpt of the results is shown in Fig. 6.
3. A general construction of the algorithm is applicable for simulating repetitive control systems for other processes. To this end, it suffices to replace (10) by another one (or by the set of differential equations).
4. The control system in Algorithm 1 is nonlinear. However, the static nonlinearity is rather weak and for verifying the system stability along the pass we can use the results form [12], Chap. 7.5 for a linearized system.

3   Tuning the Control System by Simulations

Our aim in this section is to propose the methodology of running simulations for tuning the control system, i.e., selecting parameters of PI controller and CSEWMA block.

A control quality index $J(K_I, h, D)$ depends on parameter K_I of PI controller, parameter h of CSEWMA block and on $kmax \times N$ matrix D of observation errors. This matrix consists of rows $\bar{d}^{(k} \stackrel{def}{=} [d_1^{(k)}, d_2^{(k)}, \ldots, d_N^{(k)}]$, where $d_n^{(k)}$'s are realizations of independent random variables with zero mean and a probability distribution selected by the user. For $J(K_I, h, D)$ we propose to take the following expression:

$$J(K_I, h, D) = \Delta \sum_{n=1}^{N} |y_{ref}(t_n) - \hat{y}_{kmax}(t_n, d_n)| + \gamma \Delta \sum_{n=2}^{N} |W_{kmax}(t_n) - W_{kmax}(t_{n-1})|,$$

(13)

where $\Delta > 0$ is the sampling period ($N\Delta = T$), $\gamma > 0$ is the weight of the second penalty term, while $\hat{y}_{kmax}(t_n, d_n)$ is defined as

$$\hat{y}_{kmax}(t_n, d_n^{(kmax)}) = y_{kmax}(t_n) + d_n^{(kmax)}, \quad n = 1, 2, \ldots N,$$

(14)

where $y_{kmax}(t_n)$ is obtained from the last pass of Algorithm 1 at n-th sampling instant. Notice that $\hat{y}_{kmax}(t_n, d_n^{(kmax)})$ indirectly depend on all earlier realizations of random errors, since in Algorithm 1 we use the following expression:

$$\hat{q}_k(t) = K_P \left(y_{ref}(t) - \hat{y}_k(t) \right) + K_I \int_0^t \left(y_{ref}(\tau) - \hat{y}_k(\tau) \right) d\tau,$$

(15)

instead of (11), with obvious changes also in (12). In (15) $\hat{y}_k(t)$) is a noise corrupted version of $y_k(t)$) that is obtained as follows: after calculating $y_k(t)$ (by solving (10)) this signal is sampled and corrupted by random disturbances:

$$\hat{y}_k(t_n, d_n^{(k)}) = y_k(t_n) + d_n^{(k)}, \quad n = 1, 2, \ldots, N.$$

(16)

Then, $\hat{y}_k(t)$) is obtained by interpolating $\hat{y}_k(t_n, d_n^{(k)})$.

The first term in (13) is the mean absolute deviation of the system output from the reference value. The second term in (13) is less obvious in control theory. It is a penalty for too large changes in a control signal, i.e., the laser power in our case. Notice that this term is similar to, but not the same as, the total variation, which is the norm in the space of functions with bounded variation (see, e.g., [2] for the definition and properties.).

Taking into account that D's is randomly generated, we have to average $J(K_I, h, D)$ also with respect to D. The following algorithm calculates the averaged quality index for fixed K_I and h

$$\tilde{J}(K_I, h) = j_{max}^{-1} \sum_{j=1}^{j_{max}} J(K_I, h, D^{(j)}),$$

(17)

where $D^{(j)}$ is j-th realization of random matrix D, while j_{max} is the number of samples used for averaging.

Algorithm 2 – Algorithm for Estimating Quality of a Repetitive Control System for Fixed Tuning Parameters

Step (0) Select $K_P > 0$, $K_I > 0$, $0 < h < 1$, $y_{ref}(t)$ and the number of repetitions j_{max}. Set run counter $j = 1$ and $S = 0$.

Step (1) Generate a random matrix $D^{(j)}$ and use its elements in (16).

Step (2) Run Algorithm 1 with (15) replaced by (11).

Step (3) Calculate $J(K_I, h, D^{(j)})$ according to (13) and update $S = S + J(K_I, h, D^{(j)})/j_{max}$.

Step (4) If $j < j_{max}$, set $j := j + 1$ and go to Step 1). Otherwise, STOP with S as the output.

Having Algorithm 2 at our disposal we can optimize $\tilde{J}(K_I, h)$ with respect to K_I and h (and possibly other parameters of the control system). To this end, one can use one of many available and well known global optimization algorithms, e.g., genetic or evolutionary algorithms (see, e.g., [4]) or their recently developed versions that take constraints into account by applying the Fletcher filter [9,11]. The need for using global optimization methods instead of faster but local ones stems from the fact that random errors may lead to false local minima, even if a large number of repetitions j_{max} is used.

The time of running Algorithm 2 once, for 6 cladding layers and $j_{max} = 600$ repetitions, was about 100 s. on a standard PC i7/3 GHz. In order to grasp an intuition how the landscape of $\tilde{J}(K_I, h)$ looks like, Algorithm 2 has been run on the grid for $h \in [0.1, 0.9]$ and $K_I \in [0, 10]$. The remaining parameters have been selected as follows: $K_P = K_E = 1$, $\Delta = 0.01$ s, random errors – uniformly

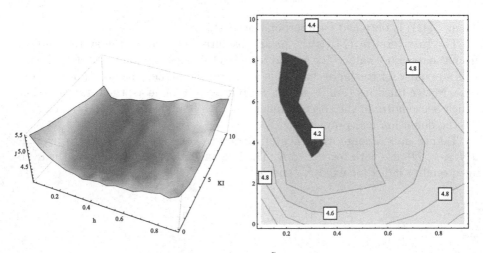

Fig. 5. Dependence of control quality criterion $\tilde{J}(K_I, h)$ on (K_I and h – 3D plot (left panel) and contour plot (right panel)

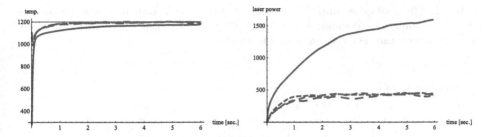

Fig. 6. Four passes of the cladding process for approximately optimal tuning of the control system. Left panel – the lake temperature vs time. Right panel – the laser power used

distributed in $[-20, 20]\,°C$. The results of the simulations are shown in Fig. 5. As one can notice, the landscape is rather flat, but the global optimum is clearly visible. Although a relatively large number of repetitions $j_{max} = 600$ has been used, one can find many local minima (see, e.g., a vicinity of $h = 0.85$, $K_I = 5$ – left panel of Fig. 5). Nevertheless, for the right panel of this figure, one can easily read out that pairs (h, K_I) in the darkest region provide the smallest $\tilde{J}(K_I, h)$, which is equal to 4.2. The larger region: $h \in [0.2, 0.55]$, $K_I \in [3.5, 8]$ provides quite good quality of about 4.4. Thus, the cladding process can be run safely in this region.

4   Selected Experimental Results

The results presented in the previous sections have been based on simulations. Here, we provide selected experimental results of using the PI-CSEWMA control system to the laser cladding robot. A 3D thin wall has been built several times, using different settings of the control system that are listed in the first and the second column in Table 1. The third column contains J criterion, as defined by (13), with $\lambda = 3$ and $\Delta = 1/6$. The reason for selecting this value is the following: the length of each pass was 6 s, but for evaluating J we have taken 2000 samples (from 5000 to 7000) in the middle of the pass, which corresponds to one second. The results displayed in the fourth column is the percentage of the improvement of J by introducing control systems in comparison to the case when constant power $W = 0.65\,kW$ was applied (first row). As one can observe, introducing the PI controller reduces J by 38 %. Additional reduction, by additional 14 % is obtained when under-smoothed ($h = 0.5$) CSEWMA filter is introduced. When properly selected smoothing ($h = 0.1$) in CSEWMA filter is applied, then we obtain the reduction of J to 65–66 % of its value without control. Notice that interchanging positions of PI and CSEWMA smoother does not influence this result. Applying other then zero initial state of CSEWMA filter also does not improve the performance, although it can be desirable in order to get even smoother control signals.

Table 1. The quality of control (3-rd column) for different control system configurations and tuning (1-st column) and the percentage of the improvement with respect to no control (constant laser power) case (4-th column)

Control syst.	Param	$J = $ eq. (13)	% improv.
None (const. W)	–	8.25	–
PI	$K_P = 0.9$, $K_I = 5.88$	5.13	38
PI + CSEWMA 1	$K_P = 0.9$, $K_I = 5.88$, $h = 0.5$, $q_0 = 0$	3.95	52
PI + CSEWMA 2	$K_P = 0.9$, $K_I = 5.88$, $h = 0.1$, $q_0 = 0$	2.88	65
PI + CSEWMA 3	$K_P = 0.9$, $K_I = 5.88$, $h = 0.1$, $q_0 = 450$	2.81	66
CSEWMA + PI	$K_P = 0.9$, $K_I = 5.88$, $h = 0.1$, $q_0 = 0$	2.78	66

5   Conclusions and the Directions ff Further Research

The methodology of simulating the dynamics of controlled repetitive processes and optimizing parameters of the control system has been presented in details. Then, this methodology has been applied to the laser power control of the cladding process. The control system consisting of PI-controller and CSEWMA filter has been tuned by the simulations. Then, the designed control system has been tested on a real-life cladding robot. The results are satisfactory in the sense that we have obtained a good performance of the system both in its pass-to-pass behavior as well as in its behavior along each pass, which is smoother then in the case when the CSEWMA filter is not used.

Further effort is needed to better control the material deposition at the end points, using images from the IR (thermovision camera), but this topic is outside the scope of this paper.

Acknowledgements. The works of Piotr Jurewicz, Jacek Reiner and Ewaryst Rafajłowicz have been supported by the National Science Center under grant: 2012/07/B/ST7/01216, internal code 350914 of the Wrocław University of Science and Technology. Wojciech Rafajłowicz has been supported by the Grant B50328 for Young Researchers from the Faculty of Electronics, Wrocław University of Science and Technology 2015/016.

References

1. Baraniecki, T., Chlebus, E., Dziatkiewicz, M., Kędzia, J., Reiner, J., Wiercioch, M.: System for laser microsurfacing of metal powders. Weld. Int. **30**(2), 98–102 (2016)
2. Benedetto, J.J., Czaja, W.: Integration and Modern Analysis. Springer Science & Business Media, Heidelberg (2010)
3. Bi, G., Gasser, A., Wissenbach, K., Drenker, A., Poprawe, R.: Investigation on the direct laser metallic powder deposition process via temperature measurement. Appl. Surf. Sci. **253**(3), 1411–1416 (2006)
4. Coello, C.A.C., Van Veldhuizen, D.A., Lamont, G.B.: Evolutionary Algorithms for Solving Multi-objective Problems, vol. 242. Springer, Heidelberg (2002)

5. Devesse, W., De Baere, D., Guillaume, P.: Design of a model-based controller with temperature feedback for laser cladding. Phys. Proc. **56**, 211–219 (2014)
6. Liu, J., Li, L.: Effects of process variables on laser direct formation of thin wall. Optics Laser Technol. **39**(2), 231–236 (2007)
7. Mandarapu, S., Lolla, S., Kumar, M.S.: Digital PI controller using anti-wind-up mechanism for a speed controlled electric drive system. Int. J. Innovative Technol. Exploring Eng. (IJITEE) 3(1) (2013). ISSN: 2278–3075
8. Picasso, M., Marsden, C., Wagniere, J., Frenk, A., Rappaz, M.: A simple but realistic model for laser cladding. Metall. Mater. Trans. B **25**(2), 281–291 (1994)
9. Rafajłowicz, E., Rafajłowicz, W.: Fletcher's filter methodology as a soft selector in evolutionary algorithms for constrained optimization. In: Rutkowski, L., Korytkowski, M., Scherer, R., Tadeusiewicz, R., Zadeh, L.A., Zurada, J.M. (eds.) EC 2012 and SIDE 2012. LNCS, vol. 7269, pp. 333–341. Springer, Heidelberg (2012)
10. Rafajłowicz, E., Wnuk, M., Rafajłowicz, W.: Local detection of defects from image sequences. Int. J. Appl. Math. Comput. Sci. **18**(4), 581–592 (2008)
11. Rafajłowicz, W.: Numerical optimal control of integral-algebraic equations using differential evolution with Fletcher's filter. In: Rutkowski, L., Korytkowski, M., Scherer, R., Tadeusiewicz, R., Zadeh, L.A., Zurada, J.M. (eds.) ICAISC 2014, Part I. LNCS, vol. 8467, pp. 406–415. Springer, Heidelberg (2014)
12. Rogers, E., Galkowski, K., Owens, D.H.: Control Systems Theory and Applications for Linear Repetitive Processes, vol. 349. Springer Science & Business Media, Heidelberg (2007)
13. Tang, L., Landers, R.G.: Melt pool temperature control for laser metal deposition processes part I: online temperature control. J. Manuf. Sci. Eng. **132**(1), 011010 (2010)

Automated Application of Inventory Optimization

Tomáš Martinovič[✉], Kateřina Janurová, Kateřina Slaninová,
and Jan Martinovič

IT4Innovations National Supercomputing Center,
VŠB – Technical University of Ostrava, 17. listopadu, 708 33 Ostrava, Czech Republic
{tomas.martinovic,katerina.janurova,katerina.slaninova,
jan.martinovic}@vsb.cz

Abstract. We present automated application of inventory optimization based on sales forecast. Inventory stock optimization is very required issue by companies recent years, however inventory models are based on the sales expectation. Therefore, the problem of optimizing inventory stock is divided into two parts, sales forecast and setting optimal inventory. We describe an automated solution to model selection for sales forecast and the inventory setting based on those predictions. In the end, we present our validation of the system through historical simulation. We compare simulations results against real inventory levels. Due to the large number of different length time series, this simulation was run in parallel on cluster and was parallelized in R. The algorithms were developed and tested on inventory time series from real data sets of the K2 atmitec company (Sales forecasting and inventory optimization are parts of ERP solution K2, which is provided by K2 atmitec s.r.o. company, http://www.k2.cz/en/).

Keywords: Inventory optimization · Sales forecasting · Model selection · Parallelization

1 Introduction

The goal of our work was the design and implementation of automated application of inventory control for optimization and simplification of the decision making process of sales managers. Models for inventory control are based on the products sales expectations. Therefore, as the first step of inventory control, the sales forecast needs to be estimated. In our application, the sales forecast can be determined by four different models applied on several modifications of sales history. The result of the model with the best prediction according to the selected measure of accuracy is used as the input for the inventory control model.

Because of the lack of information needed for the standard inventory control models like Economic Order Quantity model or newsvendor model, we had to

© IFIP International Federation for Information Processing 2016
Published by Springer International Publishing Switzerland 2016. All Rights Reserved
K. Saeed and W. Homenda (Eds.): CISIM 2016, LNCS 9842, pp. 230–239, 2016.
DOI: 10.1007/978-3-319-45378-1_21

base our approach for the second step of inventory control on a fixed time review period model with variable demand and modify it to better suit our needs. This modification was verified by the simulation, which imitates behavior of sales manager on the assumption of complete trust in our application. The results of such simulation were compared with the real historical data of inventory time series.

The simulations were parallelized in R language and run in parallel on cluster because of the large number of products used for verification and repeated model estimations.

2   Inventory Stock Optimization

As described above, the inventory stock optimization consists of the two steps: sales forecasting and optimal inventory setting.

2.1   Sales Forecasting

Sales forecasting represents a typical application of time series analysis and prediction. Classical time series analysis is based on the assumption that the time series y_t for $t = 1, 2, \ldots, n$ can be decomposed into four components: trend, cyclic, seasonal and irregular. The trend component characterizes a long-term tendency of the examined phenomenon that is influenced by factors operating in the same direction eg. production technology, demographic conditions, market conditions, etc. The first approach we used in time series modeling is based on the idea that if the long-term tendency of time series corresponds to a certain function of time eg. a linear, quadratic, exponential, S-curve etc., the trend component can be modeled using this function [1].

Assume that the time series y_t can be written as the sum of trend and residual process

$$y_t = T_t + \varepsilon_t \quad t = 1, 2, \ldots, n, \tag{1}$$

where T_t can be described by the appropriate mathematical function of the time variable t, and ε_t is the residual component with the character of white noise process.

We used three different mathematical functions for modeling the trend components in our simulation:

1. linear trend function in the form

$$T_t = \beta_0 + \beta_1 t, \quad t = 1, 2, \ldots, n, \tag{2}$$

2. quadratic trend function in the form

$$T_t = \beta_0 + \beta_1 t + \beta_2 t^2, \quad t = 1, 2, \ldots, n, \tag{3}$$

3. and cubic trend function in the form

$$T_t = \beta_0 + \beta_1 t + \beta_2 t^2 + \beta_3 t^3, \quad t = 1, 2, \ldots, n. \tag{4}$$

The regression parameters of the trend functions $\beta_0, \beta_1, \beta_2$ and β_3 were estimated by the least squares estimation method. Although this approach may appear to be too simple, in many practical cases the best solution is the simplest one.

The second approach we used in time series modeling is provided by the ARIMA model [2]. ARIMA - Autoregressive integrated moving average - is part of the Box-Jenkins methodology, which was developed for the analysis of time series, where we assume that the residual component ε_t does not have the character of white noise. Unlike the first approach, where the regression model is built only as the function of time, the Box-Jenkings models are built as the function of linear combination of p past values of the modeled variable itself, hence the term autoregressive, and regression-like model of $q + 1$ past forecast errors. In such way the ARMA(p, q) - autoregressive moving averages - model is obtained. ARIMA(p, d, q) model is then essentially an ARMA model applied to the dth difference of the original series. Such approach is used in the cases when the studied series is not stationary (it's properties depend on the time at which the series is observed). The stationarity can be achieved by applying the difference of the first or the second order, difference of the higher order are usually not used in practice.

The final sales forecast is made in four steps. At first, all the models described above are fitted to the training part of the data, y_t for $t = 1, 2, \ldots, m$, where $m < n$, then the sales forecasts $\hat{y}_t$ for $t = m + 1, m + 2, \ldots, n$ are made on the basis of fitted models. The different forecasts are compared with the test part of the data y_t for $t = m + 1, m + 2, \ldots, n$ using appropriate measure of accuracy, and finally the best forecast is chosen as the input for inventory control model. Additionally, the models are fitted simultaneously on the original daily data and data with weekly and monthly aggregation.

For the best forecast selection, several measures of accuracy eg. RMSE, MAE, MAPE, etc. were considered [3]. However, because of the different time aggregation of the compared time series, the accuracy measure, that is independent of the scale of the data, seems to be the most convenient one. This kind of accuracy measure, Mean Absolute Scaled Error, was proposed by Hyndman and Koehler [4] as

$$\text{MASE} = \text{mean} \ (|q_t|), \tag{5}$$

with the scaled error q_t defined as

$$q_t = \frac{e_t}{\frac{1}{n-m-1} \sum\limits_{i=m+2}^{n} |y_i - y_{i-1}|}, \tag{6}$$

where e_t is the forecast error defined as $e_t = y_t - \hat{y}_t, t = m + 1, m + 2, \ldots, n$.

2.2   Inventory Control

Numerous models for inventory control were developed such as Economic Order Quantity model (EOQ) or newsvendor model. Those are the basic deterministic and stochastic models for the inventory control. Based on the stochastic nature of our problem and available data we used fixed time review period model with variable demand as a basis for our solution.

It was difficult to estimate ordering costs and holding costs due to the character of the available data. Therefore, we use just quantities and we focus on providing inventory level measures based on the user specified service level in our approach. To achieve that, three measures need to be computed. The first is the safety stock, which should cover most of the uncertain demand. This uncertainty means that it would be too costly, and often impossible, to hold enough inventory to cover all the variations in demand. Therefore, the user of the software may set requested level of service. Safety stock then depends on standard deviation of sales, lead time, service level and probability distribution of sales. Assuming standard normal distribution of sales, constant lead time and constant variation of sales, we can define the safety stock [5] as

$$S = \varphi(sl)\sqrt{t_l \sigma_d^2}, \tag{7}$$

where $\varphi(sl)$ is the quantile function for normal distribution and its quantile is given by service level. Variable t_l stands for lead time and σ_d is standard deviation of demand. By leaving the assumption of constant lead time and adding uncertainty to lead time we get

$$S = \varphi(sl)\sqrt{t_l \sigma_s^2 + E(s)\sigma_l^2}, \tag{8}$$

where $E(s)$ is expected mean sales and σ_l is lead time standard deviation. Now we can define reorder point, which is the level of inventory needed to cover the demand until the arrival of the next batch of inventory plus safety stock. If we assume the constant demand and constant lead time we can define reorder point as follows

$$R = S + E(s)t_l. \tag{9}$$

The last step is to compute the order quantity. This is defined as the quantity necessary to cover the demand for the user specified time. Hence, the order quantity is affected by mean expected sales, order time, incoming goods and goods reserved in advance. Additionally, the ordered quantity should be adjusted by the difference between actual stock and reorder point. We can write this as

$$Q = E(s)t_o - G_i + G_r + R - A, \tag{10}$$

where t_o is the order time, G_i is the incoming goods quantity, G_r is reserved goods quantity and A is actual level of inventory. This definition of order quantity covers the demand for the defined time with set service level for covering the stochastic behaviour of customers.

2.3   Automated Application of Inventory Optimization

The theory described in Sects. 2.1 and 2.2 was used for development of an approach for inventory optimization that was implemented as part of ERP software by K2 atmitec company. This software can simplify the decision making process of sales managers. It includes three main parts, which are "best model selection", "sales prediction" and "inventory control".

3 Verification of Automated Application of Inventory Optimization

To evaluate our approach, we created a simulation which imitates behavior of sales manager on the assumption of complete trust in our approach. The simulation includes all three parts mentioned in previous section, which are complemented by an automatically controlled decision making process for running specific parts. We used historical time series of sales and inventory stock levels for verification of our simulation, the results are given in Sect. 3.3.

3.1 Data Description

The real historical data for our software verification was provided by the K2 atmitec company. The dataset contained the information about approximately 33 000 products in several warehouses in Czech Republic. We were not able to simulate the behavior for all of the provided products due to the small number of observations in the followed history. The software was finally verified on about 950 and 750 products in two selected warehouses, what was sufficiently large enough number.

3.2 Simulations

On the beginning of the simulation, some parameters must be set. The lead time for the given goods, order interval and maximum level of inventory. The lead time and maximum level of inventory are variable for every type of stock. The review period was set to 30 days. In addition, we had to select the service level, which was set to 95 %.

The starting point for the simulation is a year and a half. That means we take the first year and a half of sales time series and the inventory level at that time. The "best model selection" part begins with running the model selection algorithm, when the original time series is preprocessed in several steps. In order to find the best model for given data, the time series with originally daily sales is aggregated in weekly and monthly sales. There is a possibility of removing outliers for each aggregation and also filtering by Kalman [6] or Baxter-King [7] filter for weekly and monthly aggregation. At the end of preprocessing step, each original time series leads to 10 final modifications on which the four models given in Sect. 2.1 are fitted and compared by the MASE accuracy measure. This chooses a predictive model used for the next three months. Then, the simulation runs the "sales prediction" part, that calculates the predicted sales quantity on the basis of previously selected predictive model. The result of this step is

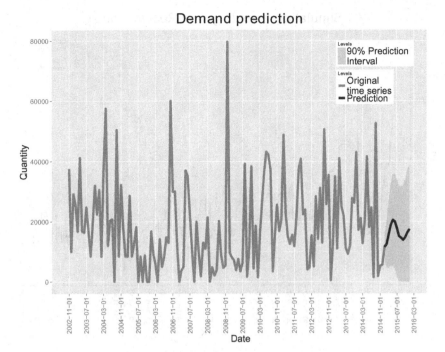

Fig. 1. Prediction of sales quantity of real inventory time series

the predicted time series, that is used as the input for the "inventory control" part, which sets the reorder point and safety stock. The visualization of such prediction is shown in Fig. 1.

After the first day, the simulation iterates by day, reducing the inventory level by the same amount as it is reduced in the real inventory time series. When it reaches the reorder point, the "sales prediction" and "inventory control" parts are run again. The reorder point and safety stock are updated according to the new results and order for the new inventory is made. The ordered inventory is added to the simulated inventory after the lead time period. Every three months new predictive model is chosen based on the "best model selection" part. This process is repeated until the end of the time series.

The main output of this simulation is simulated inventory time series. This may be compared with the actual inventory time series, as is shown in Fig. 2. In general, if the mean level of simulated inventory is less than the actual inventory and the stockout time is within boundaries of chosen service level, we can say, that the simulation is successful. In addition, to the simulated inventory time series, we have other outputs. Those are chosen predictive models, history of inventory control settings, orders history and graphical output. These outputs allow us to make a quick analysis of reasons for the success or failure of our simulation.

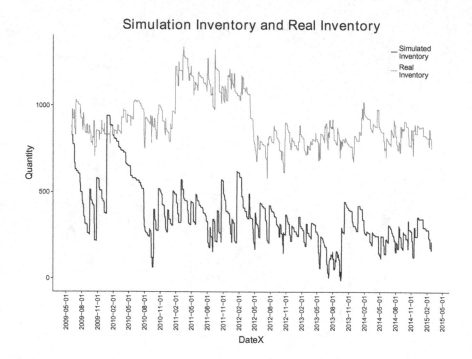

Fig. 2. Comparison of simulated inventory time series and real inventory time series

Because of a large number of products at each warehouse and repeated model estimations, we had to parallelize this algorithm. Due to the independency of simulations for specific goods, the computation was easily parallelized through Rmpi[1] package in R software. This package uses MPI for communications between nodes. Our algorithm uses distributed apply function, where a master node sends time series data to free slave nodes, which execute the simulation on given data. This method allows us to run this algorithm both single node or on the cluster and scales well, because there is minimal need for the communication. The computation was made on Salomon cluster equipped with Intel Xeon E5-2680v3 processors. We used 8 compute nodes, each with 24 cores and 128 GB RAM.

In the future, we would like to make improvements in the computations of reorder point and safety stock, since they are very susceptible to sudden changes in demand as is shown in Fig. 3. The most sensible seems to be the solution by moving averages since this will allow for changes to happen, but it would smooth them at the same time. However, this approach needs to be tested.

---

[1] Yu, H. (2002). Rmpi: Parallel Statistical Computing in R. R News 2/2:10-14.

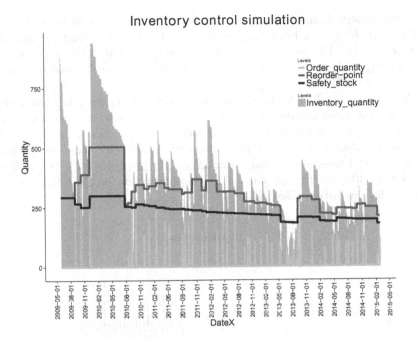

Fig. 3. Inventory quantity, safety stock, reorder point and order quantity history for inventory control simulation

3.3 Comparison of Simulation Results and Real Inventory Data

Simulations were completed on two warehouses, one with 950 products and the second with 761 products. For each simulation, the mean level of real inventory and the mean level of simulated inventory were determined, and the relative percentage difference with respect to mean level of real inventory was calculated. The higher relative percentage difference, the more successful simulation was. Stockout was calculated for the sake of real information as the number of days for which the product was unavailable. The mean and median values for the relative percentage difference as well as the mean values of stockout days for both warehouses are given in Table 1.

Table 1. Summary statistics for the comparisons of the mean level of real inventory and the mean level of simulated inventory.

	Warehouse 1	Warehouse 2
Number of products	950	761
Mean stockout [%]	2.7	3.1
Mean relative percentage difference [%]	17.4	20.0
Median relative percentage difference [%]	34.8	35.2

As can be seen from the summary statistics, the mean stouckout is within the required level of 5 % for both warehouses. The mean level of relative percentage difference was 17.4 % and 20.0 %, with the meaning that if the sales manager trusted completely in our software, the mean inventory level would be lower by 17.4 % and 20.0 %.

The values of median relative percentage difference suggest, that the decrease could be even more significant, and that the mean relative percentage difference value is influenced by several unsuccessful simulations, as can be seen from the distribution of relative percentage difference with removed outliers in Figs. 4 and 5. Those were mainly simulations on products with the lead time greater than 40 days. Improvement of the simulation on such products is one of the tasks for our future research.

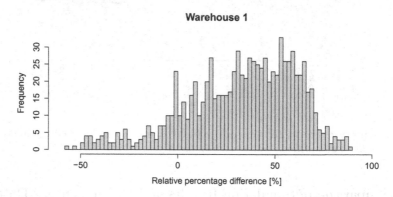

Fig. 4. Distribution of relative percentage difference with respect to real inventory in Warehouse 1

Fig. 5. Distribution of relative percentage difference with respect to real inventory in Warehouse 2

4   Conclusion

Our paper describes design, implementation and verification of the automated application of inventory control that is based on predictions of real historical sales data. The sales prediction is estimated by several approaches of time series modeling of which the best is chosen by the selected measure of accuracy. Modification of fixed time review period model with variable demand was proposed for inventory control model and verified by the described simulation process which compares inventory time series simulated by our application with the real inventory time series. The results of the simulation showed, that if the sales manager acted completely in accord with our application recommendation, the mean inventory level would decrease by 17.4 % in one tested warehouse and by 20.0 % in the second tested warehouse.

The future work in this area involves, besides the tasks mentioned in previous section, the research and the implementation of other suitable models for sales forecasting and their ensembles, an improved model selection, and alternative inventory control models.

Acknowledgment. This work was supported by The Ministry of Education, Youth and Sports from the National Programme of Sustainability (NPU II) project 'IT4Innovations excellence in science – LQ1602' and from the Large Infrastructures for Research, Experimental Development and Innovations project 'IT4Innovations National Supercomputing Center – LM2015070'.

References

1. Hyndman, R.J., Athanasopoulos, G.: Forecasting: Principles and Practice. OTexts, Melbourne (2013). http://otexts.org/fpp/. Accessed 26 April 2016
2. Asteriou, D., Hall, S.G.: Applied Econometrics, 2nd edn. Palgrave MacMillan, Basingstoke (2011)
3. Palit, A.K., Popovic, D.: Computational Intelligence in Time Series Forecasting: Theory and Engineering Applications. Springer-Verlag, London (2005)
4. Hyndman, R.J., Koehler, A.B.: Another look at measures of forecast accuracy. Int. J. Forecast. **22**, 679–688 (2006)
5. Russell, R.S., Taylor, B.W.: Operations Management. Wiley, Hoboken (2011)
6. Durbin, J., Koopman, S.J.: Time Series Analysis by State Space Methods. Oxford Statistical Science Series. Clarendon Press, Oxford (2001)
7. Baxter, M., King, R.G.: Measuring business cycles approximate band-pass filters for economic time series. Technical report, National Bureau of Economic Research (1995)

Optimal Ellipse Based Algorithm as an Approximate and Robust Solution of Minimum Volume Covering Ellipse Problem

Krzysztof Misztal[1(✉)], Jacek Tabor[1], and Jakub Hyła[2]

[1] Faculty of Mathematics and Computer Science, Jagiellonian University,
Łojasiewicza 6, 30-348 Kraków, Poland
krzysztof.misztal@uj.edu.pl, tabor@ii.uj.edu.pl
[2] The Faculty of Electrical Engineering, Automatics,
Computer Science and Biomedical Engineering,
AGH University of Science and Technology,
al. A. Mickiewicza 30, 30-059 Kraków, Poland
kuba.hyla@gmail.com

Abstract. We propose a algorithm to give a approximate solution of a minimal covering circle or ellipse of a set of points. The iterative algorithm is based on the optimal ellipse which best describe a given set of points.

Keywords: Smallest ellipse problem · Computational geometry · Optimal ellipse · Online algorithm

1 Introduction

In order to more realistically simulate the behavior of solid in games, we have to check especially if they collide with each other every time they move, and if they do, we have to do something about it. This lead us to game physics engine that gives the game's world life. Understanding collision physics in 2D and 3D games [1–3] is particularly important for game developers. The collision detection algorithms depends on the type of shapes that can collide. We can consider e.g. rectangle to rectangle or circle to circle collisions. In general case we will have a simple generic shape that covers the entity known as a "hitbox" so even though collision may not be pixel perfect, it will look good enough and be performance across multiple entities.

This problem can be also reformulated as finding the unique minimum volume covering ellipse (MVCE) problem of finite set of points in N-dimensional real space (namely in $\mathbb{R}^N$) if we consider just elliptical generic shapes. Such an ellipse has appealing mathematical properties which makes it theoretically interesting and practically useful. This convex constrained problem arises in a

K. Saeed and W. Homenda (Eds.): CISIM 2016, LNCS 9842, pp. 240–250, 2016.
DOI: 10.1007/978-3-319-45378-1_22

variety of applied computational settings, particularly in data mining and robust statistics. For example in computational statistics, the minimum-volume ellipsoid covering k of m ($0 \leq k \leq m$, $k, m \in \mathbb{N}$) given points in $\mathbb{R}^N$ is well-known for its affine equivariance and positive breakdown properties as a multivariate location and scattering estimator [4]. In the area of robust statistics and data mining, efficiently finding outliers is a challenge that has attracted much research interest [5]. Indeed, one can identify data outliers quickly if one can compute the minimum-volume ellipsoid quickly, because outliers are essentially points on the boundary of the minimum-volume covering ellipsoid.

In this paper we focus on the image data, namely the points from $\mathbb{R}^N$. The extended version for arbitrary dimension with streaming approach is prepared as a full paper and will be published in the future.

A new algorithm for finding the MVCE is based on the Mahalanobis distance [6] and uses the statistical and analytical properties of circular and elliptical objects, is proposed herein. The main advantage of the proposed method is that no complicated mathematical computation is involved in the implementation. Thus its evaluation is very fast. However the outcome ellipse is not optimal one – this will be disused in further part of this article.

We compare our algorithm with the incremental algorithm of Welzl, with move-to-front heuristic [7] – the whole implementation is described in [8].

The remainder of the paper is organized as follows: in the next section we present basics of the covariance matrix and Mahalanobis distance. In the third section we provide the algorithm for finding approximate minimal covering ellipse. The next section gives same experiments o illustrate the performance of our method. Finally, the last section contains some concluding remarks and possible directions of future work.

2   Mathematical Basis

2.1   Covariance Matrix and Optimal Ellipse

Multivariate and multidimensional analysis has been one of the most important areas in the modern statistics. Thus, the researchers have developed many useful techniques to efficiently describe the behavior of complicated data.

The definition of the covariance matrix states as follows, if set C is discrete, namely $C = \{x_i\}_{i=1}^{N} \subset \mathbb{R}^N$, then the covariance matrix equals

$$\Sigma_C = \frac{1}{N} \sum_{i=1}^{N} (x_i - \mathbf{m}_C)(x_i - \mathbf{m}_C)^T,$$

where $\mathbf{m}_C = \frac{1}{N} \sum_{i=1}^{N} x_i$ is a mean of set C. In the general case by the covariance matrix of a set we understand the covariance of the uniform normalized density on S.

Theoretically, covariance is the object which represents the true statistical independent structure of the underlying population units. On the other hand, if based solely on empirical data, only a small piece of the independent structure is obtained. It is therefore important to select the efficient representations of the data for sampling the covariance matrix.

Remark 1. In practice the mean and the covariance matrix for a given set $C \subset \mathbb{R}^N$ is unknown. Thus they must be estimated from random variables (observed samples) by well-known estimators

$$\hat{\mathbf{m}}_C = \sum_{i=1}^{n} w_i x_i,$$

$$\hat{\Sigma}_C = \frac{\sum_{i=1}^{n} w_i}{(\sum_{i=1}^{n} w_i)^2 - \sum_{i=1}^{n} w_i^2} \sum_{i=1}^{n} (x_i - \hat{\mathbf{m}}_C)(x_i - \hat{\mathbf{m}}_C)^T,$$

where $x_i \in C$ for $i = 1, \ldots, n$ and w_i – the weight of the point x_i. If all weights are the same, the weighted mean and covariance reduce to the sample mean and covariance. The weight assigned with the point of space will be used to store (and use) the information about color while the work is done with grayscale images. For a binary image a natural simplification is employed: 1 for the foreground color (usually black) and 0 for the background color (usually white).

Remark 2. The above consideration discuses discrete sets. In general case the basic definition of covariance matrix can be stated as follows. For a random variable with a probability density function $f : \mathbb{R}^N \to \mathbb{R}$ the covariance matrix of set $S \subset \mathbb{R}^N$ can be computed[1] as

$$\Sigma_S = \int_S (x - \mu)(x - \mu)^T f(x) dx,$$

where μ is an expected value (mean) of set S.

2.2   Pixels on Image as a Atomic Piece of Information in Covariance Matrix

When we apply the above investigations to image data, we shall threat a single pixel (point with coordinates $(x, y) \in ([1, w] \cap \mathbb{Z}) \times ([1, h] \cap \mathbb{Z})$, where $w \times h$ is the size of the image) like a square. It allows to convert the discrete data of an image to continuous, which is more natural and consistent with the human perception of images. To calculate the measure of such transformation we use the following remark.

Remark 3. Consider a set $P \subset \delta \cdot \mathbb{Z}^N$ which represents the set $S = P + [-\frac{\delta}{2}, \frac{\delta}{2}]^N$ for $\delta > 0$. Then, obviously, covariance matrix is

$$\Sigma_S = \Sigma_P + \Sigma_{[-\frac{\delta}{2}, \frac{\delta}{2}]^N} = \Sigma_P + \frac{1}{12} \delta^{N+2} I,$$

---

[1] If the set S is discrete, namely $S = \{x_i\}_{i=1}^{N}$, then the covariance matrix equals $\Sigma_S = \frac{1}{N} \sum_{i=1}^{N} (x_i - \mu)(x_i - \mu)^T$, where $\mu = \frac{1}{N} \sum_{i=1}^{N} x_i$ is a mean of set S.

where I denotes the identity matrix. This can be used to compute the measure and covariance of S efficiently.

In the case of the image data we set $\delta = 1$, which is because the coordinates of each pixel are integers.

In general case we have to determine the appropriate value of δ, for which investigated dataset can be threaded as a subset of $\delta \cdot \mathbb{Z}^N$.

This section is concluded with a simple, but important observation for singletons in image data, namely for $X = \{x_0\}$ we get

$$m_X = x_0,$$

$$\Sigma_X = \frac{1}{12}I,$$

$$\mathrm{card}(X) = 1,$$

where I denotes identity matrix and $x_0 \in \mathbb{Z}^2$.

2.3   An In-Place Covariance Modification

Following theorem highlights how mean and covariance matrix will change if we add same points to the set, which will be used for the algorithm in the further part of this work. While new algorithm in each step modify mean and covariance matrix respectively to added point, this theorem allows as not to recalculate the whole covariance matrix each time – we just calculate the change of covariance matrix.

Theorem 1 ([9]). *Let U, V be given finite subsets of $\mathbb{R}^N$. Assume additionally that $U \cap V = \emptyset$. Then*

$$m_{U \cup V} = p_U m_U + p_V m_V \tag{1}$$

$$\Sigma_{U \cup V} = p_U \Sigma_U + p_V \Sigma_V u + p_U p_V (m_U - m_V)(m_U - m_V)^T \tag{2}$$

where

$$p_U := \frac{\mathrm{card}(U)}{\mathrm{card}(U) + \mathrm{card}(V)}, \qquad p_V := \frac{\mathrm{card}(V)}{\mathrm{card}(U) + \mathrm{card}(V)}.$$

2.4   Mahalanobis Distance

It is well-known that the Euclidean distance between two points x and y in real space is given by

$$\|x - y\| = \sqrt{(x - y)^T(x - y)} = \sqrt{(x - y)^T I(x - y)}, \text{ for } x, y \in \mathbb{R}^N,$$

where T denotes the transpose operation and I is the identity matrix. It follows immediately that all points with the same distance from the origin $\|x - 0\| = c$

satisfy $x_1^2 + \ldots + x_n^2 = c^2$, which means that all components of the observation x contribute equally to the Euclidean distance of x from the center.

However, in statistics variability (how the set is spread out or closely clustered) is also considered. If the correlation between variables is to be taken into account when computing statistical distance, then we use Mahalanobis distance, which can be defined as follows.

Definition 1 (Mahalanobis Distance). *Let C denote the given subset of $\mathbb{R}^N$. By m_C the mean value of C is denoted, and the covariance matrix of C is denoted by Σ_C. The statistical distance or Mahalanobis distance between two points $x, y \in \mathbb{R}^N$ is defined as*

$$\|x - y\|_{\Sigma_C} = \sqrt{(x - y)^T \Sigma_C^{-1} (x - y)}. \tag{3}$$

If $y = 0$ then the Eq. (3) is the general equation of an ellipsoid centered at the origin. In practice the center of the observations will differ from the origin, thus the distance from the mass center of observed samples chosen $y = m_C$ will be of interest.

2.5 Ellipse in Mahalanobis Transformed Space

A brief summary of the Mahalanobis distance and transform properties was given in previous section. Some important observations crucial in the construction of the following algorithm with the use of Mahalanobis distance will be hereby presented.

Recall the value of the Mahalanobis distance of the unit N-dimension ball receptively to covariance matrix Σ can be calculated, namely

$$B_{\Sigma}(x_0, R) := \{x \in \mathbb{R}^N : \|x - x_0\|_{\Sigma} \leq R\}.$$

The following knowledge is crucial for the algorithm construction.

Theorem 2 ([10]). *Consider uniform probability density on the ellipse $E \subset \mathbb{R}^N$ with mean m_E and covariance Σ_E. Then*

$$E = B_{\Sigma_E}\left(m_E, \sqrt{N + 2}\right). \tag{4}$$

Theorem 2 gives the equation for optimal ellipse for given set and has the following consequences in understanding of the elliptical pattern recognition. Moreover, it describe how to reconstruct the set if we just have mean and covariance matrix.

Remark 4. Theorem 2 gives the necessary and sufficient condition for a given shape to be elliptical (generalization of plane ellipse) – general ellipse in arbitrary dimension. Namely, it can be stated that an object $E \subset \mathbb{R}^N$ is an ellipse if and only if it can be approximated by $\mathrm{B}_{\Sigma_E}\left(\mathbf{m}_E, \sqrt{N+2}\right)$ or, that is,

$$E \approx \mathrm{B}_{\Sigma_E}\left(\mathbf{m}_E, \sqrt{N+2}\right).$$

The above considerations gives us the specified condition to decide whether or not the current point x from the cluster $C \subset \mathbb{R}^N$ belong to the "elliptical" part of the cluster. Namely, the condition for point x is given by

$$\sqrt{(x - \mathbf{m}_C)^T \Sigma_C^{-1}(x - \mathbf{m}_C)} \le \sqrt{N+2},$$

where $\mathbf{m}_C$ and Σ_C denote the mean and covariance of C respectively. This gives as full necessarily information for construction the proper algorithm for finding approximate minimum volume covering ellipse.

3   The Algorithm

In this section we introduce the algorithm for finding approximate minimum volume covering ellipse. We will describe this algorithm using Fig. 1 which presents the example of investigated set (original image) and steps of the algorithm.

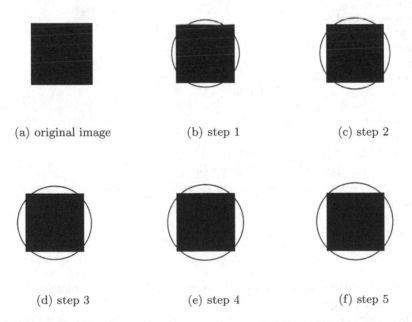

(a) original image   (b) step 1   (c) step 2

(d) step 3   (e) step 4   (f) step 5

Fig. 1. New algorithm for finding minimal covering ellipse: (a) original image and (b)-(f) steps of the algorithm.

Let consider the finite set C of which we want to calculate the smallest covering ellipse. Since C is finite we can state $C = \{x_i\}_{i=1,\ldots,M}$.

At the beginning of the algorithm we calculate the optimal ellipse for C, by calculating the mean and covariance matrix denoted m_0 and Σ_0 respectively. The optimal ellipse is current approximation of minimal covering ellipse.

Then in each i-step we proceed as follows:

- we check which of points in C are not covered by current approximation of minimal covering ellipse – we denote the set consist of such points by l_i. If the set l_i is empty we end the algorithm;
- we calculate the mean and covariance matrix for set l_i and denoted them m_i and Σ_i respectively;
- we update the current approximation of minimal covering ellipse according Theorem 1;
- then we proceed to next step.

The pseudo-code of the algorithm can be stated as follows:

Algorithm 1. Finding approximate minimum volume covering ellipse

---

initial conditions
   $C = \{x_i\}_{i=1,\ldots,M} \subset \mathbb{R}^N$
   put $l_0 \leftarrow \{x_1, \ldots, x_M\}$
   put $m_0 \leftarrow \mathbf{m}_{l_0}$
   put $\Sigma_0 \leftarrow \mathbf{\Sigma}_{l_0}$
   put $n_0 \leftarrow \operatorname{card}(l_0)$
   put $i \leftarrow 0$
repeat
   $l_{i+1} \leftarrow \emptyset$
   for each x **in** l_i **do**
      if $x \notin \mathrm{B}_{\Sigma_i}(m_i, \sqrt{N+2})$ **then**
         $l_{i+1} \leftarrow l_{i+1} \cup \{x\}$
      end if
   end for
   $m_{i+1} \leftarrow \frac{n_i}{n_i+n_{i+1}} m_i + \frac{n_{i+1}}{n_i+n_{i+1}} \mathbf{m}_{l_{i+1}}$
   $\Sigma_{i+1} \leftarrow \frac{n_i}{n_i+\operatorname{card}(l_{i+1})} \Sigma_i + \frac{n_{i+1}}{n_i+\operatorname{card}(l_{i+1})} \mathbf{\Sigma}_{l_{i+1}} +$
      $+ \frac{n_i}{n_i+\operatorname{card}(l_{i+1})} \frac{n_{i+1}}{n_i+\operatorname{card}(l_{i+1})} (m_i - \mathbf{m}_{l_{i+1}})(m_i - \mathbf{m}_{l_{i+1}})^T$
   $n_{i+1} \leftarrow n_i + \operatorname{card}(l_{i+1})$
   $i \leftarrow i+1$
until $l_i \neq \emptyset$

The outcome of this algorithm are the mean and covariance matrix of approximate covering ellipse.

The following comment are needed to clarify the algorithm statements and used notations:

- the $\mathbf{m}_i$ and $\mathbf{m}_{l_i}$ denotes the mean of current approximation of convex hull and the mean value of set l_i respectively;
- the $\mathbf{\Sigma}_i$ and $\mathbf{\Sigma}_{l_i}$ denotes the covariance matrix of current approximation of convex hull and the covariance matrix value of set l_i respectively;
- the condition $x \notin \mathrm{B}_{\Sigma_i}(m_i, \sqrt{N+2})$ means that for tested x we get

$$\sqrt{(x - \mathbf{m}_i)^T \mathbf{\Sigma}_i^{-1}(x - \mathbf{m}_i)} > \sqrt{N+2};$$

- calculation of $\mathbf{m}_{i+1}$ and $\mathbf{\Sigma}_{i+1}$ in each step are done according to Eqs. (1) and (2) from Theorem 1.

4   The New Algorithm in Simple Illustrations

Emo Welzl [7] proposed a simple randomized algorithm for the minimum covering circle problem that runs in expected $O(N)$ time, based on a linear programming algorithm of Raimund Seidel [11]. The algorithm is recursive, and takes as arguments two sets of points S and Q. The algorithm computes the smallest enclosing circle of the union of S and Q, as long as every point of Q is one of the boundary points of the eventual smallest enclosing circle. Thus, the original smallest enclosing circle problem can be solved by calling the algorithm with S equal to the set of points to be enclosed and Q equal to the empty set; as the algorithm calls itself recursively, it will enlarge the set Q passed into the recursive calls until it includes all the boundary points of the circle.

In this work we compare result of our new algorithm with the incremental algorithm of Welzl implemented in CGAL library [12]. The Fig. 2 compares the results of finding smallest enclosing ellipse for same set of image data. As we can observe the results sames to be identical. However, the time needed to calculate those results differ for both algorithm – compare with Table 1. Thus our algorithm seem to be better in time consuming tests.

To confirm this we choose the benchmark image – Fig. 3 – which has originally size 300×300 pixels and contains 8000 black pixels (points of interest). Then we

Table 1. Execution time for authors algorithm vs. CGAL implementation of the incremental algorithm of Welzl.

Image name from Fig. 2	CGAL (ms)	Authors (ms)
(a)	643	19
(b)	926	37
(c)	1126	32
(d)	542	48
(e)	958	15
(f)	294	13

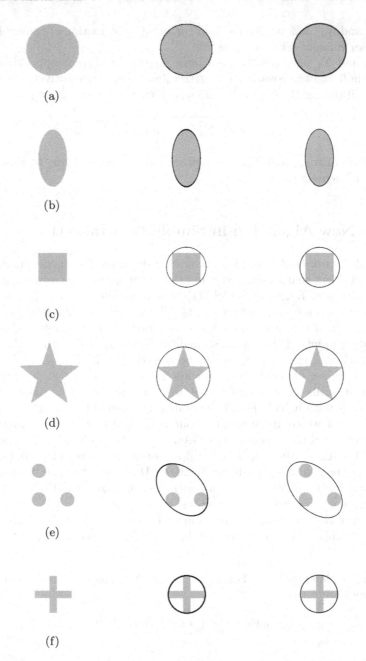

Fig. 2. Comparison of results of two algorithm: CGAL implementation of the incremental algorithm of Welzl (second column) and authors' algorithm applied for certain shapes (first column).

resize the original image according to sizes given in Table 2. For each sizes we calculate the execution time of both algorithms.

This experiments shows that indeed the authors' algorithm is faster. However it seam that the complexity of new algorithm is also $O(N)$, but this complexity in this case is realized with smaller constance then in case of Welzl algorithm.

Fig. 3. Input, output from CGAL

Table 2. Comparison of execution time for image presented on Fig. 3 for different image size (first column) calculated with CGAL implementation of the incremental algorithm of Welzl and authors' method

Image size	No. of black pixels	CGAL (ms)	Authors' (ms)
300×300	8000	1364	28
270×270	6624	1181	22
243×243	5371	777	18
219×219	4329	660	15
197×197	3465	573	14
177×177	2945	541	12
159×159	2295	379	9
143×143	1925	266	8

5   Conclusions

Int this paper the new approach for finding minimal covering ellipse was presented. This new method based on calculating the covariance matrix and interpret this according to behavior of Mahalanobis distance. The main advantage of this approach is that the results can be obtained very quickly.

We are planning to test this approach for streaming data, to detect the changes in stream data trends.

Acknowledgement. The research of Krzysztof Misztal is supported by the National Science Centre (Poland) [grant no. 2012/07/N/ST6/02192].

References

1. Lin, M., Gottschalk, S.: Collision detection between geometric models: a survey. In: Proceedings of IMA Conference on Mathematics of Surfaces, vol. 1, pp. 602–608 (1998)
2. Jiménez, P., Thomas, F., Torras, C.: 3D collision detection: a survey. Comput. Graph. **25**(2), 269–285 (2001)
3. Ericson, C.: Real-Time Collision Detection. CRC Press, Boca Raton (2004)
4. Croux, C., Haesbroeck, G., Rousseeuw, P.J.: Location adjustment for the minimum volume ellipsoid estimator. Stat. Comput. **12**(3), 191–200 (2002)
5. Knorr, E.M., Ng, R.T., Zamar, R.H.: Robust space transformations for distance-based operations. In: Proceedings of the Seventh ACM SIGKDD International Conference on Knowledge Discovery and Data Mining, pp. 126–135. ACM (2001)
6. Mahalanobis, P.C.: On the generalized distance in statistics. Proc. Nat. Inst. Sci. (Calcutta) **2**, 49–55 (1936)
7. Welzl, E.: Smallest enclosing disks (balls and ellipsoids). In: Maurer, H. (ed.) New Results and New Trends in Computer Science. LNCS, vol. 555, pp. 359–370. Springer, Heidelberg (1991)
8. Gärtner, B., Schönherr, S.: Smallest enclosing circles-an exact and generic implementation in C++ (1998)
9. Tabor, J., Spurek, P.: Cross-entropy clustering. Pattern Recogn. **47**(9), 3046–3059 (2014)
10. Misztal, K., Tabor, J.: Mahalanobis distance-based algorithm for ellipse growing in iris preprocessing. In: Saeed, K., Chaki, R., Cortesi, A., Wierzchoń, S. (eds.) CISIM 2013. LNCS, vol. 8104, pp. 158–167. Springer, Heidelberg (2013)
11. Seidel, R.: Small-dimensional linear programming and convex hulls made easy. Discrete Comput. Geom. **6**(3), 423–434 (1991)
12. The CGAL Project: CGAL, Computational Geometry Algorithms Library. http:// www.cgal.org

Process of Point Clouds Merging for Mapping of a Robot's Working Environment

Petr Olivka$^{(\boxtimes)}$, Michal Krumnikl, Pavel Moravec, and David Seidl

Department of Computer Science, FEECS, VŠB – Technical University of Ostrava,
17. listopadu 15, Ostrava, Czech Republic
{petr.olivka,michal.krumnikl,pavel.moravec,david.seidl}@vsb.cz
http://www.cs.vsb.cz

Abstract. The lidar is nowadays increasingly used in many robotic applications. Nevertheless the 3D lidars are still very expensive and their use on small robots is not economical. This article briefly introduces a construction of cheap 3D lidar for indoor usage based on the 2D laser range finder. Subsequently, this article introduces process of merging acquired point clouds. The every pair of neighboring point clouds is oriented in space to fit together in the best possible way. The result of this process is a 3D map of the robot working environment. This map can be segmented and further used for a navigation. In this way, it is also possible to map inaccessible and dangerous areas.

Keywords: Lidar · Laser range finder · Point clouds · Mapping · Robot

1 Introduction

Nowadays there are many types of laser devices for a distance measurement. Probably the best known application of this type of devices is the use of lidar in the autonomous car driving systems. For example, Google cars use lidar Velodyne HDL-64E which can be seen in Fig. 1.

It is not possible to use this type of lidar on small robots in industrial applications. There are many reasons for not using Velodyne lidar. At first, it is very expensive. The Velodyne HDL-64E price is around $8000. For small robotic applications such price is absolutely unacceptable. The next reason is the narrow measuring range. Despite this lidar measures 360° around, the vertical field of view is only 28° [12]. The visualization of the raw data from HDL-64E is in Fig. 2. The small viewing angle is suitable in traffic environment, but it is insufficient for indoor application like recognition of nearby objects and obstacles. But what is for internal use completely inappropriate is the blind space above the lidar. For the indoor robot navigation it is very important to detect space above the robot.

In contrast to this high-end devices there are several cheap devices available on the market suitable for home or office use. The first example is Kinect as depicted

D. Seidl—This work was partially supported by the Grant of SGS No. SP2016/58, VŠB - Technical University of Ostrava, Czech Republic.

© IFIP International Federation for Information Processing 2016
Published by Springer International Publishing Switzerland 2016. All Rights Reserved
K. Saeed and W. Homenda (Eds.): CISIM 2016, LNCS 9842, pp. 251–264, 2016.
DOI: 10.1007/978-3-319-45378-1_23

Fig. 1. Velodyne lidar HDL-64E [12]   **Fig. 2.** Raw data from HDL-64E [12]

in Fig. 3 and a similar device Xtion PRO can be seen in Fig. 4. The disadvantage of these devices is that they are not designed for industrial applications and they have very limited measurement field of view in vertical and horizontal axes. These devices are also not prepared for measurement in 360° range.

Because 3D lidars are nowadays still very expensive and cheap customer devices are not suitable for industrial usage, it is necessary to focus to a different device design for a reliable measurement of distances in 3D space. There is a large variety of 2D Laser Range Finders (LRF) available on the market. These devices are produced for measurement of short or long distances with different measurement precision, they are equipped with different interfaces and they are designed for indoor or outdoor use. These 2D devices can be easily used for the measurement in 3D. It is only necessary to add the third dimension. The probably first design of 3D LRF device was introduced in 2009 and it can be seen in Fig. 5. In this figure there is 2D LRF Hokuyo URG-04LX mounted on a servo in order to achieve the ability to measure in 3D.

This design has two disadvantages. The servo has a problem with precision of positioning. It is impossible to achieve the precise angular position and the repeatability of the positioning is also problematic. The second problem of this design lies in the mechanical features of the servo. The design of the servo does not handle axial and radial forces correctly. The use of this design on the robot will let to a quickly damage of the servo. The inertial forces of mounted 2D LRF will very quickly damage gears and their mounting.

Fig. 3. Kinect [http://www.microsoft. com]   **Fig. 4.** Xtion PRO LIVE [http://www. asus.com]

Fig. 5. First known design of 3D LRF with servo [10]

Fig. 6. Zebedee design of 3D LRF with 2D LRF mounted on spring [1]

Alternative design of 3D LRF was introduced by SCIRO [1]. In this design the 2D LRF is mounted on a spring and the third dimension is added by a swinging. The overall design is shown in Fig. 6. Such design has also some disadvantages. It is necessary to manually swing with the mounted LRF and maintain very precise synchronization between the gyroscope mounted under the LRF and the LRF scanning.

2   3D LRF Desing

Based on the introduced constructions and their disadvantages we have developed a new design of the 3D LRF. The diagram of this design is in Fig. 7. The 2D LRF Hokuyo URG-04LX is mounted on a step motor by a carrier. This construction guarantees the sufficient strength of the design. All inertial forces are captured in ball bearings of the step motor and the step motor also guarantees the precise positioning of the mounted LRF.

In the diagram we can see that the rotation axis of the step motor is identical with the internal axis x_i of the LRF. It simplifies the future computation. The current position of the step motor is given by angle α_r and the position and

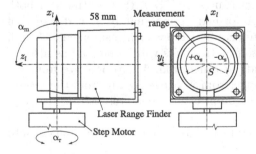

Fig. 7. 3D LFR schema

Fig. 8. 3D LRF overall design

254 P. Olivka et al.

measurement range of laser beam is defined by angle α_s. The mounting position of LRF on the step motor is marked in the diagram as the angle α_m.

Now the principle of 3D LRF measurement will be described. The 2D LRF measures distances of obstacles by a laser beam. The 2D measurement is performed in the plane $x_i y_i$. The current position of the laser beam is marked in the diagram as an angle α_s. The resolution of used 2D LRF is $360°/1024$. The angular range of the measurement is from $-120°$ to $120°$ and in this range 628 points are measured.

The carrier with 2D LRF is mounted on the step motor and is rotated around axis x_i. The rotation of the whole LRF is performed in the range of a half turn ($180°$). This rotating movement guarantees the whole coverage of the environment. The current position of the 2D LRF is marked as α_r. The resolution of the step motor is $360°/800$.

The overall design of the 3D LRF is depicted in Fig. 8. The figure shows a complete device with the control computer and the microstepping unit [8]. For the following experiment the 3D LRF was mounted on the small robotic undercarriage Roomba.

The 2D LRF measures distances in all positions and measured distances will be marked as $l_{r,s}$. This measured distances can be transformed to a position vector $\boldsymbol{l}_{r,s} = [l_{r,s}, 0, 0, 1]^T$. All measured distances can be then transformed to point cloud, where every point will be represented by its position vector $\boldsymbol{p}_{r,s}$. The computation is performed by following formula:

$$\boldsymbol{p}_{r,s} = R_z(\alpha_r) \cdot R_y(\alpha_m) \cdot R_z(\alpha_s) \cdot \boldsymbol{l}_{r,s}, \tag{1}$$

where R_y and R_z are transformation matrices for rotations.

During the single measurement the designed 3D LRF captures point clouds composed of 628×401 points. It is in total 252828 points.

Practically every manufactured LRF Hokuyo URG-04LX unit has some manufacturing inaccuracies. For the precise measurement it is necessary to calibrate every LRF. The process of calibration is described in details in [9]. Acquired results are very inaccurate without this calibration.

The set of point clouds were acquired for the following experiment. Inside the building 26 meters long corridor was selected with variety of surfaces and irregular shapes. This corridor were measured by 3D LRF four times in both directions and measurements were performed approximately at a distance of one meter. Thus 25 point clouds were acquired in every measurement. Overall 100 point clouds were acquired. These points clouds will be marked as a set of point clouds M_1 to M_{100}. Point clouds in range from M_1 to M_{25} are from the first measurement, point clouds in range from M_{26} to M_{50} are from the second measurement, etc. An example of single point cloud, concretely M_1, is visible in Fig. 9.

The following task is to merge all point clouds from every measurement into one whole.

Fig. 9. Acquired point cloud M_1

3   Point Clouds Preprocessing for Merging

Nowadays there are many preprocessing methods, algorithms, filters and analysis known. But for point clouds merging only a few of them are suitable. The main focus should be concentrated mainly on these three areas:

- features,
- keypoints,
- registration.

3.1   Features

Features is general term for many characteristics of point clouds. It is possible to compute density of points, normal vector of points, collect neighbours, compute curvature of surface etc. From this list the most suitable features for preprocessing before merging are the computation of normal vectors and curvature.

In this experiment the Point Cloud Library [11] (PCL) is used. The normal vectors are in this library computed by eigenvalues and eigenvectors. The algorithm is described in more details in [2]. The knowledge of this algorithm is very important for the computation of curvature and segmentation. Without this knowledge it is not possible to understand used terms and parameters in PCL implementation.

3.2   Keypoints

The aim of keypoints is to select a subset of points from the point cloud which will represent the whole point cloud in the processing steps. The subset selection should represent the point cloud, but the reduced amount of points will increase speed of the following processing. This is similar procedure as searching for correspondence in stereometry. The keypoints detection can be performed by many algorithms. The description and the comparison and recommendation of the best algorithms after testing were introduced by Alexandre [3] and Filipe [4].

3.3 Registration

The previous algorithms are designed for usage with single point cloud and they detect important attributes in point cloud. However, the registration is directly designed for two point clouds merging. The principles of registration process based on planar surfaces are described in [5] and advanced registration for outdoor environment was introduced in [6]. The implementation of registration is based on features and keypoints.

3.4 Preprocessing Recommendation

Even there are many algorithms for point clouds preprocessing, all of them mentioned above are designed and tested for point clouds representing the small area in front of a robotic device. The point cloud acquired by the 3D LRF introduced above captures the whole environment around robotic device, not only in front. Thus problem of merging the point clouds is more complex. The merging process should be based on main principles introduced in this section, but must be designed to accept different type of point clouds.

4 Point Clouds Segmentation

The point cloud acquired by the presented 3D LRF covers big part of the environment around the device. In this situation the point cloud contains much more information than from devices which acquire only a small range of the environment. In this case it is possible to expand small details - keypoints - to larger object. Every point cloud can be divided to separated segments. The number of segments is significantly smaller than number of points in cloud. Moreover all segments can be represented by some typical features, e.g. center of gravity, normal vector, size, etc. So the usage of segmentation for point cloud preprocessing is promising and will be consequently verified.

4.1 Segmentation Algorithms

The PCL library offers a few segmentation algorithms. Most of them are described by Rusu [2].

The algorithm *Fitting simplified geometric model* is based on searching of certain structures or patterns of points. The *Basic clustering techniques* is based on space decomposition and clustering by proximity. The *Finding edges* algorithm is complementary algorithm of the next one. It is segmentation by *Region growing*. This algorithm is well known from image processing. But the implementation for point clouds must be based on different attributes. In the PCL it is based on normal vectors and curvature.

A few additional segmentation algorithms are implemented in the PCL library. The testing of all algorithms showed that the best method for segmentation is the *Region growing*. The comparison is not presented here.

Fig. 10. Point cloud M_1 after segmentation (Color figure online)

4.2   Point Clouds Preprocessing by Segmentation

The example of the segmentation of the point cloud from Fig. 9 is visible in Fig. 10. The figure contains only large segments. The threshold for the large segment was set to 500 points and every segment is distinguished by a color.

4.3   Verification of Region Growing Algorithm

Figure 10 shows that the segmentation method *Region growing* is working well for the point cloud M_1. To be sure that this segmentation can be used for the whole data set it is necessary to apply segmentation to every point cloud from data set and create overall statistic of all segmentation results.

All segments of point clouds will be separated into six groups: left, right, front, rear, top and bottom. This separation can be based on normal vector of segments. This vector can be computed in the centroid of all segments, where the centroid can be computed by the following formula:

$$c_s = \frac{1}{N_s} \cdot \sum_{i=1}^{N_s} p_{s,i}, \tag{2}$$

where c_s is the centroid of the segment s and N_s is a number of points of that segment. Vectors $p_{s,i}$ are position vectors of all points of segment s computed by (1).

The computation of normal vector of segments in PCL library automatically orients the vector direction to half-space with the origin of coordinate system. So the largest coordinate of normal vector can divide segments to their proper group. The largest positive coordinate x of normal vector specifies rear segment, the largest positive y specifies right segment, the positive z specifies bottom segment, etc.

The segmentation of all point clouds from the data set was performed and for all large segments their proper group was determined. The overall statistic is visible in Table 1. In this table the column Minimum indicates that in all point clouds at least 1 large top, left and right segment were recognized. The median for these segments is 3. One bottom segment was also recognized in all point clouds. Only front and rear segments are not recognized in all point clouds. This is an expected result, because the measurement was performed in the long narrow corridor.

Table 1. Statistic of the whole data set segmentation

Segments	Number of segments			
	Average	Median	Minimum	Maximum
Left	3.1	3	1	7
Right	3.3	3	1	8
Top	3.2	3	1	7
Bottom	1.1	1	1	3
Front	1.2	1	0	4
Rear	1.2	1	0	4

This statistic proved that the segmentation method *Region growing* is suitable for preprocessing the whole data set of our experiment.

5   Point Clouds Merging Process

The process of point clouds merging will be performed in four stages. All of them are illustrated for clarity in Fig. 11 using a matchbox.

The sub-picture Fig. 11(a) depicts the general startup position of two neighbouring point clouds. Subsequent sub-pictures depicts following four stages of merging process:

Fig. 11. Illustration of point clouds merging stages on the process of closing a matchbox

1. Fig. 11(b) - the horizon leveling.
2. Fig. 11(c) - the direction alignment.
3. Fig. 11(d) - the centering.
4. Fig. 11(e) - the insertion.

The main advantage of proposed 3D LRF design will be used in following process. The advantage is the possibility of scanner to measure the whole environment including a space even above the scanner. Just the ceiling is the most visible part of the environment. It is flat, without obstacle and in long term in the unchanging state. Thus the ceiling will be in center of attention in the most stages of point clouds merging process.

5.1 Horizon Leveling

The measuring device does not stay during the measurement always in ideal horizontal position. The floor has minor irregularities which cause small inclination of the device. The tilt in some cases is greater than few degrees.

In this stage the horizon will be balanced according to the ceiling plane. The segment of ceiling is in all point clouds the largest segment of all. It covers the area of approximately 10 to 16 square meters. So the informative value of these segments is very high and it can be used in a simple way. The normal vector of the ceiling segment can be easily computed in centroid of the segment ceiling. This normal vector will consequently define a new direction of the vertical axis z.

The balancing of the whole point cloud will be realized by rotations around axes x and y. The necessary angles of rotations can be easy computed from the angle between the normal vector n and the axis z. All points in every point cloud will be transformed by following formula:

$$p_{r,s} = R_y(\alpha_y) \cdot R_x(\alpha_x) \cdot p_{r,s}. \tag{3}$$

5.2 Direction Alignment

In this stage the ceiling segment will be reused again. The direction of the point cloud will be based on left and right edges of the ceiling segment. The top view of this situation is depicted in Fig. 12.

The measuring device is in general position in the origin of the coordinate system O. The virtual lines, parallel with the axis y, are regularly marked at distances d on both sides of the axis y. On the left and right side these lines leaves ceiling segment in edge points L_i and R_j. The connecting lines of these points creates a set of vectors l_i and r_j. Now these vectors will be used to determine the direction in two steps: estimation of direction and improving its accuracy.

The estimation of the direction will be computed separately for the left and right side of the ceiling segment using the following formulas:

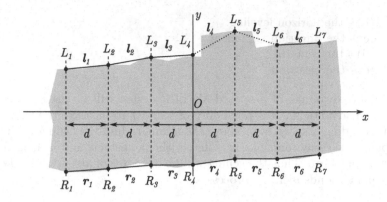

Fig. 12. The segment representing the ceiling used for the direction alignment

$$l = \frac{\sum_{i=1}^{M} l_i}{\sum_{i=1}^{M} |l_i|}, \quad r = \frac{\sum_{j=1}^{N} r_j}{\sum_{j=1}^{N} |r_j|}, \tag{4}$$

where M and N is a number of left and right vectors.

The estimation will be used for a simple filtering. Vectors from the left and right set, which divert from the vector l and r more than the given angular threshold, will be removed. In this experiment this threshold is set to 10°. This simple filtering removes bounces and niches in wall from both ceiling edges. Removed vectors are marked in Fig. 12 by dotted line.

The number of vectors will be reduced by this filtering to number M' and N' and final direction d is computed from all remaining vectors by the formula:

$$d = \frac{\sum_{i=1}^{M'} l_i + \sum_{j=1}^{N'} r_j}{\sum_{i=1}^{M'} |l_i| + \sum_{j=1}^{N'} |r_j|}. \tag{5}$$

Now it remains only to calculate the angle α_z between the vector d and the axis x. Every point cloud will be rotated around the axis z by this angle:

$$p_{r,s} = R_z(\alpha_z) \cdot p_{r,s}. \tag{6}$$

5.3   Centering

This is the first stage where a pair of neighbouring point clouds will be used. Furthermore, the odometric value of the shift between two measurements is needed. As was mentioned above, this distance is approximately 1 meter. This distance will be marked as d_o.

In this stage, two neighbouring point clouds will be placed side by side, on its joined axes x at the distance d_o. This situation is partially visible in Fig. 13. The illustration depicts only left edges of two neighbouring point clouds. Elements

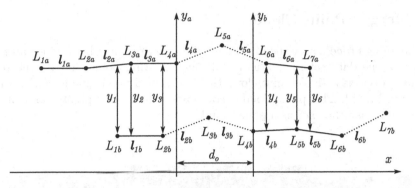

Fig. 13. The left edges of two point clouds

of the first point cloud are marked with additional index a and elements of the second point cloud with index b.

Now it is necessary to compute distances between all points L_i of cloud a and edges l_j of cloud b and vice versa. The same procedure is applied for right edges of both point clouds. The distances between points and removed edges are not computed.

The result is a set of distances y_k and the number of distances can be marked as K. The average value of all y_k can be computed by the following formula:

$$y_a = \frac{\sum_{k=1}^{K} y_k}{K}. \tag{7}$$

The average distance will be used for translation of the whole point cloud b by distance y_a:

$$\boldsymbol{p}_{r,s} = T_y(-y_a) \cdot \boldsymbol{p}_{r,s}. \tag{8}$$

5.4   Insertion

The last stage of point clouds merging will use odometric distance d_o and corresponding front and back segments of neighbouring point clouds.

The estimation of the insertion is based on the distance d_o. The improvement of accuracy is performed by measuring the distance of corresponding front and back segments. The pair of segments corresponds when the distance of their centroids is less than 20 % of d_o. The distances of centroids are only computed in the direction of the axis x. These distances are averaged in the similar way as in previous stage. The result leads to more accurate distance d_o'. This distance d_o' can be used for the translation of all points of point cloud b:

$$\boldsymbol{p}_{r,s} = T_x(d_o') \cdot \boldsymbol{p}_{r,s}. \tag{9}$$

Now it is possible to merge all points from point cloud a and b into single point cloud.

6 Merged Point Cloud

The merging process described in the previous section must be used for all point clouds in the data set as well as for all neighbouring point clouds. The result of this process is a single point cloud that merges 25 point clouds. The result is visible in Fig. 14. This point cloud is composed of 5.4×10^6 points. Thus in this figure it seems solid, not as a point cloud.

Fig. 14. The top view and the side view of the whole corridor - 25 merged point clouds

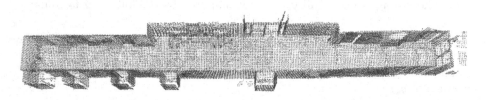

Fig. 15. The merged point cloud after voxelization (100 mm)

Figure 14 shows that the merging process did not create an exact straight object. The result is a little bit curved. But this result was achieved by using point clouds only without any additional position or incline sensors.

For further usage it is necessary to reduce the amount of points of the merged point cloud. For the reduction of points a *voxelization* algorithm is used. It this process the whole space is divided into small cubes, for this experiment the cube size is 100 mm, and all points inside every cube is reduced to a single point. Obtained results directly correspond to the Octomaps used for the robot navigation [7]. The result of this process is visible in Fig. 15. This point cloud is composed of only 46×10^3 points. It is less than 1 % of the original merged point cloud size.

The segmentation algorithm can be repeatedly applied on the merged point cloud with reduced number of points.

The result of this segmentation is visible in Fig. 16. There is clearly visible that the segmentation recognizes the ceiling very well as the single (red) segment.

Fig. 16. Side view of the resulting segmentation of the reduced point cloud (Color figure online)

Fig. 17. Top view of the resulting segmentation of the reduced point cloud (Color figure online)

The same result is for the floor which is depicted as a single (blue) segment. In Fig. 17 it is also visible that the segmentation can very well recognize niches and doors. The resulting

Based on this result, it is possible to say that the process of point clouds merging was successful.

7   Conclusion

The paper introduces a novel concept of using cheap 2D LRF as a 3D scanning device. In contrast to more advanced devices, additional procedures of calibration and point cloud merging is necessary, however the final results are comparable with the more expensive devices. This article focuses on the process of merging point clouds and describes it in more details. Special properties of indoor measurements are used as a basis for establishing merging parameters. Merged point clouds represent whole environment and can be used after the segmentation as a source for the robot navigation and environment mapping. The experiments showed that for the successful merging only a small part of raw measurements is needed (in the described example less than 1 % of acquired points were used).

References

1. Bosse, M., Zlot, R., Flick, P.: Zebedee: design of a spring-mounted 3-D range sensor with application to mobile mapping. IEEE Trans. Robot. **28**(5), 1104–1119 (2012)
2. Rusu, R.B.: Semantic 3D object maps for everyday manipulation in human living environments. Disertation, Institut für Informatik der Technischen Universität München (2009)
3. Alexandre, L.A.: 3D descriptors for object, category recognition: a comparative evaluation. In: Workshop on Color-Depth Camera Fusion in Robotics at the IEEE/RSJ International Conference on Intelligent Robots and Systems (IROS), Vilamoura, Portugal, p. 7 (2012)

4. Filipe, S., Alexandre, L.A.: A comparative evaluation of 3D keypoint detectorsin a RGB-D object dataset. In: 2014 International Conference on Computer Vision Theory and Applications (VISAPP), vol. 1, pp. 476–483. IEEE (2014)
5. Xiao, J., Adler, B., Zhang, H.: 3D point cloud registration based on planar surfaces. In: 2012 IEEE Conference on Multisensor Fusion and Integration for Intelligent Systems (MFI), pp. 40–45. IEEE, September 2012
6. Xiao, J., Adler, B., Zhang, J., Zhang, H.: Planar segment based three-dimensional point cloud registration in outdoor environments. J. Field Robot. **30**(4), 552–582 (2013)
7. Wurm, K.M., Hornung, A., Bennewitz, M., Stachniss, C., Burgard, W.: OctoMap: a probabilistic, flexible, and compact 3D map representation for robotic systems. In: Proceedings of the ICRA 2010 Workshop on Best Practice in 3D Perception and Modeling for Mobile Manipulation, vol. 2, May 2010
8. Krumnikl, M., Olivka, P.: PWM nonlinearity reduction in microstepping unit firmware. Przegld Elektrotech. **88**(3a), 232–236 (2012)
9. Olivka, P., Krumnikl, M., Moravec, P., Seidl, D.: Calibration of short range 2D laser range finder for 3D SLAM usage. J. Sens. **501**, 3715129 (2016)
10. I Heart Robotics, More Hokuyo 3D Laser Scanner Images, October 2015. http://www.iheartrobotics.com/2009/06/more-hokuyo-3d-laser-scanner-images.html
11. Point Cloud Library. http://www.pointclouds.org
12. Velodyne LiDAR, HDL-64E. http://www.velodynelidar.com/hdl-64e.html

Techniques of Czech Language Lossless Text Compression

Jiří Ševčík and Jiří Dvorský[✉]

IT4Innovations, VŠB - Technical University of Ostrava,
17. listopadu 15/2172, 708 33 Ostrava, Czech Republic
{jiri.sevcik,jiri.dvorsky}@vsb.cz

Abstract. For lossless data compression of the texts of natural language and for achieving better compression ratio we can use linguistic and grammatical properties extracted from the text analysis. This work deals with usage of word order, word categories and grammatical rules in sentences and sentence units in Czech language. Special grammatical properties of this language which are different from for example English language are used here. Further, there is an algorithm designed for searching similarities in analyzed sentence structures and its next processing to final compressed file. For analysis of the sentence units a special tool is used which allows parsing on more levels.

Keywords: Lossless data compression · Czech language · Linguistic · Morphology · Graphs

1 Introduction

Within the compression we can encounter several data types. These types can be graphic data, sound data or a text in natural language. All these types have different statistic properties and dependences following from them. In case of the text compression we can point out that the character of given language has an influence on the compression itself. From this finding we can deduce that knowledge of the language structures and rules can influence the final compression ratio if we use it properly. Our work focuses on these properties. It is not a general system which processes any kind of language, but Czech language. On account of the fact that Czech language belongs to different category than English language, there will be mentioned examples in both languages for better understanding.

2 Language Categories

Czech belongs to Slavic languages. These languages, similarly to English, belong to Indo-European languages. We can divide Czech language into two categories: standard Czech language which is used for official communication and common

© IFIP International Federation for Information Processing 2016
Published by Springer International Publishing Switzerland 2016. All Rights Reserved
K. Saeed and W. Homenda (Eds.): CISIM 2016, LNCS 9842, pp. 265–276, 2016.
DOI: 10.1007/978-3-319-45378-1_24

Czech language which is used in daily communication between people. In Czech language we can find many dialects. Czech vocabulary is mainly Slavic, but it can adopt words from other languages, for example from German or Polish.

The number of language properties which are different for described categories is higher, but it is sufficient for basic understanding. Thanks to this understanding we can point out the fact that in case of inflected languages is the word arrangement looser than in the analytic languages. The word order is mainly influenced by semantic point of view of the whole sentence or by its grammatical arrangement. Knowledge of this property is one of the crucial features of our work and the whole principle of the data preprocessing for compression is built on this property. There are many branches that deal with grammatical arrangement and with natural language analysis on different levels and its importance and contribution to this work will be mentioned in following parts.

3   Previous Work

We can find a large number of researches or works that deal with the compression which specializes on a particular language. The largest amount of them deals with English text or with Indo-European languages [1,2]. We can find also special compressing methods for different language categories such as Arabic [3] or Chinese [5] language. Since we are dealing with a compression of text only lossless principles will be mentioned. There exist also methods for loss compression with the informational content maintained but based on the aim of this work we will not deal with them.

In a number of these works we can encounter also preprocessing. It divides the compression into two sequential parts – preprocessing algorithm and compression algorithm. First algorithm transforms the input data for the compression based on its own compression scheme and these modified data he will deliver to the second algorithm which will, based on some standard or special methods, compress it. Decompression works just the opposite way. In the case of preprocessing algorithm we can encounter various general methods. The closest one to the topic of this work is the one on the level of words [4], symbols or sentential units. Another interesting method is the compression based on syllables [6,7].

4   Linguistics

The problem of compressing a natural language is therefore large and we can approach it with different perspectives. The aim of this work is to use some of these specific attributes and characteristics of Czech language and with the use of that attain a better compression ratio. Therefore we have to use possibilities of a science related to the language – linguistics. It represents a large group of sub-fields of study which deal with a large spectrum of language attributes from grammatical and syntactic parts to for example special usage related to the fields as sociology or psychology. We can divide it into general linguistics, applied linguistics or language linguistics. Further we can divide it based on its aims – in our case we will specialize in descriptive linguistics and theoretical linguistics. It, based on Czech linguistic tradition [9], incorporates many subsystems because we can understand the language as a system. On theoretical level we can divide these subsystems into three categories: phonetics, grammar and syntax. Related to the aim of this work we will specialize on the second category which is divided into morphology and syntax.

Morphology we can describe as a discipline which deals with the study of the creation of words their declension and deriving of new words. Further we analyze the structure of particular words or whole word form. For the analysis of words we use morphematics. Basic morphological unit is an component which has a particular meaning – morpheme. If standing alone it may not be even a word. In the basic division morpheme may be lexical (word base) root of the word which represents action or characteristic or morpheme grammatical (*afix*) which defines grammatical categories (*sematics*) [9].

Another characteristic which morphology deals with is the study of grammatical categories which determine the meaning of particular morphemes. The most general category is a word class which is in the Czech language divided into ten types. Those can be divided based on the mentioned possibility if the *flex* (inflected words) may be used or not (inflexible words). To inflected words belong nouns, adjectives, pronouns, numerals and verbs and to Inflexible words are adverbs, prepositions, conjunctions, particles and interjection.

Morphological analysis lies on analyzing of a particular word form without taking the context into consideration. The output of this analysis are two components. One of them is the mentioned lemma and the second one is the morphological tag which comprises of 15 symbols (in special cases even 16). Each of these 15 positions are related to a particular morphological category and to every value of this category a particular symbol corresponds to [10]. In most of the cases it is a capital letter of alphabet or another alternative is a lower case letter. The last possible characteristic is "-" when used it means that for that particular word the morphological category is not applicable which is related to the rules of Czech language and grammar. A typical example is the case in verbs. The most important categories are (the number symbolizes the position in the tag) pos, gender, number, case, person, tense and grade.

The opposite procedure of analysis is the morphological synthesis. Here, in order to acquire a particular word we need to know its basic lemma form and morphological tag. There are various morphological taggers for the Czech language and each processes the text in a different way. Among the most well-known belong Free morphology tagger of Jan Hajič [13] and Ajka system [14]. Another category is the syntactic discipline. Its primary use in linguistics is to study the relationships between the words in a single clause or the relationships of individual clauses or sentences. It can be said that it is a study of the general sentential structure and its parts.

In European linguistics the dependency description is used to describe the structure of the sentence. Here, the verb is considered to be the central part of the clause or the sentence. The whole structure of the sentence is described in the form of tree where each node represents an individual constituent. The borders between the nodes represent dependency relations and each node has only a single superordinate parent node. Here the verb is the root node. The nodes in the tree are arranged structurally according to their dependency relations and also linearly according to their sequence in the sentential word order.

5   Computer Linguistics

The described linguistic disciplines are difficult and complex field and a "handmade" analysis of the grammatical constituents or units is very demanding not only with the respect to time. Here the use of computers comes in the picture. Such processing is called Natural language processing. It is a field that links not only linguistics and informatics but also other fields such as acoustics in case of spoken word synthesis.

The corpus is the important term here. It is a structured set of texts/ literature or even transcriptions of a spoken language. This set includes other information about the linguistic informations of the given text. Such information is crucial for us because they are syntactic and morphological. Various languages, including the Czech language, have many corpuses. For our task the Prague Dependency Treebank [11] is the most interesting. It has been developed since the middle of the 1990s in Institute of Formal and Applied Linguistics, Charles University in Prague and its actual version 3.0. comprises of several millions of entries. This corpus, besides other functions, includes two aforementioned levels, that is the *morphological layer* (m-level) and *analytical/syntactic layer* (a-level). A *tectogrammatical layer* is also included, however it is not crucial for our task. The actual data is stored in the structured format *PML* (Prague Markup language) which is based on the well-known marking XML and thus the computer data processing is made easier.

The resulting dependency tree includes the description of dependencies in the line descendant – parent between the individual constituents of the sentential whole. Such analytical tag is called afun and there are twenty-eight types of them. The second most important information included is the morphological part which records the lemma form to each grammatical constituent and a complete morphological tag. The last presented tool is *Treex* [12] which is capable of processing the text, creating its morphological and syntactic analysis and generate the resulting *PML* set. The tool can be configured, schemes and required resulting layers for the output adjusted and it also allows a reverse morphological synthesis. In total, twenty-three attributes are available, the majority of which is not important for our task (for example specialized linguistic categories of particular words) but we shall deal with them in the subsequent phases of development. One of them is for example *is_spaces_after* attribute which allows a detection of whitespace after given word and use of this information in the set of resulting trees.

6   Our Work

The previous text proves that processing and analysis of the text can be done on the lowest levels even in the complex language such as Czech. It can be also said that despite the free word-order the clause or the grammatical constituent need to have a certain structure resulting from the given grammatical rules. The idea of our task, that deals with the use of the described analytical tool *Treex* as a part of the preprocessing in a compressive algorithm, is based on these premises. The progress of the preprocessing can summed up into several parts. The processing of the input text by analyser, finding similarities in tree structures while using the knowledge of grammatical rules and subsequent compression of the individual parts by compressive algorithms.

6.1   Processing of the Text

Treex analyser is to be used for the analysis of the compressed text. The program can be used in a graphic mode via web program as well as a console application. After morphological and syntactic analysis is done, the output is transferred to the next part of the algorithm. Thus the analyser runs as the individual process and later a greater integration and interconnection with the preprocessing algorithm could be one of the subsequent parts of the development. But in the current phase the manner how the analysis runs is sufficient.

6.2   Similarities in Tree Structures

In informatics and in other fields of course, the graph theory offers countless of possibilities and thus there is no need, considering the length and the character of this paper, to deal with it in-depth. For our case, the searching for similarities in graphs is the most important. The search is to be done in two, mutually collaborating levels. The algorithm works in several phases:

1. **The initial phase** takes place during the actual processing of the input text in *Treex* analyser. Here we observe whether the afun *Coord* appears in the morphological analyses because here it serves as the coordinate function for grammatical constituents; Namely the symbols "," and "*a*". In such case the whole tree is divisible into grammatical constituents. After the conclusion of this initializing phase the trees are divided in two sets (hereinafter referred to as A and B).
2. **The first similarity phase**: Here, and also in the following phase, the work is done by the general algorithm for similarity search in the graph. The manner and evaluation of similarities is to be discussed later. The algorithm first processes the set tagged as divisible i.e. A. In case there are more trees with necessary similarity, they are moved into resultant set C.
3. **The phase of division** – A division into sentential units is to be done for all the remaining trees from the set A. The division is made on the spot of the occurrence of the *Coord* afun. Thus two subtrees are created, to which we

assign the information about the linking coordinating function and which tree is their parent. The division into subtrees is done recursively because of the possibility of several *Coords* appearing in the single tree. After all subtrees are determined for the individual tree, they are moved into set B where all trees gained from the first phase can be found.

4. **The second similarity phase.** The same procedure as in the set A is used for the set B with the exception that all trees are to be moved into the resultant set.

As another possibility we have synthesis and modification of these phases in two which shall look as follows:

1. **The first phase** – after processing the text in *Treex*, the sentences where *Coord* afun occurs, will be divided into subtrees that will be saved into set together with all other trees that could not be divided.
2. **The second phase** – The similarity algorithm is applied on the whole set.

In the current phase of this work we cannot decidedly tell which procedure shall bear better results. It can be assumed that the processing of divided sentential units [8] will enhance the overall compression ratio but considering the small modification of preprocessing algorithm both alternatives shall be tested.

6.3   Comparing the Similarity in Graphs

The issue of comparing and defining the similarity of graphs is not unusual and there are many theoretical and practical works that deal with the topic. Thus there is plenty of research material and completed theoretical solutions. We are especially interested in the research group created under Czech Technical University in Prague. This group which consists of the members of well-known The Prague Stringology Club created a research group Arbology in 2008. Their work deals with the use of known algorithms from stringology for work with trees and tree-like structures [15]. The scope of their work is thus very large. In our work we can use the tree similarity on several levels which again reflect the variability of the Czech language and grammar.

Structural Similarity. A clause or a grammatical constituent can be regarded as a tree without further research of its attributes and dependency functions between the individual nodes.

Word-Order Similarity. This similarity has already been mentioned – there are certain similarities to be found even in the free word-order.
Example: "Voda je studená." (Water is cold.), "Básničky se nám líbily." ("We liked a poems.") – subject "Voda" and "Básničky" and predicates "je studená" and "se nám líbily".

Morphological Similarity. The most frequent similarity can be found in the same grammatical case of the words.
Example: "Honzík a Anička se domluvili, že se odpoledne sejdou na hřišti."

("Honzik and Anicka agreed that they will meet on the playground on the afternoon."). Subject "Honzík" and subject "Anička" are grammatically connected and both are in nominative case. Preposition "se" and adverb "hřišti" are grammatically connected and both are in accusative case.

It can be seen that the similarity of the grammatical constituents can be found on several levels. Our goal is to create such an algorithm that will be capable of processing all input trees and create the smallest possible output set of trees for them on all similarity levels. The algorithm will be capable to determine whether it is suitable for particular clause to create a new tree if there is a similarity with the already existing output tree. Or whether an existing should be used considering that the original tree is modified and the modification is saved as the additional information. The modification will be most commonly used in addition or removal of the node in the tree or change of some morphological tags.

6.4   Tag Compression

This idea of processing and subsequent compression seemed, after initial testing and several tests, very promising. However, we started encountering one significant problem with the speed of the text analysis using *Treex*. At first this did not seem as an obstacle but in case of several megabytes of input text the speed of analysis took tens of minutes. This duration was of course also caused by a non-optimized usage of the individual tool. After evaluating options and factoring that our development is at the beginning, it was decided that in the first phase of the development the morphological analysis shall be handled by a different tool called *MorphoDiTa* [18]. Another supportive argument for this choice was the fact that we needed to achieve some initial results that would allows as to verify that our input assumptions for compression based on the utilisation of knowledge of grammatical structure and rules of the Czech language are correct. This would confirm the assumption that the devised algorithm will be effectual. Therefore we decided, for the time being, to use a different tool.

Unlike *Treex*, the *MorphoDiTa* executes the text analysis only on the morphological level, ignoring the syntactic or tectogrammatical layer. Due to this focus, the tool is much faster and it can be also used for the reverse generating of the original word, if the lemma and morphological tag are known. There are more tools suitable for the operation, however *MorphoDiTa* was chosen for its simple integration into our current task. There is also a possibility to work the tool into our algorithm because it can be used as a standalone tool or a library, which was another reason for the use. Thanks to the output information that had been provided by *MorphoDiTa*, our subsequent research focused on the possible compression forms of the morphological tag (see the previous chapters). This seems sufficient because these tags are utilised very often in the complex algorithm which we already devised, and their analysis will make the following work easier.

As already described, the tag itself consists of 15 marks. Because the marks (to make things easier we shall use only this designation as the detailed description can be found here [10,13]) correspond to grammatical categories and advanced rules of the Czech language. From this knowledge we can extrapolate the fact that some marks can be used only if other signs occur or in case when we cannot use any mark in combination with the group of other – symbol "-".

The most important mark in the tag are the first (*POS*) and the second (*SUBPOS*) marks according to which it can be clearly said what combinations of marks will appear in the subsequent positions and which positions will remain empty. After applying this knowledge, it is possible to employ compression into the following form. All this on condition that in case of decompression we will be able to assemble the original tag.

Example - Original Tag: N N I P 1 - - - - - A - - - - -
Example - No Gaps: N N I P 1 A

Another possibility is the elimination of the first mark – *POS* based on the condition of its reverse deducibility from the sign *SUBPOS*.

Example - *POS* **Elimination:** N I P 1 A

These pieces of information allow us to effectively compress the whole mark. Another problem we have dealt with is the manner of how the tag is saved which went through two phases. During the course of the research we arrived to several possibilities. As the first we could name these: – Saving the whole sign as the text without compression. – Saving the mark as the text after the previous two-stage compression. This possibility seems as a very ineffective one. Given the assumption that in the each position only a limited and finite number of symbol can appear, the further research was lead in this direction. The first possibility lies in the assignment of the numerical indication of the individual signs within its category only.

Example - Numeric: 34 3 2 1 1

As evident, a greater efficiency can be achieved. However this state was not final and thanks to the extracted knowledge of the structure of the sign, it is possible to make the numerical indication even more efficient by very simple means. We know that the certain category of the signs can be used only in the case of use of the certain *POS/SUBPOS*, therefore we can divide the signs into other categories and use the numbering only within a frame of these smaller categories. This way we reduce the highest used numbers.

Example - Numeric, Reduced: 34 2 1 1 1

In the following part of the research, our concern proceeded towards the possibilities of saving the sequences of numbers that represent tags. In the current phase of the development we work with several possible variants:

– saving the number as *float/int*,
– encryption of the number using the existing coding algorithms,

– binary representation of the number,
– combination of several possibilities.

The first possibility was quickly dismissed for the inefficiency which mainly lied in the compression of small numbers. There the second option as utilized why using elias-gamma coding [16]. This manner of encoding is further used in other parts of this task and the final values are recorded using this method. Another possibility – the binary representation of the number – is currently in the phase of development but it is possible to say that this method seems applicable. The principle lies in finding of the highest possible number which needs to be encoded, then in the determination of the number of bites that represent it, thus also determining the number of bites upon which all other numbers will be represented. The last possibility related to the combination of various techniques offers a huge space for experimenting. It is for example expected that the algorithm alone will determine the most suitable methods (or the their combinations) of encoding for the given initial text.

6.5   Coding of Lemmas

The current version of the algorithm uses LZ algorithms [17] for the compression of lemmas as it currently seems as sufficient enough. However further ahead we expect to use other tests for different compression algorithms which are primarily intended for the compression of text.

6.6   Organisation of Saving

After analysis and text processing, all unique lemmas and tags are arranged according to their frequency. They are kept in the list for the final processing. Therefore it is important for us to use the optimal encoding of sequences of numbers also due to saving of position and indexes. The resulting compressed file is sorted into three parts:

1. The list of all lemmas found in the text
2. The list of all signs found in the text
3. For the every word the original text here is represented by a pair of indexes that are referring to the previous two lists.

Here, the usage of various methods of encoding will be advantageous according to the total size of lists of lemmas/tags. As already stated, in the current phase we use only one method of the numerical coding.

6.7   The Use of External Corpuses

One of the possible extensions for achieving of the best possible compression is the use of external dictionaries, both for lemmas and tags. In case of tags the use is simpler because the number of possible combinations can be unambiguously determined. According to it, all possible variations are generated. This method is rather more difficult with lemma dictionaries. As the language that is still being used, the Czech constantly develops and thus the new words and lemmas are being created. On the other hand, some words become archaic and less used. In this case, the generating of all lemmas is inefficient and insufficient. There is another factor to consider; that in various types of texts (fiction, spoken word, scientific texts) the frequency of words is vastly different. Another drawback is the non-existence of the word/lemma of the original text in the given corpus. A typical example are for example the additional postfixes of lemmas which are added by analyser for better accuracy.

The corpora are available in several categories at UCNKP [19]. Organised corpora of words and their lemmas for different categories of text and period of time can be acquired from there. On closer examination one can see that for different types of text the frequencies do differ and thus there is no universal list that could be considered as the best for all types. The initial thought of using the corpus lied in the method that the compressed file will not include the first two lists with lemmas and tags and that the pair of indexes, representing the initial text, will refer to positions in external corpora. This method should ensure the smaller size of the resulting file, however for the reverse decompression it will be necessary to use the external file with corpus which might not be really optimal.

In the initial experiment of our work, the general corpus *SYN2010* was used. The corpus includes more than 30,000 lemmas. During the tests, we compared the intersection of lemmas included in this corpus with lemmas appearing from the set of literature of fiction (which is used in our other tests). After evaluation, the corpus was found insufficient for our testing set because of the great number of missing lemmas. However, despite these initial findings we plan to use these corpora at least for the specific types of initial tests. Recently, the corpus *SYN2015* has been available which, besides morphological analysis, also includes the syntactic analysis. For the next parts of our work we shall use this corpus as it cancels the necessity to use the external tools *MorphoDiTa* or *Treex* for the creation of input text analysis during the testing.

6.8   Results

Brief characteristic of files used in the test is given in Table 1. Due to the aforementioned reasons, our tests dealt with a single method of compression which is:

- the compression of the lemma forms using LZ,
- encoding of tags using the numerical encoding,
- representation of indexes of the initial text using elias-gamma code.

After the evaluation of the results, see Table 2, we arrived at several conclusions which will assist us in our further work. The most substantial part, which influences the final size of file the most, is the encoding of indexes. The method of encoding we chose does not seem as the most suitable in case of truly huge

Table 1. File characteristics

File	File size (megabytes)	Number of words	Number of unique lemmas	Number of unique tags
A	1	359,614	14,854	574
B	5	1,764,258	34,286	718
C	10	3,578,666	41,466	733
D	50	17,874,992	110,254	911
E	100	35,635,693	162,935	981

Table 2. Compression results

File	Lemma (bits)	Lemma index (bits)	Tags (bits)	Tag index (bits)	Compression ratio ($\approx$%)
A	452,896	3,867,038	7,155	1,896,490	74
B	1,015,200	19,518,472	9,148	9,394,852	71.2
C	1,237,792	39,005,856	9,304	18,913,870	70.5
D	3,301,856	197,755,574	12,132	94,951,596	70.6
E	4,945,152	395,358,961	13,123	189,143,515	70.3

numbers which obviously results from this type of elias-code. Another crucial factor is the size of occurrence of the original tags in the text. It can be seen that if the initial set of words increases hundredfold then the number of the original tags increases only twice as much. This fact underlines the attributes of the Czech language and supports our assumptions that despite the complexity of the rules of language, the regularities in structural composition can be found. The similar ratio can be seen even in the number of the original lemmas but here the size ratio is not so prominent. But this is the result (besides other things) of the selection of the input text that was analysed and compressed.

7   Conclusion and Future Works

It can be said that the first phase of our tests met its purpose and confirmed our initial assumptions while setting the direction of further research. The results alone are not the best possible (due to the chosen methods of encoding), however the improvement of the methods and their optimization will make the main content of our work. After we finish this phase, we shall focus on the possibility of at least partial integration of external dictionaries and then on the search of similarities at several levels.

Acknowledgment. This work was supported by The Ministry of Education, Youth and Sports from the National Programme of Sustainability (NPU II) project "IT4Innovations excellence in science - LQ1602" and from the Large Infrastructures for Research, Experimental Development and Innovations project "IT4Innovations National Supercomputing Center – LM2015070".

References

1. Yuret, D.: Discovery of Linguistic relations using lexical attraction. Ph.D. thesis, Massachusetts Institute of Technology (1998)
2. Bach, J., Witten, H.: Lexical attraction for text compression. In: Proceedings of Data Compression Conference, pp. 516–516 (1999)
3. Awajan, A.: Multilayer model for Arabic text compression. Int. Arab J. Inf. Technol. **8**(2), 188–196 (2011)
4. Moffat, A.: Word-based text compression. Softw. Pract. Exp. **19**, 185–198 (1989)
5. Chang, K.Y., Yang, G.T.: A data compression system for Chinese fonts and binary images using classification techniques. Pr. Exp. **22**(12), 1027–1047 (1992)
6. Lanský, J., Zemlicka, M.: Compression of small text files using syllables. Technical report of Department of Software Engineering No. 2006-1 (2006)
7. Akman, I., Bayindir, H., Ozleme, S., Akin, Z., Misra, S.: Lossless text compression technique using syllable based morphology **8**(1), 66–74 (2011)
8. Kazik, O.: Lingvistická komprese textu. Diploma thesis, Charles University in Prague (2009)
9. Hajicova, E., Panevova, J., Sgall, P.: Úvod do teoretické a počítačové lingvistiky. I. svazek - Teoretická lingvistika, Nakladatelství Karolinum, Praha (2002)
10. Hana, J., Zeman, D.: Manual for Morphological Annotation, Revision for the Prague Dependency Treebank 2.0 (2005)
11. Honetschläger, V. a kol.: The Prague Dependency Treebank 3.0. https://ufal.mff.cuni.cz/pdt3.0
12. Treex Highly Modular NLP Framework. http://ufal.mff.cuni.cz/treex
13. Hajič, J.: Disambiguation of Rich Inflection (Computational Morphology of Czech). Karolinum, Praha (2004)
14. Sedlacek, R.: Morfologicky analyzator cestiny. Diploma thesis, Masaryk University Brno (1999)
15. Melichar, B., Janousek, J., Flouri, T.: Introduction to Arbology, Czech Technical University in Prague (2008)
16. Elias, P.: Universal codeword sets and representations of the integers. IEEE Trans. Inf. Theor. **21**(2), 194–203
17. Ziv, J., Lempel, A.: A universal algorithm for sequential data compression. IEEE Trans. Inf. Theor. **23**, 337–343 (1977)
18. Strakova, J., Straka, M., Hajic, J.: Open-source tools for morphology, lemmatization, POS tagging and named entity recognition. In: Proceedings of 52nd Annual Meeting of the Association for Computational Linguistics: System Demonstrations, June 2014
19. Ceský narodni korpus: Srovnavaci frekvencni seznamy, Ustav Ceského narodniho korpusu FF UK, Praha (2010). http://ucnk.ff.cuni.cz/srovnani10.php

Optimization of Combining of Self Organizing Maps and Growing Neural Gas

Lukáš Vojáček[1]([⊠]), Pavla Drázdilová[2], and Jiří Dvorský[2]

[1] IT4Innovations, VŠB - Technical University of Ostrava,
17. listopadu 15/2172, 708 33 Ostrava, Czech Republic
`lukas.vojacek@vsb.cz`
[2] Department of Computer Science, VŠB - Technical University of Ostrava,
17. listopadu 15/2172, 708 33 Ostrava, Czech Republic
`{pavla.drazdilova,jiri.dvorsky}@vsb.cz`

Abstract. The paper deals with the issue of high dimensional data clustering. One possible way to cluster this kind of data is based on Artificial Neural Networks (ANN) such as Growing Neural Gas (GNG) or Self Organizing Maps (SOM). Parallel modification, Growing Neural Gas with pre-processing by Self Organizing Maps, and its implementation on the HPC cluster is presented in the paper. Some experimental results are also presented. We focus on effective preprocessing for GNG. The clustering is realized on the output layer of SOM and the data for GNG are distributed into parallel processes.

Keywords: Self organizing maps · Growing neural gas · High-dimensional dataset · High performance computing

1 Introduction

Recently, several topics and issues have emerged such as availability of big and/or high-dimensional data, petascale HPC systems aiming towards exascale supercomputers and need of processing this kind of data. Large high-dimensional data collections are commonly available in areas like medicine, biology, information retrieval, web analyze, social network analyze, image processing, financial transaction analysis and many others. To process such kind of data unsupervised learning algorithms, such as *Self Organizing Maps* (SOM) or *Growing Neural Gas* (GNG), are usually used. Various aspects of parallel implementation of these algorithms on HPC were studied e.g. [12,13].

The one of still preserving issues is efficient utilization of the computation resources. When speaking on SOM or GNG learning algorithms there are two challenges. The first one is fast computation of similarity in high-dimensional space and the second one is ideally uniform distribution of computation load among individual CPU cores.

Parallel implementation usually allocates one CPU core to group of neurons, evaluate similarity of these neurons with given input vector, find local best matching neuron and then using some form of communication to find a global

© IFIP International Federation for Information Processing 2016
Published by Springer International Publishing Switzerland 2016. All Rights Reserved
K. Saeed and W. Homenda (Eds.): CISIM 2016, LNCS 9842, pp. 277–286, 2016.
DOI: 10.1007/978-3-319-45378-1_25

best matching neuron in the whole neural network. The CPU cores are allocated regularly, using some pattern [12] regardless of input vectors distribution on neurons i.e. CPU cores causing a bottleneck in the parallel learning algorithm. To reduce the bottleneck input vectors preprocessing is done using small SOM and clustering algorithm. This allows us to improve distribution of neurons over CPU cores and subsequently speed-up the learning algorithm itself.

The paper is organized as follows. The Sect. 2 briefly describes used neural networks: SOM and GNG. Input vectors preprocessing algorithm is provided in Sect. 3. Experimental results are given in Sect. 4.

2   Artificial Neural Networks

In this section we will describe two types of neural networks, the first is Self Organizing Maps and the second is Growing Neural Gas and then we present a combination of SOM and GNG.

2.1   Self Organizing Maps

Self Organizing Maps (SOMs), also known as Kohonen maps, were proposed by Kohonen in 1982 [4]. SOM is a kind of artificial neural network that is trained by unsupervised learning. Using SOM, the input space of training samples can be represented in a lower-dimensional (often two-dimensional) space [5], called a *map*. Such a model is efficient in structure visualization due to its feature of topological preservation using a neighbourhood function.

SOM consists of two layers of neurons: an *input layer* that receives and transmits the input information, and an *output layer*, the map that represents the output characteristics. The output layer is commonly organized as a two-dimensional rectangular grid of nodes, where each node corresponds to one neuron. Both layers are feed-forward connected; each neuron in the input layer is connected to each neuron in the output layer. A real number, or weight, is assigned to each of these connections.

2.2   Growing Neural Gas

The representation of Growing Neural Gas is an undirected graph which need not be connected. Generally, there are no restrictions to the topology. The graph is generated and continuously updated by competitive Hebbian Learning [7,9]. According to the pre-set conditions, new neurons are automatically added and connections between neurons are subject to time and can be removed. GNG can be used for vector quantization by finding the code-vectors in clusters [3], image compression, disease diagnosis.

GNG works by modifying the graph, where the operations are the addition and removal of neurons and edges between neurons.

To understand the functioning of GNG, it is necessary to define the learning algorithm. The algorithm published in [12] is based on the original algorithm [2,3], but it is modified for better continuity in the SOM algorithm.

Remark. The notation used in the paper is briefly listed in Table 1.

Table 1. Notation used in the paper

Symbol	Description
M	Number of input vectors
n	Dimension of input vectors, number of input neurons, dimension of weight vectors in GNG output layer neurons
N	Current number of neurons in GNG output layer
N_{max}	Maximum allowed number of neurons in GNG output layer
n_i	i-th input neuron, $i = 1, 2, \ldots, n$
N_i	i-th output neuron, $i = 1, 2, \ldots, N$
N_F	the fattest neuron
T	Number of epochs
l_{c_1}	Learning factor of BMU_1
l_{nc_1}	Learning factor of BMU_1 neighbours
e_i	Local error of output neuron N_i, $i = 1, 2, \ldots, N$
C_i	ith cluster witch contains similar input vectors
m_i	Number of input vectors in cluster C_i
$\boldsymbol{Z}_i$	Centroid of cluster C_i
α	Error e_i reduction factor
β	Neuron error reduction factor
γ	Interval of input patterns to add a new neuron
a_{max}	Maximum edge age

3   Combination of SOM and GNG

In our previous paper [12], we focused on a combination of SOM and GNG, where the basic idea was to pre-process the input data by SOM, as a result of which there are clusters of similar data. Subsequently, we created the same number of GNG network as clusters, and assigned each cluster to one GNG. Each GNG creates its own neural map and after the learning process is finished, the results are merged. The entire description above can be summarized as follows: Help speeding up computation parallelization is shown in Fig. 1 where the top layer of parallelization (SOM) is described in a previous paper [13]. In this chapter we will describe an improved method focusing on the creating clusters of input data and optimization of used resources.

To improve the efficiency of parallelization is needed to clusters of input data for GNG network contained approximately the same number of input data. Based on the fact that when the GNG assigned more input vectors, the calculation takes longer. In the past to create clusters we used to spanning tree algorithm [12] which, however, does not reflect the number of input vectors

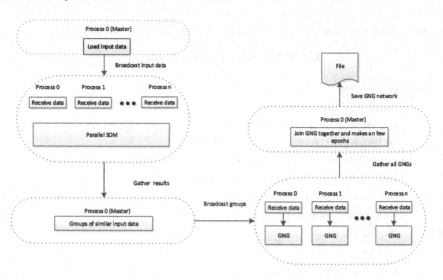

Fig. 1. Parallel algorithm

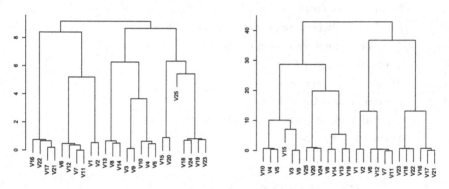

Fig. 2. Dendrograms of hierarchical clustering (Average-linkage and Ward's method) of output layer of SOM 5×5

in clusters. To obtain clusters of neurons we now use two different clustering algorithms. The first algorithm is agglomerative hierarchical clustering methods of calculation for determining the distance between clusters. Practically useful methods are *Ward's method*, *Centroid-linkage* and *Average-linkage* (AVL), see Fig. 2. The second clustering algorithm is the algorithm PAM [8], which like the above hierarchical algorithms, operates with a matrix of distances between the neurons in the output layer. The thus formed clusters are input to the following algorithm, which subdivides the neurons of the output layer SOM into clusters containing the closest possible number of the input data. The clusters are created on the basis of Algorithm 1.

We proposed an optimization for the calculation of GNG networks, which aims to optimize the maximum utilization of the allocated resources, but on

---

Algorithm 1. Calculate the distribution of neurons to efficiently parallelize

---

Input : The set of clusters $\mathbf{C}' = \{C'_1, \ldots, C'_m\}$ which contain neurons from output layers of SOM ($k \times k$ size) where training vectors are mapped to specific neurons. The clustering was done using algorithm with the best Silhouette index (Figs. 3 and 4)

Output: The new set of clusters $\mathbf{C} = \{C_1, \ldots, C_n\}$ where $m < n$

1. For $k = \{5, 6, 7, 8\}$ find in each SOM ($k \times k$) fattest neuron N_F which satisfies

$$F = \arg \max_{i=1,\ldots,N} |\mathsf{N}_i|$$

   where $|\mathsf{N}_i|$ denotes number of input vectors mapped to neuron N_i.

2. Find a $K \in \{5, 6, 7, 8\}$ for which value $\mathsf{N}_F^k - \frac{1}{k^2}M$ is minimal. So that SOM ($K \times K$) has the smallest dispersion of $|\mathsf{N}_i|$. Furthermore, we will work with SOM ($K \times K$). For sake of simplicity the index K will be omitted from N_F^K in following text.

3. Divide the cluster C'_i with the fattest neuron N_F to two clusters C_{N_F} and C_i where cluster C_{N_F} contain only one neuron N_F and cluster $C_i = C'_i \backslash \{\mathsf{N}_F\}$.

4. For others clusters C'_j verify: if number of input data $|C'_j|$ in cluster C'_j $|C'_j| > |\mathsf{N}_F|$, then split C'_j into two clusters $C_{j,1}$ and $C_{j,2}$ where cluster $C_{j,1}$ contain fattest neuron from C'_j and cluster $C_{j,2} = C'_j \backslash C_{j,1}$.

5. Return new set of cluster.

---

condition that the computing time must be similar. The principle of optimization is based on the idea that individual computing resources will count more GNG networks than only one – as it has until now. In Algorithm 2, the overall functionality is described. Here it is necessary to mention two facts regarding point 4. Firstly, it is a variation of a known problem *Subset sum* [6], which is an NP complete problem [1]. But at the beginning it was defined that the size of the output map of SOM is small and therefore the maximum possible number of clusters is also small, and therefore negligible. And secondly the maximum limit is reduced by 10 % on the grounds that to work with each GNG network time for I/O operations must be added.

Algorithm 2. Algorithm to optimize the utilization of computing resources

---

1. From the set of clusters $\mathbf{C} = \{C_1, \ldots, C_n\}$; take cluster C_{N_F} with the greatest number of input vectors.
2. Remove C_{N_F} from $\mathbf{C}$.
3. Assign cluster C_{N_F} to unused computing resource.
4. Select the set of clusters from set $\mathbf{C}$ wherein the sum of their input vectors is approaching number of input vectors in $0.9|C_{\mathsf{N}_F}|$
5. Remove used clusters from the set $\mathbf{C}$.
6. Assign selected clusters to the unused computing resource.
7. If $\mathbf{C}$ is not empty return to step 4.

---

4   Experiments

We will describe different datasets and we will provide experiments with datasets in this section.

4.1   Experimental Datasets and Hardware

Two datasets were used in the experiments. The first dataset was commonly used in Information Retrieval – *Medlars*. The second one was the test data for the elementary benchmark for clustering algorithms [11].

Weblogs Dataset. To test the learning algorithm effectiveness on high dimensional datasets, a Weblogs dataset was used. The Weblogs dataset contained web logs from an Apache server. The dataset contained records of two month's requested activities (HTTP requests) to the NASA Kennedy Space Center WWW server in Florida[1]. The standard data preprocessing methods were applied to the obtained dataset. The records from search engines and spiders were removed, and only the web site browsing was left (without download of pictures and icons, stylesheets, scripts etc.). The final dataset (input vector space) was of a dimension 90,060 and consisted of 54,961 input vectors. For a detailed description, see our previous work [10], where a web sites community behaviour was analyzed.

Medlars Dataset. The Medlars dataset consisted of 1,033 English abstracts from medical science[2]. The 8,567 distinct terms were extracted from the Medlars dataset. Each term represents a potential dimension in the input vector space. The term's level of significance (weight) in a particular document represents a value of the component of the input vector. Finally, the input vector space has a dimension of 8,707, and 1,033 input vectors were extracted from the dataset.

Experimental Hardware. The experiments were performed on a Linux HPC cluster, named Anselm, with 209 computing nodes, where each node had 16 processors with 64 GB of memory. Processors in the nodes were Intel Sandy Bridge E5-2665. Compute network is InfiniBand QDR, fully non-blocking, fat-tree. Detailed information about hardware is possible to find on the web site of Anselm HPC cluster[3].

4.2   First Part of the Experiment

The first part of the experiments was oriented towards the comparison of quality of clustering by the agglomerative hierarchical clustering and PAM Clustering. The used dataset was *Weblogs*. All the experiments were carried out for

---

[1] The collection can be downloaded from http://ita.ee.lbl.gov/html/contrib/NASA-HTTP.html.

[2] The collection can be downloaded from ftp://ftp.cs.cornell.edu/pub/smart. The total size of the dataset is approximately 1.03 MB.

[3] https://support.it4i.cz/docs/anselm-cluster-documentation/hardware-overview.

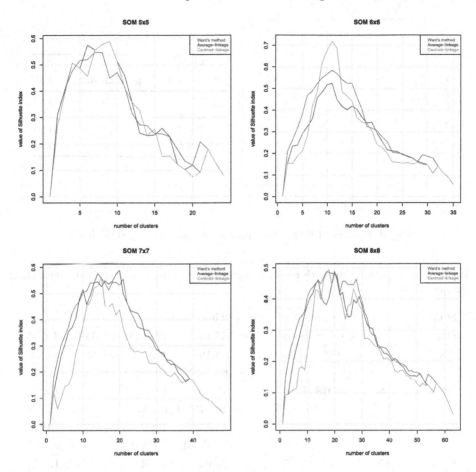

Fig. 3. Quality of hierarchical clustering of output layer of SOM k × k

20 epochs; the random initial values of neuron weights in the first epoch were always set to the same values. The tests were performed for SOM with rectangular shape 5 × 5 neurons, 6 × 6 neurons, 7 × 7 neurons and 8 × 8 neurons. The metrics used for determining the quality of clustering is *Average Silhouette Index* (ASI). The achieved quality of clustering for agglomerative hierarchical clustering is presented in Fig. 3 and for PAM Clustering is presented in Fig. 4.

4.3   Second Part of the Experiment

The second part of the experiments was oriented towards comparing the time efficiency of algorithms PAM and AVL. The GNG parameters are as follows $\gamma = 100$, $e_w = 0.05$, $e_n = 0.006$, $\alpha = 0.5$, $\beta = 0.0005$, $a_{max} = 160$, $N_{max} = 1221$, $T = 200$. The used dataset was *Weblogs*. Dimensions of SOM are 5 × 5, 6 × 6, 7 × 7 and 8 × 8. Number of cores are 32 for each group and the groups are computed sequentially (Tables 2 and 3).

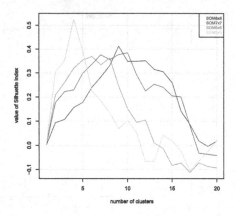

SOM dimensions	# of clusters	ASI
5 × 5	4	0.53
6 × 6	6	0.37
7 × 7	10	0.38
8 × 8	9	0.41

Fig. 4. Quality of PAM clustering of output layer of SOM k × k

Table 2. Computing time with respect to number of cores, standard GNG algorithm, dataset Medlars

SOM		Numbers of vectors		Time [mm:ss]			
Dimension	Time [s]	Max	Second max	4* PAM	10 PAM	9* AVL	4 AVL
5 × 5	13	6852	1636	14:19	14:37	14:44	14:22
				6* PAM	10 PAM	11* AVL	6 AVL
6 × 6	18	5918	1900	13:50	14:12	14:11	14:02
				10* PAM	6 PAM	20* AVL	6 AVL
7 × 7	27	5607	1795	13:57	13:47	14:26	13:48
				9* PAM	6 PAM	20* AVL	6 AVL
8 × 8	35	5192	1437	14:03	13:51	14:41	13:37

Table 3. The quality of algorithms (the lower is better)

4* PAM	10 PAM	9* AVL	4 AVL
1.24	1.23	1.24	1.2
6* PAM	10 PAM	11* AVL	6 AVL
1.22	1.24	1.22	1.26
10* PAM	6 PAM	20* AVL	6 AVL
1.14	1.38	1.4	1.18
9* PAM	6 PAM	20* AVL	6 AVL
1.24	1.04	1.3	1.18

4.4   Third Part of the Experiment

The third part of experiments was oriented towards speedup and resource optimization. The GNG parameters are as follows $\gamma = 200$, $e_w = 0.05$, $e_n = 0.006$, $\alpha = 0.5$, $\beta = 0.0005$, $a_{max} = 160$, $N_{max} = 1000$, $T = 200$. Medlars dataset was used. The tests were performed for SOM with a rectangular shape of 5×5 neurons. The achieved speedup is presented in Tables 4 and 5. Both samples have similar speedup but fundamentally differ in efficiency; in the fastest case without optimization the efficiency is 0.02, but with optimization it is 0.23.

Table 4. Combination SOM and GNG's

Cores	Time	Speedup	Efficiency
1	02:28:46	1.00	1.00
32	00:18:01	8.26	0.26
64	00:17:51	8.33	0.13
128	00:16:37	8.95	0.07
256	00:10:42	13.90	0.05
512	00:07:27	19.97	0.04
1024	00:06:37	22.48	0.02

Table 5. Combination SOM and GNG's and resource optimization

Cores	Time	Speedup	Efficiency
1	02:28:46	1.00	1.00
32	00:18:02	8.26	0.26
64	00:17:48	8.33	0.13
96	00:06:39	22.37	0.23
-	-	–	–
-	-	–	–
-	-	–	–

5   Conclusion

In this paper, we presented experiments with preprocessing of data in output layer of SOM. Different clustering algorithm was used and different quality of clusters were obtained. The global input data preprocessed on this SOM was used as an input for GNG neural network. This approach allows us almost uniformly distribute data on computation cores efficiently utilize them. The achieved speedup is also very good. In future work we intend to focus on sparse date, and improved acceleration and use Xeon phi for better speed-up.

Acknowledgment. This work was supported by The Ministry of Education, Youth and Sports from the Large Infrastructures for Research, Experimental Development and Innovations project "IT4Innovations National Supercomputing Center LM2015070" and partially supported by Grant of SGS No. SP2016/68, VŠB – Technical University of Ostrava, Czech Republic.

References

1. Carlson, J.: The Millennium Prize Problems. American Mathematical Society, Providence (2006)
2. Fritzke, B.: A growing neural gas network learns topologies. In: Advances in Neural Information Processing Systems, vol. 7, pp. 625–632. MIT Press, Cambridge (1995)

3. Holmström, J.: Growing neural gas experiments with GNG, GNG with utility and supervised GNG. Master's thesis, Uppsala University, 30 August 2002
4. Kohonen, T.: Self-organization and Associative Memory. Springer Series in Information Sciences, vol. 8, 3rd edn. Springer, Heidelberg (1984)
5. Kohonen, T.: Self Organizing Maps, 3rd edn. Springer, Heidelberg (2001)
6. Li, J., Wan, D.: On the subset sum problem over finite fields. Finite Fields Appl. **14**(4), 911–929 (2008). http://www.sciencedirect.com/science/article/pii/S1071579708000208
7. Martinetz, T.: Competitive hebbian learning rule forms perfectly topology preserving maps. In: Gielen, S., Kappen, B. (eds.) ICANN 1993, pp. 427–434. Springer, London (1993). http://dx.doi.org/10.1007/978-1-4471-2063-6_104
8. Park, H.S., Jun, C.H.: A simple and fast algorithm for k-medoids clustering. Expert Syst. Appl. **36**(2, Part 2), 3336–3341 (2009). http://www.sciencedirect.com/science/article/pii/S095741740800081X
9. Prudent, Y., Ennaji, A.: An incremental growing neural gas learns topologies. In: Proceedings of 2005 IEEE International Joint Conference on Neural Networks, 2005, IJCNN 2005, vol. 2, pp. 1211–1216, July–4 August 2005
10. Slaninová, K., Martinovič, J., Novosád, T., Dráždilová, P., Vojáček, L., Snášel, V.: Web site community analysis based on suffix tree and clustering algorithm. In: Proceedings - 2011 IEEE/WIC/ACM International Conference on Web Intelligence and Intelligent Agent Technology - Workshops, WI-IAT Workshops 2011, pp. 110–113 (2011)
11. Ultsch, A.: Clustering with SOM: U*C. In: Proceedings of Workshop on Self-organizing Maps, Paris, France, pp. 75–82 (2005)
12. Vojáček, L., Dráždilová, P., Dvorský, J.: Combination of self organizing maps and growing neural gas. In: Saeed, K., Snášel, V. (eds.) CISIM 2014. LNCS, vol. 8838, pp. 100–111. Springer, Heidelberg (2014)
13. Vojáček, L., Martinovič, J., Dvorský, J., Slaninová, K., Vondrák, I.: Parallel hybrid SOM learning on high dimensional sparse data. In: Chaki, N., Cortesi, A. (eds.) CISIM 2011. CCIS, vol. 245, pp. 239–246. Springer, Heidelberg (2011)

Scheduling in Manufacturing and Other Applications

Robust Tabu Search Algorithm for Planning Rail-Truck Intermodal Freight Transport

Wojciech Bożejko, Radoslaw Grymin$^{(\boxtimes)}$, Szymon Jagiełło,
and Jarosław Pempera

Department of Control Systems and Mechatronics,
Wrocław University of Science and Technology,
Wybrzeże Wyspiańskiego 27, 50-370 Wrocław, Poland
radoslaw.grymin@pwr.edu.pl

Abstract. In this paper a new efficient tabu search algorithm for assigning freight to the intermodal transport connections was developed. There were also formulated properties of the problem that can be used to design robust heuristic algorithms based on the local search methods. The quality of solutions produced by the tabu search algorithm and by often recommended greedy approach were also compared.

Keywords: Intermodal transport · Optimization · Tabu search

1 Introduction

Road transportation is very expensive. Because of that, carrying goods over a long distance is achieved as a combination of different types of transportation (e.g. with the use of rail, ships and trucks). Such means of transportation is called *intermodal freight transport*. The problems related to the intermodal transport are intensely studied by the Operations Research. Thanks to such activities, transport infrastructure can be better designed, vehicle routes and delivery schedules can be planned more consciously which results in savings and consequently may lead to lower prices of transported goods.

A widely used definition of intermodal freight transport was introduced at the European Conference of Ministers of Transport. It was defined as "the movement of goods in one and the same loading unit or vehicle by successive modes of transport without handling of the goods themselves when changing modes". Second commonly used definition was introduced by Macharis and Bontekoning [18]. They define it as "the combination of at least two modes of transport in a single transport chain, without the change of container for the goods, with most of the route travelled by rail, inland waterway or ocean-going vessel and with the shortest possible initial and final journeys by road". More definitions of intermodal freight transport can be found in [6].

Problems related to the intermodal transport are much more complex to solve than problems which take into consideration a fixed type of transportation (aka

© IFIP International Federation for Information Processing 2016
Published by Springer International Publishing Switzerland 2016. All Rights Reserved
K. Saeed and W. Homenda (Eds.): CISIM 2016, LNCS 9842, pp. 289–299, 2016.
DOI: 10.1007/978-3-319-45378-1_26

unimodal problems). Moreover, models used to solve unimodal problems are also applied to intermodal transport problems. For this reason, there is a group of people convinced that intermodal transportation research is emerging as a new transportation research field and it is still in the pre-paradigmatic phase and proper models are not known at the moment (see [6,18]). Bontekoning, Macharis and Trip [6] described the actual state of intermodal transport research field and marked actions which should be done to make it similar to "normal science". They proved that the intermodal transport research is in the pre-paradigmatic phase. They found plenty of small research communities that address intermodal transport problems. They proposed transformation of these small communities to one or two large research communities.

Macharis and Bontekoning [18] underlined that the intermodal transport is a very complex process that involves many decision-makers. They distinguished four types of them and emphasized that some decisions can have long-term effects (e.g. planning and building a railway infrastructure) when other can have short-term effects (temporary changes in timetable). Decision-makers should work in a close collaboration to achieve supreme results. Many decisions lead to a variety of areas where optimization can be used, whereas many authors introduced overview of articles and methods used in the intermodal transport research and classified them by the type of decision maker and by the time horizon of operations problem.

Caris, Macharis and Janssens [11] proposed new research fields regarded to decision support in intermodal freight transport. They made an overview of applied applications that support decisions of policy makers, terminal network design, intermodal service network design, intermodal routing, ICT (Information and Communication Technologies) innovations and drayage operations. They pointed out that there is no link between models for terminal network design and intermodal service network design. They recognized the need for solution methods solving intermodal freight transport optimization problems that can accept multiple objective functions, transportation mode schedules, economies of scale and demanded times of delivery.

Intermodal freight transport, due to its big complexity and plenty of constraints imposed on solutions, constitutes a challenge for many types of heuristics and metaheuristics. Caris and Janssens [10] optimized pre- and end-haulage of intermodal container terminals using heuristic approach. They modeled problem as a Full Truckload Pickup and Delivery Problem with Time Windows (FTPDPTW) where vehicles carry full truckloads to and from an intermodal terminal. Time windows were used to represent the time interval in which the service at a customer must start. They proposed two-phase insertion heuristic and the improvement heuristic with three types of neighborhood. The solution is obtained by two-phase insertion heuristic and afterwards improved by the improvement heuristic.

There are some articles devoted to comercial decision support systems (DSS). Kelleher, El-Rhalibi and Arshad [16] described features of PISCES, the integrated system for planning intermodal transport. They presented methods used in PISCES for dealing with the triangulation in the pick-up and drop scenario.

Another research on decision support system was published by Rizzoli, Fornara and Gamberdella [21]. They presented the terminal simulator component of the Platform project, funded by the Directorate General VII of the European Community. Presented software can model processes taking place in an intermodal road or rail terminal. It was designed on the basis of discrete-event simulation paradigm. Software user can define the structure of terminal and different input data. It allows us to check how changing terminal structure may have an influence on its performance.

Noteworthy are also researches on systems that support decision-making by more than one policymaker. Febraro, Sacco and Saeednia [12] proposed an agent-based framework for cooperative planning of intermodal freight transport chains. In this system, many actors can work together and negotiate their decisions to achieve a common goal.

Transport companies are not willing to share their tariffs on their websites. This information may be hidden due to many factors, e.g. cost changes. Costs can change overnight because of fluctuations of exchange rates, political situation etc. Moreover, prices vary from one company to another. Researchers need such data to develop better algorithms. Special price models come forward. Hanssen, Mathisen, Jorgensen [15] proposed a generalized transport costs model that can be used to assess mean prices of different types of transport on the given distance. Intermodal transport research field demands knowledge base that will ease scientists to conduct their researches on the real data. Experimental results will be more reliable. It should be in the interest of governments and all shipping companies to support building of such database.

2   Problem Formulation

In a planning phase, transportation management company has to realize a certain number of transport tasks. Transport task is to carry some amount of goods from suppliers to customers. Transport can be organized in two ways: (i) by a single truck, (ii) by the intermodal transport (truck-train-truck). Goods are transported in containers or semitrailers customized to rail transport.

There are known locations of customers, suppliers and intermodal terminals, distances between: (i) intermodal terminals, (ii) intermodal terminals and customers, (iii) suppliers and customers. Of course in the first case this is the length of the rail route and in the other cases it is the length of the road route. Cargo trains implementing intermodal freight transport follow the schedule of courses. Each course specifies initial and final intermodal terminal, time of delivery, unit cost of the course and the amount of free wagons. The number of free wagons is updated online based on reservations of transportation management companies. Attachment of wagons on intermediate stations is forbidden. The objective of optimization is the assignment of task to the train course simultaneously minimizing the overall costs of transport.

Let $J = \{1, \ldots, n\}$ be a set consisting of n transport tasks and let $T = \{1, \ldots, t\}$ be the set of railway courses. For each task $j \in J$ and each course $i \in T$ the distance achieved by the traffic transport $d_{j,i}$ is given. Note, that the distance $d_{j,i}$ is the result of summing distances between supplier and the initial intermodal terminal and between final intermodal terminal and the customer. The distance achieved by the traffic transport between supplier and customer for the fixed $j \in J$ is marked as $d_{j,0}$. The railway distance for the course $i \in T$ is r_i. The course $i \in T$ has $l_i \geq 0$ free cargo wagons to load. The overall price for the carriage of freight from the supplier to the customer using cargo train $i \in T$ is $c_{j,i}$. The cost of direct road transport from the supplier to the customer specified in the task j is $c_{j,0}$. Let the assignment of the course to the task j be marked as a_j, $a_j \in \{0\} \cup T$ ($a_j = 0$ if the transport is carried only by the truck). Vector $\alpha = [a_j]$ denotes the assignment of all tasks to the courses. The total cost of transport for assignment α is

$$Cost(\alpha) = \sum_{j=1}^{n} c_{j,a_j}. \tag{1}$$

We would like to find such assignment α^* that the total cost of transport is as small as possible

$$Cost(\alpha^*) = \min_{\alpha \in \Lambda} Cost(\alpha), \tag{2}$$

where Λ is the set of all possible assignments, $|\Lambda| = n^{m+1}$.

2.1 Properties of the Problem

In the current subsection we formulate certain properties of the problem, which can be used in the design of efficient heuristic algorithms based on local search methods. The first one relates to the method that allows us to determine the lower bound of the objective function value for the optimal solution, the second one allows us to reduce the number of solutions in the neighborhood by eliminating the subset with worse solutions.

Proposition 1. *Let* $u_i = \min_{k=0,...,m} c_{j,k}$, *then the lower bound*

$$LB = \sum_{j=1}^{n} u_j. \tag{3}$$

Proposition 2. *Let* α *and* β *be the assignments of tasks to the trains such that* $Cost(\beta) < Cost(\alpha)$. *Then, at least one task has lower cost of transporting in the assignment* β *than in the assignment* α.

Proposition 3. *Let* β *be the assignment of tasks to the trains resulting from* α *by the assignment of the task* j *to train* i, *then*

$$Cost(\beta) = Cost(\alpha) - c_{j,a_j} + c_{j,i}. \tag{4}$$

Proposition 4. *Let* β *be the assignment of tasks to the trains resulting from* α *by interchanging assignment of tasks* j *and* k, *then*

$$Cost(\beta) = Cost(\alpha) - c_{j,a_j} - c_{k,a_k} + c_{j,a_k} + c_{k,a_j}. \tag{5}$$

Note, if $Cost(\alpha)$ is known, expressions (4) and (5) can be determined in time $O(1)$.

2.2 Example

A certain logistic company has to realize $n = 5$ transportation tasks. Transportation may be achieved with $t = 3$ courses of cargo train. All trains have $l_i = 2$ free cargo wagons to load. The transportation costs (traffic and intermodal) are given in Table 1.

Table 1. Costs of intermodal and traffic transport

	Task 1	Task 2	Task 3	Task 4	Task 5
0-traffic	1962	1863	1879	1947	1972
1-course	1323	1276	1375	1289	1410
2-course	1328	1283	1304	1327	1184
3-course	**1057**	**1156**	**1140**	**1072**	**1047**

It is easy to see that the price of road transport is 9623 whereas, the lowest price of transport is $LB = 5472$ (marked with bold). Transport with the lowest price requires use of 5 wagons of the course 3. It is not possible because rail connection 3 has only two free wagons. In Table 1 a feasible connection (that takes into account number of free wagons) with total price 5893 was marked in bold.

Let us consider a greedy strategy that assigns tasks to the cheapest intermodal freight transport connection. In the first row, tasks with the biggest difference in price between road and rail transport will be assigned. Tasks that cannot be achieved by the rail transport with the cheapest cost will be achieved by truck transport. The described strategy is used in many logistic companies, where assignment of transport tasks is realized with the use of forwarding agents. A forwarding agent is concentrated on finding the cheapest solution of transport problem, because his salary depends (directly or indirectly) on the income that is the difference between the price of transport negotiated with a customer and the real price.

Let us assume that road transport prices were negotiated with customers, profits from the intermodal freight transport are formed respectively: 905, 707, 739, 875, 925. Tasks 1 and 5 generate the biggest profits, therefore they will be realized by the intermodal freight transport. The rest of tasks will be realized by trucks.

3 An Approximation Algorithm

In order to solve the stated problem we propose a local search algorithm based on the tabu search (TS) approach [13,14]. The tabu search is one of the best methods of constructing heuristic algorithms. This is confirmed for many optimizing problems, as a main method (for scheduling of tasks [3,4,8,19], vehicle routing [9,20], packing [17], container loading [7]), as well as a key element of higher metaheuristics, e.g. golf method [5]. Neighborhood determination in the tabu search metaheuristics is also frequently parallelized (see [1,2]).

An algorithm based on this method, in each iteration searches neighborhood of the basic solution for the solution with the best objective function value. In every iteration the best solution replaces the basic solution. To prevent searching loops, the tabu mechanism is used. It is usually implemented as a list with the limited length. In each iteration, selected attributes of subsequently visited solutions are stored. Contents of the list divide the neighborhood into two subsets: a set of forbidden and a set of feasible solutions. Forbidden solutions are not searched except the case when forbidden solution is better than the best solution found so far.

The search stops when the given number of iterations without improving the criterion value has been reached or the algorithm has performed a given number of iterations.

3.1   Moves and Neighborhood

The neighborhood of a solution is generated by moves. In our problem, the solution is represented by a vector of task assignments α. The neighborhood of the solution can be created due to exchanges of assignment of two tasks or change of assignment of a single task.

Let $v = (a, b)$ be a pair of exchanged tasks. We define a new assignment $\alpha^{(v)}$ obtained from $\alpha = (\alpha_1, \ldots, \alpha_n)$ by exchanging assignment of tasks a and b as follows:

$$\alpha^{(v)} = (\alpha_1, \ldots, \alpha_{a-1}, \alpha_b, \alpha_{a+1}, \ldots, \alpha_{b-1}, \alpha_a, \alpha_{b+1}, \ldots, \alpha_n) \ \ for \ a < b \qquad (6)$$

and

$$\alpha^{(v)} = (\alpha_1, \ldots, \alpha_{b-1}, \alpha_a, \alpha_{b+1}, \ldots, \alpha_{a-1}, \alpha_b, \alpha_{a+1}, \ldots, \alpha_n) \ \ for \ a > b. \qquad (7)$$

Let EX be a set of some such moves and $N(EX, \alpha) = \{\alpha^{(v)} : v \in EX\}$ be a neighborhood of solution α generated by a move set EX. For a feasible solution α every move $v \in EX$ generates a feasible solution.

Let $v = (a, k)$ be the move that changes the assignment of the task a to the course k. We define the new assignment α^v obtained from $\alpha = (\alpha_1, \ldots, \alpha_n)$ by execution move v in α as follows:

$$\alpha^{(v)} = (\alpha_1, \ldots, \alpha_{a-1}, k, \alpha_{a+1}, \ldots, \alpha_n). \qquad (8)$$

Let INS be a set of some such moves and $N(INS, \alpha) = \{\alpha^{(v)} : v \in INS\}$ be a neighborhood of solution α generated by a move set INS. For the feasible solution α, there are infeasible moves $v = (a, k) \in INS$ such that $\alpha_a \neq k$ and cargo train $k \in T$ has not free wagons.

Let $U = \{v : \alpha^{(v)}\ is\ feasible\ \wedge\ v \in EX \cup INS\}$ be a set of feasible moves and $N(U, \alpha)$ be a neighborhood of solution α. The neighborhood $N(EX, \alpha)$ has n^2 neighbors, while $N(INS, \alpha)$ has nm neighbors. The determination of the total cost explicitly from the Formula (1) requires $O(n)$ time for each solution, therefore the search of neighborhood can require a great computational effort. The use of expression (4) for moves from INS and expression (5) for moves from EX reduces computation time to $O(1)$ (n times) for each generated solution.

We propose a reduction of the neighborhood size to the set of promising moves. The move v is promising if its execution gives the chance to receive a better solution. From Proposition 2 we have simple conditions for obtaining a better solution:

- $c_{a,\alpha_a} > c_{a,k}$ for move $v = (a, k) \in INS$,
- $c_{a,\alpha_a} > c_{a,\alpha_b}$ for move $v = (a, b) \in EX$,
- $c_{b,\alpha_b} > c_{b,\alpha_a}$ for move $v = (a, b) \in EX$.

We will mark the reduced set of moves as V.

4   Computation Results

The main objective of experimental studies was to evaluate the usefulness of advanced heuristics in assigning transportation tasks to intermodal transport. Experimental test was carried out on the randomly generated data. The set of 120 instances is divided into 12 groups. Each group consists of 10 instances with the same number of tasks n and freight trains t. The study was conducted for groups, where the number of tasks $n \in \{50, 100, 200, 500\}$ and the number of cargo trains $t \in \{10, 20, 30\}$.

Railway distances r_i for course $i \in T$ were generated from the uniform distribution on [2000,2500], in intermodal transport the distances achieved by traffic transport $d_{j,i}$ were generated from uniform distribution on [30,200]. A traffic transport distance is usually shorter than distance of intermodal transport thus we determine this distance from the expression $d_{j,0} = \min_{i=1,...,t}(r_i - d_{j,i})$.

We assumed unit costs of traffic transport $c_{j,0} = d_{j,0}$. The cost of task $j \in J$ carried by freight train $i \in T$ includes the cost of road transport $(d_{j,i})$, the cost of handling in intermodal terminal (h_j), the cost of transporting freight train depending on the distance (r_j) and is expressed by the formula $c_{j,i} = d_{j,i} + h_j + \gamma r_j$, where γ is the factor of the cost of rail transport to the cost of traffic transport. The research was carried out for three values of factor γ (0.8, 0.65, 0.5) and $h_j = 60$. Note that for $\gamma = 0.8$ and transport distance 300 the costs of traffic and intermodal transport are comparable.

The number of free wagons was the same for each cargo train. We considered two levels of wagon availability for loading: (i) a few free wagons: $l_i = \lfloor n/t \rfloor + 1$, (ii) many free wagons: $l_i = 2 \cdot \lfloor n/t \rfloor$.

The algorithm TS was implemented with the reduced neighborhood V, written in C++ and ran on Lenovo T540p personal computer with processor i7-4710 2.5 GHz. Further, we wrote a greedy algorithm G (see Subsect. 2.2 for details)

and an algorithm R which compute the total cost of traffic transportation. The
algorithm TS performed 1000 iterations and started from the solution in which
all tasks were assigned to road transport.

Since there are no algorithms for solving the considered problem in the literature, we made a comparison of TS, G and R with lower bound LB (3). For
each instance, we defined the following values:

$Cost(\alpha^A)$ – the total cost of transportation of tasks forms set J found by the
algorithm A, $A \in \{TS, G, R\}$,
$PRD(A)$ – the mean value of the relative cost of solution found by algorithm
A with respect to the lower bound LB i.e.

$$PRD(A) = \frac{Cost(\alpha^A) - LB}{LB} \cdot 100[\%], \tag{9}$$

CPU – the mean computation time (in seconds).

The results of computer computations are summarized in Table 2. The first
column contains the number of tasks and freight trains in each instance of the
group, the second contains the average relative cost of traffic transport, the next
three columns refer to instances of the small number of available wagons and
include: the average relative cost of the solution generated by greedy algorithm
R, the average relative cost of the solution generated by tabu search algorithm
TS and the average number of transports carried out exclusively by road in
the solution generated by the algorithm TS. The other three columns refer to
instances with many free cargo wagons. The table shows the results for different
γ values.

At the beginning of the analysis of the results collected in Table 2, it should
be noted that the proposed tabu search algorithm successfully finds the task
assignments for intermodal transport. The solutions generated by TS algorithm
for the intermodal transport with a limited number of free cargo wagons are only
a few percent worse than transport with minimum cost i.e. with the unlimited
number of free cargo wagons and trucks. It is easy to notice that the algorithm
TS finds significantly better solutions for instance with a large number of wagons
to be loaded.

According to Table 2, tabu search heuristic performs significantly better than
the greedy heuristic. The average relative cost does not exceed 3.2 % for instances
with large number of free wagons and 8.3 % for instances with small number of
free wagons. In the case of greedy algorithm this cost varies accordingly from
3.2 % to 38.3 % and from 6.0 % to 52.6 %. The superiority of the algorithm TS
over the greedy algorithm R increases with decreasing γ (with increasing attrac-
tiveness of intermodal transport).

While comparing the cost of road transport and intermodal transport, it can
be noted that with decreasing γ values increases the difference between the cost
of road transport and the intermodal one. For $\gamma = 0.5$ it is close to 70 %. The
experiment shows that for the highest γ value, the profit of using intermodal
transport is admittedly less (approximately 10 %) however, in our opinion, it is

Table 2. Relative cost of traffic and intermodal costs

$n \times t$	G traffic	A few free wagons			Many free wagons		
		Greedy	TS	Use of trucks	Greedy	TS	Use of trucks
$\gamma = 0.80$							
50 × 10	10.5	6.0	3.7	25.0	3.2	1.5	8.0
50 × 20	10.5	7.4	5.3	37.0	5.4	2.5	8.8
50 × 30	10.5	7.7	5.4	32.4	5.8	2.3	2.4
100 × 10	10.7	6.4	4.3	32.0	3.6	1.3	3.5
100 × 20	10.5	7.8	5.6	38.8	5.9	3.0	10.4
100 × 30	10.4	7.7	5.5	37.8	5.9	2.7	7.3
200 × 10	10.6	6.3	4.4	33.4	3.7	1.4	6.7
200 × 20	10.7	7.5	5.1	33.7	5.4	2.4	4.7
200 × 30	10.4	7.9	6.0	45.1	6.1	3.2	12.8
500 × 10	10.4	6.9	5.2	42.7	4.6	2.5	15.4
500 × 20	10.6	7.5	5.7	42.4	5.3	2.7	12.5
500 × 30	10.7	8.1	5.9	41.6	6.2	3.0	7.8
$\gamma = 0.65$							
50 × 10	34.7	19.5	4.5	0.0	10.4	1.5	0.0
50 × 20	34.8	24.0	6.7	0.0	17.0	2.4	0.0
50 × 30	34.9	25.6	6.5	0.0	19.1	2.1	0.0
100 × 10	35.0	20.5	5.2	0.0	11.6	1.1	0.0
100 × 20	34.8	25.1	7.2	0.0	18.9	2.8	0.0
100 × 30	34.8	24.7	6.9	0.0	18.8	2.5	0.0
200 × 10	34.8	20.5	5.7	0.0	11.3	1.3	0.0
200 × 20	35.0	24.2	6.1	0.0	17.0	2.1	0.0
200 × 30	34.8	26.1	8.3	0.0	19.9	3.2	0.0
500 × 10	34.4	22.9	6.8	0.0	15.5	2.5	0.0
500 × 20	34.9	24.4	7.6	0.0	16.8	2.7	0.0
500 × 30	35.1	26.3	8.2	0.0	19.9	2.8	0.0
$\gamma = 0.50$							
50 × 10	72.4	38.1	3.9	0.0	18.7	1.1	0.0
50 × 20	72.8	47.5	6.2	0.0	32.4	2.1	0.0
50 × 30	73.3	51.1	6.0	0.0	36.6	1.8	0.0
100 × 10	73.0	39.8	4.7	0.0	20.0	0.9	0.0
100 × 20	72.8	49.2	6.6	0.0	35.4	2.4	0.0
100 × 30	73.1	49.1	6.4	0.0	35.0	2.2	0.0
200 × 10	72.8	40.7	5.2	0.0	20.7	1.0	0.0
200 × 20	73.3	47.7	5.6	0.0	31.8	1.8	0.0
200 × 30	73.2	53.2	7.8	0.0	38.8	2.9	0.0
500 × 10	71.9	44.9	6.0	0.0	28.5	1.9	0.0
500 × 20	73.2	49.0	7.1	0.0	31.7	2.3	0.0
500 × 30	73.6	52.6	7.7	0.0	38.3	2.5	0.0

Table 3. Computation time in seconds

$n \times t$	A few free wagons		Many free wagons	
	$TS(V)$	$TS(U)$	$TS(V)$	$TS(U)$
100×10	0.1	0.1	0.0	0.1
100×20	0.1	0.2	0.1	0.2
100×30	0.2	0.3	0.1	0.4
200×10	0.3	0.5	0.2	0.5
200×20	0.4	0.8	0.3	1.0
200×30	0.7	1.2	0.4	1.2
500×10	1.9	3.2	1.4	3.2
500×20	3.9	6.2	2.9	6.0
500×30	5.8	9.3	4.6	9.7

important from the standpoint of business activity. In addition, with decreasing γ, the percentage share of road transport in the solutions generated by the algorithm TS is reduced. For $\gamma = 0.8$ it varies from 25 % to 45 % and from 2.4 % to 15.4 %, for the remaining values of coefficient γ it equals 0.

Table 3 shows the average computational time for 9 groups of instances (for groups with $n = 50$ the computation time was less than 0.1). The calculations were performed for two versions of the algorithm TS: $TS(V)$ with reduced neighborhood V and $TS(U)$ with the full neighborhood U. It is easy to see that the computation time increases with the increasing number of tasks n and the number of cargo trains t. While comparing computation time $TS(V)$ and $TS(U)$, it should be highlighted that $TS(V)$ runs faster than $TS(U)$ from 30 % to 50 %. The computation time of algorithm $TS(V)$ does not exceed 6 seconds for instance with the biggest number of tasks and cargo trains.

5   Conclusion

In this paper, we developed the tabu search algorithm to minimize the total cost of transport. We have considered the intermodal transport as an alternative to the most used traffic transport. We have formulated several properties of the problem, which were used not only to increase the efficiency but also to reduce the computation time of TS algorithm. We experimentally proved that the global cost optimization of intermodal transport allows us to achieve significantly higher profits than using in practice of the greedy approach.

The results obtained and our research experience [22] encourage us to extend the ideas proposed to multi-criteria problems generated by intermodal transport.

References

1. Bożejko, W.: Parallel path relinking method for the single machine total weighted tardiness problem with sequence-dependent setups. J. Intell. Manuf. **21**, 777–785 (2010)
2. Bożejko, W.: On single-walk parallelization of the job shop problem solving algorithms. Comput. Oper. Res. **39**, 2258–2264 (2012)
3. Bożejko, W., Makuchowski, M.: A fast hybrid tabu search algorithm for the no-wait job shop problem. Comput. Ind. Eng. **56**, 1502–1509 (2009)
4. Bożejko, W., Pempera, J., Smutnicki, C.: Parallel tabu search algorithm for the hybrid flow shop problem. Comput. Ind. Eng. **65**, 466–474 (2013)
5. Bożejko, W., Uchroński, M., Wodecki, M.: The new golf neighborhood for the flexible job shop problem. In: Proceedings of the ICCS 2010, Procedia Computer Science, vol. 1, pp. 289–296 (2009)
6. Bontekoning, Y., Macharis, C., Trip, J.: Is a new applied transportation research field emerging?—A review of intermodal rail-truck freight transport literature. Transp. Res. Part A: Policy Pract. **38**(1), 1–34 (2004)
7. Bortfeldt, A., Gehring, H., Mack, D.: A parallel tabu search algorithm for solving the container loading problem. Parallel Comput. **29**, 641–662 (2003)
8. Bożejko, W., Wodecki, M.: Parallel genetic algorithm for the flow shop scheduling problem. In: Wyrzykowski, R., Dongarra, J., Paprzycki, M., Waśniewski, J. (eds.) PPAM 2004. LNCS, vol. 3019, pp. 566–571. Springer, Heidelberg (2004)
9. Bożejko, W., Wodecki, M.: Solving permutational routing problems by population-based metaheuristics. Comput. Ind. Eng. **57**(1), 269–276 (2009)
10. Caris, A., Janssens, G.K.: A local search heuristic for the pre- and end-haulage of intermodal container terminals. Comput. Oper. Res. **36**(10), 2763–2772 (2009)
11. Caris, A., Macharis, C., Janssens, G.K.: Decision support in intermodal transport: a new research agenda. Comput. Ind. **64**(2), 105–112 (2013)
12. Di Febbraro, A., Sacco, N., Saeednia, M.: An agent-based framework for cooperative planning of intermodal freight transport chains. Transp. Res. Part C: Emerg. Technol. **64**, 72–85 (2016)
13. Glover, F.: Tabu search part I. ORSA J. Comput. **2**, 190–206 (1989)
14. Glover, F.: Tabu search part I. ORSA J. Comput. **2**, 4–32 (1990)
15. Hanssen, T.E.S., Mathisen, T.A., Jørgensen, F.: Generalized transport costs in intermodal freight transport. Procedia-Soc. Behav. Sci. **54**, 189–200 (2012)
16. Kelleher, G., El-Rhalibi, A., Arshad, F.: Scheduling for intermodal transport. Logist. Inf. Manage. **16**(5), 363–372 (2003)
17. Leung, S.C., Zhou, X., Zhang, D., Zheng, J.: Extended guided tabu search and a new packing algorithm for the two-dimensional loading vehicle routing problem. Comput. Oper. Res. **38**, 205–215 (2011)
18. Macharis, C., Bontekoning, Y.M.: Opportunities for or in intermodal freight transport research: a review. Eur. J. Oper. Res. **153**(2), 400–416 (2004)
19. Nowicki, E., Smutnicki, C.: A fast taboo search algorithm for the job shop problem. Manage. Sci. **42**(6), 797–813 (1996)
20. Renaud, J., Laporte, G., Boctor, F.F.: A tabu search heuristic for the multi-depot vehicle routing problem. Comput. Oper. Res. **23**(3), 229–235 (1996)
21. Rizzoli, A.E., Fornara, N., Gambardella, L.M.: A simulation tool for combined rail/road transport in intermodal terminals. Math. Comput. Simul. **59**(1), 57–71 (2002)
22. Smutnicki, C., Pempera, J., Rudy, J., Żelazny, D.: A new approach for multi-criteria scheduling. Comput. Ind. Eng. **90**, 212–220 (2015)

Multi-machine Scheduling with Setup Times

Wojciech Bożejko[1]([✉]), Łukasz Kacprzak[1], Piotr Nadybski[2],
and Mieczysław Wodecki[3]

[1] Department of Automatics, Mechatronics and Control Systems,
Faculty of Electronics, Wrocław University of Science and Technology,
Wyb. Wyspiańskiego 27, 50-370 Wrocław, Poland
{wojciech.bozejko,lukasz.kacprzak}@pwr.edu.pl
[2] Faculty of Technical and Economic Science,
The Witelon State University of Applied Sciences in Legnica,
Sejmowa 5a, 59-220 Legnica, Poland
nadybskip@pwsz.legnica.edu.pl
[3] Institute of Computer Science, University of Wrocław,
Joliot-Curie 15, 50-383 Wrocław, Poland
mieczyslaw.wodecki@uwr.edu.pl

Abstract. In this paper we are considering the problem of tasks scheduling executed simultaneously on multiple identical machines with a cost-criterion, which is the product of the tasks execution time and the number of used machines. Moreover, it is assumed that between the tasks performed sequentially there must be setup of the machines performed. Solution to the problem comes down to a generalization of a two-dimensional packing problem. The paper presents simulated annealing algorithm with different variants of packing strategy. The conducted computational experiments proved that designated solution differs little from some lower bounds for the constraints of the objective function.

1 Introduction

In the vast majority of the considered in the literature scheduling problems, it is assumed that a task is done on a single machine. However, in many real production processes, in particular - modern computational systems - a task execution requires the use of more than one machine (CPU), Bożejko et al. [5]. Then, we can talk about systems with parallel machines and multi-machine (multiprocessor) tasks. We can meet such an approach also in cloud exploration [17]. In literature, such problems have been considered for a long time, for instance in the work of Drozdowski [8,10] and in the monograph [9], Fleitelson [11], as well as in doctoral thesis of Kramer [13] where they mainly concern computer systems.

The first applications of multi-machine models of tasks scheduling refer not only to chemical industry (Bozoki and Richard [3]) but also to projects scheduling (Vizing [18]). The natural reference for this type of tasks are, examined from decades, multiprocessor computer systems (Błażewicz et al. [1]). In the vast majority of them the completion date of the execution of all tasks ($C_{\max}$) was maximized. Today, many computer centers offer performance of calculations

© IFIP International Federation for Information Processing 2016
Published by Springer International Publishing Switzerland 2016. All Rights Reserved
K. Saeed and W. Homenda (Eds.): CISIM 2016, LNCS 9842, pp. 300–311, 2016.
DOI: 10.1007/978-3-319-45378-1_27

and the cost of the service depends not only on the duration of the computations but also on the number of required processors. Therefore, there appears a need for the construction and testing of new, corresponding to the reality models and analysis of criterion functions taking into account the overall costs. We can encouter similar issues in construction projects planning, where the simultaneous use of multiple resources is the basis for the organization of work.

The basic problem of multi-machine scheduling, $P|size_j|C_{max}$ (where P - is a symbol of multimachine, whereas $size_j$ — required number of machines) was studied mainly in reference to the approximate algorithms and the worst case scenario (Lin [15], Lloyd [16]). It has been proven that already in the case of two machines, the problem $P2|size_j|C_{max}$ is *NP-hard*. Błądek et al. [2] consider the problem with C_{max} criterion assuming further that to certain tasks there must be assigned a fixed number of neighboring machines. In addition, it is assumed that the time of task scheduling undergoes learning or aging process, depending on the start of its execution.

In this paper we consider the problem of multi-machine scheduling, in which, between the tasks performed in sequence, there are additionally setups of machines introduced. In the case of construction processes, a setup is the time required for the movement of machines, equipment and employees. However, in computer systems, the setup time is related to the exchange (update) of the software transfer data/results, synchronization calculations, etc. Apart from the execution time of machine, the criteria, taking into account also other parameters (e.g. the number of used processors) undoubtedly enable more accurate determination of the actual cost of operating of such a system.

2   Problem Definition

The considered in the work problem of multi-machine tasks scheduling can be formulated as follows.

Problem: there is a set of tasks $\mathcal{J} = \{1, 2, \ldots, n\}$, given, which should be executed on identical machines (i.e. characterized with the same functional properties and equal capacities) from the set $\mathcal{M} = \{1, 2, \ldots, m\}$. Task $i \in \mathcal{J}$ requires at the same time execution of $size_i$ machines in $p_i > 0$ time units. Machines $l, k \in \mathcal{M}$ ($l \neq k$) are called *neighbouring*, if $k = l+1$ ($l = 1, 2, ..., m-1$) lub $k = l - 1$ ($l = 2, 3, ..., m$). By $s_{i,j}$ we denote the time of machine setup after the completion of task i and before starting the task j ($i, j \in \mathcal{J}$), where both tasks are performed on the same machine. At the same time the following restrictions must be met:

(a) any machine, at any moment, cannot exercise more than one task,
(b) the task execution cannot be interrupted,
(c) each task is performed on the required number of neighboring machines,
(d) between the tasks executed sequentially there must be setup of the machine performed.

We assume further that the number of machines is $m \geqslant \max\{size_i \colon i \in \mathcal{J}\}$.

The considered in the work problem (in short denoted by **MPP**) boils down to determining, for each task, a subset of machines and the starting moments of its execution (for each machine) satisfying the constraints (a)–(d), to optimize the adopted criterion. The first solution can be represented by a pair of $\Theta = (Q, \mathcal{S})$ is such that:

- $\mathbf{Q} = [Q_1, Q_2, ..., Q_n]$, where Q_i ($Q_i \subseteq \mathcal{M}$, $|Q_i| = size_i$,) is a set of machines (assignment) on which the task $i \in \mathcal{J}$,
- $\mathcal{S} = [S_{1,1}, ..., S_{1,m}, S_{2,1}, ..., S_{2,m}, ..., S_{n,1}, ..., S_{n,m}]$, will be executed, where the element $S_{i,j}$ is the starting moment of task i execution on machine j (if $j \notin Q_i$, then we assume $S_{i,j} = -\infty$).

By Ω let us denote the set of all solutions to MPP problem.

For any solution $\Theta \in \Omega$

$$C_{\max}(\Theta) = \max\{S_{i,j} + p_i \colon i \in \mathcal{J}, j \in \mathcal{M}\}$$

is the moment of all task completion, and

$$M_{\max} = \max\{j \colon j \in Q_i, i \in \mathcal{J}\}$$

the maximum number of machine from all allocated to tasks execution. Let

$$F(\Theta) = C_{\max}(\Theta) \cdot M_{\max}(\Theta). \tag{1}$$

We consider the problem of scheduling of Textbf MPP tasks consisting in determination of solution $\Theta^* \in \Omega$ such that

$$F(\Theta^*) = \min\{F(\Theta) \colon \Theta \in \Omega\}.$$

Example. There is a set of multi-machine tasks given $\mathcal{J} = \{1, 2, 3, 4, 5, 6\}$ to be executed on $m = 4$ machines from the set $\mathcal{M} = \{1, 2, 3, 4\}$. The parameters of the individual tasks are shown in Table 1 (it is assumed that the setup times equal 0).

Table 1. Tasks parameters.

Task (j)	1	2	3	4	5	6
p_j	1	2	1	3	3	1
$size_j$	4	3	1	2	2	1

Figure 1 shows a Gantt diagram to certain solution $\Theta = (\mathbf{Q}, \mathcal{S})$, where $\mathbf{Q} = [Q_1, Q_2, Q_3, Q_4, Q_5, Q_6]$ and $Q_1 = \{1, 2, 3, 4\}$, $Q_2 = \{2, 3, 4\}$, $Q_3 =$

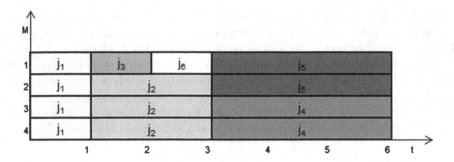

Fig. 1. Gantt diagram for solution Θ.

$\{1\}$, $Q_4 = \{3,4\}$, $Q_5 = \{1,2\}$, $Q_6 = \{1\}$. The beginning times of execution of tasks $\mathcal{S} = (0,0,0,0,-\infty,1,1,1,1,-\infty,\ -\infty,-\infty,-\infty,-\infty,3,3,3,$ $3,-\infty,-\infty,2,-\infty,-\infty,-\infty)$. For this solution

$$M_{\max}(\Theta) = 4,\ C_{\max}(\Theta) = 6,$$

therefore the value of the goal function is $F(\Theta) = 24$.

The work [14] proved that the problem of multi-machine task scheduling (without setup times) is NP-hard. Some lower and upper bound estimation of the criterion (1) were presented in work [10]. To solve the considered in the work MPP problem there was a simulated annealing algorithm presented. The starting moments of tasks execution $\mathcal{S}$, at a fixed order, will be designated with the use of the algorithm solving two-dimensional packing problem (already one-dimensional problem of packing is strongly NP-hard, Garey et al. [12]).

3   Packing Problem

Two-dimensional bin packing problem consists in such arrangement of rectangles, that the field occupied by them had minimum surface area. In the considered variant the rectangles, which contact the sides (hights) should be moved from one other to some extent. To put the matter more formally, it can be described as follows:

Problem: there is a set of rectangles $\mathcal{R} = \{r_1, r_2, ..., r_n\}$ given. The sizes of the rectangle $r_k \in \mathcal{R}$ are defined by a pair of numbers $t_k = (l_k, w_k)$, where l_k denotes the height, whereas w_k - width of the rectangle. By $d_{i,j}$ we denote the distance by which the rectangle r_i must be moved from r_j, when they are placed right next to one another.

The considered problem is to find the G shape of a minimal surface area, within which it is possible to place all rectangles, i.e. minimization of the product,

$$\Phi(G) = L \cdot W, \tag{2}$$

where L is the height and W - the width of G. shape. In short, the considered in the paper packing problem will be denoted by **BBP**.

With each rectangle located within the G shape there is identified the position, in which it was enclosed, represented by the coordinates in a Cartesian coordinate system. The rectangles should be placed inside the G shape in such a way so as not to overlap one other, whereas their edges, representing respectively their length and width, were located parallely to the edges representing the length and width of G. shape. The interval in the horizontal plane, between any two rectangles $r_i, r_j \in \mathcal{R}$ cannot be less than the value d_{r_i, r_j}. The example illustrating the above-described definitions and indications is given in Fig. 2.

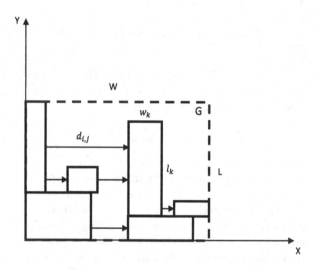

Fig. 2. G shape with enclosed rectangles

It is easy to observe the following relationship:

Corollary 1. *The problem of multi-machine task scheduling* MPP *is equivalent to the problem of two-dimensional bin packing* BBP.

3.1   Simulated Annealing Algorithm

The solution is represented in the form of a permutation (sequence) of rectangles

$$\alpha = [r_1, r_2, \ldots, r_n].$$

On its basis, using the **packing strategy** (the decoding solution), there is the value of the solution determined, i.e. the surface area of the $G(\alpha)$ shape in which rectangles are placed. Permutation Λ determines the order of rectangles in which they will be executed by the packing procedure. Let Ω be the set of all permutations of elements of $\mathcal{R}$, i.e. the set of feasible solutions. The simulated annealing algorithm (SA) will be used to search through this set.

The key elements of the algorithm are: initial temperature, probability function, with which the solutions worse than the current one, are accepted and cooling scheme (decreasing of the value) of the temperature.

In each step of the algorithm there are some elements the solutions space Λ - neighborhood of the current solution considered. It is a set of elements, generated by small modifications of the considered solution. In the case where the current solution is worse than the one drawn from the neighborhood, it is replaced by it. With some probability, it is also possible to replace the current solution with the worse solution. This strategy is used not only to prevent stagnation but also to direct the trajectory of explorations in new areas of the solution space. The selection of temperature, cooling scheme and the probability function has influence on the frequency of accepting solutions worse than the current solutions, thus not only on the ability of the algorithm to leave local minima but also on the stability of the search itself.

Let $\alpha \in \Omega$ be any starting solution. By $\mathcal{N}(\alpha)$ we denote the neighborhood, whereas by t the control parameter (temperature).

Simulated annealing algorithm

$\alpha_{best} \leftarrow \alpha$;
repeat
  repeat
    Randomly determine element β from neighborhood $\mathcal{N}(\alpha)$;
    if $G(\beta) < G(\alpha)$ then $\alpha \leftarrow \beta$
    else
      if $exp\{-(G(\beta) - G(\alpha))/t\} > random$ then $\alpha \leftarrow \beta$;
    if $G(\beta) < G(\alpha_{best})$ then
      $\alpha_{best} \leftarrow \beta$;
  until $Change\_control\_parameter$;
  Change control parameter t;
until $End\_Condition$.

Neighborhood $\mathcal{N}(\alpha)$ is generated by two types of random moves, namely - the swap and the twist type. Such neighborhoods are described in details in the works of Bożejko and Wodecki [4, 6, 7]. The temperature, in turn, is changed according to the geometric distribution, i.e. $t_{k+1} = t_k \cdot \lambda$ where lambda $0, 8 \leqslant \lambda < 1$.

3.2 Packing Strategy

In the construction of rectangle packing procedures, i.e. in the process of determination of the shape (area) within which the rectangle is enclosed, there are different strategies applied. They differ from one another in the criteria for selecting the area (coordinates), in which the considered rectangle will be placed. In each of the used strategies we consider rectangles in the order they appear in the solution (permutation), at the same time trying to designate the space of the smallest possible surface area. A general description of the rectangle packing procedure is presented below.

Let $\alpha = [r_1, r_2, \ldots, r_n]$ be a certain sequence (permutation) of rectangles. The rectangles are considered in the order they appear in α. In i-th iteration of the procedure ($i = 1, 2, \ldots, n$) we will enclose the rectangle r_i to G shape (area), in which there are already enclosed rectangles $r_1, r_2, \ldots, r_{i-1}$. The set $P_{i-1} = \{z_1, z_2, \ldots, z_s\}$, where $z_i = (x_i, y_i)$ contains positions on which the considered rectangle is inserted (we assume that at the starting moment the area $G = \emptyset$ and $P_0 = \{(0,0)\}$). Next, rectangle r_i is 'temporarily' placed into the G, area (shape) on each position from the set P_{i-1}. In this way, we generate a set of temporary areas $O = \{G_1, G_2, \ldots, G_s\}$. Depending on the used packing strategy, we choose from O corresponding area (i.e. the coordinates of the point where we insert a rectangle r_i). If the area G_l, was chosen, then:

(*i*) rectangle r_i is placed into the G shape on the position $z_l = (x_l, y_l)$,
(*ii*) the set of positions $P_i = P_{i-1} \setminus \{z_l\} \cup \{(x_l + d_{r_c,r_i} \cdot \delta, y_l), (x_l + d_{r_c,r_i} \cdot \delta, y_l + l_i)\}$,
    where $\delta \in \{0, 1\}$ and takes the value 1, if the placed rectangle r_i was moved by size d_{r_c,r_i}, and position z_l was created in the result of placing the rectangle r_c. Otherwise $\delta = 0$.

Next, we move to the next iteration. The procedure ends after placing all rectangles on their positions. When selecting position, in which the following rectangle is inserted, the following strategies were used:

1. *Minimum area* - the position, causing minimal enlargement of the area (2) is chosen, created as a result of the insertion of the considered rectangle,
2. *Area-sizes* - it is the development of the minimum area strategy. The value of the ratio is calculated, taking into account the surface area of the temporary (area) shape and the difference in the length of its sides. The purpose of application of this factor is to create areas having a uniform shape,
3. *Roulette* - the position is drawn in accordance with the principle of a roulette. The probability of drawing is proportional to the size of the temporary area,
4. *XYZ* - similarly as in the case of a roulette but the drawing is carried out according to the uniform distribution.

In the simulated annealing algorithm, each of the above-described packing strategy was implemented. For each designated by the algorithm solution G there was *packing accuracy* calculated $T/\Phi(G)$, where T is the sum of all the areas of rectangles (the lower bound of function Φ).

4   Computational Experiments

The computations were performed on a computer equipped with a 6-core Intel Core i7 X980 CPU (3.33 GHz) and Linux operating system Ubuntu 12.04.5 LTS. For the purposes of computational experiments there were test data of varying degrees of heterogeneity randomly generated. The number of possible types of rectangles is 3(107), 5(101), 8(143), 10(134), 12(142), 15(129), 20(161). The total number of rectangles is given in brackets. The following values of the SA algorithm parameters were adopted: initial temperature $t_0 = 125$, rate of temperature change $\lambda = 0, 98$, while the temperature change occurs every 100 iterations (return to the initial value every 500 iterations) and a maximum number of iterations is 5000. The results of the carried out study are presented in Tables (2, 3, 4 and 5). Each row of the table contains the results obtained for one installation of test data: the number of types of rectangles (*Types*), the accuracy of the designated solution (*Accuracy*), the surface area of the shape (area) including the considered rectangles (*Shape area*), lengths of the shorter and the longer side of the surface area (*Shorter, Longer side*), the ratio of the longer side to the shorter side(*Ratio*) and the calculations time in seconds (*Time*). By far the best results for all instances of the problem were obtained by applying the strategy of minimum area (Table 2) in the packing procedure. For each example there was the shortest time of calculations observed. The parameter values *Ratio* were much greater than the value received after the application of other packing strategies (longer side was from 12.23 to 60.00 times larger than the shorter side). This strategy shows a clear preference of the surface area of the specified space. Using the Area-sizes ratio strategy (Table 3) the results were only a little worse than those listed in the Table 2. With the use of this strategy the smallest value of the *Ratio* coefficient for the number of types 3, 8, 10, 12, 15 and 20 were obtained. For the two types 3 and 5, the values were the same as in the strategy Roulette strategy. The value of the *Ratio* parameter close to 1.00 means that shape of the designated area is close to the square.

Table 2. Minimum area strategy.

Types	Accuracy	Shape area	Shorter side	Longer side	Ratio	Time
3	0.920	489176	94	5204	55.36	56
5	0.873	677100	150	4514	30.09	37
8	0.850	766140	113	6780	60.00	117
10	0.860	641200	229	2800	12.23	162
12	0.842	689475	145	4755	32.79	171
15	0.874	699470	226	3095	13.69	102
20	0.841	892080	216	4130	19.12	160

Table 3. Area-sizes ratio strategy.

Types	Accuracy	Shape area	Shorter side	Longer side	Ratio	Time
3	0.861	522440	706	740	1.05	141
5	0.851	694540	820	847	1.03	115
8	0.832	782310	879	890	1.01	278
10	0.803	686412	828	829	1.00	217
12	0.816	711490	842	845	1.00	254
15	0.819	746496	864	864	1.00	190
20	0.804	933131	961	971	1.01	376

Table 4. Roulette strategy.

Types	Accuracy	Shape area	Shortest side	Longer side	Ratio	Time
3	0.220	2042350	1396	1463	1.05	142
5	0.303	1947150	1379	1412	1.02	121
8	0.183	3565740	1774	2010	1.13	317
10	0.256	2151000	1434	1500	1.05	268
12	0.193	3009260	1704	1766	1.04	315
15	0.201	3043580	1689	1802	1.07	238
20	0.148	5069220	2075	2443	1.18	444

Table 5. XYP strategy.

Types	Accuracy	Shape area	Shorter side	Longer side	Ratio	Time
3	0.134	3352340	1713	1957	1.14	180
5	0.244	2423280	1366	1774	1.30	154
8	0.157	4158810	1622	2564	1.58	423
10	0.182	3035430	1305	2326	1.78	354
12	0.167	3476110	1547	2247	1.45	417
15	0.168	3632800	1353	2685	1.98	315
20	0.151	4966610	1793	2770	1.54	604

The next two Tables 4 and 5 include the results obtained after application of non-deterministic packing strategy in SW algorithm. The values of the solutions obtained with the use of the Roulette strategy (Table 4) were significantly worse than ones obtained with the use of Minimum area or area-size ratio strategy. Also, the time of computations was longer. For the two types 3 and 5 there were the biggest values of the *Ratio* parameter obtained.

While applying the strategy XYP (the results - Table 5) there were the worst solutions, for the six types, obtained. This concerned both the computation time and the accuracy. Generally, deterministic strategies proved to be much better than probabilistic ones. If we take into account only the surface area, it is better to use the Minimum area strategy. On the other hand, when we are looking for an area of shape similar to a square, then it is better to use the Area-sizes strategy. For the determination of costs of multiprocessor tasks, the choice of packing strategy, depends on the relationship between the time of CPU utilization (computations time) and the number of processors used.

Simulated Annealing and Genetic Algorithm Comparison. The canonical version of the Genetic algorithm was adopted. The algorithm has been configured as follows. For crossover, the PMX method was used, the Mutation was based on random chromosome fields exchange. The stopping condition was the maximum iteration number – 5000.

Table 6. Simulated annealing and genetic algorithms comparison

	Simulated annealing			Genetic algorithm		
	Accuracy	Ratio	Time	Accuracy	Ratio	Times
Area	0.920	55.36	55.7	0.920	55.36	15
Area-sizes	0.861	1.05	140.9	0.894	1.05	16
Roullette	0.220	1.05	141.7	0.256	1.16	149
XYP	0.134	1.14	180.0	0.323	1.86	34
Area	0.873	30.09	36.5	0.872	58.11	21
Area-sizes	0.851	1.03	114.8	0.892	1.00	23
Roullette	0.303	1.02	121.1	0.346	1.22	130
XYP	0.244	1.30	154.3	0.462	1.24	37
Area	0.850	60.00	117.4	0.898	15.31	30
Area-sizes	0.832	1.01	278.1	0.866	1.00	63
Roullette	0.183	1.13	317.4	0.236	1.44	345
XYP	0.157	1.58	423.3	0.313	1.78	88
Area	0.860	12.23	161.8	0.887	11.61	44
Area-sizes	0,803	1.00	217.1	0.845	1.00	44
Roullette	0.256	1.05	268.3	0.305	1.04	322
XYP	0.182	1.78	354.2	0.418	1.22	69
Area	0.842	32.79	170.9	0.903	20.30	54
Area-sizes	0.816	1.00	254.4	0.852	1.00	52
Roullette	0.193	1.04	315.2	0.261	1.04	340
XYP	0.167	1.45	416.8	0.356	1.24	89
Area	0.874	13.69	101.6	0.903	13.79	36
Area-sizes	0.819	1.00	190.3	0.851	1.01	44
Roullette	0.201	1.07	238.3	0.306	1.03	280
XYP	0.168	1.98	315.0	0.390	1.33	60
Area	0.841	19.12	160.1	0.853	9.58	54
Area-sizes	0.804	1.01	376.1	0.835	1.01	91
Roullette	0.148	1.18	443.5	0.218	1.07	489
XYP	0.151	1.54	603.8	0.266	1.64	132

There are Accuracy, Ratio and Time results, for all strategies combined with Simulated Annealing and Genetic Algorithm compered in Table 6. The results are organized in four-row data structures, for all test data instances (3, 5, 8, 10 12, 15 and 20 types). Each row presents results for particular strategy and data set. The usage of Genetic algorithm in most cases improved the Accuracy results, especially for XYP strategy. Thirteen times the Ratio had greater value when Simulated Annealing algorithm was used, six times the result was equal. This means that structures builded with Genetic Algorithm had the shape close to square more often. The computation time was shorter in all cases for Area, Area-sized and XYP strategy combined with Genetic Algorithm. Roulette packing strategy had shorter execution time with Simulated Annealing than with Genetic Algorithm.

5   Conclusions

In the paper there was the problem of multi-machine tasks scheduling with setup times and minimizing the product of the number of machines used and the length of time of all tasks execution considered. Designation of a solution can be brought down to a two-dimensional rectangles packing problem with minimization of the surface area of the occupied area (shape). The simulated annealing algorithm using different packing strategies was presented in the work, i.e. placing rectangles within the proposed area. The conducted computational experiments showed that the designated surface area (to solve the tasks scheduling problem) are only slightly greater than the sum of surface areas of all the rectangles (i.e. the lower bound).

References

1. Błażewicz, J., Drabowski, M., Węglarz, J.: Scheduling multiprocessor tasks to minimize schedule length. IEEE Trans. Comput. **C–35**(5), 389–393 (1986)
2. Błdek, I., Drozdowski, M., Guinand, F., Schepler, X.: On contiguous and noncontiguous parallel task scheduling. J. Sched. **18**, 487–495 (2015)
3. Bozoki, G., Richard, J.-P.: A branch-and-bound algorithm for the continuous-process job-shop scheduling problem. AIIE Trans. **2**(3), 246–252 (1970)
4. Bożejko, W., Wodecki, M.: On the theoretical properties of swap multimoves. Oper. Res. Lett. **35**(2), 227–231 (2006)
5. Bożejko, W., Gniewkowski, Ł., Wodecki, M.: Solving timetabling problems on GPU. In: Rutkowski, L., Korytkowski, M., Scherer, R., Tadeusiewicz, R., Zadeh, L.A., Zurada, J.M. (eds.) ICAISC 2014, Part II. LNCS, vol. 8468, pp. 445–455. Springer, Heidelberg (2014)
6. Bożejko, W., Wodecki, M.: Solving permutational routing problems by population-based metaheuristics. Comput. Ind. Eng. **57**, 269–276 (2009)
7. Bożejko, W., Wodecki, M.: Parallel genetic algorithm for the flow shop scheduling problem. In: Wyrzykowski, R., Dongarra, J., Paprzycki, M., Waśniewski, J. (eds.) PPAM 2004. LNCS, vol. 3019, pp. 566–571. Springer, Heidelberg (2004)
8. Drozdowski, M.: Scheduling multiprocessor tasks an overview. Eur. J. Oper. Res. **94**, 215–230 (1996)
9. Drozdowski, M.: Select Problems of Scheduling Tasks in Multiprocessor Computer System. Poznań University of Technology Press, Poznań (1997). Series: Monographs, No. 321
10. Drozdowski, M.: Scheduling for Parallel Processing. Computer Communications and Network. Springer, Berlin (2009)

11. Feitelson, D.G., Rudolph, L., Schwiegelshohn, U., Sevcik, K.C., Wang, P.: Theory and practice in parallel job scheduling. In: Feitelson, D.G., Rudolph, L. (eds.) IPPS-WS 1997 and JSSPP 1997. LNCS, vol. 1291, pp. 1–34. Springer, Heidelberg (1997)
12. Garey, M.R., Johnson, D.S.: Computers and Intractability: A Guide to the Theory of NP-Completeness. Freeman, San Francisco (1979)
13. Kramer, A.: Scheduling multiprocessor tasks on dedicated processors. Ph.D. thesis, Fachbereich Mathematik/Informatik, Univeristat Osnabruck (1995)
14. Lee, C.Y., Cai, X.: Scheduling one and two-processor tasks on two parallel processors. IIE Trans. **31**(5), 445–455 (1999)
15. Lin, J., Chen, S.: Scheduling algorithm for nonpreemptive multiprocessor tasks. Comput. Math. Appl. **28**(4), 85–92 (1994)
16. Lloyd, E.: Concurrent task system. Oper. Res. **29**(1), 189–201 (1981)
17. Smutnicki, C., Pempera, J., Rudy, J., Żelazny, D.: A new approach for multi-criteria scheduling. Comput. Ind. Eng. **90**, 212–220 (2015)
18. Vizing, V.: About schedules observing deadlines. Kibernetika **1**, 128–135 (1981)

Two Step Algorithm for Virtual Machine Distributed Replication with Limited Bandwidth Problem

Wojciech Bożejko[1], Piotr Nadybski[2(✉)], and Mieczysław Wodecki[3]

[1] Institute of Computer Engineering, Control and Robotics,
Wrocław University of Technology, Janiszewskiego 11-17, 50-372 Wrocław, Poland
wojciech.bozejko@pwr.edu.pl
[2] Faculty of Technical and Economic Science,
Witelon State University of Applied Sciences in Legnica,
Sejmowa 5A, 59-220 Legnica, Poland
nadybskip@pwsz.legnica.edu.pl
[3] Institute of Computer Science, University of Wrocław,
Joliot-Curie 15, 50-383 Wrocław, Poland
mieczyslaw.wodecki@uwr.edu.pl

Abstract. This article presents a proposal of solution for the problem of optimization of the virtual machine (VM) backup or replication process in architecture with multiple locations where efficient bandwidth usage and maximal tardiness for single VM are objectives. The two step algorithm is considered, where in the first step a set of tasks is partitioned into smaller subsets for load balancing. In the second step - tabu search algorithm is used to minimize weighted sum of tardiness. The paper contains the results of computational experiments on the scalability of the presented method.

1 Introduction

In the recent years cloud computing model has became one of the most commonly used architectures for modern IT systems. Many software developers or organizational end users decide to migrate from traditional server environment to cloud based solutions. Recent experiences of customers show that products in this group of technology are now mature, reliable and can offer us many benefits: security, demanded performance and reduced costs of exploitation of IT resources. What is more, the use of such a model of IT systems development changes quite radically the way of thinking about IT tools, which, regardless of their complexity and structure, is becoming just a service to the end user instead of being just a piece of hardware and software running on it [1]. Undoubtedly, this simplicity is just a user's point of view. In fact, technical background in hardware, as well as in software layer, is much more complex and is based on many complementary technologies. The term *cloud computing* is not a name for a specific service or product. It is rather used to describe a certain model, a trend in the area of computer system engineering.

© IFIP International Federation for Information Processing 2016
Published by Springer International Publishing Switzerland 2016. All Rights Reserved
K. Saeed and W. Homenda (Eds.): CISIM 2016, LNCS 9842, pp. 312–321, 2016.
DOI: 10.1007/978-3-319-45378-1_28

One of the most commonly used technologies connected with cloud computing is *virtualization* as it most often provides technical basis for cloud computing architecture. Virtualization involves separating the software from the physical environment in which it is run. The division may occur at a few levels. Infrastructure-as-a-Service (IaaS) is one of the possibilities [8]. In this model the most important definition is a virtual machine (VM). This is a software implementation of a machine that executes programs operating systems and applications like a physical machine. Each virtual machine has its own set of virtual hardware that implements its functionality through the use of physical hardware. Essentially, many virtual machines can run on one physical computer simultaneously. The most important components of the typical platform for running virtual machines are: hardware components (a single server or a cluster of servers) delivering necessary computing power, memory and disk space for image files of virtual machines and *hypervisor (Virtual Machine Manager - process running on physical machine responsible for realization of VM instruction on physical hardware)*. To ensure reliability and performance in bigger solutions serving dozens or hundreds VMs disk space is delivered usually by dedicated storage systems.

Reliability, in addition to functionality and performance, is the most important requirement of IT systems. Redundancy is one of the best practices in this field. This means that at least two components realize a specific function. If one fails, the other provides the continuous work of the system. For example, in the case of database servers the consistency of the two copies of the data in the both databases is required. In cloud computing infrastructure with virtual machines redundancy in most situation means that there are at least two data stores and hypervisor managing virtual machines on two separated hardware platforms. Undeniably both copies should be identical. Data integrity process is known as replication. There are many strategies for data replication. Among them there are synchronous, asynchronous and *point-in-time* replications. The first two of them assume that data will be distributed to all backup storages immediately (synchronous) or as soon as possible (asynchronous). Undoubtedly this is the best strategy in case of failure, nevertheless it requires a lot of hardware resources and very fast network connection between data stores. In *point-in-time* strategy data (for example periodic *snapshots* - state of a virtual machine at a particular point in time) is copied to backup localization.

With the progress of cloud technology deployment in real business solutions, the problem of workflow scheduling became an important field of interest for researches. Many of them were described in work Wu et al. [9]. Commercial usage requires on-time resource delivery and guaranteed or predictable time of tasks processing, handling of failures, while costs of hardware resources, power consumption etc. should be reduced as much as possible. The most challenging aspect of the workflow scheduling problems solving process is the fact, that they are NP-hard, so finding optimal solution in those cases is usually impossible in acceptable time period. Problem of tasks scheduling, described in this paper is an example of this class of problems.

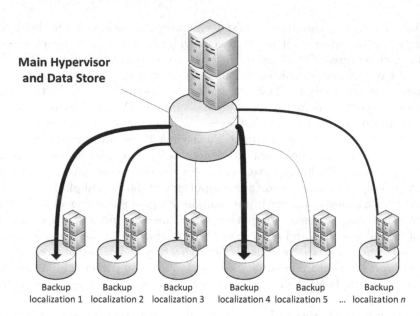

Fig. 1. Cloud architecture.

2   Problem Description and Preliminaries

There is an infrastructure for running clients virtual machines (Fig. 1). Analysis
of system load statistics shows that there are significant differences in the current use of resources in different parts of the day. In addition to the main data
store, there are m backup localizations. Each VM should have one, as actual
as possible, backup copy. During the normal system state secondary instance of
virtual machine image is immediately synchronized with primary one. Due to big
bandwidth usage a situation where users import, restore or create a new virtual
machine is more problematic. In such a situation big amount of data is generated
and needs to be replicated (Fig. 2). To avoid decrease of the system performance,
backup copies of new instances are made cyclic, only in the previously mentioned
moments when the system usage level is expected to be acceptably low.

Basic Assumptions:

- There is m backup localization and each of them is connected with primary
  location by connection of limited bandwidth. It means that in specified time
  only limited amount of data can be send. Let

  $\mathcal{L} = \{1, 2, ..., m\}$ - be a set of backup localizations, whereas
  b_l - the amount of data possible to transfer during one cycle for localization
  $l \in \mathcal{L}$.
- There are n new machines (tasks) to be transferred to secondary location. Each
  VM has specified size, so transferring it to backup location takes particular
  period of time, depending on connection bandwidth. Each newly created VM

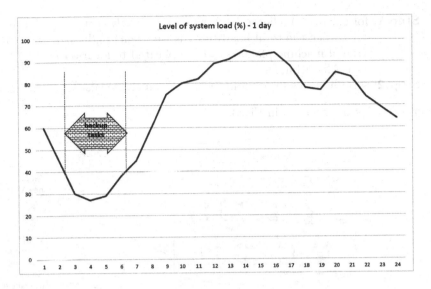

Fig. 2. Daily load condition of the system

has timer showing the period between creation moment and current time. The timer stops when backup process begins. Each machine should be replicated as soon as possible. There is due time for each new machine to be copied. If not, cost of the tardiness is counted for late replication. What is more, each virtual machine has priority, depending on customer costs plan or administrator's decision.

$\mathcal{V} = \{1, 2, ..., n\}$ - set of tasks - new virtual machines,
s_v - size of machine v $(v \in \mathcal{V})$,
d_v - due time for machine v replication,
w_v - positive weight of the virtual machine v tardiness.

– Tardiness is a time between the moment of completion the replication and due time:

$$T_v = max\{0, C_v - d_v\} \quad - \text{ tardiness, and}$$

$$w_v \cdot T_v \quad - \text{ cost of } v \text{ machine replication.}$$

– The main goal is to make a backup copy of each new virtual machine and minimize the summary cost of the replication process. Summary cost is given by formula

$$\sum_{v=1}^{n} w_v \cdot T_v.$$

As mentioned earlier in this document, finding global optimal solution due to computational complexity is not possible in most real situations where a set of solutions is too big to check all possibilities. For problem described above there is the two step algorithm proposed

Step 1: for each $v \in \mathcal{V}$ choose $l \in \mathcal{L}$ where $\sum V_j < b_l$ (this condition is true when the total bandwidth is sufficient) and j is a number true of machine planned to be replicated to location l (see Algorithm 1);

Step 2: sort the tasks for each location l to minimize cost.

General conception is shown in Fig. 3.

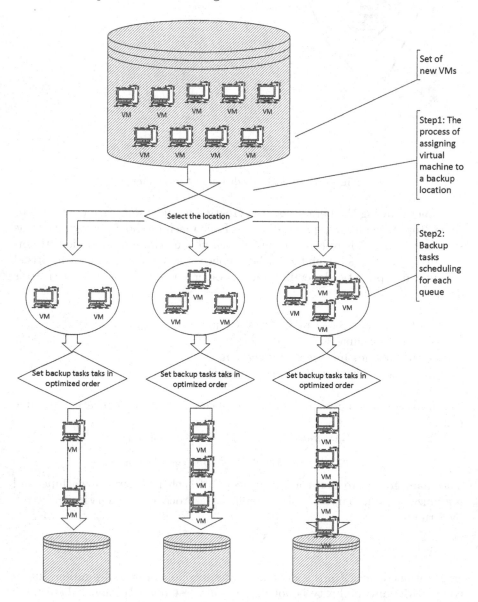

Fig. 3. Conception of backup data flow.

Algorithm 1. Pseudocode for least-used method.

```
sort V in descending order
for all v in V do
    x ← 0                                    ▷ index of least loaded location
    y ← 0                         ▷ index of least loaded and not overloaded location
    for all l in L do
        calculate CL
        if CLₗ < CLₓ then
            x ← l
        end if
        if CLₗ < CLᵧ then
            y ← l
        end if
    end for
end for
if y <> 0 then
    v ← y
else
    v ← x
end if
```

2.1   Assign Virtual Machine to Backup Location

The main goal of the first step is to provide optimal use of all available bandwidth. This is a typical problem for issues related to the load balancing in computer networks. In algorithm described in this paper *Weighted Least-Used* strategy is implemented. It means that each time when location for the single Virtual Machine is chosen, the least heavily loaded backup storage is preferred [6]. Level of load (CL) is calculated as

$$CL = \frac{\sum_{i=1}^{k+1} s_i}{b_l},$$

where k is a number of virtual machines already assigned to location l, the $k+1$ machine is the actually considered one and b_l is maximal amount of data to be transferred during one cycle without overload to location l and s_i is a size of machine i.

2.2   Tabu Search Algorithm for the Single Machine Total Weighted Tardiness Problem

As a result of *Step 1* all Virtual Machines are assigned for replication to one of the available backup locations. From this moment each channel can be considered separately and is known as The Single Machine Total Weighted Tardiness Problem $(1||\sum w_i T_i$, [10,11], see also [4,5,7]). As the problem is *NP-hard*, the heuristics algorithms are used instead of classic method. As the problem has applications in many fields of science and industry, this problem was the subject of many studies. For the purpose of this experiment classic form of the tabu search (TS) algorithm has been implemented. For neighborhood permutations generating *s-moves* there are used [2,3]. After preliminary calculations, tabu list length was set to 7.

3   Computational Experiments

Algorithm was implemented in *C#* language and tested on Intel i7 3537U (3.1 GHz) processor. In the first run the number of backup locations was set to 5. The set of VMs was randomly generated five times and the algorithm was run for each of them. Then the average time was calculated. The number of iterations for tabu search was set to 50. The operations were repeated for 100, 200 and 500 VMs. In the second run the number of backup location was set to 10. The rest of the procedure was unmodified. The results are presented in the Table 1 and Fig. 4.

On the test platform, sets of few hundreds were computed in acceptable time of few minutes, especially when the number of locations was also 10 or more. The performed experiment proved that algorithm is more efficient in cases where more backup location is available. The reason for this is the fact that in such cases the whole set is subdivided into more smaller subsets that are optimized by tabu search.

Table 1. Computing time in (*ms*) for increasing number of VMs).

VMs	Storages	Iterations	Computing time
50	5	50	294
100	5	50	2578
200	5	50	21538
500	5	50	508956
1000	5	50	6431293
50	10	50	97
100	10	50	930
200	10	50	6331
500	10	50	137865
1000	10	50	1804413
50	5	100	562
100	5	100	3320
200	5	100	45944
500	5	100	860553
1000	5	100	11504165

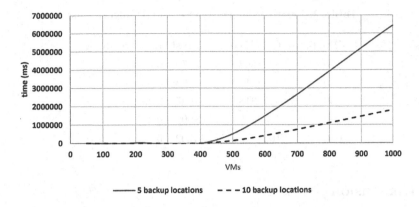

Fig. 4. Computing time in (ms) for increasing number of VMs (50 iterations).

As expected, with increasing amount of virtual machines to backup, the number of operations to be performed consequently increases very fast. It is worth mentioning that increasing number of backup location causes shorter completion time.

Table 2 contains average relative change between greedy algorithm (GREE) and tabu search optimized results for set of data used in this experiment. Due to greedy algorithm tasks are firstly ordered by d_i (due time) from the shortest time to the longest and then, one by one, assigned to remote backup location where cost for this machine would be the lowest. The method presented in this paper, compared with GREE, allowed for a 40 to 50 percent reduction of the $w_i \cdot T_i$ cost, depending on the test set of data.

Algorithm 2. Pseudocode for GREE algorithm.

---

sort $\mathcal{V}$ in ascending order by due time
for all v in $\mathcal{V}$ **do**
    $x_v \leftarrow 1$ $\triangleright$ index of optimal already found backup location for this VM
    $y \leftarrow \sum_{i=1}^{n_1}(w_i * T_i) + (w_v * T_v)$ $\triangleright$ n_1 - number of backup tasks assigned already to location 1
    for all l in $\mathcal{L}$ **do**
        calculate $C_l = \sum_{i=1}^{n_l}(w_i * T_i) + (w_v * T_v)$ $\triangleright$ Cost of tasks (vm) assigned to l location and task v
        if $C_l < y$ **then**
            $x_v \leftarrow l$
        end if
    end for
end for

Table 2. Relative change (GREE and TS algorithms)

VMs/tasks	GREE cost	TS cost	Relative change
50	1803	872	0.52
100	8911	4493	0.50
200	43318	24885	0.43
500	253636	148099	0.42
1000	1051256	624702	0.41

4   Conclusion

Strategy for scheduling backup or replication tasks in cloud computing, virtualization environment presented in this paper is based on two methods widely used for solving problems in industry and computer networks. Both of them used together as the two-step algorithm allow to improve performance and reduce time needed for operations. In the first step the size of problem is reduced by quick method, where each task is assigned to destination based on amount of data to be transferred and bandwidth usage of each available network connection. This operation reduces the size of a set processed by a more precise but also more complex algorithm used in the second step. The proposed method can produce less accurate results than in case, when classic heuristic like Tabu Search is only used, but should reduce processing delay. Further research is also possible for tabu search for or example more sophisticated method in the first step can be tested. The discussed method can be used for problems in cloud computing like non on-line replication, synchronization where many network connections, data storages or virtualization platforms are available. As the parameters of cost function are freely definable other use is also possible.

References

1. Armbrust, M., Fox, A., Griffith, R., Joseph, A.D., Katz, R., Konwinski, A., Zaharia, M.: A view of cloud computing. Commun. ACM **53**(4), 50–58 (2010)
2. Bożejko, W., Wodecki, M.: On the theoretical properties of swap multimoves. Oper. Res. Lett. **35**(2), 227–231 (2006). Elsevier Science Ltd
3. Bożejko, W., Wodecki, M.: Solving permutational routing problems by population-based metaheuristics. Comput. Ind. Eng. **57**, 269–276 (2009)
4. Bożejko, W., Wodecki, M.: Parallel genetic algorithm for minimizing total weighted completion time. In: Rutkowski, L., Siekmann, J.H., Tadeusiewicz, R., Zadeh, L.A. (eds.) ICAISC 2004. LNCS (LNAI), vol. 3070, pp. 400–405. Springer, Heidelberg (2004)
5. Bulbul, K.: A hybrid shifting bottleneck-tabu search heuristic for the job shop total weighted tardiness problem. Comput. Oper. Res. **38**, 967–983 (2011)
6. Ellrod, C.: Load Balancing - Least Connections. https://www.citrix.com/blogs/2010/09/02/load-balancing-least-connections/. Accessed 10 April 2016

7. Lin, Y.K., Chong, C.S.: A tabu search algorithm to minimize total weighted tardiness for the job shop scheduling problem. J. Ind. Manage. Optim. **12**(2), 703–713 (2016)
8. Mell, P., Grance, T.: The NIST definition of cloud computing, Recommendations of the National Institute of Standards and Technology. http://faculty.winthrop.edu/domanm/csci411/Handouts/NIST.pdf. Accessed 03 April 2016
9. Wu, F., Wu, Q., Yousong, T.: Workflow scheduling in cloud: a survey. J. Supercomput. **71**(9), 3373–3418 (2015)
10. Wodecki, M.: A branch-and-bound parallel algorithm for single-machine total weighted tardiness problem. Int. J. Adv. Manuf. Technol. **37**(9–10), 996–1004 (2008)
11. Wodecki, M.: A block approach to earliness-tardiness scheduling problems. Int. J. Adv. Manuf. Technol. **40**, 797–807 (2009)

An Optimization Based Software Tool for Individual Automated Guideway Transit Systems

Ezzeddine Fatnassi[✉]

Institut Supérieur de Gestion de Tunis, Université de Tunis,
41, Rue de la Liberté - Bouchoucha, 2000 Bardo, Tunisia
ezzeddine.fatnassi@gmail.com

Abstract. Automated Guideway Transit is a form of public transportation tools where fully driverless vehicles operate in order to move passengers between specific locations. Automated Guideway Transit includes a large variety of systems including mass transit systems and limited people automated guideway transit systems. In this paper, we focus on a specific limited people mover system called personal rapid transit. We develop in this paper an optimization based software which could manage efficiently the empty vehicles movements within the personal rapid transit system. Within this context, a branch and bound algorithm is proposed and its efficiently is proved on a set of instances taken from the literature. Our algorithm is shown to get good quality results.

Keywords: Automated guideway transit · On-demand transportation systems · Optimization · Branch and bound

1 Introduction

Personal Rapid Transit (PRT) is a relatively new mode of specific transportation system. It falls under the automated guideway transit systems (AGT). In fact and as any classic AGT, PRT uses a set of automated vehicles which run on dedicated guideways. PRT is designed to move people in urban areas. PRT vehicles move people directly from origin station to destination station with a PRT'network of guideways without intermediate stops or transfers. The transportation service in PRT is done on-demand where one or a group of passengers ask for their transportation service. Typically, the main characteristics of PRT includes: (i) Small electric driverless vehicles, (ii) Direct origin-to-destination transportation service, (iii) on demand transportation service and (iv) Exclusive use of the PRT network by the PRT vehicles.

In summary, the main characteristics of PRT includes the offer of a taxi-like transportation service by the use of driverless vehicles on a set of dedicated guideways.

As the PRT is a complex, intelligent transportation service, it consists mainly on several advances components such as electric/electronic hardware, guideways, automated vehicles, stations, power sources and software [13].

© IFIP International Federation for Information Processing 2016
Published by Springer International Publishing Switzerland 2016. All Rights Reserved
K. Saeed and W. Homenda (Eds.): CISIM 2016, LNCS 9842, pp. 322–333, 2016.
DOI: 10.1007/978-3-319-45378-1_29

Typically, a software is one of the core component of any PRT system. It includes and supervises all the other PRT'components in order to deliver a high level of mobility for its users. Central control system for PRT manages the vehicles movements, the requested trips scheduling, the response of irregular operations such as intrusion, accidents and so on. Consequently, implementing efficient softwares for PRT is of a high importance for such an intelligent transportation system. In this paper, we focus on implementing an optimization based software for PRT in order to effectively manage the empty vehicles management of PRT while reducing its total energy consumption. In fact for a on-demand transportation service such as PRT, we could get up for a high number of empty vehicles moving to take passengers from different stations in the PRT'network which represents a high level of wasted transportation capacity. Therefore including optimization module within PRT'management software is of a high importance.

In the literature, several operational optimization related studies to PRT were published such as dynamic routing [3], network design [19], simulation [5,11], optimized operational planning [6,9], energy minimization [18], total traveled distance [8,10,12], fleet size [4] and so on.

In this paper, we focus on the optimization problem related to PRT studied by Mrad and Hidri [18]. They proposed to study the routing electric vehicles with limited battery capacity in a static deterministic context. We propose a branch and bound resolution approach for that problem. We found that our branch and bound method outperforms the commercial solver Cplex' results[1] for solving the PRT'optimization problem. An specific integration of our optimization approach within a PRT'software is also proposed.

The remainder of this paper is organized as follows: Sect. 2 presents the formal problem definition. Section 3 develops our branch and bound optimization approach. Section 4 describes the computational results as well as the integration of our optimization approach within a PRT'software. Finally, Sect. 5 concludes the paper.

2   Problem Formulation

We present in this section the problem formulation as presented in the work made by Mrad and Hidri [18]. The problem treated is based on the assumption that we have a predetermined list of trips to serve.

Let us suppose that we have a set of PRT stations S, a depot D, and a PRT network that makes it possible to journey between any pair of stations. Let us also suppose that we have an unlimited number of vehicles that are initially located in the depot and have battery capacity B.

$Cost_{i,j}$ is a cost matrix that defines the cost of traveling from station i to station j. The cost of moving between station i and station j in the PRT network will be the length of the shortest path calculated using a Floyd–Warshall algorithm.

---

[1] Details about Cplex could be found in https://www-01.ibm.com/software/commerce/optimization/cplex-optimizer/.

Let us define a list of trips T that has cardinality $|T| = n$. Each trip i $(= 1, \ldots, n)$ will have its particular origin and arrival stations (OS_i, AS_i) and its particular departure and arrival times (OT_i, AT_i). We also suppose that the vehicle should return to the depot to charge its battery when necessary. The PRT problem is defined on an asymmetric graph $G = \{V, E\}$, where $V = \{v_0, v_1, v_2, ; v_n\}$ is a set of nodes for which v_0 defines the depot and $v_1, v_2, ; v_n$ defines the n different trips that the PRT system must cover. We define $V^* = V/v_0$. Moreover, $E = \{(v_i, v_j); v_i, v_j \in V\}$ is a set of arcs that is defined as follows:

- If $v_i, v_j \in V^*$ with $AT_i + Cost_{(AS_i, OS_j)} \leq OT_j$, then the arc (i, j) exists and has cost c_{ij}, which represents the energy consumed from the arrival station of trip i (AS_i) to the arrival station of trip j (AS_j). Hence, each edge will have a combined cost that includes the cost of the movement from one trip to another and the cost of a trip itself.
- For each node $i \in V^*$ we add an arc $(0, i)$. The cost of this arc is c_{0i} and represents the energy used to reach the arrival station of trip i from the depot.
- For each node $i \in V^*$ we add an arc $(i, 0)$. The cost of this arc is c_{i0} and represents the energy used to reach the depot from the arrival station of trip i.

We also define $E' = \{(v_i, v_j); v_i, v_j \in V^*\}$.

Note that G is a direct incomplete graph, because if the arc between node v_i and node v_j exists, the opposite arc does not exist. Our problem is a typical node routing problem that can be assimilated into the asymmetrical distance-constrained vehicle routing problem (ADCVRP). The main purpose in our problem is to assign trips to vehicles with respect to the battery capacity of each vehicle in order to minimize the total consumption of electrical energy.

2.1   Flow-Based Mathematical Formulation

In this section, we adapt and present a flow-based mathematical formulation of our problem. This formulation was presented in [16] for the asymmetrical distance-constrained vehicle routing problem. We first introduce the following integer variables:

$$x_{ij} = \begin{cases} 1 & \text{if node } j \text{ is visited after node } i, \\ 0 & \text{otherwise,} \end{cases}$$

$$z_{ij} = \begin{cases} \text{the shortest length traveled from the depot to customer } j, \\ \quad \text{as } i \text{ is the predecessor of } j \\ 0 \quad \text{otherwise.} \end{cases}$$

Let c_{ij} be the cost of the journey from node i to node j. Let $\delta^+(i)$ is the set of edges that have v_i as a root. Let $\delta^-(i)$ is the set of edges that have v_i as a sink.

$$\textbf{PRT(1):} \quad \text{Minimize} \sum_{(i,j)\in E} c_{ij}x_{ij} \tag{1}$$

$$\sum_{j\in\delta^+(i)} x_{ij} = 1 \quad \forall i \in V^* \tag{2}$$

$$\sum_{j\in\delta^-(i)} x_{ji} = 1 \quad \forall i \in V^* \tag{3}$$

$$\sum_{(i,j)\subset E'} z_{ij} - \sum_{(i,j)\in E'} z_{ji} - \sum_{j\in V^*} c_{ij}x_{ij} = 0 \quad \forall i \in V \tag{4}$$

$$z_{ij} \leq (B - c_{j0})x_{ij} \quad \forall(i,j) \in E' \tag{5}$$

$$z_{ij} \geq (c_{ij} + c_{0i})x_{ij} \quad \forall i \neq 0, \forall(i,j) \in E' \tag{6}$$

$$z_{0i} = c_{0i}x_{0i} \quad \forall i \in E' \tag{7}$$

The objective (1) is to minimize the total charge used to make all the trips. Constraints (2) and (3) control the assignment of trips to routes. In fact, both constraints require that each node $i \in V^*$ be visited just once. Constraint (4) ensures that the distance from node v_i to any node v_j by road is equal to the distance between the depot and node v_j plus the distance from node v_j to node v_i. Constraint (5) ensures that the different routes are generated with respect to the battery capacity. In fact, it guarantees that the amount of charge the vehicle consumes to reach node v_j from the depot is less than its battery capacity minus the charge needed for returning to the depot. Moreover, in accordance with constraint (6), the total charge used to reach node v_j from the depot is greater than or equal to the charge needed to follow the direct link between the depot and node v_j. Finally, constraint (7) provides the initial value for z_{0i}, which should be equal to the distance from the depot to node v_i.

3 Branch-and-Bound Algorithm for Static Routing Problem of Personal Rapid Transit System

For the general VRP, there exists a different method of solution that utilizes an exact algorithm. The reader is referred to [2] for a more extensive review of the exact method for the VRP. In this paper, we propose a branch-and-bound algorithm for solving the PRT problem. We present first the general framework of our branch-and-bound procedure (B&B) [7,15,17]. The branch-and-bound algorithm is an exact method of finding optimal solutions for various distinctive optimization problems. This method was first introduced by Land and Doig in 1960. Its main idea consists in enumerating all possible solutions in a search tree. The branch and bound first solves a general global problem at the root of the search tree. Then, for all the other nodes the branch and bound will solve subproblems in which some constraints are relaxed and some variables are fixed.

The branch and bound normally starts from a feasible initial solution given by an upper-bounding procedure. However, if we do not have a heuristic approach, the initial upper bound is set to infinity. Once some constraints are relaxed, we need to define a search strategy that consists of the main rules for choosing the next node to branch off and treat. There are two well-known strategies for branching: the depth-first search (DFS), which consists in solving the most recently generated nodes first; and the best-first search, which consist in solving the most promising node first [14]. Our B&B is presented in Algorithm 1. Based on Algorithm 1, there are several components that need to be defined such as the lower bounding procedure and the branching rules. In the next sections, we present details of the specific components of the B&B method. We should note that a solution S in Algorithm 1 represents a set of roads that cover each node in graph G exactly once.

3.1 Computation of Lower Bound for PRT Problem

The lower bound is one of the most important issues for the branch-and-bound algorithm. In fact, the branch and bound has to apply a lower-bounding procedure at each node of the search tree. The lower bound also has the advantage of giving a performance measure for heuristics. In the branch and bound, the lower bounds can be found by relaxing the mathematical formulation. There is a multitude of ways to relax these models. In our B&B, we decided to use the following linear model in order to generate the lower bounds.

We will first introduce the following integer variables

$$x_{ij} = \begin{cases} 1 & \text{if node of index } j \text{ is visited after node of index } i \\ 0 & \text{Otherwise} \end{cases}$$

c_{ij} define the cost of moving between nodes v_i and v_j in G.

$$\textbf{PRT:} \quad \text{Min} \sum_{(i,j) \in E} c_{ij} x_{ij} \tag{8}$$

$$\sum_{j \in \delta^+(i)} x_{ij} = 1 \forall i \in V^* \tag{9}$$

$$\sum_{j \in \delta^-(i)} x_{ji} = 1 \forall i \in V^* \tag{10}$$

$$x_{ij} \in \{0, 1\} \forall \ (i,j) \in E \tag{11}$$

In fact to generate the lower bounds, we decided to remove the battery constraints from the mathematical model presented in [18] for solving the PRT problem. The quality of this lower bound is not high, but with this lower-bounding scheme we obtain integer solutions. Solving the relaxed mathematical model, we obtained two types of cycles (routes):

- A cycle that respects the battery capacity of the PRT vehicles.
- A cycle that does not respect the battery capacity of the PRT vehicles which must be eliminated in future resolution of the relaxed linear program.

Algorithm 1. B&B

1: Compute Lower Bound of the problem
2: **if** Obtained Solution S Is Feasible **then**
3:     Solution S is Optimal
4:     Return Objective value of S
5: **else**
6:     **for all** Infeasible Routes in Solution S **do**
7:         Compute the ratio for each route
8:         Choose the route with the largest ratio
9:         **for all** Arcs in the chosen Route **do**
10:             Relax the arc by putting its value to ∞
11:             **if** We get a feasible solution **then**
12:                 Update the Upper Bound
13:             **end if**
14:             Add Node to the tree
15:         **end for**
16:     **end for**
17:     **while** ActualNode<MaxNodes **do**
18:         Choose Subproblem with the smallest value of objective function
19:         **if** There is more than one subproblem **then**
20:             choose one randomly
21:         **end if**
22:         Calculate Lower Bound
23:         **for all** Infeasible Routes in Solution S **do**
24:             Compute the ratio for each route
25:             Choose the route with the largest ratio
26:             **for all** Arcs in the chosen Route **do**
27:                 Relax the arc by putting its value to ∞
28:                 **if** We get a feasible solution **then**
29:                     Update the Upper Bound
30:                 **end if**
31:                 Add Node to the tree
32:             **end for**
33:         **end for**
34:         **if** List of infeasible nodes is empty **then**
35:             Return the upper Bound
36:         **end if**
37:     **end while**
38: **end if**
39: Return the upper Bound

3.2 Branching Rules

As mentioned in the previous section, solving of the lower bound can result in cycles that do not respect the battery capacity. Such a route is infeasible and thus should be eliminated (i.e., the cycle should not appear in any future relaxation of the problem). Accordingly, we take inspiration from previous work on solving either the asymmetric traveling salesman problem (ATSP) [14] or the ADCVRP [1]. Normally, to eliminate an infeasible route, one arc should be removed. In our branch-and-bound method, we assign a large value to the selected arc that should be removed and then solve the relaxed program again. Thus, in the future relaxations, the infeasible route will not reappear. The main disadvantage of this strategy is that the excluded edge may be present in the optimal solution, which can result in a failure of the method to find the optimal solution.

There are several ways to choose an arc to exclude from the infeasible route:

- The first way is to exclude the arc with the greatest cost.
- The second way is to exclude a random arc.
- A third way is to use the concept of the tolerance of an arc. This type of sensitivity operator will choose only one infeasible route to work on and branch from each time. Hence, for each infeasible route, the method will compute the ratio between the total electric charge used along the route and the number of arcs in that route. We then choose to work on the infeasible route with the largest ratio. For this route, we solve the different relaxation problems while eliminating one arc of the chosen route each time. We add to the tree the nodes that correspond to these different relaxations.

In this paper, we choose to work with the third way as a branching rule for our branch-and-bound algorithm.

3.3   Example

In this example, we explain the proposed B&B with the sensitivity operator. Suppose that we have 10 trips to serve and we have a battery capacity that permits the vehicle to run for 30 min. For simplicity, we assume that we have no upper bound. Therefore, the initial value of the upper bound is set to ∞. First, we solve the relaxed linear program. We obtain three routes $R1 = (D,0); (0,3); (3,7); (7,D)$, $R2 = (D,1); (1,5); (5,8); (8,9); (9,D)$, and $R3 = (D,2); (2,4); (4,6); (6,D)$ of 28, 45, and 31 min, respectively. Therefore, we have two infeasible routes $R2$ and $R3$. For each of these two routes we calculate the associated ratio ρ as follows:

–

$$\rho(R2) = \frac{45(\text{Cost of the route R1})}{5(\text{number of arcs})} = 9 \tag{12}$$

–

$$\rho(R3) = \frac{31(\text{Cost of the route R2})}{4(\text{number of arcs})} = 7.75 \tag{13}$$

The route $R2$ has the larger ratio ($\rho(R2) = 9$). Hence, we choose arcs from route $R2$ for branching. We add three nodes to the search tree, where each corresponds to solving the relaxed linear problem while excluding one arc (see Fig. 1). The node counter is increased by 3. The upper bound is not updated, since we did not find a feasible solution.

We now have three subproblems on the tree, with costs 104, 107, and 105. We choose to branch from the node with the least cost (104). Solving the new subproblem, we again have two infeasible routes $R2$ and $R3$ with costs 43 and 33. As in the previous iteration, we compute the ratio for each route:

An Optimization Based Software Tool   329

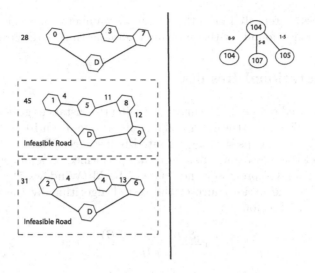

Fig. 1. First iteration of B&B

$$\rho(R2) = \frac{43(\text{Cost of the route R1})}{5(\text{number of arcs})} = 8.6 \qquad (14)$$

$$\rho(R3) = \frac{33(\text{Cost of the route R2})}{4(\text{number of arcs})} = 8.25 \qquad (15)$$

Hence, we decide to branch from route $R1$. We add additional node sub-problems to the tree, where each corresponds to excluding one of the arcs $(2,4)$ $(4,6)$, and $(6,9)$ (see Fig. 2). The node counter is updated and increased by 3. The upper bound is not updated, since we again did not find a feasible solution.

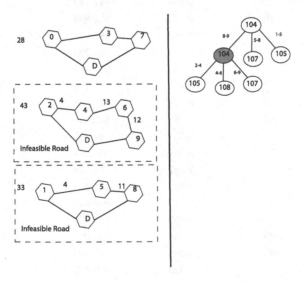

Fig. 2. Second iteration of B&B

This process is repeated until the maximum number of nodes is reached, the optimal solution is found, or the maximum running time is reached.

4   Computational Results

We have generated randomly 190 instances using the instances generator of Mrad and Hidri [18]. The size of the generated instances varies from 10 to 100 PRT'trips in steps of 5. For each trips'size, we generated 10 instances. Tests were made using a program coded in C++ and simulations are performed on a personal computer with Intel i5 2.3 GHZ processor and 6 GO of RAM (Windows 7).

We measure the performance of the tested algorithm by the GAP metric which is computed as follows:

$$GAP = (\frac{(SOL_{B\&B} - LB)}{LB}) * 100 \tag{16}$$

$SOL_{B\&B}$ represents the obtained solution for an instance using the $B\&B$ algorithm. The LB is the lower bound related to an instance of our problem. It is calculated based on the linear relaxation of the mathematical model given in [1]. All the mathematical models in this paper were coded using Cplex12.1.

Results of our algorithm are proposed in Table 1.

Table 1. Results of the B&B algorithm

Number of trips	Average gap %	Average time (s)
10	0	0.217
15	0.565	76.056
20	0.980	151.140
25	0.980	151.140
30	0.837	302.896
35	1.893	480.634
40	0.337	309.723
45	0.867	362.849
50	0.781	481.219
55	0.976	541.620
60	0.387	363.099
65	0.638	439.567
70	0.898	500.468
75	2.237	423.149
80	0.988	484.330
85	1.112	492.855
90	0.557	364.977
95	1.051	305.209
100	1.398	546.469
Average	0.920	356.717

The B&B method founds an average GAP of 0.920 % in 356.717 s which could be described as good results. In fact and in many instances, the lower-bound technique used in our B&B can find integer solutions that are very close to the optimal solution. Also one could note from Table 1 that the average computation time for B&B increases at a reasonably low rate.

We also compared the solutions obtained from B&B to those obtained by CPLEX for solving the valid mathematical model for the PRT problem [12].

Our B&B was able to find better solutions than CPLEX in 30 instances, and the results were equal in 160 instances. We also performed more extensive statistical tests to evaluate the significance of our results. In particular, we made a Wilcoxon matched-pairs signed-ranks test.

This test yielded a P-value less than 0.0001 and showed that B&B is superior to Cplex. Therefore, we can state that B&B outperforms CPLEX.

4.1   Integration of the Optimization Module Within a PRT Software

There is several ways to integrate optimization resolution techniques within intelligent mobility softwares. In our PRT context and based on our problem, we propose a full integration procedure of our optimization technique which is presented in Algorithm 2.

Algorithm 2. PRT software

1: Get the information related to the PRT network and the List of Trips
2: Construct the matrix $Cost$ and $Time$.
3: Construct the graph G.
4: Use the B&B method to generate the optimal solution
5: The PRT control system uses the obtained data related to the different obtained roads from the B&B method to manage the PRT system.

Algorithm 2 includes several steps in order to manage efficiently the PRT system. It starts by obtaining the related input such as the metric matrix related to the cost of moving between the different PRT stations and the information related to the static list of trips to serve. Next and based on these input data, the two matrix $Cost$ and $Time$ are constructed. Then, the optimization phase of our PRT software starts by building first the graph G. The optimization phase then, and using the proposed B&B method, would solve the constructed problem using the obtained input data. The last step of our algorithm includes the transmission of the obtained roads representing the solution of the B&B method to the central PRT control system in order to route efficiently the different vehicles available in the depot.

5   Conclusion

In this paper, we proposed an optimization approach to minimizing the energy consumption for PRT. While focusing on a static problem related to PRT, a

B&B resolution approach was proposed. This method adapted to the context of PRT was capable to solve various sized PRT test instances. In fact, our algorithm was shown to get a good quality results as it handles to find an average gap of 0.920 in 356.717 s.

As future works, we could implement new lower bounding procedures based on different type of relaxation. A branch and cut algorithm could also be developed in order to speed up the performance of our algorithm. Also, one could note that the implementation of efficient new meta-heuristic and solution'representation seem to be very interesting in our context in order to enhance the solution quality. New implemented meta-heuristic could also be implemented within our PRT software to solve large instances'size.

References

1. Almoustafa, S., Hanafi, S., Mladenovi, N.: New exact method for large asymmetric distance-constrained vehicle routing problem. Eur. J. Oper. Res. (2012)
2. Baldacci, R., Mingozzi, A., Roberti, R.: Recent exact algorithms for solving the vehicle routing problem under capacity and time window constraints. Eur. J. Oper. Res. **218**(1), 1–6 (2012). http://www.sciencedirect.com/science/article/pii/S0377221711006692
3. Chebbi, O., Chaouachi, J.: Modeling on-demand transit transportation system using an agent-based approach. In: Saeed, K., Homenda, W. (eds.) CISIM 2015. LNCS, vol. 9339, pp. 316–326. Springer, Heidelberg (2015)
4. Chebbi, O., Chaouachi, J.: Optimal fleet sizing of personal rapid transit system. In: Saeed, K., Homenda, W. (eds.) CISIM 2015. LNCS, vol. 9339, pp. 327–338. Springer, Heidelberg (2015)
5. Chebbi, O., Chaouachi, J.: A decentralized management approach for on-demand transit transportation system. In: Abraham, A., Wegrzyn-Wolska, K., Hassanien, A.E., Snasel, V., Alimi, A.M. (eds.) AECIA 2015. AISC, vol. 427, pp. 175–184. Springer, Heidelberg (2016). http://dx.doi.org/10.1007/978-3-319-29504-6_18
6. Chebbi, O., Chaouachi, J.: Reducing the wasted transportation capacity of personal rapid transit systems: an integrated model and multi-objective optimization approach. Transp. Res. Part E: Logistics. Transp. Rev. **89**, 236–258 (2016). http://www.sciencedirect.com/science/article/pii/S1366554515001647
7. Detienne, B., Sadykov, R., Tanaka, S.: The two-machine flowshop total completion time problem: branch-and-bound algorithms based on network-flow formulation. Eur. J. Oper. Res. **252**(3), 750–760 (2016). http://www.sciencedirect.com/science/article/pii/S0377221716300224
8. Fatnassi, E., Chaouachi, J.: VNS as an upper bound for an exact method to solve a class of on-demand transit transportation systems. Electron. Notes Discrete Math. **47**, 101–108 (2015)
9. Fatnassi, E., Chaouachi, J., Klibi, W.: Planning and operating a shared goods and passengers on-demand rapid transit system for sustainable city-logistics. Transp. Res. Part B: Methodol. **81**, 440–460 (2015)
10. Fatnassi, E., Chebbi, O., Chaouachi, J.: Discrete honeybee mating optimization algorithm for the routing of battery-operated automated guidance electric vehicles in personal rapid transit systems. Swarm Evol. Comput. **26**, 35–49 (2016). http://www.sciencedirect.com/science/article/pii/S2210650215000619

11. Fatnassi, E., Chebbi, O., Siala, J.C.: Two strategies for real time empty vehicle redistribution for the personal rapid transit system. In: 2013 16th International IEEE Conference on Intelligent Transportation Systems (ITSC), pp. 1888–1893. IEEE (2013)
12. Fatnassi, E., Chebbi, O., Siala, J.C.: Comparison of two mathematical formulations for the offline routing of personal rapid transit system vehicles. In: The International Conference on Methods and Models in Automation and Robotics (2014)
13. Furman, B., Fabian, L., Ellis, S., Muller, P., Swenson, R.: Automated transit networks (ATN): a review of the state of the industry and prospects for the future. Technical report. Mineta Transportation Institute (2014)
14. Germs, R., Goldengorin, B., Turkensteen, M.: Lower tolerance-based branch and bound algorithms for the ATSP. Comput. Oper. Res. **39**(2), 291–298 (2012). http://www.sciencedirect.com/science/article/pii/S0305054811000980
15. Kadri, A.A., Kacem, I., Labadi, K.: A branch-and-bound algorithm for solving the static rebalancing problem in bicycle-sharing systems. Comput. Ind. Eng. **95**, 41–52 (2016). http://www.sciencedirect.com/science/article/pii/S0360835216300183
16. Kara, I.: Two indexed polonomyal size formulationsfor vehicle routing problems. Technical report. Baskent University, Ankara/Turkey (2008)
17. Lee, W.C., Wang, J.Y., Lin, M.C.: A branch-and-bound algorithm for minimizing the total weighted completion time on parallel identical machines with two competing agents. Knowl.-Based Syst. **105**, 68–82 (2016). http://www.sciencedirect.com/science/article/pii/S0950705116301010
18. Mrad, M., Hidri, L.: Optimal consumed electric energy while sequencing vehicle trips in a personal rapid transit transportation system. Comput. Ind. Eng. **79**, 1–9 (2015)
19. Zheng, II., Peeta, S.: Network design for personal rapid transit under transit-oriented development. Transp. Res. Part C: Emerg. Technol. **55**, 351–362 (2015)

Determination of the Optimal Routes
for Autonomous Unmanned Aerial Vehicle
Under Varying Wind with Using
of the Traveling Salesman Problem Algorithm

Jerzy Greblicki[1] and Maciej Walczyński[2(✉)]

[1] Faculty of Electronics, Wrocław University of Technology,
Janiszewskiego 11-17, 50-372 Wrocław, Poland
jerzy.greblicki@pwr.edu.pl
[2] General Tadeusz Kościuszko Military Academy of Land Forces in Wrocław,
Czajkowskiego 109, 51-150 Wrocław, Poland
maciej.walczynski@wso.wroc.pl

Abstract. The goal of this paper is to propose and test the algorithm for traveling salesman problem (TSP) for autonomous unmanned aerial vehicles. In this paper we consider the situation when the multicopter is flying under a variable wind and is intended to visit indicated points. We analyze the efficiency of the algorithm in case of limited flying time on a constant height.

Keywords: Multicopters · UAV · Traveling salesman problem (TSP) · Drone routing problem (DRP)

1 Unmanned Aerial Vehicles

Unmanned Aerial Vehicle also known as drone is a kind of aerial machine. Drones have become one of the symbols of the global fight against terrorism. Nowdays the drones are very popular also in civil purposes. Those machines are used as a flying camera platform, platform for aerial inspection of buildings, bridges and Its hard to imagine that the history of UAV's is that long. Many of a UAVs futures are still under a laboratory experiments and the road to its commercialization and widespread use is still long.

1.1 Unmanned Aerial Vehicles in Military Solutions

The roots of Unmanned Aerial Vehicles (UAV) are strictly connected with the military solutions. One of the first UAVs was the aerial bomber balloon developed and patented in the New York in 1863 by an American inventor named Charles Parley. The idea of this solution was based on a hot-air balloon with a basket filled with explosives. This material was to be dropped on the enemy using a mechanism activated by the clock mechanism. Also, one of the first ideas of an unmanned airplane was strictly connected with army solutions in the war time. In 1916 the first airplane controlled by radio waves

© IFIP International Federation for Information Processing 2016
Published by Springer International Publishing Switzerland 2016. All Rights Reserved
K. Saeed and W. Homenda (Eds.): CISIM 2016, LNCS 9842, pp. 334–341, 2016.
DOI: 10.1007/978-3-319-45378-1_30

from the ground was created. Just a few days after the USA officially entered World War I in 1917 the American Army commissioned work on Unmanned Combat Aerial Vehicles (UCAV) [1]. Those first unmanned flying bombs based on biplane airplanes. There were several problems with those first UCAV's. One of the biggest problem was the limited aerodynamic knowledge in those times. It was almost impossible to build well flying unmanned airplane just less than twenty years after the first flight of the Wright Brothers [2] (Fig. 1).

Fig. 1. Kettering Bug one of the first UCAV's from late 1910's (https://upload.wikimedia.org/wikipedia/commons/3/35/Kettering_Bug.jpg).

The period of the 30's and 40's was a time of significant development of the technological potential of the major world powers. One of the achievements of those troubled times is the missile V-1. It is the prototype of the later unmanned airborne vehicles equipped with disposable warheads. Years of the 50's and 60's along with the Cold War between the United States of America and the Union of Soviet Socialist Republics is another period of intensive development of unmanned aerial vehicles in the history. One example is here the American MGM-1 Matador or RGM-6 Regulus I (Fig. 2).

Starting from the 90's of the twentieth century drones (due to the development of electronics and IT) began to increasingly appear more numerous and in the arenas of armed conflict. It is sufficient to mention here the participation of the Israeli-American unmanned aerial vehicles RQ-Pioneer in such operations as "Desert Shield" "Desert Storm", or "UNSOM II".

Fig. 2. RGM-6 Regulus I from 1958 (https://commons.wikimedia.org/wiki/File:USS_Tunny_SSG-282_Regulus1_launch_NAN9-58.jpg).

1.2 Unmanned Aerial Vehicles in Non-military Solutions

Today, unmanned flying platforms are becoming increasingly popular due to the significant decline in prices. The use of a no - manned airborne platforms to shoot footage in high quality becomes widespread. Increasingly used unmanned platforms to support a number of projects, such as the inspection of hard to reach places with the use of video cameras and thermal imaging (Fig. 3).

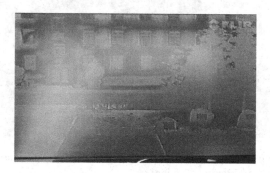

Fig. 3. Thermal image of one of the buildings in General Tadeusz Kościuszko Military Academy of Land Forces

In addition, the no - flying manned platforms begin to be used as robotic couriers carrying parcels. The number of drone applications continues to grow. List of examples of applications of drones is shown below:

- aerial photography
- building inspections
- geodesy and cartography
- delivery of packages
- meteorological measurements
- SAR – "Search and Rescue" actions
- agriculture
- mining
- study of wild life animals
- video transmission

- objects monitoring
- assessment of damages
- archeological discoveries
- emergency medical services

However, the drones are still not fully autonomous platforms capable of independent missions in varying conditions and are far from those which provide laboratories.

1.3 Autonomous Unmanned Aerial Vehicles

There are several types of civil UAV nowadays, but one of the most popular are multicopters. They are stable and easy for steering machines with the ability to hover in the given point of three-dimensional space. There are several types of multicopters but the most popular since to be quadrocopter. That is a multicopter with four vertically oriented propellers. We choose quadrocopters because of its relative low costs and the ability to immediately change the direction of flight (Fig. 4).

Fig. 4. DJI Inspire 1 quadrocopter

2 Drone Routing Problem

Drone routing problem is a variation of Vehicle Routing Problem (VRP). This is well known problem which describe a situation when we need to visit a list of points and we need to determine the optimal path. The optimization may bases on distance, cost or even other criteria. In the case of multicopters determination of the optimum flight path it is extremely important due to the very limited time to operate in the air.

2.1   Determining the Optimal Route

In many situations there is no possibility to control robots in real time. For example, control of a Martian rover must be done with using a class of offline algorithms due to a significant delay due to large distances what must overcome a radio signal from Earth to Mars and back. In addition, autonomous process of robots will need to create more and more new solutions which allows to limit the role of a man in control process. Process of determination of the optimal paths in limited time of drone flight requires a series of calculations. These calculations can be made with using a high performance workstation. That workstation may be located on ground, and path for copter flight may be send to drone with WiFi. On the other hand drones equipped with on-board computers are of considerable Capacity. An example can be DJI Matrice 600 multicopter, which can be equipped with the calculation module with 326 GigaFLOPS onboard. This computer bases on the NVIDIA Tegra K1 quad-core ARM Cortex-A15 processor with 192 GPU cores. Maximal CPU frequency is up to 2.2 GHz Such a large number of floating point operations that may be performed on -board of drone allows to make advanced signal processing from the high resolution camera, analyzing the signals from the sensors in real time. In addition, it is possible to calculate and correct the path through the drone during its flight.

2.2   Determining the Optimal Route in Variable Wind Situation

In this paper we present the method to find a good solution to TSP for modeling UAV (multirotator) vehicle in windy environment. The main deference is that distance of flight that we have to consider depends strongly on direction of flight. Upwind flight is much more expensive in terms of host because UAV have to flight against a wind. Downwind flight is respectively much more cost effective. In light of this TSP solution for UAV have to consider also wind factor.

In this paper we also presented numerical tests for route planning for UAV. By means of computer simulations on benchmarks taken from the TSPLIB we have obtained very promising results using a cluster of personal computers and the MPI library.

2.3   Definition of Problem

The classical traveling salesman problem (TSP) is defined on an undirected graph $G = (V, E)$, where $V = \{1, 2, \ldots, n\}$ is a vertex (cites) set and $E = \{\{i, j\} : i \neq j, i, j \epsilon V\}$ is an edge set. A non-negative cost (distance) matrix C is defined on E. The matrix C is symmetric $(c_{i,j} = c_{j,i}, i, j \in V)$ and satisfies the triangle inequality $(c_{i,j} + c_{i,k} \geq c_{i,k}$ for all $i, j, k \in V)$. The problem deals with finding a minimum length Hamiltonian cycle (a tour that passes through each city exactly once, and returns to the starting city) on a G.

Each feasible solution of the TSP (a cycle including all the nodes of a G) is a permutation of elements of the set V. Let

$$L(\delta) = \sum\nolimits_{j=1}^{n-1} c_{\delta(j),\delta(j+1)} + c_{\delta(n),\delta(1)} \qquad (1)$$

denotes length of traveling salesmen's tour

$$(\delta(1), \delta(2), \ldots, \delta(n), \delta(1)), \delta \epsilon \Pi, \qquad (2)$$

where Π is set of all permutations of elements of the set V.

In real environment route planning for UAV have to consider fact that UAV flows with masses of air (wind drag). We have to define ground speed of UAV. When UAV moves down wind speed of vehicle is added to speed of wind and ground speed is relatively higher. When UAV moves up wind speed of vehicle is substracted from speed of wind and ground speed is relatively lower. That means that flight distance is differs $(c_{i,j} \neq c_{j,i}, i,j \in V)$ and matrix C_{wind} is not symmetrical. Let C_{wind} denotes distance matrix in windy environment. C_{wind} can be calculated from C in following way.

Lets assume that matrix W_s denotes wind speed, and element of $w_{i,j}$ of matrix W_s denotes wind speed, on route between cities i and j. Moreover matrix W_α denotes direction (angle of wind), and element of $\alpha_{i,j}$ of matrix W_d denotes wind direction, on route between cities i and j. In light of this we may analyze influence of wind on way between cities i and j. Example situation is presented on figure when we consider downwind flight. We may see that flight time is reduced comparing to windless environment. From perspective of UAV destination city is closer than it is. Speed over the ground is called *ground speed,* speed of UAV relative to ground is called *air speed.*

Similar situation is presented on figure below when vehicle moves upwind (Figs. 5 and 6).

It is also important to note that flight time as well as drag influence depends also on speed of vehicle. More over if speed of wind is higher than speed of vehicle distance is equal to infinity (vehicle can't move that direction).

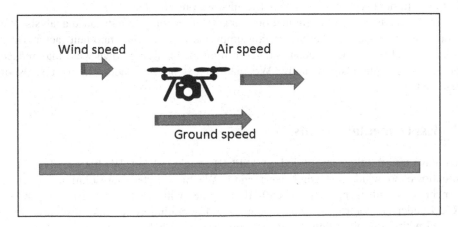

Fig. 5. Analysis of UAV speed in windy environment (downwind flight)

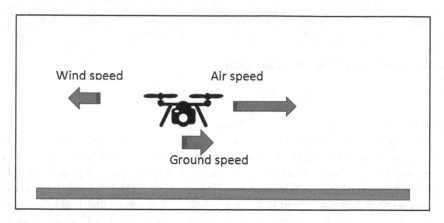

Fig. 6. Analysis od UAV speed in windy environment (up wind flight)

On this basis we are able to calculate new matrix C_{wind} in a following way.

$$c'_{i,j} = \sqrt[2]{\left(c_{i,j} * \cos(\alpha_{i,j}) + w_{i,j} * \cos(\alpha_{i,j}) * t_{i,j}\right)^2 + \left(c_{i,j} * \sin(\alpha_{i,j}) + w_{i,j} * \sin(\alpha_{i,j}) * t_{i,j}\right)^2}$$

(3)

where $t_{i,j}$ denotes flight time between cities i and j.

We may notice that during flight from j to i wind speed is the same but direction is opposite. In light of this new matrix C_{wind} is not symmetrical.

Modification of C matrix to non-symmetrical makes possible usage of almost all know methods for solving TSP problem [3–5]. In this paper we would like to focus on analysis of wind influence on solution of TSP so we decided to use deterministic approach, to find local minimum. For all test cases optimization algorithm is applied (e.g. 2-exchange Lin-Kerninghan algorithm, the so-called "2-opt") but distance matrix is C_{wind}. In next section experimental results are presented.

In this analysis we have limited our considerations only to a distance analysis. We would like to underline that power consumptions is also very important factor. Drag force depends on velocity second power in light of this flying down wind may reduce power consumption significantly. We plan to extend this model in next steps of research.

3   Experimental Results

We have tested influence of wind on TSPLIB benchmark set. We have analyzed tree situations: no wind, east wind, west wind. We have tested our solution on set of benchmarks with using Lenovo Y50-70 computer with Intel i5 processor and 8 GB RAM under the control of Linux Ubuntu 16.04 operating system. All test cases were solved with 2-opt algorithm [6]. Results are presented below (Table 1).

Table 1. Results

Name of benchmark	Number of cities	Distance		
		Windless	East wind	West wind
kroA100	100	22876	23456	25642
kroA150	150	28996	29012	27805
kroA200	200	33213	33900	33100
kroB100	100	23077	24021	23534

We may have noticed that wind has strong influence on solution. In some cases it extends length by 10 %. And the planed route differs between windless conditions and windy environment.

4 Conclusions

In this paper we proposed and tested the algorithm for traveling salesman problem (TSP) for autonomous unmanned aerial vehicles. We described and tested situations with different vectors of wind speed, air speed and ground speed with using deterministic approach, to find local minimum. For very limited time of flight of multicopters proposed method can allow for autonomous execution of the mission under varying wind. In this paper we represents only the theoretical considerations and its a starting-point for further research.

References

1. Clark, R.M.: Uninhabited Combat Aerial Vehicles: Airpower by the People, for the People, But Not with the People. CADRE Paper No. 8. Air University Press, Maxwell Air Force Base, Montgomery, AL (2000)
2. Howard, F.: Orville and Wilbur: The Story of the Wright Brothers. Hale, London (1988). ISBN 0-7090-3244-7
3. Reinelt, G.: TSPLIB - a traveling salesman problem library. ORSA J. Comput. **3**(4), 376–384 (1991)
4. Papadimitriou, C.H.: The complexity of the Lin-Kernighan heuristic for the traveling salesman problem. SIAM J. Comput. **21**(3), 450–465 (1992)
5. Johnson, D.S., McGeoch, L.A.: The traveling salesman problem: a case study in local optimization. In: Aarts, E.H.L., Lenstra, J.K. (eds.) Local Search in Combinatorial Optimization. Wiley, New York (1997)
6. Englert, M., Röglin, H., Vöcking, B.: Worst case and probabilistic analysis of the 2-Opt algorithm for the TSP. In: Proceedings of the 18th ACM-SIAM Symposium on Discrete Algorithms (SODA), pp. 1295–1304 (2007)

Cyber Security of the Application Layer of Mission Critical Industrial Systems

Rafał Kozik[1]([⊠]), Michał Choraś[1], Rafał Renk[2], and Witold Hołubowicz[1,2]

[1] Institute of Telecommunications and Computer Science,
UTP University of Science and Technology in Bydgoszcz, Bydgoszcz, Poland
`rafal.kozik@utp.edu.pl`
[2] Adam Mickiewicz University, UAM, Poznan, Poland
`renk@amu.edu.pl`

Abstract. In this paper we focus on proposing the effective methods of cyber protection of the application layer. We also discuss how this challenge is related to mission critical industrial and manufacturing systems. In this paper we propose two step HTTP request analysis method that engages request segmentation, statistical analysis of the extracted content and machine learning on the imbalanced data. In this work, we particularly addressed the segmentation technique that allows us to divide the large dataset on smaller subsets and learn the classifiers in a significantly shorter time. In our experiments we evaluated several classifiers that are popular in data mining community. The results of our experiments are obtained on a benchmark CSIC'10 HTTP dataset. The proposed approach allows us to further improve the achieved results of protecting application layer in comparison to other benchmark approaches.

Keywords: Cyber security · Anomaly detection · Pattern extraction · Application layer attacks · Web application security

1 Introduction and Rationale

The problem of cyber security in the application layer is recently more severe and challenging. In fact, top-ranked network threats and attacks e.g. on the OWASP list are those targeting application layer (such as SQLIA and XSS [2]). There are many reasons for such situation such as programmers faults, software bugs but also large number of the new applications and services being launched every day, their uniqness, lack of security standards for web applications, rapid changes in scalability etc. Another key aspect is the lack of cyber security awareness within the users and very often users are those providing access and creating security holes being the weakest link in the security chain.

On the other hand, the level of cyber security of operating systems and network protocols is constantly increasing. Therefore, for the attackers it is cheaper, easier and more effective to focus on attacks on the application layer.

K. Saeed and W. Homenda (Eds.): CISIM 2016, LNCS 9842, pp. 342–351, 2016.
DOI: 10.1007/978-3-319-45378-1_31

In this paper we focus on the effective methods of anomaly detection in the application layer. We also discuss how cyber threats and attacks in the application layer are related to mission critical industrial and manufacturing systems.

This paper is structured as follows. First, we discuss the cyber security aspects of mission critical industrial and manufacturing systems with the focus on the application layer. Later we provide an general overview of proposed method (Sect. 3). Then, the detailed description of request segmentation and feature vector encoding is given (Sect. 4). The experiments and results are given afterwards.

2 Related Work

There are many solutions (called web application firewalls - WAFs), that work as signature-based filters (e.g. set of rules) over the HTTP traffic. These signatures usually cover common web application attacks (e.g. SQL Injection, Cross Site Scripting, etc.). In example, the ModSecurity [3] plug-in for Apache web server (particularly the "OWASP ModSecurity Core Rule Set – CRS") is intended to provide defensive protection against common application layer attacks. Also the PHPIDS [4] tool is another security measure for web applications. However, in contrast to ModSecurity it can be integrated only with PHP-enabled web servers. The NAXSI [5] is a third party plug-in module for high performance Nginx [6] web server. The NAXSI stands for Nginx Anti XSS and SQL Injection and it provides low-level rules that detect keywords (symptoms) of application layer attacks. In contrast to ModSecurity and PHPIDS, NAXSI learns normal application behaviour instead of attacks patterns.

In the literature there are also methods applying anomaly detection (variety of complex schemas for learning normal/anomalous models). For instance, in [7] authors used χ^2 metric and character distribution approach to detect anomalous HTTP requests. In order to increase the attack detection effectiveness authors used a parser that splits the request into URL address and query string of attributes followed by values. Another approach to HTTP traffic anomaly detection was presented in [8]. Authors applied DFA (Deterministic Finite Automaton) to compare the requests described by the means of tokens. In contrast, in [9] authors have compared different n-grams techniques applied to application layer anomaly detection. In the literature there are also approaches combining n-grams with Self Organizing Maps [10], Bloom filters [11], and wide variety of different machine-learnt classifiers [12].

3 Can Mission Critical Industrial Systems Be Targeted by Application Layer Cyber-Attacks?

So far in computer security and critical infrastructures protection community, the focus was on cyber protection of network protocols in the lower layers. Also, after the successful attack on Ukrainian power system in December 2015, the severity of such attacks is well known. Therefore, many researchers and projects were focused on SCADA/ICS cyber protection [30–32], WSN protection etc. [33,34].

However, mission critical cyber physical systems and critical infrastructures can be also targeted by cyber attacks on the application layer and web services/applications.

The cyber attacks targeting web applications are usually cross domain, meaning that they are targeting information systems such as web servers or web services, but also indirectly can impact physical infrastructures (e.g. application controlling industrial and manufacturing processes). This happens due to the increasing interconnectivity among different systems, but also due to the fact that more and more institutions are adapting internet technologies to provide new services on top of the existing infrastructure. In many cases, the legacy systems were never expected nor designed to be connected via open network.

One example of the problems with complex interconnectivity is the Havex worm case [1]. It used the security hole in web application of company providing software solutions for SCADA systems. The attacker was able to infect genuine software installers that were used to manage the SCADA systems. The infection was part of so called "water drop" attack, where the attacker wants to remain hidden as long as possible, infecting only the interested party, in this case electrical plants.

Another examples of the successful attacks on critical infrastructures (usually databases and information systems) are attacks on Italian [27] and Turkish [28] governmental databases or alleged attack that paralysed LOT Polish Airlines [29] computer system resulting even in cancelled flights.

One of the main challenges related to the web-layer attacks is fact that those are difficult to detect with typical signature-based approaches. Therefore, there is a need for methods that will use the different approach. In this paper, we propose an anomaly-based solution that analyses the content of the HTTP payload. Upon that, data algorithm builds an model of client web browser behaviour in order to recognize possible trials of the attack.

4   The Proposed Approach

The major contribution and innovation of this paper is the segmentation approach for anomaly detection in the application layer. The proposed approach is designed to work with the typical HTTP-based, request-response web application. In the current implementation it works as additional software supporting web server administrator. It is an anomaly detection tool that receives HTTP requests, analyses their content and classifies it either as normal or anomalous. Moreover, in this approach, we do not intend to block any traffic coming from user browser to web server. Such reaction is out of scope of our work and would need to be realized in accordance to legal requirements and service level agreements.

The general overview of information flow is presented in Fig. 1.

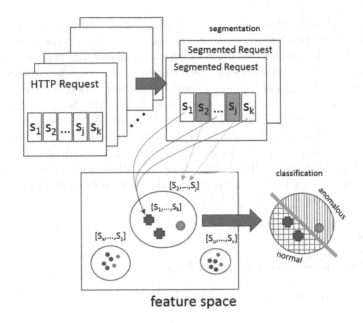

Fig. 1. The proposed two-step segmentation schema overview. The first step is a textual segmentation of similar requests. The second step is a segmentation on normal/anomalous binary class achieved with the machine-learnt classifier.

Using the available set of HTTP requests, we apply two step segmentation. The first step splits the large dataset into smaller pieces, so that further computations are executed in parallel. The segmentation uses a request segmentation method described in Sect. 4.1. It allows us to identify the possible structure of the analysed requests. The structure is described using the sequence of tokens.

The tokens (shaded boxes in Fig. 1) are used to identify clusters in our feature space that is composed of the feature vectors extracted from the data that had been tokenized (delimited by tokens). When each feature vector is extracted and assigned to the appropriate cluster, we use machine-learnt classifier to assign it to normal or anomalous class. In this research we assume that fully labelled learning dataset is available. Therefore, we can use the supervised methods.

4.1 Request Segmentation

In our work, we have proposed the technique for HTTP request segmentation. It engages dictionary of words to identify tokens (common character sequences) that appear in all the analysed request sequences. In order to find such a collection of tokens we have adapted *LZW* compression method (Lempel-Ziv-Welch [15,16]) that allows us to calculate the dictionary D containing characters sequences that appear in HTTP requests. The procedure follows the Algorithm 1.

This algorithm accepts a S set of HTTP payloads in order to produce a dictionary D, which will contain list of words (character sequences). The dictionary has a form of unordered list. Each position on that list can be taken only by one word. Obviously, using the dictionary D, one can compress the data replacing words (characters sequences) with a numbers that will correspond to the positions of that sequences in the dictionary. For efficiency reasons the D is implemented as a hash-table to provide $O(1)$ lookup time. The algorithm for establishing dictionary iteratively scans the set S of payloads until all the data is processed. In each iteration a lookup string s is built. At the beginning, it is an "empty string" that is further extended (in each step) with a single character ch read from S set. However, the s lookup string is extended with ch only if "$s+ch$" is found in the dictionary. If it is not found, the dictionary D is updated with new word "$s + ch$", s is reduced to ch and the procedure starts over.

Data: Set of HTTP payloads S
Result: Dictionary D
s = empty string
while *there is still data to be read in S* **do**
  $ch \leftarrow$ read a character ;
  if $(s + ch) \in D$ **then**
    | $s \leftarrow s+ch$;
  else
    | $D \leftarrow D \cup (s + ch)$;
    | $s \leftarrow ch$;
  end
end

Algorithm 1. Algorithm for establishing dictionary D.

In our experiments we only analyse the HTTP traffic. Therefore, we can leverage two mandatory elements of the request, namely HTTP request method (GET, POST, PUT, UPDATE, DELETE are the most frequently used ones) and the URL address of the resources the method is executed. In result, we can build the dictionary separately per different HTTP methods and URL addresses.

Additionally, in order to decrease the dimensionality of the feature vectors in a given component we post-process the dictionary eliminating (removing) those entries that are sub-sequences of other sequences. In other words, we prefer longer tokens over shorter. Once the dictionaries are established, we identify their positions in analysed requests. To correctly extract feature vector from a request, we firstly must identify the correct sequence of tokens that appears in the whole group of the analysed requests. To achieve that we use progressive multiple sequences alignment algorithm [14]. Finally, we build the feature vectors for each analysed HTTP request. However, we are using only those characters that do not belong to any token.

4.2 Parameters Encoding

In this work we have used typical approach for textual data encoding that adapts character distribution histograms (see Fig. 2). However, instead of classical byte per bin association, we count the number of characters such that the decimal value in an ASCII table belongs to following ranges: $<0,31>$, $<32,47>$, $<48,57>$, $<58,64>$, $<65,90>$, $<91,96>$, $<97,122>$, $<123,127>$, $<128,255>$. Selected ranges represent different type of symbols like numbers, quotes, letters or special characters (see Table 1). In result our histogram will have 9 bins. This is significant dimensionality reduction in contrast to sparse 256-bin histograms (one bin per byte character).

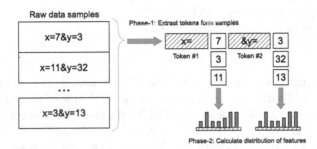

Fig. 2. The high-level overview of parameter encoding approach.

Table 1. ASCII code ranges and corresponding characters.

Group	Range	Characters
1	$< 0,31 >$	control characters
2	$< 32,47 >$	SPACE!"#$%&'()*+,-./
3	$< 48,57 >$	0123456789
4	$< 58,64 >$	:;<=>?@
5	$< 65,90 >$	ABCDEFGHIJKLMNOPQRSTUVWXYZ
6	$< 91,96 >$	[\]^_`
7	$< 97,122 >$	abcdefghijklmnopqrstuvwxyz
8	$< 123,127 >$	{~}|
9	$< 128,255 >$	special characters

5   Experiments and Results

For the experiments, the CSIC'10 dataset [18] was used. It contains several thousands of HTTP protocol requests which are organised in the form similar to the Apache Access Log. The dataset was developed at the Information Security Institute of CSIC (Spanish Research National Council) and it contains the generated traffic targeted to an e-Commerce web application. For convenience, the data was split into anomalous, training, and normal sets. There are over

Table 2. Effectiveness of the proposed approach evaluated for different classifiers

Method	TP rate	FP rate	Precision	F-measure
RandomForest	0.996	0.061	0.85	0.917
NaiveBayes	0.944	0.037	0.899	0.921
AdaBoost	0.935	0.002	0.994	0.964
PART	0.984	0.03	0.917	0.949
J48	0.991	0.05	0.873	0.928
Our previous work	0.977	0.081	0.809	0.885
Nguyen (avg.) [19]	0.936	0.069	-	-

36000 normal and 25000 anomalous requests. The anomalous requests refer to a wide range of application layer attacks, such as: SQL injection, buffer overflow, information gathering, files disclosure, CRLF injection, XSS, server side include, and parameter tampering.

Moreover, the requests targeting hidden (or unavailable) resources are also considered as anomalies. Some examples classified to this group of anomalies include client requests for: configuration files, default files or session ID in URL (symptoms of http session taking over attempt). What is more, the requests, which parameters do not have appropriate format (e.g. telephone number composed of letters), are also considered anomalous. As authors of the dataset explained, such requests may not have a malicious intention, but they do not follow the normal behaviour of the web application.

According to authors knowledge, there is no other publicly available dataset for web attack detection problem. The datasets like DARPA or KDD'99 are outdated and do not include many of the actual attacks.

The results presented in Table 2 contain measures of the following characteristics:

- *TP Rate* - True Positive Rate indicating the percentage of detected HTTP request labelled as anomalous.
- *FP Rate* - False Positive Rate indicating the percentage normal HTTP request labelled (wrongly) as anomalous.
- *Precision* - number of True Positives divided by sum of False Positives and True Positives.
- *F-Measure* - calculated according to following equation:

$$F - Measure = 2 \cdot \frac{Precision * Recall}{Precision + Recall} \tag{1}$$

In this equation *Recall* is equivalent to *TP Rate*.

The first five rows in the Table 2 refer to the proposed method, while the remaining two serve as a baseline for the measurements, namely our older previous approach [17] and the results reported by CSIC'10 dataset authors in [19].

For the proposed method we evaluated different classifiers. Herby we used RandomForest, NaiveBayes, AdaBoosting (with decision stumps as weak classifiers), PART, and J48 classifiers.

As it can be noticed, the proposed method allows us to achieve better precision in all cases. In case of [19] the values have not been provided by authors. In case of a PART and J48 tree classifier, we were able to improve the TPR and FPR values in comparison to our previous work and to results reported in [19].

6 Conclusions

In this paper we have presented the improved method of detecting attacks and anomalies in the application layer. Herby, we have proposed a two-step HTTP request segmentation. First, we apply a textual analysis of the request in order to identify the possible structure. Then, we apply feature extraction method and machine-learnt classifier.

In our work we focused on HTTP request segmentation in order to obtain better effectiveness and scalability. Conducted experiments show that this approach allows us to achieve higher recognition rates of attacks while having lower rates of false positives. Moreover, the segmentation step before the classification allows us to divide dataset on smaller ones, thus decreasing the time required for learning the classifier.

The reported results have been achieved for benchmark CSIC'10 HTTP dataset. Additionally, we have compared our results with those reported by authors of the dataset. As it was presented, our modification allows us to achieve better results.

Acknowledgments. The CIPRNet project has received funding from the European Union's Seventh Framework Programme for research, technological development and demonstration under grant agreement no 312450. The European Commission's support is gratefully acknowledged.

The work is also funded by the Polish National Centre for Research and Development (NCBiR) from funds for science in the years 2013–2016, allocated for the international projects.

References

1. F-Secure. Backdoor: W32/HAVEX description. https://www.f-secure.com/v-descs/backdoor_w32_havex.shtml
2. OWASP Top. 10 2013. OWASP project homepage. https://www.owasp.org/index.php/Top_10_2013-Top_10
3. ModSecurity project homepage. https://www.modsecurity.org/
4. PHPIDS project homepage. https://github.com/PHPIDS/PHPIDS
5. NAXSI project homepage. https://github.com/nbs-system/naxsi
6. NGINX project homepage. http://nginx.org/en/

7. Kruegel, C., Vigna, G.: Anomaly detection of web-based attacks. In: Proceedings of the 10th ACM conference on Computer and communications security, pp. 251–261 (2003)
8. Ingham, K.L., Somayaji, A., Burge, J., Forrest, S.: Learning DFA representations of HTTP for protecting web applications. Comput. Netw. **51**(5), 1239–1255 (2007)
9. Hadžiosmanović, D., Simionato, L., Bolzoni, D., Zambon, E., Etalle, S.: N-Gram against the Machine: On the Feasibility of the N-Gram network analysis for binary protocols. In: Balzarotti, D., Stolfo, S.J., Cova, M. (eds.) RAID 2012. LNCS, vol. 7462, pp. 354–373. Springer, Heidelberg (2012)
10. Bolzoni, D., Zambon, E., Etalle, S., Hartel, P.H.: POSEIDON: a 2-tier anomaly-based Network Intrusion Detection System. In: IWIA 2006: Proceedings of 4th IEEE International Workshop on Information Assurance, pp. 144–7156 (2006)
11. Wang, K., Parekh, J.J., Stolfo, S.J.: Anagram: a content anomaly detector resistant to mimicry attack. In: Zamboni, D., Kruegel, C. (eds.) RAID 2006. LNCS, vol. 4219, pp. 226–248. Springer, Heidelberg (2006)
12. Perdisci, R., Ariu, D., Fogla, P., Giacinto, G., Lee, W.: McPAD: a multiple classifier system for accurate payload-based anomaly detection. Comput. Netw. **53**(6), 864–881 (2009)
13. Lakhina, A., Crovella, M., Diot, C.: Diagnosing network-wide traffic anomalies. ACM SIGCOMM Comput. Commun. Rev. **34**, 357–374 (2004)
14. Higgins, D.G., Sharp, P.M.: CLUSTAL: a package for performing multiple sequence alignment on a microcomputer. Gene **73**(1), 237–244 (1988)
15. Welch, T.: A technique for high-performance data compression. IEEE Comput. **17**(69), 8–19 (1984)
16. Ziv, J., Lempel, A.: A universal algorithm for sequential data compression. IEEE Trans. Inf. Theory **23**, 337–343 (1977)
17. Kozik, R., Choras, M., Renk, R., Holubowicz, W.: Patterns extraction method for anomaly detection in HTTP traffic. In: Herrero, A., Baruque, B., Sedano, J., Quintan, H., Corchado, E. (eds.) CISIS 2015 and ICEUTE 2015. AISC, vol. 369, pp. 227–236. Springer, Heidelberg (2015)
18. Torrano-Gimnez, C., Prez-Villegas, A. lvarez G.: The HTTP dataset CSIC 2010 (2010). http://users.aber.ac.uk/pds7/csic_dataset/csic2010http.html
19. Nguyen, H.T., Torrano-Gimenez, C., Alvarez, G., Petrović, S., Franke, K.: Application of the generic feature selection measure in detection of web attacks. In: Herrero, Á., Corchado, E. (eds.) CISIS 2011. LNCS, vol. 6694, pp. 25–32. Springer, Heidelberg (2011)
20. Sharma, M., Toshniwal, D.: Pre-clustering algorithm for anomaly detection and clustering that uses variable size buckets. In: 2012 1st International Conference on Recent Advances in Information Technology (RAIT), pp. 515–519, 15–17 March 2012
21. Adaniya, M.H.A.C., Lima, M.F., Rodrigues, J.J.P.C., Abrao, T., Proenca, M.L.: Anomaly detection using DSNS and fireflyharmonic clustering algorithm. In: 2012 IEEE International Conference on Communications (ICC), pp. 1183–1187, 10–15 June 2012
22. Mazel, J., Casas, P., Labit, Y., Owezarski, P.: Sub-space clustering, inter-clustering results association and anomaly correlation for unsupervised network anomaly detection. In: 2011 7th International Conference on Network and Service Management (CNSM), pp. 1–8, 24–28 October 2011

23. Yang, C., FeiqiDeng, H.Y.: An unsupervised anomaly detection approach using subtractive clustering and hidden markov model. In: Second International Conference on Communications and Networking in China, CHINACOM 2007, pp. 313–316, 22–24 August 2007

24. Liang, H., Wei-wu, R., Fei, R.: An adaptive anomaly detection based on hierarchical clustering. In: 2009 1st International Conference on Information Science and Engineering (ICISE), pp. 1626–1629, 26–28 December 2009

25. Pons, P., Latapy, M.: Computing communities in large networks using random walks. J. Graph Algorithms Appl. **10**(2), 191–218 (2006)

26. Liao, Q., Blaich, A., Van Bruggen, D., Striegel, A.: Managing networks through context: graph visualization and exploration. Comput. Netw. **54**, 2809–2824 (2010)

27. Cyberattack on Italian government. http://www.lastampa.it/2015/05/19/italia/cronache/anonymous-colpisce-il-ministero-della-difesa-qlFNgswyvu20wnQiNYK1kL/pagina.html

28. Cyberattack on Turkish government. http://www.ehackingnews.com/2013/06/istanbul-special-provincial.html

29. Cyberattack on Polish Airlines LOT company. http://uk.reuters.com/article/2015/06/21/uk-poland-lot-cybercrime-idUKKBN0P10WY20150621

30. Coppolino, L., et al.: Enhancing SIEM technology to protect critical infrastructures. In: Hämmerli, B.M., Svendsen, N.K., Lopez, J. (eds.) Critical Information Infrastructures Security, vol. 7722, pp. 10–21. Springer, Heidelberg (2013)

31. Collins, S., McCombie, S.: Stuxnet: the emergence of a new cyber weapon and its implications. J. Policing Intell. Counter Terrorism **7**(1), 80–91 (2012)

32. Takagi, H., et al.: Strategic security protection for industrial control systems. In: 2015 54th Annual Conference of the Society of Instrument and Control Engineers of Japan (SICE). IEEE (2015)

33. Romano, L., D'Antonio, S., Formicola, V., Coppolino, L.: Protecting the WSN zones of a critical infrastructure via enhanced SIEM technology. In: Ortmeier, F., Daniel, P. (eds.) SAFECOMP Workshops 2012. LNCS, vol. 7613, pp. 222–234. Springer, Heidelberg (2012)

34. Formicola, V., et al.: Assessing the impact of cyber attacks on wireless sensor nodes that monitor interdependent physical systems. In: Butts, J., Shenoi, S. (eds.) Critical Infrastructure Protection VIII, vol. 441, pp. 213–229. Springer, Heidelberg (2014)

Kohonen SOM for Image Slides Sequencing

Ewa Skubalska-Rafajłowicz[✉] and Aneta Górniak

Faculty of Electronics, Department of Computer Engineering,
Wrocław University of Science and Technology, Wrocław, Poland
{ewa.rafajlowicz,aneta.gorniak}@pwr.edu.pl

Abstract. In this paper we present a new approach to sequencing of
2-D slide images with the goal of 3-D object reconstructions. We focus
our attention mostly on microscope images obtained from serial sections
of biological tissues. For adequate 3-D body reconstruction the correct
sequence of section should be available. We propose a modified SOM
Kohonen networks with open chain topology for true sequence estimation based on based on 2-D image features invariant to section image
translation and rotation, but sensitive to a scale of an object on the
slide. We provide an experimental validation of the proposed method
using artificial section images of a mechanical device and real microscopic histological section images.

Keywords: Image sequencing · SOM Kohonen map · Euclidean
travelling salesman problem · Image processing · Image registration ·
3-D image reconstruction

1 Introduction

In this paper we present a new approach to sequencing of 2-D slide images
with the goal of 3-D object reconstructions. We focus our attention on microscope images obtained from serial sections of biological tissues. It is assumed
that subsequent section images may be located inadequately in the image series.
Translations, rotations and even small non-rigid transformations of the object
of interest can occur.

Image registration is a very important step in processing sequences of images
[10]. A large number of algorithms have been developed to perform registration
of medical and biological images. Usually the image registration is the process of
aligning multiple images representing the same scene that were captured at a different time, at or by a different set of modalities, or by alignment of successive
anatomical slices [10]. We concentrate on the image registration in the case of 3-D
tissue reconstruction [17,19,23,24]. The problem becomes remarkably difficult if
the order of the slides is not known. In such a case the process involves not only
the transformation of the coordinate systems of the reference image and the input
image into the joint coordinate system, but the most important problem is determine the reference images, i.e. the nearest neighbors (the preceding and the subsequent slide image) for each section image. It is clear that aligning every pair

Published by Springer International Publishing Switzerland 2016. All Rights Reserved
K. Saeed and W. Homenda (Eds.): CISIM 2016, LNCS 9842, pp. 352–365, 2016.
DOI: 10.1007/978-3-319-45378-1_32

of slides is possible only when the number of images is small enough as it was assumed in our previous paper [12]. Otherwise, the problem of common aligning and sequencing of slide images becomes extremely expensive from computational complexity problem of view, especially when separate slide image consists of over a million pixels.

If the correct order of slides is known the reconstruction of a 3-D object body from a series of 2-D sections consists in the co-registration of any two consecutive slices. Nevertheless, the choice of the reference image has a significant impact on registration quality and 3-D reconstruction, even when the correct slide order is known, because the image chosen as a reference slide may contain distorted parts. Thus, it is advisable to repeat the registration in the reverse order and finally identify and correct possibly erroneous slides.

When we do not know which 2-D slide should be the first (the last) in the reconstructed sequence, then the performed registration may lead to undesirable slides' deformations. Thus, it is important to find possibly correct image sequence before performing precise registration. It is clear that image matching could be realized on different levels of image precision. In the paper [2] the imaging system for simultaneous morphological and molecular analysis of section images is presented, but in that approach it is also assumed that correct order of slides is given at the start of the procedure. Another worth of attention method of the automatic registration of histological slices is given in [3]. The standardized slices are divided into small groups. The best reference slice selection in every group of slides is performed. The method of selection is developed based on an iterative assessment of image entropy and mean square error of the registration process. Nevertheless, in the paper it is also assumed that the order of slides presentation have not been destroyed.

Here we concentrate on providing a method of sequencing slides which is based on 2-D image features, independent of image translation and rotation (i.e., invariant to rigid transformations), but sensitive to a scale of an object on the slide. First, in order to avoid starting a work on a cellular level, we standardize images removing intensity variations between slices and after that binarize these images providing only contours of sections at the morphological level. We assume that microscopic slides are obtained from the geometrically continuous anatomical structure [19]. Thus, simple image measurements, such as an object diameter, object area, eccentricity of the best-fit ellipse containing the object, and the mean distance of all object's pixels from the center of gravity position of the binarized image, occur highly informative and allow us not only to distinguish one slide from another but also to determine geometrical similarity between them. We propose to consider these image measurements as coordinates in an abstract Euclidean space where each slide is a point with coordinates given by mentioned image measurements. In such a way the problem of slide sequencing can be formalized as a problem of finding the shortest open path between the points. We decided to use the sum of squared Euclidean distances as an optimization criterion. However, other goal functions can also be adequate. The main reason that we prefer the sum of squared Euclidean distances criterion to the simple sum of Euclidean distances is that: the squared Euclidean distances favor the paths with more uniformly divided distances between separate points than in the case of the sum of strict Euclidean distances. Formally, we are looking for a path that visits every point once, and have separate (not-joined) endpoints, in contrast to the Hamiltonian cycle [16], where the path is closed, i.e., forms a cycle. The number of slides may vary between let say 10 to 200 (see for example [19,24]). Thus, it is important to propose any efficient method of solving this in fact combinatorial problem which is known to be NP-hard [16,20]. All method of solving the Travelling Salesmen Problem with Euclidean metric can be easily adapted to solving the open path problem. We decided to use modified version of Self-organizing Map (SOM) network with open chain topology [15], since it is fast, stable and provide very accurate solution when the number of points is not very huge. Furthermore, this method is more appropriate when the squared Euclidean distance instead of the Euclidean metric is used (see for example [6]).

Nevertheless, other general global optimization methods as simulated annealing, particle swarm optimization or genetic algorithms [13,14,22] can be also applied for solving our sequencing problem.

It should be noted that the approach for slide images sequencing proposed here will be also helpful for detection of possibly missing slides, errors in the image order or even destroyed sections.

It is clear that the method proposed here generates image sequences optimal with respect to general shape and size parameters. When sections are very similar with respect to these parameters, other, more precise and taking into account internal section details should be used. Furthermore, in the case of simple artificial 3-D bodies, for example a ball, it is obvious that the ordering may be inadequate. Fortunately, biological objects usually characterize large shape variability, allowing the method to generate sequences which with high probability are closed to the true ones. Thus, a sequence obtained on the basis of morphological parameters should be additionally inspected and corrected using internal, possibly cellular structure of subsequent sections, but this problem is outside the scope of our paper. In this paper we do not concentrate on image processing tasks. We have used image processing procedures provided by Wolfram Mathematica 10.1. These procedures occurred to be adequate to our purposes.

The paper is organized as follow. In the next Section the problem of image representation that is invariant to location and rotation on the shape and the size level is addressed. Section 3 provides a concise description of image sequencing by determining the shortest open path through a given set of points in Euclidean feature space. Section 4 presents the details of the proposed modification of the Kohonen SOM algorithm for sequencing image feature points. Section 5 describes results of two computational experiments of sequencing a set of artificial section images of a mechanical device and a set of microscopic histological slices. Finally, in Sect. 6 some brief conclusions are presented.

2   Image Representation on the Shape and the Size Level

We have assumed that each object image is represented roughly by chosen image measurements which are invariant to rigid object image transformation, i.e., are invariant to translations and/or rotations. Thus, in order to obtain exact measurements, it is important to separate precisely an object image from its background. The methods used for this task depend on the slide quality and visual inspection of results is very important [11]. In our experiments we have used algorithms supplied by Mathematica 10.1. We skip details because in every case the segmentation procedure was different. For example, in our histological sections it was important to remove images of patches used for fixing every section. After image segmentation process the background on each slide was deleted. The whole image was binarized, i.e., every object pixel intensity was set to 1 whereas the rest of pixels was set to 0. On the basis of the object silhouette we can to compute simple object features such as:

- The object area A (areas of the two largest image segments are summarized), i.e., number of object's pixels normalized by the total number of pixels forming the whole image;
- The mean distance of to the center of gravity MCD (mean distance of all object's elements from the center of gravity position) divided by number of pixels in the image column;
- Maximal perimeter distance of the object MPD (i.e., object diameter measured in pixels and divided by number of pixels in the image column);
- The eccentricity of the object E, i.e., the eccentricity of the best-fit ellipse containing the object. $E = \sqrt{1 - (b/a)^2}$, where a and b are major and minor axes of the ellipse.

We assume that subsequent slides should be characterized by similar feature values. Each image is represented by a vector of its features. We expect that good image sequence can be obtained by minimizing the sum of squared errors (distances) between image feature vectors. The good sequence means the sequence close to the true one. It is clear that in general the problem of choosing image features providing such good sequences depends on properties of object and on a quality of images.

3   Image Sequencing by Determining the Shortest Open Path Through a Given Set of Points in the Euclidean Space

Similarly as each city in the travelling-salesman problem with Euclidean distances between cities (ETSP) [16] is represented by a point on the map (usually 2-D space) also in our problem every image is represented by a point in some compact subset of R^d. We assume that this set is a unit cube $I^d = [0, 1] \times \ldots \times [0, 1]$. The problem of determining the shortest open path through a given set of N points is very close to the well known problem of finding the shortest closed path through a given set of N points, i.e., ETSP.

Let $X = \{x_1, \ldots x_N\}$ be a given set of point in I^d. Our goal is to find a sequence of points X, i.e., a permutation of points indexes $\Pi = (\pi(1), \pi(2) \ldots, \pi(N))$, such that

$$Q_P(\Pi, X) = \sum_{i=2}^{N} ||x_{\pi(i)} - x_{\pi(i-1)}||^2, \tag{1}$$

is minimized over all possible permutations. $||.||$ denotes the Euclidean norm. Due to a symmetry property of the Euclidean distance between a pair of points (and obviously also the squared Euclidean metric), there exist at most $0.5N!$ different solutions of the problem.

Testing all $0.5N!$ possible image sequences one can always find the shortest path connecting all N points, but the computational effort for this exhaustive search strategy, rises exponentially with N and rapidly becomes unmanageable. For $N = 10$ it is 1814400 different solutions, for $N = 20$ the number of solutions rises to 1216451004088320000, and for $N = 30$ it is definitely unmanageable to perform the brute force search.

Usually in the case of ETSP only the sum of Euclidean distances, and not squared Euclidean distances, is minimized:

$$C_{TSP}(\Pi, X) = \sum_{i=2}^{N} ||x_{\pi(i)} - x_{\pi(i-1)}|| + ||x_{\pi(N)} - x_{\pi(1)}||. \tag{2}$$

Furthermore, it can be assumed that $\pi(1) = 1$, so that it is possible to find only $0.5(N-1)!$ different closed paths between points from set X.

It is known that the Euclidean TSP, similarly as a more general TSP, is NP-hard [20]. There are known many exact and approximate methods of solving TSP and ETSP (see for example [22] and the literature cited in there). Most of them can be adopt to solving $\min_\Pi Q_P(\Pi, X)$. Here we concentrate on using Kohonen SOM network [15] with open chain topology since similar type SOM networks with closed chain topology used for solving ETSP [1,4–6,9,18,25] are known to minimize the sum of squared Euclidean distances (SSD) rather than the sum of Euclidean distances between TSP points [8].

In our work we have used the algorithm presented in detail in the next Section.

4   Kohonen SOM Algorithm for Sequencing Data Points

Let M denote the number of neurons. It is assumed that $M \geq N$ [1,5]. Recall that N is the number of data points in set X. Each neuron is represented by a point in R^d labeled by a number $j = 1, 2, \ldots, M$. Coordinates of such a point, let say labeled by j, form a vector $W_j \in I^d$, i.e., W_j is the j-th neuron's weight. Each data point $x_i \in X$ can be uniquely represented by neuron j^* such that

$$i^*(x_i) = arg \min_{j=1,\ldots,M} ||x_i - W_j||^2. \tag{3}$$

Such neuron is often called "a winner". In the case of ties we will randomly pick exactly one winning neuron.

As a consequence, each neuron $j \in \{1, \ldots, M\}$ may be "empty", may be closest to exactly one data point from X or it may happen that two or even more than two data points are connected to the same neuron [9]. Let $A(j)$ denote the set of data points connected to neuron j. It is clear that

$$\bigcup_{j=1}^{M} A(j) = \{1, 2, \ldots, N\}. \tag{4}$$

Furthermore, $A(j)$, $j = 1, \ldots, M$ define at least partial order in the set of data points. In the case when there exist $A(j)$ such that $|A(j)| > 1$, strict order can be obtain by random choice or using the lexicographical order defined in X. We will be represent A_j by lists rather than sets, which allows us to retain ordering. Thus, we obtain a linear order of data points from X uniquely providing sequence Π. Computational complexity of that ordering is $O(NM \log M)$ (we skip the dependence on d).

4.1 SOM Learning

Kohonen learning rule is applied for updating neuron weights (their positions in the data space). Denote by $W_j(n)$ the weight of j-th neuron in n-iteration of learning process. The process of learning is some kind of stochastic approximation process [21]. In every iteration only one data point from X is chosen at random and used for neuron position updating. Kohonen's method of learning is very efficient since not only a winning neuron selected according to (3) is updated but its neighbors in neuron's chain topology are also updated according to:

$$W_j(n) = W_j(n) + \alpha(n)h(x_i, j, n)(x_i - W_j(n)), \quad j = 1, \ldots, M \tag{5}$$

where $h(x_i, j, n)$ is a neighborhood function taking values in $[0, 1]$ and $\alpha(n)$ is a learning rate. $\alpha(n)$ is usually very small and decreases to zero with n. The common choice of the neighborhood function is the Gaussian function

$$h(x_i, j, n) = \exp\left(-\frac{|i^\star(x_i) - j|}{2\sigma(n)^2}\right), \tag{6}$$

were $\sigma(n) \to 0$ when $n \to \infty$. There could be different methods of changing σ and α. Here we will assume that the learning is performed according to the following rules of learning parameters updating:

$$\alpha(n) = 0.5 \exp\left(-n/1000\right) \tag{7}$$

and

$$\sigma(n) = \sigma_0 0.01^{n/1000}, \quad \sigma_0 = 20, \ 10, \ 5. \tag{8}$$

However, it should be noted that in the case of ETSP also other formulas are used with success [4, 6, 25].

4.2   Algorithm

Step 1. Initialization: Let n be a discrete learning time starting from 0. The algorithm inputs are points $X = \{x_1, \ldots x_N\} \subset I^d$. Choose $M \geq N$, (for example, let $M = 1.5N$). We initialize neuron's weights W at random using the uniform distribution on cube $[w_{1,min}, w_{1,max}] \times \ldots \times [w_{d,min}, w_{d,max}]$, where $w_{k,min} = Min_{1 \leq i \leq N}[x_{i,k}]$, $w_{k,max} = Max_{1 \leq i \leq N}[x_{i,k}](k = 1, \ldots, d)$, and $(x_{i,1}, \ldots, x_{i,k}, \ldots, x_{i,d})^T = x_i$, $i = 1, \ldots, N$. Set $W_{opt} = W$. Denote the value of the best sequence according to (1) by Q_{opt} and the optimal sequence consisting of N element list by Π_{opt}. Start with $Q_{opt} = 100$ and $\Pi_{opt} = (1, 2, \ldots, N)$. Let the initial value of neighborhood function parameter be $\sigma_0 = 20$. And let n_{max} be the value of the maximum number of iterations.

The main loop of the algorithm consists of the following steps:

Step 2. If $n > n_{max}$ go to Step End. Otherwise, compute parameters $\alpha(n) = 0.5 \exp(-n/1000)$ and $\sigma(n) = \sigma_0 0.01^{n/1000}$. Randomly draw point x from set of points X. Let say $x = x_i$.
Step 3. Find neuron $i^*(x_i)$ closest to x_i (3). Update weights according to (5).
Step 4. Set $A_j = \{\}$ $j = 1, \ldots, M$. For $i = 1, 2, \ldots, N$ find $j = i^*(x_i)$ and add index i to the list A_j.
Step 5. Obtain new sequence Π by concatenating lists A_j, $j = 1, \ldots, M$ (empty lists are rejected).
Step 6. Compute $Q(\Pi, X)$ according to (1). If $Q(\Pi, X) \leq Q_{opt}$ set: $Q_{opt} = Q(\Pi, X)$, $\Pi_{opt} = \Pi$ and $W_{opt} = W$. Set $n = n + 1$ and go to Step 2.
Step End Return the best results: Π_{opt} and Q_{opt}.

5   Experiments

In this section we demonstrate results of computational experiments with sequencing both artificial and natural 2-D image slides. The artificial set of slides is a part of provided by Mathematica image example *"Example-Data/CTengine.tiff"* (20 subsequent image sections from the set of 110 sections). The histological set of section images consists of 10 slides. In this case we do not know how the proper sequence should look like. The sample images of each set are shown in Figs. 1 and 6.

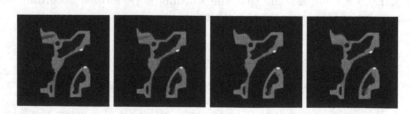

Fig. 1. The part of the image set consisting of 20 section images of a mechanical device; the size of image 256×256 pixels

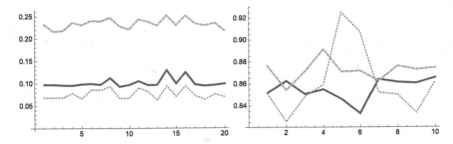

Fig. 2. Image coordinates of the randomly rearranged sequence of the mechanical device slides (see Fig. 1): area of the binarized object A (thick), maximal diameter distance of the object MPD (dashed), mean distance to the center of gravity MCD (dotted) (left panel). Image coordinates of the original (untidy) sequence of microscopy slides (see Fig. 6): area of the binarized object (thick), mean distance to the center of gravity (dashed), eccentricity of the best-fit ellipse containing the object (dotted) (right panel)

5.1 Sequencing 2-D Section Images of a Technical Device

We have 20 subsequent image sections at our disposal. Each section image is of the size 256×256 pixels. In this example the true sequence of slides is known. Thus, we have randomly changed the numbering of slides. The true sequence (after random permutations of section numbers) is

$$(20, 2, 3, 10, 9, 18, 13, 15, 5, 1, 17, 19, 4, 12, 7, 6, 11, 8, 16, 14).$$

In Fig. 1 four subsequent slides with new numbers $13, 15, 5, 1$, respectively, have been shown.

We have computed three image features: the area of the binarized object A, the maximal diameter distance of the object MPD and the mean distance to the center of gravity MCD (see Fig. 2 – left panel). The optimal sequence was obtained using the proposed here algorithm (see Sect. 4.2) as:

$$(20, 2, 3, 10, 9, 18, 13, 5, 1, 15, 17, 19, 4, 12, 7, 6, 11, 8, 16, 14).$$

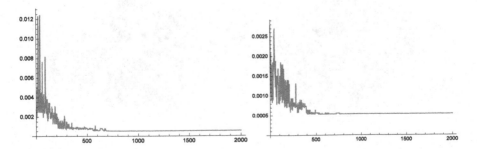

Fig. 3. The results of the section images sequencing using the proposed method. SSD obtained in the subsequent iterations of the algorithm for 20 neuron (left panel) and for 30 neuron (right panel). In the both cases the same - optimal sequence - was found

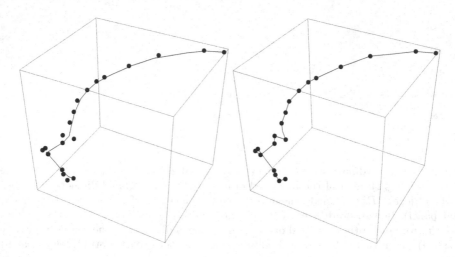

Fig. 4. The path of 20 neurons obtained for image sequence optimal with respect to SSD (left panel) and the path of 30 neurons obtained for image sequence optimal with respect to SSD (right panel). Large dots indicate position of images

This sequence differs from the true one in the position of slide 15. Its correct location is just before slides 5 and 1 (not after them). Process of Kohonen network learning was performed ten times starting from randomly chosen neuron's positions. The number of neurons was $M = 20, 30, 40$ and $\sigma_0 = 20$. In the case of $M = 30$ the optimal solution was obtained in every simulation. Otherwise, when the number of neurons was smaller or larger (i.e., $M = 20$ or $M = 40$), the network has produced also suboptimal paths. Trajectories of the sum of the squared Euclidean distances (SSD) obtained by the SOM algorithm in two exemplary runs are depicted on Fig. 3. Figure 4 shows the sketch of the neuronal paths corresponding to the obtained optimal sequence. The network equipped with $M = 30$ neurons visibly converges to the optimal solution, while in the case $M = 20$ the best sequence is computed and memorized in the Step 5 of

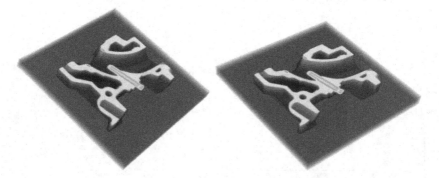

Fig. 5. 3-D image of a part of an mechanical device (left panel) 3-D reconstruction of an mechanical device object obtained on the basis of the optimal with respect to SSD section images sequence (right panel)

the algorithm, but the network further converges to the slightly worse sequence. Finally, Fig. 5 presents comparison of the 3-D image of a part of the mechanical device (on the left image) and its 3-D reconstruction obtained on the basis of the optimal with respect to SSD section sequence. The differences are not visible, although small inconsistencies can be found inside the object, since the location of section 15 should be corrected in the precise matching of neighboring slides.

5.2   Sequencing Microscopy Section Images

The analyzed set of microscopy section images contains 10 slides of the size 184×184 pixels (see Fig. 6). This time also three image features have been computed: the area of the binarized object A, the eccentricity of the best-fit ellipse containing the 2-D object E, and the mean distance to the center of gravity MCD. Due to the vary small differences between measurements and relatively large differences between mean values of the separate features, values of A and MCD features rescaled by 0.15 and 0.2, respectively. The rescaled feature values are shown on the right panel of Fig. 2. The optimal with respect to the SSD section sequence was: $(5, 6, 10, 4, 8, 7, 2, 3, 9, 1)$ with $SSD = 0.0075$ and the second best was $(5, 6, 4, 10, 8, 7, 2, 3, 9, 1)$ with $SSD = 0.0084$. Process of Kohonen network learning was performed ten times starting from randomly chosen neuron's positions. The number of neurons was $M = 10$ and $M = 15$ and $\sigma_0 = 5$ and $\sigma_0 = 20$, respectively. Trajectories of the sum of the SSD obtained by the SOM algorithm in two exemplary runs are depicted on Fig. 7. In the both cases the same - optimal sequence was found, but only for 15 neurons the networks has converged to the optimal solution. The outline of the neuronal paths corresponding to the obtained optimal sequence is shown in Fig. 8. The network equipped with $M = 15$ neurons visibly converges to the optimal solution, while in the case $M = 10$ the best sequence is computed and memorized in the Step 5 of the algorithm, but the network further converges to the slightly worse sequence. 3-D reconstruction of an biological object obtained on the basis of the optimal (with respect to SSE) section sequence is presented in Fig. 9.

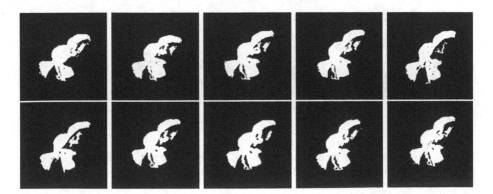

Fig. 6. The image set consisting of 10 microscopy section images of the size 184×184 pixels

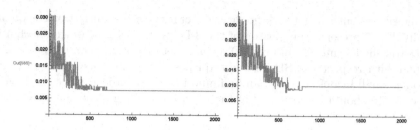

Fig. 7. The results of the section images sequencing using the proposed method. SSD obtained in the subsequent iterations of the algorithm for 15 neurons net (left panel) and for 10 neurons net (right panel)

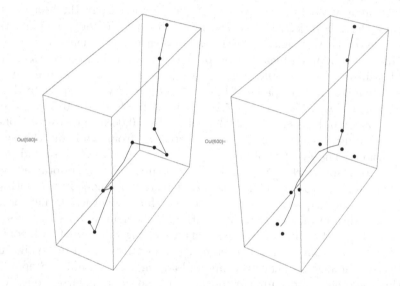

Fig. 8. The 15 neurons path obtained for optimal image sequence for starting value of $\sigma = 20$ (left panel) and $\sigma = 5$ (right panel). Large dots indicate position of images

Fig. 9. Two views of 3-D reconstruction of an biological object obtained on the basis of the optimal with respect to SSD section sequence after additional alignment

6   Conclusion

The paper presents a problem of 2-D section images ordering for 3-D body reconstruction. We propose a slightly modified SOM Kohonen networks with the open chain topology for adequate sequence specification based on 2-D image features invariant to section image translation and rotation, but sensitive to a scale of an object on the slide. This means that location and orientation of objects on slides can be coincidental and sequencing of slides at the shape and the size level is performed without precise image registration. It should be noted that the approach proposed here for slide images sequencing will be also helpful for detection of possibly missing slides, errors in the image order or even destroyed sections. The method of slide sequencing proposed here provides image orders optimal with respect to its general shape and size parameters. When sections are very similar with respect to these parameters, other, more precise and taking into account internal section details should be used. We stress that a sequence obtained on the basis of morphological parameters should be additionally inspected and corrected using internal, possibly cellular features of the subsequent sections. This problem is outside the scope of the paper and will be developed later taking into account the non-rigid registration problems.

The presented SOM algorithm is shown to perform well on artificial and on natural series section images when the number of neurons is greater than the number of slides, but not too large. $1.5N$ neurons, where N is the number of section images was a best choice. It is less than in the case of ETSP, where $2N-3N$ neurons are recommended. Inspecting sequence path picture (Figs. 4 and 8) one can observe that the points representing images are located rather regularly, also forming almost regular routes. This can be reason that a relatively small number of neuron is here needed. Due to the lack of space we have shown only the small part of experiments we have performed, but it is worth to stress that the number of iterations needed for obtaining good solution was relatively stable, independent of the number of slides. This observation agrees with experiments performed by Budinich [7] (with respect to one dimensional ordering) and indicates that properties of SOM Kohonen networks seem to be worth of further investigations.

We also hope that the proposed approach can be also usable in others sequencing problems where object of complicated structure should be ordered.

Acknowledgments. The authors express their special thanks to Dr. Agnieszka Malińska and to professor Maciej Zabel from University School of Medicine, Poznań, Poland for the microscopy section images.

This research was supported by S50242 grant at the Faculty of Electronics, Wrocław University of Science and Technology.

References

1. Angeniol, B., Vaubois, C., Texier, J.-Y.L.: Selforganizing feature maps and the traveling salesman problem. Neural Netw. **1**, 289–293 (1988)
2. Arganda-Carreras, I., Fernandez-Gonzalez, R., Munoz-Barrutta, A., Ortiz-De-Solorzano, C.: 3D reconstruction of histological sections: application to mammary gland tissue. Microsc. Res. Tech. **73**, 1019–1029 (2010)
3. Bagci, U., Bai, L.: Fully automatic 3D reconstruction of histological images. In: Proceedings of 5th IEEE International Symposium on Biomedical Imaging: From Nano to Macro, pp. 991–994 (2008)
4. Bai, Y., Zhang, W., Hu, H.: An efficient growing ring SOM and its application to TSP. In: Proceedings of the 9th WSEAS International Conference on Applied Mathematics, Istanbul, Turkey, 27–29 May 2006, pp. 351–355 (2006)
5. Bai, Y., Zhang, W., Jin, Z.: An new self-organizing maps strategy for solving the traveling salesman problem. Chaos Solitons Fractals **28**, 1082–1089 (2006)
6. Budinich, M.: A self-organising neural network for the travelling salesman problem that is competitive with simulated annealing. Neural Comput. **8**(2), 416–424 (1996)
7. Budinich, M.: Sorting with self-organising maps. Neural Comput. **7**(6), 1188–1190 (1995)
8. Budinich, M., Rosario, B.: A neural network for the travelling salesman problem with a well behaved energy function. In: Ellacott, S.W., Mason, J.C., Anderson, I.J. (eds.) Mathematics of Neural Networks: Models, Algorthms and Applications, pp. 134–139. Kluwer Academic Publishers, Boston (1997)
9. Favata, S., Walker, R.: A study of the application of Kohonen-type neural networks to the traveling salesman problem. Biol. Cybern. **64**, 463–468 (1991)
10. Flusser, J., Zitova, B.: Image registration methods: a survey. Image Vis. Comput. **21**, 977–1000 (2003)
11. Gonzalez, R.C., Woods, R.E.: Digital Image Processing. Prentice Hall, Upper Saddle River (2007)
12. Górniak, A., Skubalska-Rafajłowicz, E.: Registration and sequencing of vessels section images at macroscopic levels. In: Saeed, K., Homenda, W. (eds.) CISIM 2015. LNCS, vol. 9339, pp. 399–410. Springer, Heidelberg (2015)
13. Kennedy, J., Eberhart, R.: Particle swarm optimization. In: Proceedings of IEEE International Conference on Neural Networks, pp. 1942–1948 (1995)
14. Kirkpatrick, S., Gelatt Jr., C.D., Vecchi, M.P.: Optimization by simulated annealing. Science **220**(4598), 671–680 (1983)
15. Kohonen, T.: Self-organizing Map. Springer, New York (2001)
16. Lawler, E., Lenstra, J., Rinnooy, K.A.: The Traveling Salesman Problem: A Guided Tour of Combinatorial Optimization. Wiley, New York (1985)
17. Lippolis, G., Edsjo, A., Helczynski, L., Bjartell, A., Overgaard, N.: Automatic registration of multi-modal microscopy images for integrative analysis of prostate tissue sections. MBC Cancer **13**, 408 (2013)
18. La Maire, B.F.J., Mladenov, V.M.: Comparison of neural networks for solving the travelling salesman problem. In: IEEE Proceedings of the NEUREL 2012 (2012). doi:10.1109/NEUREL.2012.6419953
19. Ourselin, S., Roche, A., Subsol, G., Pennec, X., Ayache, N.: Reconstructing a 3D structure from serial histological sections. Image Vis. Comput. **19**(1), 25–31 (2001)
20. Papadimitriou, C.H.: The Euclidean traveling salesman problem is NP-complete. Theor. Comput. Sci. **4**, 237–244 (1978)

21. Ritter, H., Martinetz, T., Schulten, K.: Neural Computation and Self Organizing Maps: An Introduction. Addison-Wesley, New York (1992)
22. Saadatmand-Tarzjan, M., Khademi, M., Akbarzadeh-T, M.R., Moghaddam, H.A.: A novel constructive-optimizer neural network for the traveling salesman problem. IEEE Trans. Syst. Man Cybern. Part B Cybern. **37**(4), 754–770 (2007)
23. Schwier, M., Böhler, T., Hahn, H.K., Dahmen, U., Dirsch, O.: Registration of histological whole slide images guided by vessel structures. J. Pathol. Inform. **4**(Suppl. 2), S10 (2013)
24. Stille, M., Smith, E.J., Crum, W.R., Modo, M.: 3D reconstruction of 2D fluorescence histology images and registration with in vivo MR images: application in a rodent stroke model. J. Neurosci. Methods **219**, 27–40 (2013)
25. Xu, X., Jia, Z., Ma, J., Wang, J.: A self-organizing map algorithm for the traveling salesman problem. In: IEEE Proceedings of the Fourth International Conference on Natural Computation, pp. 431–435 (2008). doi:10.1109/ICNC.2008.569

An Evolutionary Approach to Cyclic Real World Scheduling

Dominik Żelazny[✉]

Department of Automatic Control and Mechatronics,
Wrocław University of Science and Technology, Janiszewskiego 11-17,
50-372 Wrocław, Poland
dominik.zelazny@pwr.wroc.pl

Abstract. Real world problems are often an inspiration for engineers to model and solve new scheduling problems. In this paper a cyclic scheduling of jobs with uncertain data is considered. A minimization of the cycle time represents an important economical factor considered by the companies. Proposed model was tested and data concerning processing times was obtained. Due to the nature of stations and human operator factor, we deal with uncertain data modeled using fuzzy numbers. For the modeled production station a fuzzy genetic algorithm was proposed and tested against deterministic algorithms. Proposed algorithm outperformed all deterministic algorithms.

Keywords: Flow shop problem · Cyclic scheduling · Real world problem · Nature-based algorithm

1 Introduction

Maintaining competitive position in fast changing market requires companies to use new methods of optimization and drives scientists to develop more efficient algorithms. Due to that competitiveness, developing effective, advanced methods is extremely important. The so-called permutation flow shop scheduling problem (PFSP) represents a class of widely studied cases based on ideas derived from production engineering.

Most of the currently researched problems consider classic criterion and data, thus are easily adaptable to real world applications, but modern scheduling problems need more advanced models. This resulted in companies switching to cyclic scheduling models, where different products are manufactured as a *Minimal Part Set – MPS*. The most common optimization of such a system is minimization of the cycle time – the time between the beginning of one MPS and the beginning of the next one.

More complex models include uncertain data, which can represent systems with tasks performed by human operators or in conditions which don't guarantee deterministic processing times. Those factors add uncertain data to the analyzed systems.

© IFIP International Federation for Information Processing 2016
Published by Springer International Publishing Switzerland 2016. All Rights Reserved
K. Saeed and W. Homenda (Eds.): CISIM 2016, LNCS 9842, pp. 366–373, 2016.
DOI: 10.1007/978-3-319-45378-1_33

In this paper a cyclic scheduling problem with uncertain data is considered. Moreover, a miniature production line (described in detail in [6]) was used to perform tests and model the problem. Fuzzy numbers are employed to identify and model the uncertain data. A meta-heuristic algorithm was developed to obtain production schedules for proposed model. The results are compared with deterministic algorithms.

2   Literature Overview

Here we present a brief overview of research considering cyclic job scheduling and fuzzy scheduling problems. We start with cyclic scheduling which received considerable attention. In paper [7] theoretical and numerical properties of methods for obtaining the minimal cycle time are studied. The cycle time is estimated through several expressions which are then compared based on their convergence speed. The distribution of the number of MPS needed to ascertain the cycle time is examined, with 3 to 4 MPS being enough almost 98 % of the time. In paper [2] graph model of the problem is employed to establish block elimination properties. Conducted research indicate improvement of the efficiency of the search process for cyclic flow shop problem. The solving methods using parallel computing have also appeared, for example, in paper [1] two parallel techniques – vector processing and multi-walk method – were employed to solve cyclic flexible job shop scheduling problem (CFJSSP). New method of computing the cycle time was also presented.

3   Problem Description

A miniature production line is considered (see Fig. 1). The model consists of five separate machines. The flow of every detail through the system can be divided into separate phases called stations. Station A consists of transportation module, production line (A1) and a pneumatic arm (A2), which transports the details from station A to station B. Station B consists of four steps: (B1) transportation module, which is supported by a human operator, (B2) lift, which transports the detail to (B3) measurement station, from where detail is taken by (B4) transportation module, which moves it to station C. Station C is our main station, where details are processed. First, they are transported by module C1, then they are processed on C2, transported by module C3 and processed for the second time on C4. At last, details are transported by module C5 to station D. First, details are transported using pneumatic arm (module D1) to module the inclined slope (module D2), which transports them to station E. Last station consists of two modules, first (E1) transports details to one of the three existing gates, while the second moves the detail from the gate to the chosen exit.

Fig. 1. Model of a production line

4   Mathematical Model

Described system can be identified as a cyclic permutation flow shop scheduling problem (CPFSP). This is the manufacturing system with sequential structure of service stages (machines). In this system following elements are defined:

- $\mathcal{M} = 1, 2, \ldots, m$ – set of machines,
- $\mathcal{J} = 1, 2, \ldots, n$ – set of jobs (details),
- $p_{i,j}$ – processing time of job j on machine i,
- $s_{i,j,k}$ – refitting time of machine i from job j to job k,
- $t_{i,j}$ – transportation time of job j from machine i to machine $i + 1$,

where $i = 1, 2, \ldots, m$, $j, k = 1, 2, \ldots, n$.

In the modeled production system following processing steps are distinguished: physical measurement (step B3), first processing (step C2), second processing (step C4) and sorting of the details (steps E1 and E2). Operation processing times p_i depend on the detail to be processed. Between each pair of subsequent machines i and $i + 1$ exists a non-zero transportation time. Refitting takes place only before first and second processing (steps C2 and C4) and depends on the details to be processed before and after the fitting.

A flow shop production system with 4 machines $\mathcal{M} = \{1, 2, 3, 4\}$ is defined. Jobs from set $\mathcal{J}$, are to be processed in non-zero processing times. Set of operations is defined as $\mathcal{O} = \{1, 2, \ldots, 4n\}$ and each job j consists of

4 operations $(\mathcal{O}_{1,j}, \ldots, \mathcal{O}_{4,j})$ processed on subsequent machines. Each machine can process only one job at the time and each job can be processed only at one machine at the same time. Moreover, interruption of processing of a operation is not allowed.

In cycle x all operations $\mathcal{O}$ for the x-th MPS must be performed. Moreover, this set can be decomposed into non-empty subsets $\mathcal{O}_k$, $k \in \{1, 2, \ldots, m\}$, containing operations from one machine k.

Schedule of jobs can be defined as a permutation $\pi = (\pi(1), \pi(2), \ldots, \pi(n))$, where $\pi(i)$ is an i-th job from permutation π.

Let $[S^x]_{m \times n}$ be a matrix of starting times of jobs on x-th MPS, where $S^x_{i,j}$ is a starting time of job j on machine i. Lets assume that the timetable of the system is fully cyclic. As such, there exists a constant $T(\pi)$ called period, such as:

$$S^{x+1}_{i,\pi(j)} = S^x_{i,\pi(j)} + T(\pi), \tag{1}$$

where $i = 1, 2, \ldots, m$, $j = 1, 2, \ldots, n$ and $x \in \mathbf{N}$. Period $T(\pi)$ depends on permutation π and is called *cycle time*. Minimal value of $T(\pi)$ will be called *minimal cycle time* and will be denoted as $T^*(\pi)$. Optimizations goal is to minimize following function:

$$T^*(\pi^*) = \min\{T^*(\pi) : \pi \in \Phi\}, \tag{2}$$

Without the loss of generality, we can assume that start and completion times of the first details on first machines are as follows: $S_{1,\pi(1)} = 0$ and $C_{1,\pi(1)} = p_{1,\pi 1}$. Completion times of details on the machines are calculated using the following recursive equation:

$$C_{i,\pi(j)} = \max \{C_{i,\pi(j-1)} + s_{i,\pi(j),\pi(k)}, C_{i-1,\pi(j)}$$
$$+t_{i-1,\pi(j)}\} + p_{i,\pi(j)}, \tag{3}$$

where $i = 1, \ldots, m$, $j = 1, \ldots, n$ and $k = 1, \ldots, n$.

Goal is to optimize following objective function:

$$T(\pi) = \max_{i \in \mathcal{M}} \{C^x_{i,\pi(n)} - S^x_{i,\pi(1)}\}. \tag{4}$$

5   Uncertain Data – Fuzzy Numbers

Fuzzy numbers [5] are a specific case of fuzzy sets [8] – which are defined through membership function $f : \mathbf{R} \rightarrow [0,1]$ – and can be viewed as generalization of the real numbers. One of the most common membership functions defines fuzzy number x as a triple (a, b, c), where $a, b, c \in \mathbf{R}$, resulting in triangular visualization.

Lets consider step B4 for some job j. The processing time of that step for job j was measured a number of times (12 in this case), creating a vector $\bar{p}_j$ with 12 elements as shown in Table 1. The estimated processing time for step B4 can be now modeled using fuzzy number $B^4 = (B^4_a, B^4_b, B^4_c)$ as follows:

$$B^4_a = \min(p_{1,j}, p_{2,j}, \ldots, p_{11,j}) = 1.20, \tag{5}$$

$$B_b^4 = \frac{p_{1,j} + p_{2,j} + \cdots + p_{11,j}}{12} = 3.30, \qquad (6)$$

$$B_c^4 = \max(p_{1,j}, p_{2,j}, \ldots, p_{11,j}) = 7.20, \qquad (7)$$

yielding $B^4 = (1.20, 3.30, 7.20)$.

Table 1. Results of measurement of $\bar{p}$ for step B4 (in seconds)

$p_{1,j}$	$p_{2,j}$	$p_{3,j}$	$p_{4,j}$	$p_{5,j}$	$p_{6,j}$	$p_{7,j}$	$p_{8,j}$	$p_{9,j}$	$p_{10,j}$	$p_{11,j}$	$p_{12,j}$
1.48	7.20	4.72	1.56	1.20	6.24	2.92	4.76	1.68	2.64	2.48	2.72

The above procedure can be applied to all steps in the production process and then be used to define all processing and transport times through fuzzy numbers. For example, transport time $t_{3,j}$ is the sum of times of steps C5, D1, D2. Thus, it can be represented as a fuzzy number computed as a sum of 3 fuzzy numbers $i.e.$ $t_{3,j} = C^5 + D^1 + D^2$. The resulting fuzzy numbers are presented in Table 2. Transport times are identical for all jobs. Fuzzy number $p_{i,j}$ represents fuzzy processing time of job j on machine i. This time is dependent on the scaling parameter γ_j which is different for various jobs. It is easily observed that the uncertainty in the considered system is significant, as the ratio $\frac{c}{a}$ can be as high as 2 or 3 for some of the presented fuzzy numbers.

Table 2. Fuzzy numbers obtained for the proposed production system

Fuzzy number	a	b	c
C^5	3.44	3.44	3.45
D^1	17.52	27.20	47.52
D^2	0.69	1.51	2.92
$t_{0,j}$	13.76	17.61	24.44
$t_{1,j}$	4.64	6.75	10.65
$t_{2,j}$	3.44	3.44	3.45
$t_{3,j}$	21.65	32.15	53.89
$p_{1,j}$	$2.32 \cdot \gamma_j$	$2.79 \cdot \gamma_j$	$3.44 \cdot \gamma_j$
$p_{2,j}$	$1.40 + \alpha_j$	$1.40 + \alpha_j$	$1.40 + \alpha_j$
$p_{3,j}$	$1.40 + \beta_j$	$1.40 + \beta_j$	$1.40 + \beta_j$
$p_{4,j}^A$	1.40	2.71	5.04
$p_{4,j}^B$	2.44	4.03	7.32
$p_{4,j}^C$	3.32	4.36	7.84

6   Proposed Method

For the purpose of this article an evolutionary method was proposed. Parameters of the algorithm were automatically adjusted (self-set parameters). Moreover, a second stop rule was implemented. When execution reaches certain (predetermined by tests) run time, the algorithm stops at current iteration.

6.1 Genetic Algorithm

Genetic Algorithm (GA) is a multi-agent method based on the evolution process found in the nature to find better solutions. Evolutionary algorithms use techniques inspired by natural occurring factors, such as inheritance, mutation, selection and crossover to generate solutions to optimization problems. Usually, the evolution starts from random initial population, which consists of individuals. In each iteration, called generation, those individuals are modified (by means of mutation and/or crossover) and their fitness is evaluated in order to select best solutions for next generation. Over the years, different approaches to the GA were proposed and tested for a variety of optimization problems. Our GA uses external Pareto archive in order to maintain non-dominated solutions through successive iterations. The individuals in population are represented by the following: jobs permutation, values of criteria functions and relative closeness indicator calculated by the TOPSIS method. Initial population includes solutions obtained from certain constructive algorithms, prepared to optimize one of the criteria. Such initialization allows faster designation of the approximation of Pareto front. Mutation is performed by interchanging two random jobs in schedule, while crossover uses a partially matched crossover (PMX) scheme. Fitness values are evaluated using the TOPSIS technique and are then used in tournament selection. After the selection, half of parent and child population is combined into new parent population. Moreover, when relative closeness values converge to zero, an anti-stagnation function is employed. Similar genetic algorithms have been proposed in [3,4].

7 Computer Experiment

All algorithms were implemented in C++ and compiled with *Embarcadero C++ Builder XE7 Professional*. The programs were tested on Intel® Core i7-3770 3400 MHz machine (8 concurrent threads) with 8 GB of RAM under the *Microsoft Windows 8.1 64 b* operating system. In order to compare the results, 3 deterministic algorithms were implemented, resulting in tests of following algorithms:

1. F – fuzzy algorithm. Based on the fuzzy problem instances with times in the form of fuzzy numbers *e.g.* $\{a, b, c\}$.
2. D_{MIN} – deterministic algorithm working on real numbers. Numbers are generated from the fuzzy instance using a value of fuzzy number.
3. D_{MID} – deterministic algorithm. Numbers are generated from the fuzzy instance using b value of fuzzy number.
4. D_{MAX} – deterministic algorithm. Numbers are generated from the fuzzy instance using c value of fuzzy number.

It can be easily observed, that fuzzy genetic algorithm (henceforth called FGA) outperformed deterministic GAs considerably. In every test, best run of the fuzzy version had best results from all of the algorithms. Its average run was

Table 3. Summary of results, instance sizes 10–25

Instance	Algorithm	Best run [%]	Average run [%]	Worst run [%]
10	F	100,00	113,91	144,43
	D_{MIN}	220,51	256,44	306,31
	D_{MID}	200,64	234,50	283,59
	D_{MAX}	202,76	234,76	278,15
15	F	100,00	113,14	148,71
	D_{MIN}	256,75	298,16	354,26
	D_{MID}	188,42	219,84	266,55
	D_{MAX}	213,44	244,54	289,41
20	F	100,00	114,58	139,31
	D_{MIN}	284,74	315,46	357,21
	D_{MID}	185,23	212,78	247,60
	D_{MAX}	211,88	241,71	278,66
25	F	100,00	124,36	155,24
	D_{MIN}	280,57	311,85	351,78
	D_{MID}	203,25	228,54	261,83
	D_{MAX}	215,68	244,37	280,67

Table 4. Summary of results, instance sizes 30–45

Instance	Algorithm	Best run	Average run	Worst run
30	F	100,00	136,01	182,08
	D_{MIN}	348,17	386,79	437,72
	D_{MID}	201,77	232,37	270,41
	D_{MAX}	272,22	308,10	354,31
35	F	100,00	149,14	204,07
	D_{MIN}	352,34	388,99	437,76
	D_{MID}	138,15	177,69	227,37
	D_{MAX}	252,77	289,37	332,77
40	F	100,00	128,40	174,28
	D_{MIN}	346,05	381,01	425,99
	D_{MID}	115,62	146,73	190,44
	D_{MAX}	220,48	262,26	311,40
45	F	100,00	117,05	144,44
	D_{MIN}	276,09	297,31	325,59
	D_{MID}	105,11	129,60	156,19
	D_{MAX}	199,96	217,35	240,55

better in most cases than the best runs of deterministic algorithms. Moreover, worst run of the fuzzy algorithm was better than best runs of D_{MIN} and D_{MAX} algorithms and, in some cases, D_{MID} deterministic algorithm.

There are 8 groups of 5 instances each, yielding 40 instances of problems for proposed problem. Groups are dependant on the number of jobs to be performed, starting from 10 up to 45. Proposed algorithm, as well as deterministic versions of GA, were tested 10 times per instance. The summarized results of first 4 groups are shown in Table 3 and last 4 groups in Table 4.

8 Conclusions and Further Research

In this paper a fuzzy genetic algorithm for a real world model of cyclic scheduling problem was proposed. The mathematical model of the problem was based on the cyclic flow shop scheduling system with uncertain (fuzzy) data. Algorithms, fuzzy and deterministic, were tested using instances with number of jobs ranging from 10 to 45. The results indicate that the proposed FGA significantly outperforms the deterministic algorithms. Each algorithm was tested under the same test conditions (maximal worktime and maximal number of iterations), so that the results were not affected by differences in test procedure.

Acknowledgements. This work is co-financed by the Młoda Kadra project, B50304.

References

1. Bożejko, W., Pempera, J., Wodecki, M.: Parallel simulated annealing algorithm for cyclic flexible job shop scheduling problem. In: Rutkowski, L., Korytkowski, M., Scherer, R., Tadeusiewicz, R., Zadeh, L.A., Zurada, J.M. (eds.) Artificial Intelligence and Soft Computing. LNCS, vol. 9120, pp. 603–612. Springer, Heidelberg (2015)
2. Bożejko, W., Uchroński, M., Wodecki, M.: Block approach to the cyclic flow shop scheduling. Comput. Ind. Eng. **81**, 158–166 (2015)
3. Bożejko, W., Kacprzak, Ł., Wodecki, M.: Parallel coevolutionary algorithm for three-dimensional bin packing problem. In: Rutkowski, L., Korytkowski, M., Scherer, R., Tadeusiewicz, R., Zadeh, L.A., Zurada, J.M. (eds.) Artificial Intelligence and Soft Computing. LNCS, vol. 9119, pp. 319–328. Springer, Heidelberg (2015)
4. Bożejko, W., Kacprzak, Ł., Wodecki, M.: Parallel packing procedure for three dimensional bin packing problem. In: Proceedings of 20th International Conference on Methods and Models in Automation and Robotics (MMAR), pp. 1122–1126 (2015)
5. Dubois, D., Prade, H.: Operations on fuzzy numbers. Int. J. Syst. Sci. **9**(6), 613–626 (1978)
6. Rudy, J.: Cyclic scheduling line with uncertain data. In: Rutkowski, L., Korytkowski, M., Scherer, R., Tadeusiewicz, R., Zadeh, L.A., Zurada, J.M. (eds.) ICAISC 2016. LNCS (LNAI), vol. 9692, pp. 311–320. Springer, Heidelberg (2016). doi:10.1007/978-3-319-39378-0_27
7. Smutnicki, C.: An efficient algorithm for finding minimal cycle time in cyclic job shop scheduling problem. In: 16th International Conference on Intelligent Engineering Systems, pp. 381–386 (2012)
8. Zadeh, L.A.: Fuzzy sets. Inf. Control **8**(3), 338–353 (1965)

Algorithms

Performance Evaluation of Probabilistic Time-Dependent Travel Time Computation

Martin Golasowski, Radek Tomis$^{(\boxtimes)}$, Jan Martinovič, Kateřina Slaninová, and Lukáš Rapant

IT4Innovations National Supercomputing Centre,
VŠB - Technical University of Ostrava, 17. listopadu 15/2172,
708 33 Ostrava, Czech Republic
{martin.golasowski,radek.tomis,jan.martinovic,
katerina.slaninova,lukas.rapant}@vsb.cz

Abstract. Computational performance of route planning algorithms has become increasingly important in recent real navigation applications with many simultaneous route requests. Navigation applications should recommend routes as quickly as possible and preferably with some added value. This paper presents a performance evaluation of the main part of probabilistic time-dependent route planning algorithm. The main part of the algorithm computes the full probability distribution of travel time on routes with Monte Carlo simulation. Experiments show the performance of the algorithm and suggest real possibilities of use in modern navigation applications.

Keywords: Probabilistic time-dependent route planning · Monte Carlo simulation · Probabilistic speed profiles · Xeon Phi · HPC

1 Introduction

Nowadays, there are many navigation services that help to find the best route to a requested destination. Drivers usually prefer the fastest route to the destination, which naturally depends on a departure time. Navigation services can find a variety of routes depending on many factors. Such factors can be map data, an algorithm used for the route planning, a possibility to use traffic data, etc. Recently, the traffic data are used extensively, because more precise results can be produced with their help. Many navigation services use traffic data to produce better and more driver friendly routes. However, such navigation services usually use only averages [6] of historic travel times on roads for computation of the routes, even though this is not sufficient in many cases. Traffic events can significantly affect the actual travel time of a route [1,2]. There can be recurrent traffic congestions at specific times which causes delays in traffic. Navigation services then should calculate with such events [3]. The probability of the traffic congestion can be low, but the delay in the case the congestion happens can be very long. Therefore, it is advantageous to count with uncertain traffic events and their probabilities in the computation of the route [4,9].

© IFIP International Federation for Information Processing 2016
Published by Springer International Publishing Switzerland 2016. All Rights Reserved
K. Saeed and W. Homenda (Eds.): CISIM 2016, LNCS 9842, pp. 377–388, 2016.
DOI: 10.1007/978-3-319-45378-1_34

Our main motivation for this paper is to give drivers some added value for suggested routes. This added value is a complete probability distribution of travel time on a suggested route. The probability distribution of travel time on a route is a valuable information, because it indicates how likely it is for the driver to reach the destination according to travel time. We use our previously developed algorithm [8] based on Monte Carlo simulation for the computation of probability distributions of travel time. The algorithm is briefly described at Sect. 2.

The added value in the form of the probability distribution of travel time brings increased computational complexity. As the first step, we suggest the best route like other navigation services, and as the second step we compute the probability distribution of travel time on this route, which requires additional computational time. The probability distribution of travel time on single route changes depending on a departure time and also on a day of the week. Traffic congestions are often connected to rush hours and some days of the week can have worse congestions than others, which is reflected in the probability distribution.

Many users might request a route at the same time and navigation services should be able to handle as many route requests at once as possible. There are two main ways to deal with a lot of route requests. The first one is to dynamically handle requests at the time they arrive and the second one is to perform the pre-processing of the probability distributions on all routes for all possible departure times and then handle requests from this precomputed data. However, it is almost impossible to cover all departure times in preprocessing, so some discretization of departure times have to be introduced. The computation time of such preprocessing is huge and depends on the number of departure times.

The main goal of this paper is to evaluate the limitations of our algorithm in a scenario with large amounts of simultaneous route requests in conjunction with a specific hardware. In other words, it would be beneficial to know how many route requests can be handled at once with different hardware. We should note that this paper evaluates only our previously developed algorithm [8] for the computation of the probability distribution of travel time, because the regular route planning used for the selection of the route is an ubiquitous topic. The organisation of the paper is as follows. Section 2 describes the tested algorithm, Sect. 3 presents experiments and an architecture overview of a testing hardware. Finally, Sect. 4 concludes the paper with final remarks.

2   Algorithm Overview

This section presents a brief description of the algorithm [8] used for the computation of the probability distribution of travel time. The input for the algorithm is some selected route and a departure time. The route is composed as a line of road segments. A Monte Carlo simulation is used for the computation of probability distributions. The simulation randomly selects probabilistic speed profiles on road segments and computes travel time at the end of the route. Probabilistic speed profiles are time-dependent sets of speeds and their probabilities assigned to road segments. Many Monte Carlo simulation iterations are needed to obtain enough travel times for the construction of the probability distribution of travel time. The number of simulation iterations greatly affects the precision of the result.

Probabilistic speed profiles present a way to state that various levels of traffic can occur with some probability. Different profile types can exist for variety of situations, e.g. free flow, congestions, traffic jams. All individual profiles are determined by belonging road segment and the time interval of its validity. Probabilistic speed profiles can be created in many ways. One way is to use Level-of-Service (LoS), which is the measured speed divided by the free flow speed. We use this method and describe it in detail at Sect. 3.

Algorithm 1 shows a pseudo code of Monte Carlo simulation. The simulation is repeated for a specified number of samples, and then the probability distribution is created from computed travel times. Time t is an actual travel time at the end of a road segment. Notice that the computation of t for a particular road segment depends on t from its preceding road segment. This makes single simulation computationally dependent and hard to parallelize. However, individual simulations are very fast and strictly independent of each other and can be run in parallel.

Algorithm 1. Monte Carlo Simulation for the Computation of the Probability Distribution of Travel Time for Given Array of Road Segments, Departure Time and Number of Samples

---

```
 1: procedure MONTECARLOSIMULATION(segments, t_d, samples)
 2:     for all samples do
 3:         t = t_d                               ▷ set time t to departure time t_d
 4:         for s in segments do
 5:             r = random number between 0 and 1
 6:             t = ComputeTravelTime(s, t, r)    ▷ speed profile is selected by r
 7:         end for
 8:         add travel time t to result
 9:     end for
10: end procedure
```

---

3 Experiment

Our algorithm is based on the well-known Monte Carlo method which is often regarded as embarrassingly parallel algorithm. The computation involves running a large number of independent instances of the algorithm with different data which makes it perfectly suitable for massively parallel computation platform such as Intel Xeon Phi. However, various problems can arise since sequential part of our implementation is memory/branch bound and is unable to fully exploit the power of vector processing unit available on the coprocessor. We expect good scalability on the coprocessor as well as on the host CPU even with this potential handicap. In this section we present results measured on the coprocessor and optimizations applied to our code to gain better speedup.

We do not try to establish a benchmark of the coprocessor since our code is not a representative sample of all Monte Carlo implementations. However, every optimization applied can improve run time on the coprocessor as well as on the host CPU. Therefore, at the end of this section we present a comparison of run times on both platforms.

3.1 Intel Xeon Phi Coprocessor Architecture Overview

The Intel Xeon Phi is a SIMD oriented coprocessor based on the many integrated core (MIC) architecture. The first version known as Knights Ferry was introduced in 2010 as a proof-of-concept targeted at high performance computing segment to counter-balance increased demand for GPGPU based architectures. The Phi has 61 x86-based cores, each core capable of running 4 threads at a time [5]. The cores are based on heavily modified P54c architecture extended by new vector processing unit (VPU) and larger cache memory. The cores communicate with the memory via ring interconnect bus based on the uncore topology introduced by Intel with the Sandy Bridge microarchitecture. It has 8 distributed memory controllers communicating with graphics double data rate (GDDR5) RAM memory. The connection with host processor is realized via 16x PCI express bus.

The main power of the Xeon Phi is in the new VPU which supports instructions from the AVX-512 instruction set. Using these instructions, each core of the Xeon Phi is able to perform arithmetical operations on either 16 single precision or 8 double precision floating point numbers at once. A theoretical speed up of 16x is achievable by correct usage of the Xeon Phi VPU. However, correct usage of the VPU depends on various factors, such as data access pattern, memory alignment, and size of the data set (ideally, the entire working data set should fit in the on-board memory, since PCIe bus introduces a significant bottleneck).

Thanks to its roots in x86 architecture, the programming model for the Phi is more or less the same as for the regular CPUs. As the card itself runs a common Linux-based operating system, standard threading models such as OpenMP, Intel TBB, or pthreads can be used, as well as MPI. Intel supplies its own SDK with optimized version of the math kernel library (MKL) and C/C++ and Fortran compilers. However, to achieve optimal exploitation of the Xeon Phi computational power, a substantial amount of attention should be paid to effective partitioning of the workload and to the overall differences of the architecture by profiling and optimization of the code.

Although cores of the Xeon Phi have superscalar properties, the cores itself are relatively slow (1.2 GHz < 2.5 GHz) compared to the Haswell CPUs and lack several features such as level 3 cache or out of order execution. Due to this deficiency, the Phi cores may perform worse in sequential or branch-heavy code compared to the host CPU (such as Haswell). On the other hand, well vectorized code can run significantly faster on the Phi than on the host CPU, thanks to the VPU and significantly larger (12 < 61) number of available cores.

3.2 Traffic Data

The data for our experiment come from motorways and 'A' roads managed by the Highways Agency, known as the Strategic Road Network, in England[1,2]. This data contain time series of average journey time, speed and traffic flow

---

[1] https://data.gov.uk/dataset/dft-eng-srn-routes-journey-times.
[2] http://www.nationalarchives.gov.uk/doc/open-government-licence/version/3/.

information for segments of various length (from few hundred meters to several kilometers) with 15-minute aggregation periods (i.e. four values for each hour). Traffic speed in these data sets is calculated using a combination of stationary sensors (Automatic Number Plate Recognition, Induction loops) and floating car data sources.

In our experiment, we used data from January to December 2014. Route from Sunderland to Thetford was chosen, because it is one of the longest direct routes contained in the data set. This data were used to calculate probabilistic speed profiles for the segments along the route and to calculate empirical free flow speed for these segments. These free flow speeds were calculated as average of top 10 % aggregated speed measurements on the chosen segment (as these speeds are most probably not influenced by the traffic density).

Profiles used for experiments were created for four LoS intervals, specifically $\langle 100; 75 \rangle$, $\langle 75; 50 \rangle$, $\langle 50; 25 \rangle$ and $\langle 25; 0 \rangle$. An example of such speed profiles for the entire route from Sunderland to Thetford, Monday 8:00 is presented in Fig. 1.

The interpretation of what these intervals mean can be as follows. The first interval $\langle 100; 75 \rangle$ represents free traffic, the second interval $\langle 75; 50 \rangle$ corresponds to light traffic, the third interval $\langle 50; 25 \rangle$ means heavy traffic, and the last one $\langle 25; 0 \rangle$ is for traffic jams.

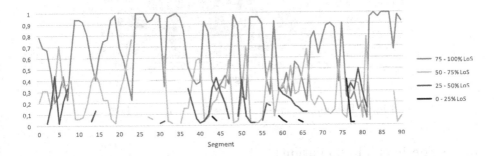

Fig. 1. Speed profiles for the selected route, monday 8:00 AM

Table 1. Example of probabilistic speed profiles

Day of week	Hour	Level of service							
		100 %		75 %		50 %		25 %	
		s [km/h]	p [%]	s [km/h]	p [%]	s [km/h]	p [%]	s [km/h]	p [%]
Monday	8:00	83.45	0.21	61.33	0.058	39.46	0.29	14.39	0.44
	8:15	83.40	0.19	56.25	0.086	36.18	0.21	15.44	0.52
	8:30	85.71	0.13	66.33	0.057	35.29	0.32	14.12	0.48
	8:45	84.00	0.17	63.08	0.230	40.23	0.25	17.05	0.34

Figure 2 shows an example of speed profiles of the segments on the whole selected route for the interval 50–75 % of LoS. The color indicates the probability that this interval of LoS occurs. The speed profiles were created on the basis of data from January to December 2014 considering days of the week. Table 1 shows example of probabilistic speed profiles for single road segment and for one hour. Each LoS is represented by two values, speed s in kilometers per hour and probability $p \in \langle 0; 1 \rangle$.

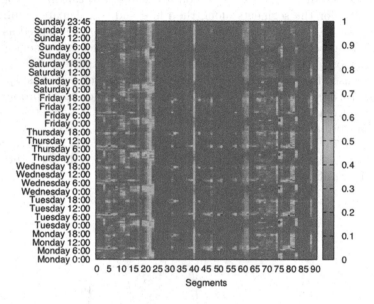

Fig. 2. Heatmap of speed profiles for 50–75 % of LoS

3.3   Experimental Simulations

The simulation was performed with the traffic data described in Subsect. 3.2 on the Salomon supercomputer operated by IT4Innovations National Supercomputing Centre, the Czech Republic. Nodes of the Salomon cluster contain a version of the Xeon Phi coprocessor based on the Knights Corner microarchitecture (7210P). This model has 16 GB of on board RAM memory, 61 compute cores, and there are 2 cards per compute node of the cluster. In total, there are 432 nodes containing 2 Xeon Phi coprocessors. Each compute node has two 12 core Haswell CPUs and 128 GB RAM.

An example of simulation output is presented in Figs. 3a and 3b. The single profile simulation (a) uses a selected profile as a starting point, then runs the simulation for the entire path. In this case, the starting point was determined by week day (Tuesday) and time (8:00 AM). The all profiles simulation (b) runs the algorithm for all available speed profiles determined by its parameters (i.e. days of the week and 15 min intervals of a single day). Both the simulations have been run with 1000 Monte Carlo samples.

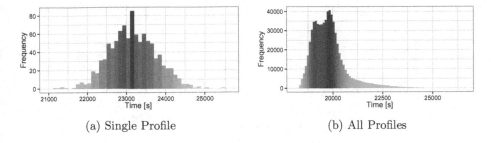

(a) Single Profile   (b) All Profiles

Fig. 3. Example of the simulation output

The first simulation provides information about the most probable travel time along the given path and for a selected time of departure. Based on results of our simulation shown in Fig. 3a, it can be said that if you drive from Sunderland to Thetford on Tuesday around 8:00 AM, you will most probably reach your destination in about 6 h and 30 min (23,200 s). By looking at results of the simulation for all profiles in Fig. 3b, it is evident that the estimated travel time can vary through the week, however the journey will most likely take no more than 5 h and 30 min (19,800 s).

3.4 Performance on the Intel Xeon Phi Coprocessor

Various other factors involving configuration of the run time environment can affect performance of the coprocessor. One of the factors in our case was thread allocation strategy. Our code is parallelized using the OpenMP standard. Intel provides its own OpenMP implementation as part of the Xeon Phi Manycore Software Stack (MPSS) toolchain. The library allows to choose between various thread allocation strategies by setting KMP_AFFINITY environment variable[3].

There are three main strategies. The *compact* strategy allocates whole cores in blocks. For example, running 40 threads on the Phi would use only 10 cores since single core runs 4 hardware threads. The *scatter* strategy assigns threads to cores evenly in round-robin fashion across all cores. The *explicit* strategy is the last one and allows explicit assignment of a given software thread to a particular core.

Measurements of the code scalability with the *compact* and *scatter* strategy are presented in Fig. 4. The *scatter* strategy is more suitable in our case since our code is memory/branch bound and running more than 2 threads per core creates unwanted congestion during memory reads.

Another factor involved is the cache hierarchy of the coprocessor. The Xeon Phi has 32 kB + 32 kB (instruction, data) L1 cache and 512 kB L2 data cache per core. The graph in Fig. 5 shows differences in performance of the code on cold and hot caches. The cold cache times were measured from single execution

---

[3] Thread affinity interface documentation: https://software.intel.com/en-us/node/522691.

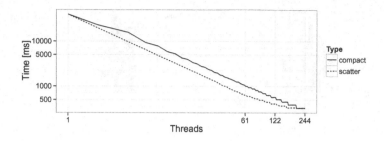

Fig. 4. Scalability of simulation for all available profiles on the Xeon Phi coprocessor

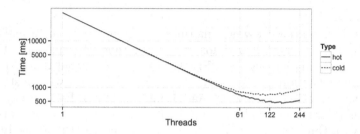

Fig. 5. Scalability of simulation for all available profiles on the Xeon Phi coprocessor

of the code on the coprocessor for different number of threads. The hot cache times were measured as average of 10 successive runs of the code.

The graphs show that proper use of the cache memory can provide significant speed up of our code. Unfortunately, the input data for single run will most likely differ each time, since most of the user requests will be computed for different road segments and start time. The real world usage of the coprocessor is reflected by the cold cache measurement which means we are able to effectively use only half of the resources available for efficient usage of the coprocessor.

Scalability of the code on the host CPU is presented in Fig. 6. The code scales very well while execution time is approx. 2 times shorter when running on single 12 core Haswell CPU that on the coprocessor. The code running on the CPU benefits from L3 data cache as well as from out-of-order execution and more sophisticated memory prefetching.

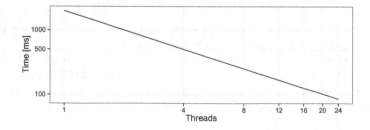

Fig. 6. Scalability of simulation for all available profiles on the host CPU

Table 2. Measured run times on the coprocessor

Threads	Times [ms]			
	Scatter	Compact	Cold	Hot
1	40,111	40,207	40,162	40,118
61	637	995	819	705
122	410	571	731	514
244	332	331	955	553

Table 3. Measured run times on the host CPU

Threads	Times [ms]
1	1,973
12 (single CPU)	166
24 (two CPUs)	85

Measured times of execution on the coprocessor are presented in the Table 2 and measured times on the host CPUs in Table 3. All measurements were performed with 1,000 samples run, threads were distributed evenly across all available cores of the target platform (except for the compact thread affinity strategy).

3.5 Code Optimization

In parallel Monte Carlo based simulations, the optimization effort usually focuses on finding a suitable method for random number generation and on optimizing data access pattern since only single synchronization occurs at the end of all runs and no data dependencies exist between the threads. The core of our algorithm relies on the selection of a speed profile given a canonical probability $p \in (0;1)$. Effective indexing of the speed profiles for a given path segment can significantly improve overall run time of the algorithm. The speed profile for single time interval (identified by a day of the week and a time) is represented by pairs of velocity and probability values (see Table 1). The velocity values are distributed in an array of fixed length according to their probability.

The size of the array determines the resolution of the probability values which can be represented by a linear index. An example of the mapping between speed profiles and the storage array is presented in Table 4. The first table shows a single probabilistic speed profile with four LoS. The second table shows the final distribution and encoding of the velocities to the linear array indexes according to their probability. All the speed profiles for single road segment are represented by matrix of the velocity arrays stored in single linear array to improve usage of the cache memory. This type of the representation lowered the amount of necessary processor instructions used for the selection of the appropriate speed from the speed profile.

Table 4. Example of probabilistic speed profile encoding

Speed	83.45	61.33	39.46	14.39					
Probability	0.21	0.058	0.29	0.442					

Index	0	1	2	3	4	5	6	7	8	9
Speed	83.45	83.45	61.33	39.46	39.46	39.46	14.39	14.39	14.39	14.39

The early version of our code computed the index of the profile in a given day from time specified in UNIX timestamp format. The computation of the profile index involved several system function calls (namely `localtime`) which posed a significant bottleneck in the multithreaded environment on the coprocessor. The next version was based on simple data types and did not use any date-time related functions from the C standard library.

However, profiling in Intel VTune[4] suggested that another bottleneck appeared as we used pseudo-random number generation routines (introduced in C++11) available in C++ Standard Library. The slowdown was apparent especially when using large number of threads such as on Xeon Phi accelerator, since the library implementation was mainly sequential and thus unsuitable for usage on the Xeon Phi due to lack of any parallelism and vectorization.

Intel provides optimized version of the math kernel library (MKL)[5] for the Xeon Phi in its SDK[6] and we have decided to use their Mersenne-Twister implementation. This implementation uses vector instructions and allows us to generate the random numbers in batches which leads to more efficient use of the coprocessor. In the current version of our code, the random number generation takes only approx. 20 % of the computation time according to the Intel VTune profiler in comparison with 90 % in the previous version of the code.

4   Conclusion

The paper evaluated the computational performance of our algorithm for the computation of probabilistic time-dependent travel time on the Intel Xeon Phi coprocessor and Haswell CPU. Various code optimizations described in Sect. 3.5 have been done with appropriate speed up. We expected good scalability on the Xeon Phi coprocessor due to large parallelization potential of the algorithm even though it was not taking any advantage of the vector processing unit, and seemed generally unsuitable for the coprocessor. However, we have been able to use the VPU by using Intel MKL Vector Statistics Library. Finally, the good scalability was achieved on the coprocessor as well as on the host CPU. Measured

---

[4] https://software.intel.com/en-us/articles/how-to-analyze-xeon-phi-coprocessor-applications-using-intel-vtune-amplifier-xe-2015.

[5] https://software.intel.com/en-us/mkl-reference-manual-for-c.

[6] https://software.intel.com/en-us/articles/intel-manycore-platform-software-stack-m-pss.

execution times and scalability graphs are presented in Sect. 3.3. By performing experiments, we estimated that it is the best to run our code on 122 threads evenly distributed across all 61 cores of the coprocessor.

The experiments met our expectations, however a number of specific optimizations had to be applied to obtain these results. Each optimization that led to the improvement for the coprocessor also improved the execution time on the CPU, often significantly. Finally, the execution time was at best 2 times slower on the coprocessor than on the single host CPU. In general, we have been able to lower the overall execution time quite significantly. The early version of the code ran for approx. 5 min on single coprocessor while optimized version of our code runs for approx. 400 ms for the same input data.

It follows that the algorithm can easily handle many simultaneous route requests and the number of requests should be large enough to utilize the full power of the available hardware. Using the current implementation we can offload half of the work to the coprocessor and efficiently utilize the entire power of the HPC infrastructure.

In the future work, we would like to focus on further optimizations related to the cache memory subsystem of the coprocessor and to finding a vectorizable version of the algorithm. Another possible area of the research emerged during the optimization process. Some of the optimization techniques can be generalized for this type of Monte Carlo based algorithms by using some type of domain specific language, for example DSL and autotuning techniques being developed within the ANTAREX[7] project [7]. This way, the specific optimizations can be applied by users without the need to perform such extensive studying of the target hardware microarchitecture.

Acknowledgment. This work was supported by The Ministry of Education, Youth and Sports from the National Programme of Sustainability (NPU II) project 'IT4Innovations excellence in science - LQ1602', from the Large Infrastructures for Research, Experimental Development and Innovations project 'IT4Innovations National Supercomputing Center - LM2015070', and co-financed by the internal grant agency of VŠB - Technical University of Ostrava, Czech Republic, under the project no. SP2016/179 'HPC Usage for Transport Optimisation based on Dynamic Routing II'.

References

1. Fan, Y., Kalaba, R., Moore I, J.E.: Arriving on time. J. Optim. Theor. Appl. **127**(3), 497–513 (2005)
2. Hofleitner, A., Herring, R., Abbeel, P., Bayen, A.: Learning the dynamics of arterial traffic from probe data using a dynamic Bayesian network. IEEE Trans. Intell. Transp. Syst. **13**(4), 1679–1693 (2012)
3. Miller-Hooks, E.: Adaptive least-expected time paths in stochastic, time-varying transportation and data networks. Networks **37**, 35–52 (2000)

---

[7] ANTAREX (AutoTuning and Adaptivity appRoach for Energy efficient eXascale HPC systems), Project Reference: 671623, Call: H2020-FETHPC-2014 - http://www.antarex-project.eu.

4. Nikolova, E., Brand, M., Karger, D.R.: Optimal route planning under uncertainty. In: ICAPS, vol. 6, pp. 131–141 (2006)
5. Rahman, R.: Intel® Xeon Phi™ Coprocessor Architecture and Tools: The Guide for Application Developers. Apress, New York (2013)
6. Rice, J., Van Zwet, E.: A simple and effective method for predicting travel times on freeways. Intell. Transp. Syst. 5(3), 200–207 (2004)
7. Silvano, C., Agosta, G., Cherubin, S., Gadioli, D., Palermo, G., Bartolini, A., Benini, L., Martinovič, J., Palkovič, M., Slaninová, K., Bispo, J., Cardoso, J.M.P., Abreu, R., Pinto, P., Cavazzoni, C., Sanna, N., Beccari, A.R., Cmar, R., Rohou, E.: The ANTAREX approach to autotuning and adaptivity for energy efficient HPC systems. In: ACM International Conference on Computing Frontiers 2016 (2016)
8. Tomis, R., Rapant, L., Martinovič, J., Slaninová, K., Vondrák, I.: Probabilistic time-dependent travel time computation using monte carlo simulation. In: Kozubek, T., Blaheta, R., Šístek, J., Rozložník, M., Cermák, M. (eds.) HPCSE 2015. LNCS, vol. 9611, pp. 161–170. Springer, Heidelberg (2016). doi:10.1007/978-3-319-40361-8_12
9. Yang, B., Guo, C., Jensen, C.S., Kaul, M., Shang, S.: Multi-cost optimal route planning under time-varying uncertainty. In: Proceedings of the 30th International Conference on Data Engineering (ICDE), Chicago, IL, USA (2014)

Flexible Global Constraint Extension
for Dynamic Time Warping

Tomáš Kocyan[1](✉), Kateřina Slaninová[1,2], and Jan Martinovič[1,2]

[1] IT4Innovations National Supercomputing Center,
VŠB – Technical University of Ostrava, 17. listopadu 15/2172,
708 33 Ostrava, Czech Republic
{tomas.kocyan,katerina.slaninova,jan.martinovic}@vsb.cz
[2] Faculty of Electrical Engineering and Computer Science,
VŠB – Technical University of Ostrava, 17. listopadu 15/2172,
708 33 Ostrava, Czech Republic

Abstract. Dynamic Time Warping algorithm (DTW) is an effective tool for comparing two sequences which are subject to some kind of distortion. Unlike the standard methods for comparison, it is able to deal with a different length of compared sequences or with reasonable amount of inaccuracy. For this reason, DTW has become very popular and it is widely used in many domains. One of its the biggest advantages is a possibility to specify definable amount of benevolence while evaluating similarity of two sequences. It enables to percept similarity through the eyes of domain expert, in contrast with a strict sequential comparison of opposite sequence elements. Unfortunately, such commonly used definition of benevolence cannot be applied on DTW modifications, which were created for solving specific tasks (e.g. searching the longest common subsequence). The main goal of this paper is to eliminate weaknesses of commonly used approach and to propose a new flexible mechanism for definition of benevolence applicable to modifications of original DTW.

Keywords: Dynamic time warping · Flexible global constraint · Longest common subsequence · Comparison of sequences

1 Introduction

Nowadays, searching and comparing time series databases generated by computers, which consist of accurate time cycles and which achieve a determined finite number of value levels, is a trivial problem. Main attention is focused rather on optimization of the searching speed. A non-trivial task occurs while comparing or searching signals with different length, which are not strictly defined and have various distortions in time and amplitude. As a typical example, we can mention the measurement of functionality of human body (ECG, EEG) or the elements (precipitation, flow rates in riverbeds), that does not contain any accurate timing for signal generation. Therefore, comparison of such sequences is significantly difficult, and almost impossible while using standard functions for

© IFIP International Federation for Information Processing 2016
Published by Springer International Publishing Switzerland 2016. All Rights Reserved
K. Saeed and W. Homenda (Eds.): CISIM 2016, LNCS 9842, pp. 389–401, 2016.
DOI: 10.1007/978-3-319-45378-1_35

similarity (distance) computation [2], such as *Euclidean distance* [3], *cosine measure* [8], *Mean Estimate Error* [16], etc. Examples of such signals are presented in Fig. 1. A problem of standard functions for similarity (distance) computation consists in sequential comparison of the opposite elements in the both sequences (comparison of elements with the identical indices). Fortunately, such lack of commonly used approach can be easily eliminated by the *Dynamic Time Warping* algorithm, which is able to percept similarity through the eyes of a domain expert, in contrast with a strict sequential comparison. However, such commonly used definition of benevolence cannot be applied on DTW modifications, which were created for solving specific tasks (e.g. searching the longest common subsequence).

The main goal of this paper is to eliminate weaknesses of commonly used approach and to propose a new flexible mechanism for definition of benevolence applicable to modifications of the original DTW. It is organized as follows: First, the DTW algorithm for comparing two distorted sequences and its several modifications will be described in Sect. 2. In Sect. 3, commonly used approaches for definition of benevolence will be introduced. It will be followed by a proposal of a new *Flexible Global Constraint*. Finally, an effect of the algorithm's settings will be visualized and the proposed solution will be discussed.

2   Dynamic Time Warping

Dynamic Time Warping (DTW) is a technique for finding the optimal matching of two warped sequences using pre-defined rules [11]. Essentially, it is a nonlinear mapping of particular elements to match them in the most appropriate way. The output of such DTW mapping of sequences from Fig. 1 can be seen in Fig. 2. At first, this approach was used for comparison of two voice patterns during an automatic recognition of voice commands [13]. Since this time, it was widely used in many domains, e.g. for efficient satellite image analysis [12], in analysis of student behavioral patterns [17] or in protein fold recognition [9]. As it is correctly noted in [5], a common problem of many DTW applications lies in the fact, that the DTW is too computationally expensive. In order to speed up the algorithm run, several lower bounding methods [4] or parallelization techniques were created [14,15]. Moreover, the DTW was modified many times for solving specific tasks (e.g. searching the longest common subsequence [7]) or for better algorithm behavior (e.g. *Derivative Dynamic Time Warping* [6]). Since the proposed approach is also an extension of this algorithm, the original DTW algorithm will be described in more detail for better understanding.

Formally, the main goal of DTW method is a comparison of two time dependent sequences x and y, where $x = (x_1, x_2, \ldots, x_n)$ and $y = (y_1, y_2, \ldots, y_m)$, and finding an optimal mapping of their elements. To compare partial elements of sequences $x_i, y_j \in \mathbb{R}$, it is necessary to define a local cost measure $c : \mathbb{R} \times \mathbb{R} \to \mathbb{R}_{\geq 0}$, where c is small if x and y is similar to each other, and otherwise it is large. Computation of the local cost measure for each pair of elements of sequences x and y results in a construction of the cost matrix $C \in \mathbb{R}^{n \times m}$ defined by $C(i, j) = c(x_i, y_j)$ (see Fig. 3(a)).

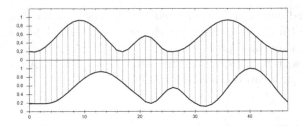

Fig. 1. Standard metrics comparison

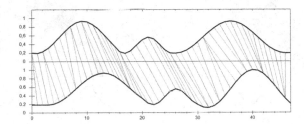

Fig. 2. DTW comparison

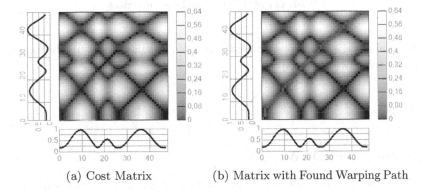

(a) Cost Matrix   (b) Matrix with Found Warping Path

Fig. 3. DTW cost matrices

Then the goal is to find an alignment between x and y with a minimal overall cost. Such optimal alignment leads through the black valleys of the cost matrix C, trying to avoid the white areas with a high cost. Such alignment is demonstrated in Fig. 3(b). Basically, the alignment (called warping path) $p = (p_1, \ldots, p_q)$ is a sequence of q pairs (warping path points) $p_k = (p_{kx}, p_{ky}) \in \{1, \ldots, n\} \times \{1, \ldots, m\}$. Each of such pairs (i, j) indicates an alignment between the ith element of the sequence x and jth element of the sequence y.

Retrieval of optimal path p^* by evaluating all possible warping paths between sequences x and y leads to an exponential computational complexity. Fortunately, there exists a better way with $O(n \cdot m)$ complexity based on dynamic programming. It involves the use of an accumulated cost matrix $D \in \mathbb{R}^{n \times m}$ described in [11].

Accumulated cost matrix computed for the cost matrix from Fig. 3(a) can be seen in Fig. 4(a). It is evident that the accumulation highlights only a single black valley. The optimal path $p^* = (p_1, \ldots, p_q)$ is then computed in a reverse order starting with $p_q = (n, m)$ and finishing in $p_1 = (1, 1)$. An example of such found warping path can be seen in Fig. 4(b).

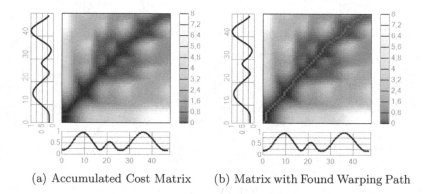

(a) Accumulated Cost Matrix   (b) Matrix with Found Warping Path

Fig. 4. DTW accumulated cost matrices

The final *DTW cost* can be understood as a quantified effort for the alignment of the two sequences (see Eq. 1).

$$DTW(x, y) = \sum_{k=1}^{q} C(x_{p_{kx}}, y_{p_{ky}}) = D(n, m) \tag{1}$$

2.1 Subsequence DTW

In some cases, it is not necessary to compare or align the whole sequences. A usual goal is to find an optimal alignment of a sample (a relatively short time series) within the signal database (a very long time series). This is very usual in situations, in which one manages with a signal database and wants to find the best occurrence(s) of a sample (query). Using the slight modification [11], the DTW has the ability to search such queries in a much longer sequence. The basic idea is not to penalize the omission in the alignment between x and y that appears at the beginning and at the end of the sequence y. Suppose we have two sequences $x = (x_1, x_2, \ldots, x_n)$ of the length $n \in \mathbb{N}$ and $y = (y_1, y_2, \ldots, y_m)$ of the much larger length $m \in \mathbb{N}$. The goal is to find a subsequence $y_{a:b} = (y_a, y_{a+1}, \ldots, y_b)$ where $1 \leq a \leq b \leq m$ that minimizes the DTW cost to x over the all possible subsequences of y. An example of such searching the best subsequence alignment can be seen in Fig. 5. Both constructed matrices including the found warping path are then shown in Fig. 6.

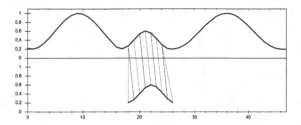

Fig. 5. Found DTW subsequence

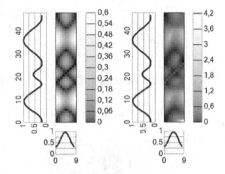

Fig. 6. Cost matrix and accumulated cost matrix for searching subsequence

Despite the fact that the DTW has its own modification for searching subsequences, it works perfectly only in case of searching an exact pattern in a signal database. However, in real situations, exact patterns are not available because they are surrounded by additional values, or even repeated several times in a sequence (see Fig. 7). Unfortunately, the basic DTW is not able to handle these situations and it fails or returns only a single occurrence of the pattern. To deal with this type of situations, several DTW modifications were created and described for example in [7] or [10] in detail.

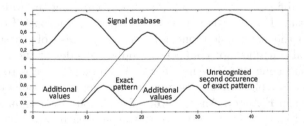

Fig. 7. Basic DTW subsequence inaccuracies

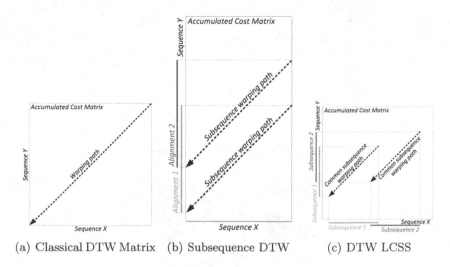

(a) Classical DTW Matrix   (b) Subsequence DTW   (c) DTW LCSS

Fig. 8. Approach for searching the warping path

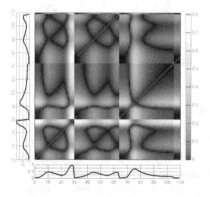

Fig. 9. Cost matrix with found warping paths

The biggest difference is in the approach for searching the warping path. In simple terms, the algorithm does not search the warping path from the upper right corner to the bottom left one (shown in the case of classical DTW in Fig. 8(a)) and also it does not connect the opposite sides of the matrix (shown in the case of subsequence DTW in Fig. 8(b)). The main idea is to find warping paths as long as possible from any element to another one, parallel to a diagonal, as it is outlined in Fig. 8(c). An example of such found common subsequences can be seen in Fig. 10. The corresponding warping paths are also visualized in the cost matrix in Fig. 9.

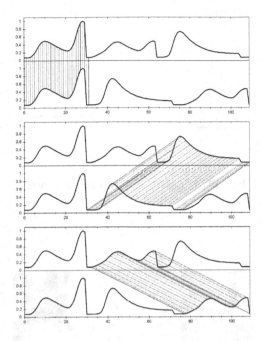

Fig. 10. Found common subsequences

3   Flexible Global Constraints

In the practical applications [1, 18–20], the construction of a warping path has to be controlled. The reason is possible uncontrolled high number of warpings, i.e. alignment of a single element to a high number of the elements in the opposite sequence [11]. In this manner, dissimilar sequences can get low *DTW Cost* and they can be evaluated as similar. This situation is demonstrated on sequences in Fig. 11, and on appropriate cost matrix in Fig. 12.

Generally, this can be easily fixed by definition of a global constraint region $R \subseteq D$. This region then determines the elements of the cost matrix, which can be used for searching the warping path. In the original paper about DTW [11], there are two global constraints for warping path mentioned - *Itakura parallelogram* (Fig. 13(a)) and *Sakoe-Chiba band* (Fig. 13(b)).

However, for purpose of searching subsequences and other DTW modifications, the Itakura parallelogram seems to be inappropriate, because it was designed to limit warpings at the start and end of the classical DTW warping path, where the first and last warping points are exactly known. Fortunately, the Saoke-Chiba band looks more preferable. The warping path respecting this band for sequences from Fig. 11 is visible in Fig. 14.

However, one may ask what width of band to choose. The width essentially defines the maximal number of warpings in a found sequence. For this reason, it is almost impossible to define a universal number applicable both on shorter and

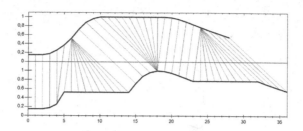

Fig. 11. Mapping of dissimilar sequences

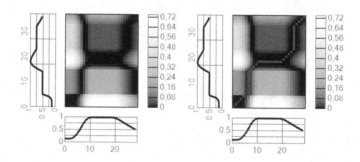

Fig. 12. Cost matrix of dissimilar sequences

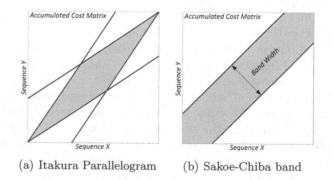

(a) Itakura Parallelogram   (b) Sakoe-Chiba band

Fig. 13. DTW global constraint regions

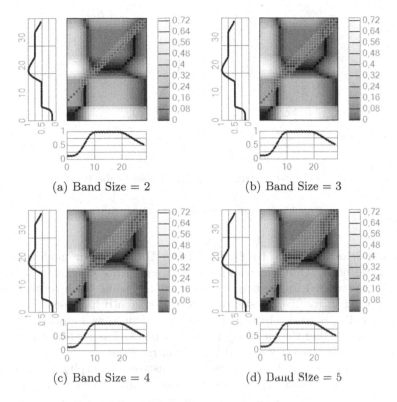

(a) Band Size = 2

(b) Band Size = 3

(c) Band Size = 4

(d) Band Size = 5

Fig. 14. Examples of applied Saoke-Chiba bands

longer sequences. It is evident that allowing five warpings on a path comparing sequences of the length ten or hundred has absolutely different meaning. In this example, the results look satisfactorily, but this belt was also designed for searching the warping path through the whole sequences. This inaccuracy is evident in the following example:

Lets have two sequences $x = (x_1, x_2, \ldots, x_n)$ and $y = (y_1, y_2, \ldots, y_{2n})$, where y is created by stretching x into the double length (i.e. $\forall i \in \{1, \ldots, 2n\} : y_i = x_{i/2}$). The matrix will stretch in one dimension and the line of minima will slightly bend (see Fig. 15(a)). It causes some warpings, but it is still acceptable. Using the standard Sakoe-Chiba band, the warping path cannot follow the minima trajectory and have to continue in straight direction, as shown in Fig. 15(b).

More elegant solution is to allow a band to bend itself and provide a warping path with reasonable freedom. For this purpose, we designed a flexible band allowing configurable bending. The band is based on Saoke-Chiba band, but it changes its position and shape according the previously constructed warping path. The center of the original Saoke-Chiba band lies exactly on cost matrix's diagonal.

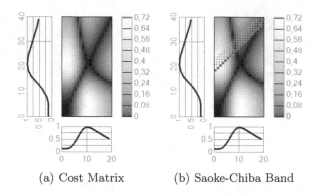

(a) Cost Matrix   (b) Saoke-Chiba Band

Fig. 15. Cost matrices for stretched sequence

Proposed Modifications to Saoke-Chiba Band. In our modification, the center of the band varies and passes through one of the previous points of the currently constructed warping path, called *control point*. Such control point is always located in the fixed distance from the currently processed point. This distance is called *control point distance* and it is defined as a number of *warping path points* preceding the currently processed point. The center of constructed band always moves to a newly established control point.

Formally, suppose we have a currently constructed warping path p defined as $p = (p_1, \ldots, p_q)$ consisting of a sequence of q path points $p_k = (p_{kx}, p_{ky}) \in \{1, \ldots, n\} \times \{1, \ldots, m\}$, $p_1 = (n, m)$. Each such pair (p_{kx}, p_{ky}) indicates an alignment between the ith element of the sequence x and jth element of the sequence y. The path point (p_{kx}, p_{ky}) lies in the Saoke-Chiba band of a width w, if $|p_{kx} - p_{ky}| < w$. With the flexible band of the width w and with a control point distance d, the path point (p_{kx}, p_{ky}) lies in the band if $|(p_{kx} - p_{(k-d)x}) - (p_{ky} - p_{(k-d)y})| < w$. The distance d of such control point from the end of the warping path defines a rigidity of the band.

Figure 16 demonstrates how the increasing distance of the control point d causes higher toughness of the band, and how the ability to bend loses. The shorter distance makes the band more flexible, the higher distance causes inflexibility. It is especially evident from Fig. 16(d) (with $d = 4$), where the band became too much tough to follow the black valleys.

An effect of predefined toughness can be also easily quantified by the received *DTW Cost* defined in Eq. 1. With an original Saoke-Chiba Band (see Fig. 13), received *DTW Cost* = 3.6433. On the other hand, with using the proposed flexible constraint (distances of the control point d) and appropriately adjusted benevolence, the sequences can be evaluated as almost equal (*DTW Cost* = 0,0182). Table 1 illustrates how the received *DTW Cost* reflects the adjusted amount of benevolence (various distances of the control point d). In order to set the *control point distance* up correctly, it is necessary to have some domain knowledge. At this point, the domain expert has to define the benevolence for the evaluation.

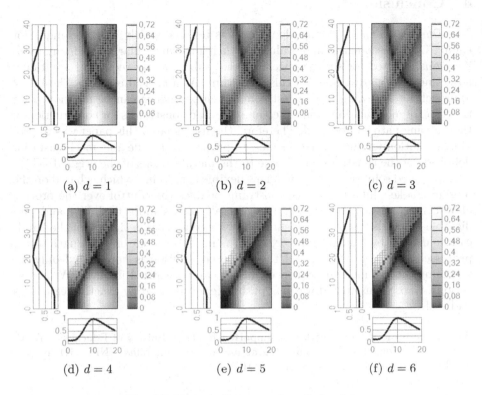

(a) $d = 1$ (b) $d = 2$ (c) $d = 3$

(d) $d = 4$ (e) $d = 5$ (f) $d = 6$

Fig. 16. Various distances of control point

Table 1. DTW costs for various control point distances

Control point distance	DTW Cost
1	0.0182
2	0.0182
3	0.0182
4	1.0329
5	2.3110
6	2.9819
7	3.1504
8	3.9598
9	3.6433
10	3.6433
Without flexible band	3.9634

4   Conclusion

The *Dynamic Time Warping* algorithm has become widely used technique for comparing two sequences and evaluating their mutual similarity. Its many modifications, created for solving specific tasks, subsequently requested additional adjustments of partial steps of this algorithm. As a typical example, the DTW approach for searching the longest common subsequence can be mentioned. In this type of modification, none of commonly used constraints for construction of the warping path can be used. Therefore, the mail goal of this paper was to provide a solution for such situations and to propose a new flexible mechanism for definition of the constraint applicable to the modifications of the original DTW. The proposed solution consists in a new flexible constraint, which is based on the original Saoke-Chiba band. The constraint enables the control over the process of warping path construction and it generally offers more flexibility and predictable behaviour. Moreover, definition of its conduct (i.e. rigidity of the band) can be defined by a single number, which is not dependent on the length of the processed sequences. The use of the proposed solution is not limited only for searching the common subsequences, but it can be utilized in all DTW modifications, whose constructed warping paths are not defined by exactly beginnings and ends.

Acknowledgment. This work was supported by The Ministry of Education, Youth and Sports from the National Programme of Sustainability (NPU II) project 'IT4Innovations excellence in science - LQ1602'.

References

1. Cheng, H., Dai, Z., Liu, Z., Zhao, Y.: An image-to-class dynamic time warping approach for both 3D static and trajectory hand gesture recognition. Pattern Recogn. **55**, 137–147 (2016)
2. Ding, H., Trajcevski, G., Scheuermann, P., Wang, X., Keogh, E.: Querying and mining of time series data: experimental comparison of representations and distance measures. Proc. VLDB Endow. **1**(2), 1542–1552 (2008)
3. Elmore, K.L., Richman, M.B.: Euclidean distance as a similarity metric for principal component analysis. Mon. Weather Rev. **129**(3), 540–549 (2001)
4. Keogh, E.: Exact indexing of dynamic time warping. In: Proceedings of the 28th International Conference on Very Large Data Bases, VLDB 2002, pp. 406–417. VLDB Endowment (2002). http://dl.acm.org/citation.cfm?id=1287369.1287405
5. Keogh, E.J., Pazzani, M.J.: Scaling up dynamic time warping for datamining applications. In: Proceedings of the Sixth ACM SIGKDD International Conference on Knowledge Discovery and Data Mining, pp. 285–289. ACM (2000)
6. Keogh, E.J., Pazzani, M.J.: Derivative dynamic time warping. In: First SIAM International Conference on Data Mining SDM 2001 (2001)
7. Kocyan, T., Martinovič, J., Slaninová, K., Szturcová, D.: Searching the longest common subsequences in distorted data. In: 27th European Modeling and Simulation Symposium, EMSS 2015, pp. 84–92 (2015)
8. Lee, D.L., Chuang, H., Seamons, K.: Document ranking and the vector-space model. IEEE Softw. **14**(2), 67–75 (1997)

9. Lyons, J., Biswas, N., Sharma, A., Dehzangi, A., Paliwal, K.K.: Protein fold recognition by alignment of amino acid residues using kernelized dynamic time warping. J. Theor. Biol. **354**, 137–145 (2014)
10. Movchan, A., Zymbler, M.L.: Time series subsequence similarity search under dynamic time warping distance on the intel many-core accelerators. In: SISAP (2015)
11. Müller, M.: Information Retrieval for Music and Motion. Springer-Verlag New York Inc., Secaucus (2007)
12. Petitjean, F., Weber, J.: Efficient satellite image time series analysis under time warping. IEEE Geosci. Remote Sens. Lett. **11**(6), 1143–1147 (2014)
13. Rabiner, L., Juang, B.H.: Fundam. Speech Recogn. Prentice-Hall Inc, Upper Saddle River (1993)
14. Rakthanmanon, T., Campana, B., Mueen, A., Batista, G., Westover, B., Zhu, Q., Zakaria, J., Keogh, E.: Addressing big data time series: mining trillions of time series subsequences under dynamic time warping. ACM Trans. Knowl. Discov. Data **7**(3), 101–1031 (2013)
15. Sart, D., Mueen, A., Najjar, W., Keogh, E., Niennattrakul, V.: Accelerating dynamic time warping subsequence search with GPUs and FPGAs. In: 2010 IEEE International Conference on Data Mining, pp. 1001–1006, December 2010
16. Singh, J., Knapp, H.V., Arnold, J., Demissie, M.: Hydrological modeling of the iroquois river watershed using HSPF and SWAT. J. Am. Water Resour. Assoc. **41**(2), 343–360 (2005)
17. Slaninová, K., Kocyan, T., Martinovič, J., Dráždilová, P., Snášel, V.: Dynamic time warping in analysis of student behavioral patterns. In: Proceedings of the Dateso 2012 Annual International Workshop on DAtabases, TExts, Specifications and Objects. CEUR Workshop Proceedings, pp. 49–59 (2012)
18. Toyoda, M., Sakurai, Y.: Discovery of cross-similarity in data streams. In: Proceedings - International Conference on Data Engineering, pp. 101–104 (2010)
19. Xu, Q., Zheng, R.: Automated detection of burned-out luminaries using indoor positioning. In: International Conference on Indoor Positioning and Indoor Navigation, IPIN 2015 (2015)
20. Zhao, J., Liu, K., Wang, W., Liu, Y.: Adaptive fuzzy clustering based anomaly data detection in energy system of steel industry. Inf. Sci. **259**, 335–345 (2014)

Orthogonal Illuminations in Two Light-Source Photometric Stereo

Ryszard Kozera$^{(\boxtimes)}$ and Alexander Prokopenya

Faculty of Applied Informatics and Mathematics,
Warsaw University of Life Sciences - SGGW, Nowoursynowska str. 159,
02-776 Warsaw, Poland
ryszard.kozera@gmail.com, alexander_prokopenya@sggw.pl

Abstract. In this paper we investigate the case of ambiguous shape reconstruction from two light-source photometric stereo based on illuminating the unknown Lambertian surface. So-far this problem is merely well-understood for two linearly independent light-source directions with one illumination assumed as overhead. As already established, a necessary and sufficient condition to disambiguate the entire shape reconstruction process is controlled by the satisfaction of the corresponding second-order linear PDE with constant coefficients in two independent variables. This work extends the latter to an arbitrary pair of light-source directions transforming the above constraint into a special nonlinear PDE. In addition, a similar ambiguity analysis is also performed for a special configuration of two light-source directions assumed this time as orthogonal and contained in the vertical plane. Finally, this work is supplemented by illustrative examples exploiting symbolic computation used within a framework of continuous reflectance map model (i.e. an image irradiance equation) and applied to a genuine Lambertian surfaces.

Keywords: Photometric stereo · Image irradiance equation · Ambiguity in shape reconstruction · Computer vision

1 Problem Formulation

The task of surface reconstruction from its image (or images) poses one of the major challenges in computer vision. There are two common approaches adopted to tackle this problem. The first one (termed *a stereo-like method*) involves projective geometry tools applied to multiple camera images [1–3]. Solving the so–called *matching problem* constitutes here the gist of the entire reconstruction process based on incorporating the triangulation-like technique [1,2,4]. The second approach, coined *shape from shading* [3–5], relies on *a priori* knowledge of the physical properties of light reflectance inherent to the specific material coating the unknown surface S. In this model the surface S is assumed to be formed as a graph $S = graph(u)$ of the unknown C^k $(k = 0, 1)$ function $u : \Omega \to \mathbb{R}$ defined over an image domain $\Omega \subset \mathbb{R}^2$. Recall that the normal $n(s) = (n_1(s), n_2(s), n_3(s))$ to S at the point $s = (x, y, u(x, y)) \in S$ (with $n_3(s) < 0$) reads as $n(s) =$

© IFIP International Federation for Information Processing 2016
Published by Springer International Publishing Switzerland 2016. All Rights Reserved
K. Saeed and W. Homenda (Eds.): CISIM 2016, LNCS 9842, pp. 402–415, 2016.
DOI: 10.1007/978-3-319-45378-1_36

$(u_x(x, y), u_y(x, y), -1)$. Assuming a distant light–source (yielding a parallel light-beam along the direction $p = (p_1, p_2, p_3)$) the so-called *image irradiance equation*

$$R(u_x(x, y), u_y(x, y)) = E(x, y) \qquad (1)$$

encapsulates the relation between reflected light from surface S and absorbed light in the image Ω - see [4]. Here $E(x, y)$ denotes the intensity of the absorbed light at the image point $(x, y) \in \Omega$. On the other hand, R called *reflectance map* refers to the intensity of the reflected light from $s \in S$ with normal $n(s)$. In the special case of a Lambertian surface S_L, R_L is proportional to $\cos(\alpha)$, where α represents the angle between the normal $n(s)$ and a given light-source direction $p = (p_1, p_2, p_3)$ - see [4]. Consequently, for S_L the corresponding image irradiance Eq. (1) (over $\Omega = \{(x, y) \in \mathbb{R}^2 : 0 \le E(x, y) \le 1\}$) reads as:

$$\frac{\langle p|n(s) \rangle}{\|p\|\|n(s)\|} = \frac{p_1 u_x(x, y) + p_2 u_y(x, y) - p_3}{\sqrt{p_1^2 + p_2^2 + p_2^2}\sqrt{u_x^2(x, y) + u_y^2(x, y) + 1}} = E(x, y). \qquad (2)$$

By Cauchy-Schwartz inequality $|E(x, y)| \le 1$ holds. The extra condition required $E(x, y) \ge 0$ excludes shadowed (x, y)-points. The Eq. (2) yields the first order non-linear PDE (in two variables) modelling *a single image shape from shading* for S_L. Commonly, in solving (2) one usually searches for $u \in C^k$ ($k = 1, 2$), modulo a vertical shift $v = u + c$ (here c is an arbitrary constant). A single image irradiance Eq. (2) renders generically *an ill-posed problem* (see [6–10]). Though various mathematical extra assumptions can disambiguate (2) or limit its number of solutions [4,11–15], they often turn unrealistic or difficult to be met from real camera images.

A feasible remedy is to employ *a photometric stereo technique* for which the unknown surface S_L (or S) is consecutively illuminated by distant multiple light–sources positioned along linearly independent directions [4,16]. In this set-up, contrary to the classical stereo method relying on images taken from multiple cameras, only a single camera is deployed.

As demonstrated in [4,16,17], *three-light source photometric stereo* suffices to guarantee a unique surface $S_L = graph(u)$ (up to a vertical shift) with $u \in C^1$ satisfying the corresponding system of three image irradiance Eq. (2) (formulated for p, q and r) over an image $\Omega = \Omega_1 \cap \Omega_2 \cap \Omega_3$. The respective right-hand sides of (2) (i.e. the intensities $E_i \ge 0$ over Ω_i, for $i = 1, 2, 3$) are obtained by consecutive illuminations of S_L along three linearly independent directions p, q $r \in \mathbb{R}^3$. The entire reconstruction process is decomposed here into two following steps:

(a) *a gradient computation (an algebraic step)*:

$$u_x(x, y) = f_1(x, y, E_1, E_2, E_3), \qquad u_y(x, y) = f_2(x, y, E_1, E_2, E_3). \qquad (3)$$

In case of three light-sources the resulting vector field $\nabla u = (u_x, u_y)$ satisfying three equations of type (2) is uniquely determined in (3) in terms of image intensities E_i ($i = 1, 2, 3$) and light-source directions p, q and r - see [4,17].

(b) *a gradient integration (an analytic step):*

$$u(x, y) = u(x_0, y_0) + \int_\gamma u_x(x, y)dx + u_y(x, y)dy, \qquad (4)$$

where $(x_0, y_0), (x, y) \in \Omega$ and $\gamma : [t_0, t_1] \to \Omega$ is an arbitrary piecewise-C^1 curve such that $\gamma(t_0) = (x_0, y_0)$ and $\gamma(t_1) = (x, y)$. Note that (x_0, y_0) is fixed here and $u(x_0, y_0)$ represents any constant c. The choice of γ joining (x_0, y_0) with varying (x, y) is arbitrary (at least in continuous model of (1)), provided Ω is simply connected and the vector field (3) fulfills the so-called *integrability condition*. The latter reads for $u \in C^2$ as

$$u_{xy}(x, y) = u_{yx}(x, y), \qquad (5)$$

and for $u \in C^1$ as

$$\int_{\gamma_c} u_x(x, y)dx + u_y(x, y)dy = 0, \qquad (6)$$

holding for any piecewise-C^1 loop $\gamma_c \subset \Omega$ (with $\gamma_c(t_0) = \gamma_c(t_1)$). Assuming E_i ($i = 1, 2, 3$) are formed by a genuine Lambertian surface $S_L = graph(u)$, a unique vector field ∇u obtained from (3) is automatically integrable and hence the formula (4) determines an unambiguous $u \in C^1$ (up to a constant).

The case of *two-light source photometric stereo* requires more intricate analysis (see [17–19]). The respective system of two image irradiance equations:

$$\frac{p_1 u_x(x, y) + p_2 u_y(x, y) - p_3}{\sqrt{p_1^2 + p_2^2 + p_3^2}\sqrt{u_x^2(x, y) + u_y(x, y)^2 + 1}} = E_1(x, y),$$

$$\frac{q_1 u_x(x, y) + q_2 u_y(x, y) - q_3}{\sqrt{q_1^2 + q_2^2 + q_3^2}\sqrt{u_x^2(x, y) + u_y(x, y)^2 + 1}} = E_2(x, y) \qquad (7)$$

is solved by the following vector field (see [17, 18]):

$$u_x = \frac{\|p\|(q_1\langle p|q\rangle - p_1\|q\|^2)E_1 + \|q\|(p_1\langle p|q\rangle - q_1\|p\|^2)E_2 + (p_3q_2 - p_2q_3)\varepsilon\sqrt{\Lambda}}{\|p\|(p_3\|q\|^2 - q_3\langle p|q\rangle)E_1 + \|q\|(q_3\|p\|^2 - p_3\langle p|q\rangle)E_2 + (p_1q_2 - p_2q_1)\varepsilon\sqrt{\Lambda}},$$

$$u_y = \frac{\|p\|(q_2\langle p|q\rangle - p_2\|q\|^2)E_1 + \|q\|(p_2\langle p|q\rangle - q_2\|p\|^2)E_2 + (p_1q_3 - p_3q_1)\varepsilon\sqrt{\Lambda}}{\|p\|(p_3\|q\|^2 - q_3\langle p|q\rangle)E_1 + \|q\|(q_3\|p\|^2 - p_3\langle p|q\rangle)E_2 + (p_1q_2 - p_2q_1)\varepsilon\sqrt{\Lambda}}, \qquad (8)$$

where

$$\Lambda = \|p\|^2\|q\|^2 \left(1 - E_1^2(x, y) - E_2^2(x, y)\right) - \langle p|q\rangle \left(\langle p|q\rangle - 2\|p\|\|q\|E_1(x, y)E_2(x, y)\right) \quad (9)$$

with the function $\varepsilon(x, y)$ taking values ± 1 so that $f(x, y) = \varepsilon(x, y)\sqrt{\Lambda(x, y)}$ is continuous (for $u \in C^1$) or smooth (for $u \in C^2$).

As discussed in [17, 18] an image domain Ω is often decomposed into $\Omega = \Omega^{(1)} \cup \Omega^{(2)} \cup \Gamma$ with $\Lambda > 0$ over disjoint sub-domains $\Omega^{(j)} \subset \Omega$ (here $j = 1, 2$)

and with $\Lambda = 0$ satisfied along some smooth curve Γ. Consequently, over each component $\Omega^{(j)}$ either $\varepsilon(x,y) \equiv 1$ or $\varepsilon(x,y) \equiv -1$ hold, yielding the respective two vector fields $(u_x^{\pm}, u_y^{\pm})$ in (8) satisfying (7). Assuming E_1 and E_2 are generated by a genuine Lambertian surface S_L, at least one of these two pairs of vector fields (over each $\Omega^{(j)}$) is integrable.

The ambiguous case of more than one integrable vector field from (8) is well-understood merely for the special configuration of light-source directions, namely when $p = (0,0,-1)$ and $q = (q_1, q_2, q_3)$ (here $q_1^2 + q_2^2 > 0$) - see [17,18]. In fact, generically there is only one integrable vector field over each $\Omega^{(j)}$ (and thus over Ω). The latter is governed by the fulfillment of the tight condition (10). Indeed, given two simply connected sub-images $\Omega^{(j)}$, a necessary and sufficient condition enforcing both vector fields (u_x^+, u_y^+) and (u_x^-, u_y^-) to be integrable (and thus yielding the existence of $u^+, u^- \in C^2(\Omega^{(i)})$ solving (7)) reads as:

$$q_1 q_2 \left(u_{yy}(x,y) - u_{xx}(x,y) \right) + (q_1^2 - q_2^2) u_{xy}(x,y) = 0, \tag{10}$$

which is to be satisfied by either u^+ or u^-. In addition (see [17,18]), if one of u^+ (or of u^-) satisfies (10) then so does the complementary one i.e. u^- (or u^+). In a rare situation of (10) holding, both pairs (u^+, u^-), determined by (4) over $\Omega^{(j)}$ ($j = 1,2$), can *bifurcate (i.e. can be glued together) along the curve Γ* to yield either zero or two or four global solutions $u \in C^2$ over the whole image Ω (see [17,18]). As it turns out, there are extra geometrical relations between both graphs of u^+ and u^-. Indeed, let $K_u(x,y)$ denote the Gaussian curvature of the surface $S_L = graph(u)$ taken at the point $(x, y, u(x,y)) \in S_L$ and determined by the formula (see [20]):

$$K_u(x,y) = \frac{u_{xx}(x,y) u_{yy}(x,y) - u_{xy}^2(x,y)}{(1 + u_x^2(x,y) + u_y^2(x,y))^2}. \tag{11}$$

Interestingly, it is proved in [17,18] that if both (7) and (10) hold then:

$$K_{u^+}(x,y) = -K_{u^-}(x,y). \tag{12}$$

Consequently, if $s_1 = (x, y, u^{\pm}(x,y)) \in S_L^{\pm}$ yields *a hyperbolic point* (having negative Gaussian curvature) then $s_2 = (x, y, u^{\mp}(x,y)) \in S_L^{\mp}$ renders *an elliptic point* (having positive Gaussian curvature). Thus for $p = (0,0,-1)$ and $q = (q_1, q_2, q_3)$ the *convexity/concavity ambiguity* is automatically excluded. Noticeably, such ambiguity eventuates for single image shape from shading with $p = (0,0,-1)$ (see e.g. [4,8]). Finally, if s_1 is *a parabolic point* (with vanishing Gaussian curvature) then so is s_2.

This paper extends the above results with the following (see Sect. 2):

1. The necessary and sufficient condition (10) for testing the ambiguity in (7) is extended to arbitrary pairs of linearly independent light-source directions $p = (p_1, p_2, p_3)$ and $q = (q_1, q_2, q_3)$. Ultimately, such general case leads to the non-linear second-order PDE (see (18)), which inherently constitutes a challenging problem.

2. To alleviate the above difficulty, special configurations of two light-source directions (different from $p = (0, 0, -1)$ and $q = (q_1, q_2, q_3)$) are here admitted. Namely, the family of orthogonal unit vectors (parallel to OXZ-plane):

$$p_\alpha = (-\sqrt{1-\alpha^2}, 0, -\alpha), \quad q_\alpha = (\alpha, 0, -\sqrt{1-\alpha^2}) \tag{13}$$

(with $0 < \alpha < 1$) is considered. The corresponding analysis for solving (7) (with $p = p_\alpha$ and $q = q_\alpha$) addresses the uniqueness issue and establishes, in rare ambiguity cases, intrinsic geometrical inter-relations between multiple solutions in two light-source photometric stereo (see also Theorem 1).

The theoretical Sect. 2 is also supplemented (see Sect. 3) by illustrative examples supported by *Mathematica* numerical and symbolic computation applied to the continuous Lambertian model with pixels represented as ideal points $(x, y) \in \Omega$ and image intensities (E_1, E_2) simulated here from u as left-hand sides in (7). Finally, the closing Sect. 4 summarizes the main thrust of this paper together with indicating its extensions and hints their possible solutions.

2   Orthogonal Illumination Directions in Vertical Plane

In the first part of this section (i.e. in *(i)*) we consider an arbitrary configuration of linearly independent light-source directions p and q with $\|p\| = \|q\| = 1$. Under such general assumption, condition (10) (testing whether the second vector field from (8) over each $\Omega^{(j)}$ is also integrable) is subsequently extended to the nonlinear PDE expressed by (18). Noticeably, the latter constitutes a difficult task for further theoretical analysis. In order to deal with the latter somehow, a special case of orthogonal vectors p and q contained in the OXZ-plane is here admitted (see *(ii)*). The analysis to follow complements already established results in [17], covering a different special choice of $p = (0, 0, -1)$ and $q = (q_1, q_2, q_3)$ with $q_1^2 + q_2^2 > 0$.

(i) Assume now that E_1 and E_2 introduced in (7) are generated by a genuine Lambertian surface $S_L = graph(u)$, where $u \in C^2$. Evidently, still by (7) both image intensities are also expressible in terms of u_x and u_y. Using symbolic computation in *Mathematica* [21–23] (or alternatively see complicated proof in [17]) one arrives at:

$$\Lambda(x, y) = \frac{(u_x(p_2 q_3 - p_3 q_2) - u_y(p_1 q_3 - p_3 q_1) + p_2 q_1 - p_1 q_2)^2}{u_x^2 + u_y^2 + 1} = \frac{(\langle p \times q | n \rangle)^2}{u_x^2 + u_y^2 + 1}. \tag{14}$$

Combining the latter with (8) (over each $\Omega^{(j)}$ determined by $\Lambda > 0$) leads to:

$$u_x = \begin{cases} u_x, & \text{if } sgn(\varepsilon)sgn(\theta) > 0; \\ \frac{(a^2 - b^2 - c^2)u_x + 2acu_y + 2ab}{2abu_x + 2bcu_y + b^2 - a^2 - c^2}, & \text{if } sgn(\varepsilon)sgn(\theta) < 0 \end{cases} \tag{15}$$

and

$$u_y = \begin{cases} u_y, & \text{if } sgn(\varepsilon)sgn(\theta) > 0; \\ \frac{2acu_x + (c^2 - a^2 - b^2)u_y + 2bc}{2abu_x + 2bcu_y + b^2 - a^2 - c^2}, & \text{if } sgn(\varepsilon)sgn(\theta) < 0, \end{cases} \tag{16}$$

where

$$a = p_3 q_2 - p_2 q_3, \quad b = p_1 q_2 - p_2 q_1, \quad \text{and} \quad c = p_1 q_3 - p_3 q_1, \quad (17)$$

and $\theta = u_x(p_2 q_3 - p_3 q_2) - u_y(p_1 q_3 - p_3 q_1) + p_2 q_1 - p_1 q_2$. Here the function $\varepsilon = \varepsilon(x, y)$ is everywhere constant taking values ± 1. The first pair (u_x, u_y) from (15) and (16) satisfies integrability condition (5) over each $\Omega^{(j)}$ as $u \in C^2$. On the other hand, the integrability of the second vector field from (15) and (16) eventuates, if and only if:

$$\left(\frac{(a^2 - b^2 - c^2)u_x + 2acu_y + 2ab}{2abu_x + 2bcu_y + b^2 - a^2 - c^2} \right)_y = \left(\frac{2acu_x + (c^2 - a^2 - b^2)u_y + 2bc}{2abu_x + 2bcu_y + b^2 - a^2 - c^2} \right)_x.$$

Upon resorting to the symbolic computation in *Mathematica*, the last equation is transformable into *the following non-linear PDE*:

$$c\left(a - bu_x(x, y)\right)u_{yy}(x, y) + \left(a^2 - c^2 + bcu_y(x, y) - abu_x(x, y)\right)u_{xy}(x, y)$$
$$+ a\left(bu_y(x, y) - c\right)u_{xx}(x, y) = 0, \quad (18)$$

which is to be satisfied by u. Evidently, the latter does not hold generically and therefore *the resulting integrability condition* (18) *disambiguates almost always two-source photometric stereo modelled by* (7) - see also Example 1. Still, in a pursue of solving a rare ambiguity in (7), one ought to deal with (18) which inevitably leads to a non-trivial task. Thus in the next step *(ii)* of this section, a tighter constraint imposed on illumination directions p and q is considered.

(ii) Suppose now that two light-source directions p_α and q_α are introduced according to (13). The resulting two image irradiance equations coincide with:

$$\frac{\alpha - \sqrt{1 - \alpha^2}u_x(x, y)}{\sqrt{u_x^2(x, y) + u_y(x, y)^2 + 1}} = E_1(x, y), \quad \frac{\alpha u_x(x, y) + \sqrt{1 - \alpha^2}}{\sqrt{u_x^2(x, y) + u_y(x, y)^2 + 1}} = E_2(x, y). \quad (19)$$

Since $p_\alpha \perp q_\alpha$ (i.e. are orthogonal), the function Λ defined in (9) simplifies into:

$$\Lambda(x, y) = 1 - E_1^2(x, y) - E_2^2(x, y) = \frac{u_y^2(x, y)}{1 + u_x^2(x, y) + u_y^2(x, y)}. \quad (20)$$

Thus $\Omega_{\Lambda > 0} = \{(x, y) \in \Omega : u_y(x, y) \neq 0\}$ and $\Omega_{\Lambda \equiv 0} = \{(x, y) \in \Omega : u_y(x, y) = 0\}$. Similarly to the special case of $p = (0, 0, -1)$ and $q = (q_1, q_2, q_3)$ discussed in [17,18], often the triples u, p_α and q_α (see Example 1) yield $\Omega_{\Lambda > 0} = \Omega^{(1)} \cup \Omega^{(2)}$, with $\Omega^{(j)}$ $(j = 1, 2)$ standing for two disjoint sub-domains of Ω and $\Omega_{\Lambda \equiv 0} = \Gamma$ representing a smooth curve in Ω. Here *a bifurcation curve* (along which solutions over $\Omega^{(1)}$ and $\Omega^{(2)}$ are glued) coincides with the curve (overlapping with $\Omega_{\Lambda \equiv 0}$):

$$\Gamma = \{(x, y) \in \Omega : u_y(x, y) = 0\}. \quad (21)$$

Furthermore in (17) , since $p_2 = q_2 = 0$ then $a = b = 0$ and since $q_1 = -p_3 = \alpha$ and $p_1 = q_3 = -\sqrt{1 - \alpha^2}$ then $c = 1$. Consequently, both Formulae (15) and (16) are reducible into:

$$u_x = \begin{cases} u_x, & \text{if } sgn(\varepsilon)sgn(\theta) > 0; \\ \\ u_x, & \text{if } sgn(\varepsilon)sgn(\theta) < 0; \end{cases} \qquad u_y = \begin{cases} u_y, & \text{if } sgn(\varepsilon)sgn(\theta) > 0; \\ \\ -u_y, & \text{if } sgn(\varepsilon)sgn(\theta) < 0. \end{cases}$$
(22)

Thus for the non-generic case of the second vector field $(u_x, -u_y)$ also integrable (over each $\Omega^{(i)}$), the function u should satisfy *the following linear PDE*:

$$u_{xy}(x, y) = 0.$$
(23)

Note that the last equation can be independently reached by substituting $a = b = 0$ and $c = 1$ into (18). The generic case of (23) not fulfilled is illustrated also in Example 1. Upon double integration (first over x and then over y) of (23), the following representation for u (if two vector fields from (22) are to be integrable over $\Omega^{(i)}$) holds:

$$u(x, y) = \phi_1(x) + \psi_1(y),$$
(24)

for some twice continuously differentiable functions ϕ_1 and ψ_1 in a single variable. It is not difficult to show that $\phi_1(x) = u(x, 0) - c$, where $\psi_1(0) = c$. Similarly, $\psi(y) = u(0, y) - \phi_1(0) = u(0, y) - u(0, 0) + c$. Naturally, an analogous argument applies to the second solution $v \in C^2$ to (19) resulting in v satisfying (23) and hence $v(x, y) = \phi_2(x) + \psi_2(y)$, where ϕ_2 and ψ_2 are defined similarly to the introduction of ϕ_1 and ψ_1. Furthermore, by (22), the second function $v \in C^2$ (over each $\Omega^{(j)}$) fulfills $(v_x, v_y) = (u_x, -u_y)$. Combining the latter with $u_x(x, y) = \phi_1'(x)$, $u_y(x, y) = \psi_1'(y)$, $v_x(x, y) = \phi_2'(x)$ and $v_y(x, y) = \psi_2'(y)$ yields *"a conjugate-like" relation* between u and v:

$$u(x, y) = \phi_1(x) + \psi_1(y), \qquad v(x, y) = \phi_1(x) - \psi_1(y) + c_1,$$
(25)

with c_1 being a constant. Formula (25) determines specific analytic representations of the solutions to (19) over each $\Omega^{(j)}$ in a rare situation of the ambiguous two light-source photometric stereo. A straightforward verification shows that the geometrical constraint from (12) is also preserved for p_α and q_α. Indeed, combining (11) with (25) leads to $K_u(x, y) = (\phi_1''(x)\psi_1''(y))(1 + (\phi_1'(x))^2 + (\psi_1'(y))^2)^{-2} = -K_v(x, y)$. Note that the condition (21) coupled with (25) implies that Γ (or more general $\Omega_{\Lambda \equiv 0}$) represents a line $L = \{(x, y*) \in \Omega : \psi_1'(y*) = 0\}$ (or a collection of lines) parallel to the OX-axis. In addition, as $\nabla u = (u_x, u_y)$ and $\nabla v = (u_x, -u_y)$ visibly any critical point of u is also a critical point of v. Moreover, if such point represents a local minimum (maximum, saddle) for u then it is also a local maximum (minimum, saddle) for v. Note also that by (21) any critical point of u (and thus of v) belongs to the set $\Omega_{\Lambda \equiv 0}$ and thus to the potential bifurcation curve Γ. The non-generic ambiguity case discussed above for p_α and q_α is illustrated in Example 2.

Evidently, as (18) or (23) are generically not fulfilled, there exists only one solution $u \in C^2$ to (7) or (19) over each $\Omega^{(j)}$. Upon gluing u together, only *one global solution $u \in C^2$ prevails over entire image Ω*. On the other hand, the rare scenario of the existence of two solutions $u, v \in C^2$ over each $\Omega^{(j)}$ (i.e. satisfying (23)) leads to *the possible bifurcations along Γ rendering 0, 2 or 4 global solutions* of class C^2 over entire image Ω. Recall that we assume here $\Omega = \Omega^{(1)} \cup \Omega^{(2)} \cup \Gamma$. The other decomposition topologies of $\Omega = \Omega_{\Lambda>0} \cup \Omega_{\Lambda=0}$ are discussed in [17]. The detailed analysis justifying necessary and sufficient conditions to guarantee successful C^k bifurcations ($k = 0, 1, 2$) (in case of $\Omega = \Omega^{(1)} \cup \Omega^{(2)} \cup \Gamma$) holding along Γ exceeds the scope of this paper and therefore is here omitted.

Taking into account the above argument, the main theoretical contribution of this paper can be summarized into the following:

Theorem 1. *Assume that $u \in C^2$ (which graph $S_L = graph(u)$ represents an illuminated genuine Lambertian surface) satisfies (19) or (7) with p_α and q_α determined by (13) (or with arbitrary linearly independent p and q). Suppose, moreover that Λ in (9) satisfies $\Lambda > 0$ over simply-connected $\Omega^{(j)}$ ($j = 1, 2$). In order that there exists only one more solution $v \in C^2$ to (19) over $\Omega^{(j)}$ it is necessary and sufficient for u to satisfy (23) or (18). In addition, the ambiguous case for p_α and q_α yields $u(x, y) = \phi(x) + \psi(y)$ and $v(x, y) = \phi(x) - \psi(y)$, with ϕ and ψ determined as in (24). Finally, the Gaussian curvatures of graphs of u and v at respective points $(x, y, u(x, y))$ and $(x, y, v(x, y))$ (see (11)) satisfy $K_u(x, y) = -K_v(x, y)$.*

As already pointed out, a local ambiguity to (19) or (7) (over $\Omega_{\Lambda>0}$) can even be more proliferated to a global one (over entire image Ω) due to possible bifurcations of u and v along $\Omega_{\Lambda\equiv0}$. The matter gets more complicated if $\Omega_{\Lambda\equiv0}$ forms an open subset of Ω (see [17,18]). The latter occurs once $\langle p \times q | n \rangle = 0$ as implied by (14). Due to these intricacies, the respective discussion on bifurcation issue in two light-source photometric stereo is here left out.

3   Experiments

This section includes two examples illustrating the main results established in Sect. 2 (see also Theorem 1). The experiments presented here are carried out with the aid of *Mathematica* symbolic computation. The corresponding pictures of images (with the respective intensities E_1 and E_1) are simulated synthetically upon admitting arbitrary or specific illumination directions and assuming a genuine u as temporarily initially given.

Example 1. (a) Consider a *Lambertian hemi-sphere* $S_L^1 = graph(u_1)$ with $u_1 \in C^2(\hat{\Omega})$ defined as $u_1(x, y) = \sqrt{R^2 - x^2 - y^2}$, where $\hat{\Omega} = \{(x, y) \in \mathbb{R}^2 : x^2 + y^2 \leq R^2\}$. For two linearly independent normalized light-source directions p and q the respective image irradiance equations read as:

$$\frac{p_1 u_x + p_2 u_y - p_3}{\sqrt{u_x^2 + u_y^2 + 1}} = E_{11}(x, y) = \frac{-p_1 x - p_2 y - p_3 \sqrt{R^2 - x^2 - y^2}}{R},$$

$$\frac{q_1 u_x + q_2 u_y - q_3}{\sqrt{u_x^2 + u_y^2 + 1}} = E_{21}(x, y) = \frac{-q_1 x - q_2 y - q_3 \sqrt{R^2 - x^2 - y^2}}{R}, \quad (26)$$

over $\Omega = \Omega_1 \cap \Omega_2 \cap \hat{\Omega}$, where $\Omega_i = \{(x,y) \in \mathbb{R}^2 : E_{i1}^1(x,y) \geq 0\}$ (for $i = 1, 2$). The negative values of E_{i1} represent shadowed subareas of $\hat{\Omega}$. The bifurcation curve Γ (see (14)) reduces into a planar quadratic determined by:

$$(p_3 q_2 - p_2 q_3)x - (p_3 q_1 - p_1 q_3)y + (p_2 q_1 - p_1 q_2)\sqrt{R^2 - x^2 - y^2} = 0. \qquad (27)$$

Furthermore, the condition (18) ascertaining the existence of exactly one solution $u_1 \in C^2(\Omega)$ (modulo its vertical shift) to (26) enforces u_1 to satisfy:

$$(cx - ay)\left(ax + cy - b\sqrt{R^2 - x^2 - y^2}\right) = 0, \qquad (28)$$

over $\Omega^{(j)}$, with a, b and c defined as in (17). Clearly, the Eq. (28) is not satisfied by u_1 for all $(x,y) \in \Omega^{(j)}$. This yields *uniqueness in solving* (26) (i.e. $u = u_1$) within $u \in C^2(\Omega)$. In particular, for p_α and q_α (see (13)), (17) combined with $a = b = 0$ and $c = 1$ reduce (27) into $y = 0$ rendering $\Gamma = \{(x,y) \in \hat{\Omega} : y = 0\}$, $\Omega^{(1)} = \{(x,y) \in \Omega : y < 0\}$ and $\Omega^{(2)} = \{(x,y) \in \Omega : y > 0\}$. The ambiguity condition (28) is transformed into $xy = 0$ merely fulfilled along both X- and Y-axes. Hence, again for arbitrary p_α and q_α, *uniqueness of u_1 prevails*. This is expected since p_α and q_α represents a special case of general positions of p and q analyzed above.

(b) Let *a Lambertian hill-like surface* $S_L^2 = graph(u_2)$ with $u_2 \in C^2(\hat{\Omega})$ be defined according to $u_2(x,y) = (2(1 + x^2 + y^2))^{-1}$, over e.g. $\hat{\Omega} = \{(x,y) \in \mathbb{R}^2 : |x| \leq 1 \text{ and } |y| \leq 1\}$. The respective two image irradiance equations read as:

$$\frac{p_1 u_x + p_2 u_y - p_3}{\sqrt{u_x^2 + u_y^2 + 1}} = E_{12}(x,y) = \frac{-p_1 x - p_2 y - p_3(x^2 + y^2 + 1)^2}{\sqrt{x^2 + y^2 + (x^2 + y^2 + 1)^4}},$$

$$\frac{q_1 u_x + q_2 u_y - q_3}{\sqrt{u_x^2 + u_y^2 + 1}} = E_{22}(x,y) = \frac{-q_1 x - q_2 y - q_3(x^2 + y^2 + 1)^2}{\sqrt{x^2 + y^2 + (x^2 + y^2 + 1)^4}}, \qquad (29)$$

over unshadowed $\Omega = \Omega_1 \cap \Omega_2 \cap \hat{\Omega}$, where $\Omega_i = \{(x,y) \in \mathbb{R}^2 : E_{i2}^1(x,y) \geq 0\}$ (for $i = 1, 2$). The bifurcation curve Γ from (14) is defined by the following equation:

$$(p_2 q_1 - p_1 q_2) + \frac{(p_3 q_2 - p_2 q_3)x}{2(1 + x^2 + y^2)^{3/2}} + \frac{(p_3 q_1 - p_1 q_3)y}{2(1 + x^2 + y^2)^{3/2}} = 0. \qquad (30)$$

On the other hand, the integrability condition (18) stipulates u_2 to satisfy

$$(cx - ay)\left(b + 6(ax + cy)\sqrt{1 + x^2 + y^2}\right) = 0, \qquad (31)$$

over $\Omega^{(j)}$, with a, b and c introduced as in (17). Again, (31) is not fulfilled by u_2 for all $(x,y) \in \Omega^{(j)}$. Hence there exists *a unique solution of class C^2* to (29) (i.e. $u = u_2$) over Ω. In the special case of p_α and q_α (see (13)), (17) coupled with $a = b = 0$ and $c = 1$ transform (30) into $y = 0$. Hence again $\Gamma = \{(x,y) \in \hat{\Omega} : y = 0\}$, $\Omega^{(1)} = \{(x,y) \in \Omega : y < 0\}$ and $\Omega^{(2)} = \{(x,y) \in \Omega : y > 0\}$.

Furthermore the ambiguity constraint (31) is reduced into $xy = 0$ which holds again only along both X- and Y-axes. Thus for p_α and q_α *the uniqueness of u_2 to (29) eventuates* (as also follows from the above general (p,q)-position analysis).

Example 2. Consider now *a Lambertian paraboloid $S_L^3 = graph(u_3)$* with $u_3 \in C^2(\hat{\Omega})$ defined as $u_3(x,y) = (x^2+y^2)/2$ over $\hat{\Omega} = \{(x,y) \in \mathbb{R}^2 : |x| \leq 1 \text{ and } |y| \leq 1\}$. For a general position of p and q, the integrability condition (18) reads here as $b(ay - cx) = 0$. Provided $b \neq 0$, such constraint never holds over any open subset of Ω and thus *uniqueness* of u_3 follows. Noticeably the bifurcation curve Γ (a line) is determined here by $p_2q_1 - p_1q_2 + (p_2q_3 - p_3q_2)x + (p_3q_1 - p_1q_3)y = 0$.

For p_α and q_α from (13) the resulting two image irradiance equations are:

$$\frac{\alpha - \sqrt{1 - \alpha^2}\, u_x(x,y)}{\sqrt{u_x^2(x,y) + u_y(x,y)^2 + 1}} = E_{13}(x,y) = \frac{\alpha - \sqrt{1 - \alpha^2}\, x}{\sqrt{x^2 + y^2 + 1}},$$

$$\frac{\alpha u_x(x,y) + \sqrt{1 - \alpha^2}}{\sqrt{u_x^2(x,y) + u_y(x,y)^2 + 1}} = E_{23}(x,y) = \frac{\alpha x + \sqrt{1 - \alpha^2}}{\sqrt{x^2 + y^2 + 1}}, \qquad (32)$$

over $\Omega_\alpha = \hat{\Omega}$ (for $\alpha = 1/\sqrt{2}$) and over $\Omega_\alpha = \{(x,y) \in \hat{\Omega}_\alpha : -1 \leq x \leq 0.204\}$ (for $\alpha = 1/5$). Figure 1 shows images of S_L^3 with $\alpha = 1/\sqrt{2}$ over $\Omega_{1/\sqrt{2}} = \hat{\Omega} = [-1,1] \times [-1,1]$. The bifurcation curve Γ_α in (21) coincides here with the X-axis (i.e. here $y = 0$) trimmed either to $-1 \leq x \leq 1$ or to $-1 \leq x \leq 0.204$, for $\alpha = 1/\sqrt{2}$ or $\alpha = 1/5$, respectively. The remaining decomposition components of Ω_α (along which $\Lambda > 0$) read as $\Omega_\alpha^{(1)} = \{(x,y) \in \Omega_\alpha : y > 0\}$ and $\Omega_\alpha^{(2)} = \{(x,y) \in \Omega_\alpha : y < 0\}$ - see Fig. 2. Furthermore, since by (17) the constant $b = 0$, the ambiguity condition $b(ay - cx) = 0$ is now satisfied. Hence, upon combining (25) with $\phi(x) = x^2/2$ and $\psi(y) = y^2/2$, *the only one another C^2 solution* to (32) equals to $u_4(x,y) = (x^2 - y^2)/2$ (modulo a vertical shift), over each $\Omega_\alpha^{(j)}$ (here $j = 1,2$). Once u_k are glued with itself ($k = 3,4$) along X-axis, *two C^2 class global solutions* to (32) over entire image Ω_α are defined (i.e. u_3 and u_4) - see Fig. 3 for $\alpha = 1/\sqrt{2}$ (with gluing curve). On the other hand the local solutions u_3 (or u_4) over $\Omega_\alpha^{(1)}$ cross-bifurcate along

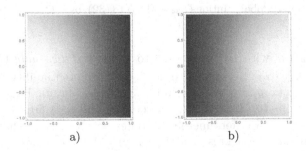

a)   b)

Fig. 1. Two images of $S_L^3 = graph(u_3)$ illuminated along $p_{1/\sqrt{2}}$ and $q_{1/\sqrt{2}}$ directions.

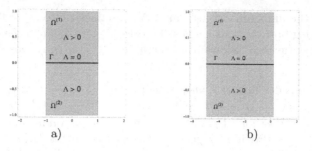

a)   b)

Fig. 2. Decomposition of $\Omega_\alpha = \Omega_\alpha^{(1)} \cup \Omega_\alpha^{(2)} \cup \Gamma_\alpha$ for (32) with (a) $\alpha = 1/\sqrt{2}$, (b) $\alpha = 1/5$.

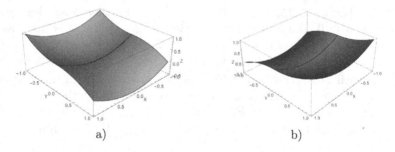

a)   b)

Fig. 3. Two C^2 class global solutions u_3 and u_4 to (32), over $\Omega_{1/\sqrt{2}} = [-1,1] \times [-1,1]$.

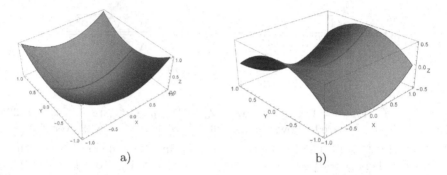

a)   b)

Fig. 4. Two C^1 class global solutions u_{34} and u_{43} to (32), over $\Omega_{1/\sqrt{2}} = [-1,1] \times [-1,1]$.

$\Gamma_{1/\sqrt{2}}$ with u_4 (or with u_3) over $\Omega_\alpha^{(2)}$ to yield *next two only C^1 class solutions* u_{34} and u_{43} to (32) over Ω_α. Indeed, a C^2 differentiability is excluded as $\lim_{(x,y)\to(x,0)} u_{3yy}(x,y) = 2 \neq -2 = \lim_{(x,y)\to(x,0)} u_{4yy}(x,y)$. The remaining two C^1 global solutions to (32) over $\Omega_{1/\sqrt{2}}$ (i.e. u_{34} and u_{43}) are plotted in Fig. 4. The case for $\alpha = 1/5$ differs merely by different $\Omega_{1/5}$. Note that by (11) the respective Gaussian curvatures yield $K_{u_3}(x,y) = 4(1+x^2+y^2)^{-2} = -K_{u_4}(x,y)$ which is consistent with Theorem 1. A unique critical point $(0,0)$ of u_3, u_4, u_{34} and u_{43} belongs, as expected to Γ.

4   Conclusion

This paper extends the claims of [17,18], where a special configuration of two light-source directions $p = (0,0,-1)$ and $q = (q_1, q_2, q_3)$ (for $q_1^2 + q_2^2 > 0$) in photometric stereo is studied. In particular, a respective integrability condition expressed by the non-linear PDE (18) is derived here for a general configuration of linearly independent p and q. Not unexpectedly, such PDE forms a difficult theoretical problem and consequently a new family of orthogonal illumination directions p_α and q_α is introduced in (13). The corresponding system of two image irradiance Eq. (19) is subsequently analyzed and the resulting ambiguity versus uniqueness question is addressed in Theorem 1. As proved in this paper, similar ambiguity results are obtainable for p_α and q_α defined in (13) (see Theorem 1 and Sect. 1) as compared to those already established in [17,18] for $p = (0,0,-1)$ and $q = (q_1, q_2, q_3)$. The experiments reported in Sect. 3 illustrate the main results from Sect. 2. *A possible extension of this paper* includes a relevant ambiguity analysis performed for the general positions of two linearly independent light-source directions. Inevitably, any pending argument would rely on characterizing the multiple solutions to the non-linear PDE defined in (18). Another worth investigation venue is to complete a global uniqueness-ambiguity analysis for two image photometric stereo over entire image Ω (see also [17,18]). The latter should first cover the case of p_α and q_α defined in (13) and then should refer to an arbitrary selection of two linearly independent illumination directions. In particular, an extra attention should be paid here in derivation of analytical and numerical methods designed to localize possible bifurcation curve(s) Γ. Some relevant clues concerning this task can be found in [24–28,30]. Finally, a similar analysis based on real Lambertian images, where pixelization and noise occur, forms another vital extension topic of this paper. Usually, handling noisy and digitized image data requires a more robust integration techniques dealing computationally with u recovery phase determined by theoretical formula (4). Such analytic step is often substituted by the pertinent optimization task designed to compute numerically *the closest discrete integrable vector field* - for more see e.g. [4,5,29].

References

1. Hartley, R., Zisserman, R.: Multiple View Geometry in Computer Vision. Cambridge University Press, Cambridge (2003)
2. Faugeras, O.: Three-Dimensional Computer Vision - A Geometric View Point. MIT Press, Cambridge (2001)
3. Trucco, E.: Introductory Techniques for 3-D Computer Vision. Prentice Hall, Englewood Cliffs (1998)
4. Horn, B.K.P.: Robot Vision. MIT Press, Cambridge (2001)
5. Horn, B.K.P., Brooks, M.J.: Shape from Shading. MIT Press, Cambridge (1989)
6. Brooks, M.J., Chojnacki, W., Kozera, R.: Shading without shape. Q. Appl. Math. **50**(1), 27–38 (1992)

7. Brooks, M.J., Chojnacki, W., Kozera, R.: Circularly symmetrical eikonal equations and non-uniqueness in computer vision. J. Math. Anal. Appl. **165**(1), 192–215 (1992)
8. Brooks, M.J., Chojnacki, W., Kozera, R.: Impossible and ambiguous shading patterns. Int. J. Comput. Vis. **7**(1), 119–126 (1992)
9. Bruss, A.R.: The eikonal equation: some results applicable to computer vision. J. Math. Phys. **5**(23), 890–896 (1982)
10. Kozera, R.: On complete integrals and uniqueness in shape from shading. Appl. Math. Comput. **73**(1), 1–37 (1995)
11. Deift, P., Sylvester, J.: Some remarks on shape-from-shading in computer vision. J. Math. Anal. Appl. **1**(84), 235–248 (1991)
12. Oliensis, J.: Uniqueness in shape from shading. Int. J. Comput. Vis. **6**(2), 75–104 (1991)
13. Chojnacki, W., Brooks, M.J.: A direct computation of shape from shading. In: Proceedings of 12-th International Conference on Artificial Intelligence and Pattern Recognition, Haifa, Israel, pp. 114–119 (1994)
14. Kimmel, R., Bruckstein, A.: Tracking level sets by level sets: a method of solving the shape from shading problem. Comput. Vis. Graph. Image Underst. **62**, 47–58 (1995)
15. Kozera, R.: Uniqueness in shape from shading revisited. Int. J. Math. Imaging Vis. **7**, 123–138 (1997)
16. Woodham, R.J.: Photometric stereo: a reflectance map technique for determining surface orientation from multiple images. Opt. Eng. **19**(1), 139–144 (1980)
17. Kozera, R.: Existence and uniqueness in photometric stereo. Appl. Math. Comput. **44**(1), 1–104 (1991)
18. Kozera, R.: On shape recovery from two shading patterns. Int. J. Pattern Recogn. Artif. Intell. **6**(4), 673–698 (1992)
19. Onn, R., Bruckstein, A.M.: Integrability disambiguates surface recovery in two-image photometric stereo. Int. J. Comput. Vis. **5**(1), 105–113 (1990)
20. Do Carmo, M.P.: Differential Geometry of Curves and Surfaces. Prentice-Hall, Englewood Cliffs (1986)
21. Wolfram Mathematica 9, Documentation Center. http://reference.wolfram.com/mathematica/guide/Mathematica.html
22. Budzko, D.A., Prokopenya, A.N.: Symbolic-numerical methods for searching equilibrium states in a restricted four-body problem. Program. Comput. Softw. **39**(2), 74–80 (2013)
23. Budzko, D.A., Prokopenya, A.N.: Symbolic-numeric analysis of the equilibrium solutions in the restricted four-body problem. Program. Comput. Softw. **36**(2), 68–74 (2010)
24. Kozera, R.: Curve modeling via interpolation based on multidimensional reduced data. Stud. Inform. **25**(4B–61), 1–140 (2004)
25. Boor, C.: A Practical Guide to Spline. Springer, Heidelberg (1985)
26. Kozera, R., Noakes, L., Klette, R.: External versus internal parameterizations for lengths of curves with nonuniform samplings. In: Asano, T., Klette, R., Ronse, C. (eds.) Geometry, Morphology, and Computational Imaging. LNCS, vol. 2616, pp. 403–418. Springer, Heidelberg (2003)
27. Kvasov, B.I.: Methods of Shape-Preserving Spline Approximation. World Scientific, Singapore (2000)
28. Kozera, R., Noakes, L.: Piecewise-quadratics and exponential parameterization for reduced data. Appl. Math. Comput. **221**, 620–638 (2013)

29. Noakes, L., Kozera, R.: Non-linearities and noise reduction in 3-source photometric stereo. J. Math. Imaging Vis. **18**(2), 119–127 (2003)
30. Atamanyuk, I.P., Kondratenko, V.Y., Kozlov, O.V., Kondratenko, Y.P.: The algorithm of optimal polynomial extrapolation of random processes. In: Engemann, K.J., Gil-Lafuente, A.M., Merigó, J.M. (eds.) MS 2012. LNBIP, vol. 115, pp. 78–87. Springer, Heidelberg (2012)

Graph Clustering Using Early-Stopped Random Walks

Małgorzata Lucińska[1]($\boxtimes$) and Sławomir T. Wierzchoń[2]

[1] Kielce University of Technology, Kielce, Poland
lucinska@tu.kielce.pl
[2] Institute of Computer Science Polish Academy of Sciences, Warsaw, Poland

Abstract. Very fast growth of empirical graphs demands clustering algorithms with nearly-linear time complexity. We propose a novel approach to clustering, based on random walks. The idea is to relax the standard spectral method and replace eigenvectors with vectors obtained by running early-stopped random walks. We abandoned iterating the random walk algorithm to convergence but instead stopped it after the time that is short compared with the mixing time. The computed vectors constitute a local approximation of the leading eigenvectors. The algorithm performance is competitive to the traditional spectral solutions in terms of computational complexity. We empirically evaluate the proposed approach against other exact and approximate methods. Experimental results show that the use of the early stop procedure does not influence the quality of the clustering on the tested real world data sets.

Keywords: Graph clustering · Random walks · Convergence rate

1 Introduction

Graph partitioning is the problem of dividing a graph into groups, with dense connections within groups and only sparser connections between them. It is an ubiquitous technique which has applications in many fields of computer science and engineering, such as image segmentation [16], in the World Wide Web [7], in biochemical neural networks [24], and in bioinformatics for protein family classification [5] among others.

Graph partitioning methods can also be categorized as either global or local optimizers. Global methods try to discover structure of the whole graph. In local partitioning, the goal is to find a group containing a given seed vertex. Hence, essentially, it is the task of finding a bipartition of the graph into two vertex sets.

A class of algorithms widely used to detect clusters in graphs is based on spectral methods, [12]. Here, to partition a graph, the eigenvectors of a suitably chosen matrix are used. This matrix represents connectivity between vertices

© IFIP International Federation for Information Processing 2016
Published by Springer International Publishing Switzerland 2016. All Rights Reserved
K. Saeed and W. Homenda (Eds.): CISIM 2016, LNCS 9842, pp. 416–428, 2016.
DOI: 10.1007/978-3-319-45378-1_37

to be grouped. The eigenvector associated to the second smallest eigenvalue of the matrix is called the Fiedler vector, named after Fiedler for his contributions to algebraic graph theory [6]. The Fiedler vector is one of the most important spectral characteristics, carrying information about structural properties of the graph.

As spectral algorithms represent global partitioning methods, they are relatively slow and thus have been mostly superseded by faster local algorithms, see e.g. [13]. Moreover, global solutions are infeasible in cases of graphs with only partly known structure, as for example the WWW network.

We propose a solution that combines the spectral method with lazy random walks. In our algorithm the Fiedler vector is approximated by running lazy random walk. After choosing a seed vertex A, for each vertex i, we update the probability of being absorbed by this A before the random walker will be captured by other distant vertex. The method is local in the sense that we obtained a rough, local approximation of the Fiedler vector by early stopping the updating process. Random walk process is not run till the convergence but stopped after the maximum probability change does not exceed an established threshold. Our method allows for bipartitioning graphs in times that scale almost linearly with their size. The procedure is motivated by machine learning practices, that try to find not an exact solution but more general one, not influenced by noise or mistakes. We have verified our approach experimentally, using real-world testing sets, including protein networks.

In Sect. 2 the notation and related terms are presented, later we give basic facts concerning random walks. The next section describes related works. Our solution is presented in details in Sect. 5. Then, in Sect. 6, we compare performance of our algorithm with another solution. Finally, in Sect. 7, the main conclusions are drawn.

2   Notation and Related Terms

Let $G = (V, E)$ be a graph with the vertex set V and the edge set $E \subseteq V^2$. The graph is undirected, i.e. each edge $e \in E$ is an unordered pair of nodes from V, and simple, i.e. the graph has no loops.

The matrix $\mathbf{S} = [s_{ij}]$ plays a role of the affinity matrix for G. The degree of a node i equals $d(i) = \sum_j s_{ij}$, and $\mathbf{D}$ is the diagonal matrix with $d(i)$'s on its diagonal. In our solution we use an adjacency matrix $\mathbf{A} = [a_{ij}]$ with $a_{ij} = 0$ if there is an edge between i-th and j-th vertex and $a_{ij} = 0$.

A clustering $\mathcal{C} = \{C_1, C_2, ...C_K\}$ is a partitioning of V into the nonempty mutually disjoint subsets $C_1, C_2, ...C_K$.

The Laplacian matrix associated with graph G is the $n \times n$ matrix $\mathbf{L} = \mathbf{D} - \mathbf{S}$. Since $\mathbf{S}$ is a symmetric matrix, $\mathbf{L}$ is also symmetric. The normalized Laplacian, is defined as: $\mathbf{L}_n = \mathbf{D}^{-1/2}\mathbf{L}\mathbf{D}^{-1/2}$. The right eigenvector associated to the second smallest eigenvalue of the Laplacian matrix is called the Fiedler vector [6]. As it carries significant structural information regarding the connectivity of the graph it forms the basis of spectral graph partitioning heuristics, see, e.g. [12] for a review. The Fiedler vector of **L** is used to produce a bipartition of the graph such that those vertices that have negative values in the eigenvector form one side of the bipartition G_S and the vertices with positive values are the other side $G\backslash G_S$. For motivation of the use of Fiedler vectors for graph bipartitioning consult e.g. [12].

3 Random Walks on Graphs

Most of the information included in this section comes from the survey of Lovász [11].

Given a graph G we can define simple random walk on G. Consider a random walker, who initially starts at the origin vertex j. At each step the walker picks uniformly at random one neighboring vertex i and moves to it with the following probability:

$$P(j,i) = \begin{cases} \frac{1}{d(j)} & \text{if } j \sim i \\ 0 & \text{otherwise} \end{cases} \tag{1}$$

Let A and B be two vertices of the graph G. The probability $p(i)$ that a random walker starting at node i reaches the node A before it reaches node B equals:

$$p(i) = \sum_{j \sim i} \frac{1}{d_i} p(j) \tag{2}$$

If we know the probability $p(j)$ that each of the neighbors of node i sent a random walker to A before B then $p(i)$ is an average of these probabilities. One can see a striking similarity between the probability vector p and the Fiedler vector. Each Laplacian eigenvalue λ and the corresponding eigenvector **f** fulfil the following equation:

$$\mathbf{Df} - \lambda \mathbf{f} = \mathbf{Sf} \tag{3}$$

and after transformation:

$$(d_i - \lambda)f_i = \sum_{j \sim i} f_j \tag{4}$$

As the second Laplacian eigenvalue is usually mach smaller than the degree of a vertex, we receive the following approximation for the i-th component of the Fiedler vector:

$$f_i \approx \frac{\sum_{j \sim i} f_j}{d_i} \tag{5}$$

Taking into consideration formulas (2) and (5) we can see that the vector p can constitute a good approximation of the Fiedler vector, especially for components corresponding to vertices with high degrees. If the second eigenvalue of the Laplacian equals zero (as in a case of two or more groups) formula 5 gives exact values of the Fiedler vector components.

This version of the random walks has one major drawback. It does not always converge: consider for instance a bipartite one-dimensional graph; the walk started at a vertex on the left will continue hopping back and forth between left and right without ever converging to any distribution.

Since $\mathbf{W} = \mathbf{D}^{-1}\mathbf{S}$ is the natural random walk transition matrix associated with a connected, undirected graph G, it follows that:

$$\mathbf{Z} = \alpha\mathbf{I} + (1-\alpha)\mathbf{W} \tag{6}$$

represents one step of the α-lazy random walk transition matrix, in which at each step there is a holding probability $\alpha \in [0,1]$. In a lazy random walk at time t the walker:

- takes a step of the original random walk with probability $1 - \alpha$,
- stays at the current vertex with probability α.

The probability that in the step $t + 1$ he is at the vertex i equals:

$$pr_{t+1}(i) = \alpha pr_t(i) + (1-\alpha)\sum_{i\sim j}\frac{1}{d_j}pr_t(j) \tag{7}$$

Regardless of starting distribution, lazy random walk always converges to stable distribution. In stable distribution, every vertex is visited with probability proportional to its degree:

$$\pi(j) = \frac{d(j)}{\sum_i d(i)}$$

The fact that $\mathbf{W}$ and $\mathbf{Z}$ are not symmetric matrices makes their analysis complicated. The normalized lazy random walk matrix is defined as:

$$\mathbf{Z_s} = \mathbf{D}^{1/2}\mathbf{Z}\mathbf{D}^{-1/2} = \alpha\mathbf{I} + (1-\alpha)\mathbf{D}^{-1/2}\mathbf{S}\mathbf{D}^{-1/2}$$

The matrices $\mathbf{Z_s}$ and $\mathbf{Z}$ have the same eigenvalues and related eigenvectors. If $\mathbf{Z}$ has eigenvalue μ_i with an eigenvector f_i, $\mathbf{Z_s}$ has the same eigenvalue with eigenvector $\mathbf{D}^{1/2}f$. Moreover the eigenvalues μ_i of the matrices $\mathbf{Z}$ and $\mathbf{Z_s}$ are related with the eigenvalues ω of the matrix $\mathbf{W}$ in the following way: $\mu_i = \alpha + (1-\alpha)\omega_i$. On the other hand matrices $\mathbf{W}$ and $\mathbf{L_n}$ have the same eigenvalues.

Let pr_0 be an arbitrary initial distribution, and pr_t be the distribution after t steps of the lazy random walk. Then the rate of convergence of the lazy random walk to the stationary distribution π [11],

$$\|pr_t - \pi\|_2 \leq (1-\lambda)^t \cdot \sqrt{\frac{\max_j d(j)}{\min_i d(i)}} \tag{8}$$

where λ is the spectral gap defined as the difference between the first and the second eigenvalues of $\mathbf{Z}$: $\lambda = \mu_1 - \mu_2$. The eigenvalues of $\mathbf{W}$ lie in $[-1,1]$, and thus those of $\mathbf{Z}$ lie in $[-1+2\alpha, 1]$. We can think of α as a constant in $[0,1]$, so the smallest eigenvalue is bounded away from -1. The largest eigenvalue is still 1. For any connected graph, the gap is simply:

$$\lambda = (1-\alpha)(\omega_1 - \omega_2) \tag{9}$$

Then for any $\epsilon > 0$ the number of steps t_ϵ for the lazy random walk distribution p_t to be within ϵ of the stationary distribution π is $O(\frac{1}{\lambda(G)} \log \frac{\bar{d}(G)}{\epsilon})$, where $\bar{d}(G) = max_{j,i \in V} \frac{d(j)}{d(i)}$ is the degree of G.

4 Literature Overview

The new trend is to replace eigenvectors with vectors obtained by running random walks. As it was showed in Sect. 3 the second eigenvector of the Laplacian can be approximately computed by iterating random walks. In a case of early stopping of distribution evaluation one does not obtain an eigenvector, but either an approximate eigenvector or a locally-biased analogue of the leading eigenvector. An important aspect of replacing an eigenvector with a random walk early distribution vector is its robustness. Mahoney [13] explained the idea on the ground of machine learning. Let us suppose that there is a "ground truth" graph that we want to partition, but the graph that we actually have available to compute with, is a noisy version of this ground truth graph. So, if we want to compute the leading nontrivial eigenvector of the unseen graph, then computing the leading nontrivial eigenvector of the observed graph is in general not a good idea. The reason is that it can be very sensitive to noise, e.g., mistakes or noise in the edges. On the other hand, if we perform a random walk and keep the random walk vector, then that is a better estimate of the ground truth eigendirection. The idea is that eigenvectors are unstable but random walks are not unstable.

One of the first early-stopped solution presented Wu and Huberman [21] in their clustering algorithm. They applied an electrical circuit analogue in order to reveal a graph structure. They imagined each edge to be a resistor with the same resistance, and connected a battery between A and B so that they have fixed electrical potentials, eg. 1 and 0. Vertices A and B belong to different clusters. Having made these assumptions the graph can be viewed as an electric circuit and current flows through each edge (resistor) as random walks. By solving Kirchhoff equations they obtained the potential value of each node. Using this information it is possible to partition the graph into two parts. A node belongs to G_1 if its electrical potential is greater than a certain threshold, and it belongs to G_2 if its potential is less than that threshold. Let us assume that C connects to n neighbors $D_1; \ldots; D_n$. According to Kirchhoff equation the total current flowing into vertex C should sum up to zero:

$$\sum_{i=1}^{n} I_i = \sum_{i=1}^{n} \frac{V_{D_i} - V_C}{R} = 0$$

where I_i is the current flowing from D_i to C, and V_C and V_{D_i} are potentials of the appropriate nodes. Thus

$$V_C = \frac{1}{n} \sum_{i=1}^{n} V_{D_i}.$$

That is, the potential of a node is the average of the potentials of its neighbors and can be computed as:

$$V_i = \frac{1}{d_i} \sum_{(i,j) \in E} V_j = \frac{1}{d_i} \sum_{j \in G} V_j s_{ij}$$

where d_i is the degree of node i and s_{ij} is the affinity matrix of the graph. There is a straight analogy between random walks and electric network. The voltage at an arbitrary vertex i equals the probability of reaching A from i before reaching B (Eq. 2).

Starting from the node with potential 1, they consecutively updated a node's potential to the average potential of its neighbors. Repeating the updating process for a finite number of rounds, one reaches an approximate solution within a certain precision, which depends on the number of iteration rounds. In other words, the obtained precision depends on number of repeated rounds and not on the size of the graph, so the total computational cost is always $O(n + m)$. Although the solution is very fast it demands answering a critical question: "How to pick the two poles so that they lie in different communities?" The authors proposed some heuristic methods to solve the problem, but they increased the computational complexity of the algorithm.

The MCL algorithm [4] simulates random walks within a graph by alternation of two operators called expansion and inflation. The first one coincides with taking the power of a stochastic matrix using the normal matrix product (i.e. matrix squaring). Inflation corresponds with taking powers entrywise of the matrix, followed by a scaling step, so that the matrix elements (on each column) correspond to probability values. The goal of the last procedure is to favor same paths inside one cluster over others leading to different clusters. Its computational complexity is of $O(md^2)$, where d represents an average number of nonzero elements in one column of the stochastic matrix.

Mathematically motivated approach showed Spielman and Teng, who introduced a local partitioning algorithm with a remarkable approximation guarantee and bound on its computational complexity [17,18]. Their algorithm has a bounded work/volume ratio, which is the ratio between the work performed by the algorithm on a given run (meaning the number of operations or computational complexity), and the volume of the set it outputs. Their algorithm computes a sequence of vectors that approximate the sequence of probability distributions of a random walk from the starting vertex. The support of these vectors is kept small by removing tiny amounts of probability mass at each step.

Their most recent algorithm uses graph sparsification [19], that is the task of approximating a graph by a sparse graph. They introduced a new notion of spectral sparsification. A spectral sparsifier is a subgraph of the original whose Laplacian quadratic form is approximately the same as that of the original graph on all real vector inputs. By applying the method inside the inverse power method, they computed approximate Fiedler vectors in time $O(m log^c m)$, where m is the number of edges in the original graph and c is some absolute constant.

Andersen, Chung, and Lang developed an improved version of the Spielman and Teng's algorithm for computing approximate PageRank vectors [1]. Instead of computing a sequence of vectors p^{t+1} they found personalized PageRank vector, which simplifies the process of finding cuts and allows greater flexibility when computing approximations. Their method allows us to find cuts using approximations with larger amounts of error, which improves the running time.

5   The ESLRW Algorithm

We have modified the method of Wu and Huberman, and according to the α-lazy random walk process, propose the following formula, describing the evolution of the distribution $p(t)$ at the vertex i:

$$p_{t+1}(i) = \alpha p_t(i) + (1 - \alpha)\frac{1}{d_i} \cdot \sum_{(i,j)\in E} p_t(j) \qquad (10)$$

Our intention was to trace the evolution of a probability distribution propagation on graph and use it for graph bipartitioning. We have focussed on the beginning stages of the process in order to observe the system before it reaches a stationary state. This way we kept a reasonably small computational cost and solution simplicity. We used the lazy random walk instead of the ordinary random walk to avoid cycling of the distribution values. Moreover we can see from equation (8) that the rate of convergence grows with increasing value of spectral gap. Taking into consideration formula (9) we decided to use α smaller then 0.5, which is the standard value for lazy random walks. Although our purpose was not to reach the convergence we just wanted to make the process a bit faster. In our experiments $\alpha = 0.3$.

Our algorithm differs from the Wu-Huberman's solution. There is no necessity to indicate two distant vertices A and B belonging to different clusters, with p values one and zero, respectively. The vertex with the highest degree was chosen as the seed vertex A, in order to make the process faster. As our algorithm runs for a small number of iterations, there are always vertices with p value equal zero, so one of them can constitute vertex B to meet the conditions of Eq. 2.

The evolution of the distribution probability is stopped when the maximum change of the vector component $p(i)$, $i \in V$, is smaller than an established threshold θ. We did not take into consideration the change of the whole vector but only of the components that fluctuate considerably during the process of evaluation. This heuristics is motivated by fact that the probability changes in the subgraph of the seed vertex are larger than in the rest of the graph. Between two not very well separated subgraphs there is a bottleneck that allows for spreading the walk, but it significantly slows down mixing. The bottleneck makes the other part of the graph difficult to reach from the location of the seed and limits the speed of convergence.

It is clear that probability distribution of random walk in the subgraph containing the seed vertex differs from those in the other subgraphs. In order to extract vertices belonging to the same subgraph as the seed vertex, we looked for the largest gap between probability values at all vertices and divide the whole set at the gap.

In our algorithm it is no necessity to give the number of clusters. We used the modularity function, a well known partitioning quality measure introduced by Newman and Girvan [9], in order to decide whether to bipartition the graph farther. After the first bipartitioning we checked with the help of the modularity, whether the next division gives better clustering. So the next stage of the ESLRW algorithm involves calculation of the modularity function.

According to Newman a good division of a graph into partitions is not merely one in which there are few edges between groups; it is one in which there are fewer than expected edges between groups. The modularity Q is, up to a multiplicative constant, the number of edges falling within groups minus the expected number in an equivalent graph with edges placed at random, or in functional form:

$$Q = \frac{1}{2m} \sum_{i,j} \left[a_{ij} - \frac{d_i d_j}{2m} \right] \delta(g_i, g_j)$$

where $\delta(g_i, g_j) = 1$ if $g_i = g_j$ and 0 otherwise, g_i stands for a group of the vertex i, and m is the number of edges in the graph. Although modularity is widely used to evaluate the cluster structure of a graph, it is prompt to increase as the number of divisions increases, including even within-cluster divisions. We assumed that a sequential division of a graph makes sense if Q increases by ten percentage of the previous modularity value. It avoids unnecessary growth of the number of clusters.

If cutting a set of vertices through a selected gap would not cause a reasonable gain of modularity, partitioning of the set is not executed and the set is labeled as complete. The algorithm finishes if all its vertices belong to complete sets.

To sum up our algorithm consists of the following steps:

– Given a graph construct its adjacency matrix
– Calculate the vector p
– Use the vector p to bipartition the graph
– Decide if the current group should be sub-divided, and recursively repartition the segmented parts if necessary.

To create the matrix $\mathbf{S}$ the k-nearest neighbors were determined for each point i on the basis of the Euclidean distance. The adjacency matrix was obtained with the help of a mutual k-nearest neighbor graph. The graph was constructed by connecting i to j if i is among the k-nearest neighbors of j and vice versa. If two vertices are connected, the appropriate value in the adjacency matrix $\mathbf{A}$ equals 1, otherwise it is 0. The parameter k was chosen experimentally.

After constructing the adjacency matrix of the graph, the vector p is calculated according to formula (10). Values of the p vector depend on the starting point of the random walk. If the starting point is located in the middle of the group and does not have connections with vertices belonging to other groups the calculation is fast and partitioning exact. To make our algorithm as simple as possible we resign from additional steps and decide to choose always the vertex with the maximum degree.

Computational complexity of the bipartitioning depends on one round complexity and the number of iterations. The round involves updating distribution probabilities at each vertex and is proportional to the number of vertices n. The random walk is executed till the maximum value, by which the distribution at one vertex is updated, exceeds a given threshold. Additionally we limited the maximum number of iterations to $itmax = 100$. To sum up the computational complexity of bipartitioning in our algorithm is $O(n \cdot it)$, where it stands for the number of iterations and is smaller than $itmax$. Taking into consideration the fact that in our experiments we used graphs with the number of nodes varying between 3000 and 20000, the number of iterations is comparably small. We can say that our solution almost linearly depends on the size of the graph. As the procedure is recursively repeated till all the clusters are found and all the vertices labeled as complete, the whole complexity of the ESLRW algorithm is $O(n \cdot it \cdot k)$, where k represents the number of clusters.

6 Experimental Results

We compared the performance of the ESLRW algorithm (implemented in MAT-LAB) to other clustering algorithms: NJW [15], K-means, K-means-based Nyström spectral clustering (K-NASP) [23], and LI-ASP [3]. The first two are popular standard algorithms and the NJW uses exact values of symmetric Laplacian eigenvectors. The last algorithm is a new approximate solution in which two improvements were made comparing to traditional spectral clustering. First, a sparse affinity graph was adopted to improve the performance of spectral clustering on a small representative dataset. Second, local interpolation was utilized to improve the extension of the clustering result. The main computation of the LI-ASP includes three parts: obtaining the representative points, running spectral clustering on the representative points and extending the clustering result by the local interpolation. The computational complexity of this solution is $O(p^3) + O(n \cdot m \cdot p \cdot k^2)$, where p stands for the number of representatives, $p \ll n$. K-means-based Nyström spectral clustering K-NASP uses Nyström law rank matrix approximation with the landmark points chosen as the K-means cluster centers. This method allows to extrapolate the complete grouping solution using only a small number of samples. The computational complexity of the algorithm is $O(m \cdot n)$.

We conducted experiments with several real-world large datasets of various sizes, described as follows:

– MNIST [20] consisting of handwritten digits, with a total of 70,000 examples; each example is a 28×28 gray-level image, and the dimensionality is 784. Considering the MATLAB memory limitation, we chose the first 2000 examples in the training set of each digit in our experiments. In addition, we also constructed two subsets of MNIST, MNIST358 and MNIST1479. MNIST358

consists of the examples of digits 3, 5, and 8, and MNIST1479 consists of the examples of digits 1, 4, 7, and 9.
- USPS [10], the US Postal Service (USPS) handwritten digit dataset, in which each sample is a 16 × 16 image. It contains ten digits 0–9. Two subsets of USPS similar to those of MNIST were also formed, which are denoted by USPS358 and USPS1479.
- Pendigit [2], a handwritten digit data set consisting of 250 samples from 44 writers. In our experiments the training and testing sets were used as two datasets, which are denoted by Pendigit train and Pendigit test, respectively.
- LetterRec [2] containing the features of 26 capital letters of the English alphabet. The character images are based on 20 different fonts. They are randomly distorted.

Table 1 summarizes basic information of these datasets. It is worth noting that the number of the instances in each dataset is more than 2000.

All the datasets are labeled, which enables evaluation of the clustering results against the labels using the accuracy of clustering (ACC) and normalized mutual information (NMI), as measures of division quality. For both measures higher number means better partitioning. We refer an interested reader to [14] for details regarding the measures. The same benchmark datasets were applied in experiments for the LI-ASP algorithm by Cao et al. We also used their results.

Table 1. A summary of datasets.

Dataset	♯ of instances	♯ of features	♯ of classes
MNIST	20000	784	10
MNIST358	6000	784	3
MNIST1479	8000	784	4
USPS	9298	256	10
USPS358	2357	256	3
USPS1479	3919	256	4
Pendigit train	7494	16	10
Pendigit test	3492	16	10
LetterRec	20000	16	26

The performance of the algorithms show Tables 2 and 3. Not all results are presented because the datasets of 20000 points were too large for NJW MATLAB implementation. We can see the superiority of the ESLRW algorithm over the other tested solutions. The results prove that the presented method is competitive to the other solutions in terms of the quality of partitioning, measured with the help of the accuracy of clustering and the NMI quality measure.

We have also applied the ESLRW algorithm to find protein complexes. In our experiments we used two well known yeast PPI datasets. The first dataset

Table 2. Comparison of K-MEANS, NJW, K-NASP, LI-ASP, and ESLRW algorithms in terms of the accuracy of clustering.

Algorithm	K-MEANS	NJW	K-NASP	LI-ASP	ESLRW
MNIST	0.4912	/	0.5284	0.6999	**0.7403**
MNIST358	0.1357	**0.7548**	0.5781	0.7175	0.7220
MNIST1479	0.3502	0.3623	0.4446	0.5032	**0.5449**
USPS	0.5921	0.6562	0.6319	0.6746	**0.9420**
USPS358	0.7170	0.9163	0.9189	0.9606	**0.9845**
USPS1479	0.5214	0.9615	0.5816	0.9446	**0.9770**
Pendigit test	0.6710	**0.8263**	0.6306	0.7705	0.8210
Pendigit train	0.6686	0.7889	0.6955	0.8113	**0.8193**
LettRec	**0.3631**	/	0.2728	0.3197	0.324

Table 3. Comparison of K-MEANS, NJW, K-NASP, LI-ASP, and ESLRW algorithms in terms of the NMI.

Algorithm	K-MEANS	NJW	K-NASP	LI-ASP	ESLRW
MNIST	0.4912	/	0.5102	0.7138	**0.7758**
MNIST358	0.1357	0.4670	0.1284	0.4284	**0.6008**
MNIST1479	0.3502	0.4700	0.3015	0.4365	**0.6491**
USPS	0.5921	0.7723	0.6178	0.7347	**0.8809**
USPS358	0.7170	0.9163	0.7224	0.8387	**0.9187**
USPS1479	0.5214	0.8662	0.5747	0.8506	**0.9066**
Pendigit test	0.6710	0.8263	0.7198	0.7793	**0.8646**
Pendigit train	0.6686	0.8008	0.7388	0.7949	**0.8623**
LettRec	0.3631	/	0.3752	0.4315	**0.4460**

(PPI-D1) is prepared by Gavin *et al.* [8] and the second dataset (PPI-D2) is a combined PPI dataset containing yeast protein interactions generated by six individual experiments [22]. The first one consists of 990 and the second one of 1440 proteins. We compared our solution with the a standard algorithm used for protein networks - the MCL algorithm. Our method outperformed the other algorithm in terms of modularity measure. For the first set PPI-D1 modularity of our algorithm was 0.8157 and of the other one 0.7692, and for the second set PPI-D2 respectively 0.8134 and 0.7835.

7 Conclusions

The computational complexity of the presented algorithm is reasonably small. It depends on the number of iterations, that never exceeds 100. The number constitutes only small percentage of iterations needed for convergence. For example in case of the Pendigit test set, the number of iterations to achieve the accuracy of 0.001 is of $3.5 \cdot 10^3$ whereas in our algorithm the early stop was made after 75 rounds.

We have presented a fast algorithm that uses random walk procedure for graph bipartitioning. The solution uses a close relation between the Fiedler vector and the vector, whose components are probabilities of reaching a seed vertex before the other distant vertex starting from i. We calculated the local rough approximation of the Fiedler vector. The vector was obtained after considerably small number of algorithm iterations. The algorithm gives promising results despite its simplicity. Our experiments show superiority of graph partitioning with the use of the local approximation of the Fiedler vector over cuts resulting from the vector itself. Because of small computational complexity our method seems to be adequate for discovering structures in large graphs.

References

1. Andersen, R., Chung, F.R.K., Lang, K.J.: Local graph partitioning using PageRank vectors. In: FOCS 2006, pp. 475–486 (2006)
2. Bache, K., Lichman, M.: UCI Machine Learning Repository (2013). http://archive.ics.uci.edu/ml
3. Cao, J.Z., Chen, P., Dai, Q., Ling, B.W.K.: Local information-based fast approximate spectral clustering. Pattern Recogn. Lett. **38**, 63–69 (2014)
4. van Dongen, S.: Graph clustering via a discrete uncoupling process. SIAM J. Matrix Anal. Appl. **30**(1), 121–141 (2008)
5. Enright, A.J., van Dongen, S., Ouzounis, C.A.: An efficient algorithm for large-scale detection of protein families. Nucleic Acids Res. **30**(7), 1575–1584 (2002)
6. Fiedler, M.: Algebraic connectivity of graphs. Czechoslovak Math. J. **23**(98), 298–305 (1973)
7. Flake, G., Lawrence, S., Lee Giles, C., Coetzee, F.: Self-organization and identification of Web communities. IEEE Comput. **35**(3), 66–71 (2002)
8. Gavin, A.C., et al.: Functional organization of the yeast protein by systematic analysis of protein complexes. Nature **415**, 141–147 (2002)
9. Girvan, M., Newman, M.E.J.: Community structure in social and biological networks. Proc. Natl. Acad. Sci. USA **99**(12), 7821–7826 (2002)
10. Hull, J.J.: A database for handwritten text recognition research. IEEE Trans. Pattern Anal. Mach. Intell. **16**, 550–554 (1994)
11. Lováasz, L.: Random walks on graphs: a survey, combinatorics, Paul Erdös is Eighty 2, pp. 146 (1993)
12. von Luxburg, U.: A tutorial on spectral clustering. Stat. Comput. **17**(4), 395–416 (2007)
13. Mahoney, M., Orecchia, L.: A local spectral method for graphs: with applications to improving graph partitions and exploring data graphs locally. J. Mach. Learn. Res. **13**, 2339–2365 (2012)
14. Manning, C., Raghavan, P., Schtauze, H.: Introduction to Information Retrieval. Cambridge University Press, Cambridge (2008)
15. Ng, A., Jordan, M., Weiss, Y.: On spectral clustering: analysis and an algorithm. Adv. Neural Inf. Process. Syst. **14**, 849–856 (2001)

16. Shi, J., Malik, J.: Normalized cuts and image segmentation. In: Proceedings of the Conference on Computer Vision and Pattern Recognition (CVPR 1997), pp. 731–752. IEEE Computer Society (1997)
17. Spielman, D.A., Teng, S.-H.: Nearly-linear time algorithms for graph partitioning, graph sparsification, and solving linear systems. In: STOC 2004, pp. 81–90. ACM, New York (2004)
18. Spielman, D.A., Teng, S.-H.: A local clustering algorithm for massive graphs and its application to nearly-linear time graph partitioning. CoRR, abs/0809.3232 (2008)
19. Spielman, D.A., Teng, S.-H.: Spectral sparsification of graphs. SIAM J. Comput. **40**, 18–025 (2011)
20. Yann, L., Corinna, C.: The MNIST database of handwritten digits (2009). http://yannlecun.com/exdb/mnist/
21. Wu, F., Huberman, B.A.: Finding communities in linear time: a physics approach. Eur. Phys. J. B **38**(2), 331–338 (2004)
22. Zaki, N.M., Lazarova-Molnar, S., El-Hajj, W., Campbell, P.: Protein-protein interaction based on pairwise similarity. BMC Bioinf. **10**, 1–12 (2009)
23. Zhang, K., Kwok, J.: Improved Nyström low rank approximation and error analysis. In: Proceedings of the International Conference on Machine Learning (ICML) (2008)
24. Zhou, H., Lipowsky, R.: Dynamic pattern evolution on scale-free networks. Proc. Nat. Acad. Sci. USA **102**(29), 10052–10057 (2005)

Methods of Synthesis of Controlled Random Tests

Ireneusz Mrozek$^{(\boxtimes)}$ and Vyacheslav Yarmolik

Faculty of Computer Science, Bialystok University of Technology,
Wiejska 45A, 15-351 Bialystok, Poland
i.mrozek@pb.edu.pl, yarmolik10ru@yahoo.com
http://www.wi.pb.edu.pl

Abstract. Controlled random tests, methods of their generation, main criteria used for their synthesis, such as the Hamming distance and the Euclidean distance, as well as their application to the testing of both hardware and software systems are discussed. Available evidences suggest that high computational complexity is one of the main drawbacks of these methods. Therefore we propose a technique to overcome this problem. A method for synthesizing multiple controlled random tests based on the use of the initial random test and addition operation has been proposed. The resulting multiple tests can be interpreted as a single controlled random test. The complexity of its construction is significantly lower than the complexity of the construction of classical random tests. Examples of generated tests as well as estimates of their effectiveness compared to other solutions have been presented in experimental studies.

Keywords: Random tests · Controlled tests · Multiple tests · Hemming distance · Euclidean distance

1 Introduction

Among the black box techniques, random testing is generally regarded as a very effective technique for testing modern hardware and software systems [1–7]. All modifications of random testing are united by the controllability principle for test pattern generation [1, 4, 7–12]. These tests are constructed based on the calculation of certain characteristics for the controlled selection of another random test set [1].

The use of controlled random tests is characterized by greater efficiency compared with other types of tests that has been confirmed in practice many times [1, 4, 12–17]. It should be noted that the need to sort potential candidates for test sets and calculate the numerical characteristics for them significantly increases the complexity of constructing controlled random tests [1, 4, 12, 13, 16].

This paper was supported by grant S/WI/3/13 from Faculty of Computer Science at Bialystok University of Technology, Ministry of Science and Higer Education, Poland.

K. Saeed and W. Homenda (Eds.): CISIM 2016, LNCS 9842, pp. 429–440, 2016.
DOI: 10.1007/978-3-319-45378-1_38

The purpose of this paper is to develop a method for constructing multiple controlled tests based on the initial controlled random test of a lesser length constructed by known methodologies [1,4,12,13,16]. The initial test is used to construct subsequent tests of multiple controlled random tests in the form of simple modifications that do not require further analysis or computational costs. The resulting multiple controlled random tests can be interpreted as a single random test or used for periodic testing in applications with time limited test procedures.

2   Analysis of Controlled Random Tests

All existing methods for constructing controlled random tests are based on the assertion which is explained below [1,12,13,15]. Each subsequent test set of the controlled random tests should be constructed such that it is as different (distant) from all previously generated test sets as possible.

For methods of controlled random testing used to test digital devices and software with m inputs and the space of input patterns consisting of 2^m binary sets (vectors), the following definitions are correct [1,7,13].

Definition 1. The test (T) is a set of $2 <= q <= 2^m$ test sets:

$$\{T_0, T_1, T_2, ..., T_{q-1}\} \text{ where } T_i = t_{i,m-1}, t_{i,m-2}, ..., t_{i,2}, t_{i,1}, t_{i,0} \text{ and } t_{i,l} \in \{0,1\}$$

Definition 2. A controlled random test, where $CRT = \{T_0, T_1, T_2, ..., T_{q-1}\}$, is a test that includes $q < 2^m$ m-bit randomly generated test patterns denoted by T_i, where $i \in \{0, 1, 2, ..., q-1\}$, and where $T_i = t_{i,m-1}, t_{i,m-2}, ..., t_{i,2}, t_{i,1}, t_{i,0}$ and $t_{i,l} \in \{0,1\}$, such that T_i satisfies some criterion or criteria obtained on the basis of previous test patterns $\{T_0, T_1, T_2, ..., T_{i-1}\}$.

Hamming distance and Euclidean distance are often used as difference measures between the test pattern T_i and previously generated patterns [1,11,18]. In this case, the measures apply to the binary test pattern T_i and T_j. The Hamming distance $HD(T_i, T_j)$ is computed as the weight $w(T_i \oplus T_j)$ of the vector $T_i \oplus T_j$ according to the following formula (1):

$$HD(T_i, T_j) = w(T_i \oplus T_j) = \sum_{l=0}^{m-1} (t_{i,l} \oplus t_{j,l}). \tag{1}$$

Euclidean distance $ED(T_i, T_j)$ is computed according to the formula (2).

$$ED(T_i, T_j) = \sqrt{\sum_{l=0}^{m-1} (t_{i,l} - t_{j,l})^2} = \sqrt{\sum_{l=0}^{m-1} (t_{i,l} \oplus t_{j,l})} = \sqrt{HD(T_i, T_j)}. \tag{2}$$

To generate the test pattern T_i, when $i > 2$, total values of the distances between T_i and all previous patterns $(T_0, T_1, T_2, ..., T_{i-1})$ are used [1,5,10,11,

16, 19]. Thus, for the next pattern T_i, the total value of the distances with respect to $(T_0, T_1, T_2, \ldots, T_{i-1})$ constitutes the following:

$$\text{THD}(T_i) = \sum_{j=0}^{i-1} \text{HD}(T_i, T_j); \quad \text{TED}(T_i) = \sum_{j=0}^{i-1} \text{ED}(T_i, T_j). \tag{3}$$

Here, $\text{THD}(T_i)$ and $\text{TED}(T_i)$ stand for the total Hamming distance and total Euclidean distance, respectively. The new pattern T_i should be chosen to make the total distances $\text{THD}(T_i)$ and $\text{TED}(T_i)$ maximal [1].

According to the methods of constructing controlled random tests outlined above, the new test set T_i is selected so that difference metrics (3) take the maximum value [1, 12, 13, 15, 16, 20]. Note that difference metrics (3) are characterized by a significant computational complexity, which increases with the growth of the index i of the test set T_i.

As shown in [14, 20], the minimum Hamming distance $\min HD(T_i, T_j)$ or the Euclidean distance $\min ED(T_i, Tj)$ is a more efficient metrics for the generation of a controlled random test. According to the method of synthesis of tests discussed in [14], the subsequent test set T_i is selected from possible candidates for the tests by the criterion of the maximum value

$$\min_{j \in \{0,1,\ldots,i-1\}} HD(T_i, T_j) \quad \text{or} \quad \min_{j \in \{0,1,\ldots,i-1\}} ED(T_i, T_j) \tag{4}$$

which provides the maximum distance (difference) of the test set T_i from all previously generated sets $\{T_0, T_1, T_2, \ldots, T_{i-1}\}$. If the maximum value of (4) is achieved, it also maximizes values $THD(T_i)$ and $TED(T_i)$ according to (3) [20].

Let us define a multiple controlled test based on the methodology of single step controlled random tests.

Definition 3. The multiple controlled random test $MCRT_r$ consists of r single step controlled random tests $CRT(0)$, $CRT(1)$, $CRT(2), \ldots, CRT(r-1)$, each of which includes q test sets. In addition, the test $CRT(0)$ satisfies Definition 2 and subsequent tests $CRT(i)$, $i \in \{1, 2, 3, \ldots, r-1\}$ are constructed according to certain algorithms such that each subsequent test $CRT(i)$ meets a certain criterion or criteria derived from previous tests $CRT(0)$, $CRT(1)$, $CRT(2)$, $\ldots$, $CRT(i-1)$.

Let us consider the Hamming and the Euclidean distance for two tests $CRT(k)$ and $CRT(l)$. Initially, we note that the Hamming distance $HD(CRT(k), CRT(l))$, which is the same as the number of distinct components $T_{k,i}$ and $T_{l,i}$ of the initial test $CRT(k)$ and the constructed one $CRT(l)$, can be considered as a prerequisite which the test $CRT(l)$ should meet. It is clear that a necessary requirement in terms of the maximum difference with which $CRT(k)$ and $CRT(l)$ should comply is the lack of matching sets $T_{k,i}$ and $T_{l,i}$ in them, which is equivalent to the inequality $T_{l,i} \neq T_{k,i}, i \in \{0, 1, 2, \ldots, q-1\}$.

The Euclidean distance for $CRT(k)$ and $CRT(l)$ is defined as:

$$ED(CRT(k), CRT(l)) = \sqrt{\sum_{i=0}^{q-1} (T_{i,k} - T_{i,l})^2}. \tag{5}$$

In order to use more effective criteria for estimating the quality of the controlled random test in the construction of the test $CRT(i)$, let us determine the maximum value of the Hamming distance $MHD(CRT(i))$ and the maximum value of the Euclidean distance $MED(CRT(i))$ as follows:

$$MHD(CRT(i)) = \max_{CRT_v(i), v \in \{0,\ldots,w\}} \{ \min_{j \in \{0,1,\ldots,i-1\}} HD(CRT_1(i), CRT(j)), \ldots,$$
$$\min_{j \in \{0,1,\ldots,i-1\}} HD(CRT_w(i), CRT(j))\};$$
$$MED(CRT(i)) = \max_{CRT_v(i), v \in \{0,\ldots,w\}} \{ \min_{j \in \{0,1,\ldots,j-1\}} ED(CRT_1(i), CRT(j)), \ldots,$$
$$\min_{j \in \{0,1,\ldots,i-1\}} ED(CRT_w(i), CRT(j))\}.$$

$$(6)$$

According to given metrics (6), the subsequent controlled random test $CRT(i)$ is selected from the set $\{CRT_1(i), CRT_2(i), \ldots, CRT_w(i)\}$ of to test candidates based on the criterion of the maximum minimum Hamming and Euclidean distances with respect to previously generated controlled random tests $CRT(j) = \{CRT(0), CRT(1), \ldots, CRT(i-1)\}$.

3   Method for Generating Multiple Controlled Random Tests

Let us use addition as the main operation in the construction of multiple random tests. It will make it possible to provide the minimal computational complexity in the construction of multiple random tests $MCRT_r$. Indeed, all subsequent tests $CRT(1), CRT(2), \ldots, CRT(r-1)$ can be easily constructed based on $CRT(0)$ by a single application of addition for each test set.

According to Definition 2, the controlled random test CRT consists of q test sets T_i, $i \in \{0, 1, 2, \ldots, q-1\}$, each of which represents a m-bit binary vector $T_i = t_{i,m-1} t_{i,m-2}, \ldots, t_{i,2}, t_{i,1}, t_{i,0}$, where $t_{i,l} \in \{0,1\}$. Thus, test sets T_i of the controlled random test CRT can be interpreted as $g = 2^m$-ary data $T_i \in \{0, 1, 2, \ldots, 2^m - 1\}$. For example, the test $CRT = \{0011, 0110, 1100, 0101, 1000\}$ can be represented as a set of 16-ary data $CRT = \{3, 6, 12, 5, 8\}$ (in the decimal system). If the initial test is $CRT(k) = \{T_0(k), T_1(k), T_2(k), \ldots, T_{q-1}(k)\}$, the ratio that is used to obtain a new test $CRT(l) = \{T_0(l), T_1(l), T_2(l), \ldots, T_{q-1}(l)\}$ takes the following form:

$$T_i(l) = T_i(k) + d \bmod 2^m; i = \overline{0, q-1}. \tag{7}$$

In the given ratio, the parameter $d \in \{1, 2, 3, \ldots, 2^m - 1\}$ is used to achieve the difference between test sets and, accordingly, between tests $CRT(l)$ and $CRT(k)$. This parameter is crucial for achieving the maximum difference of the test $CRT(l)$ from the test $CRT(k)$ in terms of the previously defined metrics. For relation (7) the following proposition is true.

Proposition 1. If the test $CRT(l)$ is derived from the initial test $CRT(k)$ based on relation (7) for the parameter $d \in \{1, 2, 3, \ldots, 2^m - 1\}$, then using the value $2^m - d$ as the parameter for the test $CRT(l)$ and using the same relation (7) we obtain the initial test $CRT(k)$. This proposition follows from the equality $d + 2^m - d \bmod 2^m = 0$.

Example 1. When $m = 4$ for the initial test $CRT(k) = \{3, 6, 12, 5, 8\}$ and the parameter $d = 8$, according to (7), we obtain $CRT(l) = \{11, 14, 4, 13, 0\}$. Using $CRT(l) = \{11, 14, 4, 13, 0\}$ as the initial test and the same value $d = 8$, we obtain the test $CRT(k) = \{3, 6, 12, 5, 8\}$, which corresponds to the Proposition 1. For the same initial test $CRT(k) = \{3, 6, 12, 5, 8\}$ and the other parameter $d = 5$, we will have a different result, namely, $CRT(l) = \{8, 11, 1, 10, 13\}$.

Example 2. For the test $CRT(k) = \{3, 7, 0, 6, 2, 5, 1, 4\}$ constructed for $m = 3$ and parameter $d = 4$, according to (7), we find that $CRT(l) = \{7, 3, 4, 2, 6, 1, 5, 0\}$. For the same initial test and parameter $d = 5$, we will have a different result, i.e., $CRT(l) = \{0, 4, 5, 3, 7, 2, 6, 1\}$. Note that, in the given example, tests include various octal data values.

In the analysis of the above examples, in each of which two new tests obtained according to (7) are represented, the question arises as to which of these two tests is more effective for multiple testing. Thus, the problem arises of determining the optimal parameter d when using the Euclidean distance as a quality metric for multiple tests. For $ED(CRT(k), CRT(l))$, where the test $CRT(l)$ is obtained according to (7) we can use the following theorem [21].

Theorem 1. The Euclidean distance $ED(CRT(k), CRT(l))$ for tests $CRT(k)$ and $CRT(l)$, where $CRT(k) = \{T_0(k), T_1(k), T_2(k), \ldots, T_{q-1}(k)\}$ consists of $q = 2^m$ m-bit nonrecurring randomly generated test sets $T_i(k) \in \{0, 1, 2, \ldots, 2^m - 1\}$, and where test sets $T_i(l)$ are obtained according to the expression $T_i(l) = T_i(k) + d \bmod 2^m, i = \overline{0, q-1}$, is calculated as

$$ED(CRT(k), CRT(l)) = \sqrt{2^m d(2^m - d)}. \qquad (8)$$

Example 3. The Euclidean distance for tests $CRT(k) = \{3, 7, 0, 6, 2, 5, 1, 4\}$ and $CRT(l) = \{7, 3, 4, 2, 6, 1, 5, 0\}$ is defined as $ED(CRT(k), CRT(l)) = [(3 - 7)^2 + (7 - 3)^2 + (0 - 4)^2 + (6 - 2)^2 + (2 - 6)^2 + (5 - 1)^2 + (1 - 5)^2 + (4 - 0)^2]^{1/2} = \sqrt{128}$ Note that the same result ($d = 4$ and $m = 3$) we obtain using 8.

Values of Euclidean distances for the case $m = 3$ and possible values of d are given in Table 1.

Table 1. Values of Euclidean distance for $m = 3$

d	1	2	3	4	5	6	7
$ED(CRT(k), CRT(l))$	$\sqrt{56}$	$\sqrt{96}$	$\sqrt{120}$	$\sqrt{128}$	$\sqrt{120}$	$\sqrt{96}$	$\sqrt{56}$

For the above Theorem 1 we have the following corollary [21].

Corollary 1. The Euclidean distance value $ED(CRT(k), CRT(l))$ will take the maximum value when $d = 2^{m-1}$, which corresponds to the solution of the equation

$$\frac{\partial \sqrt{2^m d(2^m - d)}}{\partial d} = 0$$

The validity of this corollary is confirmed by the results shown in Table 1, where for $d = 2^{m-1} = 2^{3-1} = 4$ the Euclidean distance takes the maximum value of $\sqrt{128}$.

Corollary 2. The Euclidean distance $ED(CRT(k), CRT(l))$ obtained for the parameter d is equal to the Euclidean distance of the parameter $2^m - d$, which follows from the equality

$$\sqrt{2^m d(2^m - d)} = \sqrt{2^m (2^m - d)(2^m - (2^m - d))}.$$

This property is illustrated by numerical values of the Euclidean distance shown in Table 1.

Corollary 3. The value of the Euclidean distance $ED(CRT(k), CRT(l)) = \sqrt{2^m d(2^m - d)}$ obtained according to (8) for tests $CRT(k)$ and $CRT(l)$ consisting of $q = 2^m$ m-bit data $\{0, 1, 2, \ldots, 2^m - 1\}$ can be used as the mean Euclidean distance $AED(CRT(k), CRT(l))$ equal to $\sqrt{qd(2^m - d)}$, between tests $CRT(k)$ and $CRT(l)$ that include $q < 2^m$ test sets.

For Example 1 and test $CRT(l) = \{11, 14, 4, 13, 0\}$ obtained based on the initial test $CRT(k) = \{3, 6, 12, 5, 8\}$ at $d = 8$, according to (7), we find that

$$AED(CRT(k), CRT(l)) = \sqrt{5 \times 8 \times (2^4 - 8)} = \sqrt{320}$$

Note that, for these tests, the Euclidean distance is strictly equal to its average value. Indeed, $ED(CRT(k), CRT(l)) = [(3 - 11)^2 + (6 - 14)^2 + (12 - 4)^2 + (5 - 13)^2 + (8 - 0)^2]^{1/2} = \sqrt{320}$.

Corollary 4. If the Euclidean distance $ED(CRT(k), CRT(l))$ between controlled random tests $CRT(k)$ and $CRT(l)$ according to Theorem 1 is equal to $\sqrt{2^m d_l(2^m - d_l)}$ and, for tests $CRT(k)$ and $CRT(n)$, $ED(CRT(k), CRT(n)) = \sqrt{2^m d_n(2^m - d_n)}$, then $ED(CRT(l), CRT(n)) = \sqrt{2^m d_c(2^m - d_c)}$, where $d_c = d_l - d_n \bmod 2^m$.

In accordance with Example 2 $CRT(l) = \{0, 4, 5, 3, 7, 2, 6, 1\}$ and $CRT(n) = \{7, 3, 4, 2, 6, 1, 5, 0\}$, from the Corollary 4, we obtain that $d_c = d_l - d_n \bmod 2^m = 5 - 4 \bmod 2^3 = 1$ and

$$ED(CRT(l), CRT(n)) = \sqrt{2^m d_c(2^m - d_c)} = \sqrt{2^3 \times 1 \times (2^3 - 1)} = \sqrt{56}.$$

4   Method for Generating Multiple Controlled Random Tests

As a basis for constructing multiple controlled random tests

$$MCRT_r = \{CRT(0), CRT(1), CRT(2), \ldots, CRT(r-1)\}, \qquad (9)$$

we use relation (7), which is characterized by the minimal computational complexity in obtaining subsequent tests $CRT(1), CRT(2), \ldots, CRT(r-1)$ based on the initial one $CRT(0)$.

Then, the maximum minimum Hamming distance $MHD(CRT(k), CRT(l))$ and the maximum minimum Euclidean distance $MED(CRT(k), CRT(l)), k \neq l \in \{0, 1, 2, \ldots, r-1\}$, according to (7), will be used in the construction of multiple random tests (9) as measures of efficiency.

Let us successively consider multiple controlled random tests $MCRT_r$ of various multiplicity ranging from double tests $MCRT_2$ that consist of $CRT(0)$ and $CRT(1)$, where the second test $CRT(1)$ is generated based on the initial test $CRT(0)$ according to (7). According to Corollary 1, the optimum value of the parameter d in order to obtain $CRT(1)$ is 2^{m-1}. In this case, the Euclidean distance between the tests $CRT(0)$ and $CRT(1)$ takes the maximum value that maximizes the difference between these tests and the maximum effectiveness of their joint application.

Let us consider the following theorem for tests $MCRT_r$ with the multiplicity $r > 2$ [21].

Theorem 2. The maximum value $MHD(CRT(k), CRT(l))$ with which the tests $CRT(k)$ and $CRT(l)$ ($k \neq l \in \{0, 1, 2, \ldots, r-1\}$) of the multiple controlled random test $MCRT_r$ that consists of $r > 2$ controlled random tests $\{CRT(0), CRT(1), CRT(2), \ldots, CRT(r-1)\}$, each of which contains $q \leq 2^m$ m-bit test sets, should comply is achieved in the case of the maximum minimum value $d_k - d_l$ ($k \neq l \in \{0, 1, 2, \ldots, r-1\}$), and $d_k \neq d_l \in \{1, 2, \ldots, 2^m - 1\}$.

Based on the theorem, we can conclude that for the general case of the multiple test $MCRT_r$ optimal values of parameters $d_1, d_2, \ldots, d_{r-1}$ are the values that divide the range of integers of $0 - 2^m$ into regular intervals and are calculated according to the following relation:

$$d_i = \left\lfloor \frac{i2^m}{r} + 0.5 \right\rfloor \quad i \in \{1, 2, \ldots, r-1\}. \qquad (10)$$

In the case of the triple random test $MCRT_3$, in order to obtain the second $CRT(1)$ and third $CRT(2)$ tests based on the initial test $CRT(0)$, it is necessary to use optimum combinations of parameters d_1 and d_2 according to (10) used to obtain tests $CRT(1)$ and $CRT(2)$ according to (7). Correspondingly, for triple random tests,

$$d_1 = \lfloor 1 \times 2^m/3 + 0.5 \rfloor, \; and \; d_2 = \lfloor 2 \times 2^m/3 + 0.5 \rfloor.$$

Table 2. Values of the Euclidean distance for $m = 4$

d	1	2	3	4	5	6	7	8
$ED(CRT(k), CRT(l))$	15.5	21.2	24.9	27.7	29.7	30.9	31.7	32.0
d	9	10	11	12	13	14	15	16
$ED(CRT(k), CRT(l))$	31.7	30.9	29.7	27.7	24.9	21.2	15.5	0

For $m = 3$, we find that $d_1 = 3$ and $d_2 = 5$ and, for $m = 4$, $d_1 = 5$ and $d_2 = 11$.

Let us consider $MCRT_3 = \{CRT(0), CRT(1), CRT(2)\}$ when $m = 4$ using $d_1 = 5$ and $d_2 = 11$. The Euclidean distance between the tests $CRT(0)$ and $CRT(1)$ is calculated as follows $ED(CRT(0), CRT(1)) = \sqrt{16 \times 5 \times (16 - 5)} = \sqrt{880} = 29.7$. Other values of Euclidean distances for an arbitrary value d are shown in Table 2. According to this table, the value of the Euclidean distance is $ED(CRT(0), CRT(2)) = 29.7$. At the same time, in accordance with Corollary of 4, the distance between tests $CRT(1)$ and $CRT(2)$ is determined for d equal to $d_2 - d_1 = 11 - 5 = 6$ as $ED(CRT(1), CRT(2)) = 29.7$.

The analysis of given values of Euclidean distances for the considered $MCRT_3$ indicates that $MED(CRT(k), CRT(l)) = 29.7$ for $k \neq l \in \{0, 1, 2\}$ according to (6) and $TED(CRT(2)) = ED(CRT(2), CRT(0)) + ED(CRT(2), CRT(1)) = 29.7 + 29.7 = 59.4$ according to (3) take the maximum value.

For the quadruple test $MCRT_4 = CRT(0), CRT(1), CRT(2), CRT(3)$ using (10), e.g., for $m = 4$, we find that $d_1 = 4, d_2 = 8$ and $d_3 = 12$. The values of the distances between any two tests $MCRT_4$ are given in Table 3. As can be seen from Table 3, the value $MED(CRT(k), CRT(l)), k \neq l \in \{0, 1, 2, 3\}$ for $MCRT_4$ takes the maximum possible value of 27.7.

Table 3. Values of the Euclidean distance for the test $MCRT_4$

	$CRT(0)$	$CRT(1)$	$CRT(2)$	$CRT(3)$
$CRT(0)$	–	27.7	32.0	27.7
$CRT(1)$	27.1	–	27.7	32.0
$CRT(2)$	32.0	27.7	–	27.7
$CRT(3)$	27.7	32.0	27.7	–

5   Experiments

As a measure of the effectiveness of multiple controlled random test $MCRT_r$ we used the metric $E(k, 2^m)$ introduced in [7] in order to construct subsequent test sets in the generation of the single-step controlled random test. In the case of multiple tests similar characteristic for the subsequent test $CRT(i)$ is formulated and can be determined as follows.

Definition 4. The additional number of binary combinations over all possible k out of 2^m bits generated by test sets of the test $CRT(i)$ with respect to the binary combinations generated by previous tests of the multiple test $CRT(0), CRT(1), CRT(2), \ldots, CRT(i-1)$ is the measure of effectiveness $E(k, 2^m)$ for the subsequent controlled test $CRT(i)$.

Obviously, the larger the value of this metric, the more effective is the subsequent controlled test $CRT(i)$, which together with the previous tests makes it possible to achieve maximum efficiency. Note that in previous sections it was shown that in order to achieve the maximum efficiency of multiple controlled random tests $MCRT_r$ the Euclidean distance for the test $CRT(i)$ should be maximum in relation to previously generated tests $CRT(0), CRT(1), \ldots, CRT(i-1)$.

The problem of testing storage devices was used for the comparative analysis of the effectiveness of multiple controlled random tests $MCRT_r$ [20]. First, let us consider a storage device that consists of $2^3 = 8$ memory cells. In order to test it, we used the test $CRT(0)$, which includes all possible three-bit addresses generated according to the scheme of march tests [13, 18]. In the formation of the next address the initial zero state of the memory cell is changed to a one state. Thus, the initial zero state of all cells of the storage device is changed to the one state. Note that values $ED(CRT(0), CRT(1))$ for two tests $CRT(0), CRT(1)$ and $m = 3$ are given in Table 1. The test obtained according to (7) for all possible values of the parameter d was used as the second controlled random test $CRT(1)$. The resulting values of the metric $E(k, 2^m)$ for the double test $MCRT_2$ that consists of tests $CRT(0)$ and $CRT(1)$ are shown in Table 4. As can be seen from given numerical values, the effectiveness of the double test is in strict accordance with the values $ED(CRT(0), CRT(1))$ listed in Table 1. Indeed, for $d = 1$ and $d = 7$ the Euclidean distance between $CRT(0)$ and $CRT(1)$ equals the minimum value $\sqrt{56}$ (Table 1), respectively, and the number of additional binary combinations is minimum for all the values k. At the same time, for $d = 4$ and, consequently, for the maximum value $ED(CRT(0), CRT(1)) = \sqrt{128}$

Table 4. Estimation of the effectiveness of the double test for the storage device consisting of eight memory cells ($2^m = 8$) for $k = 3, 4, 5, 6$

d	$E(k, 2^m)$ - additional number of combinations on all possible k from 2^m bits			
	$E(3,8)$	$E(4,8)$	$E(5,8)$	$E(6,8)$
1	42	105	140	105
2	72	165	200	135
3	90	195	220	140
4	96	204	224	140
5	90	195	220	140
6	72	165	200	135
7	42	105	140	105

the number of additional combinations is maximum (Table 4). The results in Table 4 confirm the validity of theoretical provisions and, above all, the validity of Theorem 1.

When using controlled random tests, in most cases, the number q of test sets is less than the total number of 2^m m-bit input patterns [1,12–15]. Accordingly, the validity of the results of Theorem 1 for the case $q < 2^m$ and, above all, for Corollary 3 is significant for the proposed method of constructing controlled random tests. According to this corollary, the Euclidean distance $ED(CRT(k), CRT(l)) = \sqrt{2^m d(2^m - d)}$ obtained for $q = 2^m$ can be used as a mean value for $q < 2^m$ and can be determined by the relation $AED(CRT(k), CRT(l)) = \sqrt{qd(2^m - d)}$. It is obvious that, according to Corollary 3, the error between the experimental values AED(CRT(k),CRT(l)), and theoretical values should decrease with increasing value of q. When $q = 2^m$, experimental and theoretical values should be equal, which is confirmed by practical results given in Fig. 1. The figure shows averaged values of deviations of the experimental data from the theoretical results depending on q. As can be seen from Fig. 1, even for $q > 100$, the experimental results hardly differ from the theoretical values, which confirms the validity of using the results of Theorem 1 to generate controlled random tests.

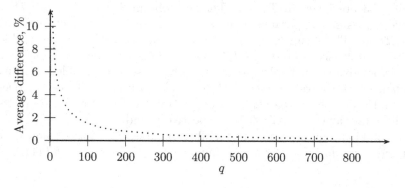

Fig. 1. Average difference value (%) of the experimental value $AED(CRT(k), CRT(l))$ from the theoretical value obtained by the formula for $m = 10$.

Finally, to confirm the proposed solution we have compared the coverage of Multiple Random Tests and Multiple Controlled Random Tests in terms of number of generated binary combinations for all arbitrary k out of N bits. Using both methods, we had generated multiple tests consisting of $r = 4$ tests with $q = 3$ subtests. In the first case all tests and subtests were generated randomly. In case of Multiple Controlled Random Tests only first test $CRT(0)$ was generated randomly whereas $CRT(1), CRT(2)$ and $CRT(3)$ were generated with respect to Theorem 2 and Eq. (7). The obtained average results for 5000 experiments are shown in the Fig. 2a and b. The x-axis represents the test number $CRT(i)$, and the y-axis – the number (in percent) of binary combinations for all arbitrary $k = 3$ and $k = 4$ out of $N = 64$ bits. For Fig. 2, we observe that in both cases

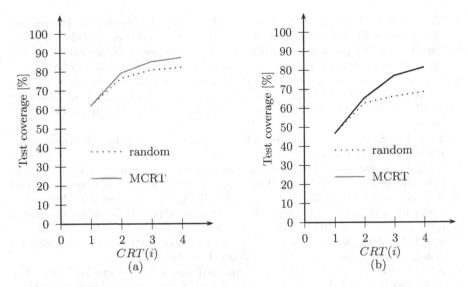

Fig. 2. The coverage of all arbitrary k out of N bits for multiple random tests and multiple controlled random test: (a) $k = 3$ and $N = 64$, (b) $k = 4$ and $N = 64$

curves rise sharply and exhibits a smooth behavior. We observe that $MCRT_r$ gives us a bit higher level of fault coverage as in case of random patterns. The same time we should noted that $MCRT_r$ is characterized by easier computational method of test patterns generation in compare to other techniques.

6 Conclusion

The concept of multiple controlled random tests has been considered. Existing solutions have been analyzed, and a formal method for generating multiple tests has been proposed. The efficiency of using the Euclidean distance to construct multiple tests has been confirmed based on the experimental results for the case of multiple tests of storage devices. Finally the efficiency of proposed Multiple Controlled Random Tests has been tested. The experimental study demonstrate a high efficiency of the proposed solution.

References

1. Anand, S., Burke, E.K., Chen, T.Y., Clark, J., Cohen, M.B., Grieskamp, W., Harman, M., Harrold, M.J., Mcminn, P.: An orchestrated survey of methodologies for automated software test case generation. J. Syst. Softw. **86**(8), 1978–2001 (2013)
2. Chen, T.Y., Merkel, R.G.: Quasi-random testing. IEEE Trans. Reliab. **56**(3), 562–568 (2007)
3. Lv, J., Hu, H., Cai, K., Chen, T.Y.: Adaptive and random partition software testing. IEEE Trans. Syst. Man Cybern.: Syst. **44**(12), 1649–1664 (2014)

4. Malaiya, Y.K., Yang, S.: The coverage problem for random testing. In: Proceedings of the 1994 IEEE International Test Conference, ITC 1984, pp. 237–245 (1984)
5. Shahbazi, A., Tappenden, A.F., Miller, J.: Centroidal voronoi tessellations – a new approach to random testing. IEEE Trans. Softw. Eng. **39**(2), 163–183 (2013)
6. Sosnowski, J., Wabia, T., Bech, T.: Path delay fault testability analysis. In: Proceedings of the 15th IEEE International Symposium on Defect and Fault-Tolerance in VLSI Systems (DFT 2000), Yamanashi, Japan, 25–27 October 2000, p. 338 (2000)
7. Yarmolik, S., Yarmolik, V.: Controlled random tests. Autom. Remote Control **73**(10), 1704–1714 (2012)
8. Kuo, F.: An indepth study of mirror adaptive random testing. In: Choi, B. (ed.) Proceedings of the Ninth International Conference on Quality Software, QSIC 2009, Jeju, Korea, 24–25 August 2009, pp. 51–58. IEEE Computer Society (2009)
9. Tappenden, A., Miller, J.: A novel evolutionary approach for adaptive random testing. IEEE Trans. Reliab. **58**(4), 619–633 (2009)
10. Wu, S.H., Jandhyala, S., Malaiya, Y.K., Jayasumana, A.P.: Antirandom testing: a distance-based approach. VLSI Des. **2008**, 1–2 (2008)
11. Xu, S.: Orderly random testing for both hardware and software. In: Proceedings of the 2008 14th IEEE Pacific Rim International Symposium on Dependable Computing, pp. 160–167. IEEE Computer Society, Washington, DC (2008)
12. Zhou, Z.: Using coverage information to guide test case selection in adaptive random testing. In: Computer Software and Applications Conference Workshops, pp. 208–213 (2010)
13. Chen, T.Y., Kuo, F.C., Merkel, R.G., Tse, T.H.: Adaptive random testing: the art of test case diversity. J. Syst. Softw. **83**, 60–66 (2010)
14. Yarmolik, S.V., Yarmolik, V.N.: The synthesis of probability tests with a small number of kits. Autom. Control Comput. Sci. **45**(3), 133–141 (2011)
15. Sahari, M.S., Aain, A.K., Grout, I.A.: Scalable antirandom testing (SAT). Int. J. Innovative Sci. Mod. Eng. (IJISME) **3**, 33–35 (2015)
16. Mrozek, I., Yarmolik, V.N.: Antirandom test vectors for BIST in hardware/software systems. Fundam. Inform. **119**(2), 163–185 (2012)
17. Mrozek, I., Yarmolik, V.N.: Iterative antirandom testing. J. Electron. Test **28**(3), 301–315 (2012)
18. Yarmolik, V.N., Yarmolik, S.V.: Address sequences. Autom. Control Comput. Sci. **48**(4), 207–213 (2014)
19. Malaiya, Y.K.: Antirandom testing: getting the most out of black-box testing. In: Proceedings of 6th IEEE International Symposium on Software Reliability Engineering, ISSRE 1995, pp. 86–95. IEEE Computer Society (1995)
20. Yarmolik, V., Yarmolik, S.: The repeated nondestructive march tests with variable address sequences. Autom. Remote Control **68**(4), 688–698 (2007)
21. Yarmolik, V.N., Mrozek, I., Yarmolik, S.V.: Controlled method of random test synthesis. Autom. Control Comput. Sci. **49**(6), 395–403 (2016)

Blocking and Deadlocking Phenomena in Two-Server Tandem Configuration with Optional Feedback – Modeling and Parameter Sensitivity Investigation

Walenty Oniszczuk[(✉)]

Faculty of Computer Science, Bialystok University of Technology,
Bialystok, Poland
w.oniszczuk@pb.edu.pl

Abstract. Tandem queues provide good mathematical models of computer systems and networks, and their detailed examination is important for theory and applications. The study presented in this paper is based on performance analysis of a two-server computer network with blocking and deadlocking. New, practical results provided describe performance of a three-node Markovian queuing network with finite capacity buffers. The results highlight an area where measures of effectiveness, such as Quality of Service (QoS) are essential. In conclusion, a two-dimensional state graph is constructed, followed by a set of steady-state equations along with their probabilities for each of the states.

Keywords: Tandem queues · Feedback · Deadlock · Blocking probability

1 Introduction

The behavior of various systems, including communication and computer systems, as well as production and manufacturing procedures, can be represented and analyzed through queuing network models to evaluate their performance [10, 25, 26]. System performance analysis consists of the derivation of a set of particular features [2, 6, 7, 9]. This usually includes the queue length distribution and various performance indicators such as response time, throughput and utilization.

Tandem queues are widely used in design, capacity planning and performance evaluation of computer and communication systems, call centers, flexible manufacturing systems, etc. Some examples of their application in real systems (two transmitter communication networks with DBA (Dynamic Bandwidth Allocation), service facility with front and back room operations) can be found in [24], [1] respectively.

The theory behind tandem queues is well developed, see, e.g. [3–5, 11, 22, 23]. However, there is still a great interest around more complicated setups involving blocking and deadlocking phenomena as well as different mechanisms for offering services. In particular, the two-node tandem queuing model with the BMAP (Batch Markovian Arrival Process) input flow and non-exponential service time distribution

K. Saeed and W. Homenda (Eds.): CISIM 2016, LNCS 9842, pp. 441–452, 2016.
DOI: 10.1007/978-3-319-45378-1_39

described in the paper [8]. Additionally, systems with finite capacity queues under various blocking mechanisms and scheduling constraints are analyzed by the author in [12–21].

In [12, 13], the closed type, multi-center computer networks with different blocking strategies are investigated and measures of effectiveness based on Quality of Service (QoS) are studied. Markovian and semi-Markovian approaches for analysis of open tandem networks with blocking are presented in [14, 16, 18, 20, 21]. Some two-stage tandem queues with blocking and an optional feedback are presented in [17, 19]. In such systems, feedback is the likelihood of a task return, with fixed probability to the first node of the tandem immediately after the service at the second one. Tandems with feedback are usually more complex than the ones without and they are mostly investigated given stationary Poisson arrival process and exponential service time distribution. Blocking and deadlocking phenomena in an open series, linked network model with HOL (head-of-line) priority feedback service was investigated and presented by the author in [15].

The rest of this paper is organized as follows: Sect. 2 presents and explains the analytical model. Section 3, analyzes a tandem network with blocking, feedback service and deadlock phenomena. Procedures for calculating performance measures and Quality of Service (QoS) parameters are presented in Sect. 4. Numerical results obtained using our solution technique is given in Sect. 5. Finally, Sect. 6 concludes the paper.

2 Model Specification and Description

The general model outline:

- The arrival process from source station is Poisson.
- Each station consists of a single server and buffer.
- Two stations provide service that is exponentially distributed.
- The deadlock resolving rate μ^d is also exponentially distributed.
- Scheduling disciplines are FCFS.
- All buffers have finite capacity $m1$ and $m2$.

Figure 1 presents a simplified two-server tandem setup of the proposed model. Tasks arrive from the source at station A according to the Poisson process with rate λ and they are processed in a FIFO manner. The service received by station A is as follows: the task first accepts an exponentially distributed service with rate μ^A, after service completion at station A, the task proceeds to station B (exponentially distributed service with rate μ^B), once it finishes at station B, it gets sent back to station A for re-processing with probability $1 - \sigma$. We are also assuming that tasks, after being processed in the station B, may leave the network with probability σ.

The successive service times at both servers are mutually independent and are not conditioned on the state of the network. A finite capacity buffers (with capacity $m1$ and $m2$) are allowed at the front of each server. A task, upon service completion at server A, attempts with probability $1 - \sigma$ to join server B. If server B at the given time is full, then the first server must hold the completed task and consequently becomes blocked (i.e., not available for service on incoming tasks) until the second server completes

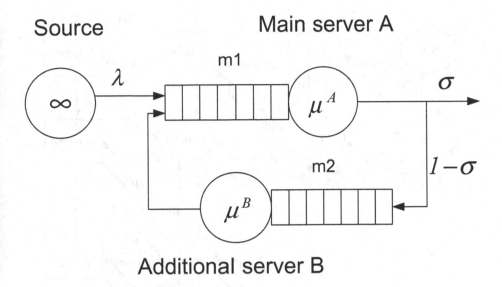

Fig. 1. Two-server tandem configuration with feedback.

service. The nature of the service process in this case depends only of the service rate at station B. It allows one to treat this task as located in additional places in the buffer B. Similarly, if the first buffer (with capacity $m1$) ahead of the first station is full, then the source station or the server B becomes blocked. In this case, the nature of the service process depends only of the service rates in station A and we can treat these tasks as located in additional places in the buffer A. There can be a maximum of $m1 + 3$ tasks assigned to the first servicing station including the tasks at the source and server B that can become blocked. Likewise, there can be a maximum of $m2 + 2$ tasks assigned to station B with a task blocked at server A (see Fig. 2).

In this special type of multi-stage network with blocking a deadlock may occur. For example, let us suppose that server A is full and server B blocks it. A deadlock will occur if the task in service at server B is sent to server A upon completion of its service. We assume that a deadlock is detected instantaneously and resolved with some delay time by simultaneously exchanging both blocked tasks at the mean rate equal to μ^d.

Generally, blocking and deadlocking phenomena is a very important mechanism for controlling and regulating intensity of arriving tasks from the source to the tandem stations. The arrival rate to the first server depends on the state of the network and blocking factor that reduces the rate at which source is sending traffic to this server.

3 Exact Analysis

Markov processes constitute the fundamental theory underlying the concept of queuing systems and provide very powerful and descriptive means for analysis of dynamic computer networks. Each queuing system can, in principle, be mapped onto an instance

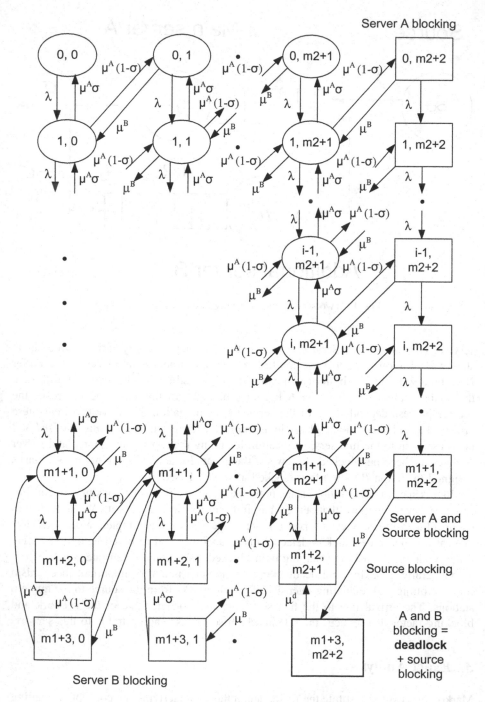

Fig. 2. State transmission diagram for tandem with blocking and deadlock

of a Markov process and then mathematically evaluated in terms of this process. According to general assumptions, a continuous-time homogeneous Markov chain can represent a tandem network. The queuing network model reaches a steady-state condition and the underlying Markov chain has a stationary state distribution. Also, such queuing network with finite capacity queues has finite state space. The solution of the Markov chain representation may then be computed and the desired performance characteristics, as queue length distribution, utilizations, and throughputs, obtained directly from the stationary probability vector. In addition, features such as deadlocks, blocking, feedback service, may be incorporated into a Markov chain representation – although the effect of doing so will increase the size of the state space.

In theory, any Markov model can be solved numerically. In particular, solution algorithm for Markov queuing networks with blocking, feedback service and deadlocks is a five-step procedure:

1. Definition of the series network state space (choosing a state space representation).
2. Enumerating all the transitions that can possible occur among the states.
3. Definition of the transition rate matrix Q that describes the network evaluation (generating the transition rate).
4. Solution of linear system of the global balance equations to derive the stationary state distribution vector (computing appropriate probability vector).
5. Computation from the probability vector of the average performance indices.

In this type of a network we may denote its state by the pair (i,j), where i represents the number of tasks in server A and j denotes the number in server B (including the tasks in service, in blocking, or in deadlock). For any non-negative integer values of i and j, (i,j) represent a feasible state of this queuing network, and $p_{i,j}$ denotes the probability for that state in equilibrium. These states and the possible transitions among them are shown in Fig. 2. The flux into a state of the model is given by all arrows into the corresponding state, and the flux out of the state is determined from the set of all outgoing arrows from the state. The arrows indicate the only transitions that are possible for this model. Transitions from top to bottom represent a change of state due to an arrival from the source station. Diagonal transitions from left to right or from right to left represent a change of state due to a task completing service at server A or at server B. Finally, transitions indicated by bottom to top arrows represent a change of state due to departures from the network, which occurs at rate $\mu^A \sigma$. The state diagram of the blocking network (see Fig. 2) contains all possible non-blocked states (marked by ovals) as well as the blocking states (marked by rectangles). Additionally, one special state, which represents deadlock state – is marked by a bold rectangle. The number of states in the blocking network is the sum of all possible non-blocking states plus all the blocking states: $(m2 + 2)(m1 + 3) + m1 + 2 + m2 + 2$. Based on an analysis the state space diagram, the process of constructing the steady-state equations in the Markov model, can be divided into several independent steps, which describe some similar, repeatable patterns. For the server A, the steady-state blocking equations are:

$$(\lambda + \mu^B) \cdot p_{0,m2+2} = \mu^A(1 - \sigma) \cdot p_{1,m2+1}$$
$$(\lambda + \mu^B) \cdot p_{i,m2+2} = \lambda \cdot p_{i-1,m2+2} + \mu^A(1 - \sigma) \cdot p_{i+1,m2+1} \quad \text{for } i = 1, \cdots, m1 \quad (1)$$
$$\mu^B \cdot p_{m1+1,m2+2} = \lambda \cdot p_{m1,m2+2} + \mu^A(1 - \sigma) \cdot p_{m1+2,m2+1}$$

For the source, the blocking equations are:

$$(\mu^A\sigma + \mu^A(1 - \sigma)) \cdot p_{m1+2,j} = \lambda \cdot p_{m1+1,j} \quad \text{for } j = 0, \cdots, m2$$
$$(\mu^A\sigma + \mu^A(1 - \sigma)) \cdot p_{m1+2,m2+1} = \lambda \cdot p_{m1+1,m2+1} + \mu^d \cdot p_{m1+3,m2+2} \quad (2)$$

For the server B, the blocking equations are:

$$(\mu^A\sigma + \mu^A(1 - \sigma)) \cdot p_{m1+3,j} = \mu^B \cdot p_{m1+1,j+1} \quad \text{for } j = 0, \cdots, m2 \quad (3)$$

For the deadlock, the steady-state blocking equation is:

$$\mu^d \cdot p_{m1+3,m2+2} = \mu^B \cdot p_{m1+1,m2+2} \quad (4)$$

The steady-state equations for all states without blocking are:

$$\lambda \cdot p_{0,0} = \mu^A\sigma \cdot p_{1,0}$$
$$(\lambda + \mu^B) \cdot p_{0,j} = \mu^A(1 - \sigma) \cdot p_{1,j-1} + \mu^A\sigma \cdot p_{1,j} \quad \text{for } j = 1, \cdots, m2+1$$
$$(\lambda + \mu^A\sigma + \mu^A(1 - \sigma)) \cdot p_{i,0} = \lambda \cdot p_{i-1,0} + \mu^B \cdot p_{i-1,1} + \mu^A\sigma \cdot p_{i+1,0} \quad \text{for } i = 1, \cdots, m1$$
$$(\lambda + \mu^A\sigma + \mu^A(1 - \sigma) + \mu^B) \cdot p_{i,j} = \lambda \cdot p_{i-1,j} + \mu^B \cdot p_{i-1,j+1} + \mu^A\sigma \cdot p_{i+1,j} + \mu^A(1 - \sigma) \cdot p_{i+1,j-1}$$
$$\quad \text{for } i = 1, \cdots, m1, j = 1, \cdots, m2+1$$
$$(\lambda + \mu^A\sigma + \mu^A(1 - \sigma)) \cdot p_{m1+1,0} = \lambda \cdot p_{m1,0} + \mu^B \cdot p_{m1,1} + \mu^A\sigma \cdot p_{m1+2,0} + \mu^A\sigma \cdot p_{m1+3,0}$$
$$(\lambda + \mu^A\sigma + \mu^A(1 - \sigma) + \mu^B) \cdot p_{m1+1,j} = \lambda \cdot p_{m1,j} + \mu^B \cdot p_{m1,j+1} + \mu^A\sigma \cdot p_{m1+2,j} + \mu^A\sigma \cdot p_{m1+3,j} + \mu^A(1 - \sigma) \cdot p_{m1+3,j-1}$$
$$\quad \text{for } j = 1, \cdots, m2$$
$$(\lambda + \mu^A\sigma + \mu^A(1 - \sigma) + \mu^B) \cdot p_{m1+1,m2+1} = \lambda \cdot p_{m1,m2+1} + \mu^B \cdot p_{m1,m2+2} + + \mu^A\sigma \cdot p_{m1+2,m2+1} + \mu^A(1 - \sigma) \cdot p_{m1+3,m2}$$
$$\quad (5)$$

A queuing network with feedback, blocking and deadlock, under appropriate assumptions, is formulated here as a Markov process. The stationary probability vector can be obtained from (1)–(5) equations, by using numerical methods for linear systems of equations. The generation of the rate matrix Q can now be accomplished by going through the list of states and generating all the feasible transitions out of each state and the associated rates of each transition. For Markov processes in steady state, we have:

$$xQ = 0 \quad (6)$$

where x is the stationary probability vector whose l-th element x_l is the steady-state probability of a system in state l. Vector x can be obtained from (6) and a normalization condition for all network states $\sum x_l = 1$, using equation-solving techniques.

4 Selected Performance Measures

When steady-state probabilities are known, one can easily obtain various performance measures. For example, the procedures for calculating the Quality of Service (QoS) parameters use the steady-state probabilities in the following manner:

1. Deadlock probability p_{dead}:

$$p_{dead} = p_{m1+3, m2+2} \tag{7}$$

2. Source node blocking probability p_{blS}:

$$p_{blS} = \sum_{j=0}^{m2+1} p_{m1+2, j} \tag{8}$$

3. Server A blocking probability p_{blA}:

$$p_{blA} = \sum_{i=0}^{m1} p_{i, m2+2} \tag{9}$$

4. Server B blocking probability p_{blB}:

$$p_{blB} = \sum_{j=0}^{m2} p_{m1+3, j} \tag{10}$$

5. Simultaneously source and node A blocking probability p_{blSA}:

$$p_{blSA} = p_{m1+1, m2+2} \tag{11}$$

6. Network blocking probability p_{bl}:

$$p_{bl} = p_{blA} + p_{blB} + p_{blS} + p_{m1+1, m2+2} \tag{12}$$

7. Idle probability p_{idle}:

$$p_{idle} = p_{0,0} \tag{13}$$

8. Server A utilization ρ_A:

$$\rho_A = \sum_{i=1}^{m1+2} \sum_{j=0}^{m2+1} 1 \cdot p_{i,j} + \sum_{j=0}^{m2} 1 \cdot p_{m1+3, j} + \sum_{i=0}^{m1+1} 1 \cdot p_{i, m2+2} \tag{14}$$

9. Server B utilization ρ_B:

$$\rho_B = \sum_{i=0}^{m1+2} \sum_{j=1}^{m2+1} 1 \cdot p_{i,j} + \sum_{i=0}^{m1+1} 1 \cdot p_{i,m2+2} + \sum_{j=0}^{m2} 1 \cdot p_{m1+3,j} \tag{15}$$

10. The mean deadlocking time:

$$t_{dead} = 2 \cdot p_{m1+3,m2+2} \cdot \frac{1}{\mu^d} \tag{16}$$

11. The mean blocking time in server A:

$$t_{blA} = \left(\sum_{i=0}^{m1+1} 1 \cdot p_{i,m2+2} \right) \cdot \frac{1}{\mu^B} \tag{17}$$

12. The mean blocking time in server B:

$$t_{blB} = \left(\sum_{j+0}^{m2} 1 \cdot p_{m1+3,j} \right) \cdot \frac{1}{\mu^A} \tag{18}$$

13. The mean blocking time in source node:

$$t_{blS} = \left(\sum_{j=0}^{m2+1} 1 \cdot p_{m1+2,j} + 1 \cdot p_{m1+1,m2+2} \right) \cdot \frac{1}{\mu^A} \tag{19}$$

14. The network blocking time:

$$t_{bl} = t_{blA} + t_{blB} + t_{blS} \tag{20}$$

5   Numerical Results

In this section, we present some numerical examples to study the effect of the parameters on the selected performance characteristics. We will concentrate on the several important performance descriptors, such as the probability that the tandem network is deadlocked or blocked, blocking probabilities for A and B servers and various time measures. Different values of the parameters are taken for task inter-arrival rates, service intensities or feedback probabilities. To demonstrate this, the following configuration was chosen: the inter-arrival rate λ from the source station to server A is changed within a range from 0.5 to 5.0. The service rates in server A and server B are equal to: $\mu^A = 10.0$, $\mu^B = 5.0$. The deadlock resolving rate μ^d is 1.5, the depart probability σ is chosen as 0.3 and the buffer capacities are equal to: $m1 = 10$, $m2 = 5$.

For this model with deadlock and blocking, the following results were obtained; the majority of them are presented in Fig. 3 and Table 1.

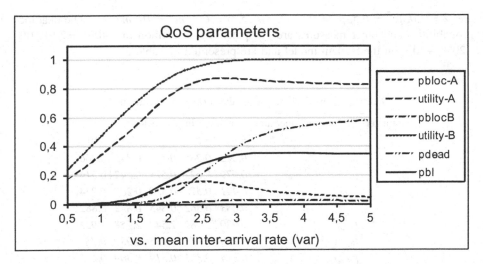

Fig. 3. Graphs of QoS parameters, where, *pbloc-A* - the server *A* blocking probability, *pblocB* - the server *B* blocking probability, *pdead* is the deadlock probability, *pbl* is the common network blocking probability, *utility-A* and *utility-B* are the servers utilization coefficients.

Table 1. The time measures versus mean inter arrival rates

λ	t_{blA}	t_{blS}	t_{blB}	t_{dead}	t_{bl}	ρ_A	ρ_B
0.5	0.000	0.000	0.000	0.000	0.000	0.167	0.233
1.0	0.001	0.000	0.000	0.000	0.001	0.337	0.467
1.5	0.008	0.000	0.000	0.004	0.008	0.534	0.694
2.0	0.024	0.001	0.001	0.069	0.028	0.746	0.869
2.5	0.031	0.004	0.002	0.277	0.045	0.859	0.959
3.0	0.025	0.008	0.003	0.523	0.051	0.868	0.991
3.5	0.017	0.009	0.003	0.660	0.049	0.851	0.998
4.0	0.013	0.010	0.003	0.719	0.046	0.839	0.999
4.5	0.011	0.011	0.002	0.752	0.045	0.832	1.000
5.0	0.009	0.011	0.002	0.773	0.045	0.828	1.000

Figure 3 and Table 1 illustrate dependencies of blocking and deadlock probabilities and their time measures given certain parameters. In this example, the utilization of the tandem network is determined only by one parameter, e.g. by increasing the inter-arrival rates for the fixed values of other parameters. Also, results in Fig. 3 and Table 1 evidently show that the deadlock and blocking phenomena must be taken into account because variation of inter-arrival rate drastically changes QoS and time measures of the tandem network with feedback.

Sensitivity analysis of the proposed tandem model is performed with respect to the effect of changes in the parameters μ^A, μ^B, μ^d, σ, $m1$ and $m2$ (without changes λ - see investigation in the previous example) on the deadlock and blocking probabilities, the time measures and the nodes utilization. The data parameters for the sensitivity analysis are: $\lambda = 1.0$, $\mu^A = 0.5$, $\mu^B = 0.5$, $\mu^d = 0.25$, $\sigma = 0.5$, $m1 = 10$, $m2 = 5$. The deadlock probabilities and other measures are computed with variation of -40%, -20%, 0%, $+20\%$, $+40\%$ on the tandem model and are presented in Table 2.

Table 2. Sensitive analysis of the proposed tandem model

Parameter	Performance measure	% change in parameter				
		−40	−20	0	+20	+40
μ^A	p_{dead}	0.242	0.285	0.319	0.345	0.366
	p_{bl}	0.679	0.622	0.578	0.542	0.514
	p_{blS}	0.441	0.378	0.328	0.288	0.254
	ρ_A	0.883	0.862	0.845	0.832	0.882
	t_{dead}	1.939	2.282	2.548	2.758	2.925
	t_{bl}	2.159	1.512	1.155	0.935	0.789
μ^B	p_{dead}	0.314	0.321	0.319	0.309	0.295
	p_{bl}	0.603	0.584	0.578	0.579	0.585
	p_{blS}	0.291	0.314	0.328	0.338	0.344
	ρ_A	0.743	0.804	0.845	0.876	0.899
	t_{dead}	2.513	2.573	2.548	2.472	2.261
	t_{bl}	1.353	1.218	1.155	1.131	1.131
μ^d	p_{dead}	0.438	0.369	0.319	0.280	0.250
	p_{bl}	0.476	0.535	0.578	0.610	0.635
	p_{blS}	0.271	0.304	0.328	0.349	0.361
	ρ_A	0.872	0.857	0.845	0.837	0.830
	t_{dead}	5.839	3.688	2.548	1.869	1.430
	t_{bl}	0.953	1.070	1.155	1.220	1.271
σ	p_{dead}	0.420	0.378	0.319	0.228	0.069
	p_{bl}	0.539	0.556	0.578	0.604	0.603
	p_{blS}	0.285	0.304	0.328	0.365	0.438
	ρ_A	0.792	0.815	0.845	0.891	0.894
	t_{dead}	3.358	3.020	2.548	1.827	0.551
	t_{bl}	1.077	1.112	1.155	1.208	1.207
$m1$	p_{dead}	0.319	0.319	0.319	0.319	0.318
	p_{bl}	0.578	0.578	0.578	0.578	0.578
	p_{blS}	0.328	0.328	0.328	0.328	0.328
	ρ_A	0.845	0.845	0.845	0.845	0.845
	t_{dead}	2.548	2.548	2.548	2.548	2.548
	t_{bl}	1.155	1.155	1.155	1.155	1.155
$m2$	p_{dead}	0.319	0.319	0.319	0.318	0.318
	p_{bl}	0.577	0.577	0.578	0.578	0.578
	p_{blS}	0.329	0.329	0.328	0.328	0.328
	ρ_A	0.845	0.845	0.845	0.845	0.845
	t_{dead}	2.553	2.550	2.548	2.548	2.547
	t_{bl}	1.153	1.154	1.155	1.155	1.155

From the Table 2 it is clear that the probability and time measures are highly effected by small changes in the parameters μ^A, μ^d, and σ. On the average effect was observed, when the μ^B parameter changes from −40% to +40% and minimal effect was observed, when parameters $m1$ and $m2$ varies from −40% to +40%.

6 Conclusions

In this paper, the problem of analytical (mathematical) modelling and calculation of the stationary state probabilities for a two-server tandem network with recycling, task blocking and deadlocking is investigated. Deadlock and task blocking probabilities and some other fundamental performance characteristics of such network are derived and followed by numerical examples. The results confirm importance of a special treatment for the models with blocking, deadlock and with feedback service, that justifies my research. The results can be used for capacity planning and performance evaluation of real-time computer networks where deadlock, blocking and feedback are present.

References

1. Arivudainambi, D., Poongothai, V.: Analysis of a service facility with cross trained servers and optional feedback. Int. J. Oper. Res. **18**(2), 218–237 (2013)
2. Atencia, I.: A discrete-time system with service control and repairs. Int. J. Appl. Math. Comput. Sci. **24**(3), 471–484 (2014)
3. Balsamo, S., De Nito Persone, V., Onvural, R.: Analysis of Queueing Networks with Blocking. Kluwer Academic Publishers, Boston (2001)
4. Clo, M.C.: MVA for product-form cyclic queueing networks with blocking. Ann. Oper. Res. **79**, 83–96 (1998)
5. Economou, A., Fakinos, D.: Product form stationary distributions for queueing networks with blocking and rerouting. Queueing Syst. **30**(3/4), 251–260 (1998)
6. Gemikonakli, E., Mapp, G., Gemikonakli, O., Ever, E.: Exploring service and buffer management issues to provide integrated voice and data services in single and multi-channel wireless networks. In: 2013 IEEE 27th International Conference on Advanced Information Networking and Applications (AINA), pp. 1056–1063. IEEE Conference Publications (2013). doi:10.1109/AINA.2013.57
7. Itoh, H., Fukumoto, H., Wakuya, H., Furukawa, T.: Bottom-up learning of hierarchical models in a class of deterministic POMDP environments. Int. J. Appl. Math. Comput. Sci. **25**(3), 597–615 (2015)
8. Kim, C.S., Klimenok, V., Tsarenkov, G., Breuer, L., Dudin, A.: The BMAP/G/1-> •/PH/1/M tandem queue with feedback and losses. Perform. Eval. **64**, 802–818 (2007)
9. Kwiecień, J., Filipowicz, B.: Firefly algorithm in optimization of queueing systems. Bull. Pol. Acad.: Tech. **60**(2), 363–368 (2012)
10. Malekian, R., Abdullah, A.H., Ye, N.: Novel packet queuing algorithm on packet delivery in mobile internet protocol version 6 networks. Appl. Math. Inf. Sci. **7**(3), 881–887 (2013)
11. Martin, J.B.: Large tandem queueing networks with blocking. Queueing Syst. **41**(1/2), 45–72 (2002)
12. Oniszczuk, W.: Quality of service requirements in computer networks with blocking. In: Saeed, K., Pejas, J. (eds.) Information Processing and Security Systems, pp. 245–254. Springer Science+Business Media, New York (2005)

13. Oniszczuk, W.: Modeling of dynamical flow control procedures in closed type queuing models of a computer network with blocking. Automat. Contr. Comput. Sci. **39**(4), 60–69 (2005)
14. Oniszczuk, W.: Tandem models with blocking in the computer subnetworks performance analysis. In: Saeed, K., Pejas, J., Mosdorf, R. (eds.) Biometrics, Computer Security Systems and Artificial Intelligence Applications, pp. 259–267. Springer Science+Business Media, New York (2006)
15. Oniszczuk, W.: Blocking and deadlock factors in series linked servers with HOL priority feedback service. Pol. J. Environ. Stud. **16**(5B), 145–151 (2007)
16. Oniszczuk, W.: Analysis of an open linked series three-station network with blocking. In: Pejas, J., Saeed, K. (eds.) Advances in Information Processing and Protection, pp. 419–429. Springer Science+Business Media, New York (2007)
17. Oniszczuk, W.: An intelligent service strategy in linked networks with blocking and feedback. In: Nguyen, N.T., Katarzyniak, R. (eds.) New Challenges in Applied Intelligence Technologies. SCI, vol. 134, pp. 351–361. Springer, Heidelberg (2008)
18. Oniszczuk, W.: Semi-Markov-based approach for analysis of open tandem networks with blocking and truncation. Int. J. Appl. Math. Comput. Sci. **19**(1), 151–163 (2009)
19. Oniszczuk, W.: Analysis of linked in series servers with blocking, priority feedback service and threshold policy. Int. J. Comput. Syst. Sci. Eng. **5**(1), 1–8 (2009)
20. Oniszczuk, W.: Loss tandem networks with blocking analysis – a semi-Markov approach. Bull. Pol. Acad.: Tech. **58**(4), 673–681 (2010)
21. Oniszczuk, W.: Open tandem networks with blocking analysis – two approaches. Control Cybern. **43**(1), 111–132 (2014)
22. Onvural, R.: Survey of closed queuing networks with blocking. Comput. Surv. **22**(2), 83–121 (1990)
23. Perros, H.G.: Queuing Networks with Blocking. Exact and Approximate Solution. Oxford University Press, New York (1994)
24. Raghavendran, Ch.V., Naga Satish, G., Rama Sundari, M.V., Suresh Varma, P.: Tandem communication network model with DBA having non homogeneous Poisson arrivals and feedback for first node. Int. J. Comput. Technol. **13**(9), 4922–4932 (2014)
25. Sunitha, G.P., Kumar, S.M.D., Kumar, B.P.V.: A pre-emptive multiple queue congestion control for different traffic classes in WSN. In: 2014 International Conference on Circuits, Communication, Control and Computing, pp. 212–218. IEEE Conference Publications (2014). doi:10.1109/CIMCA.2014.7057793
26. Tikhonenko, O., Kempa, W.M.: On the queue-size distribution in the multi-server system with bounded capacity and packet dropping. Kybernetika **49**(6), 855–867 (2013)

Mutual Information for Quaternion Time Series

Michał Piórek[✉]

Department of Computer Engineering,
Wrocław University of Science and Technology,
Wybrzeże Stanisława Wyspiańskiego 27, 50-370 Wrocław, Poland
michal.piorek@pwr.edu.pl

Abstract. Mutual Information method is a widely used method for estimation of time delay value in the process of time delay embedding. It's designed for a univariate scalar time series. In the real systems often many outputs of investigated system are available. In this case a multivariate time delay estimation method is necessary if one may require to perform the uniform time delay embedding. The special case of multivariate data is a kinematic time series(e.g. quaternion time series or Euler angles time series). The main goal of this paper is to provide a method for this case: Mutual Information method's extension for quaternion time series. The results are also compared with previously presented quaternion's angle method. The method was tested on the real kinematic data - the recordings of human gait.

Keywords: Mutual information · Quaternions · Deterministic chaos · Nonlinear time series analysis · Human motion analysis · Human gait data

1 Introduction

The time delay embedding is heavily explored area of nonlinear time series analysis and nonlinear dynamical systems areas. Usually the most common application of this method is when we want to discover the dynamics of underlying system from the univariate scalar time series created from the measurements of one of the investigated system's outputs. Taken's Embedding Theorem [18] implies, that one can reconstruct an equivalent dynamics from univariate time series using it's time delays. To carry out the embedding procedure, which should result in the reconstructed attractor in the output, two parameters need to be estimated: time delay and embedding dimension.

The time delay is a integer value describing which samples from the investigated time series we need to incorporate to time-lagged embedding vector - reconstructing the underlying phase space. There are few approaches of estimation of time delay value T_d [9]. One group of methods is series correlation approaches (autocorrelation, mutual information [8] or high order correlations [2]). Second grop are approaches of phase space extension (fillfactor [5], wavering product [4] or average displacement [17]). There are available also multiple

K. Saeed and W. Homenda (Eds.): CISIM 2016, LNCS 9842, pp. 453–461, 2016.
DOI: 10.1007/978-3-319-45378-1_40

autocorrelation and non-bias multiple autocorrelation methods [11]. The embedding dimension is an equivalent of the real underlying phase space dimension. It could be estimated using the false nearest neighbors method [3] or it's extension - Cao's method [7]. Another methods are also the saturation of system invariants method [1] or neural network approaches [13].

The popularity of the univariate embedding may be caused by the fact, that according to the embedding theorem, for recovering dynamics only a univariate time series is needed. In fact, often many time series measured in the output of the test process are available. Since in multivariate case more data is available, it helps to establish more accurate embedding - in the sense of further predictions or in the presence of data noise. However, it brings a new dilemma: which quantities from multivariate time series to use and whether is better to use constant or non-constant embedding parameters for all quantities selected to embedding vector [6].

The problem of multivariate time series embedding can be seen in terms of suitable conditioned embedding of the considered set of time series [19]. In the related work there are two approaches of multivariate time series embedding: Uniform embedding and Non-uniform embedding. The uniform embedding scheme is more popular approach and assumes that embedding parameters: the time delay and embedding dimension are selected a priori and separately for each time series. The non-uniform embedding is based on the progressive selection of time delayed values from a set of candidate values(e.g. X, Y, Z) and incorporation them to the embedding vector. In each step the most informative time delayed variables are chosen and then added to the time delay vector. As a selection criteria the mutual information between constructed embedding vector and the future state of the system is used [14,19].

A particular case of multivariate time series is a rotational data time series. There are three main parametrization of rotations: matrix of rotation, Euler angles and Quaternions. Basing on this fact one may record and construct rotational time series according to the one of the above parameterizations. In this paper quaternion rotational time series is considered.

The main goal of this work is to propose time delay estimation method for uniform time delay embedding of multivariate quaternion rotational data. The proposed approach bases on mutual information approach and it's re-designed for quaternion kinematic time series. The presented method could be used in the further time delay embedding and nonlinear analysis aimed to detect deterministic chaos properties in the investigated data. The author would like to underline that the considered method allows to estimate the time delay value staying in quaternion domain, which should help to keep physical sense of the kinematic data.

The paper is organized as following: in the second section the applicability of mutual information method for quaternion data is discussed and proposed approach is described. It also includes the information about investigated quaternion time series and how K-Means algorithm is applied. The third section presents the numerical results. The conclusions are presented in section four.

2   Mutual Information Approach for Quaternions

Quaternions are computationally efficient parametrization of rotational data. They are an extension of complex numbers defined as following:

$$q = [w, (x, y, z)] = w + ix + jy + kz \tag{1}$$

where: w represents a real part and $v = (x, y, z)$ is called a vector part (i, j and k are equivalents of imaginary unit).

The details of Quaternions algebra widely used in the parametrization of rotations is well described in the related work(e.g. [10]). In the scope of our interests are unit quaternions which describe the rotation in 3D space:

$$\|q\| = 1 \tag{2}$$

where quaternion norm is defined by:

$$\|q\| = \sqrt{w^2 + x^2 + y^2 + z^2} \tag{3}$$

We assume that the method is designed for the following quaternion time series formed by unit quaternions as following:

$$Q(n) = (q_1, q_2, ..., q_N) = (w_1 + ix_1 + jy_1 + kz_1, ..., w_N + ix_N + jy_N + kz_N) \tag{4}$$

2.1   Mutual Information - Existing Approach

The mutual information is a measure which describes the general dependence of two variables. The definition comes from Shannon's information theory, which gives the formalism of measuring information spreading. Frasser proposed to use this approach in time delay estimation process [8].

Let's assume that there are two nonlinear systems: A and B. The outputs of these systems are denoted as a and b, while the values of these outputs are represented by a_i and b_k. The mutual information factor describes how many bits of b_k could be predicted where a_i is known.

$$I_{AB}(a_i, b_k) = log_2\left(\frac{P_{AB}(a_i, b_k)}{P_A(a_i)P_B(b_k)}\right), \tag{5}$$

where $P_A(a_i)$ is the probability that $a = a_i$ and $P_B(b_k)$ is the probability that $b = b_k$ and $P_{AB}(a_i, b_k)$ is the joint probability that $a = a_i$ and $b = b_k$.

The average mutual information factor can be described by:

$$I_{AB}(T) = \sum_{a_i, b_k} P_{AB}(a_i, b_k) I_{AB}(a_i, b_k). \tag{6}$$

In order to use this method to assess the correlation between different samples in the same time series, the Average mutual information factor is finally described by the equation:

$$I(T) = \sum_{n=1}^{N} P(S(n), S(n+T)) \\ log_2\left(\frac{P(S(n), S(n+T))}{P(S(n))P(S(n+T))}\right). \tag{7}$$

Fraser and Swinney [8] propose that T_m where the first minimum of $I(T)$ occurs as a useful selection of time lag T_d. This selection guarantees that the measurements are somewhat independent, but not statistically independent. In case of absence of the average mutual information clear minimum, this criterion needs to be replaced by choosing T_d as the time for which the average mutual information reaches four-fifths of its initial value:

$$\frac{I(T_d)}{I(0)} \approx \frac{4}{5}. \tag{8}$$

2.2 Mutual Information Extension for Quaternion Time Series

The average mutual information method for univariate time series consists of 2-dimensional adaptive histogram and that is the problem in it's application to multivariate(quaternion's case). The empirical histogram is straightforward to estimate for univariate time series, however for quaternion's time series it's not trivial. Computation of multivariate histogram is exhaustive process and in the result one may obtain the histogram empty in some places.

In the current approach instead of multidimensional histogram for quaternions we propose here to use histogram based on clusters. The whole quaternion time series is initially clustered into k-groups (where k is defined a priori). The obtained clusters are treated as an equivalent of histogram bins. Further in empirical histogram estimation, instead of computing the probability of belonging to the histogram's bins, the probability of belonging to the clusters is being computed.

Algorithm 1. k Means algorithm

1: **procedure** K MEANS
2:     $X \leftarrow$ Instance set
3:     $k \leftarrow$ Number of clusters
4:     $C \leftarrow$ *Initialize clusters randomly*
5:     $i \leftarrow 0$*Number of iterations*
6:     **while** $C_i! = C_{i+1}$ **do**
7:         Assign instances to the closest cluster center
8:         Update cluster centers based on the assignment
9:     **end while**
10: **end procedure**

Data clustering as a part of machine learning and data sciences is an actively investigated field of science. There are many available clustering techniques. The review of clustering methods is presented in the related work e.g. [16]. In the presented approach K-means clustering algorithm was selected as a the simplest and commonly used method. The main goal of this work is not to examine the efficiency of clustering approaches but to provide the mutual information estimation technique used clusters based histogram. In the oder hand, the author see the underlying potential in investigation of the impact of clustering method selection on the general algorithm's performance.

The K-means algorithm was described by MacQueen [12]. It partitions the data into K clusters (C_1, C_2, ..., C_k), represented by their centers. The center of each cluster, until converge, is calculated as the mean of all the samples belonging to that cluster. Initially the centers are selected randomly. Then, in each iteration each sample is assigned to the closest cluster center according to the Euclidean distance. Then the centers are re-calculated. The whole procedure is repeated until the convergence criteria is fulfilled (e.g. there is no relocation of the centers in new iteration) [16]. The whole procedure is presented in the pseudo-code 1.

Algorithm 2. Mutual information algorithm for quaternion time series

---

1: **procedure** MUTUALINFORAMTIONQUAT(QVect,T)   ▷ Mutual information for QVec-quaternion vector and T-time delays vector
2:     $k \leftarrow$ Number of clusters
3:     $n \leftarrow$ length(QVec)
4:     $[labels, centroids] \leftarrow KMeans(QVect,k)$
5:     **for each** t in T **do**
6:         $labelsQ \leftarrow$ labels(1:n-t)
7:         $labelsQD \leftarrow$ labels(1+t:n)
8:         $mI(t) \leftarrow 0$
9:         **for** i=1:k **do**
10:             **for** j=1:k **do**
11:                 $c1 \leftarrow$ centroids(i)
12:                 $c2 \leftarrow$ centroids(k)
13:                 $jointP \leftarrow$ find(c1==labelsQ and c2==labelsQD)
14:                 $jointP \leftarrow$ length(jointP)
15:                 $c1P \leftarrow$ find(c1==labelsQ)
16:                 $c2P \leftarrow$ find(c2==labelsQD)
17:                 **if** $jointP > 0$ **then**
18:                     $jointP \leftarrow$ jointP/(n-t)
19:                     $c1P \leftarrow$ length(c1P)/(n-t)
20:                     $c2P \leftarrow$ length(c2P)/(n-t)
21:                     $mI(t) \leftarrow mI(t)+$ jointP*log2(jointP/(c1P*c2P))
22:                 **end if**
23:             **end for**
24:         **end for**
25:     **end for**
26: **end procedure**

Finally, the mutual information algorithm for a quaternion time series is described by the pseudo code 2. Initially it treats quaternion time series as a 4-dimensional time series and partitions it into K-clusters. The next step is an estimation of probability of belonging samples to the each cluster which is an equivalent of estimation of probability of belonging samples to histogram bins in a standard version of the algorithm.

The author sees the potential advance in the method using an algorithm of clustering which partitions quaternion time series staying in quaternion domain. It will be the subject of further research. It is also worth to investigate how the number of the clusters impacts the performance of the algorithm.

3 Numerical Results

The method was tested on live kinematic data recorded in the Human Motion Laboratory (HML) of the Polish-Japanese Institute of Information Technology. The recordings were performed using the Vicon Motion Kinematics Acquisition and Analysis System equipped with 10 Near InfraRed cameras. The cameras were attached to a suit which was worn by a subject.

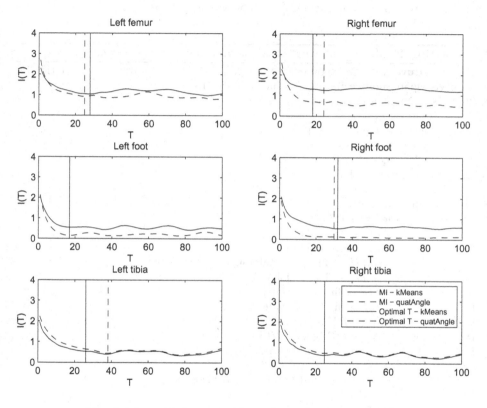

Fig. 1. Mutual information dependency for the patient A

Gait sequences were recorded in Euler angles and then converted to quaternions. Six kinds of time series were recorded - movements of femurs, tibias and feet (left and right). The method was tested on the data recorded from the treadmill walking of two healthy patients. The number of clusters in K-means algorithm was set to 7. The designed method was additionally compared with the quaternion angle method presented by the author in the same conference last year [15]. The results for the designed method are presented using solid line, where the results performed using quaternion angle method are presented using dashed line. Constantly the first local minima of the mutual information functions(time delay selection criteria) was marked by vertical lines. All estimated time delays are gathered in the Table 1.

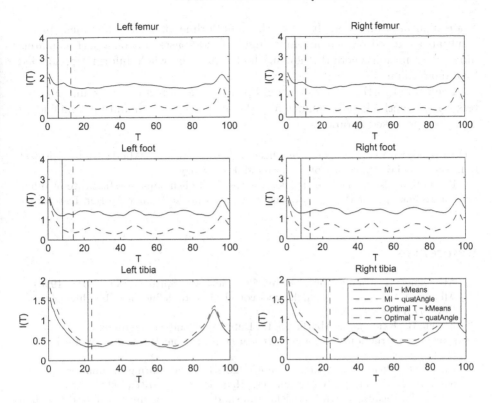

Fig. 2. Mutual information dependency for the patient B

Table 1. Time delay estimation comparison for subject A and subject B

Body part	T_d MI-angle(Patient A)	T_d MI-quat(Patient A)	T_d MI-angle(Patient B)	T_d MI-quat(Patient B)
Left femur	25	28	13	6
Right femur	24	18	11	5
Left foot	17	17	14	8
Right foot	30	32	13	8
Left tibia	38	26	24	22
Right tibia	25	25	24	22

4 Conclusion

The main goal of this article was to present a time delay estimation method for a quaternion time series. The approach extends the existing mutual information approach for quaternion time series by incorporation of K-means clustering for multivariate data instead of the empirical histogram. The method might be a first step to perform time delay embedding staying only in the quaternion domain, which will be a field of author's further research.

From visual inspection one can see that the results from the proposed method are in the same range as the results coming from previously investigated quaternion angle method. It is worth to underline that the differences in the result are expected, since quaternion angle method bases only on a part of quaternion's information where the new method utilize the whole information carried by a quaternion.

The field of further interests should be also the impact of clustering parameters on the methods performance and the analysis of the quality of embedding using the proposed approach.

Acknowledgments. This work has been supported by the "Młoda Kadra" project from the Wrocław University of Science and Technology.

The author also would like to acknowledge the Polish-Japanese Institute of Information Technology for the gait sequences recorded in the Human Motion Laboratory (HML).

References

1. Abarbanel, H.: Analysis of Observed Chaotic Data. Springer, New York (1996)
2. Albano, A.M., et al.: Using high-order correlations to define an embedding window. Phys. D **54**, 85–97 (1991)
3. Brown, R., Kennel, M., Abarbanel, H.: Determinig embedding dimension for phase-space reconstruction using a geometrical construction. Phys. Rev. A **45**(6), 3403 (1992)
4. Buzug, T., Pfister, G.: Comparison of algorithms calculating optimal embedding parameters for delay time coordinates. Phys. D **58**, 127–137 (1992)
5. Buzug, T., Pfister, G.: Optimal delay time and embedding dimension for delay-time coordinates by analysis of the global static, local dynamical behaviour of strange attractors. Phys. Rev. A **45**, 7073–7084 (1992)
6. Cao, L., Mees, A., Judd, K.: Dynamics from multivariate time series. Phys. D **121**, 75–88 (1998)
7. Cao, L.: Practical method for determining the minimum embed-ding dimension of a scalar time series. Phys. D: Nonlinear Phenom. **110**(1), 43–50 (1997)
8. Fraser, A.M., Swinney, H.L.: Independent coordinates for strange attractors from mutual information. Phys. Rev. A **33**, 1134 (1986)
9. Chong-zhao, H., Hong-guang, M.: Selection of embedding dimension and delay time in phase space reconstruction. Front. Electr. Electron. Eng. **1**, 111–114 (2006)
10. Jablonski, B.: Quaternion dynamic time warping. IEEE Trans. Sig. Process. **60**(3), 1174–1183 (2012)
11. Huang, Z., Lin, J., Wang, Y., Shen, Z.: Selection of proper time-delay in phase space reconstruction of speech signals. Sig. Process. **15**, 220–225 (1999)
12. James MacQueen et al.: Some methods for classification and analysis of multivariate observations, vol. 1(14), pp. 281–297 (1967)
13. Maus, A., Sprott, J.C.: Neural network method for determining embedding dimension of a time series. Commun. Nonlinear Sci. Numer. Simul. **16**, 3294–3302 (2011)
14. Montalto, A., Faes, L., Marinazzo, D.: Mute: a matlab toolbox to compare established and novel estimators of the multivariate transfer entropy. PloS one **9**(10), e109462 (2014)
15. Piorek, M.: Computer Information Systems and Industrial Management. Chaotic Properties of Gait Kinematic Data, pp. 111–119. Springer International Publishing, Cham (2015)

16. Rokach, L., Maimon, O.: Clustering methods, (2005)
17. Colins, J.J., Rossenstein, M.T., de Luca, C.J.: Reconstruction expansion as a geometry-based framework for choosing proper delay times. Phys. D **73**, 82–98 (1994)
18. Takens, F.: Detecting strange attractors in turbulence. Springer-Verlag, Berlin (1981)
19. Vlachos, I., Kugiumtzis, D.: Nonuniform state-space recon- struction and coupling detection. Phys. Rev. E **82**(1), 016207 (2010)

Algorithm of Allophone Borders Correction in Automatic Segmentation of Acoustic Units

Janusz Rafałko[✉]

Faculty of Mathematics and Information Science,
Warsaw University of Technology, Warsaw, Poland
j.rafalko@mini.pw.edu.pl

Abstract. In concatenative speech synthesis the fundamental factor with heavy influence on synthesized speech quality is the database of acoustic units. In case of bases received in automatic way, the key matter is suitable marking the borders of acoustic units. This article describes the algorithm of correction of acoustic units borders appointive in automatic way. It is based on two factors specified and tested here. It also describes worked out method of grade of acoustic units database, which allows to observe the influence of introduced correction on the base quality.

Keywords: Speech · Speech synthesis · Allophone · Phoneme · Text to speech · TTS · Acoustic units · Speech processing · Border correction

1 Introduction

The main goal in speech technology is to create a speech which is almost as real as a voice of a living person. One of the methods of speech synthesis based on the text (Text to Speech), which allows to reproduce the human personal speech characteristics is a concatenation method. It uses small and natural acoustic units, from which the speech is synthesized. These can be allophones, diphones or syllables. In presented system, synthesizer is based on bases composed of allophones. That type of system synthesizes the speech by joining the acoustic units in accordance to appropriate phonetic rules. The individual features of human voice are not included in this rules, but only in natural acoustic units. In order to synthesize the voice of a particular man, an acoustic units database must be created.

The acoustic units databases are the allophones bases. Preparing such base takes months and it is done by experts in a manual way. Therefore there is a demand to work out an automatic method of creating such bases e.g. presented in [1, 2]. As a result of working the system in automatic way, the borders of allophones are marked. In order to obtain the best quality of synthesized speech, the borders have to be marked in a precise way. Introduced in this paper algorithms allow to correct errors of marking these borders.

K. Saeed and W. Homenda (Eds.): CISIM 2016, LNCS 9842, pp. 462–469, 2016.
DOI: 10.1007/978-3-319-45378-1_41

2 Acoustic Units Database

Different approaches to the speech synthesis from the text are described in [3, 4]. The basic feature of concatenative approach of speech synthesis is the use of elementary pieces of natural speech [5]. In the synthesizer, the signal compiled from natural speech segments is a subject of further modification which changes the prosodic parameters of the signal.

In the [6], study shows the basic assumptions of concatenative TTS system for Polish language, based on allophones in the context of multilingual synthesis. Natural elements from which the speech is synthesized may be allophones, diphones, multi-phones as well as syllables. In concatenative method of speech synthesizing these type of basic speech units has much influence on obtaining individual speech characteristics. This paper refers to the databases of acoustic units, which include several context groups of particular phoneme, which may be identified with acoustic allophone, described in the study of Jassem [7]. The advantages of the choice of allophones as a basic units [8–11] base on the fact that firstly - speech units remain the effects of sounds interference, and secondly - the number of basic units is relatively low and holds in the range of 400–2000 in different systems. The difficulty posing in this approach is a necessity of precise allophones marking during the segmentation of natural speech signal.

3 Automatic Segmentation of Natural Speech Signal

If in the speech synthesis the compilation elements contain only the phonetical and acoustical characteristics, the segmentation task is about to "cut" the basic segments from the speech stream and place them into the database. The main stages of this algorithms include:

1. Selection and preparation of text and acoustic corpuses.
2. The automation of creation of acoustic units databases of the particular speaker voice.

As a result of this work system, we get many of the same units, but we need only one piece of each element to our base. In order to create an acoustic database it is necessary to analyze received units in details and delete those phonetic units in which the acceptable error during reading or automatic segmentation was exceeded and save only the best of them. If there are more than one identical allophones, we choose the best one. Finally we must perform the control of quality of each element that left, marking deviations and perform the correction of segments parameters with noticed deviations.

4 Correction Algorithm

The "correction" operation is performed for those segments, which are obtained in accordance to the ways mentioned above. The segments with inaccurately defined limits are subject to correction using proper procedures, involving removing the inaccurate periods of basic tone and inserting the missing terminal periods of basic tone. The diagnosis of determining the limits of units is performed by determining the level of time between periods and acoustic signal characteristics similarities on the first and the second period of basic tone, as well as on the penultimate and the last one. Both cases of periods: first, second and penultimate, the last, will be described as terminal and pre-terminal. The correction is performed only in the case of voiced units.

To determine the level of similarity of terminal and pre-terminal period of acoustic characteristics, the formula 1(a) is used. The distance between time characteristics is calculated as a ratio of duration of these periods (formula 1b).

$$(a), \ L_A = 1 - \frac{\sum\limits_{i=1}^{N} |s_i^G - s_i^P|}{\sum\limits_{i=1}^{N} (|s_i^G| + |s_i^P|)} \qquad (b), \ L_T = 1 - \frac{\min(T^G, T^P)}{\max(T^G, T^P)} \qquad (1)$$

where:

S_i^G – value of the signal at the "i" segment of terminal period

S_i^P – value of the signal at the "i" segment of pre-terminal period

T^G, T^P – duration of periods, both the terminal and the pre-terminal

These factors assume value of range 0–1. The factor of the time adjustment L_T is constructed in such a way, that it takes low value for similar duration of terminal and pre-terminal period of acoustic unit, achieving value 0 when these periods are identical. When the durations differ from each other, this factor grows up to value 1. On the contrary factor L_A vice versa, similar periods - value close to 1.

"Correction" consists of removing terminal period and duplicating pre-terminal one. In result the number of periods of segment basic tone does not change. The second case of "correction" is an absolute rejection of terminal period. Whereas in case of the correct marking of border unit, such period remains. In order to find the appropriate values of the factors by which terminal period should be remove or improve by replacing them with pre-terminal, it was analyzed various bases received as a result of automatic segmentation.

It was set experimentally, that when factor $L_T < 0, 2$ it means, that terminal and pre-terminal periods have similar durations and terminal period might be left without changes. Example of such situation is presented on Fig. 1.

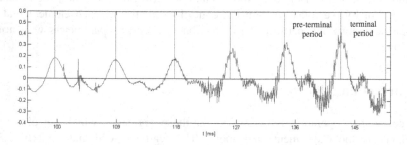

Fig. 1. Terminal and pre-terminal periods of "wi03" unit, $L_T = 0.19$.

If value of factor L_T is between 0.2 and 0.7 terminal period should be replaced by pre-terminal. Example of such situation is presented on next Fig. 2. We can notice here that border was marked in mid-period, therefore it should be replaced by pre-terminal period.

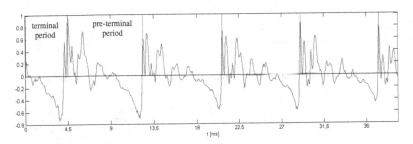

Fig. 2. Terminal and pre-terminal periods of "a0130" unit, $L_T = 0.44$.

Third case refers to factor $L_T > 0.7$. It means that terminal period is too short. Figure 3 shows that the border of unit is marked just behind the border of pre-terminal period. In such cases terminal period is removed.

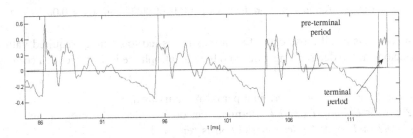

Fig. 3. Terminal and pre-terminal periods of "e1001" unit, $L_T = 0.92$.

In case of factor L_A we can also distinguish three cases. First of them, when L_A is larger ($L_A > 0.6$) means, that terminal and pre-terminal periods are similar in acoustic consideration to each other. In such case operation depends on ad valorem factor L_T. Examples are presented on previous Fig. 3 illustrates case, when $L_A = 0.89$ but nevertheless, terminal period is removed because of high value of factor L_T. On Fig. 2 terminal period is replaced at high value $L_A = 0.72$. In turn Fig. 1 shows the case when both factors have very good value ($L_A = 0.79$, $L_T = 0.19$) and terminal period remains firm.

When L_A is in range $0.4 < L_A < 0.6$ terminal period is replaced by pre-terminal period. We can see it on Fig. 4. The value $L_A = 0.57$ means that period will be replaced by pre-terminal. We can see (Fig. 4) that terminal period is different from other periods of allophone unit therefore it should be replaced.

If $L_A < 0.4$ terminal period should be removed without any regard to value of factor L_T. Example is presented on next Fig. 5. We can see that the algorithm of border marking is marked incorrectly in the last period.

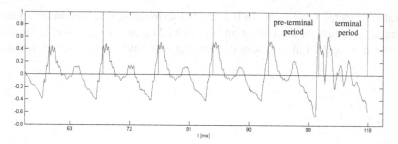

Fig. 4. Terminal and pre-terminal periods of "n03" unit, $L_A = 0.57$.

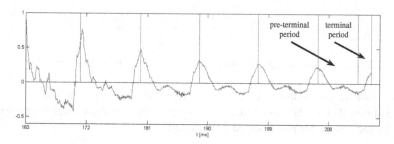

Fig. 5. Terminal and pre-terminal periods of "l02" unit, $L_A = 0.06$.

The analysis of all those cases for various bases led to defining required values of these factors and to determining when and how an allophone is a subject to a correction. If:

- $L_T < 0.2$ and $L_A > 0.6$ – terminal period remains firm;
- $0.2 < L_T < 0.7$ and $L_A > 0.4$ – terminal period is replaced by pre-terminal;
- $L_T > 0.7$ or $L_A < 0.4$ – terminal period is removed;

The first and the third cases are trivial. The replacement of terminal period by pre-terminal is a second case of correction. Figure 6 presents the allophone before

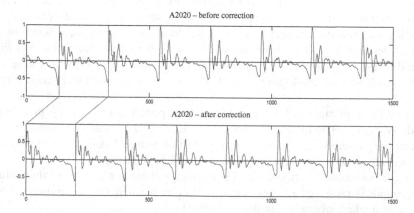

Fig. 6. Unit "a2020" before and after replacement terminal period by pre-terminal period.

correction of primary border period and the same unit after correction. The correction coefficients of initial border periods of this element are $L_T = 0.3$ and $L_A = 0.63$.

5   The Base Correctness Ratio

Taking into account parameters L_T and L_A it is possible to construct the ratio showing the correctness of cutting an acoustic unit, and after averaging - the ratio showing the correctness of whole base. Obviously, it will be showing only correctness of cutting voiced units. We can introduce the summary degree of similarity of terminal periods appointed as:

$$L = \frac{L_A + L_T}{2} \tag{2}$$

Factors L_A and L_T are constructed in such a way, that for correctly cut allophone L_A the value will be close to 1, but L_T close to 0. So total ratio for correctly cut segments should have the value approximate to 0.5. Upon introducing the average for this grade of similarity for all units in base we can receive the base correctness ratio:

$$L_{BCR} = \frac{1}{N} \sum_{i=1}^{N} \frac{L_A^i + L_T^i}{2} \tag{3}$$

Figure 7 presents the ratio L histogram of acoustic units of voice standard base prepared manually. The average value that is the ratio of correctness for this base is $L_{BCR} = 0.48$. We can see that this ratio distribution is similar to Gaussian distribution.

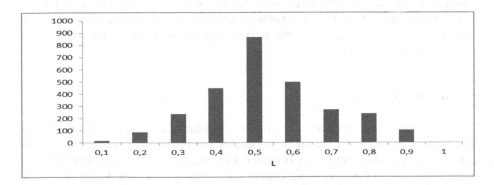

Fig. 7. Histogram of the factor L of the standard base.

Next graphs show histograms of ratio L before correction (Fig. 8) and after correction (Fig. 9). It is a base obtained in automatic way, for the same voice that standard base.

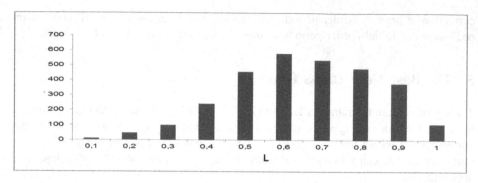

Fig. 8. Histogram of the factor L of automatic base before borders correction.

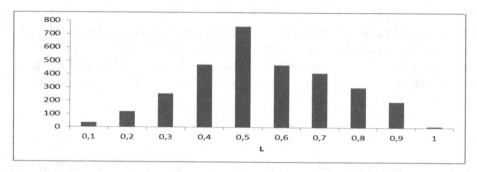

Fig. 9. Histogram of the factor L of automatic base after borders correction.

In this case the base correctness ratio is about $L_{BCR} = 0.51$. There can be many reasons why the value of ratio L had deviated from 0.5 for the unit. The reason might be incorrectly marked borders of periods by implemented algorithm. However basic cause is the fact that terminal and pre-terminal periods in allophone need not and in practice cannot be identical.

6 Summary

Research shows, that presented correction algorithms of borders of allophones appointed in automatic way improve the quality obtained base. Feedback from subjective researches also confirms it. It turns out that analytic base correctness ratio is a useful tool which, in numerical way, defines the quality of allophonic bases. Drawback of this approach and simultaneously drawback of this ratio, is the fact that it is possible to apply it only to voiced units of speech signal. However theoretically it is possible to use it in order to describe the quality of bases composed of other acoustic units than allophones.

References

1. Almpanidis, G., Kotropoulos, C.: Automatic phonemic segmentation using the Bayesian information criterion with generalised gamma priors. In: Proceedings of EUSIPCO (2007)
2. Szklanny, K., Oliver, D.: Creation and analysis of a Polish speech database for use in unit selection speech synthesis. In: LREC Conference, Genova (2006)
3. Dutoit, T.: An Introduction to Text-to-Speech Synthesis. Kluwer Academic Publishers, Dordrecht (1997)
4. Taylor, P.: Text-to-Speech Synthesis. Cambridge University Press, Cambridge (2009)
5. Van Santen, J.P.H., Sproat, R., Olive, J., Hirshberg, J.: Progress in Speech Synthesis. Springer, New York (1997)
6. Szpilewski, E., Piórkowska, B., Rafałko, J., Lobanov, B., Kiselov, V., Tsirulnik, L.: Polish TTS in multi-voice slavonic languages speech synthesis system. In: Proceedings of 9th International Conference Speech and Computer, SPECOM 2004, Saint-Petersburg, Russia, pp. 565–570 (2004)
7. Jassem, W.: Podstawy fonetyki akustycznej, wyd. PWN, Warszawa (1973)
8. Lobanov, B., Piórkowska, B., Rafałko, J., Cyrulnik, L.: Реализация межъязыковых различий интонации завиершённости и незавиершённости в синтезаторе русской и полской речи по тексту. In: Proceedings of International Conference on Computational Linguistics and Intellectual Technologies, Dialogue 2005, Zvenigorod, Russia, pp. 356–362 (2005)
9. Matoušek, J.: Building a new czech text-to-speech system using triphone-based speech units. In: Sojka, P., Kopeček, I., Pala, K. (eds.) TSD 2000. LNCS (LNAI), vol. 1902, pp. 223–228. Springer, Heidelberg (2000)
10. Rafalko, J.: The algorithms of automation of the process of creating acoustic units databases in the Polish speech synthesis. In: Atanassov, K.T., et al. (eds.) Novel Developments in Uncertainty Representation and Processing. AISC, vol. 401, pp. 373–383. Springer, Heidelberg(2015)
11. Skrelin, P.A.: Allophone-based concatenative speech synthesis system for Russian. In: Matoušek, V., Mautner, P., Ocelíková, J., Sojka, P. (eds.) TSD 1999. LNCS (LNAI), vol. 1692, pp. 156–159. Springer, Heidelberg (1999)

Decisions

Ensemble of Classifiers with Modification of Confidence Values

Robert Burduk$^{(\boxtimes)}$ and Paulina Baczyńska

Department of Systems and Computer Networks, Wroclaw University of Technology,
Wybrzeze Wyspianskiego 27, 50-370 Wroclaw, Poland
{robert.burduk,paulina.baczynska}@pwr.edu.pl

Abstract. In the classification task, the ensemble of classifiers have attracted more and more attention in pattern recognition communities. Generally, ensemble methods have the potential to significantly improve the prediction base classifier which are included in the team. In this paper, we propose the algorithm which modifies the confidence values. This values are obtained as an outputs of the base classifiers. The experiment results based on thirteen data sets show that the proposed method is a promising method for the development of multiple classifiers systems. We compared the proposed method with other known ensemble of classifiers and with all base classifiers.

Keywords: Multiple classifier system · Decision profile · Confidence value

1 Introduction

For several years, in the field of supervised learning a number of base classifiers have been used in order to solve one classification task. The use of the multiple base classifier for a decision problem is known as an ensemble of classifiers (EoC) or as multiple classifiers systems (MCSs) [12,15]. The building of MCSs consists of three main phases: generation, selection and integration (fusion) [4]. When injecting randomness into the learning algorithm or manipulating the training objects is done [3,11], then we are talking about homogeneous classifiers. In the second approach the ensemble is composed of heterogeneous classifiers. It means, that some different learning algorithms are applied to the same data set.

The selection phase is related to the choice of a set of classifiers from the whole available pool of base classifiers [14]. Formally, if we choose one classifier then it is called the classifier selection. But if we choose a subset of base classifiers from the pool then it is called the ensemble selection or ensemble pruning. Generally, in the ensemble selection, there are two approaches: the static ensemble selection and the dynamic ensemble selection [2,4].

© IFIP International Federation for Information Processing 2016
Published by Springer International Publishing Switzerland 2016. All Rights Reserved
K. Saeed and W. Homenda (Eds.): CISIM 2016, LNCS 9842, pp. 473–480, 2016.
DOI: 10.1007/978-3-319-45378-1_42

A number of articles [7,16,21] present a large number of fusion methods. For example, in the third phase the simple majority voting scheme [19] is most popular. Generally, the final decision which is made in the third phase uses the prediction of the base classifiers and it is popular for its ability to fuse together multiple classification outputs for the better accuracy of classification. The fusion methods can be divided into selection-based, fusion-based and hybrid ones according to their functioning [6]. The fusion strategies can be also divided into fixed and trainable ones [7]. Another division distinguishes class-conscious and class-indifferent integration methods [16].

In this work we will consider the modification confidence values method. The proposed method is based on information from decision profiles. The decision scheme used in training phase is created only from these confidence values that concern to the correct classification.

The remainder of this paper is organized as follows. Section 2 presents the concept of the base classifier and ensemble of classifiers. Section 3 contains the proposed modification confidence values method. The experimental evaluation, discussion and conclusions from the experiments are presented in Sect. 4. The paper is concluded by a final discussion.

2   Supervised Classification

2.1   Base Classifiers

The aim of the supervised classification is to assign an object to a specific class label. The object is represented by a set of d features, or attributes, viewed as d-dimensional feature vector x. The recognition algorithm maps the feature space x to the set of class labels Ω according to the general formula:

$$\Psi : X \to \Omega. \tag{1}$$

The recognition algorithm defines the classifier, which in the complex classification task with multiple classifiers is called a base classifier.

The output of a base classifier can be divided into three types [16].

- The abstract level – the classifier ψ assigns the unique label j to a given input x.
- The rank level – in this case for each input (object) x, each classifier produces an integer rank array. Each element within this array corresponds to one of the defined class labels. The array is usually sorted and the label at the top being the first choice.
- The measurement level – the output of a classifier is represented by a confidence value (CV) that addresses the degree of assigning the class label to the given input x. An example of such a representation of the output is a posteriori probability returned by Bayes classifier. Generally, this level can provide richer information than the abstract and rank level.

In this work we consider the situation when each base classifier returns CVs. Additionally, before the final combination of base classifiers' outputs the CVs modification process is carried out.

2.2   Ensemble of Classifiers

Let us assume that $k \in \{1, 2, ..., K\}$ different classifiers $\Psi_1, \Psi_2, \ldots, \Psi_K$ are available to solve the classification task. The output information from all K component classifiers is applied to make the ultimate decision of MCSs. This decision is made based on the predictions of all the base classifiers.

One of the possible methods for integrating the output of the base classifier is the sum rule. In this method the score of MCSs is based on the application of the following sums:

$$s_\omega(x) = \sum_{k=1}^{K} p_k(\omega|x), \qquad \omega \in \Omega, \tag{2}$$

where $p_k(\omega|x)$ is CV for class label ω returned by classifier k.

The final decision of MCSs is made following the maximum rule:

$$\Psi_S(x) = \arg\max_\omega s_\omega(x). \tag{3}$$

In the presented method (3) CV obtained from the individual classifiers take an equal part in building MCSs. This is the simplest situation in which we do not need additional information on the testing process of the base classifiers except for the models of these classifiers. One of the possible methods in which weights of the base classifier are used is presented in [5].

Decision template (DT) is another approaches to build the MCSs. DT was proposed in [17]. In this MCS model DTs are calculated based on training set. One DT per class label. In the operation phase the similarity between each DT and outputs of base classifiers for object x is computed. The class label with the closest DT is assigned to object x. In this paper algorithm with DT is labelled Ψ_{DT} and it is used as one of the reference classifiers.

3   Modification of Confidence Values Algorithm

3.1   Training Phase

The proposed algorithm of the modification CVs values uses DPs. DP is a matrix containing CVs for each base classifier, i.e.:

$$DP(x) = \begin{bmatrix} p_1(0|x) & \ldots & p_1(\Omega|x) \\ \vdots & \ldots & \vdots \\ p_K(0|x) & \ldots & p_K(\Omega|x) \end{bmatrix}. \tag{4}$$

In the first step of the algorithm we remove CVs which relate to the misclassification on the training set. This set contains N labelled examples $\{(x_1, \overline{\omega}_1), ..., (x_N, \overline{\omega}_N)\}$, where $\overline{\omega}_i$ is the true class label of the object described by feature vector x_i. CVs are removed according to the formula:

$$p'_k(\omega|x) = \begin{cases} p_k(\omega|x), & \text{if} \quad I(\Psi(x), \overline{\omega}) = 1 \\ 0, & \text{if} \quad I(\Psi(x), \overline{\omega}) = 0. \end{cases} \tag{5}$$

where $I(\Psi(x), \overline{\omega})$ is an indicator function having the value 1 in the case of the correct classification of the object described by feature vector x, i.e. when $\Psi(x) = \overline{\omega}$.

In the next step, our algorithm, the decision scheme (DS) is calculated according to the formula:

$$DS(\beta) = \begin{bmatrix} ds(\beta)_{10} & \cdots & ds(\beta)_{1\Omega} \\ \vdots & \cdots & \vdots \\ ds(\beta)_{K0} & \cdots & ds(\beta)_{K\Omega} \end{bmatrix}, \tag{6}$$

where

$$ds(\beta)_{k\omega} = \overline{ds}_{k\omega} + \beta \sqrt{\frac{\sum_{n=1}^{N} (p'_k(\omega_n|x_n) - \overline{ds}_{k\omega})^2}{N-1}} \tag{7}$$

and

$$\overline{ds}_{k\omega} = \frac{\sum_{n=1}^{N} p'_k(\omega_n|x_n)}{N}. \tag{8}$$

The parameter β in our algorithm determines how we compute DS elements. For example, if $\beta = 0$, then $ds_{k\omega}$ is the average of appropriate DFs received after the condition (5).

3.2 Operation Phase

During the operation phase the modification of CVs is carried out using $DS(\beta)$ calculated in the training phase. For the new object x being recognized, the outputs of the base classifiers construct $DP(x)$ as in (4). The modification CVs from $DP(x)$ is performed with the use of $DS(\beta)$ calculated in (6) according to the formula:

$$p'_k(\omega|x) = \begin{cases} \overline{m} * p_k(\omega|x) & \text{if } p_k(\omega|x) \geq ds(1)_{k\omega} \\ m * p_k(\omega|x) & \text{if } ds(0)_{k\omega} < p_k(\omega|x) < ds(1)_{k\omega}, \\ \underline{m} * p_k(\omega|x) & \text{if } p_k(\omega|x) \leq ds(0)_{k\omega} \end{cases} \tag{9}$$

where $\overline{m}$, m and $\underline{m}$ define how ordinal CVs are modified. The modification process taking into account the Eq. (9) causes the ensemble of the classifier method to use the modified CVs. The algorithm using the proposed method is denoted as Ψ^{MCV}. In the experiment modified CVs are combined according to the sum method (3).

4   Experimental Studies

In the experiments we use 13 data sets. Nine of them come from the Keel Project [1] and four com from UCI Repository [9] (Blood, Breast Cancer Wisconsin, Indian Liver Patient and Mammographic Mass UCI). The details of the data sets are included in Table 1. In the experiment 16 base classifiers were used from four different classification models. The first group of four base

Table 1. Description of data sets selected for the experiments

Data set	Example	Attribute	Ration (0/1)
Cylinder bands	365	19	1.7
Haberman's survival	306	3	2.8
Hepatitis	80	19	0.2
Mammographic mass	830	5	1.1
Parkinson	197	23	0.3
Pima Indians diabetes	768	8	1.9
South African hearth	462	9	1.9
Spectf heart	267	44	0.3
Statlog (heart)	270	13	1.3
Blood	748	5	3.2
Breast cancer Wisconsin	699	10	1.9
Indian liver patient	583	10	0.4
Mammographic mass UCI	961	6	1.2

classifiers works according to $k - NN$ rule, the second group uses the Support Vector Machines models. The next group uses the Neural Network model and the last group uses the decision trees algorithms. The base classifiers are labelled as $\Psi_1, ..., \Psi_{16}$.

The main aim of the experiments was to compare the quality of classifications of the proposed modification CVs algorithms Ψ_{MCV} with the base classifiers $\Psi_1, ..., \Psi_{16}$ and their ensemble without the selection Ψ_{DT} and Ψ_S. The parameters of Ψ_{MCV} algorithm were established on $\overline{m} = 1.25$, $m = 1$ and $\underline{m} = 0.75$. In the experiments the feature selection process [13,18] was not performed and we have used the standard 10-fold-cross-validation method.

The classification error with the mean ranks obtained by the Friedman test for classification algorithms used in the experiments are presented in Table 2. Considering only the mean ranks obtained by the Friedman test the best result achieved proposed in the work algorithm labelled Ψ_{MCV}. The obtained results were compared also by the post-hoc test [20]. The critical difference (CD) for this test at $p = 0.05$ is equal to $CD = 7.76$ – for 19 methods used for classification and 13 data sets. We can conclude that the post-hoc Nemenyi test detects significant differences between the proposed algorithm Ψ_{MCV} and the four base classifiers Ψ_4, Ψ_6, Ψ_8, and Ψ_{14}. The classifier method labelled Ψ_S is statistically better than the three base classifiers Ψ_6, Ψ_8 and Ψ_{14}. This confirms that the proposed algorithm is better than the ensemble of classifiers with the used sum method. It should be noted, however, that the difference in average ranks is not large enough to point to the significant differences between Ψ_{MCV} and Ψ_S algorithms.

Table 2. Classification error and mean rank positions for the base classifiers $(\Psi_1, ..., \Psi_{16})$, algorithms Ψ_S, Ψ_{DT} and the proposed algorithm Ψ_{MCV} produced by the Friedman test

Clas.	Data set													Rank
	Bands	Blood	Cance	Haber	Heart	Hepat	Liver	MamU	Mam	Park	Pima	Sahea	Spectf	
Ψ_1	0.62	0.77	0.95	0.75	0.68	0.83	0.69	0.81	0.79	0.86	0.73	0.67	0.80	10.70
Ψ_2	0.56	0.79	0.96	0.76	0.69	0.83	0.70	0.81	0.77	0.81	0.73	0.69	0.78	10.58
Ψ_3	0.61	0.80	0.96	0.74	0.68	0.84	0.70	0.81	0.78	0.80	0.74	0.68	0.77	10.50
Ψ_4	0.63	0.76	0.95	0.75	0.70	0.84	0.65	0.81	0.77	0.86	0.72	0.64	0.80	11.81
Ψ_5	0.64	0.80	0.98	0.74	0.79	0.85	0.73	0.80	0.78	0.91	0.67	0.69	0.80	7.31
Ψ_6	0.64	0.74	0.87	0.69	0.56	0.84	0.28	0.70	0.74	0.45	0.66	0.66	0.25	16.54
Ψ_7	0.64	0.79	0.94	0.75	0.56	0.84	0.73	0.79	0.79	0.73	0.59	0.67	0.80	11.50
Ψ_8	0.64	0.77	0.93	0.71	0.56	0.84	0.74	0.80	0.76	0.74	0.66	0.66	0.80	13.04
Ψ_9	0.64	0.81	0.96	0.74	0.77	0.76	0.70	0.83	0.81	0.87	0.64	0.66	0.78	9.66
Ψ_{10}	0.65	0.81	0.95	0.72	0.77	0.76	0.70	0.84	0.81	0.88	0.65	0.66	0.78	9.47
Ψ_{11}	0.65	0.81	0.94	0.71	0.73	0.79	0.68	0.83	0.81	0.87	0.65	0.66	0.76	11.31
Ψ_{12}	0.66	0.80	0.96	0.71	0.77	0.85	0.69	0.82	0.81	0.93	0.66	0.66	0.79	8.27
Ψ_{13}	0.63	0.80	0.94	0.74	0.82	0.84	0.69	0.84	0.81	0.91	0.73	0.73	0.73	7.81
Ψ_{14}	0.61	0.78	0.94	0.67	0.74	0.85	0.62	0.82	0.80	0.85	0.72	0.66	0.75	12.85
Ψ_{15}	0.63	0.79	0.94	0.70	0.79	0.81	0.65	0.84	0.80	0.90	0.70	0.68	0.76	11.20
Ψ_{16}	0.66	0.80	0.94	0.73	0.80	0.85	0.66	0.83	0.80	0.88	0.72	0.72	0.69	8.50
Ψ_{DP}	0.65	0.69	0.97	0.73	0.78	0.89	0.64	0.81	0.79	0.84	0.71	0.65	0.78	10.89
Ψ_S	0.67	0.82	0.96	0.75	0.84	0.82	0.72	0.84	0.81	0.94	0.73	0.70	0.79	4.39
Ψ_{MCV}	0.68	0.82	0.97	0.74	0.83	0.84	0.70	0.84	0.81	0.93	0.74	0.71	0.80	3.74

5   Conclusion

In this paper we have proposed the methods that use information from the decision profiles and modified CVs received from the base classifiers. The aim of the experiments was to compare the proposed algorithm with all base classifiers and the ensemble classifiers based on the sum and decision profile methods. The experiments have been carried out on 13 benchmark data sets. We can conclude that the post-hoc Nemenyi test detects significant differences between the proposed algorithm Ψ_{MCV} and four base classifiers. While the algorithm Ψ_S classification results are statistically different from the three base classifiers. The obtained results show an improvement in the quality of the classification proposed algorithm Ψ_{MCV} with respect to all the base classifiers and the used reference ensemble of the classifiers' methods. Future work might involve the application of the proposed methods for various practical tasks [8,10,22] in which base classifiers are used. Additionally, the advantage of the proposed algorithm can be investigated as well as its ability to work in the parallel and distributed environment.

Acknowledgments. This work was supported by the Polish National Science Center under the grant no. DEC-2013/09/B/ST6/02264 and by the statutory funds of the Department of Systems and Computer Networks, Wroclaw University of Technology.

References

1. Alcalá, J., Fernández, A., Luengo, J., Derrac, J., García, S., Sánchez, L., Herrera, F.: Keel data-mining software tool: data set repository, integration of algorithms and experimental analysis framework. J. Mult.-Valued Logic Soft Comput. **17**(2–3), 255–287 (2010)
2. Baczyńska, P., Burduk, R.: Ensemble selection based on discriminant functions in binary classification task. In: Jackowski, K., et al. (eds.) IDEAL 2015. LNCS, vol. 9375, pp. 61–68. Springer, Heidelberg (2015). doi:10.1007/978-3-319-24834-9_8
3. Breiman, L.: Randomizing outputs to increase prediction accuracy. Mach. Learn. **40**(3), 229–242 (2000)
4. Britto, A.S., Sabourin, R., Oliveira, L.E.: Dynamic selection of classifiers–a comprehensive review. Pattern Recogn. **47**(11), 3665–3680 (2014)
5. Burduk, R.: Classifier fusion with interval-valued weights. Pattern Recogn. Lett. **34**(14), 1623–1629 (2013)
6. Canuto, A.M., Abreu, M.C., de Melo Oliveira, L., Xavier, J.C., Santos, A.D.M.: Investigating the inuence of the choice of the ensemble members in accuracy and diversity of selection-based and fusion-based methods for ensembles. Pattern Recogn. Lett. **28**(4), 472–486 (2007)
7. Duin, R.P.: The combining classifier: to train or not to train? In: Proceedings of the 16th International Conference on Pattern Recognition, 2002, vol. 2, pp. 765–770. IEEE (2002)
8. Forczmański, P., Łabedź, P.: Recognition of occluded faces based on multi-subspace classification. In: Saeed, K., Chaki, R., Cortesi, A., Wierzchoń, S. (eds.) CISIM 2013. LNCS, vol. 8104, pp. 148–157. Springer, Heidelberg (2013)
9. Frank, A., Asuncion, A.: UCI Machine Learning Repository (2010)
10. Frejlichowski, D.: An algorithm for the automatic analysis of characters located on car license plates. In: Kamel, M., Campilho, A. (eds.) ICIAR 2013. LNCS, vol. 7950, pp. 774–781. Springer, Heidelberg (2013)
11. Freund, Y., Schapire, R.E., et al.: Experiments with a new boosting algorithm. In: ICML, vol. 96, pp. 148–156 (1996)
12. Giacinto, G., Roli, F.: An approach to the automatic design of multiple classifier systems. Pattern Recogn. Lett. **22**, 25–33 (2001)
13. Inbarani, H.H., Azar, A.T., Jothi, G.: Supervised hybrid feature selection based on PSO and rough sets for medical diagnosis. Comput. Methods Programs Biomed. **113**(1), 175–185 (2014)
14. Jackowski, K., Krawczyk, B., Woźniak, M.: Improved adaptive splitting, selection: the hybrid training method of a classifier based on a feature space partitioning. Int. J. Neural Syst. **24**(03), 1430007 (2014)
15. Korytkowski, M., Rutkowski, L., Scherer, R.: From ensemble of fuzzy classifiers to single fuzzy rule base classifier. In: Rutkowski, L., Tadeusiewicz, R., Zadeh, L.A., Zurada, J.M. (eds.) ICAISC 2008. LNCS (LNAI), vol. 5097, pp. 265–272. Springer, Heidelberg (2008)
16. Kuncheva, L.I.: Combining Pattern Classifiers: Methods and Algorithms. Wiley, Hoboken (2004)
17. Kuncheva, L.I., Bezdek, J.C., Duin, R.P.: Decision templates for multiple classifier fusion: an experimental comparison. Pattern Recogn. **34**(2), 299–314 (2001)
18. Rejer, I.: Genetic algorithm with aggressive mutation for feature selection in BCI feature space. Pattern Anal. Appl. **18**(3), 485–492 (2015)

19. Ruta, D., Gabrys, B.: Classifier selection for majority voting. Inf. Fusion **6**(1), 63–81 (2005)
20. Trawiński, B., Smęetek, M., Telec, Z., Lasota, T.: Nonparametric statistical analysis for multiple comparison of machine learning regression algorithms. Int. J. Appl. Math. Comput. Sci. **22**(4), 867–881 (2012)
21. Xu, L., Krzyżak, A., Suen, C.Y.: Methods of combining multiple classifiers and their applications to handwriting recognition. IEEE Trans. Syst. Man Cybern. **22**(3), 418–435 (1992)
22. Zdunek, R., Nowak, M., Pliński, E.: Statistical classification of soft solder alloys by laser-induced breakdown spectroscopy: review of methods. J. Eur. Optical Soc.-Rapid Publ. **11**(16006), 1–20 (2016)

Fuzzy Random Forest with C–Fuzzy Decision Trees

Lukasz Gadomer[✉] and Zenon A. Sosnowski

Faculty of Computer Science, Bialystok University of Technology,
Wiejska 45A, 15-351 Bialystok, Poland
{l.gadomer,z.sosnowski}@pb.edu.pl
http://www.wi.pb.edu.pl

Abstract. In this paper a new classification solution which joins C–Fuzzy Decision Trees and Fuzzy Random Forest is proposed. Its assumptions are similar to the Fuzzy Random Forest, but instead of fuzzy trees it consists of C–Fuzzy Decision Trees. To test the proposed classifier there was performed a set of experiments. These experiments were performed using four datasets: Ionosphere, Dermatology, Pima–Diabetes and Hepatitis. Created forest was compared to C4.5 rev. 8 Decision Tree and single C–Fuzzy Decision Tree. The influence of randomness on the classification accuracy was also tested.

Keywords: Fuzzy tree · C–Fuzzy Decision Tree · Fuzzy random forest

1 Introduction

Authors propose a new kind of classifier which joins C–Fuzzy Decision Trees and Fuzzy Random Forest. In this paper the construction of this ensemble classifier is presented. It is built similar to the Fuzzy Random Forest but instead of Janikow Fuzzy Trees [7] it uses C–Fuzzy Decision Trees [9]. The first part of this paper consists of all of the techniques connected with the proposed ensemble classifier: Fuzzy Decision trees, C–Fuzzy Decision Trees and Ramdom Forests. In the next part the details of Fuzzy Random Forest with C–Fuzzy Decision Trees classifier are described. After that, the experiments are described their results are presented. The quality of classification acquired using Fuzzy Random Forest with C–Fuzzy Decision Trees is compared with C–Fuzzy Decision Trees working singly. Also, the strength of randomness is tested by comparing results obtained using random node selection with the results achieved without it.

2 Related Work

The idea of Fuzzy Random Forest with C–Fuzzy Decision trees is based on the Fuzzy Random Forest. Before presenting this issue it is worth to take a look at two classifiers which are the fundaments of the mentioned forest. The first one is the Fuzzy Tree, the second one is the Random Forest. Both of these issues are described in following paragraphs.

© IFIP International Federation for Information Processing 2016
Published by Springer International Publishing Switzerland 2016. All Rights Reserved
K. Saeed and W. Homenda (Eds.): CISIM 2016, LNCS 9842, pp. 481–492, 2016.
DOI: 10.1007/978-3-319-45378-1_43

2.1   Fuzzy Decision Trees

Fuzzy trees are modification of traditional decision trees. The characteristic feature of this kind of trees is the fact of using fuzzy logic in their construction, learning and decision making process. There are a lot of works which concern this issue, for example [11] or [6]. One of the most popular articles about fuzzy trees is C.Z. Janikow's paper [7]. This article is described in following paragraphs.

C.Z. Janikow created fuzzy trees [7] in order to join advantages of fuzzy logic and decision trees. This kind of trees have simple, clear and intelligible knowledge structure, which is characteristic for decision trees and they can deal with noises, imprecise information etc., which is possible thanks to the fuzzy logic. It allows for using fuzzy decision trees at areas where decision trees didn't work well.

Fuzzy decision trees [7] are based on two popular decision tree creation algorithms: CART [4] and ID3 [10]. C.Z. Janikow decided to build his version of tree following assumptions of ID3, but modifying them in the way that allows for successful working with both discrete and continuous values. Proposed tree differs from the traditional one in two ways. First of them is the fact it uses the different inference procedures. The second one is about using node division criterions based on the fuzzy relations.

2.2   Random Forests

Random forest was created by L. Brieman and presented in [5]. A forest is classifier which consists of many trees. Each of these trees makes its own decision about assigning the object to the given class. After that, forest decides about the class where the object belongs, using to all of the decisions made by single trees. The thing which differs random forest from the standard one is the fact of using randomness during the tree construction process. It reduces correlation between trees with keeping the accuracy of classification. L. Briemann proposed two methods of using randomness to create random forest.

First method is based on random set of attributes selection before the node split. The nubmer of elements in this set is constant and equal for the each tree. When attributes are selected, the best candidate to divide the node is chosen. The choice is performed from the mentioned set. Brieman tested two sizes of attributes sets used to random selection. The first set's size is one, which means that from available attributes there is randomly chosen one in order to divide the node. The second set's size is the biggest number lower than $log_2 M + 1$ where M is a total number of attributes in the dataset. Tree growth is performed according to the assumptions of CART method [4], trees are not pruned. L. Brieman called the structure created the described way Forest–RI.

The second proposed method can be used when the dataset has relatively small number of features. In such situation the random choice is being made from linear combinations of attributes instead of the attributes. The structure created that way was called by its author Forest–RC.

2.3 Fuzzy Random Forests

The classifier with joins two solutions described in previous paragraphs was first presented in [1] and then widely described in [3] and [2]. The mentioned classifier was based on two papers cited before: [7] and [5]. Fuzzy random forest, according to its assumptions, combines the robustness of ensemble classifiers, the power of the randomness to decrease the correlation between the trees and increase the diversity of them and the flexibility of fuzzy logic for dealing with imperfect data [2].

Fuzzy random forest construction process is similar to Forest–RI, described in [5]. After the forest is constructed, the algorithm begins its working from the root of each tree. First, a random set of attributes is chosen (it has the same size for each node). For each of these attributes information gain is computed, using all of the objects from training set. Attribute with the highest information gain is chosen to node split. When the node is splitted, selected attribute is removed from the set of attributes possible to select in order to divide the following nodes. Then, for all of the following tree nodes, this operation is repeated using a new set of randomly selected attributes (attributes which were used before are excluded from the selection) and the same training set.

During the tree construction process, when the node is dividing, the given object's membership degree to the given node is computed. Before the division, for each node the membership degree is 1. When the division is completed, each object can belong to any number of created leaves (at least one). If the object belongs to one leaf, its membership degree to this leaf achieves 1 (for the other leaves it is equal to 0). If it belongs to more than one leaf, the membership degree to each leaf can take values between 0 and 1 and it sums to 1 in the set of all children of the given node. If the division is performed using attribute with missing value, the object is assigned to each split node with the same membership degree.

According to described algorithm trees are constructed. Each tree is created using randomly selected set of attributes, different for each tree, which ensures diversity of trees in the forest.

Bonissone et al. proposed two fuzzy random forest decision making strategies. First of them assumpts making decisions by each tree separately – then, using achieved results, forest is making its final decision about the class where the object belongs. The second strategy is about making one common decision by the forest using all of the information collected by all of the trees. For each of these strategies authors proposed several decision making methods.

2.4 C–Fuzzy Decision Trees

In [9] W. Pedrycz and Z.A. Sosnowski proposed the new kind of decision trees, called C–Fuzzy Decision Trees. This class of trees was created in order to deal with the main problems of traditional trees. There are some fundamentals of decision trees. They usually operate on a relatively small set of discrete attributes. To split the node in the tree construction process, the single attribute which brings the most information gain is chosen. In their traditional form decision trees are designed to operate on discrete class problems – the continuous problems are handled by regression trees. These fundamentals bring some problems. To handle continuous values it is necessary to perform the discretization. It can impact on the overall performance of the tree negatively. What is more, information bringed by the nodes which were not selected to split the node is kind of lost.

C–Fuzzy Decision Trees were developed to deal with these problems of traditional trees. The idea of this kind of trees assumed treating data as collection of information granules. These granules analogous to fuzzy clusters. Authors decided to span the proposed tree over them. The data is grouped in such multivariable granules characterized by high homogenity (low variablity) which are treated as generic building blocks of the tree.

The construction of C–Fuzzy Decision Tree starts from grouping the data set into c clusters. It is performed in the way that the similar objects should be placed in the same cluster. Each cluster is characterized by its prototype (centroid), which is randomly selected first and then improved iteratively during the tree construction process. When objects are grouped into clusters, the diversity of the each of these clusters is computed using the given heterogenity criterion. The computed diversity value decides if the node is selected to split or not. From all of the nodes the most heterogenous is chosen to split. The selected node is divided into c clusters using fuzzy clustering. Then, for the newly created nodes, the diversity is computed and the selection to split is performed. This algorithm works until it achieves the given stop criterion. The growth of the tree can be deep or breadth intensive. Each node of such tree has 0 or c children.

To make the paper self contained we describe the tree construction process in a formal way. Let's do the following assumptions:

- c is a number of clusters,
- $i = 1, 2, ..., c$,
- N is a number of training instances,
- $k = 1, 2, ..., N$,
- d_{ik} is a distance function between the ith prototype and the kth instance,
- m is a fuzzification factor (usually $m = 2$),
- $U = [u_{ik}]$ is a partition matrix,
- $Z = \{x(k), y(k)\}$ is an input–output pair of data instances,
- $z_k = [x_1(k)x_2k...x_n(k)y(k)]^T$,
- f_i is the prototype of the cluster.

Constructing clusters and grouping objects into them is based on Fuzzy C–Means technique (FCM), which is an example of a fuzzy clustering. Clusters are built through a minimization of objective function Q, which assumes the format:

$$Q = \sum_{i=1}^{c} \sum_{k=1}^{N} u_{ik}^m d_{ik}^2 \tag{1}$$

During the iterations of Fuzzy C–Means process partitions u_{ik} and prototypes f_i are updated. For partitions it is performed according to the following equation:

$$u_{ik} = \frac{1}{\sum_{j=1}^{c}(\frac{d_{ik}}{d_{jk}})^{2/(m-1)}} \quad (2)$$

Prototypes are updated using the following expression:

$$f_i = \frac{\sum_{k=1}^{N} u_{ik}^m z_k}{\sum_{k=1}^{N} u_{ik}^m} \quad (3)$$

In order to describe the node splitting criterion let's do the following assumptions:

- V_i is the variability of the data in the output space existing at the given node,
- m_i is the representative of this node positioned in the output space,
- $\mathbf{X}_i = \{\mathbf{x}(k)|u_i(\mathbf{x}(k)) > u_j(\mathbf{x}(k))$ for all $j \neq i\}$, where j pertains to the nodes originating from the same parent, denotes all elements of the data set which belong to the given node in virtue of the highest membership grade,
- $\mathbf{Y}_i = \{y(k)|\mathbf{x}(k) \in \mathbf{X}_i\}$ collects the output coordinates of the elements that have already been assigned to $\mathbf{X}_i$,
- $\mathbf{U}_i = [u_i(\mathbf{x}(1))u_i(\mathbf{x}(2))...u_i(\mathbf{x}(\mathbf{Y}_i))]$ is a vector of the grades of membership of the elements in $\mathbf{X}_i$,
- $\mathbf{N}_i = <\mathbf{X}_i, \mathbf{Y}_i, \mathbf{U}_i>$,

According to these notation, m_i is the following weighted sum:

$$m_i = \frac{\sum_{(\mathbf{x}(k),y(k))\in \mathbf{X}_i\times\mathbf{Y}_i} u_i(\mathbf{x}(k))y(k)}{\sum_{(\mathbf{x}(k),y(k))\in \mathbf{X}_i\times\mathbf{Y}_i} u_i(\mathbf{x}(k))} \quad (4)$$

The variability is computed as follows:

$$V_i = \sum_{(\mathbf{x}(k),y(k))\in \mathbf{X}_i\times\mathbf{Y}_i} u_i(\mathbf{x}(k))(y(k) - m_i)^2 \quad (5)$$

The tree growth stop criterion could be, for example, defined in the following way: [9]

- There aren't enough elements in any node to perform the split. The minimal number of elements in the node which allows for the split is c. Normally the boundary number of the elements in each node would be the multiplicity of c, for example $2 \times c$ or $3 \times c$,

- All nodes achieve lower diversity than assumed boundary value,
- The structurability index achieves the lower value than assumed boundary value,
- The number of iterations (splits) achieved the assumed boundary value.

When the tree is constructed it can be used for classification. Each object which has to be classified starts from the root node. The membership degrees of this object to the children of the given node are computed. These membership degrees are the numbers between 0 and 1 and they sum to 1. The node where the object belongs with the highest membership is chosen and the object is getting there. The same operation is repeated as long as the object achieves to the node which has no children. The classification result is the class assigned to achieved node.

3   Fuzzy Random Forest with C–Fuzzy Decision Trees

To describe created classifier we used the following notations (based on [2,9]):

- T is the number of trees in the C–FRF ensemble,
- t is the particular tree,
- N_t is the number of nodes in the tree t,
- n is a particular leaf reached in a tree,
- I is the number of classes,
- i is a particular class,
- C_FRF is a matrix with size $(T \times MAX_{N_t})$ with $MAX_{N_t} = max\{N_1, N_2, ..., N_t\}$, where each element of the matrix is a vector of size I containing the support for every class provided by every activated leaf n on each tree t; this matrix represents C–Fuzzy Forest or Fuzzy Random Forest with C–Fuzzy Decision Trees,
- c is the number of clusters,
- E is a training dataset,
- e is a data instance,
- $V = [V_1, V_2, ..., V_b]$ is the variability vector.
- $U = [U_1, U_2, ..., U_{|E|}]$ is the tree's partition matrix of the training objects,
- $U_i = [u_1, u_2, ..., u_c]$ are memberships of the ith object to the c cluster,
- $B = \{B_1, B_2, ..., B_b\}$ are the unsplitted nodes,

We propose creating the new kind of classifiers: Fuzzy Random Forest with C–Fuzzy Decision Trees. It is the forest, based on the idea of Fuzzy Random Forest, which consists of C–Fuzzy Decision Trees. The Fuzzy Random Forest uses randomness to improve the classification quality while C–Fuzzy Decision Tree is constructed randomly by definition – centroids of its clusters (the partition matrix) are selected randomly first. Combination these two structures is expected to give promising results.

The randomness in Fuzzy Random Forest with C–Fuzzy Decision Trees is ensured by two main aspects. The first of them refers to the Random Forest.

During the tree's construction process, node to split is selected randomly. This randomness can be full, which means selecting the random node to split instead of the most heterogenous, or limited, which assumpts selecting the set of nodes with the highest diversity, then randomly selecting one of them to perform the division (the size of the set is given and the same for the each split). The second aspect refers to the C–Fuzzy Decision Trees and it concerns the creation of partition matrix. At first, the centroid (prototype) of the each cluster selection is fully random. Objects which belong to the parent node are divided into clusters grouped around these centroids using the shortest distance criterion. Then the prototypes and the partition matrix are being corrected as long as they achieve the stop criterion. Each tree in the forest, created the described way, can be selected from the set of created trees. To create the single tree which will be chosen to the forest there can be build the set of trees. Each tree from such set is tested and the best of these trees (the one which achieved the best classification accuracy for the training set) is being chosen as the part of forest. The size of the set is given and the same for the each tree in the forest.

The split selection idea is similar to the one used in Fuzzy Random Forest. The difference is about the nature of tree used in the classifier. In Fuzzy Random Forest, the random attribute was being chosen to split. The node which was chosen to split was specified by tree growth strategy. In Fuzzy Random Forest with C–Fuzzy Decision Trees there isn't any attribute chosen – for each of the splits all of the attributes are considered. The choice concerns the node to split selection which means some nodes does not have to be splitted (when the stop criterion is achieved). The same idea is expressed in two completely different ways of building trees. Each C–Fuzzy Decision Tree in the forest can be completely different or very similar – it depends on the stop criterion and the number of clusters. The influence of randomness can be set using algorithm parameters which allows classifier to fit the given problem in a flexible way.

Prototypes of each cluster are selected randomly and then corrected iteratively, which means some of created trees can work better than others. Diversity of trees created that way depends on the number of the correction process' iterations. It is possible to build many trees and choose only the best of them to the forest in order to achieve better results. The diversity of the trees in the forest can be modified by changing the size of the set from which the best tree is chosen and the number of iterations. These parameters specify the strength of randomness in the classifier. Operating on these values also allow to fit to the given problem to improve the classification quality.

3.1 Fuzzy Random Forest with C–Fuzzy Decision Trees Learning

The process of Fuzzy Random Forest with C–Fuzzy Decision Trees learning is analogous to the learning of Fuzzy Random Forest, proposed in [2]. The differences concern two aspects. First is about the kind of trees used in the forest. In the proposed classifier there are used C–Fuzzy Decision Trees instead of Janikow's Fuzzy Trees. The second aspect refers to the way of random selection of the node to split, which was described before.

The Fuzzy Random Forest with C–Fuzzy Decision Trees is created using Algorithm 1.

Algorithm 1. Fuzzy Random Forest with C–Fuzzy Decision Trees learning

1: **procedure** FRFwC–FDTLEARNING
2:    **for** 1 to T **do**
3:        1. Take a random sample of $|E|$ examples with replacement from the dataset E
4:        2. Apply Algorithm 2 to the subset of examples obtained in the previous step to construct C–Fuzzy Decision Tree
5:    **end for**
6: **end procedure**

Each tree in Fuzzy Random Forest with C–Fuzzy Decision Trees is created using Algorithm 2.

Algorithm 2. C–Fuzzy Decision Tree learning

1: **procedure** C–FDTLEARNING
2:    1. Start with the examples in E
3:    2. Create the partition matrix U randomly
4:    3. Perform FCM
5:    **while** Stop criterion is not satisfied **do**
6:        4. Divide the samples belonging to the splitted node into its children
7:        5. Make a random selection of nodes from the set of unsplitted nodes B
8:        6. Compute the variability matrix V
9:        7. Choose the node with maximum variability to split nodes
10:       8. Perform FCM
11:   **end while**
12: **end procedure**

3.2 Fuzzy Random Forest with C–Fuzzy Decision Trees Classification

After the Fuzzy Random Forest with C–Fuzzy Decision Trees is constructed it can be used for new object's classification. The decision–making strategy used in the proposed solution assumes making decision by forest after each tree's decisions are made.[1] It is performed according to the Algorithm 3. It can be described by equation, similar to the one presented in [2]:

---

[1] There is also another decision–making strategy which assumpts making the single decision by the whole forest. It is described in [2].

$$D_F RF(t,i,C\_FRF) = \begin{cases} 1 \text{ if } i = arg \max_{j,j=1,2,...,I} \left\{ \sum_{n=1}^{N_t} C\_FRF_{t,n,j} \right\} \\ 0 \text{ otherwise} \end{cases}$$

Algorithm 3. Fuzzy Random Forest with C–Fuzzy Decision Trees classification

---

1: **procedure** FRFwC–FDTCLASSIFICATION
2:     DecisionOfTrees
3:     DecisionOfForest
4: **end procedure**
5: **procedure** DECISIONOFTREES
6:     **for** 1 to T **do**
7:         1. Run the example e to obtain the tree's partition matrix U_i
8:         2. Choose the class c where $c = arg \max_{i,i=1,2,...,I} D\_FRF_{t,i,C\_FRF}$
9:     **end for**
10: **end procedure**
11: **procedure** DECISIONOFFOREST
12:     Assign to class according to the simple majority vote of trees decisions
13: **end procedure**

---

4   Experimental Studies

To test a quality of created classifier there were performed several experiments. These experiments were performed on four popular datasets from UCI Machine Learning Repository [8]:

- Ionosphere,
- Dermatology,
- Pima–Diabetes,
- Hepatitis.

Each dataset was divided into five parts with equal size (or as close to the equal as it's possible) randomly. Each of these parts had the same proportions of objects representing each decision class as it is in the whole dataset (or as close to the same as it's possible). There were no situations when in some of parts there weren't any objects representing some of decision classes. This random and proportional division was saved and used for each experiment.

Each experiment was performed using 5–fold crossvalidation. Four of five parts were used to train the classifier, one to test the learned forest. This operation was repeated five times, each time the other part was excluded from training and used for testing the classifier. After that, classification accuracy of all five out of bag parts were averaged.

For each dataset there were performed researches for both Fuzzy Forest with C–Fuzzy Decision Trees and Fuzzy Random Forest with C–Fuzzy Decision Trees. For each of these configurations there were performed experiments with 2, 3, 5, 8, 13 and 20 clusters. Each forest were consisting of 50 trees.

The objective of the research is to test how randomness influences the classification accuracy of the forest. There is also checked how the classification accuracy changes with the different number of clusters.

All of the results are presented in Sect. 5. They are all compared with themselves and also with single C–Fuzzy Decision Tree and C4.5 rev. 8 tree.

5   Results and Discussion

Classification accuracies part consists of the following information:

– Classification accuracy achieved using C4.5 rev. 8 Decision Tree,
– Classification accuracy achieved using a single C–Fuzzy Decision Tree,
– Classification accuracies achieved using Fuzzy Forest with C–Fuzzy Decision Trees,
– Classification accuracies achieved using Fuzzy Random Forest with C–Fuzzy Decision Trees.

The results for tested datasets are presented in the following tables:

– Ionosphere – Table 1,
– Dermatology – Table 2,
– Pima–Diabetes – Table 3,
– Hepatitis – Table 4.

The general tendention that can be observed in all of those results is decreasing the classification accuracy with increasing the number of clusters. In most cases results were the best for around 5 clusters, a bit worse for 2–3 clusters and significantly worse for 13–20 clusters. This dependence is a bit different for each dataset, which means the number of clusters should be chosen according to the given problem.

In most cases Fuzzy Random Forests with Fuzzy Decision Trees achieved better results than Fuzzy Forests with Fuzzy Decision Trees. The exception was

Table 1. Results – Ionosphere

Number of clusters	2	3	5	8	13	20
C4.5 rev. 8	13,54					
Single C–Fuzzy Tree	15,1	15,68	14,82	17,11	38,71	36,17
Fuzzy Forest with C–Fuzzy Decision Trees	15,1	15,39	13,39	15,67	29,93	30,19
Fuzzy Random Forest with C–Fuzzy Decision Trees	14,25	14,82	12,24	13,96	26,2	25,92

Table 2. Results – Dermatology

Number of clusters	2	3	5	8	13	20
C4.5 rev. 8	5,98					
Single C–Fuzzy Tree	6,02	6,3	5,47	17,46	39,36	48,42
Fuzzy Forest with C–Fuzzy Decision Trees	6,02	6,3	2,99	6,01	34,64	38,82
Fuzzy Random Forest with C–Fuzzy Decision Trees	6,02	6,3	2,18	5,17	31,86	34,65

Table 3. Results – Pima–Diabetes

Number of clusters	2	3	5	8	13	20
C4.5 rev. 8	27,95					
Single C–Fuzzy Tree	30,08	30,21	27,08	27,74	32,23	31,78
Fuzzy Forest with C–Fuzzy Decision Trees	28,52	29,68	26,31	27,47	29,03	29,43
Fuzzy Random Forest with C–Fuzzy Decision Trees	28,65	29,16	26,96	26,56	28,52	30,07

Table 4. Results – Hepatitis

Number of clusters	2	3	5	8	13	20
C4.5 rev. 8	43,86					
Single C–Fuzzy Tree	34,84	41,93	37,42	41,29	44,51	51,61
Fuzzy Forest with C–Fuzzy Decision Trees	34,19	38,06	37,42	36,77	34,19	43,87
Fuzzy Random Forest with C–Fuzzy Decision Trees	34,19	37,42	36,13	38,06	41,29	40

Pima–Diabetes dataset, where at the same number of cases the results were better or worse, depending on the number of clusters. It means that randomness generally increased the classification accuracy.

For each dataset there was at least one number of clusters which in almost all cases allowed to achieve better result that C4.5 rev. 8 Decision Tree. For Hepatitis dataset the better result was achieved independently from the number of clusters (exception was 20 clusters), but for the rest of datasets there were only one or two number of clusters, where these results were better. It shows how important is the choice of the proper number of clusters for C–Fuzzy Decision Trees used in Fuzzy Forests with Fuzzy Decision Trees and Fuzzy Random Forests with Fuzzy Decision Trees.

In almost all of the cases (unusual exceptions) results achieved using Fuzzy Forest with Fuzzy Decision Trees and Fuzzy Random Forest with Fuzzy Decision Trees were better than using single C–Fuzzy Decision Tree. It clearly shows the strength ensemble classifier build of this kind of trees. They achieve much better results when working together that when working as a single classifier.

6   Conclusion

In the previous paragraphs of this article there was proposed Fuzzy Random Forest with Fuzzy Decision Trees classifier. The created solution was checked on four datasets. Ionosphere, Dermatology, Pima–Diabetes and Hepatitis. There were tested how successfully the classifier works in comparison to the C4.5 rev. 8 Decision Tree and a single C–Fuzzy Decision Tree. There were also tested how randomness affects achieved classification quality.

Performed experiments proved than in most cases Fuzzy Random Forest with C–Fuzzy Decision Trees classifier gives better results than C4.5 rev. 8 Decision Tree and single C–Fuzzy Decision Tree classifiers. They also demonstrated that using randomness in the forest can increase the classification quality.

Acknowledgment. This work was supported by the grant S/WI/1/2013 from Bialystok University of Technology founded by Ministry of Science and Higher Education.

References

1. Bonissone, P.P., Cadenas, J.M., Garrido, M.C., Diaz-valladares, R.A.: A fuzzy random forest: fundamental for design and construction. In: Proceedings of the 12th International Conference on Information Processing and Management of Uncertainty in Knowledge-Based Systems (IPMU 2008), pp. 1231–1238 (2008)
2. Bonissone, P.P., Cadenas, J.M., Garrido, M.C., Diaz-Valladares, R.A.: A fuzzy random forest. Int. J. Approximate Reasoning **51**(7), 729–747 (2010)
3. Bonissone, P.P., Cadenas, J.M., Garrido, M.C., Diaz-Valladares, R.A.: Combination methods in a fuzzy random forest. In: IEEE International Conference on Systems, Man and Cybernetics, SMC 2008, pp. 1794–799, October 2008
4. Breiman, L., Friedman, J., Olshen, R., Stone, C.: Classification and Regression Trees. Wadsworth and Brooks, Monterey (1984)
5. Breiman, L.: Random forests. Mach. Learn. **45**(1), 5–32 (2001)
6. Chang, R.L.P., Pavlidis, T.: Fuzzy decision tree algorithms. IEEE Trans. Syst. Man Cybern. **7**(1), 28–35 (1977)
7. Janikow, C.Z.: Fuzzy decision trees: issues and methods. IEEE Trans. Syst. Man Cybern. Part B (Cybern.) **28**(1), 1–14 (1998)
8. Lichman, M.: UCI machine learning repository (2013)
9. Pedrycz, W., Sosnowski, Z.A.: C-fuzzy decision trees. IEEE Trans. Syst. Man Cybern. Part C (Appl. Rev.) **35**(4), 498–511 (2005)
10. Quinlan, J.R.: Induction of decision trees. Mach. Learn. **1**(1), 81–106 (1986)
11. Yuan, Y., Shaw, M.J.: Induction of fuzzy decision trees. Fuzzy Sets Syst. **69**(2), 125–139 (1995)

On Using Speed as the Criteria of State Selection for Minimization of Finite State Machines

Adam Klimowicz[✉]

Bialystok University of Technology, Bialystok, Poland
a.klimowicz@pb.edu.pl

Abstract. This paper presents a heuristic method for minimization of incompletely specified Mealy finite state machines. In this method, such optimization criteria as the speed and possibility of merging other states are taken into account already at the stage of minimizing internal states. Algorithms for the estimation of optimization criteria values are described. The proposed method is based on two states merging. Experimental results for two styles of state encoding and two types of programmable structures are presented. The results show that this approach to minimization of FSM in most of cases is more effective than classical methods in respect of FSM performance.

Keywords: Finite state machine (FSM) · State minimization · High speed

1 Introduction

The problem of increase of performance of electronic equipment becomes especially actual. It is connected to an acceleration of rate of human life, broad implementation of products of electronics to all spheres of human life and complication of the tasks solved by electronic equipment. High-speed performance of electronic projects is important in such spheres as computers, robotics, telecommunication, embedded systems, wired and wireless networks, transport, military and etc.

The high-speed performance of the electronic system directly depends on performance of the main control unit (system clock frequency) and also on the control units of the separate parts of the system. Generally the control unit represents the sequential circuit which mathematical model is the finite state machine (FSM). There are some approaches to increase the performance of the electronic equipment:

- the technological: using the elements with a high-speed performance;
- the system: using a piping and multi-core processors;
- the circuitry: increase of a supply voltage;
- the logical: using the synthesis methods allowing to build FSMs and control units with the maximum high-speed performance, etc.

Today the large number of scientific researches is devoted to the first three directions (especially to the first) while to the fourth direction, according to author, insufficient attention is paid. At the same time, the methods of a logic synthesis can be used

© IFIP International Federation for Information Processing 2016
Published by Springer International Publishing Switzerland 2016. All Rights Reserved
K. Saeed and W. Homenda (Eds.): CISIM 2016, LNCS 9842, pp. 493–503, 2016.
DOI: 10.1007/978-3-319-45378-1_44

for any technological basis, can be applied together with system methods, and do not depend on supply voltage.

The first attempts to combine minimization and state assignment procedures were made in [1–3]. In [1], the problem was considered for asynchronous FSMs so as to minimize the state code length. The method proposed in [2] was applicable only to state machines where the number of states did not exceed 10. In paper [3], a program for concurrent state minimization and state assignment was presented, which made it possible to form incompletely specified state codes.

The problem of the simultaneous minimization of area and signal delay on the critical path is considered in [4–7]. In [4], a structural model of the FSM called MAR model is proposed, which consists of an FSM and a combinational circuit with flip-flops in the feedback loops. In [5], codes with two unities (two-hot) and three unities (three-hot) are used. In [6], the minimization of power consumption and delay is considered for asynchronous FSMs. The concept of a low power semi-synchronous FSM operating on a high frequency is proposed that can be implemented and tested as an ordinary synchronous FSM. In [7], a two-level structural model is proposed to minimize the power consumption, area and delay. The first level of this model consists of sequential units, while the second level consists of combinational units of limited size.

The paper [8] presents a new technique for improving the performance of a synchronous circuit configured as a look-up table based FPGA without changing the initial circuit configuration; only the register location is altered. It improves clock speed and data throughput at the expense of latency. In [9] a new sequential circuit synthesis methodology is discussed that targets FPGAs and reconfigurable SoC platforms. The methodology is based on the information-driven approach to circuit synthesis, general decomposition and the previously developed theory of information relationship measures.

The paper [10] proposes a timing optimization technique for a complex finite state machine that consists of not only random logic but also data operators. The proposed technique, based on the concept of catalyst, adds a functionally redundant block – which includes a piece of combinational logic and several other registers - to the circuits under consideration so that the timing critical paths are divided into stages.

The paper [11] proposes to use the evolutionary methodology to yield optimal evolvable hardware that implements the state machine control component. The evolved hardware requires a minimal hardware area and introduces a minimal propagation delay of the machine output signals. The paper [12] is concerned with the problem of state assignment and logic optimization of high speed finite state machines. The method is designed for PAL-based CPLD implementation.

The analysis of available studies showed that there are no works in which the number of internal states and the speed of FSM are simultaneously minimized. In this paper, we propose an heuristic method for minimization of incompletely specified Mealy FSMs with unspecified values of output variables. This method is based on an operation of two states merging, where such optimization criteria as the speed (critical delay path) and possibility of merging other states are taken into account already at the stage of minimizing internal states. In addition to reduction of internal states this method minimizes the number of FSM transitions and FSM input variables.

2   Preliminaries

An ISFSM can have incompletely specified outputs and incompletely specified transitions. In practice, designers usually redefine the unspecified transitions by transitions to the present state or to the reset state. Sometimes they use transitions to an additional state, where an error signal is generated, what makes it possible to increase the functional reliability of the digital systems. In the presented approach we define the unspecified values only for the output variables and do not change the unspecified transitions.

Let us denote by L the number of FSM input variables of a set $X = \{x_1, ..., x_L\}$, by N the number of FSM output variables of a set $Y = \{y_1, ..., y_N\}$, by M the number of FSM internal states of a set $A = \{a_1, ..., a_M\}$, and by R the minimal number of bits required to encode internal states, where $R = \mathrm{int}\log_2 M$.

A FSM behavior can be described by the *transition list*. The transition list is a table with four columns: a_m, a_s, $X(a_m, a_s)$, and $Y(a_m, a_s)$. Each row of the transition list corresponds to one FSM transition. The column a_m contains a *present state*, the column a_s contains a *next state*, the column $X(a_m, a_s)$ contains a *transition condition* (an *input vector*), and the column $Y(a_m, a_s)$ contains an *output vector*. An ISFSM output vector is represented by ternary vector. For example, $Y(a_m, a_s) = $ "01-0", where 0 denotes zero value, 1 denotes unity value, and dash ("-") denotes a don't care value of the corresponding output variable.

The transition condition may be described in the column $X(a_m, a_s)$ in the form of conjunction of FSM input variables. The transition condition can also be represented by a ternary vector. Since the FSM behavior is deterministic, all the transition conditions from every FSM state should be mutually orthogonal. Two transition conditions are orthogonal if they have different significant values (0 or 1) at least in one position.

Two FSM states a_i and a_j can be merged, i.e. replaced by one state a_{i_j}, if they are equivalent. Equivalency of two FSM states means that FSM behavior does not change when these states are merged in one. FSM behavior does not change after merging, if the transition conditions from the states a_i and a_j that lead to different states are orthogonal. If there are transitions from states a_i and a_j that lead to the same unique state, then the transition conditions for such transitions should be equal. Moreover, the output vectors that are generated at these transitions should be not orthogonal. Note also that in case of two FSM states merging *wait states* can be formed. The detailed conditions of the states merging procedure are precisely described in paper [13].

Under FSM states merging the output vectors with unspecified values can be merged only if they are not orthogonal. Thus the significant values (0 or 1) remain without changes, and the unspecified values are replaced by the corresponding significant values. For example, let $Y(a_i, a_s) = $ "1-0-0" and $Y(a_j, a_s) = $ "-1010", and let the states a_i and a_j assume merging, then the output vector $Y(a_{i_j}, a_s) = $ "11010" will be formed at the transition from the new state a_{i_j} to the state a_s.

3   Main Minimization Algorithm

The main strategy of the proposed method consists in finding the set G of all the pairs of FSM states satisfying the merging conditions. Then for each pair of states from set G the trial merging is performed. Finally a pair (a_i, a_j) is selected for merging in such a way that leaves the maximal possibilities for other pairs of FSM states merging. This process repeats as long as there exists a possibility of merging for at least one pair of FSM states. The method was described more precisely in paper [13].

In distinction from [13], in the present paper we chose for merging at each step the pair (a_i, a_j) that best satisfies the optimization criteria in terms of speed, and leaves the maximum possibilities for merging other pairs of states. This procedure is repeated while at least one pair of states can be merged.

Let (a_s, a_t) be a pair of states in G, where S_{st} is the estimate of speed (critical delay path), and M_{st} is the estimate of the possibility to merge other states. Regarding to the above considerations, the FSM minimization algorithm can be described as follows.

Algorithm 1 (General Algorithm for FSM Minimization)

1. Using the method described in [13], form the set G of pairs of states that admit merging. If $G = \varnothing$ (no pairs can be merged), go to step 5
2. For each pair of states (a_s, a_t) in G, calculate the estimates S_{st}, and M_{st} of the optimization criteria.
3. Choose a pair of states (a_i, a_j) for merging. Among all the pairs in G, choose a pair (a_i, a_j) for which $S_{ij} = \min$; if there are several such pairs, then choose among them the one for which $M_{ij} = \max$.
4. Merge the pair of states (a_i, a_j). Store the results of minimization (transition list and corresponding S_{st} value). Go to step 1.
5. Among all saved results of minimization select one with minimal S_{st} value.
6. Minimize the number of transitions in the FSM.
7. Minimize the number of input variables in the FSM.
8. Stop.

Merging of the states a_i and a_j (step 4 of Algorithm 1), minimization of the number of transitions (step 6 of Algorithm 1) and minimization of the number of input variables (step 7 of Algorithm 1) are performed as described in [13].

Algorithms of minimization of the number of transition an input variables are based on some observations. Suppose, for instance, that one transition from a state a_1 under condition x_1 leads to a state a_2 and the second transition from a_1 under condition $\bar{x}_1$ leads to another state a_3 and on each of these transitions not orthogonal output vectors are formed ($\bar{x}_1$ is an inversed form of the variable x_1). Suppose that the states a_2 and a_3 can be merged. After merging a_2 and a_3, a new state a_{23} is formed. Now two transitions lead from a_1 to a_{23}, one under condition x_1 and the second under condition $\bar{x}_1$. The latter means that the transition from a_1 to a_{23} is unconditional and two transitions can be replaced by one unconditional transition. Notice that in general transition conditions from a state a_1 can be much more complicated.

At minimization of the number of FSM input variables can be performed at a situation when certain input variables have no impact on the transition conditions. Suppose, for instance, that one transition from a state a_1 under condition x_1 leads to a state a_2 and another transition from a_1 under condition $\bar{x}_1$ leads to a state a_3 and the variable x_1 does not meet anywhere else in transition conditions of the FSM. Suppose that after the states a_2 and a_3 have been merged, the transition from the state a_1 to the state a_{23} becomes unconditional, i.e. it does not depend on values of input variables. The latter means that the variable x_1 has no impact on any FSM transition and therefore it is redundant.

4 Estimation of Optimization Criteria

To estimate the optimization criteria, all pairs of states in G are considered one after another. For each pair of states (a_s, a_t) in G, a trial merging is performed. For the resultant FSM, its internal states are encoded using one of the available methods that will later be used in the synthesis of the FSM, and the system of Boolean functions corresponding to the combinational part of the FSM is built. Next, for the pair (a_s, a_t), the speed S_{st}, and the possibility of minimizing other states M_{st} are estimated. The optimization criteria for each pair of states (a_s, a_t) in G are estimated at step 2 of Algorithm 1 using the following algorithm.

Algorithm 2 (Estimation of Optimization Criteria)

1. Sequentially consider the elements of the set G.
2. For each pair of states $(a_s, a_t) \in G$, make a trial merging.
3. Perform the internal states assignment using one of the available methods.
4. Build the system of Boolean functions W corresponding to the combinational part of the FSM.
5. Estimate the critical delay path (speed) S_{st}.
6. Estimate the possibility of other states minimization M_{st}.
7. Return to the original FSM (before merging at step 2).
8. Execute steps 2–7 for all pairs of states in G.
9. Stop.

The speed of operation of an FSM is determined by the length of the critical path of its combinational part, which is equal to the number of CPLD macrocells or FPGA logic elements involved in the critical path.

The CPLD architecture is a set of functional units of which each consists of two programmable arrays - AND and OR. The outputs of the array AND are connected to the inputs of the array OR; they are called terms. Typically, the number of inputs of functional blocks in CPLDs is sufficiently large (16–54) and it usually exceeds the number of arguments of the functions implemented by the combinational part of the FSM. If the FSM is implemented on the basis of CPLD, then the cause of the decomposition of the system of Boolean functions corresponding to the combinational part of the FSM can be a large number of minterms in the DNF of a function and a large number of arguments of a function. For that reason, when the FSM is implemented on the basis of CPLD, two critical paths are found, and the longest of them is chosen.

In the case of a large number of minterms in the DNF of a function, the linear decomposition with respect to the minterms is used. The number of inputs of the OR gates is restricted by the parameter q_{max} - the maximum number of terms that can be connected to one CPLD macrocell (typically, q_{max} for different families of CPLDs is between 12 and 90). In the case of a large number of arguments, linear decomposition of the Boolean function with respect to the arguments is used, where the number n_{FB} of inputs of CPLD functional blocks is used as the restriction (for different families of CPLDs, n_{FB} is between 16 and 54).

In the general case, the architecture of modern FPGAs can be represented as a set of logic elements based on Look-Up Tables (LUT). A feature of LUTs is that they can realize any Boolean function but with a small number of arguments (typically, 4–6 and more often 4). In the case when the number of arguments of functions to be realized exceeds the number of LUT inputs n_L, the Boolean function must be decomposed with respect to the number of arguments [14]. Among the great number of decomposition methods for Boolean functions with respect to the number of arguments, linear decomposition methods are most popular. They are used in the majority of industrial EDA tools. When the FSM is implemented on the basis of FPGA, the length of the critical path depends only on the maximum number of arguments of the realized functions.

Algorithm 3 (for the Estimation of the FSM Speed of Operation)

1. Find the maximum number L_{max} of arguments of the functions realized by the combinational part of the FSM. For each pair of states (a_s, a_t) in G, calculate the estimates S_{st}, and M_{st} of the optimization criteria

$$L_{\max} = \max_{w_i \in W} |L(w_i)|, \tag{1}$$

where $L(w_i)$ is a set of arguments of the function w_i. If the FSM is implemented on the basis of CPLD, then additionally the maximum number of minterms in the DNFs of the functions realized by the combinational part of the FSM is determined:

$$Q_{\max} = \max_{w_i \in W} |Q(w_i)|, \tag{2}$$

where $Q(w_i)$ is a set of minterms in the DNF of the function w_i.
2. Calculate the length of the critical path in the combinational part of the FSM.
   2.1. If the FSM is implemented on the basis of CPLD, then the lengths of two critical paths are found: one (S_L) depending on the maximum number of arguments (]x[is the minimal integer greater than or equal to x):

$$S_L = 1 +](L_{\max} - n_{FB})/(n_{FB} - 1)[\tag{3}$$

   and the other (S_Q) depending on the maximum number of terms:

$$S_Q = 1 +](Q_{\max} - q_{\max})/(q_{\max} - 1)[. \tag{4}$$

   Set $S_{st} = max(S_L, S_Q)$.
   2.2. If the FSM is implemented on the basis of FPGA, the length of the critical path is determined only based on the maximum number of arguments:

$$S_{st} = 1 +](L_{max} - n_L)/(n_L - 1)[. \tag{5}$$

3. Stop.

The estimate M_{st} is determined by the number of pairs of the FSM that can be merged after merging the pair (a_s, a_t). To provide the best possibilities for merging other states, M_{st} should be maximized. With regard to the above considerations, the algorithm for estimating the FSM speed of operation is as follows.

Algorithm 4 (for Estimation of Possibility of Merging Other States)

1. Using the method described in [13], find the set G_{st} of pairs of states that can be merged upon merging the pair (a_s, a_t). For each pair of states $(a_s, a_t) \in G$, make a trial merging.
2. Set $M_{st} = |G_{st}|$.
3. Stop.

5 Experimental Results

The method for minimization was implemented in a program called ZUBR. The ZUBR system is the scientific-industrial software developed for design of digital systems based on programmable logic. To estimate the efficiency of the offered method we used MCNC FSM benchmarks [15]. Each of tested FSM benchmarks was encoded using binary and one-hot encoding. The speed was calculated for the initial FSM, the STAMINA program [16] and the method described in this paper.

Two models of programmable structures were used for experiments. The CPLD device model has following parameters, which can affect synthesis result: $q_{max} = 5$ and $n_{FB} = 54$. It corresponds to real CPLD devices, such as XC9500XL from Xilinx. The FPGA device model has only one parameter, which can affect synthesis result: $n_L = 4$. It corresponds to most of real FPGA devices, such as Virtex and Spartan from Xilinx or Cyclone and Stratix from Altera.

The experimental results for binary encoding and synthesis using the CPLD device are presented in Table 1, where M_0 and S_0 are, respectively, the number of internal states and signal delay critical path (the number of logical levels after synthesis) of the initial FSM; M_1 and S_1 are, respectively, the same parameters after minimization using STAMINA and M_2, and S_2 are, respectively the same parameters after minimization using proposed method (with taking in consideration speed of FSM). S_0/S_2 and S_1/S_2 are ratios of the corresponding parameters; and *Mean* is the geometric mean value.

The analysis of Table 1 shows that application of the proposed method using binary encoding allows to reduce the number of internal states of the initial FSM. Similarly, the average reduction of the critical delay path of the FSM makes 1.44 times, and on occasion (example *train11*) 2.5 times. In comparison to STAMINA the number of states is higher in 1 case but the average reduction of the critical delay path of the FSM makes 1.67 times, and on occasion (example *bbsse*) 2.89 times.

The experimental results for one-hot encoding and CPLD device are presented in Table 2, where all parameters have the same meaning as in Table 1. The analysis of

Table 1. The experimental results for binary encoding and CPLD device

Name	M_0	S_0	M_1	S_1	M_2	S_2	S_0/S_2	S_1/S_2
bbara	10	7	7	4	7	4	1,75	1,00
bbsse	16	10	13	26	13	9	1,11	2,89
beecount	7	5	4	4	5	4	1,25	1,00
lion9	14	4	4	3	4	2	2,00	1,50
s27	6	7	5	6	5	5	1,40	1,20
sse	16	10	13	26	13	9	1,11	2,89
tma	20	6	18	16	18	6	1,00	2,67
train11	12	5	4	3	4	2	2,50	1,50
Mean							1,44	1,67

Table 2 shows that application of the proposed method using one-hot encoding allows to reduce the number of internal states of the initial FSM. Similarly, the average increase of the speed of the FSM makes 1.38 times, and on occasion (example train11) 2.5 times. In comparison to STAMINA the number of states is higher in 1 case but the average reduction of the critical delay path of the FSM makes 1.43 times, and on occasion (example tma) 2.17 times.

Table 2. The experimental results for one-hot encoding and CPLD device

Name	M_0	S_0	M_1	S_1	M_2	S_2	S_0/S_2	S_1/S_2
bbara	10	3	7	2	7	2	1.50	1.00
bbsse	16	7	13	12	13	7	1.00	1.71
beecount	7	5	4	4	5	4	1.25	1.00
lion9	14	4	4	3	4	2	2.00	1.50
s27	6	7	5	6	5	5	1.40	1.20
sse	16	7	13	12	13	7	1.00	1.71
tma	20	6	18	13	18	6	1.00	2.17
train11	12	5	4	3	4	2	2.50	1.50
Mean							1.38	1.43

The experimental results for binary encoding and FPGA device are presented in Table 3, where all parameters have the same meaning as in Tables 1 and 2.

The analysis of Table 3 shows that the average reduction of the critical delay path of the FSM makes 1.25 times, and on occasion (examples *lion9* and *train11*) 2 times. In comparison to STAMINA the number of states is higher in one case and speed of FSM for both methods is equal.

The experimental results for one-hot encoding and FPGA device are presented in Table 4, where all parameters have the same meaning as in above tables. The analysis of Table 4 shows that application of the proposed allows to reduce the critical delay path 1.27 times, and on occasion even 2 times. In comparison to STAMINA the number of states is higher in one case (example *beecount*). The average reduction of the critical delay path of the FSM is almost equal (in extreme cases - for *tma* benchmark reduction ratio is equal 1.33, but for *beecount* - 0.67).

Table 3. The experimental results for binary encoding and FPGA device

Name	M_0	S_0	M_1	S_1	M_2	S_2	S_0/S_2	S_1/S_2
bbara	10	3	7	2	7	2	1.50	1.00
bbsse	16	3	13	3	13	3	1.00	1.00
beecount	7	2	4	2	5	2	1.00	1.00
lion9	14	2	4	1	4	1	2.00	1.00
s27	6	2	5	2	5	2	1.00	1.00
sse	16	3	13	3	13	3	1.00	1.00
tma	20	3	18	3	18	3	1.00	1.00
train11	12	2	4	1	4	1	2.00	1.00
Mean							1.25	1.00

It can be noticed that the reduction of states in most of cases leads to critical path reduction of FSMs. But for 3 cases, if using STAMINA minimization program, there was a longer critical delay path than for the FSM without using minimization. These results were obtained when minimization for CPLD was performed.

Table 4. The experimental results for one-hot encoding and FPGA device

Name	M_0	S_0	M_1	S_1	M_2	S_2	S_0/S_2	S_1/S_2
bbara	10	5	7	4	7	4	1.25	1.00
bbsse	16	7	13	6	13	6	1.17	1.00
beecount	7	3	4	2	5	3	1.00	0.67
lion9	14	4	4	2	4	2	2.00	1.00
s27	6	3	5	3	5	3	1.00	1.00
sse	16	7	13	6	13	6	1.17	1.00
tma	20	6	18	8	18	6	1.00	1.33
train11	12	4	4	2	4	2	2.00	1.00
Mean							1.27	0.99

Table 5 presents the average speed for two used encoding styles for CPLD device. S_{AV0}, S_{AV1} and S_{AV2} parameters stand for the average speed of the initial FSM, the FSM after minimization using the STAMINA program and the method from this paper accordingly.

Table 5. Average speed comparison for tested encodings for CPLD device

Encoding	S_{AV0}	S_{AV1}	S_{AV2}
Binary	6.75	11.0	5.125
One-hot	5.5	6.875	4.375

The analysis of the Table 5 shows that results obtained using presented approach are better than results obtained from the STAMINA in all styles of encoding used. Also, the one-hot encoding style was the better than binary in terms of FSM speed for all considered cases for CPLD devices.

Table 6 presents the average speed for two used encoding styles for FPGA device, where all parameters have the same meaning as in Table 5.

Table 6. Average speed comparison for tested encodings for FPGA device

Encoding	S_{AV0}	S_{AV1}	S_{AV2}
Binary	2.5	2.125	2.125
One-hot	4.875	4.125	4.0

The analysis of the Table 6 shows that results obtained using presented approach are equal or better than results obtained from the STAMINA in both of styles of encoding used. Also, the binary encoding style was the better than one-hot in terms of FSM speed for all considered cases for FPGA devices.

It can be noticed, that in terms of speed, the binary encoding is more effective for FPGA devices and the one-hot encoding – for CPLD. It is related to fact, that the key parameters for FPGA devices is the number of arguments of each function, which is often higher than the number of minterms in tested benchmarks. The last mentioned parameter is a key parameter in synthesis on CPLD. To increase speed in FPGA implementation we can use other methods of decomposition, e.g. functional decomposition [17].

6   Conclusion

In this paper an efficient method for ISFSM minimization was presented. In this method, the critical delay path is taken into account already at the stage of the minimization of the number of internal states. The presented method allows to reduce the number of internal states of FSM and additionally it allows to increase a speed of FSMs comparing to STAMINA program. The proposed method also allows to reduce the number of FSM transitions and input variables. The time of execution of presented algorithm do not exceed 20 s on the computer with Intel i3 processor for FSMs having more than 200 states and 1500 transitions.

In future, more experiments with real digital systems will be performed using industrial EDA tools and specific programmable devices. In the offered approach to FSM minimization only two states merging is considered. The presented method can be modified to join a group of states containing more states. Proposed method is only the part of work on the complex minimization method [18], where speed, power consumption and area parameters are taken in consideration. In future, this method will serve to minimize power, cost and increase speed for FSM realization on programmable logic devices.

Acknowledgements. The research was done in the framework of the grant S/WI/1/2013 and financed from the funds for science by MNiSW.

References

1. Hallbauer, G.: Procedures of state reduction and assignment in one step in synthesis of asynchronous sequential circuits. In: 1974 Proceedings of the International IFAC Symposium on Discrete Systems, Riga, Pergamons, pp. 272–282 (1974)
2. Lee, E.B., Perkowski, M.: Concurrent minimization and state assignment of finite state machines. In: 1984 Proceedings of the IEEE International Conference on Systems, Man and Cybernetics, Minneapolis. IEEE Computer Society (1984)
3. Avedillo, M.J., Quintana, J.M., Huertas, J.L.: SMAS: a program for concurrent state reduction and state assignment of finite state machines. In: 1991 Proceedings of the IEEE International Symposium on Circuits and Systems (ISCAS), Singapore, pp. 1781–1784. IEEE (1991)
4. Rama Mohan, C., Chakrabarti, P.: A new approach to synthesis of PLA-based FSM's. In: 1994 Proceedings of the 7th International Conference on VLSI Design, Calcutta, India, pp. 373–378. IEEE Computer Society (1994)
5. Gupta, B.N.V.M., Narayanan, H., Desai, M.P.: A state assignment scheme targeting performance and area. In: 1999 Proceedings of the Twelfth International Conference on VLSI Design, Goa, India, pp. 378–383. IEEE Computer Society (1999)
6. Lindholm, C.: High frequency and low power semi-synchronous PFM state machine. In: 2011 Proceedings of the IEEE International Symposium on Digital Object Identifier, Rio de Janeiro, pp. 1868–1871. IEEE Computer Society (2011)
7. Liu, Z., Arslan, T., Erdogan, A.T.: An embedded low power reconfigurable fabric for finite state machine operations. In: 2006 Proceedings of the International Symposium on Circuits and Systems (ISCAS), Island of Kos, Greece, pp. 4374–4377. IEEE Computer Society (2006)
8. Miyazaki, N., Nakada, H., Tsutsui, A., Yamada, K., Ohta, N.: Performance improvement technique for synchronous circuits realized as LUT-Based FPGA's. IEEE Trans. Very Large Scale Integr. VLSI Syst. 3(3), 455–459 (1995)
9. Jozwiak, L., Slusarczyk, A., Chojnacki, A.: Fast and compact sequential circuits through the information-driven circuit synthesis. In: Proceedings of the Euromicro Symposium on Digital Systems Design, Warsaw, Poland, 4–6 September 2001, pp. 46–53
10. Huang, S.-Y.: On speeding up extended finite state machines using catalyst circuitry. In: Proceedings of the Asia and South Pacific Design Automation Conference (ASAP-DAC), Yokohama, January–February 2001, pp. 583–588
11. Nedjah, N., Mourelle, L.: Evolutionary synthesis of synchronous finite state machines. In: Proceedings of the International Conference on Computer Engineering and Systems, Cairo, Egypt, 5–7 November 2006, pp. 19–24
12. Czerwiński, R., Kania, D.: Synthesis method of high speed finite state machines. Bull. Pol. Acad. Sci. Tech. Sci. 58(4), 635–644 (2010)
13. Klimowicz, A., Solov'ev, V.V.: Minimization of incompletely specified mealy finite-state machines by merging two internal states. J. Comput. Syst. Sci. Int. 52(3), 400–409 (2013)
14. Zakrevskij, A.D.: Logic Synthesis of Cascade Circuits. Nauka, Moscow (1981). [in Russian]
15. Yang, S.: Logic synthesis and optimization benchmarks user guide, version 3.0. Technical report, North Carolina, Microelectronics Center of North Carolina (1991)
16. Rho, J.-K., Hachtel, G., Somenzi, F., Jacoby, R.: Exact and heuristic algorithms for the minimization of incompletely specified state machines. IEEE Trans. Comput.-Aid. Des. 13, 167–177 (1994)
17. Luba, T., Selvaraj, H.: A general approach to boolean function decomposition and its applications in FPGA-based synthesis. VLSI Des. 3(3-4), 289–300 (1995)
18. Solov'ev, V.V.: Complex minimization method for finite state machines implemented on programmable logic devices. J. Comput. Syst. Sci. Int. 53(2), 186–194 (2014)

PLACE_SUBST Transformation of P/T Petri Process Nets and Its Properties

Ivo Martiník[(✉)]

Faculty of Economics, VŠB-Technical University of Ostrava,
Sokolská třída 33, 702 00 Ostrava 1, Czech Republic
ivo.martinik@vsb.cz

Abstract. Petri nets is one of mathematical modeling languages for the description of all kind of parallel systems. Property-preserving Petri net process algebras (PPPA) were originally designed for the specification and verification of Petri net processes representing the manufacturing systems. PPPA does not need to verify the composition of Petri net processes because all their algebraic operators preserve the specified set of the properties. These original PPPA are generalized for the newly introduced class of the P/T Petri process nets (PTPN) in this article. The only one PLACE_SUBST transformation is defined for the class of PTPN and its chosen properties are presented. The PTPN can be with the support of the PLACE_SUBST transformation easily applied into the area of design, simulation and verification of multithreading programming systems executed in parallel or distributed environment. This fact is demonstrated on the simple example of the client-server distributed programming system.

Keywords: P/T Petri process net · Well-formed process net · Property preservation · PLACE_SUBST transformation · Parallel systems modeling

1 Introduction

Petri nets [1–4] is one of mathematical modeling languages for the description of all kind of parallel systems and they represent a popular formalism connecting advantages of the graphic representation of a modeled system with the possibilities of its simulation and the formal analyzability. Property-preserving Petri net process algebras (PPPA) [6] were originally designed for the specification and verification of manufacturing systems. PPPA also follows many ideas that can be originally seen in the class of workflow nets [5]. The elements of PPPA are the Petri net processes, an ordinary connected Petri nets with a unique entry place, a unique exit place and a set of places for handling resource sharing with their initial marking allowed. Among other features, PPPA does not need to verify composite components because all of their operators preserve many properties. PPPA have five types of operators: extensions, compositions, refinements, reductions and place-merging. All the operators can preserve about twenty properties (some under additional conditions), such as liveness, boundedness, reversibility, traps, siphons, proper termination, etc. Hence, if the primitive modules satisfy the desirable properties, each of the composite components, including the system itself, also satisfies these properties.

© IFIP International Federation for Information Processing 2016
Published by Springer International Publishing Switzerland 2016. All Rights Reserved
K. Saeed and W. Homenda (Eds.): CISIM 2016, LNCS 9842, pp. 504–515, 2016.
DOI: 10.1007/978-3-319-45378-1_45

In this article we will generalize PPPA for the special class of the P/T Petri process nets (PTPN), define the only one PTPN transformation called **PLACE_SUBST** and present its base characteristic of the well-formedness and purely-formedness properties preservation. This class of PTPN with the support of the **PLACE_SUBST** transformation can be then successfully used in the area of design, simulation and verification of programming systems executed in distributed or parallel environment. This fact is then demonstrated on the simple example of the distributed programming system based on the client-server architecture.

2 P/T Petri Process Nets and Their Properties

Let N denotes the set of all natural numbers, $N: = \{1, 2, ...\}$, N_0 the set of all non-negative integer numbers, $N_0: = \{0, 1, 2, ...\}$, $\emptyset$ the empty set, $\ulcorner$ the logical negation operator, $|A|$ the cardinality of the given set A, where $|N| = \aleph_0$.

Let A be a non-empty set. By the (non-empty finite) **sequence** σ over the set A a function σ can be understood, $\sigma: \{1, 2, ..., n\} \rightarrow A$, where $n \in N$. The function $\varepsilon: \emptyset \rightarrow A$ is called the **empty sequence** over the set A. The sequence $\sigma: \{1, 2, ..., n\} \rightarrow A$ is usually represented by the notation $\sigma = a_1\, a_2\, ...\, a_n$ of the elements of the set A, where $a_i = \sigma(i)$ for $1 \leq i \leq n$.

Let $A = \{a_1, a_2, ..., a_n\}$, where $n \in N$, is a finite non-empty set. **Vector** V is a function $V: A \rightarrow N_0$. We will denote a vector V by the statement $V = (V(1), V(2), ..., V(n))$.

Let $\mathbf{V} = \{(V(1), V(2), ..., V(n)) \mid V(i) \in N_0 \text{ for } 1 \leq i \leq n\}$ and $\mathbf{W} = \{(W(1), W(2), ..., W(m)) \mid W(j) \in N_0 \text{ for } 1 \leq j \leq m\}$. Then

$$\mathbf{V} \otimes \mathbf{W} = \{(V(1), ..., V(n), W(1), ..., W(m)) \mid V(i) \in N_0 \text{ for } 1 \leq i \leq n,\ W(j) \in N_0 \text{ for}$$
$$1 \leq j \leq m\},\ \text{if}\ (\mathbf{V} \neq \emptyset) \wedge (\mathbf{W} \neq \emptyset),$$
$$= \mathbf{V},\ \text{if}\ (\mathbf{V} \neq \emptyset) \wedge (\mathbf{W} = \emptyset),$$
$$= \mathbf{W},\ \text{if}\ (\mathbf{V} = \emptyset) \wedge (\mathbf{W} \neq \emptyset),$$
$$= \emptyset,\ \text{if}\ (\mathbf{V} = \emptyset) \wedge (\mathbf{W} = \emptyset).$$

It is clear that the $\otimes$ is an associative operation (i.e., $(\mathbf{V} \otimes \mathbf{W}) \otimes \mathbf{U} = \mathbf{V} \otimes (\mathbf{W} \otimes \mathbf{U})$).

Process net (PN) is an ordered 9-tuple $PN: = (P, T, A, AF, TP, RP, IP, OP, RM_s)$, where

- P is a finite non-empty set of **places**,
- T is a finite set of **transitions**, $P \cap T = \emptyset$,
- A is a finite set of **arcs**, $A \subseteq (P \times T) \cup (T \times P)$,
- AF is the **arc function**, $AF: (P \times T) \cup (T \times P) \rightarrow N_0$, $AF(x, y) \in N$ iff $(x, y) \in A$, $AF(x, y) = 0$ iff $(x, y) \notin A$,
- TP is a **transition priority** function, $TP: T \rightarrow N$,
- RP is a finite set of **resource places**, $RP \subset P$,
- IP is the **input place**, $IP \in (P \setminus RP)$, it is the only one place such that $\bullet IP = \emptyset$,

- OP is the **output place**, $OP \in (P \setminus RP)$, it is the only one place such that $OP\bullet = \emptyset$,
- RM_s is the set of all **allowed resource places static markings**, $RM_s \subseteq \mathbf{M_s}$, where $\mathbf{M_s}$ is the set of all the static markings M_s of the PN (see below),
- (P, T, A) is a **connected net**.

We will denote the class of all the PNs by the symbol $\boldsymbol{PNET}$. The given PN is then described with a bipartite graph containing a finite non-empty set P of places used for expressing of the conditions of a modeled process (we usually use circles for their representation), a finite set T of transitions describing the changes in the process (we usually draw them in the form of rectangles), a finite set A of arcs being principally oriented while connecting the place with the transition or the transition with the place and we usually draw them as lines with arrows, the arc function AF assigning each arc with a natural number (such number has the default value of 1, if not explicitly indicated in the PN diagram) expressing the number of removed or added tokens from or to the place associated with that arc when executing a particular transition. Transition priority function TP assigns with each transition the natural number value expressing its priority (with the default value of 1). The finite set RP of resource places is used for expressing conditions of a modeled process containing some initial resources and we use circles with the double line for their representation. The input place IP is the only one non-resource place of PN PN with no input arc(s) and the output place OP is the only one non-resource place of PN PN with no output arc(s). RM_s is the set of all the allowed resource places static markings that is subset of the set $\mathbf{M_s}$ of all the static markings M_s of the PN PN (the term static marking M_s of PN PN will be explained below). The net (P, T, A) must be connected.

Some commonly used notations for PNs are $\bullet y = \{x \mid (x, y) \in A\}$ for the **preset** and $y\bullet = \{x \mid (y, x) \in A\}$ for the **postset** of a PN element y (i.e., place or transition).

Marking M of the PN PN is a mapping $M: P \rightarrow N_0$. Marking M then expresses the current status of a modeled process. Marking M can be written as a $|P|$-vector $M: = (M(IP), M(P_1), M(P_2), \ldots, M(P_k), M(R_1), M(R_2), \ldots, M(R_m), M(OP))$, where $P: = (IP, P_1, P_2, \ldots, P_n, R_1, R_2, \ldots, R_m, OP)$, $RP: = \{R_1, R_2, \ldots, R_m\}$, $n \in N_0$, $m \in N_0$.

The transition $t \in T$ is **enabled** in the marking M of the PN PN if at each input place of the transition t are in the marking M at least as many tokens as required by the value of the arc function AF of the particular input arc of the transition t, i.e., if $\forall p \in \bullet t$: $M(p) \geq AF(p, t)$. If the transition t is enabled in the marking M of the PN PN, we denote that fact in the form of t **en** M. **Firing of the transition** $t \in T$ itself consists in the removal of as many tokens from each preset place of the transition t as required by the value of the arc function AF of the particular input arc of the transition t, and adding of as many tokens into each of the postset places of the transition t as required by the value of the arc function AF of the particular output arc of the transition t, i.e., it results in changing the marking M into the marking M', where $\forall p \in P$: $M'(p) = M(p) - AF(p, t) + AF(t, p)$, that is denoted by $M[t\rangle M'$.

We say that the marking M'' is reachable from the marking M iff there exists a finite sequence $\sigma: = t_1 t_2 \ldots t_n, n \in N$, of the transitions $t_1, t_2, \ldots, t_n$, such that $M[t_1 t_2 \ldots t_n\rangle M''$. The set of all the PN's markings reachable from its given marking M will be denoted by the symbol $[M\rangle$, the set of all the transition sequences $\sigma: = t_1 t_2 \ldots t_n, n \in N$, of the transitions that are fireable from the marking M will be denoted by the symbol $[M\rangle\rangle$, i.e., $[M\rangle\rangle := \{t_1t_2\ldots t_n | \exists M'' \in [M\rangle : M[t_1t_2\ldots t_n\rangle M'', n \in N\}$.

Let $k \in N$. The following special markings of the PN $PN: = (P, T, A, AF, TP, RP,$ $IP, OP, RM_s)$ are defined:

- **static marking** M_s: $\forall p \in RP$: $M_s(p) \geq 0$; $\forall p \notin RP$: $M_s(p) = 0$; $\forall t \in T$: $\ulcorner(t\ en\ M_s)$,
- **entry marking** M_e: $M_e(IP) = k$; $\forall p \in (P \setminus \{IP\})$: $M_e(p) = M_s(p)$,
- **exit marking** M_x: $M_x(IP) = 0$; $M_x(OP) = M_e(IP) = k$; $\forall p \notin (RP \cup \{OP\})$: $M_x(p) = 0$; $\forall t \in T$: $\ulcorner(t\ en\ M_x)$.

For the given PN PN we will denote the set of all its static markings M_s by the symbol $\mathbf{M_s}$, the set of all its entry markings M_e by the symbol $\mathbf{M_e}$ and the set of all its exit markings M_x by the symbol $\mathbf{M_x}$.

Figure 1, illustrates the PN $PROC: = (P, T, A, AF, TP, RP, IP, OP, RM_s)$, where $P = \{IP, P1, R1, OP\}$, $T = \{T1, T2, T3\}$, $A = \{(IP, T1), (IP, T2), (T1, P1), (T2, P1),$ $(R1, T1), (P1, T3), (T3, R1), (T3, OP)\}$, $AF = \{((IP, T1), 1), ((IP, T2), 1), ((T1, P1), 1),$ $((T2, P1), 1), ((R1, T1), 1), ((P1, T3), 1), ((T3, R1), 2), ((T3, OP), 1)\}$, $TP = \{(T1, 1),$ $(T2, 1), (T3, 1)\}$, $IP = IP$, $OP = OP$, $RM_s = \{(RM_s(R1))\} = \{(n) \mid n \in N\}$, in its static M_s, entry M_e and exit M_x markings where $k = 3$ (note the resource place R1 with the initial token in the static marking M_s and the fact that no transition must be enabled in (any) static M_s or exit M_x markings) where the notation $RM_s = \{(RM_s(R1))\} = \{(n) \mid n \in N\}$ means that in any allowed resource static marking M_s the resource place R1 must contain at least one token.

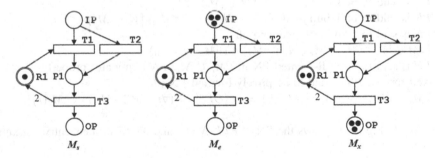

Fig. 1. Static, input and output markings of the PN $PROC$

A **P/T Petri process net** (PTPN) is an ordered couple $PTPN = (PN, M_e)$, where PN is a PN and M_e is an entry marking of the PN PN. We will then denote a PTPNs by an ordered 10-tuple $PTPN: = (P, T, A, AF, TP, RP, IP, OP, RM_s, M_e)$ and the class of all the PTPNs by the symbol $\boldsymbol{PTPNET}$.

When enabling individual transitions of a given PTPN so called **conflicts** can originate in its certain markings (or **conflict transitions**). At the enabling of the transitions t_1 and t_2 of the given PTPN in its marking M the conflict occurs, if both transitions t_1 and t_2 have at least one input place, each of the transitions t_1 and t_2 is individually enabled in the marking M, but the transitions t_1 and t_2 are not in the marking M enabled in parallel and enabling of one of them will prevent enabling the other (i.e., ($\bullet t_1 \cap \bullet t_2 \neq \varnothing$) $\wedge$ (t_1 *en M*) $\wedge$ (t_2 *en M*) $\wedge$ $\ulcorner$($\{t_1, t_2\}$ *en M*)). The term of conflict transitions can be obviously easily generalized for the case of a finite set $t_1, t_2,$ ..., t_n ($n \in N$) of the transitions of a given PTPN.

A typical example of the conflict transitions in the particular marking of the PTPN is shown in Fig. 2, where transitions T1 and T2 have a common input place IP, both are enabled, but they are not enabled in parallel. When solving such transitions conflict we will therefore follow the rule which determines, informally said, that from the set of conflict transitions the one will be enabled, whose value of the transition priority function *TP* is the highest. If such transition from the set of conflict transitions does not exist, the given conflict would have to be solved by other means. The transition T2 is then enabled on the basis of that rule in our studied example (because $TP(T1) = 1$ and $TP(T2) = 2$).

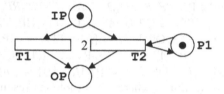

Fig. 2. Conflict transitions in P/T Petri process net

Definition 1. Let *PN*: $= (P, T, A, AF, TP, RP, IP, OP, RM_s)$ be a PN, M_e be its entry marking. Then:

- *PN* is said to be **safe** iff $\forall p \in P \, \forall M \in [M_e\rangle : M(p) \leq 1$,
- *PN* is said to be *k*-**bounded** iff $\exists k \in N \, \forall p \in P \, \forall M \in [M_e\rangle : M(p) \leq k$,
- *PN* is said to **terminate properly** iff
  $(\forall M \in [M_e\rangle \, \exists M_x \in \mathbf{M}_x : M_x \in [M\rangle) \wedge (|[M_e\rangle\rangle| \neq \aleph_0)$,
- *PN* is said to be **well-formed** PN iff $\forall M_e \in \mathbf{M}_e$: *PN* terminates properly,
- well-formed *PN* is said to be **purely-formed** PN iff
  $\forall M_e \in \mathbf{M}_e \forall M_x \in \mathbf{M}_x : ((M_e(IP) = M_x(OP)) \Rightarrow (\forall r \in RP : M_e(r) = M_x(r))$.

Example 1. Figure 3, shows the PNs *NET1*, *NET2* and *NET3* in their entry markings M_e, where:

- PN *NET1* does not terminate properly, because there exists the infinite sequence of reachable markings $M_e[T1\rangle M_1[T1\rangle M_2[T1\rangle\ldots$, and so the PN *NET1* is not a well-formed PN,
- PN *NET2* terminates properly for every of its entry markings M_e (and so it is a well-formed PN), but it is not purely-formed PN, because $\exists M_e \in \mathbf{M}_e$ $\exists M_x \in \mathbf{M}_x : (M_e(IP) = M_x(OP) \wedge (\exists R1 \in RP : M_e(R1) \neq M_x(R1))$, where $M_e = (1, 0, 1, 0)$ and $M_x = (0, 0, 2, 1)$,
- PN *NET3* is a purely-formed PN.

Lemma 1. Let *PN*: $= (P, T, A, AF, TP, RP, IP, OP, RM_s)$ be a PN. Then (*PN* is well-formed PN) $\Rightarrow$ ($\forall M_e \in \mathbf{M}_e \, \exists k \in N$: *PN* is *k*-bounded).

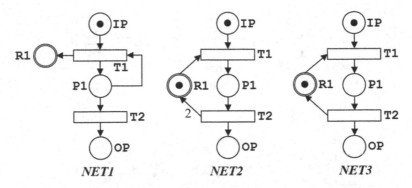

Fig. 3. PNs *NET1*, *NET2* and *NET3* in their entry markings M_e

Proof. Clear. (*PN* is well-formed PN) $\Rightarrow$ ($\forall M_e \in \mathbf{M}_e$: *PN* terminates properly) $\Rightarrow$ ($\forall M_e \in \mathbf{M}_e$: (($\forall M \in [M_e\rangle \exists M_x \in \mathbf{M}_x : M_x \in [M\rangle) \wedge (|[M_e\rangle| \neq \aleph_0)))$ $\Rightarrow$ ($\forall M_e \in \mathbf{M}_e$: (($(|[M_e\rangle|$ is finite) $\wedge$ ($\forall M \in [M_e\rangle : M$ is finite marking of *PN*))) $\Rightarrow$ ($\forall M_e \in \mathbf{M}_e \exists k \in N$: *PN* is k-bounded). $\qquad\square$

3   Base P/T Petri Process Nets and Their Properties

As it was mentioned in the introduction of this article we want to generalize the PPPA for the class of the PNs. From many properties of PNs we are especially interesting in their well-formedness, resp. purely-formedness, property (in the terminology of programming systems well-formedness property informally means that the programming system modeled by a given PN will not cause deadlock and memory or device overflow and purely-formedness property informally means that given well-formed programming system will not have any side effects). It is of course possible to inspect the properties of traps, siphons, P- and T-invariants etc., of a given PN but it is outside the scope of this article. We will then represent given multithreading programming system by the PN, i.e., programming systems that will be executed in parallel environment by k programming threads, where $k \in N$. These programming threads will be represented by k tokens in the input place *IP* of given PN in its entry marking M_e.

We start our generalization of PPPA for the class of PNs by introduction of so called **base PNs** (BPN). BPNs represent the subclass of PNs that are elementary purely-formed, (i.e., purely-formedness of these PNs can be trivially proved).

Figure 4, shows six simple BPNs in their static markings M_s (i.e., the letter m in every of their resource places denotes m tokens, $m \in N$). The BPN *BASE1* is the simplest purely-formed BPN at all and it contains only one place IOP that is simultaneously its input and output place (definition of PN allows this case). Purely-formed BPN *BASE3* can be used for the modeling of the programming statement IF ... THEN ... ELSE ... (note that the value of the transition priority function $TP(T2) = 2$ and it helps to solve potential conflict in the firing of the transitions T1 and T2), purely-formed BPN *BASE4* represents the model of the programming critical section, where typically $m = 1$ in the resource place R1. Purely-formed BPN *BASE5* then

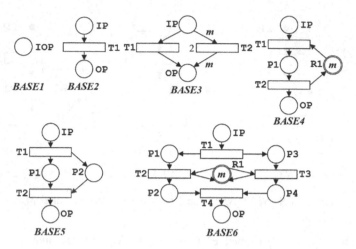

Fig. 4. Examples of BPNs

represents the synchronous programming method calling mechanism, where the called method is represented by the place P2. Purely-formed BPN *BASE6* can be then used for the modeling of the programming barrier.

Figure 5, shows purely-formed BPN *BASE7* that represents the programming statement PARALLEL FOR i: = 1 TO m DO ..., where $m \in N$. Very interesting purely-formed BPN *BASE8* will be used in the next paragraph for the purpose of the multiple-readers/single-writer lock modeling in the multithreading programming environment. Its purely-formed property can be easily proved for instance with using of the PN marking graph construction (see [1, 3, 7]).

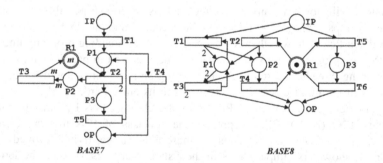

Fig. 5. Examples of BPNs

4   PLACE_SUBST Transformation and Its Properties

The only one transformation **PLACE_SUBST** (i.e., place substitution transformation) is defined for the class of all PNs and it is shown to be preserving the well-formedness and purely-formedness properties. The well-formed, resp. purely-formed, PNs form a closed set (i.e., informally said, the result of an application of the **PLACE_SUBST** transformation onto any two well-formed, resp. purely-formed, PNs will result into another well-formed, resp. purely-formed, PN). The design of a given programming system will typically starts with the BPN *BASE1* and it then follows with the several **PLACE_SUBST** transformations (i.e., substitutions of the selected BPN over the non-resource place of the actual PN) that result into the complex well-formed, resp. purely-formed, PN that models the whole programming system.

We will denote the set of all ordered pairs (PN, p) where $PN \in \textbf{PNET}$, $PN: = (P, T, A, AF, TP, RP, IP, OP, RM_s)$, $p \in (P \setminus RP)$, by the symbol **PNETPL**. We will then denote the members of the set **PNETPL** (i.e., ordered pairs (PN, p)) by the shortened notation *PN.p*.

Definition 2. Let $PN1: = (P_1, T_1, A_1, AF_1, TP_1, RP_1, IP_1, OP_1, RM_{s1})$ and $PN2: = (P_2, T_2, A_2, AF_2, TP_2, RP_2, IP_2, OP_2, RM_{s2})$ are the PNs, let $p \in (P_1 \setminus RP_1)$ is a non-resource place of the PN *PN1*. The transformation **PLACE_SUBST**: $\textbf{PNETPL} \times \textbf{PNET} \rightarrow$ **PNET** of the PN *PN2* substitution over the place p of the PN *PN1* resulting into the new PN $PN: = (P, T, A, AF, TP, RP, IP, OP, RM_s)$ will be denoted by the statement

$$PN := PN1.p <] PN2, \text{ where:}$$

- $P: = (P_1 \setminus \{p\}) \cup P_2$,
- $T: = T_1 \cup T_2$,
- $A: = A_2 \cup \{(x, y) \in A_1 \mid (x \neq p) \vee (y \neq p)\} \cup \{(x, IP_2) \mid (x, p) \in A_1\} \cup \{(OP_2, y) \mid (p, y) \in A_1\}$,
- $AF: = AF_2 \cup \{((x, y), v) \in AF_1 \mid (x \neq p) \vee (y \neq p)\} \cup \{((x, IP_2), v) \mid ((x, p), v) \in AF_1\} \cup \{((OP_2, y), v) \mid ((p, y), v) \in AF_1\}$,
- $TP: = TP_1 \cup TP_2$,
- $RP: = RP_1 \cup RP_2$,
- $IP: = IP_1$, if $p \neq IP_1$; $IP = IP_2$, if $p = IP_1$,
- $OP: = OP_1$, if $p \neq OP_1$; $OP = OP_2$, if $p = OP_1$,
- $RM_s: = RM_{s1} \otimes RM_{s2}$.

Example 2. The result of the **PLACE_SUBST** transformation *BASE5*.P2 <] *BASE2* where the place P2 of the BPN *BASE5* (see Fig. 4) was substituted by the BPN *BASE2* can be shown in Fig. 6.

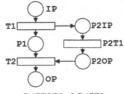

BASE5.P2 <] BASE2

Fig. 6. Result of **PLACE_SUBST** transformation *BASE5*.P2 <] *BASE2*

Lemma 2. Let $PN1$: $= (P_1, T_1, A_1, AF_1, TP_1, RP_1, IP_1, OP_1, RM_{s1})$, $PN2$: $= (P_2, T_2, A_2, AF_2, TP_2, RP_2, IP_2, OP_2, RM_{s2})$ and $PN3$: $= (P_3, T_3, A_3, AF_3, TP_3, RP_3, IP_3, OP_3, RM_{s3})$ are the PNs. Let $p1 \in (P_1 \setminus RP_1)$ is a non-resource place of the PN $PN1$ and $p2 \in (P_2 \setminus RP_2)$ is a non-resource place of the PN $PN2$. Then:

$$PN1.p1 <] (PN2.p2 <] PN3) = (PN1.p1 <] PN2).p2 <] PN3.$$

Proof. Follows directly from the *Definition 2.*   □

Lemma 3. Let $PN1$: $= (P_1, T_1, A_1, AF_1, TP_1, RP_1, IP_1, OP_1, RM_{s1})$ is a well-formed, resp. purely-formed, PN and $PN2$: $= (P_2, T_2, A_2, AF_2, TP_2, RP_2, IP_2, OP_2, RM_{s2})$ is a well-formed, resp. purely-formed, PN. Let $p \in (P_1 \setminus RP_1)$ is a non-resource place of the PN $PN1$. Let $(\forall t \in p\bullet: (p, t) \in A_1 \Rightarrow \bullet t \times p\bullet \subseteq A_1) \wedge (\forall t \in p\bullet: AF_1(p, t) = 1))$.
   Then $PN1.p <] PN2$ is a well-formed, resp. purely-formed, PN.

Proof. Clear. Because both PN $PN1$ and $PN2$ are well-formed, i.e., $(\forall M_e \in \mathbf{M}_e: PN1$ terminates properly$) \wedge (\forall M_e \in \mathbf{M}_e: PN2$ terminates properly$)$, then for the PN $PN1$ holds true that $\forall M \in [M_e\rangle, M(p) > 0, \exists M_x : M_x \in [M\rangle$, and for the PN $PN2$ holds true that $\forall M \in [M_e\rangle, M(IP_2) > 0, \exists M_x : M_x \in [M\rangle)$, then the whole PN $PN1.p <] PN2$ must also terminate properly for any of its input markings M_e. The property of purely-formedness of the resulting PN $PN1.p <] PN2$ can be proved similarly.
   The necessity of the condition $(\forall t \in p\bullet: (p, t) \in A_1 \Rightarrow \bullet t \times p\bullet \subseteq A_1)$ fulfilment is presented in Fig. 7, where both $PN1$ and $PN2$ are purely-formed PN but the resulting PN $PN1.P2 <] PN2$ is not any more purely-formed PN. This fact can be seen for instance from the transition sequence $(1, 0, 0, 0, 0)[T1\rangle(0, 1, 1, 0, 0)[T2\rangle(0, 0, 0, 1, 1)$ that causes deadlock. This problem follows from the fact that for the PN $PN1$ is not satisfied the condition $(P2, T3) \in A_1 \Rightarrow (P2, T2) \in A_1$. Satisfaction of this condition that is well-known from the class of free choice Petri nets (see [8]) implies of the purely-formedness of the resulting PN $PN1.P2 <] PN2$.
   The necessity of the condition $(\forall t \in p\bullet: AF_1(p, t) = 1)$ fulfilment is presented in Fig. 8, where both $PN3$ and $PN4$ are purely-formed PN but the resulting PN $PN3.P1 <] PN4$ is not any more purely-formed PN. This fact can be seen for instance from the transition sequence $(1, 0, 0, 0, 1, 0)[T1\rangle(0, 3, 0, 0, 1, 0)[T4\rangle(0, 2, 1, 0, 0, 0)[T5\rangle(0, 2, 0, 1, 1, 0)[T3\rangle(0, 2, 0, 1, 1, 0)$ that causes impossibility of reaching of the

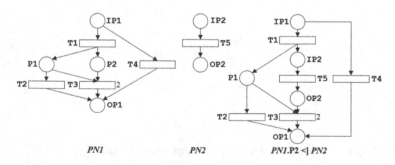

Fig. 7. Place substitution operation $PN1.P2 <] PN2$

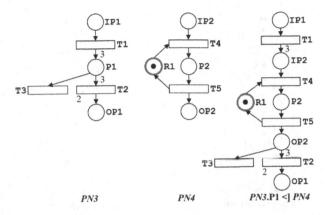

Fig. 8. Place substitution operation *PN3*.P1 <] *PN4*

exit marking M_x of the PN. This problem follows from the fact that for the PN *PN1* is not satisfied the condition $AF(P1, T2) = 1$. Satisfaction of this condition implies of the purely-formedness of the resulting PN *PN3*.P1 <] *PN4*. □

5 An Example of PLACE_SUBST Transformation Application at the Modeling of Distributed Programming System

In the following simple example we will develop a design of a PN modeling the distributed programming system operating on the client and application server side and realizing reading and writing procedures from the given database system on the basis of a client requests. Individual client requests are executed via a finite set of programming threads on the server side (in our model of that programming system we assume availability of totally three server side programming threads) stored in the created pool of threads. At the moment of accepting the user request is for the needs of its responding a free thread randomly selected in pool which realizes such request, i.e., it will ensure execution of reading or writing data into the database system. In so doing it is required that in the case of realization of the request for the writing of the database no other thread can access the database environment and in the case of request for the reading any finite number of threads realizing reading of data can access the database.

Figure 9a, shows the PN *BASE7*.P3 <] *BASE5* in its entry marking M_e (where $M_e(R1) = 4$) that represents the client side of the whole distributed programming system. Client side will perform PARALLEL FOR cycles with two programming threads (the tokens in the input place IP) requesting the read and write server side database operations (firing of the transition T6). Server side database service is represented by the place P4 and will be requested by synchronous manner.

Figure 9b, shows the PN *BASE4*.P1 <] *BASE8* determined for the execution of user requirements on reading or writing into the database while using three common accessible programming threads located in the common programming pool (see the

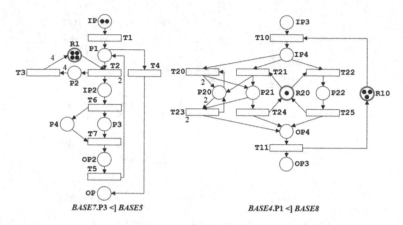

BASE7.P3 <] BASE5   BASE4.P1 <] BASE8

Fig. 9. a, b. PNs modeling client and server side of distributed programming system

resource place R10). The respective threads realize either reading (firing of the transition T20, resp. T21) or writing (firing of the transition T22) of the data from or to the database via the mechanisms of BPN *BASE8* (see Fig. 5) that models the access into the database environment with the support of multiple-readers/single-writer lock. The token in the resource place R20 represents single lock determined for obtaining the multiple-readers/single-writer access of the database environment. Following realization of the relevant event the programming thread will be returned back into the common pool of threads represented by the resource place R10 and it will be ready for the execution of the next user request.

We will obtain the resulting PN that represents the whole distributed programming systems as shown in Fig. 10, by applying the following **PLACE_SUBST** transformation: (*BASE7.P3 <] BASE5*).P2 <] (*BASE4.P1 <] BASE8*). This resulting PN is

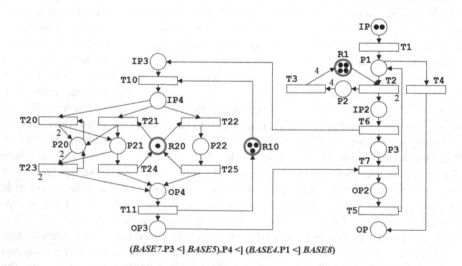

(*BASE7.P3 <] BASE5*).P4 <] (*BASE4.P1 <] BASE8*)

Fig. 10. Resulting PN modeling distributed programming system

according to *Lemma 3* (because the BPNs *BASE4*, *BASE5*, *BASE7* and *BASE8* are purely-formed PNs) purely-formed PN.

6 Conclusions

There is an opportunity to define additional transformations and operators for the class of PNs and to generalize it (for instance transformations for connecting two or more PNs). Selected PN then represents typically a method in the model of the programming system realized with the support of the Petri nets formalism. PNs can be thus successfully applied also in the area of the bi-relational P/T Petri nets [9] that represent an interesting modification of conventional P/T Petri nets.

The principles introduced in the class of PNs can be further generalized and implemented in the definition of the class of high-level Petri nets called the sequential object Petri nets [10, 11] which differ from PNs mainly by mutually differentiable tokens. The tokens alone are formed by non-empty sequences over the set of all integer numbers (this is also where the name of this Petri nets class came from). Sequential object Petri nets are then specially determined for the design, modeling and verification of distributed multithreading programming systems based on the object oriented and functional paradigms.

This paper has been elaborated in the framework of the project CZ.1.07/2.3.00/ 20.0296 supported by the European Social Fund.

References

1. Reisig, W., Rozenberg, G. (eds.): APN 1998. LNCS, vol. 1491. Springer, Heidelberg (1998)
2. Diaz, M.: Petri Nets: Fundamental Models, Verification and Applications. Wiley, ISTE Ltd., New York (2009)
3. Reisig, W.: Elements of Distributed Algorithms. Springer, Heidelberg (1998)
4. David, R., Alla, H.: Discrete, Continuous and Hybrid Petri Nets. Springer, Heidelberg (2010)
5. van der Alst, W., van Hee, K.: Workflow Management: Models, Methods and Systems. The MIT Press, Massachusetts (2002)
6. Huang, H., Jiao, L., Cheung, T., Mak, W.M.: Property-Preserving Petri Net Process Algebra in Software Engineering. World Scientific Publishing Co. Pte. Ltd, Singapore (2012)
7. Martiník, I.: Modeling of distributed programming systems with using of property-preserving petri net process algebras and P/T petri net processes. In: ICIA 2013 Proceedings: The Second International Conference on Informatics & Applications (ICIA2013), pp. 258–263. Lodz University of Technology, IEEE (2013)
8. Desel, J., Esparza, J.: Free Choice Petri Nets. Cambridge University Press, New York (1995)
9. Martiník, I.: Bi-relational P/T petri nets and the modeling of multithreading object-oriented programming systems. In: Snasel, V., Platos, J., El-Qawasmeh, E. (eds.) ICDIPC 2011, Part I. CCIS, vol. 188, pp. 222–236. Springer, Heidelberg (2011)
10. Martiník, I.: Sequential object petri nets and the modeling of multithreading object-oriented programming systems. In: Petri Nets - Manufacturing and Computer Science, pp. 195–224. InTech, Rijeka (2012)
11. Martiník, I.: Modeling of object-oriented programming systems with using of petri nets. SAEI, vol. 5. VŠB-TU Ostrava, Ostrava (2015)

Fuzzy Dempster-Shafer Modelling and Decision Rules

Zenon A. Sosnowski[(✉)] and Jarosław S. Walijewski

Faculty of Computer Science, Bialystok University of Technology,
Wiejska 45A, 15-351 Bialystok, Poland
z.sosnowski@pb.edu.pl

Abstract. In this study, we discuss the use of Dempster-Shafer theory as a well-rounded algorithmic vehicle in the construction of fuzzy decision rules. The concept of fuzzy granulation realized via fuzzy clustering is aimed at the discretization of continuous attributes. Detailed experimental studies are presented concerning well-known medical data sets available on the Web.

Keywords: Dempster-Shafer theory · Fuzzy modelling · Fuzzy decision rules

1 Introduction

Fuzzy modeling is regarded to be one of the possible classification architecture of machine learning and data mining. There have been a significant number of studies devoted to generating fuzzy decision rules from sample cases or examples. These include attempts to extend many classical machine learning methods to learn fuzzy rules. One very popular approach is decision trees [10]. Since the inception of this concept, it has been extended for the construction and interpretation of more advanced decision trees [3, 5–7, 9, 13, 15, 18]. Although the decision trees based methods can extract a set of fuzzy rules which works well, a problem is that the lack of backtracking in splitting the node leads to lower learning accuracy comparing to other machine learning methods. Another widely used machine learning method is artificial neural network. In recent years enormous work has been done in attempt to combine the advantages of neural network and fuzzy sets [14]. Hayashi [4] has proposed to extract fuzzy rules from trained neural net. Lin [8], on the other hand, introduced a method of directly generating fuzzy rules from self-organized neural network. The common weakness of neural network, however, is a problem of determination of the optimal size of a network configuration, as this has a significant impact on the effectiveness of its performance.

The objective of this paper is to employ the Dempster-Shafer theory (DST) as a vehicle supporting the generation of fuzzy decision rules. More specifically, we concentrate on the role of fuzzy operators, and on the problem of discretization of continuous attributes. We show how they can be effectively used in the quantization of attributes for the generation of fuzzy rules.

The material is arranged in the following way. First, we summarize the underlying concepts of the Dempster-Shafer theory and briefly discuss the nature of the underlying

K. Saeed and W. Homenda (Eds.): CISIM 2016, LNCS 9842, pp. 516–529, 2016.
DOI: 10.1007/978-3-319-45378-1_46

construction. By doing so, the intension is to make the paper self-contained and help identify some outstanding design problems emerging therein. In Sect. 4 we explain essentials of our model. Finally, in Sect. 5, we report exhaustive experimental studies.

This paper is a continuation of our earlier work [12]. Here we apply theoretical vehicle, introduced in previous research, to the new input data in order to find possible area of application. Our important objective here is to reveal a way in which this approach becomes essential to a more comprehensive treatment of continuous attributes.

2 Dempster-Shafer Theory

The Dempster-Shafer theory starts by assuming a Universe of Discourse Θ also called **Frame of Discernment**, which is a finite set of mutually exclusive alternatives. The frame of discernment may consist of the possible values of an attribute. For example, if we are trying to determine the disease of a patient, we may consider Θ being the set consisting of all possible diseases.

For each subset S of Θ it is associated:

- a basic probability assignment $m(S)$
- a belief $Bel(S)$
- a plausible belief $Pla(S)$

$m(S)$, $Bel(S)$ and $Pla(S)$ have value in the interval [0,1], and $Bel(S)$ is not greater than $Pla(S)$.

In particular, m represents the strength of some evidence. For example, in rule-based expert system, m may represent the effect of applying of a rule. $Bel(S)$ summarizes all our reasons to believe S. $Pla(S)$ expresses how much we should believe in S if all currently unknown facts were to support S. Thus the true belief in S will be somewhere in the interval $[Bel(S), Pla(S)]$. More formally, a map

$$m : 2^{\Theta} \to [0, 1] \qquad (1)$$

such that for each $A \in 2^{\Theta}$ (where 2^{Θ} is set of all subsets of Θ)

1. $m(\emptyset) = 0$
2. $\sum_{A \subseteq \Theta} m(A) = 1$

is called a *basic probability assignment* for Θ.

Subset A is called a *focal element* of m if $m(A) > 0$.

For a given *basic probability assignment* m, the *Belief* of a subset A of Θ is the sum of $m(B)$ for all subsets B of A, so

$$Bel : 2^{\Theta} \to [0, 1] \qquad (2)$$

such that $Bel(A) = \sum_{B \subseteq A} m(B)$.

The **Plausibility** of a subset A of Θ is defined as $Pla(A) = 1 - Bel(A')$, where A' is the complement of A in Θ.

If we are given two basic probability assignments m_1 and m_2, we can combine them into a third basic probability assignment $m : 2^{\Theta} \rightarrow [0, 1]$ in the following way.

Let us consider frame of discernment Θ and two belief functions Bel_1 and Bel_2. We denote focal elements of Bel_1 as $A_1...A_K$ and focal elements of Bel_2 as $B_1...B_L$ respectively and the basic probability assignments as m_1 and m_2. Then we can show graphically this combination as an orthogonal sum of m_1 and m_2.

The mass of probability of the interval $A_i \cap B_j$ expressed as a measure $m_1(A_i) \cdot m_2(B_j)$ is illustrated in Fig. 1.

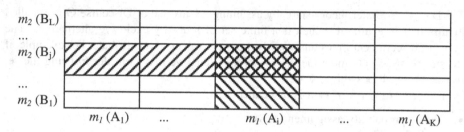

Fig. 1. Orthogonal sum of m1 and m2

Of course, more intersections can give the same focal element A. In general the mass of probability of set A is defined as:

$$m(A) = \sum_{\substack{i,j \\ A_i \cap B_j = A}} m_1(A_i) \cdot m_2(B_j) \qquad (3)$$

Then we find a problem with an empty set. It is possible that sets with empty intersection exist. We can meet this normal situation in many combinations. Then the mass of $\emptyset$, according to above definition, will be greater than zero, but according to the definition of basic probability assignment, it is not possible.

We assume that

$$\sum_{\substack{i,j \\ A_i \cap B_j = \emptyset}} m_1(A_i) \cdot m_2(B_j) < 1 \qquad (4)$$

to define the orthogonal sum m_1 and m_2, and denote it as $m_1 \oplus m_2$.

Then it is necessary to change the definition (3) of the formula of the basic probability assignment of the combination as follows:

1. $m(\emptyset) = 0$

2. $m(A) = \dfrac{\displaystyle\sum_{\substack{i,j \\ A_i \cap B_j = A}} m_1(A_i) \cdot m_2(B_j)}{1 - \displaystyle\sum_{\substack{i,j \\ A_i \cap B_j = \emptyset}} m_1(A_i) \cdot m_2(B_j)}$ for non-empty $A \subset \Theta$

We call this as an orthogonal sum of Bel_1 and Bel_2, and denote as $Bel_1 \oplus Bel_2$.
    This is the **Dempster Rule for Combining** of Beliefs [11].

For Θ we have $m(\Theta) = \sum_{A \subseteq \Theta} m(A) = 1$ and for combination if

$$\sum_{\substack{i,j \\ A_i \cap B_j = \emptyset}} m_1(A_i) \cdot m_2(B_j) = 0$$

we have

$$m(\Theta) = \sum_{A \subseteq \Theta} m(A) = \sum_{A \subseteq \Theta} \sum_{\substack{i,j \\ A_i \cap B_j = A}} m_1(A_i) \cdot m_2(B_j) = \sum_{i,j} m_1(A_i) \cdot m_2(B_j) = 1$$

3 Fuzzy Modelling

Fuzzy set theory is widely known and we do not introduce its underlying concepts essential to understand this framework. Readers interest themselves we refer to [16] and [17].
    Fuzzy Modeling is applied in those areas where the model of the system cannot be described precisely because of many reasons. The input data received by the system may not be completely reliable, may contain noise, or may be inconsistent with other data or with expectation about these data. The system is described by the set of linguistic rules. Let D denotes an output variable of the system, and $X_1, X_2, \ldots, X_n$ denote an input variables. The linguistic rules have the following format:

$$If (X_1 \ is \ A_{k,1,j1}) \ And \ \ldots And \ (X_n \ is \ A_{k,n,jn}) \ Then \ (D \ is \ S_{k,p}) \tag{5}$$

where $(X_i \ is \ A_{k,i,ji})$ are the fuzzy antecedents, $A_{k,i,ji}$ ($1 \leq j_i \leq |A_i|$) are values of the i-th input variable, and $S_{k,p}$ ($1 \leq p \leq |S|$) is the value of output variable in k-th rule.
    The rules are implemented as fuzzy relation according to the formula:

$$R_k = A_{k,1,jl} \times A_{k,2,jl} \times \cdots \times A_{k,n,jl} \times S_{k,p} \tag{6}$$

where $\times$ denotes the fuzzy Cartesian product.

Then all rules are aggregated to relation R described as:

$$R = \bigcup_{k=1}^{M} R_k \qquad (7)$$

where M is the number of rules.

The conclusion is based on the compositional rule of inference

$$S' = \left(A'_{1,j1} \times A'_{2,j2} \times \cdots \times A'_{n,jn} \right) \circ R \qquad (8)$$

where $A'_{1,j1}, A'_{2,j2}, \cdots, A'_{n,jn}$ are input values, S' is a conclusion (decision class), and $\circ$ denotes the composition of fuzzy relation.

In fuzzy modeling we can assume that expert defines the rule set, or we can automatically generate them from the set of samples describing the behavior of the system being modeled.

4 Fuzzy Dempster-Shafer Model

In Fuzzy Dempster-Shafer (FDS) model [2] we consider rules R_r as:

$$\textit{If } \left(X_1 \textit{ is } A_{r,1,j_1} \right) \ldots \textit{And} \ldots \left(X_n \textit{ is } A_{r,n,j_n} \right) \quad \textit{Then} \quad (D \textit{ is } m_r) \qquad (9)$$

where X_i and D stand for input and output respectively, and m_r is a fuzzy belief structure, that is a standard belief structure with focal elements $S_{r,p}$ as fuzzy subset of frame of discernment Θ with basic probability assignment $m_r(S_{r,p})$, and $m_r(S_{r,p})$ is the believe that the conclusion should be represented as class $S_{r,p}$.

4.1 Learning – Rules Construction

In antecedent construction, let us assume that we have n features (attributes) in antecedents of testing example. We consider a collection of m generic linguistic terms characterized by membership functions defined in a universe of discourse being a domain of each attribute. The conclusion belongs to decision class S.

For each element of data t we build a collection:

$$
\begin{matrix}
A_{1,1,t} & A_{2,1,t} & \cdots & A_{n,1,t} \\
A_{1,2,t} & A_{2,2,t} & \cdots & A_{n,2,t} \\
\vdots & \vdots & \ddots & \vdots \\
A_{1,m,t} & A_{2,m,t} & \cdots & A_{n,m,t}
\end{matrix}
\qquad (10)
$$

where $A_{i,j,t}$ are the values of j-th membership function for i-th feature and for t-th element of data.

Example 1. We demonstrate the calculations on the set of synthetic data presented in Table 1.

Table 1. Sample data set

Item	F1	F2	F3	F4	Class
L1	1	1	1	1	1
L2	9	8	8	9	2
L3	1	1	3	4	1
L4	2	1	2	2	1
L5	2	2	2	2	2
L6	5	6	7	8	2
T1	3	3	3	2	1
T2	1	2	2	1	1
T3	4	7	7	9	2
T4	2	8	7	8	2

First six rows (L1–L6) will constitute learning data, while the remaining ones (T1–T4) will form testing data. All the features are numbers from the <0; 9> interval. The last column represents the decision class equal to 1 or 2. We will consider four membership quadratic functions uniformly distributed along the space of all attributes. Other membership functions will be discussed in the next section.

According to (10) for row T1 we have:

$$
\begin{matrix}
1.0 & 1.0 & 0.0625 & 0.0156 \\
0 & 0 & 0.9375 & 0.9844 \\
0 & 0 & 0 & 0 \\
0 & 0 & 0 & 0
\end{matrix}
$$

■

On the base of (10), for a given data point t we can calculate two vectors:

$$A_{\mu,t}: \quad A_{1,\max_1,t} \quad A_{2,\max_2,t} \quad \cdots \quad A_{n,\max_n,t} \tag{11}$$

and index of membership functions

$$I_{c,t}: \quad I_{1,\max_1,t} \quad I_{2,\max_2,t} \quad \cdots \quad I_{n,\max_n,t} \tag{12}$$

where $A_{i,\max_i,t}$ is a maximum value of all membership functions designed for the feature i and $I_{i,\max_i,t}$ is the number of the best membership function for feature i.

Then we have the following candidate for a rule

$$R_t: \quad I_{1,\max_1,t} \quad I_{2,\max_2,t} \quad \cdots \quad I_{n,\max_2,t} \tag{13}$$

The firing level of the rule is calculated according to the following formula

$$\tau_t = \overset{n}{\underset{i=1}{\phi}} \left(A_{i,\max_i,t}\right) \tag{14}$$

where ϕ means the operator of fuzzy matching. See Sect. 5.2. for details.

The rule candidate is added to rules set if $\phi[\tau_r, m_r] \geq Th$ (where Th threshold value, and ϕ matching operator). This can help to eliminate bad rules from the final rule set.

More ten one rule can have the same antecedent part but it is also possible that conclusion of these rules are different. Then we have to use appropriate counters $c_{t,1},\dots,$ $c_{t,|S|}$, where $|S|$ denotes the power of decision class set. These counters can show us how many data, according to rule pattern, vote for each decision class.

Example 2. In our sample (T1) the vectors are:

$A_{\mu,1}$: 1.0000, 1.0000, 0.9375, 0.9844
$I_{c,1}$: 1, 1, 2, 2 with counters vector 1, 0

In our sample matching value equals to 0.9229, were multiplication was used as the matching operator (1.0000* 1.0000* 0.9375* 0.9844 = 0.9229). For the threshold set on 0.75, we obtain a new rule.

■

The product is a new belief structure on X

$$\hat{m}_r = \tau_r \wedge m_r \tag{15}$$

Focal elements are fuzzy subset given as

$$F_{r,p}(x) = \tau_r \wedge S_{r,p}(x) \tag{16}$$

and appropriate distributions of new focal elements are defined as:

$$\hat{m}_r(F_{r,p}) = m_r(S_{r,p}) \tag{17}$$

So we can build an aggregate:

$$m = \bigcup_{r=1}^{R} \hat{m}_r \tag{18}$$

Then for each collection

$$\Im = \left\{ F_{r_1,p_1}, F_{r_2,p_2}, \dots, F_{r_R,p_R} \right\} \tag{19}$$

where F_{r_t,p_t} are focal elements of $\hat{m}_r$ we have focal element E of m described as

$$E = \bigcup_{t=1}^{R} F_{r_t,p_t} \tag{20}$$

with appropriate probability distribution

$$m(E) = \prod_{t=1}^{R} m(F_{r_t,p_t}) \qquad (21)$$

At this point, the rule generation process is complete.

Example 3. Our sample data produce the following rule set.

	I_{1max}	I_{2max}	I_{3max}	I_{4max}	C_1	C_2	m
R1 :	1	1	2	2	1	0	2.5000
R2 :	1	1	4	1	2	1	2.0833
R3 :	4	4	4	4	0	1	1.2500
R4 :	2	3	3	4	0	1	1.2500

The first four elements are numbers of the best membership function for proper features, the next two are counters for decision classes and the last one is a probability distribution.

Let us observe that rule R2 covers the data L1, L4 and L5. L1 and L4 produce decision class C_1 but L5 decision class C_2.

∎

Now we can move to the testing of new rules.

4.2   Test

In testing we ignore the value from the last column in Table 1, that is decision class number, because our goal is to calculate it.

To compute the firing level of a rule k for a given data

$$X_k : \quad X_{1,k} \quad X_{2,k} \quad \ldots \quad X_{n,k} \quad D_k \qquad (22)$$

where $X_{i,k}$ – feature's value, D_k – conclusion decision class that we have to compare with the result of inference; we build a rule matrix

$$\mu_{k,t} = \overset{n}{\underset{i=1}{\Phi}} \left(A_{i,l,k}(X_{i,t}) \right), \quad l = I_{i,max,k} \qquad (23)$$

We are interested only in active rules i.e. rows with matching value $\mu_{k,t} > 0$.

Example 4. In test we will demonstrate calculations on

$$L5. 2 \quad 2 \quad 2 \quad 2$$
$$T1. 3 \quad 3 \quad 3 \quad 2$$

For sample data L5 we have two active rules:

```
R1:1 1 2 2      1 0      0.859375 0.859375 0.609375 0.609375 0.274242
R2:1 1 1 1      2 1      0.859375 0.859375 0.859375 0.859375 0.54542
```

The first four elements are the rule pattern, the next two are the counters for decision classes. The next four numbers are the values of appropriate membership function. The number 0.859375 is the value of the first membership function, according to the first number in the rule, on the first feature. The next three numbers are calculated in the same way.

The last numbers in the above rows are the matching value for the rule. It has been calculated by matching operator for the values of membership function.

We focused only on the rows with matching value grater then zero.

For sample data T1 we have:

R1: 1 1 2 2   1 0   0.4375 0.4375 0.9375 0.6094 0.1093
R2: 1 1 1 1   2 0   0.4375 0.4375 0.4375 0.8594 0.0720

∎

For each collection of F_{r_t,p_t} focal elements $\hat{m}_r$ we define an aggregate

$$E = \cup_{t=1}^{R} F_{r_t,p_t} \tag{24}$$

with basic probability assignment

$$m(E) = \prod_{t=1}^{R} m(F_{r_t,p_t}) \tag{25}$$

The results of classification are D is m, with focal elements $E_k(k = 1,...,R^{|S|})$ and distribution $m(E_k)$. That results are calculated using focal elements and appropriate counters $c_{t,1},..., c_{t,|S|}$.

Example 5. For sample point L5 and T1 the counters are 3, 1, and 3, 0 respectively

∎

Then we perform defuzzification according to COA method [1].

$$\bar{y} = \sum_{k=1}^{R^{|S|}} \bar{y}_k m(E_k) \tag{26}$$

where $\bar{y}_k$ are defuzzified values for focal element E_k defined as

$$\bar{y}_k = \frac{\sum\limits_{1 \leq t \leq n} x_t \mu_{k,t}(x_t)}{\sum\limits_{1 \leq t \leq n} \mu_{k,t}(x_t)} \tag{27}$$

In the next step, the rules structure is simplified to

If Antecedent$_r$ Then $(D$ is $H_r)$,

where $H_r = \left\{ \frac{1}{\gamma_r} \right\}$ is a singleton fuzzy set for factor $\gamma_r = \sum\limits_{p=1}^{|S|} \bar{y}_p m_r(S_{r,p})$.

Example 6. For both L5 and T1 we calculate decision class 1. It is correct in case of T1, but wrong for L5. The values of H_r are 0.4283 and 0.4800 respectively.   ∎

5 Empirical Learning for FDS Model

In this section we compare and analyze the performance of several membership functions and matching operators. We start from a standard solution used in the introduction to fuzzy modeling, then we consider more complicated models. We compute results for the following membership function: *Linear, Quadratic, Gaussian,* and *FCM*. We concentrate on *Minimum, Multiply* and *Implication* as a matching operators. The most valuable is comparing the results of all calculations. In the end of this section we show some results of experimental research.

5.1 Membership Functions

The membership function makes possible the division of data into *n* intervals. It is a way of discretization of the input data. Hence, we get the best result for continuous data or for data with several discrete (nominal) values. If we have discrete or binary data then results of the proposed model are not good enough.

The choice of membership function has a great influence on the quality of rules. Although the quantity of rules is different, the quality of classification is comparable.

The most interesting membership function was generated by Fuzzy c-Means (FCM) algorithm [1]. The results of experimental research with membership functions have been summarized in Table 2.

Table 2. Membership functions

	Function	Formula	Features
1	*Linear triangle*	F1: $Y = (X - x_{i+1})/$ $(x_i - x_{i+1})$ F2: $Y = (X - x_i)/$ $(x_{i+1} - x_i)$	The simplest, The result are not so good;
2	*Quadratic*	$Y = 1 - (X - x_i)^2/$ $(x_{i+1} - x_i)^2$	Still simply calculated function, The result are better than in the case of Linear function;
3	*Gaussian*	$y = e^{-\left(\frac{X-x_i}{x_{i+1}-x_i}\right)^2}$	Exponential function, Using it leads in general to proper conclusions especially in learn sample;
4	*FCM*	FCM algorithm	The complex algorithm – values of function have to be previously generated. In general proper conclusion

5.2   Matching Operators

It was shown in our experiments that a matching operator applied to data sample with existing rules plays the very important role in the accuracy of diagnoses. It occurred as early as the rules were generated. A matching operator influences the quality of the generated rules. Of course, this quality has secondary means, but in general, the more rules the better accuracy.

From the analysis of the results of experiments in Table 4, we can infer that the most powerful operator is implication. This is not all the true, because Table 4 shows the results only for one fixed threshold value. It is not optimal in all instances, especially in multiply operator. The change of the threshold value (e.g. to 0.25) gives almost the same results as for implication operator. Anyway, the choice of the threshold value is of minor importance here, but it can have influence on the result of the receiving of rules. Of course, we cannot analyze the threshold value without keeping in mind the features of the membership function and the number of intervals. The choice of the threshold value will be subject of future works.

The results of the investigation of various matching operators are collected in Table 3.

Table 3. Matching operators

	Name	Formula	Features
1	Minimum	$\text{Max}(0,\min(x,y))$	The simplest case In many experiments the results are good
2	Multiply	$\text{Max}(0, x*y)$	It's case of *implication*, with $\alpha = -1$. The results are better than in the case of Minimum operator. Important setting of threshold value
3	Implication	$\text{Max}(0,(\alpha+1)* (x + y-1)$ $- \alpha*x*y)$	Function seems to be complex. The best results. Setting constant α - direction for future research

6   Experimental Studies

Some results of experimental research are shown in Table 4. We fixed here count of membership functions on 6 and threshold value on 0.75. All data sets have been divided into two parts: learning (training) data (about 2/3 of the entire data set) and testing data (remaining 1/3). The learning data has been used to generate the rule set. Testing data has been applied to test the produced rule set. To obtain reliable results, we carried out the experiment several times.

That formulation does not show the most favorable case but it is allowed to see the part of real results with using different methods for generalizing rules. These results can be comparable.

Table 4. Experimental results

		Linear			Quadratic			Gaussian			FCM			Decision Trees	
		Rules	Learn	Test	Rules	Learn	Test	Rules	Learn	Test	Rules	Learn	Test	Learn	Test
Minimum															
	Iris	15	93.80	97.50	41	97.50	97.50	41	93.75	100.00	-	-	-	94.00	91.30
	Ulcers	43	66.25	9.52	79	93.75	28.57	79	87.50	52.38	76	78.75	57.14	-	-
	Diabetes	0	0.00	0.00	58	94.29	37.84	23	87.14	56.76	9	47.14	24.32	-	-
	BCW	2	59.66	73.73	203	91.63	85.71	203	40.56	24.42	201	95.28	91.71	96.00	90.30
	Derm.	0	0.00	0.00	244	100.00	86.89	244	100.00	50.82	241	100.00	73.77	94.00	87.50
	EKG	1	2.27	5.56	44	100.00	38.89	44	100.00	66.67	43	100.00	72.22	76.00	59.00
Multiply															
α = -1	Iris	0	0.00	0.00	18	95.00	97.50	19	95.00	100.00	-	-	-		
	Ulcers	0	0.00	0.00	2	35.00	2.38	2	70.00	2.38	74	65.00	54.76		
	Diabetes	0	0.00	0.00	35	82.86	29.73	25	80.00	54.05	9	47.14	24.32		
	BCW	2	59.66	73.73	30	81.33	79.72	33	95.06	97.24	17	60.30	82.95		
	Derm.	0	0.00	0.00	230	95.08	86.89	235	99.18	51.64	13	9.84	24.59		
	EKG	1	2.27	5.56	6	45.45	5.56	6	50.00	11.11	35	56.82	55.56		
Implication															
α = -20	Iris	35	83.75	97.50	39	97.50	97.50	40	96.25	100.00	-	-	-		
	Ulcers	43	61.25	9.52	75	90.00	28.57	75	85.00	52.38	75	80.00	59.52		
	Diabetes	31	0.00	0.00	58	94.29	37.84	58	87.14	56.76	9	47.14	24.32		
	BCW	15	40.34	46.08	203	91.63	85.71	103	62.02		203	97.21	93.55		
	Derm.	0	0.00	0.00	233	99.18	86.89	243	99.59	50.82	200	95.90	90.16		
	EKG	22	70.45	0.00	41	100.00	38.89	43	100.00	66.67	39	100.00	77.78		

The methods of automatically generated decision rules that are described in this paper have the best results on *Iris* data set. In a few points, reach a destination 100 % of the decision accuracy. This set consists of all data as continuous values. In other cases, the construction of the data discretization caused a little worse results. In spite of the fact that in the case of *Ulcers* data set, for which over the half features was discrete, the results on the learning data was nearly the same like in the case of *Iris* data.

Diabetes data set is a sample of testing proposed algorithms on discrete data. The results of rules accuracy are not satisfactory. It has shown the case when the method of generating and verifying decision rules ineffectual as only one.

Another observation is that, the smaller number of binary data in antecedent, then the better accuracy of our rules. If the features have no binary data or if number of it is strongly less, then others then our rules can be applicable. We can see that during analyzing *Breast Cancer Wisconsin* and *Dermatology* data sets. In *Echocardiogram* data set, when number of binary data is equal to three the results are worse.

In all the instances, intermediate reports were stored in disk data files. It was used to compute results with the FCM algorithm. It also made possible to connect described method with others.

In our research, the proper choice of threshold value gave us information if rule is valuable or not. The importance of this value has been shown in the case of *Multiply* operator. The result presented in Table 4 could suggest less "weight" of this operator, but it is not true. If we change threshold value, we notice that it has almost the same occurrence as more complied in calculations *Implication* operator. *Implication* is a sample of a very interesting and powerful operator of fuzzy relation.

We compare the results of our research with standard decision trees algorithm [10]. For all data sets, we get better results using *Gaussian* function or *FCM* algorithm [1], and in a few points of *Quadratic* function, we obtained also better accuracy.

In *Dermatology* and *Echocardiogram* data sets, we removed records with missing input features, because we concentrate only on complete data.

7 Conclusions

The study has focused on the use of Fuzzy Dempster-Shafer model for generating of fuzzy decision rules. Fuzzy sets are useful in discretization of continuous attributes. The approach is discussed in the concrete applications of two real medical data sets (especially to problems of identification of diseases) and several well-known data sets available on the Web. The results are used to classify objects. It has been found through series of experiments that this approach outperforms the results of the C4.5 algorithm in terms of higher classification accuracy.

Acknowledgement. This work was supported by the grant S/WI/1/2013 from Bialystok University of Technology founded by Ministry of Science and Higher Education.

References

1. Bezdek, J.C., Sabin, M.J., Tucker, W.T.: Convergence theory for fuzzy c-means: counterexamples and repairs. IEEE Trans. Syst. Man Cybern. **smc-17**(5), 873–877 (1987)
2. Binaghi, E., Gallo, I., Madella, P.: A neural model for fuzzy Dempster-Shafer classifiers. Int. J. Approx. Reason. **25**, 89–121 (2000)
3. Chiang, I.J., Hsu, J.Y.J.: Integration of fuzzy classifiers with decision trees. In: Proceedings of 1996 Asian Fuzzy Systems Symposium, pp. 266–271 (1996)
4. Hayashi, Y., Imura, A.: Fuzzy neural expert system with automated extraction of fuzzy if-then rules from a trained neural network. In: 1st International Symposium on Uncertainty Modeling and Analysis, pp. 489–494, December 1990
5. Hayashi, A., Maeda, T., Bastian, A., Jain, L.C.: Generation of fuzzy decision trees by fuzzy ID3 with adjusting mechanism of AND/OR operators. In: Proceedings of 1988 International Conference on Fuzzy Systems (FUZZ-IEEE 1998), pp. 681–685 (1998)
6. Ichihashi, H., Shirai, T., Nagasaka, K., Miyoshi, T.: Nero-fuzzy ID3: a method of inducing fuzzy decision trees with linear programming for maximizing entropy and an algebraic method for incremental learning. Fuzzy Sets Syst. **81**(1), 157–167 (1996)
7. Janikow, C.Z.: Fuzzy decision trees: issues and methods. IEEE Trans. Syst. Man Cybern. Part B (Cybern.) **28**(1), 1–14 (1998)
8. Lin, C.T., Lee, C.S.: Neural-network-based fuzzy logic control and decision system. IEEE Trans. Comput. **12**, 1320–1336 (1991)
9. Pedrycz, W., Sosnowski, Z.A.: C-fuzzy decision trees. IEEE Trans. Syst. Man Cybern. Part C Appl. Rev. **35**(4), 498–511 (2005)
10. Quinlann, J.R.: Induction of decision trees. Mach. Learn. **1**, 81–106 (1986)
11. Shafer, G.: Mathematical Theory of Evidence. Princeton Univ. Press, Princeton (1976)
12. Sosnowski, Z.A., Walijewski, J.S.: Generating fuzzy decision rules with the use of Dempster-Shafer theory. In: ESM 1999, pp. 419–426, Warsaw (1999)
13. Umano, M., Okamoto, H., Hatono, I., Tamura, H., Kawachi, F., Umedzu, S., Kinoshita, J.: Generation of fuzzy decision trees by fuzzy ID3 algorithm and its application to diagnosis by

gas in oil. In: Proceedings of 1994 Japan-USA Symposium on Flexible Automation, pp. 1445–1448 (1994)

14. Viharos, Z.J., Kis, K.B.: Survey on neuro fuzzy systems and their applications in technical diagnostics. Measurement **67**, 126–136 (2015)
15. Weber, R.: Fuzzy ID3: a class of methods for automatic knowledge acquisition. In: Proceedings of 2nd International Conference on Fuzzy Logic and Neural Networks, Iizuka, Japan, pp. 265–268 (1992)
16. Yager, R., Filev, D.: Essentials of Fuzzy Modeling Control. Wiley, New York (1994)
17. Yager, R., Filev, D.: Including probabilistic uncertainty in fuzzy logic controller modeling using Dempster-Shafer theory. IEEE Trans. Syst. Man Cybern. **25**(8), 1221–1230 (1994)
18. Yun, J., won Seo, J., Yoon, T.: The new approach on fuzzy decision trees. Int. J. Fuzzy Logic Syst. **4**(3) (2014)

Classification of Protein Interactions Based on Sparse Discriminant Analysis and Energetic Features

Katarzyna Stąpor and Piotr Fabian[✉]

Faculty of Automatic Control, Electronics and Computer Science,
Silesian Technical University, Akademicka 16, Gliwice, Poland
{Katarzyna.Stapor,Piotr.Fabian}@polsl.pl

Abstract. Prediction of protein-protein interaction (PPI) types is an important problem in life sciences because of fundamental role of PPIs in many biological processes. In this paper we propose a new classification approach based on the extended classical Fisher linear discriminant analysis (FLDA) to predict obligate and non-obligate protein-protein interactions. To characterize properties of the protein interaction, we proposed to use the binding free energies (total of 282 features). The obtained results are better than in the previous studies.

Keywords: Sparse discriminant analysis · Feature selection · Protein-protein interaction

1 Introduction

Prediction of protein-protein interaction (PPI) types is an important problem in life sciences because of fundamental role of PPIs in many biological processes [6]. PPIs have been investigated in various ways, involving both experimental (in vivo or in vitro) and computational (in silico) approaches [2, 10]. Experimental approaches tend to be costly, labor intensive and suffer from noise. Therefore, using computational approaches for prediction of PPIs is a good choice for many reasons.

PPIs can be divided into non-obligate and obligate complexes (binding components can/cannot form stable functional structures). Based on the duration and life time of the interactions, there are transient complexes and permanent ones. Although interfaces have been the main subject of study to predict protein-protein interactions, an accuracy of 70 % has been independently achieved by several different groups [9, 10, 13, 14]. These approaches have been carried out by analyzing a wide range of parameters, including solvation energies, amino acid composition, conservation, electrostatic energies, and hydrophobicity.

These includes a method based on PCA combined with Chernoff extension of Fisher linear discriminant analysis [9]. PCA is necessary to reduce the dimensionality of the input feature space (i.e. to be less than the sample size). As a consequence some important information is lost.

In this paper, we propose a new classification approach based on sparse discriminant analysis [12] to predict obligate (permanent) and non-obligate (transient) protein-protein

K. Saeed and W. Homenda (Eds.): CISIM 2016, LNCS 9842, pp. 530–537, 2016.
DOI: 10.1007/978-3-319-45378-1_47

interactions. To characterize properties of protein interaction, we proposed to use the binding free energies.

2   Fisher and Sparse Regularized Linear Discriminant Analyses

Fisher Linear Discriminant analysis (FLDA) [5, 11] is a multivariate technique which is concerned with the search for a linear transformation that reduces the dimension of a given p-dimensional statistical model to q ($q < p$) dimensions, while maximally preserving the discriminatory information for the several classes within the model.

Formally, suppose that there are k classes and let $x_{ij}, j = 1, \ldots, n_i$ be vectors of observations from the i-th class, $i = 1, \ldots, k$. Set $n = n_1 + \ldots + n_k$ and let $X_{n \times p} = (x_{11}, \ldots, x_{1n_1}, \ldots, x_{k1}, \ldots, x_{kn_k})^T$, where p is the dimensionality of the input space. FLDA determines a linear mapping L, i.e. a $q \times p$ matrix A, that maximizes the so-called Fisher criterion J_F:

$$J_F(A) = tr((AS_W A^T)^{-1}(AS_B A^T)) \tag{1}$$

where $S_B = \sum_{i=1}^{k} p_i (m_i - \bar{m})(m_i - \bar{m})^T$ and $S_W = \sum_{i=1}^{k} p_i S_i$ are the between-class and the average within-class scatter matrix, respectively; $S_i = \frac{1}{n_i - 1} \sum_{j=1}^{n_i} (x_{ij} - m_i)(x_{ij} - m_i)^T$ is the within-class covariance matrix of class i, m_i is the mean vector of class i, p_i is it's *a priori* probability, and $\bar{m} = \sum_{i=1}^{k} p_i m_i$ is the overall mean. FLDA maximizes the ratio of between-class scatter to average within-class scatter in the lower-dimensional space. Optimizing (1) comes down to determining an eigenvalue decomposition of $S_W^{-1} S_B$, and taking the rows of A to equal the q eigenvectors corresponding to the q largest eigenvalues. There are no more than $\min(p, k-1)$ eigenvectors corresponding to nonzero eigenvalues.

When the number of variables exceeds the sample size, i.e., in the high-dimensional, low-sample size (HDLSS) settings, the within-class covariance matrix S_W is singular and the classical FLDA breaks down. Several extensions have been proposed to overcome this problem but all of them possess the data pilling problem [8]. To ameliorate this problem, some sparse version of LDA have been proposed.

In our approach, to circumvent this problem, we adapt the sparse linear discriminant approach (slda) from [12] that incorporates feature selection in FLDA. The term "sparse" means that the discriminant vectors have only a small number of nonzero components. The underlying assumption is that, among the large number of variables there are many irrelevant or redundant variables for the purpose of classification. This method is based on the connection of FLDA and a generalized eigenvalue problem, stated formally by the following theorem:

Theorem [12]:
Suppose S_w is a positive definite matrix and denote its Cholesky decomposition as $S_w = R_w^T R_w$ (R_w is an upper triangular matrix). Let H_b be $k \times p$ matrix, $V_1, \ldots,$

V_q ($q < \min(p, k - 1)$) denote the eigenvectors of $S_W^{-1} S_B$ corresponding to the q largest eigenvalues $\lambda_1 \geq \ldots \geq \lambda_q$, $A = [\alpha_1, \ldots, \alpha_q]$, $B = [\beta_1, \ldots, \beta_q]$. For $\lambda > 0$ let $\hat{A}, \hat{B}$ be the solution to the following problem:

$$\min_{A,B} \sum_{i=1}^{k} \left\| R_w^{-T} H_{b,i} - A B^T H_{b,i} \right\|^2 + \lambda \sum_{j=1}^{q} \beta_j^T (S_w) \beta_j \text{ subject to } A^T A = I_{p \times q},$$

where:

$H_{b,i} = \sqrt{n_i} (\bar{x}_i - \bar{x})^T$ is the i-th row of the matrix

$H_b = \left(\sqrt{n_1} (\bar{x}_1 - \bar{x}), \ldots, \sqrt{n_k} (\bar{x}_k - \bar{x}) \right)^T$,

e^{n_i} is a vector of ones with length n_i,

Then $\hat{\beta}_j, j = 1, \ldots q$, span the same linear space as $V_j, j = 1, \ldots, q$.

The following method of regularization is applied in [12] to circumvent the singularity problem and to obtain the sparse linear discriminants: i.e. the first q sparse discriminant directions $\beta_1, \ldots, \beta_q$ are defined as the solutions to the following optimization problem:

$$\min_{A,B} \sum_{i=1}^{k} \left\| R_w^{-T} H_{b,i} - A B^T H_{b,i} \right\|^2 + \lambda \sum_{j=1}^{q} \beta_j^T \left(S_w + \gamma \frac{tr(S_w)}{p} I \right) \beta_j + \sum_{j=1}^{q} \lambda_{1,j} \|\beta_j\|_1$$

subject to $A^T A = I_{p \times q}$, where $B = [\beta_1, \ldots, \beta_q]$, $\|\beta_j\|_1$ is the 1-norm of the vector β_j, the same λ is used for all q directions, different $\lambda_{1,j}$'s are allowed to penalize different discriminant directions.

Our empirical study suggests that the solution is very stable when λ varies in a wide range, for example in (0.01, 10000). We can use K-fold cross validation (CV) [11] to select the optimal parameters $\lambda_{1,j}$, but when the dimension of the input data is very large, the numerical algorithm becomes time consuming and we can let $\lambda_{1,1} = \ldots = \lambda_{1,q}$. The tuning parameter γ controls the strength of the regularization of the matrix S_w, the large values will bias too much S_w towards identity matrix (high degree of regularization). In our empirical studies, we find that the results are not sensitive to the choice of γ if a small value that is less than 0.1 is used, in our studies we set $\gamma = 0.05$. More careful studies of choice of γ are left for future research.

The above problem can be numerically solved by alternating optimization over A and B [12] and the resulting algorithm is summarized below.

* * *

Regularized sparse LDA (rSLDA) algorithm (based on [12]):

1. Form the matrices from the input data:

$$H_w = X - \begin{pmatrix} e^{n_1} (\bar{x}_1)^T \\ \vdots \\ e^{n_K} (\bar{x}_K)^T \end{pmatrix}$$

$$H_b = \left(\sqrt{n_1}(\bar{x}_1 - \bar{x}), \ldots, \sqrt{n_k}(\bar{x}_k - \bar{x})^T \right)$$

2. Compute upper triangular matrix R_w from the Cholesky decomposition of:

$$\left(S_w + \gamma \frac{tr(S_w)}{p} I \right) \quad \text{such that} \quad \left(S_w + \gamma \frac{tr(S_w)}{p} I \right) = R_w^T R_w$$

3. Solve the q independent optimization problems

$$\min_{\beta_j} \beta_j^T (\tilde{W}^T \tilde{W}) \beta_j - 2 \tilde{y}^T \tilde{W} \beta_j + \lambda_1 \| \beta_j \|_1, \ j = 1, \ldots, q$$

where

$$\tilde{W}_{(n+p) \times p} = \begin{pmatrix} H_b \\ \sqrt{\lambda} \cdot R_w \end{pmatrix} \quad \tilde{y}_{(n+p) \times 1} = \begin{pmatrix} H_b R_w^{-1} \alpha_j \\ 0 \end{pmatrix}$$

4. Compute SVD:

$$R_w^{-T}(H_B^T H_B)B = UDV^T \text{ and let } A = UV^T$$

5. Repeat steps 3 and 4 until converges.

*** * ***

3   Protein-Protein Interaction Classification Method

To characterize properties of protein interaction, we proposed to use the binding free energies. These were computed using FastContact [4], which obtains their fast estimates. FastContact delivers the electrostatic energy, solvation free energy, and the top 20 maximum and minimum values for:

1. residues contributing to the binding free energy,
2. ligand residues contributing to the solvation free energy,
3. ligand residues contributing to the electrostatic energy,
4. receptor residues contributing to the solvation free energy,
5. receptor residues contributing to the electrostatic energy,
6. receptor-ligand residue solvation constants,
7. receptor-ligand residue electrostatic constants.

Thus, all these values and the total solvation and electrostatic energy values compose a total of 282 features characterizing interaction.

To create a dataset for classification, we used the pre-classified dataset from previous study [9] containing 62 transient and 75 obligate complexes as two different classes for classification. Each complex is listed in the form of chains for ligand and receptor respectively. The relevant data about the structure of each complex was obtained from the Protein Data Bank (PDB) [1] and then obtaining the 282 features by invoking FastContact.

Due to the fact that the number of features (282) is greater than the number of samples in a dataset (137), we have HDLSS setting, so we apply sparse regularized linear discriminant analysis for the calculation of discriminant directions, i.e. the algorithm sparsed rLDA described above.

For the classification of the samples in the new discriminant space, we applied the nearest centroid method [11] as the classification algorithm.

4   Rapid Estimation of Contact and Binding Free Energies

The estimation of contact and binding free energies may be in general a time con-suming job. One of components of the binding energy is electrostatic energy. This term applies to a system of charges and is defined as the work necessary to move all the electric charges from infinity to positions occupied in the analyzed system. This work does not depend on the path traveled by the charges and is one of properties of a static arrangement of charges in space. Electrostatic interaction works on relatively long distances [7]. For proteins, it refers to the interaction between electrically charged atoms in different proteins or interactions between charges in the surface of the protein and charges in the environment. The exact computation of this energy for each possible conformation would be time consuming.

We have used a method called FastContact, developed by Camacho et al. [3, 4]. The binding energy is computed as a sum of the electrostatic potential and the des-olvation free energy in proteins: $G_{\text{binding}} = E_{\text{electrostatic}} + G_{\text{desolvation}}$. In this formula, $E_{\text{electrostatic}}$ is the standard intermolecular Coulomb electrostatic potential with relative permittivity varying with the distance r and equal to $4r$. The term $G_{\text{desolvation}}$ includes basic features of the desolvation free energy in proteins: hydrophobic interactions, self-energy change resulting from desolvating charge on polar atom groups and side-chain entropy loss. The $G_{\text{desolvation}}$ term is calculated as a sum of atomic contact potentials (ACP) between all pairs of atoms, where the first atom belongs to the receptor, the second to the ligand. Each term of this sum is additionally multiplied by a function $g(r)$ depending on the distance r between involved atoms. For $r > 7$ Å the value is 0, for $r < 5$ Å is 1 and between 5 Å and 7 Å $g(r)$ is a smooth function. These ACPs are defined for 18 atom types. The function $g(r)$ makes possible faster compu-tation by zeroing interactions between distant atoms.

5   Experimental Results

In our experiments we have used the dataset of 137 protein complexes described in [13]. 75 samples in this dataset belong to the first class (i.e. "obligate interactions") and 62 samples to the second class (i.e. "non-obligate interactions"). This dataset is ran-domly divided into a "training set" and "testing set" in a ratio of 4:1.

As we have only two classes ($k = 2$), there is only one discriminant direction β_1 ($q = 1$). Using all variables in constructing the discriminant vector β_1 might cause the overfitting of the training data, resulting in high testing error rate. Moreover it is computationally demanding, so sparsification would be a good choice.

Denote the number of significant variables involved in specifying the discriminant direction β_1 (i.e. giving the best prediction), to be m. To find these most significant variables we have performed the experiment with varying values of m. For a given value of m, only the m maximum values of the coordinates of the vector β_1 (so called beta values) are left, the rest is zeroed.

After computing the components of the β_1 vector withthe SLDA algorithm, taking their absolute values and sorting them in ascending order, we have found out, that they rise slowly to about 0.3 of the maximum value at the element 230 and then grow more rapidly within last 52 components.

We leave only m biggest values, zeroing all others. We keep track of indices of these biggest values and modify the original β_1 leaving only m biggest values. These values are used to cast the original 282-dimensional vector onto a one-dimensional space. The projection of the samples from the protein dataset uses only these m non-zero coefficients.

Then, classification is performed in such new discriminant space by the nearest centroid method.

The results are shown in Fig. 1. We can observe that the error rate of the nearest mean classifier grows rapidly and then decreases with the rise of m, up to 28 (error = $\sim 25\,\% \pm 5$ measured on the testing set). Then, for bigger values of m, almost a constant error rate was observed.

From the plot it is clear that if we specify m = 28 as the number of component variables in discriminant vector β_1 - sparse LDA algorithm can discriminate the two classes fairly well (the classifier performance = $\sim 75\,\% \pm 5$).

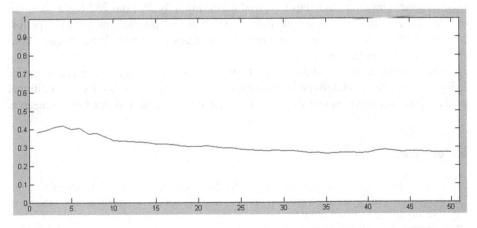

Fig. 1. The average classification error rate as a function of the number of variables using nearest centroid method [10] on the projected data (based on 5 random partitions of the dataset into training and test) – the local minimum is at 28

These 28 input features ("selected" by the rslda algorithm) are the most significant for classification. These are the following (corresponding to the ascending order of the absolute value of the coefficients composing vector β_1):

$$202\ 198\ 281\ 200\ 48\ 42\ 243\ 203\ 47\ 133\ 128\ 121\ 161\ 160$$
$$157\ 132\ 49\ 156\ 46\ 134\ 241\ 131\ 155\ 158\ 127\ 119\ 135\ 41$$

Among these 28 features – 13 are from the receptor residues contributing to the desolvation free energy, but these are not from the beginning of the above list. It can be observed that in each of the 7 groups of energetic features – only features with extreme (min or max) contribution to the energy are always selected. The features from the beginning of the list are those from the receptor residues contributing to the electrostatics energy. One may conclude that electrostatic energy is the most important in the prediction of obligate/non-obligate protein-protein interactions. Electrostatic energy involves a long-range interaction and occur between charged atoms of two interacting proteins.

Thus, the rslda algorithm does suggest which constituents are the most important in the classification of interactions.

6   Conclusions

We have proposed a classification approach for obligate/non-obligate (transient) protein-protein complexes. We have used regularized version of sparse linear discriminant analysis algorithm [12] for feature extraction as well as for input variable selection. To discriminate between two types of protein interactions: obligate and non-obligate, we have used the "energetic features". These are based on the binding free energy defined as the sum of the desolvation and electrostatic energies. These were computed effectively using the package FastContact [4]. The results on the protein-protein interactions dataset showed that using only 28 from 282 input variables enables the classification of the mentioned two types of interactions with the performance of 75 %. Among the most important features are those from residues contributing to the electrostatic energy.

The hypothesis on the importance of the electrostatic energy in the prediction of obligate/non-obligate protein-protein interactions should be confirmed by the additional experiments on bigger protein datasets. This will be the subject of our future research.

References

1. Berman, H., et al.: The protein data bank. Nucleid Acid Res. **28**, 235–242 (2000)
2. Bordner, A., Abagyan, R.: Statistical analysis and prediction of protein-protein interfaces. Proteins **60**(3), 353–366 (2005)
3. Camacho, C.J., Gatchell, D.W., Kimura, S.R., Vajda, S.: Scoring docked conformations generated by rigid-body protein-protein docking. PROTEINS: structure. Funct. Genet. **40**, 525–537 (2000)

4. Camacho, C., Zhang, C.: FastContact: rapid estimate of contact and binding free energies. Bioinformatics **21**(10), 2534–2536 (2005)
5. Fukunaga, K.: Introduction to Statistical Pattern Recognition. Academic Press, New York (1990)
6. Jones, S., Thornton, J.M.: Principles of protein-protein interactions. Proc. Natl. Acad. Sci. U.S.A. **93**(1), 13–20 (1996)
7. Maleki, M., Vasudev, G., Rueda, L.: The role of electrostatic energy in prediction of obligate protein-protein interactions. Proteome Sci. **11**(Suppl. 1), S11 (2013)
8. Marron, J., et al.: Distance-weighted discrimination. J. Am. Stat. Assoc. **102**, 1267–1273 (2007)
9. Rueda, L., Garate, C., Banerjee, S., Mominul Aziz, M.: Biological protein-protein interaction prediction using binding free energies and linear dimensionality reduction. In: Dijkstra, T.M., Tsivtsivadze, E., Marchiori, E., Heskes, T. (eds.) PRIB 2010. LNCS, vol. 6282, pp. 383–394. Springer, Heidelberg (2010)
10. Skrabanek, L., et al.: Computational prediction of protein-protein interactions. Mol. Biotechnol. **38**(1), 1–17 (2008)
11. Stąpor, K.: Classification methods in computer vision. PWN, Warszawa (2011) (in Polish)
12. Qiao, Z., Zhou, L., Huang, J.: Sparse linear discriminant analysis with applications to high dimensional low sample size data. IAENG Int. J. Appl. Math. **39**, 1 (2009)
13. Zhou, H., Shan, Y.: Prediction of protein-protein interaction sites from sequence profile and residue neighbor list. Proteins **44**(3), 336–343 (2001)
14. Zhu, H., et al.: NoxClass: prediction of protein-protein interaction types. BMC Bioinform. **7**, 27 (2006)

Ensembles of Heterogeneous Concept Drift Detectors - Experimental Study

Michał Woźniak[1]([✉]), Paweł Ksieniewicz[1], Bogusław Cyganek[2], and Krzysztof Walkowiak[1]

[1] Department of Systems and Computer Networks, Faculty of Electronics, Wrocław University of Technology, Wybrzeże Wyspiańskiego 27, 50-370 Wrocław, Poland
{michal.wozniak,pawel.ksieniewicz,krzysztof.walkowiak}@pwr.edu.pl
[2] AGH University of Science and Technology, Al. Mickiewicza 30, 30-059 Kraków, Poland
cyganek@agh.edu.pl

Abstract. For the contemporary enterprises, possibility of appropriate business decision making on the basis of the knowledge hidden in stored data is the critical success factor. Therefore, the decision support software should take into consideration that data usually comes continuously in the form of so-called *data stream*, but most of the traditional data analysis methods are not ready to efficiently analyze fast growing amount of the stored records. Additionally, one should also consider phenomenon appearing in data stream called *concept drift*, which means that the parameters of an using model are changing, what could dramatically decrease the analytical model quality. This work is focusing on the classification task, which is very popular in many practical cases as fraud detection, network security, or medical diagnosis. We propose how to detect the changes in the data stream using combined concept drift detection model. The experimental evaluations confirm its pretty good quality, what encourage us to use it in practical applications.

Keywords: Data stream · Concept drift · Pattern classification · Drift detector

1 Introduction

The analysis of huge volumes and fast arriving data is recently the focus of intense research, because such methods could build a competitive advantage of a given company. One of the useful approach is the data stream classification, which is employed to solve problems related to discovery client preference changes, spam filtering, fraud detection, and medical diagnosis to enumerate only a few.

However, most of the traditional classifier design methods do not take into consideration that:

© IFIP International Federation for Information Processing 2016
Published by Springer International Publishing Switzerland 2016. All Rights Reserved
K. Saeed and W. Homenda (Eds.): CISIM 2016, LNCS 9842, pp. 538–549, 2016.
DOI: 10.1007/978-3-319-45378-1_48

- The statistical dependencies between the observations of the given objects and their classifications could change.
- Data can arrive so quick that labeling all records is impossible.

This section focuses on the first problem called *concept drift* [23] and it comes in many forms, depending on the type of change. Appearance of concept drift may potentially cause a significant accuracy deterioration of an exploiting classifier. Therefore, developing positive methods which are able to effectively deal with this phenomena has become an increasing issue. In general, the following approaches may be considered to deal with the above problem.

- Frequently rebuilding a model if new data becomes available. It is very expensive and impossible from a practical point of view, especially when the concept drift occurs rapidly.
- Detecting concept changes in new data, and if these changes are *sufficiently* significant then rebuilding the classifier.
- Adopting an incremental learning algorithm for the classification model.

Let's firstly characterize shortly the probabilistic model of the classification task [4]. It assumes that attributes $x \in \mathcal{X} \subseteq \mathcal{R}^d$ and class label $j \in \mathcal{M} = \{1, 2, ..., M\}$ are the observed values of a pair of random variables $(\mathbf{X}, \mathbf{J})$. Their distribution is characterized by *prior* probability

$$p_j = P(\mathbf{J} = j), \; j \in \mathcal{M} \tag{1}$$

and conditional probability density functions[1]

$$f_j(x) = f(x|j), \; x \in \mathcal{X}, \; j \in \mathcal{M}. \tag{2}$$

The classifier Ψ maps feature space $\mathcal{X}$ to the set of the class labels $\mathcal{M}$

$$\Psi : \mathcal{X} \to \mathcal{M}. \tag{3}$$

The optimal Bayes classifier Ψ^* minimizes probability of missclassification according to the following classification rule[2]:

$$\Psi^*(x) = i \text{ if } p_i(x) = \max_{k \in \mathcal{M}} p_k(x), \tag{4}$$

where $p_j(x)$ stands for *posterior* probability

$$p_i(x) = \frac{p_i f_i(x)}{f(x)} \tag{5}$$

and $f(x)$ is unconditionally density function.

$$f(x) = \sum_{k=1}^{M} p_k \, f_k(x) \tag{6}$$

---

[1] We assume continuous attributes, but for discrete ones we have to take into consideration corresponding conditional probabilities $p(x|j)$.

[2] We assume so-called 0–1 loss function. For different loss function the optimal algorithm minimizes so-called overall risk [4].

Backing to the concept drift problem we may distinguished two types of drifts according its influence into probabilistic characteristics of the classification task [5]:

- *virtual concept drift* means that the changes do not have any impact on decision boundaries (some works report that they do not have an impact on *posterior* probability, but it is disputable), but they change unconditionally density functions [22].
- *real concept drift* means that the changes have an impact on decision boundaries, i.e., on *posterior* probabilities [19,23].

Considering the classification task, the real concept drift is the most important, but detecting the virtual one could be useful as well, because in the case if we are able not only to detect the drift, but also distinguish between virtual and real concept drift, then we may decide if classifier's model rebuilding is necessary or not. Another taxonomy of concept drift bases on its impetuosity. We may distinguish:

- Slow changes (*gradual or incremental drift*). For the gradual drift for a given period of time examples from different models could appear in the stream concurrently, while for incremental drift the model's parameters are changing smoothly.
- Rapid changes (*sudden drift, concept shift*).

A plethora of solutions have been proposed how to deal with this phenomena. Basically, we may divide these algorithms into four main groups:

1. Online learners [24]
2. Instance based solutions (also called sliding window based solutions)
3. Ensemble approaches [11,13,16]
4. Drift detection algorithms

In this work we will focus on the drift detectors which are responsible for determining whether two successive data chunks were generated by the same distribution [9]. In the case the the change is detected the decision about collecting new data to rebuild new model could be made.

2   Concept Drift Detection

As we mentioned above the appearance of concept drift may potentially cause a significant accuracy deterioration of an exploiting classifier [15], what is shown in Fig. 1.

Concept drift detector is an algorithm, which on the basis of incoming information about new examples and their correct classification or a classifier's performance (as accuracy) can return information that data stream distributions are changing. The currently used detectors return only signal about drift detection, which usually requires a quick classifier's model updating or that warning

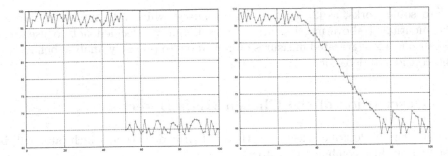

Fig. 1. Exemplary deterioration of classifier accuracy for sudden drift (left) and incremental one (right).

level is achieved, which is usually treated as a moment that new learning set should be gathered (i.e., all new incoming examples should be labeled). The new learning set is used to update the model is drift is detected. The idea of drift detection is presented in Fig. 2

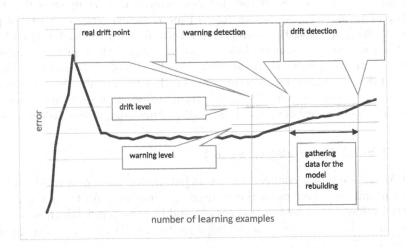

Fig. 2. Idea of drift detection.

The drift detection could be recognized as the simple classification task, but from practical point of view detectors do not use the classical classification model. The detection is hard, because on the one hand we require quick drift detection to quickly replace outdated model and to reduce so-called restoration time. On the other hand we do not accept false alarms [8], i.e., when detector returns that change appears, but it is not true. Therefore to measure performance of concept drift detectors the following metrics are usually used:

– Number of correct detected drifts.
– Number of false alarms.
– Time between real drift appearance and its detection.

In some works, as [2], aggregated measures, which take into consideration the mentioned above metrics, are proposed, but we decided not to use them because using aggregated measures do not allow to precisely analyse behavior of the considered detectors.

3   Description of the Chosen Drift Detectors

Let us shortly describe selected methods of drift detection, which later will be used to produce combined detectors.

3.1   DDM (*Drift Detection Method*)

This algorithm [6] is analyzing the changes in the probability distribution of the successive examples for different classes. On the basis of the mentioned above analysis DDM estimates classifier error, which (assuming the convergency of the classifier training method) has to decrease, what means the probability distribution does not change [18]. If the classifier error is increasing according to the number of training examples then this observation suggests a change of probability distribution and the current model should be rebuilt. DDM estimates classification error, its standard deviation and stores their minimal values. If estimated error is greater than stored minimal value of error and two times its standard deviation then DDM returns signal that the warning level is achieved. In the case if estimated error is greater than stored minimal value of error and three times its standard deviation then DDM returns signal that drift is detected.

3.2   CUSUM (*CUmulative SUM*)

CUSUM [17] detects a change of a given parameter value of a probability distribution and indicated when the change is significant. As the parameter the expected value of the classification error could be considered, which may be estimated on the basis of labels of incoming objects from data stream. The detection condition looks as follows

$$g_t = max(0, g_{t-1} + \epsilon_t - \xi) > treshold \qquad (7)$$

where $g_0 = 0$ and ϵ_t stands for observed value of a parameter in time t (e.g., mentioned above classification error). ξ describes rate of change. The value of *treshold* is set by an user and it is responsible for detector's sensitivity. Its low value allows to detect drift quickly, but then a pretty high number of false alarms could appear [2,5].

3.3   Test PageHinkley

It is modification of the CUSUM algorithm, where the cumulative difference between observed classifier error and its average is taken into consideration [20].

3.4 Detectors Based on Hoeffding's and McDiarmid's Inequalities

The interesting drift detectors based on non-parametric estimation of classifier error employing Hoeffding's and McDiarmid's inequalities were proposed in [3].

4 Combined Concept Drift Detectors

Let's assume that we have a pool of n drift detectors

$$\Pi = \{D_1, D_2, ..., D_n\} \tag{8}$$

Each of them returns signal that warning level is achiever or concept drift is detected, i.e.,

$$D_i = \begin{cases} 0 \ if \ drift \ is \ not \ detected \\ 1 \ if \ warning \ level \ is \ achieved \\ 2 \ if \ drift \ is \ detected \end{cases} \tag{9}$$

As yet not so many papers deal with combined drift detectors. Bifet et al. [2] proposed the simple combination rules based on the appearance of drift once ignoring signals about warning level. The idea of combined drift detector is presented in Fig. 3.

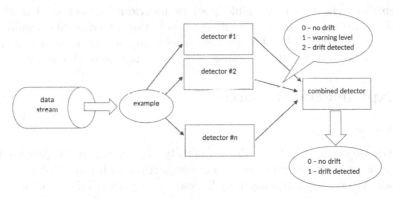

Fig. 3. Idea of combined drift detector.

Let's present three combination rules which allow to combine the concept drift detector outputs. Because this work focuses on the ensemble of heterogeneous detectors, therefore only the combination rules using drift appearance signal are taken into consideration.

4.1 ALO (*At Least One Detects Drift*)

Committee of detectors makes a decision about drift if at least one individual detector returns decision that drift appears (not all of the detectors can return warning signal).

$$ALO(\Pi, x) = \begin{cases} 0 \ \sum_{i=1}^{n} [D_i(x) = 2] \\ 1 \ \sum_{i=1}^{n} [D_i(x) = 0] \end{cases} \tag{10}$$

where [] denotes Iverson bracket.

4.2 ALHD (*At Least Half of the Detectors Detect Drift*)

Committee of detectors makes a decision about drift if at half of individual detectors return decisions that drift appears.

$$ALHWD(\Pi, x) = \begin{cases} 0 & \sum_{i=1}^{n}[D_i(x) = 2] < \frac{n}{2} \\ 1 & \sum_{i=1}^{n}[D_i(x) = 2] \geqslant \frac{n}{2} \end{cases} \tag{11}$$

4.3 AD (*All Detectors Detect Drift*)

Committee of detectors makes a decision about drift if each individual detector returns decisions that drift appears.

$$ALHWD(\Pi, x) = \begin{cases} 0 & \sum_{i=1}^{n}[D_i(x) = 2] < n \\ 1 & \sum_{i=1}^{n}[D_i(x) = 2] \geqslant n \end{cases} \tag{12}$$

Let's notice that proposed combined detectors are *de facto* classifier ensembles [25], which use deterministic (untrained) combination rules. They do not take into consideration any additional information as about individual drift detector's qualities. In this work, we also do not focus on the very important problem how choose the valuable pool of individual detectors. For classifier ensemble such a process (called ensemble selection or ensemble pruning) uses diversity measure [14], but for the combined detectors the measures have been using, thus far is impossible, because of different nature of the decision task.

5 Experimental Research

5.1 Goals

The main objective of the experimental study was evaluating the proposed combined concept drift detectors and their comparison with the well-known simple methods. To ensure the appropriate diversity of the pool of detectors we decided to produce an ensemble on the basis of five detectors employing different models presented in the previous section. For each experiment we estimated detector sensitivity, number of false alarms and computational complexity of the model, i.e., commutative running time.

5.2 Set-Up

We used the following models of individual detectors:

- DDM with window includes 30 examples.
- HDDM_A - detector based on McDiarmid's inequality analysis with the following parameters: drift confidence 0.001, warning confidence 0.005, and one-side t-test.
- HDDM_W - detector based on Hoeffding's inequality analysis with the following parameters: drift confidence 0.001, warning confidence 0.005, and one-side t-test.

- Cusum with window includes 30 examples, $\delta = 0.005$ and $lambda = 50$
- Page-Hinkley test with window includes 30 examples, $\delta = 0.005$, $lambda = 50$, and $\alpha = 1$

As we mentioned above we use the individual detectors to build three combined ones based on the ALO, ALHD, and AD combination rules.

All experiments were carried out using MOA (*Massive Online Analysis*)[3] and our own software written in Java according to MOA's requirements [1].

For each experiment 3 computer generated data streams were used. Each of them consists of 10 000 examples:

- Data stream with sudden drift appearing after each 5 000 examples.
- Data stream with gradual drift, where 2 concept appear.
- Data stream without drift.

The stationary data stream (without drift) was chosen because we would like to evaluate the sensitivity of the detector, i.e., number of false alarms.

5.3 Results

The results of experiment were presented in Tables 1, 2 and 3.[4]

5.4 Discussion

Firstly we have to emphasize that we realize that the scope of the experiments was limited therefore drawing the general conclusions is very risky. For each experiments the detector based on Hoeffding's inequality (HDDM_W) [3] outperformed other models. The combined detectors have not behaved well for sudden and frequent drift (see Table 1), because some of them (as ALO) has

Table 1. Results of experiment for data stream with sudden drift

Detector	No. of real drifts	No. of corrected detected drifts	Average detection delay	No. of false detections	Time
DDM	20	20	71.45	0	1.47
HDDM_A	20	19	19	1	1.79
HDDM_W	20	20	11.65	0	1.71
PageHinkley	20	1	102	0	1.61
CUSUM	20	20	141.95	0	1.59
ALO	20	0	-	78	4.93
ALHD	20	1	102	0	4.76
AD	20	20	29.8	6	4.85

[3] http://moa.cms.waikato.ac.nz/.
[4] The detailed results of the experiments could be found https://drive.google.com/drive/u/0/folders/0B8ja_TIQel7KbnJMblJJUzltNzQ.

Table 2. Results of experiment for data stream with gradual drift

Detector	No. of real drifts	No. of corrected detected drifts	Average detection delay	No. of false detections	Time
DDM	1	1	235	2	1.44
HDDM_A	1	1	310	1	1.65
HDDM_W	1	1	242	1	1.62
PageHinkley	1	1	340	1	1.59
CUSUM	1	1	346	1	1.62
ALO	1	1	235	10	4.89
ALHD	1	1	346	1	4.86
AD	1	1	299	2	4.95

Table 3. Results of experiment for data stream without drift

Detector	No. of real drifts	No. of corrected detected drifts	Average detection delay	No. of false detections	Time
DDM	0	0	-	0	1.4
HDDM_A	0	0	-	0	1.65
HDDM_W	0	0	-	0	1.59
PageHinkley	0	0	-	0	1.53
CUSUM	0	0	-	0	1.61
ALO	0	0	-	0	7.79
ALHD	0	0	-	0	4.84
AD	0	0	-	0	4.92

to low sensitivity or so high sensitivity (as for AD) caused a high number of false alarms. The computation time of AD detector was similar as in the case of HDDM_A or HDDM_W, but as we mentioned before the number of false alarms was not acceptable. For gradual drift the combined detectors ALHD and AD behaved similar as individual detectors. For stationary stream they have not presented so high sensitivity (similar as individual detectors). Probably, not so impressive results of combined detectors have been caused by the fact that we nominated the the individual models arbitrary and we did not check how adding or removing detector from the pool could impact on the combined detector quality. Additionally, HDDM_W and HDDM_A detectors strongly outperformed other models, what could cause that the decision of the detector ensemble was the same as the dominant models. The similar observation has been reported for the classifier ensemble using deterministic combination rules. On the basis of the experiment we are not able to say expressly if the combined concept drift detectors are promising direction. Nevertheless, we decided to continue the works on such models, especially for a pool of homogeneous detectors and method which are able to prune the detector ensemble. We have also to notice the main drawback of the proposed models, which are more complex than single ones. On the other hand we have to notice that using the proposed method of parallel interconnection is easy to parallelize and could be run in a distributed computing environment.

6 Final Remarks

In this work three simple combination rules for combined concept drift detectors were discussed and evaluated on the basis of the computer experiments for different data streams. They seem to be an interesting proposition to solve the problem of concept drift detection, nevertheless the results of experiments do not confirm their high quality, but as we mentioned above it is probably caused by very naive choice of the individual models of the detector ensemble.

It is worth noticing that we assume the continue access to class labels. Unfortunately, from the practical point of view it is hard to be granted that labels are always and immediately available, e.g., for credit approval task the true label is usually available ca. 2 years after the decision, then such labeled example could be worthless as come from outdated model. Therefore, during constructing the concept drift detectors we have to take into consideration the cost of data labeling, which is usually passed over. It seems to be very interesting to design detectors on the basis of a partially labeled set of examples (called *active learning*) [7] or unlabeled examples. Unfortunately, unsupervised drift detectors can detect the virtual drift only, but it is easy to show that without access to class labels (then we can analyse the unconditionally probability distribution only $f(x)$) the real drift could be undetected [21].

Let's propose the future research directions related to the combined concept drift detectors:

- Developing methods how to choose individual detectors to a committee, maybe dedicated diversity measure should be proposed. In this work the diversity of the detectors was ensured by choosing different detector's models, but we may also use the same model of detector but with different parameters, e.g., using different drift confidences and warning confidences for detector based on McDiarmid's inequality.
- Proposing semi-supervised and unsupervised methods of combined detector training.
- Proposing trained combination rule to establish the final decision of the combined detector and to fully exploit the strengths of the individual detectors.
- Developing the combined local drift detectors, probably employing the clustering and selection approach [10, 12], because many changes have the local nature and touch the selected area of the feature space or selected features only.
- Employing other interconnections of detectors (in this work the parallel architecture was considered only) including serial one.

Acknowledgements. This work was supported by the statutory funds of the Department of Systems and Computer Networks, Faculty of Electronics, Wroclaw University of Science and Technology and by the Polish National Science Centre under the grant No. DEC-2013/09/B/ST6/02264. This work was also supported by the AGH Statutory Funds No. 11.11.230.017. All computer experiments were carried out using computer equipment sponsored by ENGINE project (http://engine.pwr.edu.pl/).

References

1. Bifet, A., Holmes, G., Kirkby, R., Pfahringer, B.: MOA: massive online analysis. J. Mach. Learn. Res. **11**, 1601–1604 (2010)
2. Bifet, A., Read, J., Pfahringer, B., Holmes, G., Žliobaitė, I.: CD-MOA: change detection framework for massive online analysis. In: Tucker, A., Höppner, F., Siebes, A., Swift, S. (eds.) IDA 2013. LNCS, vol. 8207, pp. 92–103. Springer, Heidelberg (2013)
3. Blanco, I.I.F., del Campo-Avila, J., Ramos-Jimenez, G., Bueno, R.M., Diaz, A.A.O., Mota, Y.C.: Online and non-parametric drift detection methods based on Hoeffding's bounds. IEEE Trans. Knowl. Data Eng. **27**(3), 810–823 (2015)
4. Duda, R.O., Hart, P.E., Stork, D.G.: Pattern Classification, 2nd edn. Wiley, New York (2001)
5. Gama, J., Zliobaite, I., Bifet, A., Pechenizkiy, M., Bouchachia, A.: A survey on concept drift adaptation. ACM Comput. Surv. **46**(4), 44:1–44:37 (2014)
6. Gama, J., Medas, P., Castillo, G., Rodrigues, P.: Learning with drift detection. In: Bazzan, A.L.C., Labidi, S. (eds.) SBIA 2004. LNCS (LNAI), vol. 3171, pp. 286–295. Springer, Heidelberg (2004)
7. Greiner, R., Grove, A.J., Roth, D.: Learning cost-sensitive active classifiers. Artif. Intell. **139**(2), 137–174 (2002)
8. Gustafsson, F.: Adaptive Filtering and Change Detection. Wiley, New York (2000)
9. Harel, M., Mannor, S., El-yaniv, R., Crammer, K.: Concept drift detection through resampling. In: Jebara, T., Xing, E.P. (eds.) Proceedings of the 31st International Conference on Machine Learning (ICML 2014), JMLR Workshop and Conference Proceedings, pp. 1009–1017 (2014)
10. Jackowski, K., Krawczyk, B., Woźniak, M.: Improved adaptive splitting and selection: the hybrid training method of a classifier based on a feature space partitioning. Int. J. Neural Syst. **24**(03), 1430007 (2014)
11. Krawczyk, B.: One-class classifier ensemble pruning and weighting with firefly algorithm. Neurocomputing **150**, 490–500 (2015)
12. Kuncheva, L.I.: Clustering-and-selection model for classifier combination. In: Proceedings of the Fourth International Conference on Knowledge-Based Intelligent Engineering Systems and Allied Technologies, vol. 1, pp. 185–188 (2000)
13. Kuncheva, L.I.: Classifier ensembles for changing environments. In: Roli, F., Kittler, J., Windeatt, T. (eds.) MCS 2004. LNCS, vol. 3077, pp. 1–15. Springer, Heidelberg (2004)
14. Kuncheva, L.I.: Combining Pattern Classifiers: Methods and Algorithms. Wiley-Interscience, Hoboken (2004)
15. Lughofer, E., Angelov, P.P.: Handling drifts and shifts in on-line data streams with evolving fuzzy systems. Appl. Soft Comput. **11**(2), 2057–2068 (2011)
16. Ouyang, Z., Gao, Y., Zhao, Z., Wang, T.: Study on the classification of data streams with concept drift. In: FSKD, pp. 1673–1677. IEEE (2011)

17. Page, E.S.: Continuous inspection schemes. Biometrika **41**(1/2), 100–115 (1954)
18. Raudys, S.: Statistical and Neural Classifiers: An Integrated Approach to Design. Springer Publishing Company, London (2014). Incorporated
19. Schlimmer, J.C., Granger Jr., R.H.: Incremental learning from noisy data. Mach. Learn. **1**(3), 317–354 (1986)
20. Sebastiao, R., Gama, J.: A study on change detection methods. In: Progress in Artificial Intelligence, 14th Portuguese Conference on Artificial Intelligence, EPIA, pp. 12–15 (2009)
21. Sobolewski, P., Wozniak, M.: Concept drift detection and model selection with simulated recurrence and ensembles of statistical detectors. J. Univers. Comput. Sci. **19**(4), 462–483 (2013)
22. Widmer, G., Kubat, M.: Effective learning in dynamic environments by explicit context tracking. In: Brazdil, P.B. (ed.) ECML 1993. LNCS, vol. 667, pp. 227–243. Springer, Heidelberg (1993)
23. Widmer, G., Kubat, M.: Learning in the presence of concept drift and hidden contexts. Mach. Learn. **23**(1), 69–101 (1996)
24. Wozniak, M.: A hybrid decision tree training method using data streams. Knowl. Inf. Syst. **29**(2), 335–347 (2011)
25. Wozniak, M., Grana, M., Corchado, E.: A survey of multiple classifier systems as hybrid systems. Inf. Fusion **16**, 3–17 (2014). Special Issue on Information Fusion in Hybrid Intelligent Fusion Systems

Intelligent Distributed Systems

Harmony Search for Data Mining
with Big Data

Jerzy Balicki[1]([⊠]), Piotr Dryja[2], and Waldemar Korłub[2]

[1] Faculty of Mathematics and Information Science, Warsaw University of
Technology, Koszykowa St. 75, 00-662 Warsaw, Poland
j.balicki@mini.pw.edu.pl
[2] Faculty of Telecommunications, Electronics and Informatics,
Gdańsk University of Technology, Narutowicza St. 11/12,
80-233 Gdańsk, Poland
piotrdryja83@gmail.com, waldemar.korlub@pg.gda.pl

Abstract. In this paper, some harmony search algorithms have been proposed for data mining with big data. Three areas of big data processing have been studied to apply new metaheuristics. The first problem is related to *MapReduce* architecture that can be supported by a team of harmony search agents in grid infrastructure. The second dilemma involves development of harmony search in preprocessing of data series before data mining. Moreover, harmony search as a classification algorithm is studied as the third application. Finally, some outcomes for numerical experiments are submitted.

1 Introduction

A goal of this paper is to describe an approach based on harmony search (an acronym HS) for data mining with Big Data (BD). Although, there are several data mining algorithms, including back-propagation neural networks or locally weighted linear regression, we can extend these set to better support of parallelism in Big Data processing and to avoid some limitations of well-known machine learning procedures like k-Means, or support vector machines [5].

We assume that data is usually gathered from multiple sources, which may be heterogeneous and spread geographically across the world. Also, the collected data may be stored in distributed facilities. Data mining algorithms can be applied for large-scale multimedia applications, in massive parallel way, to ensure higher capacity of training. In fact, both logistic regression and Gaussian discriminant analysis can be used concurrently for different parts of images to make decision for the whole pattern. Similarly, naive Bayes or the independent variable analysis can be developed, simultaneously [12].

A motivation for this paper is fact that a quality of BD processing mainly depends on services provided by some public cloud computing platforms. Especially, BigQuery service that is delivered by Google Cloud can be applied to analyze data in the cloud by SQL-like queries. A query for BD is usually performed for multi-terabyte datasets in 1–2 s. This service is easy to use and it is scalable. In consequence, BD services provided by some public cloud computing platforms can offer real-time insights about large-scale multimedia data [11].

© IFIP International Federation for Information Processing 2016
Published by Springer International Publishing Switzerland 2016. All Rights Reserved
K. Saeed and W. Homenda (Eds.): CISIM 2016, LNCS 9842, pp. 553–565, 2016.
DOI: 10.1007/978-3-319-45378-1_49

MapReduce is a batch-oriented parallel cloud computing model and it can be applied to some machine learning algorithms because they regularly prerequisite to probe through the training data. It needs exhaustive computing to entrance the large-scale data recurrently. It is important that MapReduce has still got a certain advantage in performance over some relational databases [16].

In this paper, related work is described in Sect. 2. Then, MapReduce architecture is characterized in Sect. 3. Next, Sect. 4 presents some studies under intelligent agents in data mining. Genetic programming in data mining is discussed in Sect. 5. Moreover, some harmony search algorithms for data series are studied in Sect. 6. We focus on time series during experiments. A description of parallelism in big data is included in Sect. 7. Furthermore, harmony search for big data preprocessing and some outcomes for numerical experiments with harmony agents are submitted in Sect. 8.

2 Related Work

Main characteristics of dynamic data streams are continuity and unpredictability. What is more, some crucial features are quickness and infinity, too. It is worth to underline that above features of dynamic data streams can loss some valuable information. Data streams are extensively applied in medical testing, online trading, and financial analysis. Chang, Bai and Zhu proposed some parallel algorithms for mining large-scale rich-media data that can be treated as the massive, multisource, and dynamic Big Data [13]. Some data mining methods have been extended from the single-source knowledge discovery methods.

Moreover, Chen, Sivakumar and Kargupta studied collective mining of Bayesian networks from distributed heterogeneous data [14]. Especially, they analyzed stream data that are dynamic and the other approach for data mining should be applied. Similarly, Domingos and Hulten extended a mining method on high-speed data streams that can be applied to visual information processing on large-scale [17].

Big Data are gathered from different sources. Due to some computer hardware improvements, some new knowledge discovery algorithms can be developed for massive data. That is why, there has been constructed a logical framework for identifying quality knowledge from different data sources. Besides, some data mining algorithms have been studied for a multisource massive data.

Some crucial differences between multisource data withdrawal and single-source knowledge mining are related to massive characteristics of multisource data. So, we can distinguish some characteristics for heterogeneous and real-time data. Some characteristics of flow and a data stream require some knowledge mining algorithms. Recently, the theory of local pattern analysis has been introduced to avoid centralized computing.

Banerjee and Agarwal studied collective behavior from blogs using swarm intelligence [7]. On the other hand, it has been proposed a paralleled big data algorithm with MapReduce framework for mining data from Twitter [10]. MapReduce is adopted to parallelize the mining algorithm as well as to ensure scalability of knowledge discovery system. A performance can rise despite growths in data set size. A performance ratio raises as the size of the dataset growths, and as the number of data nodes rises. Several

millions of active users of Twitter post over 140 million messages every day and a big
data set may contains billions of records. So, a new architecture to process the data
mining algorithm is required [19].

On this background, harmony search can be applied for big data mining in different
areas [6]. In this evolutionary-based metaheuristic, an optimization problem is imitated
as a melody performance procedure with searching for a good harmony. HS models
how an orchestra conductor or a music composer optimizes a melody performance to
achieve good harmony music. Similarly to jazz improvisation when musicians seek a
best harmony by artistic intelligence, some outcomes from an optimization algorithm
tend to a global optimum regarding objective function.

3 Hadoop and MapReduce Architecture

MapReduce has recently gained in popularity as one of the key concepts related to BD.
It was introduced by Dean and Ghemawat as a distributed and scalable solution for
parallel processing and large data sets on clusters [16]. Many different commercial and
non-commercial products offer a variety of different implementations of MapReduce
making the everyday use relatively easy. The most popular open-source implementation is Apache Hadoop, embraced by companies such as Adobe or Amazon [1].

MapReduce can be perceived as a universal model which can be used in a variety of
scenarios. This is due to the fact that the model requires two custom functions to be
provided by a user. These functions, known as map and reduce, are responsible for
domain-specific computation not covered by the model. The map function takes the pair
(key, value) as an input, then it performs computation and returns a set of other intermediate pairs (key, value). The key is not unique and it is even usually expected to be
many pairs with the same key. The reduce function is executed after the map function in
the logical. Usually, the role of the reduce function is to merge the input values to a smaller
set. It is therefore possible to define the map and reduce functions, as follows [26]:

$$map(k1, v1) \rightarrow list(k2, v2)$$
$$reduce(k2, list(v2)) \rightarrow list(v2)$$

An execution flow in MapReduce model consists of four major phases (Fig. 1). The
first phase is dedicated to splitting the input required to be processed. Let the text with
random words be considered. Each of the splits can then be processed by the map
function in parallel. The particular word is the key and the '1' is the value. Some
intermediate pairs (key, value) must be then sorted and grouped by a key. This is
because the particular key and its values are passed to the reduce function in the next
phase. The reduce function can be also run in parallel and after computation results are
being sent to output. In this case the reduce function's responsibility is to sum the each
key's values (Fig. 1) [29].

Apache Hadoop is a widely known open-source project that offers the set of
libraries with the MapReduce implementation and own implementation of the distributed file system – Hadoop Distributed File System (HDFS). These two modules can

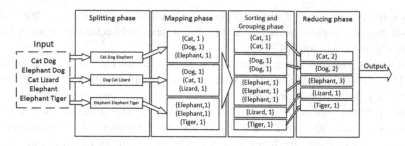

Fig. 1. MapReduce execution flow illustrated with the case of counting the number of occurrences of each word

be perceived as one core. However, Hadoop with other related projects offer much more additional functionality nowadays. Some the Hadoop ecosystem solutions are worth mentioning such as Apache Pig, which offers custom scripting language and Apache HBase – a non-relational distributed database which can serve as a data input for MapReduce.

MapReduce is applied to solve several problems like large-scale machine learning or clustering problems for the Google News. Moreover, an extraction of data is used to produce reports of popular queries and extraction of geographical locations from a large corpus of web pages for localized search. In 2004, Google changed an indexing system that produces data used for web search service to system that used MapReduce. The new indexing system takes input documents that have been retrieved from a crawling system store as a set of files, and then they are processed by from five to ten MapReduce operations. That system gives them many benefits like simpler, smaller, easier to understand code, simplicity to change entire indexing process. Moreover, it is easier to operate because of automatic resolving problems like machine failures, slow machines and networking hiccups [1].

In 2008, New Your Times released service web-based archive of scanned issues from 1851 till 1980. To create that archive company had to convert 405,000 large TIFF images, 3.3 million SGML files, and 405,000 XML files. Output consisted on 810,000 PNG images and 405,000 JavaScript files. To speed up this process they applied Amazon Elastic Compute Cloud and Hadoop. Regarding to hundreds of machines, the process took less than 36 h [16].

4 Intelligent Agents and Genetic Programming in Data Mining

We consider agents that are based on harmony search, generally. There are several traits of multiagent systems that make them suitable for BD acquisition and processing. One of them is mobility of agents, which translates into an ability to move between different data facilities and processing nodes constituting the system that deals with BD. Software agent is not bound to any particular machine or execution container [24]. By migrating to different machines, agents can get closer to the source of an online data stream or closer to the data storage they are about to process. Instead of having to provide the data to the system, data administrators can rely on agents that acquire it on their own. It reduces bandwidth requirements and communication delays [22]. Another important factor is the ability of agents to react upon sudden changes of the environment in which they reside. It provides means for handling changes in the availability of data sources. An agent can make decision about moving to another set of data [28].

Agents are designed with heterogeneous environments in mind [25]. It translates to capability of integrating with different data sources. Agents can integrate with multiple different data stores and handle online streams of information. Acquired data can be later delivered to the processing algorithm in a unified form without the need to use internal storage mechanisms of any particular software framework, e.g. distributed file system of the aforementioned Hadoop platform. One trait of agents that aids the integration with online data streams is their reactive nature. Each new information fragment delivered in the stream becomes an event that agent should react upon.

However, agents can not only react upon external events but also take actions on their own, which is an effect of their pro-activeness. Knowledge extraction from BD is one of the fields, where this trait is particularly important. As there are often no clues in advance about possible interrelationships in BD, the final result is heavily influenced by the decisions made during the actual analysis. Pro-active architectures provide foundation for agents that need to work under uncertainty and act without complete knowledge about their environment.

As was previously mentioned, agents can easily handle acquisition of data from both offline datasets and online streams. Agents can be also deployed inside the lambda architecture to aid actual analysis of data coming from those two distinctive types of sources. The lambda architecture itself is built of three layers: the batch layer, the serving layer and the speed layer. The batch layer is responsible for offline data processing and uses solutions like the MapReduce architecture. Batch view produces by this layer are exposed to external clients by the serving layer. The speed layer is responsible for real-time processing of data streams. It analyses data that was not yet processed by the batch layer. Speed layer produces real-time views that can be merged with batch views to create complete representation of the extracted knowledge.

The main motivation for employing agents is the fact that implementation of a system based on lambda architecture requires integration of several heterogeneous components: one for batch processing, another one for serving views, a different solution for real-time stream analysis, and a component that merges real-time views with batch views. The use of multiagent environment provides a common ground for information exchange between different component and a common execution model.

Agents can improve efficiency of data mining compared to centralized approaches. Multiagent systems have been applied in different domains showing promising results for further research, e.g. banking and finance domain or resource allocation in distributed environments [4, 22].

Some special sort of intelligent agents are based on genetic algorithms that have several advantages in data mining. One of them is its feature of automated searching for optimized solutions without a need for prior knowledge of data. Evolutionary computing also constantly evaluates created models as a whole, which is not a case with most traditional machine learning algorithms. It should be mentioned that this approach is easily adapted to suit researcher needs by changing it evaluation method or tree representation. Genetic programming is being used in wide range of data mining techniques like classification [23].

Although traditional solutions like C4.5 are usually faster than genetic programming, its execution time can be improved by removing parts of decision tree that do not contribute to overall result of evaluation. These parts are named introns [30].

Genetic programming performance can be improved by using some optimization techniques. One of them is search space refinement by dividing existing search space into smaller groups. Researchers may also extend tree representation by using fuzzy logic to improve created models [18]. When compared genetic programming solutions are often better than traditional data mining tools including simple genetic algorithm.

5   Harmony Search for Data Series

Big data requires some database capacities from terabytes to even zetabytes. Capacity of big data depends on the sort of application, e.g. capacity of five terabytes is a great enough for a banking transaction system, but too small to test a web search engine. BG are uncooperative with using some relational database management systems RDBMS, too [8].

Parallelism for big data can be supported by using open grids instead of clouds. In the grids like BOINC, Comcute@home, or SETI@Home data sets are transformed into several millions of subsets that are executed parallel by thousands of computers. In grid, we can use a massively parallel system with lots of CPUs, GPUs, RAM and disks to obtain a high performance by data-based parallelism. So, maximal performance can be estimated at PFLOPS [9].

That is why, we suggest using grid as virtual supercomputer to data mining of big data. In an experimental grid called Comcute, a dilemma with capacity of BD appears if we study some simulations of fire spread to find some strategies. So, we design some intelligent agents for support parallelism in BD queries [15].

Two kinds of intelligent agents act in a middleware layer. Managing agents send data series from distributed sources to distribution agents that cooperate with web computers to calculate outcomes and return them to managing agents, and then to users. Both types of agents can autonomously move from one host to another to improve quality of grid resource using [2].

Moreover, two groups of the other agents based on harmony search as well as genetic programming, optimize a resource usage. A set of agents designed for local optimization consists of some harmony search schedulers. They cooperate with distributors and managers to give them information about optimal workload in some parts of grid. Finally, genetic programming has been applied for finding the compromise configurations of the whole grid. These agents cooperate with harmony search schedulers to correct some local timetables.

Crucial difficulties in parallelism of Comcute are data capture, regarding different sources: sensors, smartphones, cameras, tablets, microphones, computer simulations, satellites, and social networks via some wireless sensor networks. Moreover, data storage, their visualization, analysis and search are still some open problems.

BD is not convenient to the most RDBMS. Advantage of grid development for data basis is related to a fact that an intensive progress in data communication capacity is observed. For instance, the dilemma of finding the optimal strategy against a fire spread can be identified as the 4Vs model described by: high volume, extraordinary velocity, great data variety, and veracity.

In data mining for BD, harmony search can be used to find predictions for data series. Most of methods in data mining for time series consider some discrete time series. On the other hand, some analog time series are discretized with floating-point values. Moreover, time series discretization for knowledge discovery method like artificial neural network can be optimized [27].

Time series values can be represented by a multi connected graph. Under this representation, similar time series can be grouped into a graphical model. However, this approach works with one time series at a time, only. In result, it is inconvenient for parallel processing.

A symbolic representation of time series called SAX allows on dimensionality reduction, and it also allows distance measures to be defined on the symbolic approach where the lower bound corresponding distance measures is defined on the original series. Moreover, Genetic Entropy Based Linear Approximation GENEBLA can be used for time series discretization. For this approach, the EBLA3 algorithm is based on the simulated annealing and it permits on finding an alphabet size and word size to maximize accuracy in classification [20].

Some data mining algorithms for discrete time series require a word size to separate the length of time series, and also an alphabet size to reduce the series. Therefore, a harmony search algorithm can be used to find an optimal word size and alphabet size. Then, they can be used by SAX process to discrete time series for big data sets. So, the question is how to maximize both word size and alphabet size for given data sets. It permits to compress data sets and improve classification accuracy. In this approach, we protect some essential data and hidden patterns.

6 Parallelism in Big Data

Big data applications can develop Hadoop or NoSQL cluster like MongoDB with different nodes to deal with online transaction processing OLTP. Additionally, low response time for decision-support queries is related to online analytical processing OLAP to answering multi-dimensional analytical queries. A required reliability can be obtained through data replication [21].

Figure 2a shows a case for concurrent and different queries that operate on the same data.

The second case (Fig. 2b) is related to complex query that is divided on some parallel operations acting on diverse data. Architecture with shared-disk cluster is much more prepared for big data processing than NUMA Non-Uniform Memory Access architecture. A crucial feature of BD is related to intensive reading from hard disks and then processing, instead of processing and then intensive writing. If we consider no sharing of memory or disks across nodes (Fig. 3), this system requires data partitioning of database like in server DB2.

a)   b)

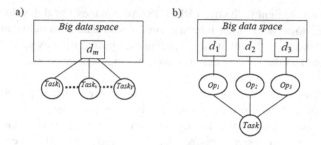

Fig. 2. Two cases of data-based parallelism

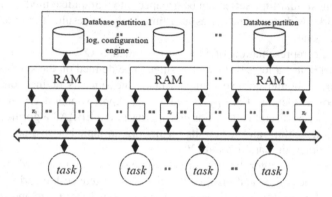

Fig. 3. Shared-nothing cluster architecture for big data [1]

Big data is spread over some partitions that run on some separate servers with own table spaces, logs, and configurations. A query is performed in parallel on all partitions. Such architecture can support Google search engine.

7   HS for BD Preprocessing and Task Optimization

To avoid the predefinition of alphabet size and word size the entropy measure can be used. Entropy minimization heuristic EMH divides continuous value and minimum description length criteria to control the number of interval produced on continuous space. The stopping criterion for this technique is minimum description length principle MDLP.

We have M time series of data. If the length of time series is equal to N, then a word size α_m is a decision variable that cannot exceed N. We can vary a word size from 1 to N. So, we can introduce the inequality constraint, as below:

$$\alpha_m \leq N, \ m = \overline{1, M}. \tag{1}$$

The maximum entropy is based on information gain and the objective function can be defined, as follows:

$$f(x) = \frac{\sum\limits_{m=1}^{M} g_m(x)}{M}, \tag{2}$$

where

M – the time series length;
$g_m(x)$ – the gain between time series value TSV and the mth class value CV_m;
$x = (\alpha_1, \beta_1, \ldots, \alpha_m, \beta_m, \ldots, \alpha_M, \beta_M)$;
α_m – a word size for the mth series;
β_m – an alphabet size for the mth series.

The characteristics of time series value TSV is given:

$$Ent(TSV) = p(S|v)_m \log_2 p(S|v)_m. \tag{3}$$

The time series value TSV can be characterized by tsv - the number of time series with value in S. The characteristics of time series class TSC is given, as follows:

$$Ent(TSC) = -\sum_{j=1}^{J} p_j \log_2 p_j, \tag{4}$$

where

J - the number of classes;
p_j - the probability of class j in TSC.

It is important to remark that the entry time series is considered as one attribute and that the discretization scheme is considered for the whole dataset. It allows harmony search to find a good global solution that maximizes the entropy on data.

For the mth time series HS algorithm is applied to obtain the word size α_m. This the mth time series is formulated regarding new word size αm. Next, against harmony search is used to obtain the alphabet size β_m. Afterwards, the SAX procedure is developed to convert the values of time series to symbolic representation using new alphabets size β_m. Finally, any classification algorithm is applied to evaluate the performance of new data representation.

Figure 4 shows architecture of the grid Comcute with two agents AHS1 and AHS2 that are based on harmony search. One AHS can find suboptimal configuration for at most 15 nodes, 50 tasks and 15 alternatives of resource sets ARS. It represents a volunteer computer.

Figure 5 shows an example of finding the compromise configuration by $AHS1$. The first criterion is the CPU workload of the bottleneck computer ($\hat{Z}_{max}$), and the second one is the communication workload of the bottleneck server ($\tilde{Z}_{max}$) [2]. This problem is the constrained bi-criteria optimization dilemma with integer decision variables [2]. There are presented Pareto-optimal evaluations obtained by harmony search during 10^6 iterations (Fig. 5).

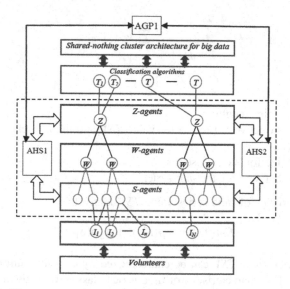

Fig. 4. Harmony search agents HAS in the grid for big data processing

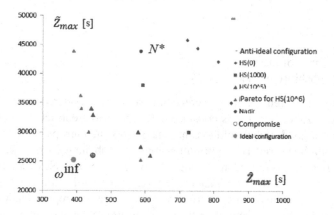

Fig. 5. Finding a compromise configuration by AHS1 in the Comcute grid

The harmony search algorithm has been used with some tuned parameters: *HMCR = 0.9, PAR = 0.5, BW1 = 3, BW2 = 4, HMS = 30* and *HMS2 = 20*. The run time for 1 000 000 updating of the harmony memory HM was 5 h on PC *Windows 7/ Intel Core i7-2670 QM 2,2* GHz. An algorithm during one run found an ideal point $\omega^{inf} = (411; 25\ 221)$ [s], the nadir point $N^* = (587; 43\ 863)$ [s] and the anti-ideal point $\omega^{sup} = (850; 49\ 577)$ [s]. Then, the criterion space is normalized that permits on finding the compromise solution. The distance $\varsigma_2(\bar{\omega}^{Sal}) = \inf_{\bar{\omega} \in \overline{\Omega}} \xi_2(\bar{\omega})$ is equal to 0,127. In the normalized criterion space $\overline{\Omega}$, there is $\bar{\omega}^{Sal} = (0,124;\ 0,030)$, and the compromise evaluation ω^{Sal} is (448; 25 952) [s] in the criterion space Ω. A new solution x^{Sal}

has the following characteristics: $Z_{suma} = 318\,001$ [s], $\Delta_{max} = 13\,200$[s] for $\rho_1 = 0,5$ $\rho_2 = 0,5$, $\Theta = 453\,450$ in units of the CPU *Mark*, $\Xi = 325\,875$ [$], $\upsilon = 856$ and $E = 19\,240$ [W].

Moreover, there are satisfied constraints on RAM and HDD. An encoded configuration is as follows: $X^\alpha = [10,7,12,4,1,11,12,10,5,8,3,14,7,13,11,9,8,5,6,6,1,3,14,10,11,$ $6,13,2,4,5,9,13,9,7,9,4,6,2,2,5,3,1,4,12,2,]^T$, $X^\beta = [3,8,3,9,8,9,8,3,9,3,3,3,3,0]^T$. If $X^\alpha[1] = 10$, the module with the index 1 is assigned to the node number 10. So, some clusters of software modules in nodes can be obtained from X^α. If $X^\beta[1] = 3$, the computer number 3 is assigned to the node number 1. In a compromise solution, there are considered three from twelve possible computers that are assigned to fourteen nodes. The new grid consists on 8 servers *BizServer* E5-2660v2, 3 servers HP *ProLiant* E5-2695, and 3 servers HP *ProLiant* E5-2697.

8   Concluding Remarks and Future Work

Intelligent agents based on harmony search in the middleware of grid can significantly support efficiency of the proposed approach. Multi-objective harmony search can be used for the self-reconfiguration of the grid. Agents based on harmony search can optimize a problem of grid resource using.

Our future work will focus on testing the harmony search to find the compromise configurations for different criteria and constraints. Moreover, quantum-inspired algorithm can be analyzed due to supporting big data, too [3].

References

1. Apache Hadoop. http://hadoop.apache.org/. Accessed 8 Mar 2016
2. Balicki, J.: Negative selection with ranking procedure in tabu-based multi-criterion evolutionary algorithm for task assignment. In: Alexandrov, V.N., van Albada, G.D., Sloot, P.M., Dongarra, J. (eds.) ICCS 2006. LNCS, vol. 3993, pp. 863–870. Springer, Heidelberg (2006)
3. Balicki, J.: An adaptive quantum-based multiobjective evolutionary algorithm for efficient task assignment in distributed systems. In: Mastorakis, N. et al. (eds.) Proceedings of the 13th WSEAS International Conference on Computers Recent Advances in Computer Engineering, Rhodes, Greece, pp. 417–422 (2009)
4. Balicki, J., Kitowski, Z.: Multicriteria evolutionary algorithm with tabu search for task assignment. In: Zitzler, E., Deb, K., Thiele, L., Coello Coello, C.A., Corne, D.W. (eds.) EMO 2001. LNCS, vol. 1993, pp. 373–384. Springer, Heidelberg (2001)
5. Balicki, J., Korłub, W., Szymanski, J., Zakidalski, M.: Big data paradigm developed in volunteer grid system with genetic programming scheduler. In: Rutkowski, L., Korytkowski, M., Scherer, R., Tadeusiewicz, R., Zadeh, L.A., Zurada, J.M. (eds.) ICAISC 2014, Part I. LNCS, vol. 8467, pp. 771–782. Springer, Heidelberg (2014)

6. Balicki, J., Korlub, W., Krawczyk, H., et al.: Genetic programming with negative selection for volunteer computing system optimization. In: Paja, W.A., Wilamowski, B.M. (eds.) Proceedings the 6th International Conference on Human System Interactions, 2013, Gdańsk, Poland, pp. 271–278 (2013)
7. Banerjee, S., Agarwal, N.: Analyzing collective behavior from blogs using swarm intelligence. Knowl. Inf. Syst. **33**(3), 523–547 (2012)
8. Birney, E.: The making of ENCODE: lessons for big-data projects. Nature **489**, 49–51 (2012)
9. BOINC. http://boinc.berkeley.edu/. Accessed 25 Feb 2015
10. Bollen, J., Mao, H., Zeng, X.: Twitter mood predicts the stock market. J. Comput. Sci. **2**(1), 1–8 (2010)
11. Bughin, J., Chui, M., Manyika, J.: Clouds, big data, and smart assets: ten tech-enabled business trends to watch. McKinSey Q. (2010)
12. Cao, L., Gorodetsky, V., Mitkas, P.A.: Agent mining: the synergy of agents and data mining. IEEE Intell. Syst. **24**, 64–72 (2009)
13. Chang, E.Y., Bai, H., Zhu, K.: Parallel algorithms for mining large-scale rich-media data. In: Proceedings of the ACM International Conference on Multimedia, pp. 917–918 (2009)
14. Chen, R., Sivakumar, K., Kargupta, H.: Collective mining of Bayesian networks from distributed heterogeneous data. Knowl. Inf. Syst. **6**(2), 164–187 (2004)
15. Comcute. http://comcute.eti.pg.gda.pl/. Accessed 25 Jan 2016
16. Dean, J., Ghemawat, S.: MapReduce: simplified data processing on large clusters. Commun. ACM **51**, 1–13 (2008)
17. Domingos, P., Hulten, G.: Mining high-speed data streams. In: Proceedings of the Sixth ACM SIGKDD International Conference on Knowledge Discovery and Data Mining, pp. 71–80 (2000)
18. Eggermont, J.: Data mining using genetic programming: classification and symbolic regression. Ph.D thesis (2005)
19. Gillick, D., Faria, A., DeNero, J.: MapReduce: distributed computing for machine learning. Berkley, 18 December 2006
20. Gunarathne, T., et al.: Cloud computing paradigms for pleasingly parallel biomedical applications. In: Proceedings of the 19th ACM International Symposium on High Performance Distributed Computing, Chicago, Illinois, pp. 460–469 (2010)
21. Guojun, L., Ming, Z., Fei, Y.: Large-scale social network analysis based on MapReduce. In: Proceedings of the International Conference on Computational Aspects of Social Networks, 2010, pp. 487–490 (2010)
22. Jennings, N.R., Wooldridge, M.: Applications of intelligent agents. In: Jennings, N.R., Wooldridge, M. (eds.) Intelligent Agents, pp. 3–28. New York, Springer (1998)
23. Koza, J.R., et al.: Genetic Programming IV. Routine Human-Competitive Machine Intelligence. Kluwer Academic Publishers, New York (2003)
24. Leyton-Brown, K., Shoham, Y.: Multiagent Systems: Algorithmic, Game-Theoretic, and Logical Foundations. Cambridge University Press, Cambridge (2008)
25. Li, H.X., Chosler, R.: Application of multilayered multi-agent data mining architecture to bank domain. In: Proceedings of the International Conference on Wireless Communications, Networking and Mobile Computing, pp. 6721–6724 (2007)
26. Mardani, S., Akbari, M.K., Sharifian, S.: Fraud detection in process aware information systems using MapReduce. In: Proceedings on Information and Knowledge Technology, pp. 88–91 (2014)
27. Marz, N., Warren, J.: Big Data - Principles and Best Practices of Scalable Realtime Data Systems. Manning Publications Co., New York (2014)
28. O'Leary, D.E.: Artificial intelligence and big data. IEEE Intell. Syst. **28**, 96–99 (2013)

29. Ostrowski, D.A.: MapReduce design patterns for social networking analysis. In: Proceedings of the International Conference on Semantic Computing, pp. 316–319 (2014)
30. Raymer, M.L., Punch, W.F., Goodman, E.D., Kuhn, L.A.: Genetic programming for improved data mining: application to the biochemistry of protein interactions. In: Proceedings of the 1st Conference on Genetic Programming, pp. 375–380. MIT Press, Cambridge (1996)

Harmony Search for Self-configuration of Fault–Tolerant and Intelligent Grids

Jerzy Balicki[1(✉)], Waldemar Korłub[2], Jacek Paluszak[2], and Maciej Tyszka[2]

[1] Faculty of Mathematics and Information Science,
Warsaw University of Technology, Koszykowa St. 75, 00-662 Warsaw, Poland
balicki@eti.pg.gda.pl
[2] Faculty of Telecommunications, Electronics and Informatics,
Gdańsk University of Technology, Narutowicza St. 11/12,
80-233 Gdańsk, Poland
waldemar.korlub@pg.gda.pl,
jpaluszak@gmail.com, tyszka.maciej@gmail.com

Abstract. In this paper, harmony search algorithms have been proposed to self-configuration of intelligent grids for big data processing. Self-configuration of computer grids lies in the fact that new computer nodes are automatically configured by software agents and then integrated into the grid. A base node works due to several configuration parameters that define some aspects of data communications and energy power consumption. We propose some optimization agents that are based on harmony search to find a suboptimal configuration of fault–tolerant grids processing big data. Criteria such as probability that all tasks meet their deadlines and also a reliability of grid are considered. Finally, some experimental results have been considered.

1 Introduction

An intelligent grid is supposed to manage its resources to meet the task requirements on the way to achieving the common objective. Self-configuration of computer grids lies in the fact that new computer nodes are automatically configured by software agents and then integrated into the grid. The whole process of self-configuration is similar to the "plug-and-play" rule for some operating systems. However, configuring agents launch connectivity and download some configuration parameters. If a new computer node is added to the middleware layer and powered on, it is instantly identified and registered by configuration agents.

A base node works due to several configuration parameters that define some aspects of data communications and energy power consumption. These parameters can be improved to change grid behavior, based on some administrator observations. Another way is to delegate this competences to optimization agents they find the most adjusted configuration to the workload and resource using. One of the most commonly used criterion of grid behavior is its reliability that should be maximized. The main dilemma is the fact that this problem is NP-hard and it is impossible to find an optimal configuration for hundreds of nodes.

K. Saeed and W. Homenda (Eds.): CISIM 2016, LNCS 9842, pp. 566–576, 2016.
DOI: 10.1007/978-3-319-45378-1_50

In the presented model, we propose some optimization agents that are based on harmony search to find a suboptimal configuration of fault–tolerant grids processing big data. A fault-tolerant grid deals with failures of its nodes and software where each node has some duplicated servers associated with its [38]. One node is the primary, and some associated nodes are dedicated for backup [18]. Tasks are performed by primary and backup servers, concurrently. Another model of grid is based on assumption that there are no fault-tolerant nodes. A grid node cooperates with other nodes as backups. In case of a node failing, all tasks allocated to this server are re-allocated to one of its backups. Some algorithms of resource using take into account the failure/repair rates and the fault-tolerant overheads. These algorithms can improve the grid performance mean-ingfully, but the quality of configuration and delay for its founding are still under construction [20, 42].

In this paper, an outlook of harmony search metaheuristics is discussed in Sect. 2. Moreover, specific aspects for big data are presented in Sect. 3. Especially, *Map-Reduce* model for BD processing is studied in Sect. 4. Then, intelligent agents based on harmony search for improvement of fault-tolerant measure are described in Sect. 5. Moreover, some outcomes from numerical experiments are interpreted in Sect. 6.

2   Outlook of Harmony Search Metaheuristics

Harmony search can be applied for self-configuration support of some fault-tolerant grids. Harmony search metaheuristics HS models phenomena related to the process of playing on musical instruments [41]. An optimization process can be compared to a process of selection the best sound while improvising jazz musicians. Similarly, a conductor of orchestra searches the best harmony of several instruments or a com-positor creates the best melody for different music lanes [1]. The HM concept was suggested by Geem [15, 45]. Figure 1 shows a diagram of the basic version of the HS metaheuristics [2].

The HS algorithm determines a solution for one-criterion optimization problem with continuous decision variables that can be formulated, as follows [4]:

$$\min_{x \in X} f(x), \tag{1}$$

where:

$f(x)$ – a value of an objective function f for solution $x \in X, f : \boldsymbol{R}^{J_{max}} \to \boldsymbol{R}$;

x – a vector of decision variables, $x = [x_1, \ldots, x_j, \ldots, x_{J_{max}}]^T$ for $l_j \leq x_j \leq u_j$, $j = \overline{1, J_{max}}$;

J_{max} – a number of decision variables;

X – a set of decision variables.

The lower limit vector is $l = [l_1, \ldots, l_j, \ldots, l_{J_{max}}]^T$ and the upper limit vector is $u = [u_1, \ldots, u_j, \ldots, u_{J_{max}}]^T$, wherein $l_j \in \boldsymbol{R}, u_j \in \boldsymbol{R}, l_j \leq u_j$ for $j = \overline{1, J_{max}}$. An initializa-tion the harmonic memory HM (Fig. 1) occurs after setting the following parameters:

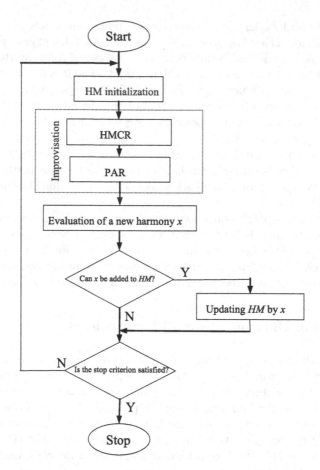

Fig. 1. A diagram of the harmony search algorithm [29]

- *HMS - Harmony Memory Size* [24];
- *HMCR - Harmony Memory Considering Rate* is the probability of a random event that the value of the decision variable during improvisation (constructing a solution) is drawn from the memory HM; an uniform distribution is assumed to draw;
- *PAR - Pitch Adjusting Rate* is the rate of the randomly selected decision variable;
- *NGmax - Number of Generations* (Improvisations);
- *BW - Bandwidth of Generations* that is the width of the interval to modify the value of the decision variable that is randomly selected from memory; the new value of the decision variable is modified by adding the value from the range $[-BW, BW]$.

In memory *HM*, there are stored *HMS* randomly generated solutions with J_{max} coordinates and the corresponding fitness function values *fitness(x)*. If restrictions are imposed on the solution, its efficiency is reduced by the appropriate punishment in case of violation of restrictions. The efficiency of each solution can be increased by an amount such that the accepted value of non-negative. The basic version of the harmony search algorithm has been repeatedly modified to adjust to solve some optimization problems [22].

3   Intelligent Agent Architecture for Big Data

Big data (an acronym BD) is related to databases with petabyte capacities 10^{15} B. 10 terabytes is a large capacity for a financial transaction system, but it is too small to test a web search engine. BD is uncooperative to work with using some relational database management systems like DB2, INGRES, Oracle, Sybase or SQL Server. Big data requires hundred thousand processors for data processing like supercomputers [36], grids [11] or clouds [8]. Especially, cloud architectures are preferred to BD processing because of commercial data centers with expensive information.

Tasks developed SQL-like queries to BD are massive parallel because the short time of a query performing is required. For instance, a query for multi-terabyte datasets at *BigQuery* service in *Google Cloud* is performed during few seconds. *BigQuery* service is scalable cloud like *IaaS Infrastructure as a Service*. Furthermore, this *RESTful* web service enables interactive analysis cooperating with *Google Storage* [16]. The most important tasks are related to analytics, capture, search, sharing, storage, and visualizing. Moreover, some BD mining tasks can be used to find predictions as well as some descriptive statistics tasks can be developed for business intelligence [23].

BD can be characterized by the 4Vs model due to high *volume*, extraordinary *velocity*, great data *variety*, and *veracity*. Data can be captured via Internet of Things from different sensors like smartphones, tablets, microphones, cameras, computers, radars, satellites, radio-telescopes and the other sensors. Moreover, data can be captured from social networks. A storage capacity can achieve many petabytes for one volume that is *high volume* [26]. *MongoDB* is one of perspective solutions for BD because the *NoSQL* database supports data stored to different nodes. Mongo DB can cooperate with massively parallel cluster with lots of CPUs, GPUs, RAM units and disks [27]. A crucial problem with BD is related to reading from a storage system to obtain the rapid answer on a complex query that is divided on some parallel operations acting on diverse data. Big data can be spread over some partitions that run on some separate modes with own table spaces, logs, and configurations. In that case, a query is performed on all partitions concurrently [35, 44].

In an experimental grid called *Comcute*, two kinds of intelligent tasks have been considered to implement a middleware layer [13]. This grid is dedicated to parallel computing with using volunteer computing. Agents for data management send data from source databases to distribution agents. Then, distribution agents cooperate with web computers to calculate results and return them to management agents. Both types of agents can autonomously move from one host to another to improve quality of grid resource using. Moreover, the other agents based on harmony search have been introduced to optimize big data processing regarding some fault-tolerant aspects. These harmony search schedulers can cooperate with distributors and managers to give them information about optimal workload in a grid [9, 10].

The lambda architecture is developed for real-time BD analysis [26]. The batch layer of this architecture supports offline data processing by *MapReduce* framework [39]. This layer produces batch views of data, which can be exposed to external applications (Fig. 2). The serving layer offers prepared views to clients. The speed layer is responsible for real-time processing of data streams. It analyses data that was not yet processed

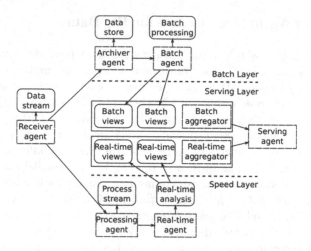

Fig. 2. Multi-agent real-time processing utilizing lambda architecture [37]

by the batch layer. Speed layer produces real-time views that can be coupled with batch views to create complete representation of the extracted knowledge [19].

The lambda architecture can be defined in terms of a heterogeneous multiagent system [37]. An implementation requires integration of a few components: one for batch processing, another one for serving views, a different solution for real-time stream analysis and a component that merges real-time views with batch views [43].

The use of multiagent environment will provide a common way for information exchange between different component and a common execution model [40]. The differences between individual components of the lambda architecture lead to inherently heterogeneous realizations so the ability to handle diversity in agent systems in another motivation for this approach [22].

4   Map-Reduce Model for Fault-Tolerant Grid

Grid and volunteer computing systems are different from super-computing systems because inexpensive hardware commodities have been widely deployed, which is helpful to the scalability. But it also brings a large number of hardware failures. Moreover, many machines constantly restart to update systems, which cause huge software failures [14]. Similarly, the popular cloud computing model *MapReduce* also has to overcome the failures [5, 7].

When a job consists of thousands tasks, the possibility of a few failed tasks is very high. Several fault-tolerant applications can be executed in the platform, which can use the result despite of some failed tasks. To support such fault-tolerant computing, an open source implementation of *MapReduce* can be applied. *Hadoop* has already provided the interface, by which the job can tolerate a given percentage of failed tasks. It was observed that optimizing the availability of individual task is not an effective approach for ensuring the high availability of these multi-task jobs [30].

However, *Hadoop* implicitly assume the nodes are homogeneous, but it doesn't hold in practice. These motivate to propose an optimal multi-task allocation scheme towards heterogeneous environments, which can tolerant a given percentage of failures to total tasks [28]. In this case the *reduce* function's responsibility is to sum the each *key's values* [34].

MapReduce is applied to solve several problems like large-scale machine learning for the *Google News*. Moreover, an extraction of data is used to produce reports of popular queries and extraction of geographical locations from a large corpus of web pages for localized search. In 2004, *Google* changed an indexing system that produces data used for web search service to system that used *MapReduce*. The new indexing system takes input documents that have been retrieved from a crawling system store as a set of files, and then they are processed by from five to ten *MapReduce* operations. It is easier to operate because of automatic resolving problems like machine failures, slow machines and networking hiccups [17, 25].

5 Harmony Search Agents for Local Grid Self-configuration

Intelligent agents can optimize a grid resource management for tasks related to big data queries. An agent based on harmony search metaheuristics AHS can reconfigure a local part of a grid. The whole grid is divided on zones and the AHS is assigned to its grid zone to support self-optimization of a system. The main part of AHS is a multi-objective scheduler for tasks from a middleware layer. This scheduler optimizes a probability that all tasks meet their deadlines, and the grid reliability [12]. We assume that each computer and each link between them are assumed to fail independently with exponential rates. It is preferred to allocate modules to computers on which failures are least likely to occur during the execution of task modules [3]. The rationale assumption is that repair and recovery times are largely implementation-dependent. Moreover, repair and recovery routines usually introduce too high time overheads to be used on-line for time-critical applications [6].

The overhead performing time of the task T_v by the computer $\pi_j \in \Pi = \{\pi_1, \ldots, \pi_j, \ldots, \pi_J\}$ is represented by t_{vj}. Let the computer π_j be failed independently due to an exponential distribution with rate λ_j. Computers can be allocated to nodes and also tasks can be assigned to them in purpose to maximize the reliability function R, as below [21]:

$$R(x) = \prod_{v=1}^{V} \prod_{i=1}^{I} \prod_{j=1}^{J} \exp(-\lambda_j t_{vj} x_{vi}^m x_{ij}^\pi), \tag{2}$$

where

$$x_{ij}^\pi = \begin{cases} 1 & \text{if } \pi_j \text{ is assigned to the } w_i, \\ 0 & \text{in the other case.} \end{cases}$$

$$x_{vi}^m = \begin{cases} 1 & \text{if task } T_v \text{ is assigned to } w_i, \\ 0 & \text{in the other case,} \end{cases}$$

$$(x^m, x^\pi) = [x_{11}^m, \ldots, x_{1I}^m, \ldots, x_{vi}^m, \ldots, x_{VI}^m, x_{11}^\pi, \ldots, x_{1J}^\pi, \ldots, x_{ij}^\pi, \ldots, x_{I1}^\pi, \ldots, x_{Ij}^\pi, \ldots, x_{IJ}^\pi]^T.$$

Figure 3 shows the relation between the measure of system reliability R and time of using this system for the chosen two-computer system for $\lambda_1 = 0.001$ [TU^{-1}] and $\lambda_2 = 0.002$ [TU^{-1}].

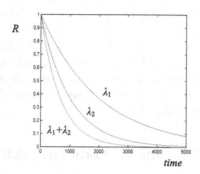

Fig. 3. The time-depended reliability of two-computer system

6 Task Scheduling Algorithm

Let the distributed application A_n starts running after λ_n and complete it before δ_n [31]. Figure 4 shows an example of the task flow graph for two applications. Task m_2 is performed with the probability q in a sub-graph denoted as OR (Fig. 4) and task m_3 – with the probability $(1-q)$. Task may be performed at the most L_{max} times in a sub-graph denoted as $Loop$, and each repetition of this module is performed with the probability p. The task flow graph is split on some instances to schedule tasks if the sub-graph OR appears. There are $2L_{max}$ instances for the task graph from Fig. 4. The instance, where task m_2 appears and task m_5 runs k times, occurs with the probability:

$$p_i = q(1-p)p^{k-1} \tag{3}$$

An allocation of modules to computers (x^m, x^π) creates possibility to schedule tasks for each computer. Times of task completions $(C_1, \ldots, C_v, \ldots, C_V)$ can be calculated for scheduled allocation modules to computers x. Let d_v represents the completion deadline for the vth task. If $C_v \leq d_v$, then the time constraint is satisfied what can be written as $\xi(d_v - C_v) = 1$. The state of deadline constraints regarding the ith instance of the flow graph with the set of tasks marked M_i is determined, as below [32]:

$$S_i = \prod_{m_v \in M_i} \xi(d_v - C_v(x)). \tag{4}$$

Probability that all tasks meet their deadlines for K instances of the flow graph is calculated, as follows [33]:

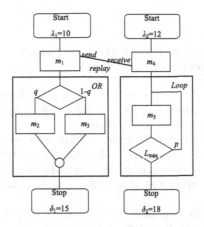

Fig. 4. A flow graph for two applications

$$P_D(x) = \sum_{i=1}^{K} p_i \prod_{m_v \in M_i} \xi(d_v - C_v(x)).\tag{5}$$

Figure 5 shows an example of a compromise configuration for its middleware zone in the *Comcute* grid that was found by the agent based on the harmony search for its area consisted on 14 modules divided among 2 computers.

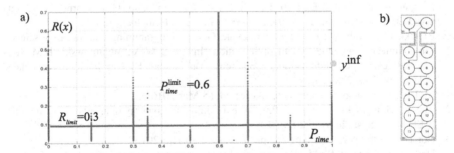

Fig. 5. A compromise configuration in the Comcute grid: (a) criterion space (b) a solution

7 Concluding Remarks and Future Work

Intelligent agents in the middleware of grid can significantly support efficiency of fault-tolerant self-configuration in grids. Agents based on harmony search can solve NP-hard multi-objective optimization problem of grid resource using to improve the level of fault-tolerance.

Our future works will focus on testing the other AI algorithms to find fault-tolerant configurations. Moreover, quantum-inspired algorithm can support big data, too [7].

References

1. Afshari, S., Aminshahidy, B., Pishvaie, M.R.: Application of an improved harmony search algorithm in well placement optimization using streamline simulation. J. Petrol. Sci. Eng. **78**, 664–678 (2011)
2. Ahmed, A.M., Bakar, A.A., Hamdan, A.R.: Harmony search algorithm for optimal word size in symbolic time series representation. In: Proceedings of Conference on Data Mining and Optimization, Malaysia, pp. 57–62 (2011)
3. Ajith, A.P., Murthy, C.S.R.: Algorithms for reliability-oriented module allocation in distributed computing systems. J. Syst. Softw. **40**, 125–138 (1998)
4. Al-Betar, M.A., Khader, A.T., Zaman, M.: University course timetabling using a hybrid harmony search metaheuristic algorithm. IEEE Trans. Syst. Man Cybern. Part C Appl. Rev. **42**, 66–681 (2012)
5. Apache Hadoop. http://hadoop.apache.org/. Accessed 15 Mar 2016
6. Balicki, J.: Negative selection with ranking procedure in tabu-based multi-criterion evolutionary algorithm for task assignment. In: Alexandrov, V.N., Albada, G.D., Sloot, P.M., Dongarra, J. (eds.) ICCS 2006. LNCS, vol. 3993, pp. 863–870. Springer, Heidelberg (2006)
7. Balicki, J.: An adaptive quantum-based multiobjective evolutionary algorithm for efficient task assignment in distributed systems. In: Mastorakis N., et al. (eds.) Recent Advances in Computer Engineering. Proceedings of the 13th WSEAS International Conference on Computers, Rhodes, Greece, pp. 417–422 (2009)
8. Balicki, J., Korłub, W., Szymański, J., Zakidalski, M.: Big data paradigm developed in volunteer grid system with genetic programming scheduler. In: Rutkowski, L., Korytkowski, M., Scherer, R., Tadeusiewicz, R., Zadeh, L.A., Zurada, J.M. (eds.) ICAISC 2014, Part I. LNCS, vol. 8467, pp. 771–782. Springer, Heidelberg (2014)
9. Balicki, J., Kitowski, Z.: Multicriteria evolutionary algorithm with tabu search for task assignment. In: Zitzler, E., Deb, K., Thiele, L., Coello Coello, C.A., Corne, D.W. (eds.) EMO 2001. LNCS, vol. 1993, pp. 373–384. Springer, Heidelberg (2001)
10. Balicki, J., Korlub, W., Krawczyk, H., et al.: Genetic programming with negative selection for volunteer computing system optimization. In: Paja, W.A., Wilamowski, B.M. (eds.) Proceedings the 6th International Conference on Human System Interactions, Gdańsk, Poland, pp. 271–278 (2013)
11. BOINC. http://boinc.berkeley.edu/. Accessed 15 Mar 2016
12. Cao, L., Gorodetsky, V., Mitkas, P.A.: Agent mining: the synergy of agents and data mining. IEEE Intell. Syst. **24**, 64–72 (2009)
13. Comcute. http://comcute.eti.pg.gda.pl/. Accessed 25 Apr 2016
14. Dean, J., Ghemawat, S.: MapReduce: simplified data processing on large clusters. Commun. ACM **51**, 1–13 (2008)
15. Geem, Z.W., Kim, J.H., Loganathan, G.V.: A new heuristic optimization algorithm: harmony search. Simulation **76**, 60–68 (2001)
16. Gunarathne, T., et al.: Cloud computing paradigms for pleasingly parallel biomedical applications. In: Proceedings of International Symposium on High Performance Distributed Computing, Chicago, Illinois, pp. 460–469 (2010)
17. Guojun, L., Ming, Z., Fei, Y.: Large-scale social network analysis based on MapReduce. In: Proceedings of International Conference on Computational Aspects of Social Networks, pp. 487–490 (2010)

18. Huang, Z., Wang, C., Liu, L., Peng, Y.: Improve availability of fault-tolerant computing: optimal multi-task allocation in MapReduce. In: Proceedings of International Conference on Computer Science and Education, pp. 249–254 (2012)
19. Jennings, N.R., Wooldridge, M.: Applications of intelligent agents. In: Jennings, N.R., Wooldridge, M. (eds.) Agent Technology, pp. 3–28. Springer, New York (1998)
20. Kafil, M., Ahmad, I.: Optimal task assignment in heterogeneous distributed computing systems. IEEE Concurr. 6, 42–51 (1998)
21. Kartik, S., Murthy, C.S.R.: Task allocation algorithms for maximizing reliability of distributed computing systems. IEEE Trans. Comput. 46, 719–724 (1997)
22. Leyton-Brown, K., Shoham, Y.: Multiagent Systems: Algorithmic, Game-Theoretic, and Logical Foundations. Cambridge University Press, Cambridge (2008)
23. Li, H.X., Chosler, R.: Application of multilayered multi-agent data mining architecture to bank domain. In: Proceedings of International Conference on Wireless Communications, Networking and Mobile Computing, pp. 6721–6724 (2007)
24. Manjarres, D., et al.: A survey on applications of the harmony search algorithm. Eng. Appl. Artif. Intell. 26, 1818–1831 (2013)
25. Mardani, S., Akbari, M.K., Sharifian, S.: Fraud detection in process aware information systems using MapReduce. In: Proceedings on Information and Knowledge Technology, pp. 88–91 (2014)
26. Marz, N., Warren, J.: Big data - Principles and best practices of scalable realtime data systems (2014)
27. O'Leary, D.E.: Artificial intelligence and big data. IEEE Intell. Syst. 28, 96–99 (2013)
28. Ostrowski, D.A.: MapReduce design patterns for social networking analysis. In: Proceedings of International Conference on Semantic Computing, pp. 316–319 (2014)
29. Paluszak, J.: Optimizing the use of resources in distributed systems with grid architecture. Ph.D. dissertation, Gdańsk University of Technology, Gdańsk (2015). (in Polish)
30. Qiu, X., et al.: Using MapReduce technologies in bioinformatics and medical informatics. In: Proceedings of the International Conference for High Performance Computing, Networking, Storage and Analysis, Portland (2009)
31. Sarvari, H., Zamanifar, K.: A self-adaptive harmony search algorithm for engineering and reliability problems. In: Second International Conference on Computer Intelligence, Modelling and Simulation, pp. 59–64 (2010)
32. Schneidewind, N.: Allocation and analysis of reliability: multiple levels: system, subsystem, and module. Innov. Syst. Softw. Eng. 2, 121–136 (2006). Springer, London
33. Shatz, S.M., Wang, J.P.: Models and algorithms for reliability-oriented task-allocation in redundant distributed-computer systems. IEEE Trans. Reliab. 38, 16–27 (1989)
34. Shvachko, K., et al.: The Hadoop distributed file system. In: MSST, pp. 1–10 (2010)
35. Snijders, C., Matzat, U., Reips, U.-D.: 'Big Data': big gaps of knowledge in the field of Internet. Int. J. Internet Sci. 7, 1–5 (2012)
36. Shwe, T., Win, A.: A fault tolerant approach in cluster computing system. In: The 5th International Conference on Electrical Engineering/Electronics, Computer, Telecommunication and Information Technology, vol. 1, pp. 149–152 (2008)
37. Twardowski, B., Ryzko, D.: Multi-agent architecture for real-time big data processing. In: Proceedings of International Conference on Web Intelligence and Intelligent Agent Technologies, vol. 3, pp. 333–337 (2014)
38. Varvarigou, T., Trotter, J.: Module replication for fault-tolerant real-time distributed systems. IEEE Trans. Reliab. 47(1), 8–18 (1998)
39. Vavilapalli, V.K.: Apache Hadoop Yarn: yet another resource negotiator. In: Proceedings of the 4th Annual Symposium on Cloud Computing, New York, USA, pp. 5:1–5:16 (2013)

40. Verbrugge, T., Dunin-Kêplicz, B.: Teamwork in Multi-Agent Systems. A formal Approach. Wiley, London (2010)
41. Wang, L., Li, L.P.: A coevolutionary differential evolution with harmony search for reliability-redundancy optimization. Expert Syst. Appl. **39**, 5271–5278 (2012)
42. Wêglarz, J., Błażewicz, J., Kovalyov, M.: Preemptable malleable task scheduling problem. IEEE Trans. Comput. **55**, 486–490 (2006)
43. Wooldridge, M.: Introduction to MultiAgent Systems. Wiley, London (2002)
44. Zhou, D., et al.: Multi-agent distributed data mining model based on algorithm analysis and task prediction. In: Proceedings 2nd International Conference on Information Engineering and Computer Science, pp. 1–4 (2010)
45. Zou, D., et al.: A novel global harmony search algorithm for reliability problems. Comput. Ind. Eng. **58**, 307–316 (2010)

A Study on Fuzzy Cognitive Map Optimization Using Metaheuristics

Aleksander Cisłak[1]([⊠]), Władysław Homenda[2], and Agnieszka Jastrzębska[1]

[1] Faculty of Mathematics and Information Science,
Warsaw University of Technology,
ul. Koszykowa 75, 00-662 Warsaw, Poland
{a.cislak,a.jastrzebska}@mini.pw.edu.pl
[2] Faculty of Economics and Informatics in Vilnius, University of Bialystok,
Kalvariju g. 135, LT-08221 Vilnius, Lithuania
homenda@mini.pw.edu.pl

Abstract. Fuzzy Cognitive Maps (FCMs) are a framework based on weighted directed graphs which can be used for system modeling. The relationships between the concepts are stored in graph edges and they are expressed as real numbers from the $[-1, 1]$ interval (called weights). Our goal was to evaluate the effectiveness of non-deterministic optimization algorithms which can calculate weight matrices (i.e. collections of all weights) of FCMs for synthetic and real-world time series data sets. The best results were reported for Differential Evolution (DE) with recombination based on 3 random individuals, as well as Particle Swarm Optimization (PSO) where each particle is guided by its neighbors and the best particle. The choice of the algorithm was not crucial for maps of size roughly up to 10 nodes, however, the difference in performance was substantial (in the orders of magnitude) for bigger matrices.

1 Introduction

Real-world phenomena modeling requires a framework that would not be hindered a by variety and diversity of relevant information. Standard methods, for instance for time series modeling, are predominantly numerical and are not well-fitted to process data in a form different than a sequence of numbers. An impressive range of fuzzy and granular models has emerged as a remedy for such issues. Fuzzy Cognitive Maps (FCMs) have been proposed by Kosko[11] in 1986 as an alternative framework for phenomena modeling.

FCMs represent knowledge in the form of a directed graph. Phenomena are stored in vertices, while edges represent their relationships. These relationships are expressed as real numbers from the $[-1, 1]$ interval. Weight matrix (or connection matrix) is a formal representation of each FCM as it gathers all weights in the map. In our research we focus on the application of FCMs to time series modeling, a domain relatively new as it has emerged in the 2000s [20].

In this paper, we present a study on a very important aspect of modeling with FCMs, namely on weight matrix learning procedures. In general, the core of each FCM, the weight matrix, can be constructed in three ways: (a) manually,

K. Saeed and W. Homenda (Eds.): CISIM 2016, LNCS 9842, pp. 577–588, 2016.
DOI: 10.1007/978-3-319-45378-1_51

by human experts; (b) automatically, using optimization algorithms; (c) with the combination of the two aforementioned options.

The first and the last option often turn out to be inapplicable, as they require human expert knowledge. A convenient alternative is offered by automated approaches that are able to determine the shape of the weight matrix. In particular, the literature of the topic recommends the application of various metaheuristic optimization procedures [15,19]. Inspired by the current developments in the studies on FCM optimization, we present a comparative study on various algorithms, which are presented later in this paper.

The study is supported by a series of empirical experiments that let us investigate and compare the quality of obtained maps. The experiments were conducted for a few time series data sets (containing both real-world and synthetic data) and for maps of various sizes. In contrast to the studies on FCM optimization reported in the literature, in our experiments we also process very large maps, with up to 27 nodes (which turned out to be crucial in terms of algorithm performance). The key novel element introduced in this paper is a thorough comparison of the effectiveness of various optimization methods. Also, to the best of our knowledge, this is the first paper where we apply Harmony Search and Improved Harmony Search to FCM optimization.

2 Related Works

The need for automated methods for FCM weight matrix construction coincided with a rapid development of various search metaheuristics. Researchers recognized opportunities offered by this family of algorithms and applied them to FCM optimization.

Indeed, there are several important arguments speaking in favor of this approach. First, FCMs are fuzzy models and the key limitation of search metaheuristics, which is a lack of guarantee for the global optimal solution, is not a major concern. Hence, when it comes to FCMs, it is common to model phenomena with an "acceptably" good accuracy. In other words, there is no need for the best solution as long as we can arrive at a one which is "good enough". Secondly, weight matrix optimization is a difficult problem and standard optimization procedures are inadequate to handle it. Last but not least, metaheuristics are attractive: they are easy to use, they make few or no assumptions about the problem being optimized, and they provide a relatively good performance. Having the above in mind, more and more heuristic search algorithms have been adapted to FCM optimization. However, many of the latest contributions mostly build on the first methodologies that have been proposed.

The objective is to form a weight matrix by an iterative search procedure. The initial weight matrix is filled in randomly, which eliminates the necessity for involving human experts in the learning process. Algorithms explore the search space in order to find a weight matrix that satisfies to the greatest extent given fitness criterion. Usually, such fitness criterion is expressed as an error between map's responses and target values:

$$\min_{\mathbf{W}=[w_{ij}],\,w_{ij}\in[-1,1],\,i,j=1,\ldots,c} error\,(\mathbf{Y},\mathbf{T}) \tag{1}$$

where $\mathbf{Y} = [y_{ij}]$, $y_{ij} \in [0,1]$, $i = 1,\ldots,c$, $j = 1,\ldots,N$ is map's output. $error$ is a measure of discrepancy between FCM's outputs ($\mathbf{Y}$) and desired target values, $\mathbf{T} = [t_{ij}]$, $t_{ij} \in [0,1]$, $i = 1,\ldots,c$, $j = 1,\ldots,N$. N is the number of observations, and c is the number of nodes in the map. The literature-based approaches often use Mean Squared Error (MSE) [15,19]:

$$MSE = \frac{1}{N \cdot c} \cdot \sum_{j=1}^{N}\sum_{i=1}^{c}(y_{ij} - t_{ij})^2, \tag{2}$$

where y_{ij} denotes map's ij-th response and t_{ij} is a corresponding target value.

Koulouriotis et al. [12] proposed the first methodology in 2001 that joined search heuristics with FCM learning. The authors applied Evolution Strategies to FCM learning in a case study of two FCMs, both with 6 nodes. Stach et al. [21] published in 2005 another important attempt at employing search heuristics for the benefits of FCM learning. Cited authors applied Real-coded Genetic Algorithm (RCGA) to develop FCM weight matrix. Presented results for maps with up to 10 nodes confirm the soundness of this approach.

Briefly after the appearance of FCM learning algorithms employing genetic approaches, Parsopoulos et al. [17] applied Particle Swarm Optimization (PSO) to automated FCM learning. The authors modeled an exemplary industrial control problem: a tank and three valves that guard the level of a liquid. The fitness function was determined accordingly to fit the application domain and it represented a combination of conditions for the tank and the valves that stabilize the industrial process. Further applications of PSO and related swarm intelligence algorithms to FCM learning have been documented [13,15]. Also, a few other successful methods for FCM learning using heuristics other than ones already discussed have been proposed, e.g., Big Bang-Big Crunch [16].

3   Approach

Our goal was to determine the performance of various non-deterministic algorithms in the context of optimizing FCM weight matrix. Regular approaches turn out to be rather ill-suited to this problem. Let us clarify that we used a popular classical algorithm Limited-memory BFGS-B [4]. The limitations concern first and foremost large maps, with 17 nodes (289 weights) and more. In our experiments we have observed that as we add more nodes, a classical optimization algorithm starts to set more and more weights to its pre-defined upper and lower bounds (-1 and 1). Such a result is not acceptable for the model assumptions of FCMs and it produces high error values. Hence, a more suited approach is required.

The challenge is caused by the lack of a feasible exact algorithm that could ensure reaching a *global* minimum (using, e.g., an exhaustive combinatorial search) owing to the complexity of the problem. However, with metaheuristic approaches there still exists a risk of reaching a *local* minimum, and there is no a priori approach to determine which evolutionary approach is better suited, which is the motivation behind our experimental evaluation.

All algorithms which were used for the optimization fall into the category of *population-based* algorithms, and most of them can be also described as *evolutionary*, since they feature operations such as breeding, mutation, and selection based on utility. Popular terms include a population, which describes a set of all individuals (candidate solutions) that are considered during a current iteration of the algorithm, and fitness, which describes the utility of an individual. An individual is essentially a multidimensional vector $V = [v_1, \ldots, v_d]$ which consists of a fixed number of features. The number of dimensions, d, usually corresponds to certain properties of real-world objects, or, in our case, the size of the FCM.

Since in our case the fitness describes an average error, we deal with a minimization problem. When we mention a better or worse fitness value, it means that it is associated with a lower or a higher fitness value, respectively (the terms error and fitness are used interchangeably). Similarly, a better individual is the one associated with a lower fitness.

Typical operation of a population-based algorithm proceeds as follows:

1. The initial population containing n random individuals is created.
2. The fitness of each individual is calculated.
3. A predefined number (e) of individuals with the best fitness is preserved (so-called elite). Afterwards, the population is refreshed, i.e. typically $n - e$ individuals are replaced with new (random) ones, although this might depend on fitness values (e.g., new individuals might enter the population only if they are better than the previous ones).
4. The population is updated using algorithm-specific tools – this can consist in, e.g., mutating the features, that is introducing random changes.
5. The search continues until a desired number of iterations is performed. In the end, the individual with the overall best fitness is returned.

Specific algorithms which were evaluated are listed below:

- **Artificial Bee Colony (ABC)** [10]
  ABC is based on the behavior of bees in their natural habitat. Each individual is called a bee, and a current state of the feature vector is referred to as a position. There exist 3 kinds of bees:
  - Employed bees: they modify their positions by mutating single features.
  - Unemployed bees: they randomly select one of the positions of the employed bees (the better the fitness of the position, the higher the probability that this position is selected) and mutate it.
  - Scout bees: they try to occupy a new random position.
    Each new position in the ABC algorithm is retained only if it turns out to be better than the original one. Main parameters include the ratios of the number of bees of each kind in the population.

- **Differential Evolution (DE)** [22]
  DE is closely related to the Genetic Algorithm, however, it uses various strategies for crossing individuals rather than the standard crossover operation, and explicit mutation is usually omitted. These differ mostly in the number of selected individuals, sampling strategies, as well as the method for combining the features. After testing selected strategies, we have decided to opt for the one which combines 3 individuals (V_1, V_2, V_3) sampled randomly from the current population. With a given probability, each feature is replaced with a new value according the following formula: $V[i] = V_1[i] + \delta(V_2[i] - V_3[i])$, where δ is a fixed parameter.
- **Genetic Algorithm (GA)**
  GA is based on two basic operations – crossover, which takes two individuals and combines them into one by mixing their features together, and mutation, which assigns a random value to one of the features. These operations correspond directly to changes in the genetic material which happen in the real world. The parameters consist of a probability of a crossover between an individual and another randomly selected individual, and a probability that an element is mutated.
- **Harmony Search (HS)** [8]
  HS was inspired by a group of musicians who use improvisation (that is, essentially, mutations of musical notes) in order to find the optimal sound combination. During a single iteration, each harmony (individual) is improvised (mutated) and it replaces the current worst harmony if it produces a better fitness score. Each feature $V[i]$ is then either replaced with a random value, or it is replaced with another feature $V_x[i]$ from a randomly selected harmony V_x from the current generation. Moreover, if one of the existing features is selected, its value is changed (it is "pitch-adjusted") by a random value from a given interval of size $\delta(max - min)$ (in our case $min = -1$ and $max = 1$). The parameters describe the probabilities of mutations.
- **Improved Harmony Search (IHS)** [14]
  IHS is based directly on harmony search and it strives to fine-tune its parameters. According to authors, effectiveness of the original algorithm might be improved when, for each consecutive iteration, the probability that a mutation occurs increases, however, the rate of change decreases. This means that at the beginning the algorithm causes the features to take fewer longer leaps, and at the end there are more frequent but smaller changes.
- **Particle Swarm Optimization (PSO)** [5]
  PSO consists of multiple particles (individuals), which change the position in the search space. The maximum value of this change is determined by the speed of a particle in question, and it can be influenced by other particles (e.g., k of its neighbors or the best particle found so far). We have investigated a simple PSO variant, where the particles explore the search space on their own, that is they are not influenced by other particles, as well as a more complicated variant from the cran library [3] (we refer to it as informed PSO), which takes into account both the position of the best particle as well as k neighbors (where $k = \lfloor 1 - (1 - (1 - \frac{1}{n}))^3 \rfloor$ for the population of size n).

4   Time Series Modeling with Fuzzy Cognitive Maps

In this section we briefly present the necessary formalisms related to FCM construction in order to present a self-contained experimental study on FCM optimization.

In a nutshell, FCM is represented by its weight matrix $\mathbf{W}$ which is used to iteratively model the behavior of phenomena. On the input to the map we pass current activation values, and the map responds with an output. Ideally, map's response is as close to the actual state of phenomena (the target) as possible. The input corresponds to the i-th discrete time point, while the output corresponds to the $i + 1$-th time point.

A single run of an FCM (single input-output) is described with an input activation vector $\mathbf{x}$, $\mathbf{x} = [x_1, x_2, \ldots, x_c]^T$, $x_i \in [0, 1]$. Map's response is a vector $\mathbf{y} = [y_1, y_2, \ldots, y_c]^T$, $y_i \in [0, 1]$. In order to calculate the i-th element of the output vector we apply the following formula:

$$y_i = f\left(\sum_{j=1}^{c} w_{ij} \cdot x_j\right) \tag{3}$$

for $i = 1, 2, \ldots, c$. f is a sigmoid function endowed with a steepness parameter $\tau > 0$:

$$f(u) = \frac{1}{1 + e^{-\tau u}} \tag{4}$$

The greater the τ, the more the shape of f resembles the unit step function. Here, $\tau = 5$ was assumed, which was based on experimental studies and on the literature review, where the majority of researchers assume the same settings [19, 20].

When the processing concerns a sequence of N activation vectors (N observations), we gather them in an activation matrix that is denoted as $\mathbf{X} = [\mathbf{x}_1, \ldots, \mathbf{x}_N]$, where $\mathbf{x}_i$ is an i-th activation vector. Consistently, the FCM responds with matrix of outputs ($\mathbf{Y} = [\mathbf{y}_1, \ldots, \mathbf{y}_N]$), which is of size $c \times N$.

Modeling with an FCM consists of the following steps:

1. FCM design,
2. FCM optimization,
3. FCM interpretation.

The first step revolves around the process of node extraction for the map, and it is a crucial point which determines the quality of the map. A general concern is that the more nodes we have in a map, the more specific model we obtain. A corollary of this is that when we add a node to the map, we should expect that its numerical accuracy will increase. The downside of an increased map size is that it affects not only the ease of interpretation, but also a computational effort needed to optimize such a map. Let us stress that number of edges (elements in the weight matrix) grows quadratically, but an average time needed to optimize such map using any metaheuristic algorithm grows faster than quadratically.

There exists a key parameter of a time series representation for modeling with FCMs: concept's dimensionality. Dimension corresponds to the number of consecutive time points represented by each concept. For instance, if the dimensionality is equal to 2, then each concept represents a pair: current time series value ($z_i \in \mathcal{R}$, $i = 2, \ldots$) and change ($\delta z_i = z_i - z_{i-1}$). If dimensionality equals 3, then each concept represents current value (z_i), change (δz_i), and change of change ($\delta\delta z_i = \delta z_i - \delta z_{i-1} = z_i - 2z_{i-1} + z_{i-2}$). The same representation has been applied by Stach et al. [20], who published a fundamental paper for the time series modeling method analyzed in this study.

Our previous research shows that the larger the dimension, the better numerical accuracy of predictions. However, the gain diminishes as the dimensionality grows. Having in mind that FCMs are models constructed to be interpreted and applied by human beings, concept dimensionality equal to 2 or 3 is a very reasonable choice, especially since we may easily represent such a space visually.

A detailed elaboration on the issues of FCM design has been presented in our previous paper [9]. At this point let us assume that we are proceeding with a task of time series modeling and we are equipped with the following: (a) a set of c concepts and (b) a set of training and testing data sets consisting of input activations $\mathbf{X}$ and targets $\mathbf{T}$.

In this paper we do not dwell further on this topic, as the focus in on the second step: FCM optimization. The aim is to construct a weight matrix $\mathbf{W}$ of size $c \times c$ that provides the smallest possible MSE (as defined in Formula 2). FCM exploration is as described in Formula 3. The time series that we model was elevated to the level of concepts and hence the modeling procedure operates on the level of concepts. In a typical scenario (as in this paper), concepts are realized with fuzzy sets, and we predict membership degrees to the extracted concepts in each discrete time point. With such assumptions we move towards the empirical section of this article, where we employ and compare a suite of different heuristic search algorithms in order to construct FCM weight matrix.

5   Experimental Results

Let us note that the problems in question are very demanding from the computational point of view, as a single run on all 4 of our data sets requires at least several days even on a modern multithreaded machine. Still, the experiments were conducted a few times and the results were consistent with one another. In fact, the relative differences between consecutive runs were surprisingly small, namely less than a few percent, and they were often negligible.

Our implementation is mostly based on the tools provided by the DEAP library [7] for Python. Moreover, we have also implemented the Genetic Algorithm from scratch in order to rule out a possible dependency on the library, and the results turned out to be similar. We have investigated 4 data sets, two of which represent real-world data (Bicup, Rainfall), and 2 synthetic ones (Synth3, Synth10); see Appendix A for more information. As regards the parameters, we have used similar values to those suggested in the literature [8, 10, 14, 18]; consult Appendix B for a complete list.

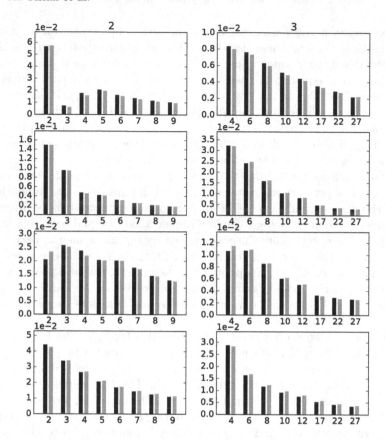

Fig. 1. Results for Differential Evolution (DE) which managed to minimize the error as the matrix size increased. Four consecutive rows correspond to each of the data sets: Synth3, Synth10, Bicup, and Rainfall (top to bottom), whereas the columns correspond to the dimensionality of data samples (consult Sect. 4 for more information). Values on the x-axis of each subplot refer to matrix sizes, and values on the y-axes describe the error (i.e. fitness in our case). Training set errors are indicated with black bars, and test set errors are indicated with grey bars.

Our results can be summarized as follows: for this particular problem class, the best effectiveness was achieved by *Differential Evolution* (DE, consult Fig. 1) and *informed PSO*. We also present the results for Improved Harmony Search (IHS) in Fig. 2. Results for other algorithms are omitted, since they demonstrate the same tendencies as the ones presented in the figures, but with higher error values (informed PSO with respect to DE and the remaining algorithms with respect to IHS).

It is worth noticing that the algorithms which managed to continue decreasing the error value as the matrix size increased were also the ones which reported overall the smallest error values. Moreover, let us note that almost all algorithms (with the exception of ABC) managed to decrease the error up to a certain point,

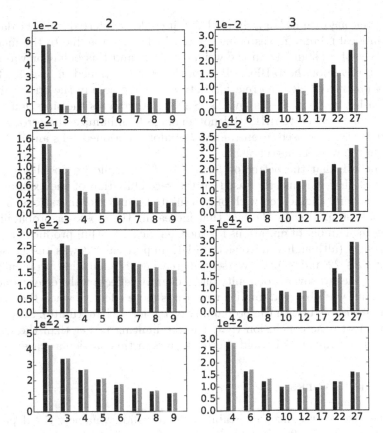

Fig. 2. Results for Improved Harmony Search (IHS) which was mostly successful only up to the matrix size of 10. Four consecutive rows correspond to each of the data sets: Synth3, Synth10, Bicup, and Rainfall (top to bottom), whereas the columns correspond to the dimensionality of data samples (consult Sect. 4 for more information). Values on the x-axis of each subplot refer to matrix sizes, and values on y-axes describe the error (i.e. fitness in our case). Training set errors are indicated with black bars, and test set errors are indicated with grey bars.

roughly matrix size 10, and in these cases the relative differences between error values were rather insignificant. This observation is consistent with the results reported by other authors, referred to in Sect. 2. Beyond this point, and especially for the largest matrices, the error value actually increased, despite a larger (i.e. more precise, at least in theory) amount of information describing the model. This leads us to the conclusion that the choice of the optimizing algorithm is not significant for smaller matrix sizes (in which case even the aforementioned L-BFGS-B approach was successful, while also being faster than population-based algorithms), however, it can be a true game changer for bigger matrices. The biggest relative differences in error values were observed for the 27-node matrix, and for some algorithms they ranged up to two orders of magnitude.

For some algorithms (e.g., simple PSO) it could be inferred from the data that a certain local minimum was being approached. This was due to the increasing appearance of -1 s and 1 s in the weight matrix, and this behavior was similar to one observed for the L-BFGS-B algorithm (as mentioned in Sect. 3). In that case, we observed a clear correlation between an increase in the error value and an increasing number of -1 s and 1 s. Still, in other cases the situation was not so clear, for instance the IHS did not manage to minimize the error value as the matrix size increased, even though the aforementioned -1 s and 1 s did not appear in the weight matrix at all.

We believe that the better performance of DE could be possibly explained by the fact that it is mostly based on the recombination of the existing population members, augmented with only a limited number of mutations. This can be partially supported by the fact that increasing the crossover probability and lowering the number of mutations for the Genetic Algorithm produced relatively better results (although still worse than DE, in particular it was unsuccessful for maps of sizes 22 and 27). Conversely, increasing the mutation probability and decreasing the crossover probability had a negative effect on the error value. Similar behavior was observed for HS, which was more effective when the mutation was almost disabled (with the probability of 1 % for each attribute). Surprisingly, this leads us to the conclusion that it is the limiting rather than the widening of the search radius which yields better results in this particular case.

6   Future Works

We would like to recognize a certain threat to validity, namely the dependence on parameter values. It is not feasible to perform exhaustive parameter tuning for this particular problem due to computational constraints. Moreover, there exist certain drawbacks associated with such tuning, explored in detail by, e.g., Eiben et al. [6]. For this reason, we plan to investigate certain parameter control methods [6] (one of the algorithms that we have evaluated, namely IHS, is an example of such a method) as future work. It would be also advantageous to extend the scope of the study onto other real-world as well as synthetic time series data samples.

Appendix A

The following data sets were used in the empirical study:

- synthetic time series (**Synth3**) based on sequence (2,6,8),
- synthetic time series (**Synth10**) based on sequence (1,5,7,3,9,9,3,7,5,1),
- real-world time series **Bicup**,
- real-world time series **Rainfall**.

Synthetic time series were constructed by replication of a base sequence so that the entire set had 3,000 elements. Then, a random distortion taken from the normal distribution with mean 0 and standard deviation 0.7 was added to each value.

Bicup time series describes the number of passenger arrivals at a subway bus terminal. Rainfall time series contains information on daily precipitation [1,2].

Appendix B

This appendix describes parameter values for each evaluated algorithm; for detailed information regarding these parameters we refer the reader to original articles. For the description of the algorithms, consult Sect. 3. The number of iterations was set to 200 for all algorithms (a larger number was unnecessary, since in most cases the improvements in fitness values were non-existent or negligible beyond this point), and the population size was equal to 100 individuals (with the exception of informed PSO, which uses its fine-tuned, custom parameters).

- **ABC**: employed bee ratio = 0.5, abandon limit = 3.
- **DE**: $\delta = 0.25$, mutation probability = 0.5.
- **GA**: two-point crossover probability = 0.2, attribute mutation probability = 0.05, tournament size = 10, elitism rate = 0.25.
- **HS**: random value probability = 0.1, pitch adjustment probability = 0.3, $\delta = 0.01$.
- **IHS**: pitch adjustment probability $\in [0.1, 0.9]$, delta $\in [0.0001, 0.75]$.
- **PSO (simple)**: minimum speed = $min/4$, maximum speed = $max/4$, (where $min = -1$ and $max = 1$), $\phi = 1.5$.

References

1. Bicup time series. http://robjhyndman.com/tsdldata/data/bicup2006.dat. Accessed 11 Jan 2016
2. Rainfall time series. http://robjhyndman.com/tsdldata/data/rainfall.dat. Accessed 11 Jan 2016
3. Bendtsen, C.: Package 'PSO'. https://cran.r-project.org/web/packages/pso/pso.pdf. Accessed 1 Apr 2016
4. Byrd, R.H., Lu, P., Nocedal, J., Zhu, C.: A limited memory algorithm for bound constrained optimization. SIAM J. Sci. Comput. **16**, 1190–1208 (1995)
5. Eberhart, R., Kennedy, J.: A new optimizer using particle swarm theory. In: Proceedings of the Sixth International Symposium on Micro Machine and Human Science, New York, NY, vol. 1, pp. 39–43. (1995)
6. Eiben, A.E., Hinterding, R., Michalewicz, Z.: Parameter control in evolutionary algorithms. IEEE Trans. Evol. Comput. **3**(2), 124–141 (1999)
7. Fortin, F.-A., De Rainville, F.-M., Gardner, M.-A., Parizeau, M., Gagné, C.: DEAP: evolutionary algorithms made easy. J. Mach. Learn. Res. **13**, 2171–2175 (2012)
8. Geem, Z.W., Kim, J., Loganathan, G.V.: A new heuristic optimization algorithm: harmony search. Simulation **76**(2), 60–68 (2001)

9. Homenda, W., Jastrzebska, A., Pedrycz, W.: Design of fuzzy cognitive maps for modeling time series. IEEE Trans. Fuzzy Syst. **24**(1), 120–130 (2016)
10. Karaboga, D., Basturk, B.: A powerful and efficient algorithm for numerical function optimization: artificial bee colony (ABC) algorithm. J. Global Optim. **39**(3), 459–471 (2007)
11. Kosko, B.: Fuzzy cognitive maps. Int. J. Man-Mach. Stud. **24**, 65–75 (1986)
12. Koulouriotis, D., Diakoulakis, I., Emiris, D.: Learning fuzzy cognitive maps using evolution strategies: a novel schema for modeling and simulating high-level behavior. In: Proceedings of IEEE Congress on Evolutionary Computation (CEC 2001), pp. 364–371 (2001)
13. León, M., Mkrtchyan, L., Depaire, B., Ruan, D., Bello, R., Vanhoof, K.: Learning method inspired on swarm intelligence for fuzzy cognitive maps: travel behaviour modelling. In: Villa, A.E.P., Duch, W., Érdi, P., Masulli, F., Palm, G. (eds.) ICANN 2012, Part I. LNCS, vol. 7552, pp. 718–725. Springer, Heidelberg (2012)
14. Mahdavi, M., Fesanghary, M., Damangir, E.: An improved harmony search algorithm for solving optimization problems. Appl. Math. Comput. **188**(2), 1567–1579 (2007)
15. Papageorgiou, E.: Learning algorithms for fuzzy cognitive maps - a review study. IEEE Trans. Syst. Man Cybern. Part C: Appl. Rev. **42**(2), 150–163 (2012)
16. Papageorgiou, E.: Maps, Fuzzy Cognitive Maps for Applied Sciences and Engineering: From Fundamentals to Extensions and Learning Algorithms. Springer Science & Business Media, Heidelberg (2013)
17. Papageorgiou, E., Parsopoulos, K., Stylios, C., Groumpos, P., Vrahatis, M.: Fuzzy cognitive maps learning using particle swarm optimization. J. Intell. Inf. Syst. **25**(1), 95–121 (2005)
18. Poli, R., Kennedy, J., Blackwell, T.: Particle swarm optimization. Swarm Intell. **1**(1), 33–57 (2007)
19. Stach, W., Kurgan, L., Pedrycz, W.: A survey of fuzzy cognitive map learning methods. Issues Soft Comput.: Theor. Appl., 71–84 (2005)
20. Stach, W., Kurgan, L., Pedrycz, W.: Numerical and linguistic prediction of time series. IEEE Trans. Fuzzy Syst. **16**(1), 61–72 (2008)
21. Stach, W., Kurgan, L., Pedrycz, W., Reformat, M.: Genetic learning of fuzzy cognitive maps. Fuzzy Sets Syst. **153**, 371–401 (2005)
22. Storn, R., Price, K.: Differential evolution - a simple and efficient heuristic for global optimization over continuous spaces. J. Global Optim. **11**(4), 341–359 (1997)

Pattern Recognition with Rejection
Combining Standard Classification Methods with Geometrical Rejecting

Wladyslaw Homenda[1,2], Agnieszka Jastrzebska[2(✉)], Piotr Waszkiewicz[2], and Anna Zawadzka[2]

[1] Faculty of Economics and Informatics in Vilnius,
University of Bialystok, Kalvariju g. 135, LT-08221 Vilnius, Lithuania
[2] Faculty of Mathematics and Information Science,
Warsaw University of Technology, ul. Koszykowa 75, 00-662 Warsaw, Poland
A.Jastrzebska@mini.pw.edu.pl

Abstract. The motivation of our study is to provide algorithmic approaches to distinguish proper patterns, from garbage and erroneous patterns in a pattern recognition problem. The design assumption is to provide methods based on proper patterns only. In this way the approach that we propose is truly versatile and it can be adapted to any pattern recognition problem in an uncertain environment, where garbage patterns may appear. The proposed attempt to recognition with rejection combines known classifiers with geometric methods used for separating native patterns from foreign ones. Empirical verification has been conducted on datasets of handwritten digits classification (native patterns) and handwritten letters of Latin alphabet (foreign patterns).

Keywords: Pattern recognition · Classification · Rejecting option · Geometrical methods

1 Introduction

The task of pattern recognition is a classical machine learning problem. As an input we pass a training dataset, consisting of labelled patterns belonging to c classes. In the process we expect to form a model that assigns correct labels to new patterns (new observations).

It is important to have in mind that patterns in their original form are often some sort of signal, for instance images or voice recordings. Due to the fact that the original patterns are often collected using some signal-acquiring devices, we may encounter patterns that do not belong to any of the proper classes. Such situation may happen, when the device that we have used to acquire data has been automatically reset due to power outage and poor default calibration distorts the segmentation process. Another scenario is when we collect data in a noisy (out of lab) environment and apart from proper patterns there are a lot

© IFIP International Federation for Information Processing 2016
Published by Springer International Publishing Switzerland 2016. All Rights Reserved
K. Saeed and W. Homenda (Eds.): CISIM 2016, LNCS 9842, pp. 589–602, 2016.
DOI: 10.1007/978-3-319-45378-1_52

of unexpected residual ones. The problem with such patterns, say – garbage patterns, is that we cannot predict their characteristics and therefore we cannot include information about them in the model training process.

The motivation for our study is to provide algorithmic approaches used for distinguishing proper patterns, that we call *native patterns* from garbage and erroneous patterns, that we call *foreign patterns*. The task described in this paper we call *foreign patterns rejection*. The design assumption is to provide methods based on native patterns only. In this way the framework that we propose is truly versatile and it can be adapted to any pattern recognition problem in an uncertain environment, where foreign patterns may appear.

The study focuses on designing methods for recognition with rejection and employs them to (a) distinguish native patterns from foreign ones and (b) improve classification quality of native patterns. A specific objective of this study is to examine the cooperation of various standard classifiers (SVMs, random forests and kNNs) with geometric methods used for rejection. We focus on the influence of rejection mechanisms on native patterns classification, i.e., improvement of Fine Accuracy measure. The proposed methods are empirically verified on datasets of handwritten digits (native patterns) and handwritten Latin letters (foreign patterns).

We would like to emphasise that the novelty of the contribution presented in this paper is not in the methods that we use, but in how we employ them and on what we achieve with them.

The remainder of this paper is organized as follows. Section 2.1 presents the background knowledge on foreign patterns detection present in the literature. Sections 2.2 and 2.3 address background algorithms, present in the literature. Section 3 presents the proposed approach. In Sect. 4 we discuss experiments. Section 5 concludes the paper and highlights future research directions.

2   Preliminaries

Data collection and processing are vital study problems across multiple domains of science. Along with a substantial automation of data acquisition we face difficulties that appear due to poor data quality. The research we present in this paper has been motivated by the issue of contaminated datasets, that apart from proper patterns contain garbage.

In this section we start the discussion with a review of relevant literature positions in machine learning that tackle the issue of contaminated datasets. Then, in order to provide a self-contained description of the employed methods we present backbone literature algorithms applied. In what follows we present the Minimum Volume Enclosing Ellipsoid (MVEE) algorithm and a suite of three classification methods: Random Forests (RF), Support Vector Machines (SVM), and K-Nearest Neighbors algorithm (kNN). Listed methods are employed in various configurations to native patterns classification with foreign patterns rejection. Our approach, based on those algorithms, is discussed in Sect. 3.

2.1   Literature Review

The rejecting option in pattern recognition problem has gained a rather weak attention despite its importance in practice. Also, there is a relatively short list of papers raising the problem of rejecting foreign patterns, cf. [8] for a short survey. Here we only hint some issues present in literature. Due to space limitations we are neither able to comprehensively cover the subject, nor can we provide a deep background of the methods employed in this study.

Discussion on approaches related to foreign patterns rejection may start with one-class classification methods. Especially, there are two noteworthy examples: centroid-based methods and One-Class Support Vector Machine.

Centroid-based methods rely on distinguishing cluster centres (centroids). Region reserved for proper patterns is usually defined by the distance between centre and the furthest proper pattern.

One-Class SVM has been introduced in [12]. While "regular" SVM algorithm forms hyperplane separating two classes, the One-Class SVM separates data points from the entire feature space. Notably, the One-Class SVM provides a soft decision rules, as there is a ν parameter determining the fraction for outliers.

When it comes to the study on actual foreign patterns rejection, there are relatively few papers to review. This issue, in spite of its importance, remains somehow neglected. Among notable studies one may mention rank-based methods, for instance ones described in [2, 4, 6, 7, 11, 13, 15]. In a nutshell, mentioned papers propose to attach confidence scores along with class labels. Rejection occurs when none of native class labels was assigned with a satisfying confidence.

2.2   Ellipsoids for Foreign Patterns Rejection

Both native and foreign patterns are represented with a vector of features extracted from the pattern of interest. Features are usually real numbers, therefore every pattern is a point in a multidimensional Euclidean space. What is more, we may propose a hypothesis that the set of native patterns belonging to the same class forms a cluster in the feature space. Assuming that this assumption is correct, we may be able to find minimal enclosing boxes for each native class.

In computational geometry, the smallest enclosing box problem is that of finding the oriented minimum bounding box enclosing a set of points. As opposed to convex hull, which is the most accurate point set container with smallest volume and which is enclosed by linear hyperplanes. Bounding boxes are far less complex. In many cases, when there is a need for computing convex hull and testing inclusions of other points, an approximation of such hull can be used, which helps in reducing time needed for computations, since most of alternative methods have lower construction and inclusion-testing complexities. Some of such approaches include using figures like hypercubes, diamonds, spheres or ellipsoids to successfully enclose given set of points.

When comparing highlights and drawbacks of each method from two perspectives: computational complexity and ease of point inclusion testing, ellipsoids seem to be a reasonable choice. Constructed ellipsoid is superior to the minimal cuboid in many ways. It is unique, gives better approximation of the object it contains and if $E(S)$ is the bounding ellipsoid for a point set S with convex hull $C(S)$ in dimension d, then: $\frac{1}{d}E(S) \subseteq C(S) \subseteq E(S)$, where scaling is with respect to the centre of $E(S)$.

To sum up, adaptation of the smallest enclosing box problem to foreign patterns rejection, or native patterns identification, seems to be a very natural approach. The justification is fairly simple: if we enclose patterns belonging to native classes, using for instance ellipsoids, formed geometrical model will discriminate a region of the features space reserved for native patterns between a region where we may encounter foreign patterns. With this premise in mind, let us present a detailed description of the MVEE algorithm.

MVEE problem is solved by several known algorithms that can be categorized as first-order, second-order interior-point or combination of the two. For small dimensions d, the MVEE problem can be solved in $O(d^{O(d)}m)$ operations using randomized or deterministic algorithms [14]. In this paper the algorithm based on Khachiyan solution is used.

An ellipsoid in its centre form is given by the formula:

$$E = \{x \in \mathbb{R}^n | (x - c)^T A(x - c) \le 1\}$$

where $c \in \mathbb{R}^n$ is the centre of the ellipse E and $A \in \mathbb{S}_{++}^n$ is a positive definite matrix. Points lying inside the ellipsoid satisfy $(x_i - c)^T A(x_i - c) \le 1 + \varepsilon$, where ε parameter defines the error margin in determining point belonging to ellipsoid, i.e. it allows to enlarge the ellipsoid.

However, constructing minimal volume bounding ellipsoid is not a convex optimization problem. It turns out that the solution is not easily obtainable so the dual problem has to be found. For a more precise and in depth solution description see [14]. The main problem, when using ellipsoids as identifiers, lies in constructing them. Two main factors that decide about identification effectiveness are tolerance and acceptance parameters. Tolerance can be viewed as a threshold for ellipsoid construction accuracy. The lower the parameter is, the better minimal volume ellipsoid is created. On the other hand, even with a good training set, there is a risk of including native patterns that lie outside of the created ellipsoid. Acceptance parameter has been introduced to prevent such unwanted behaviour. It defines a threshold for point rejection for points lying outside of the created figure.

2.3   Native Patterns Classification

The task of native patterns classification relies on forming a model based on a labelled training dataset that assigns proper class labels to new patterns. There is a multitude of classification algorithms, among which we have selected three different ones that are used in our methods. It is necessary to emphasize that if someone would like to adapt our method to their own domain, those algorithms could be substituted with some other classification tools that may be more efficient in that domain. Without further ado let us move towards a brief description of the methods that we apply in our study.

Support Vector Machines are a set of supervised learning methods used for classification, regression and outliers detection. The SVM algorithm relies on a construction of hyperplane with a maximal margin that separates patterns of two classes [5]. SVMs are effective in high dimensional spaces, memory efficient, and quite versatile with many kernel functions that can be specified for the decision function. Although in some cases, where the number of features is much greater than the number of samples, this method can give poor results, and is not cost-efficient when calculating probability estimates. However, it is well suited for the problem presented in this paper. For a multi-class classification "one-against-one" approach is used. For c classes $c \cdot (c-1)/2$ classifiers are constructed, each one is trained with data from two different classes. In our study we use decimal digits as classes. Therefore, the following 45 class-against-class SVMs are built: "0 vs 1", "0 vs 2", ... "0 vs 9", "1 vs 2", ... "1 vs 9", ... "8 vs 9". Classification decision is taken by a voting method, i.e. a new pattern subjected to classification is counted to the most frequent class among these 45 binary classifiers. The case when two or more classes are most frequent, a second choice decision is made for actual classification. For instance, the closest pattern from most popular classes or minimal sum of distances from the processed pattern to ones from most popular classes may decide.

Random Forests is a popular ensemble method. The main principle behind ensemble methods, in general, is that a group of "weak learners" can come together to form a "strong learner". In the Random Forests algorithm [3] the weak learners are decision trees, which are used to predict the membership of objects in the classes. For vector of independent variables representing one object they calculate the value of the class the object belongs to by dividing value space into two or more subspaces. More precisely, an input data is entered at the top of the tree and as it traverses down the tree the data gets bucketed into smaller and smaller sets. In this method a large number of classification trees is generated. To grow each tree a random selection with replacement is made from the examples in the training set D. Those subsets D_k are called bootstrap training sets. At each node m variables are selected at random out of the set of input variables and the best split on these m is used to split the node. After a relatively large number of trees is generated, they vote for the most popular class. Random Forests join few important benefits: (a) they are relatively prone to the influence of outliers, (b) they have an embedded ability of feature selection, (c) they are prone to missing values, and (d) they are prone to overfitting.

k-Nearest Neighbors is an example of a "lazy classifier", where the entire training dataset is the model. There is no typical model building phase, hence the name. Class membership is determined based on class labels encountered in k closest observations in the training dataset [1]. In a typical application, the only choice that the model designer has to make is selection of k and distance metrics. Both are often extracted with a help of supervised learning procedures.

3   Methodology

In general, there are two approaches that could be used to determine whether an object is rejected (classified as foreign). The first one assumes use of classification methods, which originally were not designed for rejecting. In the second approach classifiers are used only as a classification tool, whereas rejecting is realized by other methods, for instance geometrical figures or unsupervised cluster analysis. In this paper let us focus on the latter.

3.1   External Global and Local Rejecting

While ellipsoids are good for identification of native patterns region, they lack in pattern classification quality. This is caused by the fact that ellipsoids may overlap with each other, which results in conflicts when we want to univocally assign class labels. Although this can be solved by calculating distance between those patterns and each ellipsoid's centre, or by taking the value of ellipsoid-inclusion equation as a classification measure, tests have proven that such approaches

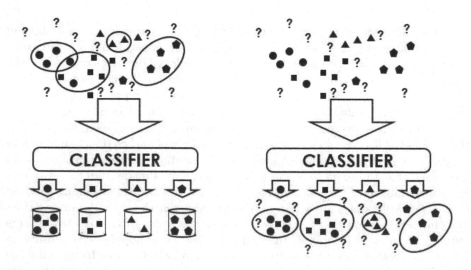

Fig. 1. Ellipsoids employed for rejecting: global rejection (left part) and local rejecting (right part). Questions marks (?) stand for foreign patterns, circles, squares, triangles and pentagons – for native patterns.

are more prone to errors than other "standard" classifiers mentioned in this paper. Considering both strengths and weaknesses of classifiers and identifiers (for native region identification), the combined solution has been prepared that employs both tools (classifiers and ellipsoids), making use of their advantages.

Classifiers have high success rate, but cannot distinguish between foreign patterns and native ones. Contrary to that, ellipsoids tend to be better in rejecting foreign patterns, what makes them good at identifying patterns that should not be classified. The natural way of dealing with that problem would be to use ellipsoids as first-entry identifier that purifies input set by removing foreign patterns. The result of such rejection would be sent to the chosen classifier that would classify remaining native patterns. Due to the order of actions in this processing scenario we call this *global rejection* scheme. Schema of this method is presented in the left part of Fig. 1. Please note that we show there a case of imperfect rejection/classification task, i.e. rejected and misclassified native patterns, as this is typically the case in real-world problems.

Another way of using ellipsoids as identifiers is to treat them as correction tools for an already classified dataset. This means that foreign patterns are not removed before classification. Instead, class-corresponding ellipsoid are employed to reject foreign patterns classified to the corresponding class. This is somewhat different from the previous approach because patterns can be rejected even if there is an ellipsoid that would pass inclusion test. The schema of this classification/rejection scenario can be seen in the right side of Fig. 1. Because rejection occurs at the local level of each native class we call this approach a *local rejection* scheme.

3.2   Quality Evaluation

In order to evaluate the quality of the proposed methods patterns from the following groups are counted:

- CC (Correctly Classified) – the number of correctly classified patterns, i.e. native patterns classified as native ones with correct class label,
- TP (True Positives) – native patterns classified as native (no matter, into which native class),
- FN (False Negatives) – native patterns incorrectly classified as foreign,
- FP (False Positives) – foreign patterns incorrectly accounted as native,
- TN (True Negatives) – foreign patterns correctly accounted as foreign.

These numbers are then used to form measures reflecting specific aspects of classification and rejection, cf. Table 1. Notions that we use are well-known in the domain of pattern recognition, cf. [8]:

- *Strict Accuracy* measures classifier's performance. It is the ratio of the numbers of all *correctly classified* patterns to all ones being processed.
- *Accuracy* is a "softer" characteristic derived from the Strict Accuracy. Accuracy describes the ability to distinguish between native and foreign patterns. The difference is that we do not require that the native patterns are labelled with their proper class label.

- *Native Precision* is the ratio of the number of not rejected native patterns to the number of all not rejected patterns (i.e. all not rejected native and foreign ones). The higher the value of this measure, the better ability to distinguish foreign patterns from native ones. Native Precision does not evaluate how effective identification of native patterns is.
- *Native Sensitivity* is the ratio of the number of not rejected native patterns to all native ones. The higher the value of Native Sensitivity, the more effective identification of native patterns. Unlike Native Precision, this measure does not evaluate separation between native and foreign patterns.
- *Strict Native Sensitivity* takes only correctly classified native patterns and does not consider native patterns, which are not rejected and assigned to incorrect classes, unlike Native Sensitivity, where all not rejected native patterns are taken into account.
- *Fine Accuracy* is the ratio of the number of native patterns classified to correct classes, i.e. assigned to their respective classes, to the number of all native patterns not rejected. This measure conveys how precise is correct classification of not rejected patterns.
- *Foreign Precision* corresponds to Native Precision, i.e. it is the ratio of the number of rejected foreign patterns to the number of all rejected elements.
- *Foreign Sensitivity* corresponds to Native Sensitivity.
- Precision and Sensitivity are complementary and there exists yet another characteristic that combines them: the *F-measure*. It is there to express the balance between precision and sensitivity since these two measures affect each other. Increasing sensitivity can cause a drop in precision since, along with correctly classified patterns, there might be more incorrectly classified.

Table 1. Quality measures for classification and rejection.

$$\text{Native Precision} = \frac{\text{TP}}{\text{TP+FP}} \qquad\qquad \text{Accuracy} = \frac{\text{TP+TN}}{\text{TP+FN+FP+TN}}$$

$$\text{Foreign Precision} = \frac{\text{TN}}{\text{TN+FN}} \qquad \text{Strict Accuracy} = \frac{\text{CC+TN}}{\text{TP+FN+FP+TN}}$$

$$\text{Native Sensitivity} = \frac{\text{TP}}{\text{TP+FN}} \qquad\qquad \text{Fine Accuracy} = \frac{\text{CC}}{\text{TP}}$$

$$\text{Foreign Sensitivity} = \frac{\text{TN}}{\text{TN+FP}} \qquad \text{Strict Native Sensitivity} = \frac{\text{CC}}{\text{TP+FN}}$$

$$\text{F-measure} = 2 \cdot \frac{\text{Precision} \cdot \text{Sensitivity}}{\text{Precision} + \text{Sensitivity}}$$

4   Experiments

In this section we move towards description of a series of experiments where we apply rejection strategies discussed theoretically in Sect. 3.1. In what follows we describe datasets, experiments' settings, and results.

4.1   Datasets

We present a study on handwritten digits recognition and handwritten letters (from the Latin alphabet) rejection. In other words, native patterns set is made of digits (it is a ten class problem), while foreign patterns are 26 different handwritten letters. The justification to assume such foreign dataset for testing purposes is that appearance of other real-world symbols, but not belonging to any proper class, is a common issue in a character recognition problem.

We would like to stress again, that foreign patterns do not participate in the model building phase. The entire scheme is based on native patterns only. Handwritten letters are used only for rejection mechanisms quality evaluation. Samples of processed patterns are displayed in Fig. 2.

The native training dataset consisted of 10,000 handwritten digits with approximately 1,000 observations in each class taken from publicly available MNIST database [9]. We split each class in proportion ca. 7:3 and as a result we got two sets. The first one includes 6,996 patterns and is used for training. The second set, the test set, contains 3,004 patterns. The dataset of foreign patterns contains 26,383 handwritten Latin letters, ca. 1,000 letters in each class. This dataset was created by 16 students, writing about 70 copies of each letter.

All patterns were normalized and feature vectors comprising of 106 numerical features were created. Examples of features are: maximum/position of maximum values of projections, histograms of projections, transitions, offsets; raw moments, central moments, Euler numbers etc. The best first search for the optimal feature subset has been performed using FSelector R package [10] and then analysis of variance was employed to select good features. The final feature vector contained 24 elements. We considered features standardization but the training data is sufficiently consistent (there are no outliers), so we normalized those features to bring linearly all values into the range [0,1].

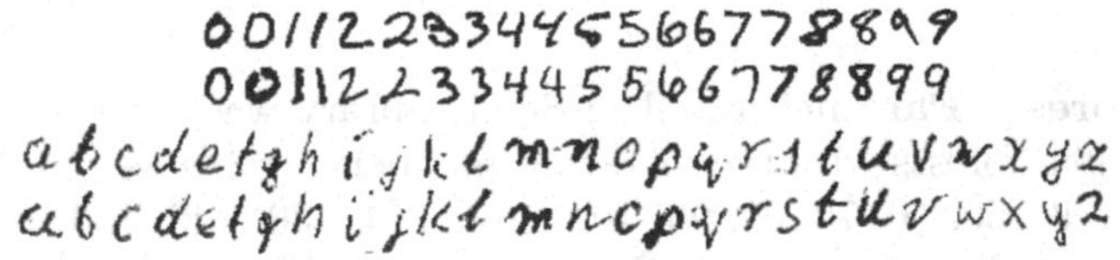

Fig. 2. Sample of: native patterns (top) and foreign patterns (bottom).

4.2   Experimental Settings

Solutions presented in this paper have been implemented in Python programming language, using scientific libraries [16–18]. The MVEE algorithm, available as MATLAB code has been rewritten in Python language, using NumPy library for matrix representation and operations. Several tests have been performed in order to find best suited method parameters for both classifiers and identifiers. For finding those values the Grid Search [18] has been used for SVM and RF.

MVEE Parameters. Each ellipsoid was created and used with two parameters: tolerance and acceptance. The tolerance argument was used during creation phase, as "accuracy measurement". Lower value means that created enclosing figure is more fitted to the construction set. Acceptance parameter defines how far can a point lie outside the ellipsoid to still be identified as belonging to it. In other words, it treats enclosing ellipsoid as being bigger than it really is. Parameters tests involved computing effectiveness of MVEE algorithm for certain tolerance and acceptance values. We tested values from such ranges:

- tolerance $= [0.5, 0.2, 0.1, 0.01]$
- accuracy $= [0.1, 0.01, 0.001, 0.0005]$

The results revealed that for the given training and test sets the best parameter combination was tolerance $= 0.5$ and accuracy $= 0.1$ and those values were used in the final, combined method described later in this document.

SVM Parameters. SVM method available in the Scikit package offers a few built-in kernels that were used during computations: radial basis function and polynomial. Additionally, there are two more parameters that were tested: C (described as penalty parameter C of the error term), and γ (known as kernel coefficient). Values that were tested:

- kernel $= [\text{'rbf', 'poly'}]$
- C $= [1, 2, 4, 5, 16]$
- $\gamma = [2^{-1}, 2^{-2}, 2^{-3}, 0, 00025]$

The best found combination of those parameters used rbf kernel along with C $= 8$ and $\gamma = 2^{-1}$ values.

Random Forests Parameters. The Scikit library was used to test random forests. Random forests with the following number of trees were tested: 1, 2, 3, 5, 10, 20, 30, 40, 50, 60, 70, 80, 90, 100, 110, 120, 130, 140, 150. It turned out that the best number of trees to build the forest was 100.

kNN Parameters. We tested the following values of k (the number of neighbours): 1, 2, 3, 4, 5, 10, 20, 30, 40, 50. The best found value of k was four. There is also one parameter – metric, but we use the standard Euclidean metric.

4.3 Results of Experiments

In this section we present the results of our experiments. We use quality measures presented in Sect. 3.2. We investigate classification quality, rejection quality and rejection's impact on classification quality. We compare two scenarios: global (rejection on is the entire dataset) and local (rejection mechanism is separate for each native class).

Influence of Rejection on Native Patterns Classification. Adding a rejection mechanism, ideally, may be a method for improvement of classification rates. It would be perceived as a positive side of the rejection mechanism, if it would be able to reject those native patterns, which would be incorrectly classified when there is no rejection mechanism at all.

Trained models partially fulfill this wish. Conducted tests, reported in Table 2, show that Fine Accuracy improved for both local and global rejection schemes and for all classifiers. This means that we have a better recognition rate (the proportion of correctly classified patterns) in the data that was accounted as native. However, we have to notice that both rejection mechanisms rejected some native patterns. Hence, Strict Accuracy and Strict Native Sensitivity are slightly higher when we do not have any rejection mechanism.

Results indicate that performing pattern rejection after their initial classification (the local rejection scheme), brings better results than using the global scheme. This could be explained by the fact that in the local rejection scheme we use one ellipsoid per each class and we apply those ellipsoids after classification. In contrast, in the global scheme we have a joint set of ellipsoids that we apply to the entire dataset. In the local rejection scenario native patterns identification regions are applied individually to each subset obtained from the classifier.

Table 2. Classification with random forests, SVMs and kNN and rejection with ellipsoids on the set of native patterns: no rejection vs. local and global rejections. Notice that all three measures turn to the same proportion CC/TP for no rejection mode.

Basic classifier	No rejection			Global rejection			Local rejection		
	RF	SVM	kNN	RF	SVM	kNN	RF	SVM	kNN
Data Set	Native Patterns, Train Set								
Strict Accuracy	1	0.985	0.955	0.941	0.938	0.936	0.942	0.942	0.942
Fine Accuracy	1	0.985	0.955	1	0.987	0.972	1	0.989	0.984
Strict Native Sens.	1	0.985	0.955	0.879	0.852	0.854	0.864	0.857	0.845
Data Set	Native Patterns, Test Set								
Strict Accuracy	0.952	0.966	0.930	0.946	0.946	0.944	0.951	0.952	0.953
Fine Accuracy	0.952	0.966	0.930	0.972	0.982	0.959	0.977	0.985	0.976
Strict Native Sens.	0.952	0.966	0.930	0.842	0.852	0.831	0.837	0.845	0.825

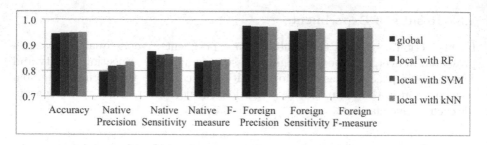

Fig. 3. Quality evaluation for global and local rejection schemes realized with ellipsoids with different classifiers: random forests, SVMs, and kNNs.

As a result there is a chance that classification would contribute to foreign patterns filtration. The same conclusion, about superiority of local rejection over global one concerns strict classification error ratios.

When comparing the overall quality achieved by mechanisms based on different classifiers we see a slight advantage of SVM.

Separating Letters from Digits. Figure 3 presents rejection results. We compare various quality measures for models constructed based on random forests, SVM, and kNN with ellipsoids for the global and the local rejection schemes.

First, let us mention that for the global rejection all rejection rates are the same for all classifiers. This is due to the specificity of this model, where rejection occurs first, so classification procedure does not modify the content of the set subjected to rejection. However, the global approach turned out to be slightly worse than the local approach.

Results show that in the local rejection model all classifiers combined with ellipsoids behave well and provide similar quality of rejection.

5   Conclusions

Enhancing classifiers' ability to classify objects by coupling them with ellipsoids for foreign patterns rejection has proven to yield good results. Conducted experiment on handwritten digits contaminated with handwritten letters showed that the local rejection scenario with fine-grained rejection ellipsoids one per each native class perform better than the global approach with a single, but less fine-grained rejection mechanism. We also report that the differences in classification ratios in the local rejection model coupled with different classifiers turned out to be very slight. SVM turned out to be the best, and its advantage is visible when we evaluate the rate of native patterns that were rejected that wanted to reject, because otherwise they would have been classified into incorrect class.

We are aware that to truly confirm obtained results, test should be repeated on different data sets. Described in this paper set consisting of letters and digits, although being very large, might not match wide spectrum of problems.

Let us conclude this paper by saying that various adaptations of the idea of foreign patterns rejection have a vital role in modern machine learning. It is needless to mention areas such as text mining, fraud detection, or medical diagnosis systems where we deal with various reincarnations of the foreign patterns. From this perspective we believe that the study in this direction is worth further efforts.

Acknowledgment. The research is partially supported by the National Science Center, grant No. 2012/07/B/ST6/01501, decision No. DEC-2012/07/B/ST6/01501.

References

1. Altman, N.S.: An introduction to kernel and nearest-neighbor nonparametric regression. Am. Stat. **46**(3), 175–185 (1992)
2. Bertolami, R., Zimmermann, M., Bunke, H.: Rejection strategies for offline handwritten text line recognition. Pattern Recogn. Lett. **27**(16), 2005–2012 (2006)
3. Breiman, L.: Random forests. Mach. Learn. **45**(1), 5–32 (2001)
4. Burger, T., Kessentini, Y., Paquet, T.: Dempster-Shafer based rejection strategy for handwritten word recognition. In: Proceedings of the International Conference on Document Analysis and Recognition, pp. 528–532 (2011)
5. Cortes, C., Vapnik, V.: Support-vector networks. Mach. Learn. **20**(3), 273–297 (1995)
6. Elad, M., Hel-Or, Y., Keshet, R.: Pattern detection using a maximal rejection classifier. In: Arcelli, C., Cordella, L.P., Sanniti di Baja, G. (eds.) IWVF 2001. LNCS, vol. 2059, pp. 514–524. Springer, Heidelberg (2001)
7. Hempstalk, K., Frank, E., Witten, I.H.: One-class classification by combining density and class probability estimation. In: Daelemans, W., Goethals, B., Morik, K. (eds.) ECML PKDD 2008, Part I. LNCS (LNAI), vol. 5211, pp. 505–519. Springer, Heidelberg (2008)
8. Homenda, W., Jastrzebska, A., Pedrycz, W.: Rejecting foreign elements in pattern recognition problem. Reinforced training of rejection level. In: Proceedings of ICAART 2015, pp. 90–99 (2015)
9. LeCun, Y., Cortes, C., Burges, C.: The MNIST database of handwritten digits. http://yann.lecun.com/exdb/mnist
10. Romanski, P., Kotthoff, L.: Package FSelector. http://cran.r-project.org/web/packages/FSelector/FSelector.pdf
11. Scheme, E.J., Hudgins, B.S., Englehart, K.B.: Confidence-based rejection for improved pattern recognition myoelectric control. IEEE Trans. Biomed. Eng. **60**(6), 1563–1570 (2013)
12. Scholkopf, B., Williamson, R., Smola, A., Shawe-Taylort, J., Platt, J.: Support vector method for novelty detection. Adv. Neural Inf. Process. Syst. **12**, 582–588 (1992)
13. Tax, D.M.J., Duin, R.P.W.: Growing a multi-class classifier with a reject option. Pattern Recogn. Lett. **29**, 1565–1570 (2008)
14. Todd, M.J., Yildirim, E.A.: On Khachiyan's Algorithm for the Computation of Minimum Volume Enclosing Ellipsoids, 30 September 2005. http://people.orie.cornell.edu/miketodd/TYKhach.pdf

15. Wang, Y., Casasent, D.: A support vector hierarchical method for multi-class classi-
    fication and rejection. In: Proceedings of International Joint Conference on Neural
    Networks, pp. 3281–3288 (2009)
16. http://www.mathworks.com/
17. http://www.numpy.org/
18. http://scikit-learn.org/stable/

Connecting Household Weather Sensors to IoT World

Pavel Moravec[1,2]([✉]), Michal Krumnikl[1,2], Petr Olivka[1], and David Seidl[1]

[1] Department of Computer Science, FEECS VŠB – Technical University
of Ostrava, 17. Listopadu 15, 708 33 Ostrava-Poruba, Czech Republic
{pavel.moravec,michal.krumnikl,petr.olivka,david.seidl}@vsb.cz
[2] IT4Innovations National Supercomputing Center, VŠB – Technical University
of Ostrava, 17. Listopadu 15, 708 33 Ostrava-Poruba, Czech Republic

Abstract. As the Internet of Things applications become more wide-spread, we face the need to replace existing implementations with Internet-enabled sensors. However, these sensors often provide worse battery life, have higher costs per unit and are not backward-compatible with existing weather stations. This paper concentrates on the possibility of decoding the weather station data by a cheap device which would forward them to the Internet of Things frameworks. The basics steps of receiving and decoding of the wireless weather sensor data are discussed together with the common problems which are associated with their capture and processing.

Keywords: Wireless sensor · Modulation · OOK · On-Off Keying · Internet of things · IoT

1 Introduction

Wireless weather stations with external sensors have become a part of many households, after their prices dropped to reasonable levels. Whilst the base weather station is placed inside, the sensors are battery-powered and have to withstand the outside environment. They are able to work unattended for several months or years without user interaction and forward data to the base station. Unfortunately, there is no common standard for the communication protocol and due to the limited storage of the base station only some of the measured values are kept (e.g. the maximum and minimum of measured values). Only the more expensive weather stations offer a way to connect the station to a computer, often by a serial connection and with a custom application and communication protocol. This means that a computer must be running all the time. Whilst it is possible to connect several wireless sensors to the base station (typically up

This work has been supported by The Ministry of Education, Youth and Sports from the National Programme of Sustainability (NPU II) project "IT4Innovations excellence in science – LQ1602" and from the Large Infrastructures for Research, Experimental Development and Innovations project "IT4Innovations National Supercomputing Center – LM2015070".

K. Saeed and W. Homenda (Eds.): CISIM 2016, LNCS 9842, pp. 603–616, 2016.
DOI: 10.1007/978-3-319-45378-1_53

to 3), they do not build a traditional sensor network by themselves, because the
sensors are just simple transmitters, unlike in [10].

In recent years, there were several papers and projects trying to receive data
from wireless sensors by a PC using software-defined radio, e.g. [9], the RTL 433
project[1], reverse-engineering the serial line protocol of common weather stations
with a USB or serial port and recording data on a PC or Raspberry Pi (e.g. [1],
Weather Station Data Logger[2], wview[3] or fowsr[4]). There were also a few projects
building a custom weather station (with wired and optional wireless sensors) e.g.
the WeatherDuino Pro2 project[5], WxShield[6], or the SparkFun Weather Shield[7].
Some resources describing the serial protocols of more expensive weather stations
may be found, e.g. [7].

In this paper, we will concentrate on the preliminaries of building a wireless
weather sensor receiver, which would pre-process the data and send them to a
one of the *Internet of Things* [5] (*IoT*) enabled platforms. We will discuss several
weather stations which use 434 MHz band and analyze the modulation, encoding
and data frame structure. It should be mentioned that some wireless sensors use
a different frequency range, typically 868 MHz or in case of the US 915 MHz,
which would require a drop-in replacement or secondary receiver.

The rest of the paper is organized as follows: In next section, we will discuss the basics of communication with wireless sensors in 434 MHz range and
their specifics. In Sect. 3 we will discuss the modulation techniques and encoding schemes. In Sect. 4 we will address some of the common protocol features.
In Sect. 5 we will disseminate actual protocols we have managed to capture and
provide a description of common frame formats. In Sect. 6, we will mention our
prototype solution, concentrating on cheap and available components, designing
the device so that its cost does not exceed €10 (not considering the router to
which it may be connected).

2   Wireless Weather Stations

The weather stations have been used for several tens or hundreds of years. With
the advent of electronic measurement, personal weather stations operated by private individuals became cheaper and more widespread. They typically measure
at least temperature, atmospheric pressure and humidity, more advanced ones
also contain an anemometer to measure the wind speed and direction (also the
wind gust measurement may not record really short wind gusts) and rain gauge.
Some personal weather stations may also measure solar radiation, UV index
or soil moisture. However, most of the cheaper models cannot be connected to
personal computers or Internet.

---

[1] https://github.com/merbanan/rtl_433.
[2] http://wmrx00.sourceforge.net/.
[3] http://www.wviewweather.com/.
[4] https://github.com/ajauberg/fowsr.
[5] http://goo.gl/3InBIq.
[6] http://www.osengr.org/WxShield/Web/WxShield.shtml.
[7] https://www.sparkfun.com/products/12081.

Most of the current wireless personal weather station systems presently consist of a base station placed indoors, which measures internal temperature and humidity as well as the atmospheric pressure, the changes of which are being recorded and used for the prediction of the weather in following 24–48 h. The base stations may also provide additional functions – local time (sometimes radio-controlled clock adjustment is possible), alarm(s), moon phase and sunrise/sunset times. Since the cheaper base stations do not offer a possibility to access data stored on them from a computer, our solution will have to replace the base station as well.

The wireless sensors are placed outside, they have to withstand harsher environmental conditions and they must co-exist together with other systems which are using the same frequency band. Typically, the base stations support up to 3 wireless temperature (or based on the type of the weather station either the temperature and humidity or temperature and soil moisture) sensors, one rain gauge and one anemometer.

As we have already stated in the Introduction, there are many incompatible protocols for data transmission from the wireless sensor to the weather station. We can compare this situation to the issues some of the Bluetooth Smart accessory is currently facing with incompatible protocols for devices which do not have a common standardized profile.

On one hand, this leads to compatibility issues, on the other hand, it should be possible to operate several sets of wireless sensors and wireless weather stations from different vendors independently in the same area. The wireless sensors use one of the free ISM (Industrial, Science, Medicine) bands for the data transmissions. In central Europe, they mainly operate in the 433,92 MHz band, which they share with some remote control devices such as car keys, garage door openers, wireless doorbells and remotely-controlled electric sockets. Alternatively, some manufacturers use the 868 MHz band, which however starts to be extensively used by home monitoring devices and Internet of Things technologies (e.g. SIGFOX). In some countries, especially in North America, the 915 MHz band is also used (but it is not possible to use it in Europe due to the collision with GSM-900 frequency range).

3 Modulation Techniques

There are many modulation techniques used in wireless transfers for binary data, which are being used nowadays. Ranging from the On-off keying to complex modulation schemes using 256-QAM (Quadrature Amplitude Modulation), OFDM (Orthogonal Frequency Division Multiplexing) and guard intervals. However, in the case of wireless external sensors, we typically encounter simple modulation techniques, which require a less complex hardware, cheaper circuitry and less power consumption.

The circuitry of the wireless meteorological sensors typically uses the *On-Off Keying (OOK)* – a simple variant of *Amplitude Shift Keying (ASK)* – which represents the transmitted binary data as a presence of the carrier wave. This modulation technique is similar to the old Morse code transfers, in the basic case representing binary 1 as the presence of the carrier wave and binary 0 as the absence of the carrier wave. Whilst this technique is very easy to implement, it is typically not used just by itself, because the noise and collisions of multiple transmissions would be hard to filter out.

A smaller number of devices (e.g. Fine Offset WH1080 Weather Station sensors) use *Frequency Shift Keying (FSK)* or Gaussian GFSK by using two frequencies for representing binary 0 and 1. There is also a possibility of future sensors using the *Frequency Hopping Spread Spectrum (FHSS)*. Decoding data from such sensors would require the knowledge of the hopping patterns and is out of scope of this paper.

So far, we have identified following modulation techniques used in combination with the OOK variant of amplitude modulation:

1. *Pulse Width Modulation (PWM)* – the logical zeros and ones are defined by the actual width of the pulse generated by the transmitter.
2. *Pulse Distance Modulation (PSM)* – the short pulses have a constant duration and the delay (or distance, space) between them defines logical zeros and ones. Sometimes, the tertiary duration is also being used as a special symbol for signaling (Start of frame, spacer, etc.) or synchronization pulses are sent, to signal the start of the frame.
3. *Return to Zero Encoding (RZ)* – a specific variant of return to zero is being used by some transmitters (since standard RZ would require three signal levels). In the middle of the bit interval, the signal is always turned off [2].
4. *Manchester Encoding* – the demodulated signal level is shifted in the middle of the bit interval based on the transmitted symbol – binary 0 is encoded as a shift from high to low and binary 1 as a shift from low to high or vice versa in some implementations. If the level in the beginning of the bit interval is already in the level to which it would be shifted, additional shift in the beginning of the bit interval occurs.
5. Modified *Differential Manchester Encoding* – uses level shift in the beginning of each bit interval for each bit and the presence or absence of level shift in the middle of the bit interval to encode binary 0 and 1.

In the rest of the paper, we will be concentrating on the devices which use the On-Off Keying, because they require a cheaper receiver module and there are many ready-made receivers available. Automatic detection of used modulation is also possible, see [3, 6, 13].

4   Weather Station Data Transmission

In this section, we will describe some common frame formats used to transmit data from a wireless sensor to the weather station.

The wireless sensor circuity is generally as simple and as cheap as possible. To save money, the sensor contains only a transmitter (unlike the wireless sensor network nodes, which provide both transmitter and receiver). As a result, the measured data transmissions are unacknowledged, and it is not possible to sense multiple access on medium, i.e. methods such as CSMA (carrier sense multiple access) are out of question. To improve a chance of successful data delivery, the frame – which is quite short, consisting of only a few nibbles[8] or bytes – is usually repeated several times during the transmission.

Two good sources of this information are available on-line [2, 12]. Whilst [12] contains incomplete information, it is a good starting point for further analysis. In fact, we have encountered a clone of such station when analyzing the data. We independently deciphered the data frame structure finding some extra information which was not part of the original document, as shown in following section.

For all weather stations mentioned in the following text, we were able to identify a set of parameters which play an important role for correct decoding of transmitted data besides the modulation scheme used, which was mentioned in previous section:

1. General transmission speed based on the pulse width and distance. Since some of the line codes do not use same length of time intervals for binary 0 and binary 1, we will rather speak about the on and off pulse lengths for individual symbols in the rest of the paper and not the bit speed.
2. *Bit ordering* of the transmitted data, both for the whole frame and for the bits in individual nibbles (4-bit sequences). There are two ways how to transmit data – the first one sends the least significant bit of a nibble (*LSB*) first, whilst the second sends the most significant bit first (*MSB*). From the global point of view, we may also send either the most or the least significant nibble first.
3. *Preamble format* differs for different implementations. The preamble is placed before the frame to synchronize the transmitter and the receiver. It is often followed by one or more synchronization bits.
4. *Number of synchronization bits* (*sync bits*) which are often placed between the preamble and the first frame and between individual frame repetitions.
5. *Frame check sequence* (*FCS*) is generally transmitted after the data frame and it is checked before the frame is processed further. However, some transmitters do not use FCS at all, other include a simple FCS inside of data portion of the frame and other combine both variants. In case of simple implementations, it is possible to determine the checksumming algorithm and verify that the data in the frame appears intact. However, if the formula is not possible to determine, we may have to use other ways how to check for data validity.
6. *Number of bits in a single frame* is the last but not least indicator which helps us to detect if the whole frame has been received. Some sensors may even stop the transmission in the middle of the last frame repetition.

The data encoded in the data frame will usually include the random sensor IDs, the channel ID for temperature and humidity measurements, battery state information, a simple abovementioned checksum and sometimes an indication that a measurement was forced manually (e.g. by pressing a button).

---

[8] A nibble consists of 4 bits, and can be represented as a hexadecimal digit.

Fig. 1. The wireless sensors used for the evaluation (left-to right): H13716A-TX, Z31130-TX and Z31915-TX

The temperature and humidity sensors – which will be mostly discussed in this paper – will also provide the temperature (3–4 nibbles) and humidity (typically 2 nibbles) measurements, and sometimes the temperature trend as well.

The measured values stored in the data frame may also use different representations of measured data, sometimes even in the same frame. The values may be stored by individual digits (*binary-coded decimal – BCD*) or a signed or unsigned binary value. The signed values may encode the numbers with a sign bit (typically the most significant bit), or use either one's complement or two's complement representation.

In case of values with decimal places, the value is multiplied by some coefficient (e.g. 10, 4, 2) and sent as an integer. So far, we have not identified a sensor, which would use floating-point number representation, possibly due to the measured ranges not requiring values which would mandate the mantissa and exponent approach, or the problematic (or missing) implementation of floating-point operations on such simple hardware.

5   Decoding Captured Sensor Data

In this section, we will discuss data captured from several different weather station wireless sensors Fig. 1, which use individual protocols. We will also describe how to decode them.

Three weather stations were available, the data from the fourth were decoded its sensor transmissions have been captured "in the wild".

The first sensor has been manufactured in 2008, contains an LCD display showing temperature and humidity values and has a type number H13716A-TX placed inside on the PCB. After decoding its data, we found document [12], which describes the same protocol (but is missing some fields). It provides both temperature and humidity data.

The second sensor has been manufactured in early 2013, it does not have an LCD display. The sensor has a type number Z31130-TX on a sticker outside and HQ-TX001 (MB) R-1 printed inside on the PCB. It also provides both temperature and humidity data.

The third sensor has been manufactured in late 2013 or early 2014. It does not have an LCD display, either. The sensor has a type number Z31915-TX on a sticker outside and TX06K-THC V2 printed inside on the PCB. It also provides both temperature and humidity data.

The last sensor has not been physically available to us, but it provides only the temperature data. We will label it UWTT (unknow wireless temperature transmitter) in the following text.

The weather stations using the second and third sensor look almost the same, they were sold under the same brand and use the same set of functions and graphics on LCD screen. One would expect that the sensors use same or similar protocols, but as we will show later, this is not the case.

In Fig. 2, we can see the I component of the analog signal, normalized to $\langle -1, 1 \rangle$ range. The samples for individual sensors were taken over a longer period of time, so the actual measured values will differ from each other. In the following text, we will address the individual steps needed for decoding of the signal.

5.1   Decoding the Demodulated Signal

The samples provided in Fig. 2 show, that all sensors in our evaluation use Pulse Distance Modulation and tri-state encoding (0, 1, space between the frames – S).

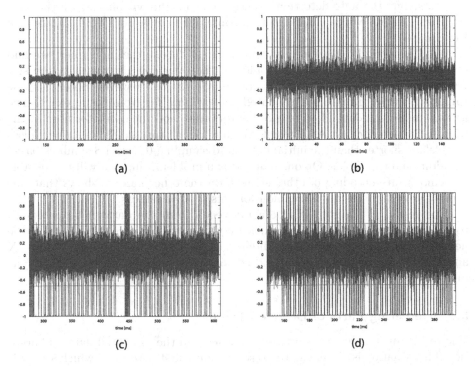

Fig. 2. Captured analog signal (I component) – first two complete frame repetitions: (a) H13716A-TX, (b) Z31130-TX, (c) Z31915-TX, (d) UWTT

The receiver circuity will demodulate the signal and provide either an analog signal, based on the input voltage, which would correspond to the non-negative part of examples shown in Fig. 2, or digital TTL levels represented by 0 or 1 values.

Table 1. Approximate timing of sensor transmissions

Sensor	Pulse	0 delay	1 delay	S delay	Sync. bit on/off	Synchronization pattern
H13716A-TX	0.4 ms	2 ms	4 ms	9 ms	–	S bit
Z31130-TX	0.5 ms	1 ms	2 ms	4 ms	–	S bit
Z31915-TX	0.75 ms	1.75 ms	4 ms	7.75 ms	1/1 ms	(2×S delay) + 4 sync bits + S bit
UWTT	0.5 ms	1 ms	2 ms	3.75 ms	0.5/0.5 ms	1 sync bit + S bit/S bit[a]

[a]First frame in sequence has the delay after sync bit (2 × S delay), the repetitions do not have a sync bit.

When processing such signal, we have to determine the pulse lengths and distances first. This may be tried semi-automatically, which will work for many receivers, but the auto-detection process may be thrown off e.g. by the synchronization bits, which can be seen in some of the measured data samples see Fig. 2(c),(d).

After successful detection of pulses, we may decode the individual bits and detect the frame length, which should be the same for all frames in the single transmission, creating the super-frame. We should, however, note, that the timings (show in Table 1 for evaluated sensors) are far from being exact. The actual timing will depend on outside temperature and the oscillator used in the wireless sensor circuity. As a result we may define thresholds, ignoring pulses and delays shorter than the initial delay and sampling 0, 1 and S symbols based on additional thresholds. On one hand, it is a problem, since we will not be able to demonstrate decoding of other signals, on the other hand it shows that this type of modulation is quite common for this type of sensors.

The result of this step will be a bit vector with the data to be processed together with meta-information which may be used for correct selection of the decoder (there may be several candidates based on the timing, e.g. Z31130-TX and UWTT use the same timing and the only difference is the presence of sync bit before S bit in UWTT).

5.2 Detecting Parts of Decoded Frame

The results of the previous step are processed and the measured data and additional information is obtained. To do so, we must first determine which sensor is being used to obtain correct frame format and interpretation. This may be done

Table 2. Basic frame information and decoded data (MSB and LSB first)

Sensor	Frame	MSB first data	LSB first data	Temperature	Humidity	Channel
H13716A-TX	36 bits	0x7DAFB004C	0x3*200*DF5BE	22.3 °C (**0x0DF**)	*20* (0x14)	3
Z31130-TX	36 bits	0x64810FF*29*	0x94FF08126	27.1 °C (**0x10F**)	41 (*0x29*)	1
Z31915-TX	40 bits	0xD262552*69*2	0x4964AA464B	7.8 °C (0x04E)	*69* (0x45)	*2*
UWTT	36 bits	0x4A8**076**F00	0x00F6E0152	11–13 °C	N/A	N/A

directly on the device which captures data, or the frame may be submitted to the server for further processing.

The decoded data is shown in Table 2, which provides both basic variants of data organization: LSB and MSB for the whole frame. We have marked the identifiable temperature data in bold, channel IDs in italics and humidity data in bold italics. We could also provide data reordered by individual bytes/nibbles, or bit-inverted data (in the case when a manufacturer would decide to use longer delay for 0 and shorter for 1), but it was not necessary in this case.

To find which parts of the frame/bits represent the measured values, it is best if we have access to the base station which should display the transmitted value (or a value close to it) on screen. The temperature is typically multiplied by 10 and stored as an 12-bit integer, so we may use its value to find the position in the frame, if available. The same way, we may look for humidity, which will be typically a 8-bit value (unless decimal places are used), channel number, or some other type of measured value which can be displayed on screen of the base station (wind speed and gust, total rainfall, etc.). The transmitted data may be further analyzed for low battery data, button pushed indication, etc.

In our case, we were directly able to identify the temperature and humidity positions for H13716A-TX, which uses LSB ordering, 12-bit temperature value and BCD-encoded humidity value. The Z31130-TX also provides both the temperature and humidity values, but in MSB order – both are hexadecimal values.

We may also expect, that UWTT temperature was 11.8 °C and the transmitter uses MSB ordering, however more measurements had to be gathered to make sure of our calculation.

5.3   Interpreting the Data Fields

Even if we were successful in identifying the data fields, at least one measurement with a negative temperature should be also made in most cases to detect the signed value representation used for temperature measurement. Example of such data is shown in Table 3. Other samples with different channel ID settings should provide the place of the channel number and battery low/high indication.

However, we have encountered a problem – the Z31915-TX did not provide any meaningful values for the temperature measurement. On the other hand, we were able to identify that data uses the MSB first order and find the positions of channel number and humidity value.

Table 3. Decoded data – subzero temperatures

Sensor	Data (in MSB format)	Temperature	Signed value	Channel	ID	Battery
H13716A-TX	0xD20FF35A0	−1.3 °C (0xFF3)	2-complement	1	0xA0	Low
Z31130-TX	0x7A9FE5F14	−2.7 °C (0xFE5)	2-complement	2	0x7A	OK
Z31915-TX	0x8B624A8383	−1.5 °C	N/A	3	0x8B	N/A

After gathering tens of samples and recording the displayed temperature, the trend started to appear. We were able to find the position of temperature measurement and determine, that the values follow a formula similar to Fahrenheit to Celsius conversion ($y = (x - 32) \cdot \frac{5}{9}$, where x is the temperature in Fahrenheit and y in Celsius).

There were however two problems – the value had still to be divided by 10 and the basic value did not match. Finally, we were able to find the correct formula for temperature calculation, which was (due to integer-based calculations prior the final step) defined as follows:

$$y = \frac{\lfloor (z - 1220) \cdot \frac{5}{9} \rfloor}{10} \quad [°C]. \tag{1}$$

The z stands for the measured value obtained from received frame and y for the temperature in Celsius.

All four evaluated sensors had a floating ID, which has been changed each time the batteries have been replaced (it means that a new scan for sensors has to be executed after battery change). The random ID allows the coexistence of different sensors with the same protocol and same channel number (or without a support for channel numbers) and ensures that the stored base values have to be reset after sensor reinitialization (e.g. for rainfall gauge). For all four sensors, the random ID has been recorded in the first two transmitted nibbles (first byte).

The frame check sequence (FCS) is often present, but unless a simple calculation has been used (like in the case of Z31130-TX), we may not be able to verify it. The channel number may appear in data directly, as a bit flag on given position, or as a value decreased by 1 (e.g. Z31130-TX uses 0 for channel 1).

There are a few additional observations to make. When using sensors other than temperature/humidity with the base station, the basic frame format (timing, repetitions, bit ordering, etc.) stays generally the same, but the sync bits and checksum calculation may change, as seen in [12].

5.4   Determined Frame Formats

In the following text, we will describe the final decoded frame formats. The following notation will be used: CH is the *channel number*, V is a bit flag indicating *low voltage*, $\overline{V}$ is a bit flag indicating that *voltage is OK*, TR indicates the *temperature trend* calculated from last measurements (00 – stable, 01 – increasing, 10 – decreasing), B indicates that a *button on the sensor has been pushed or the batteries were changed*, FCS is the *frame check sequence*.

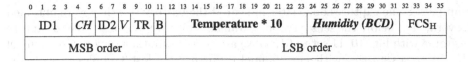

Fig. 3. Frame sent by H13716A-TX

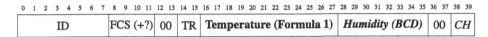

Fig. 4. Frame sent by Z31130-TX

0 1 2 3 4 5 6 7	8 9 10 11	12 13 14 15 16 17 18 19 20 21 22 23 24 25 26 27	28 29 30 31 32 33 34 35 36 37 38 39
ID	FCS (+?) 00 TR	Temperature (Formula 1) *Humidity (BCD)*	00 *CH*

Fig. 5. Frame sent by Z31915-TX

Figure 3 depicts the frame format for H13716A-TX. Detailed examination has shown, that only data from fourth nibble onward are ordered in LSB order, i.e. the channel number and trend are encoded in MSB order. The FCS is calculated (in LSB order) as

$$\mathrm{FCS_H} = 0\mathrm{xf} - (\sum_{i=0}^{7} \mathrm{nibble}_i) \ \& \ 0\mathrm{xf} \tag{2}$$

Figure 4 depicts the frame format for Z31130-TX. We were not able to find the FCS field, moreover the sensor is not equipped with a button, but there is a possibility that bit 9 is reserved for button press indication, but we were not able to verify this. The channel numbers start with 0 (for channel 1).

Figure 5 depicts the frame format for Z31130-TX. The sensor is not equipped with a button (there is a possibility that one of the bits 8–13 is reserved for button press indication, but we were not able to verify this). Also, we were not able to figure out the FCS calculation formula even with a lot of captured samples. Although it is not needed for temperature decoding, it would help us to check for erroneous frames. When we simulated the transmissions, the FCS was checked and frames with invalid FCS were dropped by the base station. However, in some cases the base station emitted a beep, so we suppose that the "button push" event may also be encoded in the, FCS but we were not able to pin it to any specific bit.

Lastly, we will describe the last weather sensor, which we were able to capture "in the wild". Figure 6 shows the sensor data we were able to obtain from several

0 1 2 3 4 5 6 7 8 9 10 11	12 13 14 15 16 17 18 19 20 21 22 23	24 25 26 27	28 29 30 31	32 33 34 35
ID $\overline{V}$ 0 *CH?*	Temperature * 10	1111	0000	0000

Fig. 6. Frame sent by unknown wireless temperature transmitter (UWTT)

samples. Some captures done later indicated the battery bit, they were obtained several days before the sensor stopped transmitting. We were also able to capture a frame with bits 10–11 set to 01, so we are pretty sure that they record channel ID, its values starting with 0 for channel 1. Further, the last 3 nibbles of the frame always read 0xf00, so there is a possibility, that this is a preset reserved value for transmitter without a humidity sensor and two of these three last nibbles in the frame may be used for humidity value in other sensors.

6   Providing the Captured Data to Internet of Things Applications

In this section, we will describe the prototype solution, which has been used to send data to the home server and to the ThingsSpeak IoT API.

The prototype implementation uses an OOK/ASK 433 MHz receiver (two possible receiver modules (the smaller one using Synoxo SYN470R [11] ASK receiver) are shown in Fig. 7 in top left corner), which are connected to the orange marked connector on the prototype board which uses a widespread cheap 8-bit microcontroller ATMEGA 328P [4].

To simulate fully the base station, we have also included humidity, barometric pressure and temperature sensors. The prototype has been connected to a router running OpenWRT firmware, which reads data from the serial port emulated by the USB-to-serial converter (top right corner). In our case we have used TP-LINK TL-WR703N. We could connect the TTL levels to on-board serial port,

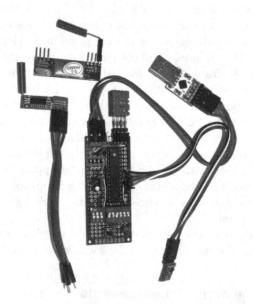

Fig. 7. Disassembled first prototype solution using ATMEGA 328P

but decided against it. It would be also possible to use a PC or Raspberry Pi instead of the router, but then we would have to solve the connectivity anyway.

The prototype has preset hard-coded parameters for individual sensors, with the possibility to replace the parameters for the first three sensors with a new custom code. There are separate configurations for both the general frame format and individual wireless sensor to make it possible to define other data types. The DIP switches in the bottom part of the prototype PCB allow us to enable/disable individual decoders (red DIP switch) and channel IDs (blue DIP switch). We have also added a LED indicating that the frame has been received, which can be disconnected (bottom right corner).

We were able to extract individual frames from the receiver and send the signal with meta-information for the processing to the router for all abovementioned wireless sensors. We are currently working on the second prototype, which uses ESP8266 SoC [8] solution with a built-in WiFi functionality, which would make the selection of wireless sensors and general configuration much easier. The device would be able to operate in a true IoT fashion, not needing the router for data preprocessing. However, the disadvantage is the increased power consumption. We are also considering the hybrid approach, with the basic decoding still done by the ATMEGA 328P processor which would provide the last captured codes on-demand when the ESP8266 module wakes from sleep, reducing the overall power consumption.

7 Conclusion

In this paper, we have provided a groundwork for the solution which would allow us to connect existing cheap home wireless weather sensors to the IoT world. We have discussed the ways how to extract data from their transmission, concentrating on the possible modulations, frame formats and data organization specifics. The paper discussed mainly the temperature and humidity sensors, but we can easily add other types of sensors as well. We have also provided examples of the frames both for the transmitters with known measured data and for a captured transmission with unknown values.

In future, we plan to build a custom solution, which would allow users to select the decoder from one of the pre-defined formats or auto-detect the possible modulation and encoding schemes and data formats. Some features, for example the used modulation, the pulse lengths and delays and used scheme, may be auto-detected when using software-defined radio to capture the sensor data. Also, we should be able to use the proposed solution together with the sensor placed in the same area to auto-detect the parameters of wireless temperature (and humidity) sensors by obtaining the data from built-in sensors and trying to match them to the received transmissions.

References

1. WMR918 PCLINK Protocol (2005). http://www.netsky.org/WMR/Protocol.htm
2. Oregon Scientific RF Protocol Description (2012). http://www.osengr.org/WxShield/Downloads/OregonScientific-RF-Protocols-II.pdf
3. Ahn, W., Choi, J., Park, C., Seo, B., Lee, M.: Automatic modulation classification of digital modulation signals based on Gaussian mixture model. In: UBICOMM 2014: The Eighth International Conference on Mobile Ubiquitous Computing, Systems, Services and Technologies. pp. 275–280 (2014)
4. Atmel Corporation: ATmega48A/PA/88A/PA/168A/PA/328/P DATASHEET (2015)
5. Atzori, L., Iera, A., Morabito, G.: The internet of things: a survey. Comput. Netw. **54**(15), 2787–2805 (2010)
6. Azzouz, E., Nandi, A.: Automatic Modulation Recognition of Communication Signals. Springer Science & Business Media, Berlin (2013)
7. Davis Instruments Corp.: Vantage Pro^{TM}, Vantage Pro2^{TM} and Vantage Vue^{TM} Serial Communication Reference Manual (2013). http://www.davisnet.com/support/weather/download/VantageSerialProtocolDocs_v261.pdf
8. Espressif Systems IOT Team: ESP8266EX Datasheet, Version 4.3 (2015). https://cdn-shop.adafruit.com/product-files/2471/0A-ESP8266_Datasheet_EN_v4.3.pdf
9. Ferrari, P., Flammini, A., Sisinni, E.: New architecture for a wireless smart sensor based on a software-defined radio. IEEE Trans. Instrum. Measur. **60**(6), 2133–2141 (2011)
10. Mainetti, L., Patrono, L., Vilei, A.: Evolution of wireless sensor networks towards the internet of things: a survey. In: 19th International Conference on Software, Telecommunications and Computer Networks (SoftCOM), pp. 1–6, September 2011
11. Synoxo: SYN470R Datasheet (300–450 MHz ASK Receiver) (2010). http://www.jmrth.com/download.asp?n=470R.pdf
12. TFD: RF transmission protocol of Auriol H13726 Ventus WS155, Hama EWS 1500, Meteoscan W155/W160 wireless weather stations v2.0 (2011). http://www.tfd.hu/tfdhu/files/wsprotocol/auriol_protocol_v20.pdf
13. Thakur, P.S., Madan, S., Madan, M.: Trends in automatic modulation classification for advanced data communication networks. Int. J. Adv. Res. Comput. Eng. Technol. (IJARCET) **4**, 496–507 (2015)

An Electronic Document for Distributed Electronic Services

Gerard Wawrzyniak and Imed El Fray[(✉)]

Faculty of Computer Science and Information Technology,
West Pomeranian University of Technology in Szczecin,
ul. Zolnierska 52, 71-210 Szczecin, Poland
gwawrzyniak@ebstream.com, ielfray@zut.edu.pl

Abstract. The paper presents the role of documents in the implementation of various types of transactions. The main features of the document determining its usefulness in the effective exchange of legal information, ensuring the authenticity, integrity and non-repudiation of origin are presented. Considering the general background of the document, the concept of an electronic document having significant (in terms of legal effectiveness) features of traditional document as well as those features that allow its operation and processing in the virtual space has been presented. An example of the use of an electronic document in the implementation of typical transactions, which are reflecting traditional electronic transaction will be discussed as well.

Keywords: Traditional document · Electronic document · Electronic transaction · XML · Electronic services

1 Introduction

Every business, regardless of the area in which it is conducted (business, administration, etc.) apart from the flow of material goods or performance of services, is associated with transfer of capital and information.

From the nature of things, the production and delivery of products and service delivery are a tangible – real. The flow of capital used to be implemented in the real world as the physical transfer of money in the past, now is almost completely dominated by the flow of information in virtual reality (electronic). The exchange and processing of information accompanying the economic processes, administrative processes etc., at all stages of their execution is carried out in many ways: talking, letters, faxes, e-mail - can be enumerated, but the importance of information is relevant to from the point of view of legal effectiveness [1–3]. At some stage of the business process execution there is a need to ensure the legal effectiveness of information being exchanged at least for purposes of legal proceedings, in case of differences in the interpretation of events and commitments undertaken by parties. Such possibility is provided by document that regardless of its form (technical implementation) must ensure authenticity, non-repudiation of origin, integrity and privacy [4–6].

Furthermore, the document as an electronic document must ensure the possibility of electronic transport, storage, and first of all the processing using electronic means.

© IFIP International Federation for Information Processing 2016
Published by Springer International Publishing Switzerland 2016. All Rights Reserved
K. Saeed and W. Homenda (Eds.): CISIM 2016, LNCS 9842, pp. 617–630, 2016.
DOI: 10.1007/978-3-319-45378-1_54

The existing formats of electronic documents actually files, do not meet requirements discussed above.

For example, the format of Microsoft Office "*.doc, .docx" or Libre Office (Open Office) does not provide legal effectiveness (no electronic signatures applied), it also do not give the possibility of electronic data processing.

Adobe format *.pdf in its basic form provides the ability to sign a document (whole content) using number of signatures - but it can not generate the signatures of various parts of a document by different people. These forms do not reflect the real (paper) forms in which it is possible to perform such signatures. It is also possible to use XFDF format, based on XML and representing data and annotations, which are included in PDF form file. Automatic processing of data from a PDF document requires a conversion (data mining) document into an XML data file (XFDF).

Electronic document, especially the one that is used by human is composed of presentation layer and data layer. It should reflect the traditional documents and forms in which these two layers are contained in a single object - a piece of paper (or multiple pages) - this is the immanent feature of a document. Mentioned above formats of documents meet this requirement. However, as already mentioned, do not meet critical requirements (legal effectiveness, ease of electronic processing). Such requirements would meet the electronic document based on XML (ease and interoperability of processing, with legal efficiency provided by electronic signatures (many signatures covering different parts of the document, done by many people) with the use of PKI, including in its structure both description of visualization and introduced by human data.

A similar solution is presented in the XFDL form (Extensible Forms Description Language) proposed by Canadian company Pure Edge [7]. In XFDL forms both data and presentation of data is stored in one XML file which syntax described using the DTD. This solution does not provide the possibility to define and then implement such features: as default values of each form field, validation rules of the data, help messages and hints. In the XFDL forms it is not possible to define a method to build XML messages based on data stored in the form, and support protocols to exchange information with network services (e.g. SOAP), which would allow to build messages, sending them to the server, receiving a response in real time as synchronous mode and present (update) data in a form for presentation.

The aim of the article is to present, with regard to described above drawbacks, the format of an electronic form with syntax formally described using XML Schema XSD. The form contains description of the form visualisation, data types of form fields, and electronic signatures with indication of elements sign by each signature, calculation rules and also the following new features (relating to the XFDL), such as definitions of default values, validation rules, mechanisms for building XML messages, descriptions how to send XML (or the entire form) using SOAP or SMTP (the list of recipients, encryption) protocols, a mechanism for interpreting XML messages received in SOAP response. These features enable to implement electronic services of transactions in real time.. Other aim of the paper is to show possibility an benefits of such document in distributed services definition and execution.

2 Document in Electronic Service Delivery

On behalf of the European Commission, the company Cap Gemini Ernst & Young, has developed a 4-point scale assessment of the progress of the e-Europe initiative for evaluating the availability of online services for citizens and businesses [8]:

0 – The service is not (in any form) provided electronically:
   – no publicly accessible website/s, or those websites does not meet the criteria for levels 1–4;

1 – Information:
   – publication of electronic information on the service provided;

2 – One-way interaction:
   – the possibility to download forms;

3 – Two-way interaction
   – the possibility to fill out forms or electronic submission of the application or requests;

4 – Transaction
   – full electronic execution of the case, taking into account the decision, informing the recipient, delivery and payment if applicable;

Levels of electronic services maturity are shown in the Fig. 1.

Achieving the highest level does not always mean executing the service at the transaction level, for example, some services are one-sided information reported to the authority and do not require a decision. Therefore, also among the criteria's for assessing the progress of e-Europe, used by the Commission of the European Union a key place takes accessibility for citizens and businesses to public services and the quality of these services. However, you can see that the achievement of 3rd and especially 4th maturity level requires:

– ensure the authenticity, integrity and non-repudiation of origin of exchanged information it means the legal effectiveness of that information, and
– the need for automation of the service and hence the need to automate the processing of information associated with the service execution.

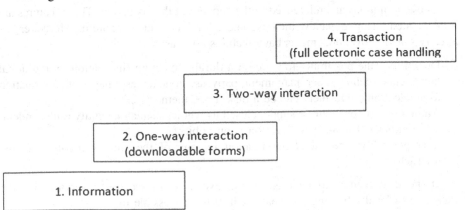

Fig. 1. Maturity levels of electronic services

Public services should therefore be considered in these two dimensions: in terms of legal regulations and technical implementation.

3   Document and Its Features

The document is any tangible or symbolic indication, fixed or saved in order to prove the phenomenon of physical or mental [9], it means that document is a resource used as evidence. However, the concept of the document in the language of computer makes some problems, it is commonly equated - the concept of electronic document and the concept of the file.

The file is a collection of data stored in permanent memory (hard disk or other media), which can be seen by the user of the operating system as a unitary, indivisible, closed as a whole, having a distinct name and a specific structure. It is the result of working with a computer program, writable and then readable.

It seems that the most preferred would be to combine the two approaches, and without changing the concept of the primary document concept, state that:

- An electronic document is a document in the form of a file, which has all the features of the document and all the features of the file.
- Data are stored on a medium. In the case of electronic information the data can be processed, communicated and interpreted by computer. A set of data may sometimes constitute a record [10].
- The international Council on Archives [10] Committee on electronic records defines a record as 'a specific piece of recorded information generated, collected or received in the initiation, conduct or completion of an activity and that comprises sufficient content, context and structure to provide proof or evidence of that activity'.

Legal effectiveness of the document is ensured by document features:

- integrity - the immutability of content (document content),
- authenticity - by knowledge of the origin of the document,
- non-repudiation - no possibility to denial of the document authorship.

These definitions and referenced to the concept of the document. These features are implemented using a handwritten signature or electronic signature. Moreover, as already stated above, documents have features such as:

- Durability - the possibility to store on a durable medium (in relation to traditional documents, such as paper, parchment, papyrus, stone tables, images etc., in relation to an electronic document can be a disk, tape, memory, etc.)
- Autonomy - it constitutes a single, closed as whole, standalone entity (independent, autonomous - data and visualization is one object).
- Interoperability - readable/interpretation by any of the entities involved in the transaction

If the document is to be used in the execution of electronic services for the exchange of legally binding information, it must be possible to.

- its transmission in electronic form,
- automatic reading and writing of data in file, automatic processing across different systems,
- automatic verification of features for its legal effectiveness,
- recording and storing in electronic warehouses (databases, file systems).

General features of document and specific features of electronic document are depicted on the following Fig. 2.

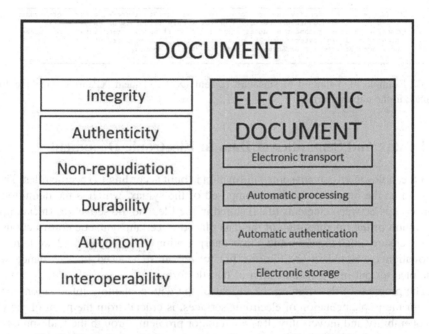

Fig. 2. Each electronic document is a document and has all of its features

The European Union Directive [11] and its national implementations in the form of national acts [12], equates in terms of legal effectiveness, the handwritten signature and the electronic signature. Thus electronic signature plays a key role in ensuring the legal effectiveness of an electronic document. In addition, it is possible and even desirable to implement other features of the handwritten signature in electronic signatures, such as:

- the possibility of signing one or more parts of the document by one signature,
- ability to place in the document number of signatures (signing - including the indicated part of the document)
- possibility of countersigning.

Such possibilities are given by XML Signature format – XMLdSig [13] and its development – XAdES [14]. Below, see Figs. 3 and 4, the example of modelling the contents of signature in electronic ebForm document is presented (ebForm is xml format of electronic document in the shape of electronic form defined by author.

```
<ds:XPath>(ancestor::*/parent::value or ancestor-or-
self::ds:Signature/ancestor::signature//parent::ebForm or
ancestor::content/ancestor::attachment or ancestor::*/ancestor::*/ancestor::mailStatus or ances-
tor::*/ancestor::value/ancestor::soap-RPC or ancestor::body/ancestor::request or ances-
tor::header/ancestor::request or ancestor::body/ancestor::response)or (ances-
tor::*/parent::value/ancestor-or-self::*/signedBy/signer[text()='clientsignature'] or ancestor-
or-self::ds:Signature/ancestor::signature/countersignedBy/signer[text()='clientsignature']
)</ds:XPath>
```

Fig. 3. Example of definition of signature content (XML element XPath) signing the client signature (one of the many users) in the ebForm form)

```
<ds:XPath>(ancestor::*/parent::value or ancestor-or-self::ds:Signature/ancestor::formSignature
or ancestor-or-self::ds:Signature/ancestor::signature//parent::ebForm or ances-
tor::content/ancestor::attachment or ancestor::*/ancestor::*/ancestor::mailStatus or ances-
tor::*/ancestor::value/ancestor::soap-RPC or ancestor::body/ancestor::request or ances-
tor::header/ancestor::request or ancestor::body/ancestor::response)
</ds:XPath>
```

Fig. 4. Example of definition of signature content (XML element XPath) signing the form template in the ebForm form

4   Syntax and Semantics of Data in Electronic Document

Each file, holds in its content some information is built according to specific rules. These rules define the file format and are composed of the syntax, which is the definition of relationships between elements (data) stored in the file, and the semantics (meaning), a description of the interpretation of the data placed in certain syntactic constructions.

To ensure unambiguous and clear interpretation (by peoples and systems) of information contained in the file, the file format must be used in accordance with principles set out in the specification of the file format.

The problem of determining the format of the data containing information necessary for the implementation of electronic services, is crucial from the point of view of interoperability and universality. It is not a major problem, through the widespread use for this purpose XML. XML has become the informal but extremely popular and the applicable standard [15–17].

In addition to many features of XML, such as:

- platform independence and software being applied using,
- support for a universal set of national characters UNICODE
- clarity and ease of processing.

Special attention should be payed to:

- the ability to define the syntax and automatic verification of information structure with the syntax,
- the ability to import syntactic structures defined in another place that is possibility to use data structures already defined,
- the ability to identify both the document and components imported using namespace (namespace) [18].

At present the centralized model of electronic services implementation and execution is used in Poland.

This is such approach to the construction of electronic public services, in which the document formats, data dictionaries and ways of delivering services are defined, implemented and executed by a designated central organization and other organizations have to subordinate to this central organization. This approach causes the separation of the responsibility for the implementation of services in its real terms from implementing the same services in the electronic (virtual) dimension. The model is complicated by the possibility of existing a few centers (tax authorities, local authorities and government) responsible for different areas of activity This is shown in the Fig. 5.

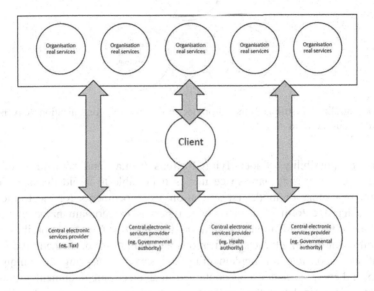

Fig. 5. The centralized model of electronic services - the existence of several different centers is possible

Considerations in the area of syntax and semantics of the data in an electronic document and the features and capabilities of XML are of particular importance in light of the concept of decentralization of public services and posting obligation to implement them to the places (institutions, organizations), where those services are actually carried out – see Fig. 6.

The decentralized model of defining the specifications and publishing electronic documents, is presented in this article assumes that:

- document formats (syntax and meaning) are defined and published by these organizations, which are responsible for the implementation of electronic service using defined document,
- data structures and data are defined in organizations using namespace that has the form of a URL, as in the domain name owned by the organization responsible for implementing the service. This provides a unique and unambiguous terms used in the exchange of documents.
- Appearance (visualization of the document), taking into account specific regulations as well as freedom of visualization within a certain range (tax form, invoice)

Fig. 6. Decentralized (distributed) model of electronic services – organization delivers services in real and electronic form

Using the possibility of identifying formats (syntax and semantics) of specific documents and data using namespace makes it possible to avoid the need for a use the central repository of model (specifications) of documents (or electronic forms). Namespace has the form of a URL, which part is the domain name owned entity responsible for the specification of certain documents. It is therefore possible "exit" the responsibility for defining these specifications and definitions of the central office to the organization responsible for implementing the service, ensuring the uniqueness of identifiers and compliance concepts contained in an electronic document with the terms defined in the act regulating the implementation of the service.

Practical use of the principles presented above, would be the universal application of the rule of expansion of legal acts which describe the public service, by the entity implementing this service by the syntax definition of electronic documents (in the form of a DTD or XML Schema) with a description of its meaning. A description of the syntax and semantics would be a complement to this part of the act, where documents and forms in its traditional form are described.

Such an approach would at the same time the specification of requirements for software vendors in regards not only to data formats and visualization, but also the acceptable range of visualization freedom (e.g. strictly defined tax form, or the appearance of freeform invoice).

The decentralization of the electronic services execution is:

- reflection of the actual geographical and functional decentralization of services delivery;
- linking responsibility for the electronic dimension of the service with the real service (one entity responsible for the execution of services in real and electronic dimension);
- The implementation of electronic services, complementary/extension services in a manner consistent with local customs and requirements.

Easier and unambiguous definition of the concepts related to the particular service - these definitions, as a part of the act regulating the implementation of services are created in the same place and in the same act.

A special, very important role in the exchange of information associated with the delivery of services regardless of method of realization: whether it is e-service, or provided traditionally, regardless of the model - the central or decentralized, regardless of the area (industry), plays the form. Natural need to enter data in the appropriate space limits the possibilities of interpreting the meaning of these data so that the form is a convenient means to collect the data necessary for the service, as well as the processing of these data, which is important especially for automatic execution of these processes. Taking into account the fact that the currently performed service may be fully or partially carried out automatically and partially, by human it would be relevant to make use of such an electronic document (form), with the use of suitable software, which could be used by a man and simultaneously processed in computer systems.

5 Electronic Form

Electronic document containing the information necessary to execute the service is processed automatically. Identification of the document type and the particular data using namespace allows unambiguous interpretation of these data (interpretation is published in the type specification document and published in the act of describing the realization of the service as described in the discussion on the implementation of services in the decentralized model) by all entities taking part in the service. The use of a document in XML format syntax as XML schema, makes possible to automatic verification of document syntax and automatic document processing.

If documents are exchanged between systems that implement the services (or services that form part of other service), then visualization of the data is not necessary, because the machine executing the service has been implemented in accordance with publicly available specifications described above.

However, if the party taking part in the execution of the service is the human, the document must be presented to the user. Human must understand the document, type the information to it and consciously sign this document.

Similar to the traditional paper document, the most convenient form of the document for this purpose is the form. The electronic form it is a document containing free places for data representing desired information, and to ensure the characteristics of the document - signature. The data are entered in the form in which the appearance of the form and arrangement of fields for entered data determine the semantics of these data. In terms of the form it is a document in which visualization and data are one inseparable entity, in which the semantics of data is determined by the graphical environment of the data. Thus, if an electronic document will contain both the data and its presentation it will be electronic implementation - a metaphor of the traditional paper form readable/understandable by man and at the same time possible to automatic processing using commonly available tools.

It should be noted that the concept of an electronic form presented above, in accordance with its traditional understanding deviates from the currently existing electronic forms, in which an separation of presentation layer and the data layer is implemented (e.g. An HTML in which "forms" are used to collect data to be sent to the server, or separating data from presentation of XML documents with reference to the transformation file XSLT). Visualization layer is responsible for presenting the form view, the user enters the required data, which are sent to the service provider (after separating them from the presentation layer - the graphical environment determining the semantics of these data). This approach prevents a uniform semantic interpretation of the transmitted (stored) data.

In the proposed solution the form is an electronic document based on XML, with syntax defined using XSD [XML Schema Definition], applying electronic signatures based on XMLDSig/XAdES [XML Advanced Electronic Signatures], containing both the data and the description of the presentation (visualization) of the form in one single file – see Fig. 7.

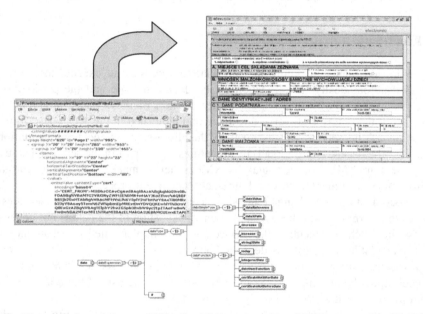

Fig. 7. Electronic form (syntax - XSD, data XML, presentation XML) – example of Polish tax declaration form

6   Features of Electronic Form

In addition to its "traditional functionality" electronic form can and should be enhanced with the features offered by the Information Technique such as:

- possibility to verify the formal validity of data,
- possibility to define default values,
- possibility to define of help and tips,
- providing a dynamic (or lock) input fields.

– calculating the value of each field based on the data entered into other fields.
– ability to define the mechanisms of communication and ways of exchanging data between the form and the environment through a well known protocols as email or web services protocols.

All these features are part of the form and are part of the document together with the data and presentation. This is due to the need to ensure that the description of the method of processing and presentation of data is accessible and known to all users in order to avoid doubts in interpretation.

In the following Fig. 8 the example of definition of text field ("textField" element) with its properties is presented (ebForm format).

```xml
<textField X="0" Y="2" height="20" horizontalAlignment="Right"
id="Pismo.MiastoPowstania.Komponent" width="175" xsi:type="stringField">
        <value>
                    <stringValue id="Pismo.MiastoPowstania">Łęczna</stringValue>
        </value>
        <defaultValue>
                    <substring>
                            <stringReference>Urzad.KodMiasto</stringReference>
                            <beginIndex>
                                        <integerValue>7</integerValue>
                            </beginIndex>
                            <endIndex>
                                        <stringLength>
            <stringReference>Urzad.KodMiasto</stringReference>
                                        </stringLength>
                            </endIndex>
                    </substring>
        </defaultValue>
        <background>
                    <colorValue id="Kolor.Pol">218 231 248</colorValue>
        </background>
        <helpText>
                    <stringValue>Należy wpisać nazwę miejscowości.</stringValue>
        </helpText>
        <tipText>
                    <stringValue>Należy wpisać nazwę miejscowości.</stringValue>
        </tipText>
        <validity id="Pismo.MiastoPowstania.Poprawnosc">
                    <rule>
                            <condition>
                                    <not>
                                            <isEmpty>
            <dateReference>Pismo.MiastoPowstania</dateReference>
                                            </isEmpty>
                                    </not>
                            </condition>
                            <description title="Brak miejscowości przy dacie">Należy wpisać
nazwę miejscowości przy dacie powstania dokumentu.</description>
                    </rule>
        </validity>
    </textField>
```

Fig. 8. Example of defining the features in the form (value, default value, background, help text, text, hints, validation rules)

Form features defined in this way, make it possible to use the form as an information medium that is synonymous with the traditional document (form) and to use the form as a intelligent interface to services, where form is a generator of messages sent out, or processor of message received from service, and involving human.

Very wide range applications of electronic forms could be enumerated. Such forms is a generic solution with can be used in different areas regardless of business area – form small companies for ordering and invoicing, thru activities associated with internal company management up to support for Client – Business, Client – Administration and Business – Administration operations. It can be applied wherever legally effective information is required or forms are being used (exchanged) both by human and machines, or by human only.

7 The Use of Electronic Forms – Applications/Implementations

Electronic forms based on the concept presented in the article can be used wherever legal effectiveness is required, regardless of the area of activity and the size of the business.

Electronic form looks exactly like its traditional counterpart. The logic of usage is also identical.

It can be transferred/delivered to recipient using widely known mechanisms like: simple mail as attachment to mail message or SOAP as Soap envelope content. It also can be transferred as ordinary file.

It can be simply processed by information systems using standard XML parsers and then integrated with internal organization's systems including data retrieval and transferring data to internal databases. For example:

- Exchange documents (agreements, orders, others) using SMTP, as attachment,
- Implementation of simple document flow even composed of few steps of document exchange within company or between companies (holiday arranging, internal reports etc....) and integration with internal systems and databases using SMTP or services implemented using SOAP protocol.
- Legally effective delivery of a document to the public authority with the official synchronous (immediately) confirmation of delivery/reception. The confirmation is digitally signed part of the document, and document is automatically integrated with internal authority system,
- Legally effective delivery of a document to recipient (human) using SMTP with confirmation signature of recipient (client) returned to sender.
- Implementation of fiscal charges undeniably linked with the document.

This shows, that presented concept of the form, in contrast to formats presented in the introduction (.doc, odt, pdf/xfdf, xfdl), allows:

- exact implementation of traditional documents.
- automatic document processing.
- automatic signatures verification (authorization, authentication).
- document integration with existing systems.
- ensuring the legal effectiveness of the document.

8 Summary

Electronic services are typically implemented using dedicated, closed - demanding and accounts of users. Legal effectiveness of documents used for the transaction is provided only in the space of the system. The autonomy and interoperability of document is violated - it can not exist out of dedicated system.

Another way to implement such transactions is the use of signed PDF documents and PDF forms. The use of such documents is a source of serious problems and costs associated with processing its.

In turn, the use of e-mail (SMTP) does not provide legal effectiveness and also creates serious problems with messages processing.

The proposed concept of electronic documents in the shape of forms using the XML format, containing both a description of visualization and data input, signed with electronic signatures and containing other elements (calculations, verification rules, defaults, etc.).

The concept of electronic form presented in this paper is a subject of work in progress at the stage of wide testing. Results of work will be presented in future papers.

References

1. Veseláa, L., Radiměřská, M.: The development of electronic document exchange. Procedia Econ. Finance **12**, 743–751 (2014)
2. Guidclines on best practices for using electronic information. How to deal with machine-readable data and electronic documents, Brussels (1997)
3. Petermann, R.: Electronic Document. ArchNet, Lodz (1998)
4. Chen, Y.-C., Horng, G., Huang, C.-C.: Privacy protection in on-line shopping for electronic documents. Inf. Sci. **277**, 321–326 (2014)
5. Sion, R., Carbunar, B.: On the computational practicality of private information retrieval. In: Proceedings of Network and Distributed System Security Symposium (2007)
6. Sakurai, K., Yamane, Y.: Blind decoding, blind undeniable signatures, and their applications to privacy protection. In: Anderson, R. (ed.) IH 1996. LNCS, vol. 1174, pp. 257–264. Springer, Heidelberg (1996)
7. Extensible Form Description Language (XFDL) 4.0, W3c Note, September 1998. https://www.w3.org/TR/1998/NOTE-XFDL-19980902
8. Digitizing Public Services in Europe: Putting ambition into action 9th Benchmark Measurement, December 2010, Capgemini, IDC, Rand Europe, Sogeti and DTi for: European Commission, Directorate General for Information Society and Media, December 2010
9. Briet, S.: Qu'est-ce que la documentation? Documentaires Industrielles et Techniques, Paris (1951)
10. International council on archives ICA.ORG. www.ica.org
11. Directive of the European Parliament and Council 1999/93/ EC of 13 December 1999. On a Community framework for electronic signatures
12. Act of 18 September 2001. On electronic signature. OJ 2001 No. 130, item. 1450
13. XML Signature Syntax and Processing. http://www.w3.org/TR/xmldsig-core/
14. XML Advanced Electronic Signatures (XAdES). http://www.w3.org/TR/XAdES

15. Extensible Markup Language (XML). http://www.w3.org/XML/
16. Blake Dournaee XML Security. McGraw-Hill Osborne Media (2002)
17. Hassler, V.: Security Fundamentals for E-Commerce. Artech House (2001)
18. Namespaces in XML. http://www.w3.org/TR/REC-xml-names/

Biometrics, Identification, Security

FE8R - A Universal Method for Face Expression Recognition

Majida Albakoor[1], Khalid Saeed[2], Mariusz Rybnik[3($\boxtimes$)],
and Mohamad Dabash[4]

[1] Artificial Intelligence Department, Faculty of Information Engineering,
Damascus University, Damascus, Syria
krsten2007@hotmail.com
[2] Bialystok University of Technology, Bialystok, Poland
k.saeed@pb.edu.pl
[3] University of Bialystok, Bialystok, Poland
mariuszrybnik@wp.pl
[4] Mathematics Department, Faculty of Science, Aleppo University, Aleppo, Syria
sfmad@yahoo.com

Abstract. This paper proposes a new method for recognition of face
expressions, called FE8R. We studied 6 standard expressions: *anger, disgust, fear, happiness, sadness, surprise*, and additional two: *cry* and *natural*. For experimental evaluation samples from *MUG Facial Expression
Database* and *color FERET Database* were taken, with addition of *cry*
expression. The proposed method is based on the extraction of characteristic objects from images by gradient transformation depending on the
coordinates of the minimum and maximum points in each object on the
face area. The gradient is ranked in $[-15, +35]$ degrees. Essential objects
are studied in two ways: the first way incorporates slant tracking, the
second is based on feature encoding using *BPCC algorithm* with classification by *Backpropagation Artificial Neural Networks*. The achieved
classification rates have reached 95 %. The second method is proved to be
fast and producing satisfactory results, as compared to other approaches.

Keywords: Face expression · Feature extraction · Feature encoding ·
Slant tracking · Artificial Neural Networks

1 Introduction

Face recognition is one of the most intensively searched topics in biometrics. Its
applications are among others behaviour interpretation, human-machine interaction and interfaces. Various data representations and classification methods
were proposed [1,2]. A derivation of the topic is recognition of psychological
emotions with the use of face image or video [3].

The problem was addressed by different approaches using various data representations and classifiers [1,4,5]. The efforts in face recognition have been
largely motivated by industrial interests [6]. Many algorithms were proposed, the

© IFIP International Federation for Information Processing 2016
Published by Springer International Publishing Switzerland 2016. All Rights Reserved
K. Saeed and W. Homenda (Eds.): CISIM 2016, LNCS 9842, pp. 633–646, 2016.
DOI: 10.1007/978-3-319-45378-1_55

majority of the proposed methods, however, fail to achieve satisfactory performance level for face expressions [7], especially for the recognition of face expressions [7, 8].

The authors propose a new feature extraction algorithm to recognize eight facial expressions: *anger, disgust, fear, happiness, natural, sadness, surprise* and *cry*, called FE8R algorithm. The data is from *MUG Facial Expression Database* [9] and *color FERET Database* [10], with addition of *cry* expression. The proposed approach relies on *essential object detection* then *geometric feature analysis* using directional encoding to feed Artificial Neural Network classifiers.

The paper is organized as follows: Sect. 2 presents state of the art in the area, Sect. 3 describes the proposed approach in detail, Sect. 4 presents some experiments and result discussion, finally Sect. 5 discusses the conclusions and future work.

2   State of the Art

Face expression recognition is a problem closely related to *segmentation* (finding the face in the image) and *facial feature extraction* (selection of characteristic points, shapes or areas). Face expression recognition may be defined as the analysis of selected facial features to detect predefined face expression classes, like *anger* or *smile*. Therefore it could be seen as a classification problem [11]. Commonly recognized emotions are {*anger, disgust, fear, happiness, sadness, surprise*} as seen in [12,13]. In this paper the authors distinguish also two other expressions: *cry* and *natural*.

2.1   Similar Approaches

Many approaches depend on feature extraction to produce a feature vector. It may consist of two types of features: *geometric features* (shape and location of segmented features) [14] or *appearance features* (based on the texture properties of the skin in certain areas) [2,15]. Appearance features may be seen as a template matching problem, applied to the emotion recognition area [16].

In [17] authors use *feature vectors* as an input to the *Artificial Neural Network* with *Radial Basis Function* neurons (*RBF*) in order to recognize facial expressions. The face image is divided into three regions of interest: mouth, nose and eyes with eyebrows. After applying *unsharpen filter* using certain threshold, the facial characteristic points (*FCPs*) are detected. *FCPs* lengths are calculated using Euclidean distance. Two angles in the mouth area are computed to represent geometric features, similarly the two remaining regions, the nose and the eyes. 19 geometric features and 64 appearance features form the input for the *RBF* neural network.

Authors in [18,19] propose an approach for coding facial expressions using *Gabor wavelets*. *Gabor filters* are applied to each image, featured by 34 fiducial points to produce *Gabor filter* bank response. This results in a feature vector of length 612 (34 fiducial points with 18 filter responses per point) that represents the facial expressions. *PCA* (*Principal Component Analysis*) technique [20] is used to arrange the feature vector in order of descending variance and is truncated at desired length. This is to find out, if the length of feature vector is sufficient for correct recognition of facial expressions. Input vectors are classified by *LVQ* neural network. In the study, the length of the feature vector was set to 90 and the sub-class size varied from 35 to 77 to classify seven different expressions.

Authors in [21] recognize 7 expressions: *angry, disgust, fear, happy, natural, sad,* and *surprise*. They use Gabor filters for facial feature extraction and 6 classification methods. Their major contribution is the analysis of the behaviour of various classifiers (simplified Bayes, AdaBoost, FDLP, SVM, FSLP) in the case of small number of training examples per class. The method proposed by authors (FSLP) reached 92.4 % of correct emotion recognition over 213 images of 10 people in this case.

Authors in [22,23] use neuro-fuzzy approach to recognize the following expressions: *happy, fear, sad, angry, disgust* and *surprise*. The image is segmented into three regions, from which the uniform *Local Binary Pattern* (*LBP*) texture features distributions are extracted and represented as a histogram descriptor. *LBP* is called uniform if the binary pattern contains at most two bitwise transitions from 0 to 1 or vice versa. When it is considered circular, the operator labels of each pixel in a Gray-level image are considered, with the pixel in question at the center and 3×3 neighborhood pixel variations formed to 8-bit binary code. The facial expressions are then recognized using *Multiple Adaptive Neuro-Fuzzy Inference System* (*MANFIS*) [24].

This paper algorithm recognizes the largest amount of expressions. It is based on geometric feature extraction and encoding, with ANN used as classifiers. Detailed results are given in Sect. 4.

2.2 Comparison

A short comparison of the authors' approach in this paper and similar approaches is presented in Table 1, with additional remarks below.

1. The approach described in [17], based on geometric and appearance features, uses as input images scaled to an array of 300 by 300 pixel with 8-bit precision for grayscale values. The recognition rate reported is between 93.5 % to 96 %.
2. In the approach with Gabor wavelets [18], generalization accuracy is reported to be from 87.51 % to 90.22 %. The recognition rate is close to uniform for all expressions including *fear*. The network does not acquire 100 % correct classifications, even for training database.
3. In the approach [21] the emphasis is put on the small number of cases in the learning database. The reported accuracy for small number of classes (10 people) is 92.4 %.
4. In the approach [22], using neuro-fuzzy and LBP, a classification accuracy rate of 94.29 % is reported.

Table 1. Comparison with other approaches

Ref.	Approach	Input	Expr.	Recogn. rate
[17]	Geometric and appearance features	300 × 300, grayscale	6	96 %
[18]	Gabor wavelets, LVQ	Grayscale	7	90 %
[21]	Gabor wavelets, various classifiers	256 × 256, grayscale	7	92.4 %
[22]	Neuro-fuzzy and LBP	Binary	7	94.29 %
This paper	FE8R	Various, unscaled	8	~95 %

The work presented in this paper does not require input image scaling. The obtained rate of recognition is comparable, despite the fact that number of recognized expressions increases to 8.

3 The Proposed Approach: FE8R Algorithm

The authors propose a complex approach to face expression classification, called FE8R algorithm. The proposed approach relies on the selection of so called *essential objects (EO)* and analysis of geometric features using either directional encoding or direct feed to Artificial Neural Network classifier. Translation and scaling issues need to be dealt with at (mostly automated) preprocessing stage.

The face image is converted into grayscale. The image is normalized if required, by adjusting the intensity using minimum and maximum of intensity values in the image. The contrast is enhanced by histogram equalization. Filtration using median filtering is used to reduce the noise and preserve the edges. The image is rotated by a suitable angle degree. Also the image edges are detected. The work area and its center are calculated depending on dividing the image into four quarters and the characteristic objects are detected using the coordinates of the minimum and maximum points of each object and the object perimeter is larger than the major-axis of the formed ellipse for the studied object. The characteristic object is reduced to get *EO*, by applying the gradient value between the x-axis and the major axis ranked in $[-15, +35]$ degrees. The number of *EO* is reduced by at least 80 %. Two methods are applied, the first method is depending on the slant, we fix the center of the object and study the slant from the starting-point. We consider the slant changing is acting so that the slant changing is examined by testing the alternate of slant sign. By slant progression analysis, one can consider the face expression as happy or sad. The second method uses feature coding, we extract the objects important points. These points are coded by BPCC algorithm [25]. Filtered code is dealt with to form an array of 81 elements. Then the array is scaled to consider as the input of ANN backpropagation network.

Two classification methods are used: the first tracks points on the basis of fixed slant, where the slant is calculated depending on the object center point and the face center, whilst the second encodes the data for ANN.

Two ways are applied the first is by slant variation after fixing the object center based on its starting-point. If the slant variation is clear without alternating slant sign compared with its preceding value, then noticeably, the face is classified as *happy*. If we have variation with slant sign alternating, the face is *sad*. The second way considers extracting the characteristic points by defining the end-points, start-points, branch, and turning pixels. The object is coded depending on the detected pixels using eight digit pairs with two passes counterclockwise. Code is filtered according to eight chosen basic pairs. Calculations are made to form an array of 9×9 elements added to the percentage of distributed points in each part of the studied character. Hence the resulting matrix is formed by 85 elements. Finally, the matrix is passed to ANN for classification.

Subsequent phases of the algorithm are detailed in the following sections.

3.1 Face Image Preprocessing

Face image requires preprocessing to improve the image quality [26–29]. The first step is converting the color image into grayscale image, as shown in Fig. 1a. The second step is image normalization with two phases [30]: first by adjusting the intensity regarding minimum and maximum intensity values, second by enhancing the contrast with histogram equalization, as shown in Fig. 1b, c. The third step is filtering using median filter in order to reduce noise, as presented in Fig. 1d. A median filter is considered more effective than convolution, when the goal is to simultaneously preserve the edges [31]. In the fourth step, if required,

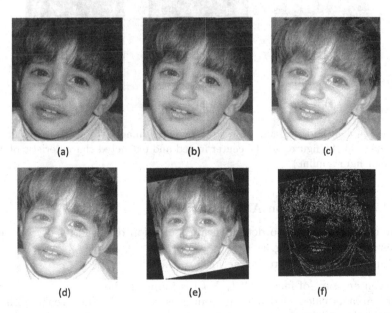

Fig. 1. Face image preprocessing: (a) color image, (b) normalized image, (c) image after histogram equalization, (d) image after median filter, (e) rotated image, (f) edge detection

the image is rotated by a suitable angle around its center (the rotation procedure in [28] is used), as shown in Fig. 1e. The fifth step is detecting the edges by Canny method [32] with the threshold 0.08 and sigma 1 (determined empirically), as depicted in Fig. 1f.

3.2   Extraction of Characteristic Objects

The authors consider that the horizontal lines (or edges) are more influential for face expressions, so the idea is to find this type of edges. After the edges are detected, the work area and its center are determined and represented as 16×8 squares. Studied object is enclosed in ellipse and the characteristic objects are extracted using the minimum and maximum coordinates of each object [1,33] and the gradient between the x-axis and major axis [29], as shown in Fig. 2. The characteristic objects boundaries are drawn in blue. Among all characteristic objects some are labeled as *essential objects*, depending on the slant. The authors have considered that the difference between the x-axis and major ellipse axis is between -15 and $+35$ degrees (determined empirically). Two methods are applied; the first is slant analysis of *ConvexHullK* [34] points to transform them into suitable input of ANN, the second method is encoding the important points of basic objects depending on *BPCC algorithm* to recognize *anger, disgust, fear, happiness, natural, sadness, surprise* and *cry* expressions.

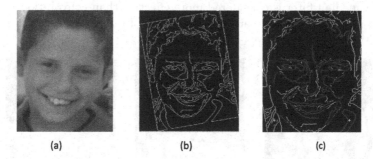

(a)   (b)   (c)

Fig. 2. An image and its boundaries; (a) primary image; (b) work area defined by yellow points in the figure, (c) the center in red and extracted characteristic objects in blue (Color figure online)

3.3   Feature Extraction Algorithm

Feature extraction leads to detection and selection of *essential objects*. This is given as a flowchart in Fig. 3.

Detailed steps of feature extraction are as follows:

1. The center point of face $M(X\_k, Y\_k)$ is found in the image.
2. Work area is calculated and its center is detected. The area is defined as the middle of face space containing the eyes, nose and mouth. That space is represented by about three-quarters of the face. This area is divided into 16×8 squares. The square length is denoted as $Square\_line\_Y$.

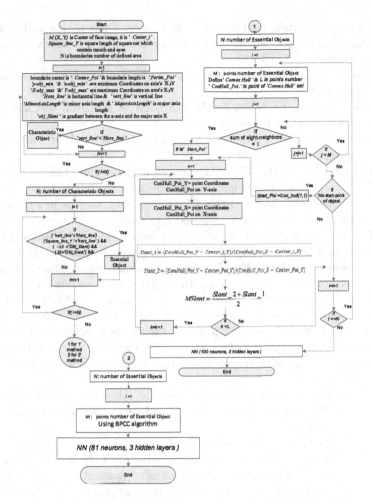

Fig. 3. The flowchart of the *essential objects* detection and selection

3. Exterior boundaries of objects are traced, with any holes inside these objects neglected. These objects are parents while their children boundaries represent continuous regions in the studied image.

4. For each object and its boundaries, the analysis is performed as follows:
   (a) The center of object is located and denoted by *Center_Poi*.
   (b) The minima of coordinates on X-axis and Y-axis are calculated, they are denoted respectively by *X-obj_min* and *Y-obj_min*. Similarly, the maxima are denoted by *X-obj_max* and *Y-obj_max*.
   (c) The horizontal line *horz_line* is represented by the difference of maximum and minimum in Y axis.
   (d) The vertical line *vert_line* is represented by the difference of maximum and minimum in X axis.

(e) An ellipse containing the object is formed, then major and minor axis ellipse lengths are calculated and denoted by *MinorAxisLength* and *MajorAxisLength*.

(f) The slant between the x-axis and the major axis of the ellipse is calculated, called *obj_slant*.

5. If the *horz_line* or the *MajorAxisLength* is larger than the *vert_line* then the object is *a characteristic object*.

6. *Characteristic object* is promoted to *an essential object* if at least one of the following conditions applies:

   (a) The *horz_line* or the *MajorAxisLength* is larger than the *vert_line*

   (b) The *horz_line* is larger than the *Square_line_Y*

   (c) The *Obj_Slant* is larger than −15 and the *Obj_Slant* is less than 35

7. Two algorithm variations were studied for classification of *essential objects*:

   (a) The first one is applied on the slant, which is calculated starting from the fixed point being the object center and the second point is the face center. The images are from *Mug Database* [9] (plus a set of images prepared by the authors for *cry* expression) and applied for 8 expressions (*anger, cry, disgust, fear, happiness, natural, sadness, surprise*). Then the *characteristic points* of *essential objects* are computed by two different ways and processed by ANN as 100 features for the first method and 81 for the second. It was applied also on *FERET Database* [10] for 4 expressions (*cry, sad, laugh and smile*) and the recognition accuracy was over 90 % in this way.

      (i) For each detected essential object the following steps are performed:
         - *The Convex Hull points* [6] are found. They are denoted by *ConHull_Poi*.
         - The search for start and end point of object starts from the first-quarter and goes counterclockwise, after the face image is divided into four-quarters. The point is considered as start point or end point if the sum of the 8-neighboring pixels of the tested point is equal to 1. They are denoted by *Start_Poi* and *End_Poi*.

      (ii) The slant between *ConHull-point* and the face center is calculated as in Eq. 1.

$$Slant_1 = \frac{(ConHull\_Poi\_Y - Center\_i\_Y)}{(ConHull\_Poi\_X - Center\_i\_X)} \tag{1}$$

      (iii) The slant between *ConHull-point* and the object center is formed as in Eq. 2.

$$Slant_2 = \frac{(ConHull\_Poi\_Y - Center\_Poi\_Y)}{(ConHull\_Poi\_X - Center\_Poi\_X)} \tag{2}$$

      (iv) The slant average *Mslant* is calculated as in Eq. 3:

$$MSlant = (Slant_2 + Slant_1)/2 \tag{3}$$

(v) The steps from (ii) to (iv) are repeated for all *ConHull-points* of the object. Figure 4(b, c, d, e, f) present the *ConvexHull points*, *essential objects* and face center as well as the way to perform required calculations.

(vi) The steps from (i) to (v) are repeated for each *essential object*. The result is a *slant vector* that is scaled up to 100, to be the input of ANN.

(b) The second way is to use feature encoding by extracting the important points (*start-point* and *end-point* of straight piece, *start-point* and *end-point* of object) of *essential objects*. These points are encoded using the *BPCC algorithm* consideration. Figure 4(h–j) present these points. *Essential objects* are formed into an array of 81 elements. The array is then considered as the input to *Backpropagation ANN*. The recognition accuracy in its maximum possibly achieved value was 95 %.

3.4 Selecting *Essential Objects* from *Characteristic Objects*

Less important characteristic objects detected in the image (about 80 %) are eliminated, leaving only *essential objects*. An example for detected *essential objects* is depicted in Fig. 4.

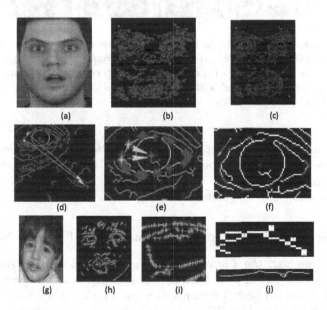

Fig. 4. Characteristic points of *essential objects* detected in the image (a): (b) Convex Hull points in blue, essential objects center in red, (c) two points of ConHulks points in cyan, (d–f) present the distance between the ConHulks and its object center (face center) shown by yellow arrows, movement goes counterclockwise. (h–j) present essential points: start-point and end-point of straight piece in green, start-point and end-point of object in red and branch point in magenta. (Color figure online)

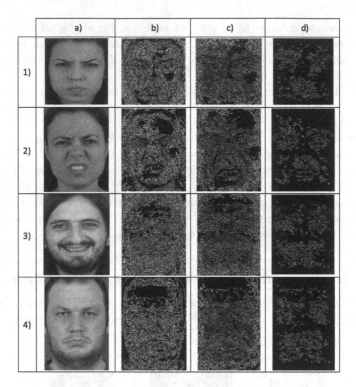

Fig. 5. Four images from MUG database [9]. Examples of *characteristic* and *essential objects*. Consequent columns are: (a) Original color image, (b) Black and white image after edge-detection, (c) Image with detected *Characteristic object* boundaries in blue and yellow, face center is marked with the red point (d) *essential objects* in green with centers in red. (Color figure online)

Figures 5 and 6 present examples of *characteristic* and *essential objects*, *characteristic object* boundaries are blue and yellow whilst the *essential object* boundaries are green. Four images from MUG database [9] are shown in Fig. 5, a sample 'cry' image produced by the first author is presented in Fig. 6.

3.5   Configuration of Backpropagation Artificial Neural Networks

For the first method, the *Convex Hull points* are defined, the slant between points and the center of objects, then face center are found. The average of slant is calculated, scaled to be 100 features as a good input to ANN.

For the second case, *FBPCC method* [25] is applied on the *essential objects*, the important points (start, end and branch points) are detected. These points are coded during two counterclockwise passes: first diagonal, then perpendicular. Eight sets of binary pairs are used to filter the resulted objects. Filtered data is formed into an array of 81 elements.

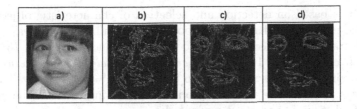

Fig. 6. A sample 'cry' image prepared by the first author. Examples of *characteristic* and *essential objects*. Consequent columns are: (a) Original color image, (b) Black and white image after edge-detection, (c) Image with detected *Characteristic object* boundaries in blue and yellow, face center is marked with the red point (d) *essential objects* in green with centers in red. *Characteristic object* boundaries are blue and yellow and the *essential* are in green. (Color figure online)

The neural network contains 81 neurons in the input layer, and {550; 350; 250} neurons in the 3 hidden layers. The number of neurons in the output layer is 8 neurons to indicate various face expressions *anger, cry, disgust, fear, happiness, natural, sadness, surprise*. The training parameters of the ANN are set up according to these values: the momentum coefficient is 0.25, the learning rate is 0.05 and the sum square error is 0.00000585. This ANN uses bipolar function as an activation function. The ANN weights and biases are generated randomly. The value range of the input vector is between -1 and $+1$.

4   Results and Discussion

ANN is trained on 52 faces, 4 images, 8 expressions with 184273 epochs. The faces are taken from *MUG Facial Expression Database* [9] and *color FERET Database* [10] with different face expressions. After training, the ANN is tested on a new set of faces (generalization database).

We tested the ANN on 32 new samples that can be split into 8 groups. We noticed some errors of ANN recognizing of facial expressions which is improved using FBPCC method [25].

By comparing the results of the two methods, we noticed there were some error rates in the possibility of distinguishing between the *angry, disgusted* and *fear* expressions, also between *sad* and *cry* expressions, between *happy, natural* and *disgusted*. The main reason for such errors comes from the fact that the work is neglecting the vertical objects and focusing on the horizontal characteristic objects. The range therefore is raised sometimes and decreased other times.

5   Conclusions and Future Work

This paper proposes a new approach for classification of eight face expressions: *anger, cry, disgust, fear, happiness, natural, sadness, surprise*. Most important paper contribution is the design and implementation of a feature extraction method. It is based on detection and selection of characteristic objects in the image. The preselected characteristic objects are studied in two ways: the first uses slant tracking, the second is based on feature encoding using *BPCC algorithm* with classification by *Backpropagation Artificial Neural Networks*. The correct classification rates were close to 50 % and 95 % respectively. The second method was proved to be fast and produced promising results. The method is unsupervised, flexible and can be adopted to recognize even more face expressions. The proposed method provides high efficiency for face expression and could be recommended for further research and studying. Future works in this area will include increasing the number of classes (various face expressions), application of other, possibly more viable, classification methods, and testing proposed approach on other databases, preferably with many subjects. Moreover, the authors are working on the ways of considering vertical oriented objects in order to increase the distinguishing rate of the similar expression features like those of *sad* and *cry*.

Acknowledgments. This work was supported by grant number S/WI/1/2013 from Bialystok University of Technology and funded from the resources for research by Ministry of Science and Higher Education. The work was also partially supported by NeiTec.

References

1. Gu, H., Su, G., Du, C.: Feature points extraction from face. In: Proceedings of Conference on Image and Vision Computing (2003)
2. Zeng, Z., Pantic, M., Roisman, G.I., Huang, T.S.: A survey of affect recognition methods: audio, visual, and spontaneous expressions. IEEE Trans. Pattern Anal. Mach. Intell. **31**, 39–58 (2009)
3. Hedaoo, S.V., Katkar, M.D., Khandait, S.P.: Feature tracking and expression recognition of face using dynamic Bayesian network. Int. J. Eng. Trends Technol. (IJETT) **8**(10), 517–521 (2014)
4. Gao, J., Fan, L., Li-zhong, X.: Median null(s_w)-based method for face feature recognition. Appl. Math. Comput. **219**(12), 6410–6419 (2013)
5. Cui, Y., Fan, L.: Feature extraction using fuzzy maximum margin criterion. Neurocomputing **86**, 52–58 (2012)
6. Gordon, G.: Face recognition based on depth maps and surface curvature. In: SPIE Geometric Methods in Computer Vision, pp. 234–247 (1991)
7. Saeed, K.: Object classification and recognition using toeplitz matrices. In: Sołdek, J., Drobiazgiewicz, L. (eds.) Artificial Intelligence and Security in Computing Systems. The Kluwer International Series in Engineering and Computer Science, vol. 752, pp. 163–172. Kluwer Academic Publishers, Massachusetts (2003)
8. Saeed, K., Albakoor, M.: Region growing based segmentation algorithm for typewritten and handwritten text recognition. Appl. Soft Comput. **9**(2), 608–617 (2009)
9. Aifanti, N., Papachristou, C., Delopoulos, A.: The MUG facial expression database. In: Proceedings of the 11th International Workshop on Image Analysis for Multimedia Interactive Services (WIAMIS), Desenzano, Italy, April 2010
10. Phillips, P.J., Moon, H., Rauss, P.J., Rizvi, S.: The FERET evaluation methodology for face recognition algorithms. IEEE Trans. Pattern Anal. Mach. Intell. **22**(10), 1090–1104 (2000)

11. Pantic, M.: Facial expression recognition. In: Li, S.Z., Jain, A. (eds.) Encyclopedia of Biometrics, pp. 400–406. Springer, Heidelberg (2009)

12. Keltner, D., Ekman, P.: Facial expression of emotion. In: Lewis, M., Haviland-Jones, J.M. (eds.) Handbook of Emotions, pp. 236–249. Guilford Press, New York (2000)

13. Chen, Y., Zhang, S., Zhao, X.: Facial expression recognition via non-negative least-squares sparse coding. Information 5, 305–331 (2014). Open Access

14. Lin, K., Cheng, W., Li, J.: Facial expression recognition based on geometric features and geodesic distance. Int. J. Sig. Process. 7(1), 323–330 (2014)

15. Kumbhar, M., Jadhav, A., Patil, M.: Facial expression recognition based on image feature. Int. J. Comput. Commun. Eng. 1(2), 117–119 (2012)

16. Brunelli, R., Poggio, T.: Face recognition: features versus templates. IEEE Trans. Pattern Anal. Mach. Intell. 15(10), 1042–1052 (1993)

17. Youssif, A., Asker, W.A.A.: Automatic facial expression recognition system based on geometric and appearance features. Comput. Inf. Sci. 4(2), 115 (2011). Canadian Center of Science and Education

18. Bashyal, S., Venayagamoorthy, G.K.: Recognition of facial expressions using Gabor wavelets and learning vector quantization. J. Eng. Appl. Artif. Intell. 21, 1056–1064 (2008)

19. Kumbhar, M., Patil, M., Jadhav, A.: Facial expression recognition using gabor wavelet. Int. J. Comput. Appl. 68(23), 0975–8887 (2013)

20. NabiZadeh, N., John, N.: Automatic facial expression recognition using modified wavelet-based salient points and Gabor-wavelet filters. In: Stephanidis, C. (ed.) HCII 2013, Part I. CCIS, vol. 373, pp. 362–366. Springer, Heidelberg (2013)

21. Guo, G., Dyer, C.R.: Learning from examples in the small sample case: face expression recognition. IEEE Trans. Syst. Man Cybern. Part B Cybern. 35(3), 477–488 (2005)

22. Gomathi, V., Ramar, K., Jeevakumar, A.S.: Human facial expression recognition using MANFIS model. Int. J. Electr. Electron. Eng. 3(6), 335–339 (2009)

23. Gomathi, V., Ramar, K., Jeevakumar, A.S.: A neuro fuzzy approach for facial expression recognition using LBP histograms. J. Comput. Theory Eng. 2(3), 245–249 (2010)

24. Khandait, S.P., Thool, R.C., Khandait, P.D.: Comparative analysis of ANFIS and NN approach for expression recognition using geometry method. J. Adv. Res. Comput. Sci. Softw. Eng. 2(3), 169–174 (2012)

25. Albakoor, M., Albakkar, A.A., Dabsh, M., Sukkar, F.: BPCC approach for Arabic letters recognition. In: Arabnia, H.R. (ed.) IPCV, pp. 304–308. CSREA Press (2006)

26. Saeed, K., Tabedzki, M., Rybnik, M., Adamski, M.: K3M: a universal algorithm for image skeletonization and a review of thinning techniques. Int. J. Appl. Math. Comput. Sci. 20(2), 317–335 (2010)

27. Mancas, M., Gosselin, B., Macq, B.: Segmentation using a region growing thresholding. In: Proceedings of the SPIE, vol. 5672, pp. 388–398 (pp. 12–13) (2005)

28. Tremeau, A., Borel, N.: A region growing and merging algorithm to color segmentation. Pattern Recogn. 30(7), 1191–1203 (1997)

29. Gottesfeld Brown, L.: A survey of image registration techniques. ACM Comput. Surv. 24, 325–376 (1992)

30. Saeed, K., Albakoor, M.: A new feature extraction method for TMNN-based Arabic character classification. Comput. Inform. 26(4), 403–420 (2007)

31. Delac, K., Grgic, M.: Face Recognition. I-Tech Education and Publishing, Vienna (2007)

32. Canny, J.: A computational approach to edge detection. IEEE Trans. Pattern Anal. Mach. Intell. **8**(6), 679–698 (1986)

33. Hess, M., Martinez, M.: Facial feature extraction based on the smallest univalue segment assimilating nucleus (SUSAN) algorithm. In: Proceedings of Picture Coding Symposium (2004)

34. Barber, C.B., Dobkin, D.P., Huhdanpaa, H.: The quickhull algorithm for convex hulls. ACM Trans. Math. Softw. **22**(4), 469–483 (1996)

A Fault-Tolerant Authenticated Key-Conference Agreement Protocol with Forward Secrecy

Tomasz Hyla[✉] and Jerzy Pejaś

Faculty of Computer Science and Information Technology,
West Pomeranian University of Technology, Szczecin, Poland
{thyla, jpejas}@zut.edu.pl

Abstract. In conference channels, users communicate with each other using a conference key that is used to encrypt messages. There are two basic approaches in which the key can be established. In the first one, a central server is used (with a chairman role). The server generates the key and distributes it to participants. The second approach is that all participants compute a key without a chairman. In this paper, we introduce a special type of group authentication using secret sharing, which provides an efficient way to authenticate multiple users belonging to the same group without the chairman. Our proposed protocol is a many-to-many type of authentication. Unlike most user authentication protocols that authenticate a single user each time, our proposed protocol authenticates all users of a group at once.

Keywords: User authentication · Conference-key agreement · Group communication · Forward secrecy · Fault tolerance

1 Introduction

In the era of mobile devices and cloud computing, millions of documents and messages are continuously exchanged over the Internet. The communication channels built using the Internet require security measures that will ensure confidentiality and entities' authentication. Communication channels can be divided into three types: one-to-one, one-to-many (broadcast channels) and many-to-many (conference channels) allowing message exchange between all participants.

Several protocol allowing mutual user authentication and key derivation exists. One of the most popular TLS (Transport Layer Security) is widely used in many kinds of different applications. Situation is more complicated when we need a conference channel. Of course, protocols like TLS can be used to simulate a conference channel by creating independent channels between users. However, when a number of users increases this starts to be infeasible, because the number of channels and exchanged messages increase quadratically.

In conference channels, users communicate with each other using a conference key K that is used to encrypt messages [1]. There are two basic approaches in which the key K can be established. In the first one, a central server is used (with a chairman role).

© IFIP International Federation for Information Processing 2016
Published by Springer International Publishing Switzerland 2016. All Rights Reserved
K. Saeed and W. Homenda (Eds.): CISIM 2016, LNCS 9842, pp. 647–660, 2016.
DOI: 10.1007/978-3-319-45378-1_56

The server generates the key and distributes it to participants. The second approach is that all participants compute a key without a chairman. The first approach is simpler and easier to implement, but it lacks of flexibility and requires an additional service. The second approach is a special case of a secure multiparty computation in which a group of people evaluate securely a function to $f(k_1, k_2, ...)$, with each person possessing a private input k_i. The conference key agreement protocols have a few different features in comparison with secure multiparty computation. Firstly, private channels between participants are not available. Secondly, the main goal of an adversary is to disrupt the protocol between honest participants. Thirdly, a cheater is excluded from participating when is found (the cheater secret is not necessary to compute the conference key) [1].

The conference-key agreement protocols have several properties [2, 3]:

(a) Forward confidentiality– *subsequent conference keys cannot be obtained by participants who left the conference sessions* [3, 4].
(b) Backward confidentiality – *former conference keys cannot be obtained by participants who joined the conference session* [3, 4].
(c) Key freshness – *If a conference-key agreement protocol achieves both backward and forward confidentiality, then the key generated using this protocol is called fresh* [3, 4].
(d) Forward secrecy - *A conference-key agreement protocol provides forward secrecy if the long-term secret key x_i of any participant U_i is compromised, but will not result in the compromise of previously established conference keys* [5–7]. Forward secrecy is different from forward confidentiality as it is related to a long-term key in opposite to forward confidentiality that is related to a short term conference key K.
(e) Authentication – the protocol is called an authenticated protocol when it contains mechanism allowing detect if the participant is a member of the conference [2].
(f) Fault tolerance – the protocol is called fault-tolerant when it detects faulty broadcast messages during the communication of participants. The sender of the faulty message is marked as possible malicious one. Faulty messages are re-verified and in a case of a negative result, the participant is excluded from the set of participants [2]. Such property allows honest participant to establish a conference key, even in malicious participant are trying to disrupt it [1, 8, 9].
(g) Dynamic settings – The dynamic group operations supported by the protocol (i.e.: single or mass join, single or mass leave, merge or divide groups) [2].

Several conference protocols have been proposed in recent years. However, the DKCAP protocol with all mentioned above properties was presented in 2015 by Ermiş et al. [2]. Also, they have provided comprehensive comparison of the protocols. The protocol proposed by Chung in 2013 [10] have all the properties except fault tolerance and supports only two dynamic operations. In contrast, Cheng et al. [11] proposed a protocol that is fault tolerant, but does not provide forward secrecy. Zhao et al. [12] proposed protocol that is authenticated, fault tolerant, provides forward secrecy and key freshness, but does not have dynamin operations.

Authenticated, fault tolerant and providing key freshness protocols, without the forward secrecy and dynamin operations have been proposed by Huang et al. [13],

Wu et al. [14], Wang [15]. Katz and Yung [16] proposed an authenticated protocol with forward secrecy and key freshness, but without fault tolerant property and dynamic operations. Tseng proposed two protocol, first one [17] with all the properties except dynamic operations and second one [3] with two dynamic operations, but without key freshness.

1.1 Objective

In this paper, we propose the improved authenticated conference key agreement protocol, called Forward-secrecy and Fault-tolerance Authenticated Conference-Key Agreement (FF-ACKA) protocol. FF-ACKA protocol is a modified version of an improved conference-key agreement protocol with forward secrecy (hereinafter in short ICKAP [2, 17]) for the static group of participants. The protocol is a provable secure conference-key agreement protocol with fault tolerance and forward secrecy. In addition, because the security of ICKAP protocol is preserved, FF-ACKA protocol is resistant against known attacks of a passive and an active adversary.

FF-ACKA protocol requires only a constant size message to be sent by each participant and has two rounds. Both rounds are authenticated by means of long-term certified asymmetric keys of participants. Hence, FF-ACKA protocol is resistant against a classic man-in-the-middle attacks.

Another contribution of this work is to provide a truly contributory group conference key, i.e., in the protocol, the conference key is established jointly by all members of the conference, and not by any single member. Furthermore, the calculation of each participant contribution, in contrast to other protocols (e.g., [2, 17]), is much less time-consuming.

1.2 Paper Organisation

The remainder of this paper is organized as follows. Section 2 contains description of a security model, definitions and notations. In Sect. 3 is described the proposed FF-ACKA protocol (A Fault-Tolerant Authenticated Key-Conference Agreement Protocol with Forward Secrecy). Next, in Sect. 4 the security analysis of FF-ACKA protocol is provided. The paper ends with conclusion.

2 Preliminaries

We adopt the system and security model, definitions, and notations similar to Tseng's works ([3, 17], see also [2]).

2.1 System Model

In the system, each participant has a long-term private key and a corresponding public key. The public system parameters and each participant's public key information with its certificate are stored in a public directory. All participants are connected using a broadcast network and can distribute messages to each other. The transmission between them should be protected and needs to establish a conference key to encrypt their communications. Below, we present two definition which is strongly related to FF-ACKA protocol given in Sect. 3.

Definition 1 (Conference Participants, [2]). Participant, participant set and their properties:

(a) Each conference participant is an entity and denoted as U_i.
(b) The participant list is represented as $(U_1, U_2, ..., U_n)$. Each participant knows all participants and theirs identities.
(c) Participants in a conference session can be categorized in two groups. If a participant fully follows the protocol, it is called a honest participant, or if a participant tries to cheat other participants to miscalculate the key is called a malicious participants.

Definition 2 (Verification Matrix, [2]). Let $U = \{U_1, U_2, ..., U_n\}$ be the set of participants. During the execution of the protocol, participant U_j, which for $1 \leq i \leq n$ and $i \neq j$ has at least one verification matrix entry $V_{i,j} = $ '*Step4:failure*' or $V_{i,j} = $ '*Step5:failure*' with the proper credentials, is defined as a potential malicious participant until its malicious behaviour is proved in a fault detection and correction step. Otherwise, i.e., if the verification matrix entry $V_{i,j} = $ '*Step4:success*' or $V_{i,j} = $ '*Step5:success*', the participant is defined as honest participant.

2.2 Security Properties

Under the same definitions as used in Tzeng's protocol [1], there are malicious adversaries. The first is a passive adversary (an eavesdropper) who is not a participant, but who tries to learn the conference key from the broadcast messages. The conference-key agreement protocol is secure against a passive attack, if a selected random value and the established conference key are computationally indistinguishable for an adversary. The second is an active adversary. This is an adversary that is also a participant and who tries to disrupt the establishment of a conference key among the honest participants. A conference-key agreement protocol is secure against an active adversary. Even if the adversary does not follow the protocol in any way, he still cannot disrupt the establishment of the conference key. The security of the conference key protocol discussed in the paper is based on the Discrete Logarithm (DL) problem.

3   The Proposed Protocol with Forward Secrecy

Our Forward-secrecy and Fault-tolerance Authenticated Conference-Key Agreement (FF-ACKA) protocol consists of three phases, including a parameter generation phase, long-term keys and a certificates' generation phase, a temporary public-key distribution phase, a secret distribution and commitment phase, a sub-key computation and verification phase, a fault detection phase, and a conference key computation phase. These phases and theirs detailed structures are explained below.

The FF-ACKA protocol with a forward secrecy property uses a temporary public key to distribute keys, thus even the disclosure of the user's secret key will not result in the compromise of previously established conference keys. The authenticity of the user's temporary key can be verified by checking the signature on the key (hereinafter referred as a temporary certificate) generated with the long-term private key. Hence, each instance of the protocol uses both the static long-term public keys as well as the temporary public keys, which makes the protocol forward secure.

Without loss of generality, let $U = \{U_1, U_2, ..., U_n\}$ be the initial set of participants that want to establish a common conference key. Each U_i ($i = 1, ..., n$), knows the set U. In FF-ACKA protocol, we assume that a conference can be started by the creator of U set who as a member of this set plays a role of a conference initiator.

3.1   Step 1: Setup

On input a security parameter $\lambda \in Z$, this algorithm runs as follows (see [18, 19]):

(a) generates a random $(\lambda + 1)$-bit prime number p;
(b) calculates a prime q number equal to $q = (p - 1)/2$;
(c) chooses an arbitrary $x \in Z_p^*$ with $x \neq \pm 1 \mod p$ and sets $g = x^2 \mod p$; g is a generator for the subgroup $G_q \subset Z_p^*$;
(d) chooses cryptographic hash functions (like as in [28]): $H : \{0, 1\}^* \to Z_q$, $G : \{0, 1\}^* \to Z_q$.

Hence, the system parameters are $params = \{G_q, Z_p, Z_q, p, q, g, H\}$.

3.2   Step 2: Keys and Long-Term Certificates Generation

We assume that each user U_i in the system makes the following operations:

(a) picks an random integer $x_i \in Z_q^*$ as a private key and computes a public key y_i such that $y_i = g^{x_i} \mod p \in Z_p^*$;
(b) sends a certificate signing request to a certificate authority (CA) in order to apply for a digital identity certificate (e.g., in X.509 format) with the U_i's certificate information CI_i, containing the CA's identifiers ID_{U_i} and ID_{CA} of the user U_i and the TA, respectively, and the time period $\Delta\tau$ for which the information CI_i is valid;
(c) takes his certificate $cert_i$ which was issued by CA.

The resulting public key is (p, q, g, y_i), while the private key has a form of (p, q, g, x_i). The authenticity of this key pair confirms the certificate $cert_i$ issued by the CA. The protocol is started by the initiator who calls for a conference by initializing a set of participants U. In addition, the function of time stamp T is required, and it will be updated to a new one for each conference session.

3.3   Step 3: Temporary Public-Key Distribution

Each from n participants belonging to a set U generates a temporary key pair and issues certificate related to the key pair. The temporary certificate is signed by the user using his private key and is valid only for a period of the key establishment phase in the conference protocol.

We use the Galindo-Garcia signature scheme given in [20, 21] to generate a temporary certificate. This signature scheme is based on the discrete logarithm problem and is secure against the adaptively chosen message attack in the random oracle model.

The algorithm described below is executed by all users $U_i \in U$:

(a) a user U_i select a short-term private key $t_i \in Z_q^*$ and an integer $v_i \in Z_q^*$ as a private key, and then computes a temporary public key $T_i = g^{t_i} \bmod p$ and $V_i = g^{v_i} \bmod p$;

(b) a user U_i composes the user's certificate information tCI_i, including the U_i's public keys T_i, its identifier ID_i and the short period $\Delta\tau$ for which the information tCI_i is valid;

(c) U_i computes a temporary certificate:

$$tCert_i = (t_i + (v_i + x_i h_i)\, g_i)\ mod\ q, \tag{1}$$

where $h_i = H(tCI_i, V_i, T)$ and $g_i = G(T_i, T, tCI_i, h_i)$ with the U_i's certificate temporary information tCI_i and broadcasts a message $tM_i = (tCert_i, tCI_i, T_i, V_i, T, \Delta\tau)$ to each U group member.

Finally, the $tCert_i$ can be called as a certificate for the temporary public key T_i or a temporary certificate in short.

3.4   Step 4: Secret Distribution and Commitments

Upon receiving all messages $tM_j = (tCert_j, tCI_j, T_j, V_j, T, \Delta\tau)$, $j = 1, ..., i - 1, i + 1, ..., n$, each user U_i ($1 \le i \le n$) validates that t_j is really issued by U_j, i.e., U_i verifies the time stamp T, computes $h_j = H(tCI_j, V_j, T)$, $g_j = G(T_j, T, tCI_j, h_j)$ and checks whether:

$$g^{tCert_j} \equiv T_j \left(V_j (y_j)^{h_j} \right)^{g_j} (mod\ p) \tag{2}$$

The user U_i also validates whether:

(a) the long-term certificate $cert_j$ related to the public key y_j is authentic and unrevoked.

(b) T_j is a generator of a subgroup G_q, i.e., if $2 \le T_j \le p - 1$ and $(T_j)^q \bmod p = 1$.

If any check for tM_j of U_j does not hold, then the participant U_i sets $V_{i,j} = $ 'Step4:failure', otherwise $V_{i,j} = $ 'Step4:success'. For both cases, the participant U_i computes credentials:

$$h_{k,i} = H\big((T_k)^{x_i} \bmod q, \; V_{i,j}, \; T\big), \quad k = 1, \ldots, n; \; k \neq i, \tag{3}$$

and broadcasts a tuple $vM_{i,j} = (V_{i,j}, \; h_{1,i}, \; \ldots, \; h_{i-1,i}, \; h_{i+1,i}, \; \ldots, \; h_{n,i}, \; T)$. Next, if $V_{i,j} = $ 'Step4:failure', the participant U_i goes to Step 6 for fault detection and correction. Otherwise, each participant U_i:

(a) randomly selects a sub-key $K_i \in Z_q^*$ and a random linear function $f_i(z)$ over Z_q:

$$f_i(z) = K_i + a_i z \in Z_q, \tag{4}$$

where the coefficient a_i is in Z_q;

(b) calculates $\gamma_{i,0} = f_i(1)$, generates random numbers $\alpha_i, \; \beta_i \in Z_q^*$, calculates $\Gamma_i = g^{\alpha_i} \bmod p$ and $B_i = g^{\beta_i} \bmod p$, subsequently calculates for each $j = 1, \ldots, n; \; j \neq i$:

$$z_{i,j} = (T_j)^{\alpha_i} \bmod q$$

$$\gamma_{i,j} = f_i(z_{i,j}) \oplus H(z_{i,j}, \; tCert_i, \; tCert_j)$$

(c) issues an attestation in a form:

$$\sigma_i = (\alpha_i + (\beta_i + t_i c_i)\, d_i)\, mod\, q \tag{5}$$

where $c_i = H(B_i, \; T)$, and $d_i = G(\Gamma_i, T, K_i, c_i)$; then sends each participant j $(j \neq i)$ a message $M_i = (\sigma_i, \; cert_i, \; tCert_i, \; \gamma_{i,0}, \; \gamma_{i,1}, \; \gamma_{i,2}, \; \ldots, \; \gamma_{i,n}, \; \Gamma_i, \; B_i)$.

Similarly as in step 3 (see Eq. 2), to issue a certificate a Galindo-Garcia signature scheme [20, 21] was used.

3.5 Step 5: Subkey Computation and Verification

Upon receiving message $M_j = (\sigma_j, \; cert_j, \; tCert_j, \; \gamma_{j,0}, \; \gamma_{j,1}, \; \gamma_{j,2}, \; \ldots, \; \gamma_{j,n}, \; \Gamma_j, \; B_j)$ from U_j $(1 \leq j \leq n)$, each participant U_i for $j \neq i$ uses his short-term private key t_i to reconstruct the sub-key K_j as follows:

(a) checks the time stamp T;

(b) computes $z_{j,i} = (\Gamma_j)^{t_i} \bmod q$ and $f_j(z_{j,i}) = \gamma_{j,i} \oplus H(z_{j,i}, \; tCert_j, \; tCert_i)$;

(c) calculates a sub-key:

$$K'_j = f_j(1)\frac{z_{j,i}}{z_{j,i} - 1} + \frac{-1}{z_{j,i} - 1} f_j(z_{j,i}) \in Z_q \tag{6}$$

(d) checks if the following equality is fulfilled:

$$g^{\sigma_j} = \Gamma_j \left(B_j(T_j)^{c_j'} \right)^{d_j'} \pmod{p} \tag{7}$$

where $c_j' = H(B_j, T)$ and $d_j' = G\left(\Gamma_j, T, K_j', c_j' \right)$.

If it holds, a user U_i accepts a sub-key $K_j = K_j'$ and sets $V_{i,j} =$ 'Step4:success'. Otherwise, a participant U_i sets $Vi,j =$ 'Step5:failure'. For both cases the participant U_i computes the credentials:

$$r_{k,i} = H(z_{k,i}, V_{i,j}, T), \; k = 1, \ldots, n; \; k \neq i, \tag{8}$$

and broadcasts a tuple $rM_{i,j} = (V_{i,j}, r_{1,i}, \ldots, r_{i-1,i,}, r_{i+1,i}, \ldots, r_{n,i}, T)$.

3.6 Step 6: Fault Detection

All faults messages broadcasted by participants in steps 4 and 5 should be verified and corrected. Each participant Uj, which does not follow the protocol in any way, should be treated as possible malicious participants and marked as $Vi,j =$ 'StepX:failure' in the verification matrix, where $X = 4$ or 5. Such approach is reasonable, because any malicious participant U_j can try to send the wrong evidences to other participants and disrupt the establishment of a conference key among the honest participants. The broadcast messages of possible malicious participants are re-verified by honest participants.

The broadcast messages of participants are verified in both secret distribution and commitment step (Step 4) and the sub-key computation and verification step (Step 5). Therefore, the fault messages in the FF-PA protocol that are sent by any malicious participant to other participants should be re-verified by honest ones.

Before the proper fault detection phase is started, each participant U_i $(1 \leq i \leq n)$ on receiving the message $vM_{j,m}$ or/and $rM_{j,m}$ (see respective Step 4 and Step 5), first computes (for $i \neq j \neq m$):

$$h_{i,j}' = H\left((y_j)^{t_i} \bmod q, \; V_{j,m}, \; T \right), \tag{9}$$

or/and

$$r_{i,j}' = H\left((\Gamma_j)^{t_i} \bmod q, \; V_{j,m}, \; T \right), \tag{10}$$

and then verifies whether holds the equations $h_{i,j}' \equiv h_{i,j}$ or/and $r_{i,j}' \equiv r_{i,j}$. If the equation (s) are satisfied, then U_i starts the execution of the fault detection phase, or else, sets U_j as a malicious participant and restarts the protocol for new honest participant group $U = U \backslash \{U_i\}$.

To detect and correct the faults, each participant $U_i \in U$ $(i \neq j \neq m)$ receiving $V_{j,m}$ acts in accordance to the following rules (compare also [2, 13, 22]):

(a) if $V_{j,m}$ = 'Step4failure' for any participant U_m, then other honest participants U_l, where $1 \leq l \leq n$, re-verify the broadcast messages tM_m and if the verification result is still $V_{l,m}$ = 'failure:Step4' (for any participant U_l), the participant U_l sets U_m as a malicious participant and goes to the step (c);

(b) otherwise, if $V_{j,m}$ = 'Step5:failure', the participants U_i knows that according to U_j the source of faulty is U_m ($m \neq i$); hence U_i:

   (i) waits for the fault detection message (α_m, a_m, K_m) from U_m;

   (ii) sets U_m as a malicious participant and goes to the step (c), if no one receives the fault detection message from U_m;

   (iii) checks whether previously distributed values $(V_m, T_m, tCert_m, \gamma_{m,0}, \gamma_{m,j}, \Gamma_m, B_m, \sigma_m)$ are correct, i.e.:

- checks whether α_m satisfies $\Gamma_m \equiv g^{\alpha_m} \bmod p$;
- checks whether Eq. (1) holds for V_m, T_m and $tCert_m$;
- inputs (a_m, K_m) into Eq. (4), calculates $z_{m,j} = (T_j)^{\alpha_m} \bmod q$ and checks whether:

$$\gamma_{m,0} \equiv f_m(1)$$
$$\gamma_{m,j} \equiv f_m(z_{m,j}) \oplus H(z_{m,j}, tCert_m, tCert_j)$$

- verifies whether $(\Gamma_m, B_m, \sigma_m)$ is the right signature on a sub-key K_m made by U_m (see Eq. (7)); if Eq. (7) holds, sets U_j as a malicious participant, otherwise, the malicious one is U_m.

(c) removes the malicious participant (U_i or U_m) from the group U, i.e., the set of users is updated as $U = U \backslash \{U_j\}$; similar operations are made by the other honest participants and finally the protocol is restarted.

3.7 Step 7: Conference-Key Computation

If no more faults are detected and all malicious participants are excluded from U, each honest participants U_i in the set of $U' = \{ U_{i,1}, U_{i,2}, \ldots, U_{i,m}\}$, where $m \leq n$, may calculate the conference key K as follows:

$$K = (K_{i,1} + K_{i,2} + \ldots + K_{i,m}) \bmod q. \tag{11}$$

4 Security Analysis

In this section, we give the security analysis of FF-ACKA protocol in fault tolerance and its forward secrecy. In the paper, a formal security analysis of the protocol is omitted. The formal analysis includes protocol resistance to passive and active attacks. Because of the similarity of the structures of the FF-ACKA and DCKAP [2] protocols, the security proof is similar to analysis presented in [2, 3].

For the fault tolerance analysis of FF-ACKA protocol we use the same approach as given in [1, 2, 13]. Let's consider two general attack scenarios on FF-ACKA protocol (compare also [22]). In the first scenario, all participants may generate different conference keys, while in second one the honest participants can be excluded from the conference. Furthermore, we assume that an adversary A is able to alter the exchanged messages in the sub-key computation and verification phase.

Given the first scenario, the participant U_i is a malicious participant who sends a wrong message tM_j (Step 4) or M_j (Step 5). Suppose, that one of the honest participants U_j broadcasts message $V_{j,i} =$ 'Step4:failure' or $V_{j,i} =$ 'Step5:failure' after verifying the digital signature $tCert_j$ (Eq. (3)) or σ_i (Eq. (8)). However, an adversary A modifies the intercepting message $V_{j,i} =$ 'Step4:failure' or $V_{j,i} =$ 'Step5:failure' to $V_{j,i} =$ 'Step4:success' or $V_{j,i} =$ 'Step5:success' and broadcasts it to other participants. As a result, all participants compute and accept different conference keys.

For the second scenario, both U_i and U_j are honest participants in the set U. In Step 4 or Step 5 the participant U_j verifies receiving message tM_j (Step 4) or M_j (Step 5). If check holds, U_j broadcasts $V_{j,i} =$ 'Step4:success' or $V_{j,i} =$ 'Step5:success'. However, like as in the first scenario, any adversary A can intercept this message and modify it to $V_{j,i} =$ 'Step4: failure' or $V_{j,i} =$ 'Step5: failure'. It is obvious that all participants start the fault detection procedure and although the participants U_i is honest all participants remove it from the set of honest participants. Of course participant U_i should be removed from a set of honest participants, but only if U_i is indeed a malicious participant and sends out the fake message $V_{i,j} =$ 'Step4: failure' or $V_{i,j} =$ 'Step5: failure', declaring U_j who is actually honest as a malicious one.

In the following theorem, we demonstrate that the proposed protocol can provide fault tolerance.

Theorem 1 (Fault tolerance, [1, 2, 22]). If honest participants follow the protocol, they may compute the same conference key even if:

(i) A malicious participant cheats the honest participants by sending wrong key values, and

(ii) A malicious participant cheats the honest participants by identifying an honest participant as a possible malicious participant.

Proof. For the first condition, assume that the participant U_i is a malicious participant and attempts to disrupt the establishment of a conference key among honest participants. The malicious participant U_i can use two methods of attacks. In first one, U_i broadcasts wrong messages in Step 4 or Step 5, while in second one U_i broadcasts the message $V_{i,j} =$ 'Step4: failure' or $V_{i,j} =$ 'Step5:failure' to claim that U_j is a malicious participant, although U_j is indeed a honest participant.

If U_i tries to cheat other honest participants in Step 4, then the broadcast messages $tM_i = (tCert_i, tCI_i, T_i, V_i, T, \Delta\tau)$ are validated by each honest participant by checking whether $g^{tCert_i} \equiv T_i \left(V_i(y_i)^{h_i} \right)^{g_i} \pmod{p}$, where $h_i = H(tCI_i, V_i, T)$, $g_i = G(T_i, T, tCI_i, h_i)$, holds or not. If the message tM_i of U_i is wrong, at least one honest participant U_j ($j \neq i$) is able to claim $V_{j,i} =$ 'Step4:failure', because the wrong messages tM_i are unable to pass the validation. If U_i broadcasts wrong messages M_i in Step 5, each honest participant U_j can also validate the message M_i and concludes if the equations

$$g^{\sigma_i} = \Gamma_i \left(B_i(T_i)^{c_i'} \right)^{d_i'} (mod\, p), \text{ where } c_i' = H(B_i,\, T) \text{ and } d_i' = G(\Gamma_i, T, K_i', c_i'), \text{ holds or}$$

not. If the K_i' value is wrong the validations do not hold, and so any honest participant U_j can claim that $V_{j,i} = $ 'Step5:failure'.

Additionally, for both above presented forgeries assume that one of the honest participant U_j broadcasts message $V_{j,i} = $ 'Step4: failure' or $V_{j,i} = $ 'Step5:failure' after verifying the wrong message tM_i or M_i. However, an adversary A can intercept the message $vM_{j,i}$ or $rM_{j,i}$ sent by U_j and modify this message to $V_{j,i}' = $ 'Step4:success' or $V_{j,i}' = $ 'Step5:success', and then broadcasts it to all other participants.

Let's take a closer look at above described adversary attack. It is easy to see that this type of attack is detected in the early stage of the fault detection phase. To show this, suppose that an adversary A replaces $V_{j,i}$ with $V_{j,i}'$ and resends it to all other participants. On receiving $V_{j,i}'$ and $h_{k,j}$ (Eq. (4)) or $r_{k,j}$ (Eq. (8)), any U_k ($k \neq i \neq j$) first computes

$$h_{k,j}' = H\left((y_j)^{t_k} mod\, q,\, V_{j,i}',\, T \right) \text{ or } r_{k,j}' = H\left(z_{k,j},\, V_{j,i}',\, T \right) \text{ and checks whether } h_{k,j}' \equiv$$

$h_{k,j}$ or $r_{k,j}' \equiv r_{k,j}$ holds or not. It is obvious that if these equations holds, an adversary should be able to compute $w_{k,j} = (T_k)^{x_j} mod\, q$ or $z_{k,j} = (\Gamma_j)^{t_k} mod\, q$. However, it is well known that a problem of finding $w_{k,j}$ or $z_{k,j}$ values is computationally hard, i.e., to obtain these values we need to solve DL problem for the equations $y_j = g^{x_j} mod\, p$ and $T_k = g^{t_k} mod\, p$ or $\Gamma_j = g^{\alpha_j} mod\, p$.

In the second method of attacks, a malicious participant U_i broadcasts the message $V_{i,j} = $ 'Step4: failure' or $V_{i,j} = $ 'Step5:failure' to claim that U_j is a malicious participant, while U_j is actually an honest participant. In such case, U_j resends message tM_j (for Step 4) or M_j and (α_j, a_j, K_j) (for Step 5) to prove his honesty. Next, other honest participants validate message tM_j by checking $g^{tCert_j} \equiv T_j \left(V_j(y_j)^{h_j} \right)^{g_j} (mod\, p)$ (see point (a) of Step 6) or messages M_j and (α_j, a_j, K_j) according to the point (b) of Step 6.

The information about any malicious attempt of U_i or an adversary A who eavesdrops on the broadcast channel and tries to alter the exchanged messages in Step 4 or Step 5, is placed in $V_{j,i}$ element of the verification matrix, for all $1 \leq j \leq n$, $j \neq i$. On receiving such fault messages, all honest participants start the fault detection phase and decide that U_i is indeed malicious participant. As a result, a participant U_i will be proved to be the malicious participant and then be removed from the set of honest participants.

Now, consider second condition (ii). Since in this case, where any honest participants U_i and U_j follow the protocol and broadcast valid messages, all participants can properly compute the same sub-key K_i. This is truth even if a malicious participant U_m sends out the failure message to convince other honest participants that U_i and U_j are dishonest or if an adversary A intercepts the message $V_{i,j} = $ 'Step4:success' or $V_{i,j} = $ 'Step5:success' sent from U_i and changes it to $V_{i,j} = $ 'Step4: failure' or $V_{i,j} = $ 'Step5: failure'. It can be noticed, that as above, these attacks are detected in fault detection phase.

Because these two conditions hold, our FF-ACKA protocol satisfies the fault-tolerance property. The last security property in this section is the forward secrecy. Below, we demonstrate that the proposed protocol has the forward secrecy property. Forward secrecy should protect the previously established conference keys and all its components against compromises, even if the long-term private key is compromised.

Theorem 2 (Forward Secrecy, [17]). If solving the discrete logarithm problem is computationally infeasible, the FF-CKAP provides forward secrecy.

Proof. The proof of Lemma 2 is similar to the proof of [17]. Suppose that adversary A compromises at time $(\tau + 1)$ the long-term private key x_i of any participant U_i and can obtain the conference key K at time τ, where K is composed of all participants' sub-keys K_i ($1 \leq i \leq n$). Because each K_i is distributed to other participants U_j ($1 \leq j \leq n, j \neq i$) using their temporary public keys $T_j = g^{t_j} \bmod p$, an adversary A should be able to obtain the short-term private key t_j. The adversary can try to get t_j directly from $T_j = g^{t_j} \bmod p$ or indirectly either form $tCert_j = \left(t_j + \left(v_j + x_j h_j\right) g_j\right) \bmod q$ or $\sigma_j = \left(\alpha_j + \left(\beta_j + t_j c_j\right) d_j\right) \bmod q$ (see respective Eq. (1) and Eq. (4)). For the first case, it is obvious that the calculation of t_j is equivalent to solving the discrete logarithm problem. However, DL problem is nevertheless considered to be computationally hard. For the second case, even if the adversary knows x_j, the solving of $tCert_j = \left(t_j + \left(v_j + x_j h_j\right) g_j\right) \bmod q$ to obtain t_j is also discrete problem [20]. In the last case, the adversary with U_j's secret key x_j tries to recover t_j form $(T_j, \Gamma_j, B_j, \sigma_j)$, where $\Gamma_i = g^{\alpha_i} \bmod p$, $B_i = g^{\beta_i} \bmod p$ and $\sigma_j = \left(\alpha_j + \left(\beta_j + t_j c_j\right) d_j\right) \bmod q$. The value σ_j (like $tCert_j$) is short signature computed using a signature scheme considered in [20]. According to Theorem 1 in [20] this signature scheme is existentially unforgeable under a chosen message attack in the random oracle model, assuming that DL problem is believed to be computationally hard. As a result, the proposed protocol FF-CKAP satisfies the forward secrecy under the difficulty of computing the discrete logarithm problem.

5   Conclusion

In this paper, we proposed an improved authenticated conference-key agreement protocol (FF-ACKA) for a static set of participants. The protocol provides important security properties like forward secrecy and fault-tolerance. Due to the last properties it is possible to ensure that all participants can obtain the same conference key. The proposed protocol uses only two rounds to generate a conference key and enables the efficient detection and elimination of malicious participants from the set of honest participants. Nevertheless, the size of messages exchanged during protocol is proportional to the number of participants.

The FF-ACKA protocol was developed to meet requirements that emerged while we have been developing MobInfoSec project [23–27]. We have needed an authenticated conference channel between mobile devices. We have achieved such channel using several one-to-one channels with a chairman. Such solution was working, but it was not scalable and generated some efficiency and security issues related to the service implementing a chairman role. The FF-ACKA protocol is designed to solve that two problems: to improve overall speed and to improve security by eliminating the necessity to have trust service that plays a chairman role. Preliminary analysis has shown that our protocol should have similar efficiency or in some situations should be faster than protocols proposed by [1, 2, 16, 22]. We are planning to implement the protocol during our future works and test it in several practical scenarios.

References

1. Tzeng, W.G.: A secure fault-tolerant conference-key agreement protocol. IEEE Trans. Comput. **51**(4), 373–379 (2002)
2. Ermiş, O., Bahtityar, S., Anarim, E., Çağlayan, M.U.: An improved conference-key agreement protocol for dynamic groups with efficient fault correction. Secur. Commun. Netw. **8**(7), 1347–1359 (2015)
3. Tseng, Y.M.: A communication-efficient and fault-tolerant conference-key agreement protocol with forward secrecy. J. Syst. Softw. **80**(7), 1091–1101 (2007)
4. Rhee, K.H., Park, Y.H., Tsudik, G.: An architecture for key management in hierarchical mobile ad-hoc networks. J. Commun. Netw. **6**(2), 1–7 (2004)
5. Bellare, M., Pointcheval, D., Rogaway, P.: Authenticated key exchange secure against dictionary attacks. In: Preneel, B. (ed.) EUROCRYPT 2000. LNCS, vol. 1807, pp. 139–155. Springer, Heidelberg (2000)
6. ANSI X9.63: Public key cryptography for the financial services industry: key agreement and key transport using Elliptic Curve cryptography. ANSI (2001)
7. Tseng, Y.M.: A robust multi-party key agreement protocol resistant to malicious participants. Comput. J. **48**(4), 480–487 (2005)
8. Katz, J., Shin, J.S.: Modelling insider attacks on group key exchange protocols. In: ACM Conference on Computer and Communications Security, pp. 180–189 (2005)
9. Tang, Q., Mitchell, C.J.: Security properties of two authenticated conference key agreement protocols. In: Qing, S., Mao, W., López, J., Wang, G. (eds.) ICICS 2005. LNCS, vol. 3783, pp. 304–314. Springer, Heidelberg (2005)
10. Chung, Y.F.: The design of authentication key protocol in certificate-free public key cryptosystem. Secur. Commun. Netw. **7**(11), 2125–2133 (2013)
11. Cheng, Z.Y., Liu, Y., Chang, C.C., Guo, C.: A fault-tolerant group key agreement protocol exploiting dynamic setting. Int. J. Commun. Syst. **26**(2), 259–275 (2013)
12. Zhao, J., Gu, D., Li, Y.: An efficient fault-tolerant group key agreement protocol. Comput. Commun. **33**, 890–895 (2010)
13. Huang, K.H., Chung, Y.F., Lee, H.H., Lai, F., Chen, T.S.: A conference key agreement protocol with fault-tolerant capability. Comput. Stand. Interfaces **31**(2), 401–405 (2009)
14. Wu, Q., Mu, Y., Susilo, W., Qin, B., Domingo-Ferrer, J.: Asymmetric group key agreement. In: Joux, A. (ed.) EUROCRYPT 2009. LNCS, vol. 5479, pp. 153–170. Springer, Heidelberg (2009)
15. Wang, Z.: Improvement on the fault-tolerant group key agreement protocol of Zhao et al. Sec. Commun. Netw. **9**(2), 166–170 (2016)
16. Katz, J., Yung, M.: Scalable protocols for authenticated group key exchange. J. Cryptol. **20**(1), 85–113 (2007)
17. Tseng, Y.M.: An improved conference-key agreement protocol with forward secrecy. Informatica **16**, 275–284 (2005). Lithuania Academy of Sciences

18. Ryabko, B., Fionov, A.: Basics of Contemporary Cryptography for IT Practioners. World Scientific Publishing Co. Pte. Ltd., Hackensack (2005)
19. Katz, J., Lindell, Y.: Introduction to Modern Cryptography: Principles and Protocols. Chapman and Hall/CRC, Boca Raton (2007)
20. Chatterjee, S., Kamath, C., Kumar, V.: Galindo-Garcia identity-based signature revisited. In: Kwon, T., Lee, M.-K., Kwon, D. (eds.) ICISC 2012. LNCS, vol. 7839, pp. 456–471. Springer, Heidelberg (2013)
21. Chatterjee, S., Kamath, Ch.: A closer look at multiple forking: leveraging (in)dependence for a tighter bound. Algorithmica **74**(4), 1–42 (2015)
22. Lee, C.C., Li, C.T., Wu, C.Y., Huang, S.Y.: An enhanced fault-tolerant conference key agreement protocol. Int. J. Comput. Electr. Autom. Control Inf. Eng. **8**(12), 2231–2235 (2014)
23. El Fray, I., Hyla, T., Kurkowski, M., Maćków, W., Pejaś, J.: Practical authentication protocols for protecting and sharing sensitive information on mobile devices. In: Kotulski, Z., Księżopolski, B., Mazur, K. (eds.) CSS 2014. CCIS, vol. 448, pp. 153–165. Springer, Heidelberg (2014)
24. El Fray, I., Hyla, T., Chocianowicz, W.: Protection profile for secure sensitive information system on mobile devices. In: Saeed, K., Snášel, V. (eds.) CISIM 2014. LNCS, vol. 8838, pp. 636–650. Springer, Heidelberg (2014)
25. Hyla, T., Pejaś, J.: Certificate-based encryption scheme with general access structure. In: Cortesi, A., Chaki, N., Saeed, K., Wierzchoń, S. (eds.) CISIM 2012. LNCS, vol. 7564, pp. 41–55. Springer, Heidelberg (2012)
26. Hyla, T., Pejaś, J.: A practical certificate and identity based encryption scheme and related security architecture. In: Saeed, K., Chaki, R., Cortesi, A., Wierzchoń, S. (eds.) CISIM 2013. LNCS, vol. 8104, pp. 190–205. Springer, Heidelberg (2013)
27. Hyla, T., Maćków, W., Pejaś, J.: Implicit and explicit certificates-based encryption scheme. In: Saeed, K., Snášel, V. (eds.) CISIM 2014. LNCS, vol. 8838, pp. 651–666. Springer, Heidelberg (2014)
28. IEEE Standard 1363.3 – 2013 – IEEE Standard for Identity-Based Cryptographic Techniques Using Pairings (2013)

Towards Generating a Unique Signature for Remote User by Keystrokes Dynamics

Puja Mukherjee and Rituparna Chaki[(✉)]

A.K. Choudhury School of IT, University of Calcutta, JD Block,
Sector III, Salt Lake City, Kolkata 700098, West Bengal, India
pujamukherjee2014@gmail.com1, rituchaki@gmail.com2

Abstract. Keystrokes dynamics has been used for quite sometimes in authentication of users. The technique has immense possibilities due to ease of implementation and un-obtrusive nature. Researchers have been working for attaining improved accuracy rate of user identification. Such techniques are validated using standard data-set. As it turns out, the quality of input data is very much important for generating an accurate use pattern vector. In this paper, an application for data collection has been presented. The application, besides creating a user data-set, also generates a signature vector database.

Keywords: Keystrokes · Remote user · Free-text · Key hold time and key dwell time · Signature vector · Authentication

1 Introduction

In this era enormous use of automated system together with the cloud based means gives a broader perspective to end user for storing as well as accessing data in an efficient manner. However it throws a big challenge to security and authentication domain. Prior to access the secured data, it is essential to verify the authenticity of the user. Determining the relevancy of the user with respect to the data is foremost agenda of authentication. Most of the advanced systems in different application working with distributed workstations (servers) deployed over different geographic region. The security of user and his/her data becomes more vulnerable in the wireless medium as there is no dedicated link or method specified over there. We need a foolproof measure against unauthorized access to computer resources and data. The traditional authentication techniques were mostly depended on password based methods. The traditional techniques fail to provide enough protection to the user data. This has prompted the researchers to identify a new area of authentication known as Biometrics, which include finger prints, palm veins; face recognition, DNA, palm print, hand geometry, iris recognition, pattern of human behavior, like- key typing rhythm, ETC. Keystroke dynamics [1, 6] or typing dynamics is a behavioral biometric, refers to the automated method of identifying or confirming the identity of an individual based on the manner and the rhythm of typing on a keyboard. The keystroke techniques are of two type - Keystroke Static authentication (KSA) and Keystroke dynamic authentication (KDA).

K. Saeed and W. Homenda (Eds.): CISIM 2016, LNCS 9842, pp. 661–671, 2016.
DOI: 10.1007/978-3-319-45378-1_57

In Static keystroke based technique, user authentication is done at a particular time instance. The continuous/ dynamic keystroke method is more effective than KSA and it requires the verification process to be continued during the entire session of user interaction. The raw measurements used for keystroke dynamics are dwell time and flight time.

The rest of the paper is organized as follows. In Sect. 2, we review various approaches in keystroke biometrics briefly and analyze their error rates. In Sect. 3, our proposed approach is described. We give a full detail of the implementations of the approaches and provide experimental results in Sect. 4. Finally, Sect. 5 concludes the paper with suggestions for future work (Fig. 1).

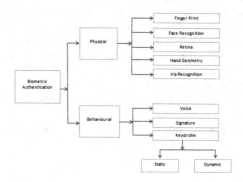

Fig. 1. Classification of biometric authentication

2 Literature Review

Most of the existing approaches focus on static verification, where a user types specific pre-enrolled string, e.g., a password during a login process, and then their keystroke features are analyzed for authentication purposes [1]. Pin et al. [2] proposed a solution with EER of 1.401 % for strengthening existing password based authentication system by using two layer fusion approach. Using classification techniques based on template matching and Bayesian likelihood models Fabian Monrose [3] achieved accuracy level of 83.22–92.14 %. Yu et al. [4] recommended nearest neighbor classifier with the new distance metric in order to identify a legitimate user with respect to a threshold value; this system achieved EER of 8.7 %. Kenneth Revett et al. [5] achieved 95 % of accuracy in user authentication by inventing software based module where combination of the typing speed and the first and last few characters of the login ID is enough to identify an authenticate user. Wang et al. [7] introduced a new user authentication approach by using keystroke dynamic method. This method includes training and authentication. It showed better performance in term of FAR and FRR. Babaeizadeh [8] suggested a KDA based system for verifying a user while requesting for services via CSP in Mobile cloud computing (MCC) environment. The proposed ECC crypto-graphic algorithm along with keystroke duration attribute was proved to defend

97.33 % of efforts for an imposter attack. The data quality, uniqueness and consistency of typing pattern can be improved by using artificial rhythms and tempo cues [9].

3 The Proposed System

Biometric authentication systems usually have two phases for verification purpose-Enrolment Phase and Authentication Phase. In enrolment phase user data is gathered, processed and stored in a database. This becomes a template for future authentication phase. In authentication phase, the user data is acquired and processed. A matching process is there to check the authenticity of the user based on his pre-stored reference templates.

Our fundamental objective is to generate a unique signature for each individual way by analyzing his/her typing behavior. The proposed system will capture user data on a continuous basis and it use the concept of free-text (i.e. no dedicated text to be provided by the user in order to create individual's profile). In brief, the characteristics of the proposed model are:

1. Keystrokes based continuous authentication.
2. Dynamic (all text editor based data collection.
3. Unique signature vector for each user.

The proposed logic has three sub-phases for identifying a user's unique behavior, these are: data collection, Preprocessing of stored data and signature vector generation.

Our proposed system depicted in Fig. 2 focused on generating a unique typing behavior of each individual.

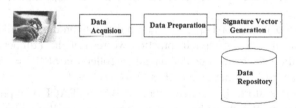

Fig. 2. Block diagram of the proposed system.

Here is a brief description of each sub-phase:

Data Acquisition: Here raw keystroke data of individuals are collected via various input devices. These may consist of normal computer keyboard, customized pressure sensitive keyboard, virtual keyboard etc [10, 11, 12]. The output of this phase is a text file of an individual's typing behavior with key dwell time and key hold time.

Data Preparation: Pre-processing procedures such as feature selection, dimension reduction, and outlier detection [13] are to be applied to the collected samples prior to feature extraction to ensure or to increase the quality of feature data. A substantial number of data samples are collected for each individual.

Signature Vector Generator: The output of phase II is used as input in this phase. This file is used to generate a unique signature for each individual by applying some rules on the identified features and store them in database for future classification.

3.1 Data Acquisition

For the purpose of the work we have designed a routine to collect user data (key typing behavior). This routine aims to collect events generated by individuals (operators of computer systems) while using a keyboard. At present, the system works on the MS-Windows platform and does not require any additional libraries. The proposed logic works continuously in background and records a user's activity associated with a keyboard. The events are captured on the fly and saved in text files user character [user_id, vi] in a database. A sample of collected input data is presented below.

Input data collection is carried out for each user user_id separately. We can represent each key event as a vector with 5 tuples. On ith Session the key pressed event represented with vector vi is as follows,

$$v_i = \{Session\_ID,\ key\_name_i,\ hold\_time_i,\ dwell\_time_i,\ sys\_time_i\}$$

where, key_namei is the name of the ith key pressed event, naming convention is according to standard QWERTY keyboard interface on the session with Session_ID; hold_timei is the timestamp difference between key pressed and key released; dwell_timei is the timestamp difference between $(i-1)$ th key release and ith key pressed; sys_timei is the system generated time in hour and minute when the event occur.

V is the composite vector $\{v_1, v_2 \ldots v_n\}$; n depends on the overall key press occur on each session on a single day. In practice we restrict the number of sample data collected from the user hence our database is a collection of $SV = \{V_1, V_2 \ldots, V_m\}$ where m is number of sample data collected for each uid.

Additionally we store the total number of BACKSPACE key-press during each session the user interact with his/her machine. The sample collected for each session for the BACKSPACE key can be described with a vector $TB = \{TB_1, TB_2 \ldots TB_l\}$; where L = number of sessions on a single day, and$TB_j = \{session_j, backspace\_count_j\}$;

where backspace_countj is the total number of times BACKSPACE key is pressed in sessionj. Then we compute the average number of BACKSPACE key-press on a single day and store them into the database with day_id. The average number of the BACKSPACE key-press (AB) on k^{th} day is calculated as follows;

$$AB_k = \frac{1}{L} \sum_{j=1}^{L} TBj,\ \text{where L is the total number of sessions on } k^{th} \text{day.}$$

All AB_k will constitute a vector $A_i = \{uid, day_i, AB_i\}$ describe the average number of BACKSPACE key-press on ith day by the user u_{id} (Table 1).

Table 1. Key_event_recoder

Input: The key pressed (K) from any text editor, like: Word Pad, Note pad, Facebook, etc.
Output: a) A text file key_detail{Session_ID, key pressed, system time of key press, k_hold, k_dwell} **b)** N=Total number of session on a particular day.

1. Initialize count = 0, k_hold = 0, k_dwell = 0, session_counter = 0;
2. Assume a threshold TH_D in milliseconds for dwell time.
3. For   K
   - a. K_pressed =Time duration (in millisecond) of key pressed.
   - b. K_released = Time duration (in millisecond) of key released
   - c. Compute k_hold = K_pressed- K_released.
   - d. count=count+1; //count total number of key pressed
   - e. Compute k_dwell = K_released[i] - K_pressed[i+1];
     - i. If   k_dwell> TH_D then   Session_counter=Session_counter+1;
   - f. Continue till closing of all editors.
4. Compute the total number of sessions on each day (N) of interaction with the dedicated machine for each individual.
5. Stop.

3.2 Data Preparation

In this phase we select unique features for generating individual signature. For this, key_hold_time and key_dwell_time are selected for analysis. We aim to generate a specific range for each key event for these two features.

Our database stored the collected sample in the form of vector SV = {V_1, V_2 ..., V_m} where m is total number of session for each u_{id} on a particular day. The pre-processing done on Vi, where Vi = {v1, v2 ... vn}; n = number of key pressed on ith session.

We sort the key pressed event in a session and measure the maximum and minimum holding time of the key event (k). Store the range of key holding time and check for update on next sessions. Finally we get a list for each key_event (k) for Day (d) with specified range for user u_id and store them into database in the form of vector K_H {day_id, key_event$_k$, max_hold_time$_k$, min_hold_time$_k$}. max_hold_time$_k$ and min_hold_time$_k$ defines the range for key holding time for kth key_event on day day_id.

For key_dwell_time feature, we make a pairing between adjacent keys (k, k + 1) and store the pair-wise dwell time. In each session, we select the same pairs and list all the dwell_time values. This way, a range for all possible key-pairs is obtained for a day, and stored as vector K_D {day_id, key_pair$_j$, max_dwell_time$_j$, min_dwell_time$_j$} per user (Tables 2 and 3).

Table 2. Key_Hold_Time

Input: The text file containing the key press event with hold time for each user U for a particular day D.

Output: The sample file containing the range for key hold time feature for all possible key on day D.

1. For each $s \in Session\_Id$
   a. Sort all the keys pressed and group the similar keys into K_{group}.
   b. For each $k \in K_{group}$,
      Find the $k\_MAX_{hold\_time}(s)$ and $k\_MIN_{hold\_time}(s)$ for k.
2. Check for the re-occurrence of the same key(k) in all sessions of day D.
3. If $k\_MAX_{hold\_time}(s) >= k\_MAX_{hold\_time}(s+1)$ replace $k\_MAX_{hold\_time}(s)$ with $k\_MAX_{hold\_time}(s+1)$.
   If the $k\_MIN_{hold\_time}(s) <= k\_MIN_{hold\_time}(s+1)$ replace the $k\_MIN_{hold\_time}(s)$ with $k\_MIN_{hold\_time}(s+1)$.
4. Stop.

Table 3. Key_dwell_Time

Input: The text file containing the key press event (K) with dwell time (k_D) for each user (u_id) for a particular day D.

Output: The sample file containing the time range of key dwelling period for all possible pairs of keys on D day.

1. Initialize an array K_D [], where K_D[i] = dwell time for a pair of keys.
2. For $\forall s \in Session\_Id$
   a. For each $k \in K$
      i. Group k^{th} & $(k+1)^{th}$ into a pair $P_{(k, k+1)}$ and store the respective dwell time (k_D) into K_D.
      ii. Search for the re-occurrence of $P_{(k, k+1)}$. Store all the k_D values in K_D.
3. Combine all the sessions on day D and check for the re-occurrence of the similar key pair.
4. Find the maximum and minimum k_D value in the K_D array and define it as the range for all pairs of keys.
5. Stop.

3.3   Signature Vector Generator

In order to generate a template for individual uid we constructed a unique signature vector for each individual. Our feature space has 3 attributes (features); key_hold_time (kh), key_dwell_time (kd) and Backspace_key_count (bkc). For template creation we consider first two features from the feature space.

After the preprocessing of the input data stored in the form of K_H and K_D vector in our repository we proceed to generate a signature vector S_V for each user.

$$U\_V = \{u\_id, \ Avg\_hold\_time, \ Avg\_dwell\_time\}$$

Avg_hold_time derived from max_hold_time, min_hold_time$k \in$ K_H vector for $\forall k \in Key$, Key comprises of all key event possessed by the user for the entire sample collection period. Similarly, max_dwell_time$_j$, min_dwell_time$_j \in$ K_D used for obtaining Avg_dwell_time for $\forall k_p \in Key\_Pair$.

Table 4. Signature_vector_generator

Input: Hold time range for all key $K_{(Hold)}$ and pair-wise dwell time range for all possible key pair $\in K_{(Pair)}$ day D.
Output: A signature vector U_V = {u_id, (Avg_hold_time ,key), (Avg_dwell_time, key_pair)} for each user (u_id).
1. Initialize maximum_hold = 0, minimum_hold = 0, max_dwell = 0, min_dwell = 0;
2. For $\forall d \in$D, (D= No. of days of collection)
    a. For $\forall$ k $\in K_{(Hold)}$,
       i. Set maximum = k_MAX$_{hold\_time}$ (d) and minimum= k_MIN$_{hold\_time}$ (d).
       ii. Update maximum and minimum if k_MAX$_{hold\_time}$ (d+1) > maximum and k_MIN$_{hold\_time}$ (d) < minimum respectively.
    b. For $\forall$ ($l, l + 1$) $\in K_{(Pair)}$,
       i. Set max_dwell = l_MAX$_{dwell\_time}$ (d) and min_dwell= l_MIN$_{dwell\_time}$ (d).
       ii. Update max_dwell and min_dwell if l_MAX$_{dwell\_time}$ (d+1) > max_dwell and l_MIN$_{dwell\_time}$ (d+1) < min_dwell respectively.
3. Compute the Avg_hold_time from max_dwell and min_dwell value and store in U_V with corresponding key set pairs (K_{Pair}).
4. Stop.

4 Experimental Results

We collected the data-sets from 10 participants for 10 days. The sample data-set collected for each individual shown in Table 4.1 based on session on a day. The users were asked to run our proposed application in background during the entire period of interaction with their dedicated machine. The sample data collected from different machine having different configuration.

The users were not bound to press any dedicated text string and there is no additional interface for capturing data. All the active windows accessed by the users were taken into consideration for generating sample data-set.

Table 5. Sample collected for an individual on a session.

Session_Id	Key_Name	Hold_Time (sec)	Dwell_Time (sec)	System_Time
1	E	0.140	0.281	23:37
1	X	0.109	0.407	23:37
1	T	0.094	0.125	23:37
1	Space	0.094	0.062	23:37
1	F	0.109	0.266	23:37
1	I	0.062	0.141	23:37
1	M	0.047	0.188	23:37
1	Backspace	0.094	0.312	23:37
1	L	0.016	0.281	23:37

Table 6. Processed data for key hold time feature per user

Day_ID	Key	Min_Hold_Time	Max_ Hold_Time
1	A	0.031	0.266
1	B	0.079	0.122
1	Backspace	0.031	0.344
1	C	0.078	0.188
1	Comma	0.125	0.125
1	D	0.078	0.156
1	Delete	0.031	0.110
1	Down	0.062	0.125

The collected samples for each user on a particular day then sorted in alphabetic order of key events. The processed samples depicted in Tables 4.2 and 4.3 for hold time and dwell time features respectively (Tables 5, 6, 7 and 8).

Table 7. Processed data-set for key dwell time feature per user

Day_ID	Key-Pair	Min_Dwell_time	Max_ Dwell_time
1	Space-Backspace	0.0203	0.844
1	D-Space	0.016	0.141
1	E-S	0.156	0.203
1	E-Space	0.031	0.110
1	G-Space	0.032	0.047
1	I-M	0.172	0.188
1	M-E	0.063	0.172
1	N-D	0.094	0.125
1	O-N	0.218	0.297

Table 8. Signature vector set for a particular user in the enrolled data-set.

U_ID	Avg_hold_time	Key	Avg_dwell_time	Key-pair
U1	0.1485	A	0.4321	Space-Backspace
U1	0.1005	B	0.0785	D-Space
U1	0.1875	Backspace	0.1795	E-S
U1	0.133	C	0.0705	E-Space
U1	0.125	Comma	0.0395	G-Space
U1	0.117	D	0.18	I-M
U1	0.0705	Delete	0.1175	M E
U1	0.0935	Down	0.1095	N-D

We differentiate the user behavior based on the two unique feature discussed so far, i.e., hold time and dwell time. [Tables 4.2 and 4.3] illustrate the comparative analysis of two user *USER1 and USER2* depending on key Hold time and key dwell time feature (Figs. 3 and 4).

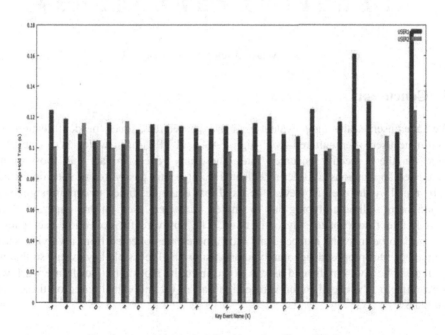

Fig. 3. Average key holding time for all possible keys

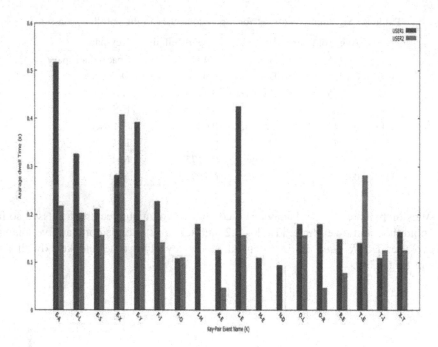

Fig. 4. Average dwell time for a key pair

5 Conclusion

We have observed that the prevalent biometrics based techniques for identification of a legitimate user often suffered from high FAR and FPR rates, which had a negative effect on the respective accuracy rate. The study reveals a fact that most of the developed applications consider a dedicated text (mainly passwords of specific format) to be typed by the user. However, the fixed text examples failed to capture significant variations in individual typing due to limited characters used. In this paper, we have used free-text concept to solve this issue. The software for collecting user data is designed to be machine independent, and samples are collected from a varying set of computers. Our proposed signature vectors deal with all possible key events so that the aggregated behavior of the end user is stored in to the repository. Our future work will concentrate on the classification verification part of the individual based on these store templates.

References

1. Umpires, D., Williams, G.: Identity verification through keyboard characteristics. Int. J. Man-Mach. Stud. **23**(3), 263–273 (1985)
2. Teh, P.S., Theo, A.B.J., Tee, C., Ong, T.S.: Keystroke dynamics in password authentication enhancement. Expert Syst. Appl. Int. J. **37**, 8618–8627 (2010)

3. Monroe, F., Rubin, A.D.: Keystroke dynamics as a biometric for authentication. Elsevier-Future Gener. Comput. Syst. **16**(4), 351–359 (2000)

4. Hong, Y., Deng, Y., Jai, A.K.: Keystroke dynamics for user authentication. In: IEEE Computer Society Conference on Computer Vision and Pattern Recognition Workshops (CVPRW), pp. 117–123 (2012)

5. Revert, K., de Magadhães, S.T., Santos, H.: Data mining a keystroke dynamics based biometrics database using rough sets. University of Technology of Compiegne (2005)

6. Karnana, M., Akilab, M., Krishnarajc, N.: Biometric personal authentication using keystroke dynamics: a review. Appl. Soft Comput. **11**(2), 1565–1573 (2011)

7. Wang, X., Fangxia, G., Jian-feng, M.: User authentication via keystroke dynamics based on difference subspace and slope correlation degree. Digit. Signal Process. **22**(5), 707–712 (2012)

8. Babaeizadeh, M., Bakhtiari, M., Maarof, M.A.: Authentication method through keystrokes measurement of mobile users in cloud environment. Int. J. Advance Soft Comp. Appl. **6**(3) (2014)

9. Hwang, S.-S., Lee, H.-J., Cho, S.: Improving authentication accuracy using artificial rhythms and cues for keystroke dynamics-based authentication. Expert Syst. Appl. ELSEVIER **36**(7), 10649–10656 (2009)

10. Kotani, K., Horii, K.: Evaluation on a keystroke authentication system by keying force incorporated with temporal characteristics of keystroke dynamics. Behav. Inf. Technol. **24** (4), 289–302 (2005)

11. Hwang, S.S., Cho, S., Park, S.: Keystroke dynamics-based authentication for mobile devices. Comput. Secur. **28**(1–2), 85–93 (2009)

12. Nauman, M., Ali, T., Rauf, A.: Using trusted computing for privacy preserving keystroke-based authentication in smartphones. Telecommun. Syst. **52**(4), 2149–2161 (2011)

13. Kaneko, Y., Kinpara, Y., Shiomi, Y.: A hamming distance-like filtering in keystroke dynamics. In: Proceedings of the 9th Annual International Conference on Privacy, Security and Trust (PST 2011), pp. 93–95 (2011)

14. Lee, W., Choi, S.-S., Moon, B.-R.: An evolutionary keystroke authentication based on ellipsoidal hypothesis space. In: Proceedings of the 9th Annual Conference on Genetic and Evolutionary Computation, pp. 2090–2097 (2007)

15. Hosseinzadeh, D., Krishnan, S.: Gaussian mixture modelling of keystroke patterns for biometric applications. IEEE Trans. Syst. Man Cybern. Part C Appl. Rev. **38**, 816–826 (2011)

A Multimodal Biometric User Identification System Based on Keystroke Dynamics and Mouse Movements

Piotr Panasiuk[1(✉)], Maciej Szymkowski[2], Marcin Dąbrowski[2], and Khalid Saeed[1,2]

[1] Faculty of Mathematics and Information Science,
Warsaw University of Technology, Warsaw, Poland
{p.panasiuk,k.saeed}@mini.pw.edu.pl
[2] Faculty of Computer Science, Bialystok University of Technology,
Bialystok, Poland
szymkowskimack@gmail.com, marcin.dabrowski@poczta.fm

Abstract. In this work it is shown how the behavioral biometrics allows to strengthen security of a personal computer during casual use. The user does not have to be even aware of verification system running in the background. Unfortunately, short passwords do not supply enough data for keystroke dynamics algorithms to be precise enough to keep the way and level the biometrics system requires. Behavioral biometrics cannot grant such authentication level as the other physiological biometric methods, e.g. fingerprint or retina scan. However, their transparency in analyzing data allows to merge methods into multimodal systems with a minimal cost. The benefit of keystroke dynamics is that it can be easily connected with some other biometric methods, especially with other human input interface devices. In this paper an approach to analyze keystroke dynamics along with mouse movement is presented. Even though both of the features are of behavioral character and hence with low repeatability, the results are good and promising for further research and modification.

Keywords: Keystroke dynamics · Mouse · Biometrics · Behavioral biometrics · Authentication · Systems security · Multibiometrics · Fusion · Multimodal system

1 Introduction

Today data safety is one of the most discussed terms. People need to prove who they really are at every turn. This includes banking, healthcare, communication and much more. *Something you know* and *something you have* - these are the most common methods used to prove your identity. You know your password, but you may forget it if you are not using it often or have too many of them to remember. Things such as tokens or cards can be used instead and they let you free of remembering sophisticated sequences of various letters, numbers and other special characters. The thing is, tokens and cards can be lost, stolen or even destroyed quite easily. Thus, another way for authentication is needed. Here comes biometrics. *Something you are* cannot be lost or

© IFIP International Federation for Information Processing 2016
Published by Springer International Publishing Switzerland 2016. All Rights Reserved
K. Saeed and W. Homenda (Eds.): CISIM 2016, LNCS 9842, pp. 672–681, 2016.
DOI: 10.1007/978-3-319-45378-1_58

forgotten. These are based on human behavioral and physical characteristics that can be measured and cannot be easy to imitate. Physiological features may include fingerprint, DNA, hand geometry, retinal scan and others that come from how organisms are built. Behavioral features on the other hand are based on how people do things, for example voice (the way one talks), gait (the way one walks) or keystroke dynamics (the way one strikes or touches the keys on the keyboard), and so on.

This paper focuses on behavioral methods. They are cheaper in implementation, usually do not require specialized hardware and often work without bothering or notifying the user. On the other hand these features are often hard to repeat in exactly the same way. This introduces information noise. Both valid users may find it difficult to repeat the activity in the same manner to fit into their patterns and from the other side impostors may also be close to imitate valid data and be falsely accepted. The goal is to find a method that despite those difficulties will make the right decision with the highest possible accuracy.

One of the ways to make biometric algorithms more robust is to join multiple biometric features. This way the algorithm gets more data to analyze what helps it in correct classification. Thus this paper proposes a method to combine multiple behavioral features to provide greater reliability and safety in computer systems. In this particular case mouse movement and keystroke dynamics were chosen as they are not very involving to the user and are often naturally used together. What is more they use standard equipment of every personal computer nowadays.

2 Known Approaches

Lately more interest in the field of behavioral biometrics has been observed. To account this, the authors of this paper decided to present some of the recent approaches in mouse and keystroke dynamics.

In [1] an interesting approach regarding mouse movement has been described. Authors analyzed user online activities by tracking mouse movements across web interfaces in certain areas of interest. One of three user activities was being recognized. Hidden Markov Models and Conditional Random Fields were used in the process. 51 students performed one of three tasks twice. Tasks were based on memorizing graphical representation of a given quadratic equation or discovering and memorizing intersection coordinates of two given quadratic equations. HMM and CRF models performance was evaluated using ratio of ground truth matches number of observation sequences to whole number of test sequences. Distance in pixel of the vicinity extent has been found accuracy determining as its higher value generally resulted in improved accuracy. For distance equal 0, HMM and PCRF models using classical observation sequences gave recognition rate of 88.24 %.

Another interesting approach regarding mouse movement has been described in [2]. Authors presented a method for user emotional state prediction basing on mouse dynamics. To collect data, authors created a simple computer game that required users to click differently sized and colored rectangles in correct order since they were placed randomly. Samples from 262 users were gathered of which 44 users were asked after session, about their emotions during task. Two different states were distinguishable.

Features including distance and direction were extracted from mouse logs among others. Classification was performed using: Logistic regression, Support Vector Machine, Random Forest, and C4.5. Authors used 10 fold cross validation for evaluation, dividing whole data into 10 random parts of same size, next using 9 for training and remaining one for validation. This setup allowed authors to obtain accuracy of 94.61 % (for SVM) in prediction of user emotional state basing on mouse movement and knowing target. Without knowledge of user emotional state during collecting data, accuracy dropped to 82.38 %.

Authors of [3] proposed a novel multimodal biometrics user verification technique based on keystroke dynamics and mouse movement. They focused on several layers of mouse events. This aspect seems interesting and worth further research. Authors claim that they have very good accuracy. The technique seems to be advanced however not all tests were performed and authors do not present the FAR level of the solution. FRR is quite low at range of 3.2 % but in case of verification system, this value may be adjusted to any level by the cost of increasing the opposite metric - FAR. The classification method of the presented solution is not precisely described. Moreover, the results were calculated on unknown database that is not publicly available (state for April 23, 2016). Thus the results and accuracy cannot be confirmed.

A fuzzy approach based method on commands typed by users was considered by the authors in [4]. Authors presented a way to detect impostor by creating two different user activity profiles, local one based on recent activity of the user and one combining multiple local profiles representing user general computer behavior. Authors used publicly available SEA data set consisting of system calls made by 70 users, giving a total of 15000 recorded commands. 50 randomly chosen users were considered legitimate, and 20 were taken as impostors. The lowest FRR ratio of 0.8 % paired with FAR equal to 70.1 was obtained by the mentioned method. Taking low computational complexity into account, this method can successfully be used in real-time.

Another keystroke dynamics based approach was presented by authors of [5]. In that paper user password typing dynamics was observed. Fuzzy sets were used to construct user model. Data for 51 users, each one typing the same password 400 times in 8 sessions of 50 tries, contained in publicly available database *Keystroke Dynamics Benchmark Data Set* by Kevin Killourhy and Roy Maxion [6] was used to perform experiments. Using proposed method allowed to obtain EER value of 9.2 % - an improvement over original [6] methods giving best EER of 9.6 %. According to authors, results improved greatly due to data normalization.

The authors of this paper also have achievements in the field of biometric methods. Apart from the algorithms suggested on the basis of physiological features, which is not the subject of this paper, many other behavioral approaches were introduced [7–14]. The mouse movement was considered for the first time in 2005 [7]. The work introduced then comprised a new method for analyzing biometric features for human authentication. The rhythm of the movement is individual and characteristic for each person, so it can be used for identification in small defined groups or verification for larger groups of users. The method analyzes the dynamics of the mouse cursor movement. The processed signal is the cursor changing speed obtained during the random movement of the mouse. This signal is transformed into frequency domain with Discrete Fourier Transform and then analyzed by Toeplitz matrix minimal eigenvalues method [7]. The resulting feature vector is used for classification performed by two methods: k-nearest neighbors and NN - artificial neural networks. The obtained results were promising and showed a large possibility of integrating the method with other features in multimodal biometrics systems.

The authors' team performed other multiple approaches on keystroke dynamics user identification over the past few years. Algorithms take into account many features including: dwell and flight times, average keystrokes per minute, overlapping specific keys, typing errors, the way of error correction and others. Using simple 1-NN classifier resulted in accuracy of 75.68 % on 37 users [8]. Later approach used improved algorithm based on k-NN classifier on authors' database consisting of samples left by over 250 individuals. Gathered samples included one-word phrase and longer sentences in Polish and English. It was proven that even small number of samples may be enough for successful recognition with the high user amount and right choice of phrase. Best classification accuracy of 90.83 % was obtained with 21 users [9]. Other algorithm modifications were conducted in the next works. On fixed-text approach high accuracy of 98.78 % was obtained for 16 users, although decreasing with greater number of users (e.g. 72.3 % for 79 individuals) [10]. Database quality, however, was taken into account in the following approaches.

In [11] the authors used their own and Maxion-Killourhy's [6] databases with self-developed improved algorithm allowing to discard samples with errors. Said method allowed accuracy increase of 3.6 % for Maxion's data and increase of 5.6 % for authors' database in comparison to initial values. Next [12] authors further analyzed database impact on results. Data gathering precision and conditions along with various algorithm modifications allowed authors to deeply compare mentioned databases and classification methods. This research lead to conclusion that databases with longer samples are more suitable for user identification than authentication and inclusion of user-specific imperfect samples can improve FRR. Additionally, updating training set over time is believed to affect classification accuracy in a positive way. Authentication by non-fixed text of various length was also taken into consideration by the authors [13]. Data were gathered over the Web using browser application and also locally with the use of dedicated applications. Sample length provided to be vital on recognition accuracy as longer texts generally allowed to obtain better results. Using statistical characteristics of the sample gave better outcome than using raw sample data, eventually leading to EER value of 6.1 % for 200-keystroke long samples. Comparison of the Keystroke Dynamics databases was conducted by the authors in [14]. In said work newly-gathered database was presented and compared with existing one which is publicly available [6]. Authors collected it in the way it can be directly compared with *Keystroke Dynamics Benchmark Data Set*. That led to two databases being almost identical. It was possible by using the same phrase typed equal number of times by every user of both databases, i.e., 400 valid samples in 8 sessions. Main difference introduced with authors' database was that its data were collected in unsupervised, less restrictive conditions with the use of commonly available devices when Maxion's database was supervised and used specific high-precision devices. The use of the same algorithms on both databases resulted in differences in the outcome ranging up to about 30 % in some situations, which led to the conclusion that new algorithms should be tested on multiple databases, including publicly available ones and not limiting to the ones gathered by the authors' for the specific research purpose. Moreover, less restrictive method of collecting data allowed to obtain generally higher recognition accuracy.

3 Proposed Approach

In order to get data a web application has been created. It is located under the Internet address [15]. Users have to register in order to create their unique account. During the registration process no biometric data are being collected. Then after logging in they can leave their biometric samples. Authors encourage everyone to visit our system and contribute to the database. User details like email address are stored only to remember the user and allow him to reset the password. The database is meant to be published online. More details will be available on the mentioned website in the near future as the samples set grows rapidly.

A sample in our database consists of two phrases that a user has to type and the mouse data recorded as an interaction with the user interface. The first phrase is a fixed text. It imitates fairly strong password "_Y9u3elike22". It is common for all users. The second phrase is a free-text phrase that a user comes up with spontaneously while typing it. Its only limitation is that it has to be not shorter than 80 characters and not longer than 4000. When it comes to mouse movement data are gathered in a raw form - events like button press, button release and move. Each data has a timestamp from the beginning of the sample and coordinates of a cursor on the web page. Keystroke events are recorded within each text field; however mouse events are being recorded for whole duration of leaving a complete sample. This means since pressing the first button, through selecting each text field and pressing additional button, until submitting a form by clicking the last button on the data acquisition web page.

Data examined during this research were only fixed phrase and mouse activity. From these data authors had to extract the most valuable features. Samples were gathered in unsupervised conditions so an algorithm for various corner-cases was applied. When it comes to mouse data single mouse moves are being extracted. Mouse move is considered as cursor position change from the beginning of a move until button press. Due to unwanted cursor movements during releasing the mouse by the user, authors decided to ignore move events after mouse click and before typing a text. Finally, the authors examined few mouse movement features - move time, move speed (in pixels per second) and move distance. As a separate feature mouse button dwell times while clicking buttons or text fields are accounted. When it comes to keyboard data we have tried to extract flight times and dwell times as they are the most common keystroke features, but to our surprise they did not perform well with success rate at about 11 % using approach and setup presented in the following paragraph. It might be the case that the sample was really difficult, especially the first half of it. Some additional difficulties came up with shift key being pressed different amount of times. Authors tried to implement an algorithm that would deal with those differences however the overall recognition rate was really affected by those artifacts. So the dwell times of specific key presses were analyzed instead. They have proven to give really good accuracy which is presented in the next chapter.

After defining feature vectors our next step was the identification process. In this purpose authors used fast and simple *k*-NN algorithm. The most important part is the distance calculation. There are three features that are being extracted from both keystroke and mouse data. A *keyboardDistance* (1) is a distance calculated using Manhattan metrics between corresponding dwell times of a training and a testing sample. In a case of mouse data represented by *mouseDistance* (2) there are mouse key dwell times, the metric used is Manhattan metric as well. The last feature is *moveDistance* (3) which proved to be the best metric to calculate the moves and is defined by the Euclidean distance from the move start point to the move end point in a two-dimensional space according to the move definition in a foregoing paragraph.

$$keyboardDistance = \frac{1}{k}\sum_{i=0}^{k}|dwellA_i - dwellB_i| \tag{1}$$

$$mouseDistance = \frac{1}{m}\sum_{i=0}^{m}|mouseDwellA_i - mouseDwellB_i| \tag{2}$$

$$moveDistance = \frac{1}{n}\sum_{i=0}^{n}dist(moveA_i, moveB_i) \tag{3}$$

As one can see each distance is normalized. To calculate the final distance between two samples authors use Eq. (4). What should be explained is that *keyboardWeight* is the importance factor of keyboard event. Mouse events importance factor is *mouseWeight* and the *moveWeight* is the importance factor of the mouse moves.

$$distance = \frac{kD \cdot kW + mD \cdot mW + moveD \cdot moveW}{kW + mW + moveW} \tag{4}$$

where:
  kD - keyboardDistance
  kW - keyboardWeight
  mD - mouseDistance
  mW - mouseWeight
  moveD - moveDistance
  moveW - moveWeight

Mentioned weights have been selected empirically. The detailed information about the experiment setup and preparation is described in the following chapter. After defining the distance the classic *k*-NN algorithm is being followed.

4   Results of the Experiment

Authors' database has irregular amount of samples per user. This is due to constant growth of the dataset. Because of this the users that does not get sufficient amount of samples have been removed from the experimental setup. In our *k*-NN-based method

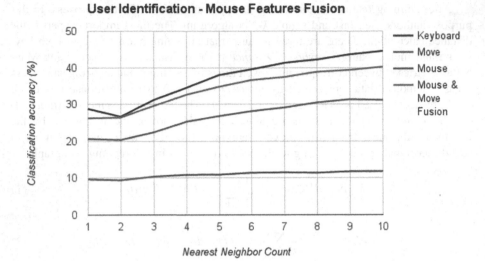

Fig. 1. Influence of joining mouse button dwell times and mouse moves on algorithm accuracy.

the minimum number of samples per user is k. This number allows to prepare a valid training set having exactly k samples for each user. The rest of remaining user samples are used for a testing purpose. Finally for a $k = 10$ there are 50 valid classes in each of the experiments. This is why all setups has been limited to those 50 classes. So the users set among all experiment runs are the same. To get reliable results each experiment was repeated 100 times for each setup, every time using randomly selected training and testing samples.

At the beginning authors had to select proper feature weights to get the best results. This way the algorithm has been run for each of three features separately and authors got the information about accuracy of each of the methods. The weakest method was mouse dwell times alone with average success rate of about 12 %. The second one that was mouse move distances gave the success rate around 31 %. It is worth mentioning that while analyzing move speeds in pixels per second instead of move distances the accuracy has dropped to the level of 8 %. Finally the best was keystroke dynamics with around 44 % of accuracy. In order to obtain the best weight values authors picked the two weakest features and joined them using different weight ratio.

After conducting the experiment with weights ranging from 0.0 to 1.0 with step of 0.05, the best ratio proved to be 0.8 for *mouseWeight* vs. 0.2 for *moveWeight* that returned the accuracy of around 40 % for mouse data only.

Figure 1 presents the results of classification accuracy after joining mouse dwell times and mouse movement features in comparison to keystroke dynamics alone. Having these results authors tested different *moveWeight* values and the results shown that the big increase can be gained. The accuracy of the algorithm in a setup where *keyboardWeight* = 2, *mouseWeight* = 0.4, and *moveWeight* = 0.1 returned the identification accuracy of 68.8 % for 50 classes. This result has exceeded authors' expectations for such little of data. In Fig. 2 one can see results of our experiments. Different

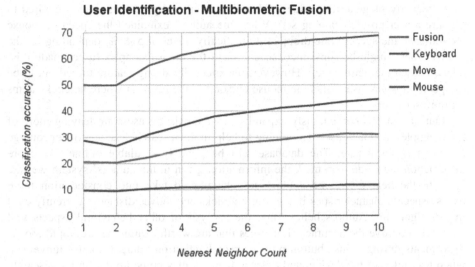

Fig. 2. Chart presenting classification accuracy using different approaches along with different *k*-nearest neighbor value used.

values of parameter *k* (from 1 to 10) were taken into account whereas count of classes was stable and equal to 50. Each method accuracy has been marked separately and the optimal fusion method results are also presented.

5   Conclusions and Future Work

Biometric methods present a very convenient way to harden the computer system security. Even if the user knows the password it is really hard for him to repeat it in the same manner to breach the security. If it comes to identification, it is even a harder task because a user does not claim his identity. Thus the whole database has to be searched for matching the user pattern. Identification algorithms have to be fast and robust. Presented in this paper *k*-NN algorithm perfectly matches these requirements.

As it was presented, user identification by using mouse button dwell is not very reliable. When mouse moves are analyzed, the accuracy increases significantly. When both mouse button press and mouse move features are used together they are almost as effective as keystroke dynamics using dwell times. What was surprising in this experiment is the fact that flight times and dwell times which usually make the user typing features more persistent in time, resulted in a huge accuracy drop (from 44 % to merely 11 %). This is possible due to the short sample length and few ways to type the phrase correctly (using the shift key).

As expected, combining both keystroke dynamics and mouse features allowed to obtain much better recognition ratio than relying on them separately. Accuracy of 68.8 % as a result of fusion is quite impressive, taking into account the high number of users in relation to quite short samples. Fusion of different biometric algorithms gives us a great advantage at low values of k which significantly decreases time required to prepare a user profile (training set). When the authors examined the speed of mouse movements, the success rate dropped dramatically (level of 5–8 %, depending on the setup). There might be some inconsistencies in the mouse samples (users made mistakes, missed the button, etc.). However, unexpectedly strong feature turned out to be the position where user parks the mouse cursor and the position where he clicks items on the user interface.

Our database is continuously expanding as the existing users are leaving more of their samples, and new users are willing to help in the research. The authors encourage everyone to participate. The database will be publicly available online. For more information the reader can track the information given in the authors' system website [15]. In the near future the authors are planning to take into consideration more mouse-specific characteristics in addition to clicks and moves distances currently used in our algorithm. Authors believe that the analysis of other behavioral aspects will definitely improve the accuracy. Examples that are worth examining are: rapid mouse movements during mouse button press, cursor fixation on a target, mouse movement when user releases the device, and other issues that may come up during the research. Additionally, as an extension to this research authors would like to introduce some decision algorithm and understand user mistakes for better handling of unusual users and data anomalies.

Acknowledgments. This work was partially supported by grant number S/WI/1/2013 from Bialystok University of Technology and funded from the resources for research by Ministry of Science and Higher Education. It was also partially supported by Neitec company.

References

1. Elbahi, A., Omri, M.N., Mahjoub, M.A., Garrouch, K.: Mouse movement and probabilistic graphical models based e-learning activity recognition improvement possibilistic model. Arab. J. Sci. Eng. **41**(8), 2847–2862 (2016). Springer, Heidelberg
2. Pentel, A.: Patterns of confusion: using mouse logs to predict user's emotional state. In: 5th International Workshop on Personalization Approaches in Learning Environments in conjunction with 23rd Conference on User Modelling, Adaptation and Personalization, Dublin, Ireland. CEUR Workshop Proceedings, vol. 1388, pp. 40–45 (2015)
3. Motwani, A., Jain, R., Sondhi, J.: A multimodal behavioral biometric technique for user identification using mouse and keystroke dynamics. Int. J. Comput. Appl. **111**(8), 15–20 (2015)
4. Kudłacik, P., Porwik, P., Wesołowski, T.: Fuzzy approach for intrusion detection based on user's commands. Soft Comput. **20**(7), 2705–2719 (2015). Springer, Heidelberg
5. Kaganov, V.Y., Korolev, A.K., Krylov, M.N., Mashechkin, I.V., Petrovskii, M.I.: Machine learning methods in authentication problems using password keystroke dynamics. Comput. Math. Model. **26**(3), 398–407 (2015)
6. Killourhy, K.S., Maxion, R.A.: Comparing anomaly-detection algorithms for keystroke dynamics. In: Dependable Systems & Networks, Lisbon, Portugal, pp. 125–134. IEEE (2009)

7. Tabędzki, M., Saeed, K.: Nowa metoda do badania dynamiki ruchów myszy komputerowej do celów identyfikacji. In: Krajowa Konferencja Naukowa – KBIB 2005, tom I, Systemy Informatyczne i Telemedyczne, Wydawnictwa Politechniki Częstochowskiej, Częstochowa, Poland, pp. 467–472 (2005) (in Polish)
8. Rybnik, M., Tabedzki, M., Saeed, K.: A keystroke dynamics based system for user identification. In: Computer Information Systems and Industrial Management Applications, pp. 225–230. IEEE (2008)
9. Rybnik, M., Panasiuk, P., Saeed, K.: User authentication with keystroke dynamics using fixed text. In: International Conference on Biometrics and Kansei Engineering, Cieszyn, Poland, pp. 70–75. IEEE (2009)
10. Panasiuk, P., Saeed, K.: A modified algorithm for user identification by his typing on the keyboard. In: Choraś, R.S. (ed.) Image Processing and Communications Challenges 2. AISC, vol. 84, pp. 113–120. Springer, Heidelberg (2010)
11. Panasiuk, P., Saeed, K.: Influence of database quality on the results of keystroke dynamics algorithms. In: Chaki, N., Cortesi, A. (eds.) CISIM 2011. CCIS, vol. 245, pp. 105–112. Springer, Heidelberg (2011)
12. Rybnik, M., Panasiuk, P., Saeed, K., Rogowski, M.: Advances in the keystroke dynamics: the practical impact of database quality. In: Cortesi, A., Chaki, N., Saeed, K., Wierzchoń, S. (eds.) CISIM 2012. LNCS, vol. 7564, pp. 203–214. Springer, Heidelberg (2012)
13. Rybnik, M., Tabedzki, M., Adamski, M., Saeed, K.: An exploration of keystroke dynamics authentication using non-fixed text of various length. In: International Conference on Biometrics and Kansei Engineering, pp. 245–250. IEEE (2013)
14. Panasiuk, P., Dąbrowski, M., Saeed, K., Bocheńska-Włostowska, K.: On the comparison of the keystroke dynamics databases. In: Saeed, K., Snášel, V. (eds.) CISIM 2014. LNCS, vol. 8838, pp. 122–129. Springer, Heidelberg (2014)
15. Authors' system website. http://www.ikds.metna.nct. Accessed 26 Apr 2016

An Efficient Three Factor Based Remote User Authentication Protocol for Distributed Networks

Ashish Singh[(✉)] and Kakali Chatterjee

Department of Computer Science and Engineering,
National Institute of Technology Patna, Patna 800005, Bihar, India
ashish.cse15@nitp.ac.in

Abstract. In distributed networks, one major security drawback is to identify the legitimate remote users of a web service on the Internet. To eliminate this security problem, many researchers have been proposed smart card based remote user authentication for secure communication in wireless networks. The wireless networks mostly use password based protocols that are based on two factors-smart card and PIN. But, this type of authentication protocols are susceptible to password guessing attack, stolen verifier attack, replay attack etc. In this paper, we propose a three factor based mutual authentication protocol using smart card in distributed networks, which resists all possible attacks. This protocol is suitable for hand held devices due to the low computational and communicational cost.

Keywords: Mutual authentication · Smart card · Diffie-Hellman key exchange

1 Introduction

Modern day's Internet is connecting different types of devices which are communicating with each other in different types of distributed networks. In distributed networks secure communication is challenging as the network is based on client server model where the server may possibly be distributed and replicated. Thus, if a remote user wants to get services, he must authenticate himself in the network.

On the basis of the Lamport's [1] authentication scheme, many single servers authentication protocols are found in the literature. However, his scheme required verification tables, which can be hacked by hackers. When the user access services from more than one server, the single-server authentication schemes become highly inconvenient in a distributed environment. Hence, many multi-server user authentication schemes have been proposed by the researchers [2–12]. Among these protocols, some suffers from the parallel session attack [10,12] and the server spoofing attack and some does not resist replay attack,

© IFIP International Federation for Information Processing 2016
Published by Springer International Publishing Switzerland 2016. All Rights Reserved
K. Saeed and W. Homenda (Eds.): CISIM 2016, LNCS 9842, pp. 682–693, 2016.
DOI: 10.1007/978-3-319-45378-1_59

impersonation attack and fails to proof perfect forward security [9,11]. The concept of dynamic ID-based authentication scheme are found in literature [13–17]. These schemes uses smart cards for distributed systems. Sood et al. scheme [15] is based on elliptic curve cryptography which protects all such attacks. Such authentication schemes based on public key cryptography are very difficult to comprise because of the inherent strength of public key systems, but these schemes are very expensive as the use of public key cryptography involves calculation of exponential operations, which needs a lot of processing time. So, the computational cost and efficiency will increases in such cases.

From the literature, it can be summaries that a multi-server authentication scheme must have mutual authentication with no verification table and low computation and communication cost. Also, the remote user authentication will able to resist following security attack such as insider attack, impersonation attack, replay attack, password guessing attack, stolen-verifier attack and server spoofing attack.

To support these features, the paper proposes a multi-server authentication scheme for remote user, which utilizes three factor- a smart card, a password and a token for authenticating user. It also provide easy password change phase to user without replacing card. This scheme can resist many attacks such as insider attack, impersonation attack, replay attack, password guessing attack, stolen-verifier attack and server spoofing attack.

The rest of the paper is organized as follows: Sect. 2 discusses cryptanalysis of Chen et al. scheme, Sect. 3 discusses proposed mutual authentication protocol based on Diffie-hellman key agreement, Sect. 4 discusses the security and performance of the recommended system. Finally, the paper concludes in Sect. 5.

2 Cryptanalysis of Chen et al. scheme

The section of this paper discusses cryptanalysis of Chen et al. scheme [9], that is shown in Figs. 1 and 2. Researchers assumed that two main capabilities must be considered while check the security strength of the smart-card based authentication. First, the communication link is under the control of the adversary so that he can insert, delete, and modify messages and second, the attacker will able to extracts the secrets of the smart card or both of them.

Impersonation Attack. This protocol fails to protect from impersonation attack. During registration process the attacker extracts the user identity ID_u and password PW_u. Now from the next communication, he extracts $C_1=h(SID_j||R_u)\oplus N_c=h(SID_j||h(ID_u||X))\oplus N_c$. He keep this values. Now, the attacker sends ID_u, SID_j, C_1 to AC and ID_u, C_1 to the server S_j. After that the attacker receives the token from AC and from $C_3= N_{rc1}\oplus h(SID||h(ID||X))$ he get N_{rc1}. Now he generates $C_7= h(N_{rc1}||N_c||ID)$ and verify himself to AC. After that he receives $C_9= h(ID||h(SID||Y)|| N_s+1||N_{rc2}+2)\oplus h(SID||h(ID||X)||N_c+1||N_{rc1}+2)$. After completing the mutual authentication he can generate the session key which is equal to $h(ID||h(SID||Y)||N_s+1||N_{rc2}+2)||h(SID||h(ID||X)||N_c+1||N_{rc1}+2||N_{s2}+1||N_{c2}+2)$.

After that the attacker can impersonate as a valid user and exchange messages with server.

Replay Attack. This protocol fails to resist replay attack. The protocol does not check the validity of the nonce C_1, C_2 which are coming from the user and target server respectively. Also, AC uses these nonce C_1, C_2 for the generation of two other nonce N_c, N_s. If the attacker manages to know the value of R_u, then he can able to know the value of N_c. All other nonce values can be retrieved from this value. Later, by the attacker can replay the message C_1 for further authentication. There is no validity checking of each message packet. So, he can easily perform replay attack to gather the knowledge of authentication exchange.

Man-in-Middle Attack. This attack can easily perform in this scheme. Suppose, an attacker listen all the communication between the user and AC. Also, he has capture the message carrying the token $C_9 = h(ID||h(SID||Y)||N_s+1||N_{rc2}+2) \oplus h(SID||h(ID||X)||N_c+1||N_{rc1}+2)$. Now, he wants to set the session key for communication. The attacker also captures the message $C_{10} = N_{s2} \oplus h(SID||h(ID||X)||N_c+1||N_{rc1}+2)$ and $C_{11} = N_{c2} \oplus h(ID||h(SID||Y)||N_s+1||N_{rc2}+2)$ which user and server exchanged during mutual authentication phase. Now following operations, he performed for getting the value of N_{c2}, N_{s2}. He can perform $C_9 \oplus C_{10} \oplus C_{11}$ to get the value of $N_{s2} \oplus N_{c2}$. Now using differential cryptanalysis he can able to find the value of N_{s2}, N_{c2}. After that he can easily get: $C_{10} \oplus N_{s2} = h(SID||h(ID||X)||N_c+1||N_{rc1}+2)$, $C_{11} \oplus N_{c2} = h(ID||h(SID||Y)||N_s+1||N_{rc2}+2)$ Hence, can calculate session key: $K_s = h(ID||h(SID||Y)||N_s+1||N_{rc2}+2)||h(SID||h(ID||X)||N_c+1||N_{rc1}+2||N_{s2}+1||N_{c2}+2)$ Now, all the encrypted message will come to the attacker, he can modify and send to the server.

Dictionary Attack. This protocol cannot resist the off line dictionary attack. Suppose, an attacker capture the smart card of the user, now the attacker is interested in finding the password. For example, he gathers the information, the password is 6 digits. He can list of numbers and then apply hash function to every number. A rainbow table is used to attack a hashed password in reverse. That means the attacker has a table with possible hashes and look up a matching password. After a match, the attacker goes for online and use the password to access the system. So, require a password change phase for changing the password.

Perfect Forward Secrecy. In this scheme, we have seen that if the attacker knows the password and stole the smart card, he can retrieve the value $R_u = h(ID_u||X)$ from $C_0 = R_u \oplus h(PW_u)$. Now from previous session, he can get the nonce value N_c from $C_1 = h(SID_j||h(ID_u||X)) \oplus N_c$. Similarly, he can get N_s from $C_2 = h(ID_u||h(SID_j||Y)) \oplus N_s$ and from $C_3 = N_{rc1} \oplus h(SID||h(ID||X))$ he get N_{rc1}. In such a way the attacker extract all the nonce and calculate the session key. Hence, no perfect forward secrecy is maintained in this protocol.

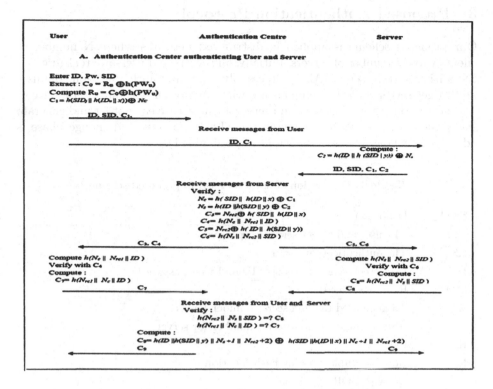

Fig. 1. Message transfer in authentication process in Xie et al. scheme

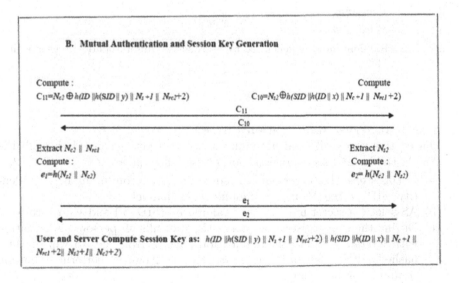

Fig. 2. Message transfer in mutual authentication in Xie et al. scheme

3 Proposed Authentication Protocol

Our proposed scheme is applied in distributed networks where N number of clients with M number of servers. Initially, all servers and users are registered on the authentication server. After successfully login and authentication, the user and target server directly communicate with each other without interference of authentication server. The user and server authenticate each other and generate the session key for secure communication. Lastly, a password change phase is added. The whole scheme is shown in Fig. 3 (Table 1).

Table 1. Description of notation used in proposed scheme

Symbol	Definition
U, S	The user and target server, respectively
AS	The authentication server
UID, PW	User credentials means user ID and user password
SID	Remote server ID
X	AS generated random secret number for user
Y	AS generated random secret number for server
R	User salt
h(.)	Non-invertable one-way hash function
$\oplus$	Bit-wise XOR operation
P	Large positive natural number called prime number
G	Generator of order p-1 in the field $Z_p{}^*$
T	Timestamp
ΔT	Network delay
a, b, c, d	Random integers generated by user, server and authentication server in $\{1,\ldots\ldots,p\text{-}1\}$

1. **User and Server Registration Phase**

   During this phase all legal users and all servers get registered through the AS. At the time of server registration phase, all steps are given in Table 2.

   (a) In this steps, the server sends a request message containing her/his identity 'SID' to the AS by a communication channel.

   (b) AS selects a secret number Y to calculate h(SID||Y) and send it to S.

   (c) During the user registration phase, the user fills all personal information with UID and PW to the application page of AS. The AS will produce hashed salted password, but never store it. Now AS performs following computation on them.

   (d) On receiving the UID and hashed salted password AS computes: $R_u = h(UID||X)$ and $C_0 = R_u \oplus h(PW \oplus R)$. Now, AS stores R_u in a smart card

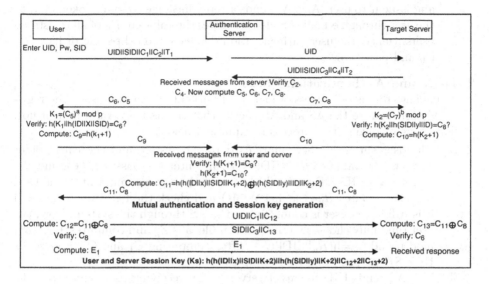

Fig. 3. Proposed mutual authentication protocol

Table 2. Flow of proposed mutual authentication scheme

Steps	Message flow	Message format	Message contains
Registration phase			
1	S → AS	Server_Req_Msg	SID
2	AS → S	Server_Reply_Msg	$h(SID||Y)$
3	U → AS	User_Req_Msg	$UID||h(PW \oplus R)$
4	AS → U	User_Reply_Msg	$UID||C_0$
Login and authentication phase			
1	U → AS	User_Req_Login	$UID||SID||C_1||C_2||T_1$
2	S → AS	Server_Req_Login	$UID||SID||C_3||C_4||T_2$
3	AS → U	User_Grant_Login	$C_5||C_6$
4	AS → S	Server_Grant_Login	$C_7||C_8$
5	U → AS	User_Challenge	$UID||C_9$
6	S → AS	Server_Challenge	$SID||C_{10}$
7	AS → S	Server_Response	$UID||C_{11}||C_6$
8	AS → U	User_Response	$SID||C_{11}||C_8$
Mutual authentication phase			
1	U → S	User_Req_Msg	$UID||C_1||C_{12}$
2	S → U	Server_Reply_Msg	$SID||C_3||C_{13}$
3	U → S	User_Response	e_1

and issue it to user. Also AS sends a reply message contains token (C_0) to the user through e-mail. AS also preserves the values of R_u of all registered users. Hence, the user authentication depends upon three factor like, R_u, C_0 and password.

2. **Login and Authentication Phase**
   This phase discusses process of login and authentication of a user. The registered user login to the AS and AS checks that the user is a valid user or not. The steps involve in this process is explained below:
   (a) The user enters his/her smart card to the system and the card reader extracts the value of R_u, UID. Now, he enter the password, C_0 and the target server ID SID with which user desires to communicate. The card reader computes $R_u = C_0 \oplus h(PW \oplus R)$ and check the two values of R_u. If it is valid then user is connected to the AS through the system. Now, the user randomly chooses a random variable 'a' $\in Z_p^*$ and computes: $C_1 = (g^a)$ mod p and $C_2 = h(R_u||SID||C_1)$. After computing C_1 and C_2, user sends UID, SID, C_1, C_2 and timestamp to AS.
   (b) The AS sends UID to target server S. On receiving user request, in the form of UID, the server 'S' randomly selects 'b'$\in Z_p^*$ and compute: $C_3 = (g^b)$ mod p and $C_4 = h(h(SID||Y)||UID||C_3)$. After that target server S sends UID, SID, C_3, C_4 to the AS.
   (c) On receiving messages from user and the server, AS first calculate the timestamp values. If $T_2 - T_1 \leq \Delta T$, then the AS checks whether h $(h(UID||X)||SID||C_1)$ is equal to C_2 and $h(h(SID||Y)||UID||C_3)$ is equal to C_4 or not. If two values are equal, then AS authenticates the user and the server, otherwise AS terminates the session. After authenticating, AS chooses randomly 'c'$\in Z_p^*$ and 'd'$\in Z_p^*$ computes: $C_5 = (g^c)(\text{mod } p)$, $K_1 = (C_1)^c(\text{mod } p) = (g^{ac})(\text{mod } p)$, $C_6 = h(K_1||h(UID||X)||SID)$, $C_7 = (g^d)(\text{mod } p)$, $K_2 = (C_3)^d(\text{mod } p) = (g^{bd})(\text{mod } p)$, $C_8 = h(K_2||h(SID||Y)||UID)$. Then, AS transfers C_5, C_6 to the user and C_7, C_8 to the target server 'S'. Each message contains present timestamps value.
   (d) After receiving the messages from AS, the user checks timestamp and calculates K_1 as, $K_1 = (C_5)^a(\text{mod } p) = (g^{ac})(\text{mod } p)$. Now user verifies received C_6 as follows, $h(K_1||h(UID||X)||SID) = C_6$?. If the two values are equal, the user authenticates AS, the user computes C_9 and send it to AS. $C_9 = h(K_1 + 1)$. Similarly, the target server 'S' checks timestamp and computes K_2: $K_2 = (C_7)^b(\text{mod } p) = (g^{bd})(\text{mod } p)$. Now, server verifies received C_8 as follows: $h(K_2||h(SID||Y)||UID) = C_8$?. If the two values are equal, the server authenticates the AS and computes C_{10}: $C_{10} = h(K_2 + 1)$. After completion of above operation, server sends C_{10}.
   (e) When AS receives C_9 and C_{10}, it verifies and calculates: $h(K_1 + 1) = C_9$? $h(K_2 + 1) = C_{10}$?. If the two values are equal, AS ensures authenticity and calculates: $C_{11} = h(h(UID||X)||SID||K_1 + 2) \oplus h(h(SID||Y)||UID||K_2 + 2)$. Once the C_{11} is computed, AS sends it to user and server with timestamp. This step marks the end of AS involvement.

3. **Mutual Authentication and Session Key Generation Phase**

In the session key generation phase, the authenticate user and target server communicate directly and generate secure session key given in Table 2. Details of each step are as follows:

(a) On receiving C_{11} from AS, the user checks timestamp and computes $C_{12}=C_{11}\oplus C_6$. The user transmits $(UID||C_1||C_{12})$ to server S through the public network.

(b) Receiving C_{12} target server computes C_6 from $C_{12}=C_{11}\oplus C_6$ and compare the received value of C_6' with the stored value C_6 which AS has sent previously. If it matches than the target server 'S' computes, $C_{13}=C_{11}\oplus C_8$. The server transmits $(SID||C_3||C_{13})$ to user through the public network. It also calculates secret key $K= (C_1)^b \bmod p$.

(c) When user receives C_{13}, it computes C_8 from $C_{13}=C_{11}\oplus C_8$ and compare the received value of C_8' with the stored value C8 which AS has sent previously. If it matches than the user computes: $E = h\,(C_{12}\oplus C_{13})$ and send the response message to target server S. It also calculate secret key $K= (C_3)^a \bmod p$. After mutual authentication both of them generate common session key:

$$K_s=h(h(ID||X)||SID||K+2)||h(h(SID||Y)||K+2)||C_{13}+2||C_{12}+2)$$

Now user and target server will exchange messages using symmetric encryption (AES) where they use session key K_s for encryption for session time T_s.

4. **Password Change Phase**

The user insert the card, the values UID, R_u is retrieved from the card and C_0, PW is taken from user. The card reader computes R_u, and also compute $R_u'=C_0\oplus h(PW\oplus R)$ from stored value. It compares the stored value with the computed value and if $R_u=R_u'$, then the system will accept the user as a valid user. Now, after entering the new password the system will generate the new $X_{new}=h(PW_{new}\oplus R)$ and sends it to AS. As the value of R_u remain unchanged, so no new card will be issued to the user. Only AS compute new $C_0= R_u\oplus h(PW_{new}\oplus R)$, send it to user's e-mail. Next time the user will authenticate himself by using the new C_0. In this way the user can change the password without involving AS.

4 Security and Performance of the Proposed Authentication Scheme

This section discusses the security of the proposed authentication protocol, which resists the following attacks:

Dictionary Attack. The system will give limited chances for login. After that it will lock the system for security. Moreover, it is not possible to guess token and password correctly at the same time. During login, the user enters UID, her/his password (PW) and the target server ID (SID). The user terminal computes R_u, where $R_u= C_0 \oplus h(PW \oplus R)$. Even if the attacker knows C_0, then also very difficult to calculate password and salt. Hence, this protocol will resist offline and online password guessing attack.

Replay Attack. The valid and fresh messages completely resists the replay attack. The freshness in messages is because of the use of randomly chosen a, b, c, d, from Z^*_p. Also each message carrying a fresh nonce which is checked the validity of the message. For example, the AS perform following calculation for user and server authentication. $h(h(UID||X)||SID||C_1) =? C_2$ and $h(h(SID||Y)||UID||C_3) =? C_4$. The user verifies received C_6 as follows, $h(K_1||h(UID||X)||SID)=C_6?$. Also the server verifies received C_8 as follows, $h(K_2||h(SID||Y)||UID)=C_8?$. So, the proposed remote user authentication scheme can withstand replay attack till the adversary doesn't know the value of $h(SID||Y)$ or $h(ID||X)$.

Impersonation Attack. Suppose, the attacker track the message $(UID||C_0)$, which the AS sends the user where $C_0=R_u \oplus h(PW \oplus R)$. Now, the attacker has to insert the correct password to the card reader. The terminal calculate the value of R_u. It is impossible for the attacker to show as a valid user. The attacker can done the mutual authentication, but not able to set the key K_1, K_2. Hence, if the attacker imitates as the valid user, he cannot get the session key without knowing the $h(SID||Y)$ or $h(ID||X)$ values. Thus, the attacker will not get a correct authentication key. So, the proposed protocol resists impersonation attack.

Insider Attack. During user registration with the authentication server the user provide her/his password in the form of $(PW \oplus R)$ instead of simply providing as (PW). The value of 'R', generated randomly by the application site. The AS never stores the token $C_0 = R_u \oplus h(PW \oplus R)$ or the salted password. So, any insider in the AS won't be able to know the actual password as well as salted password. Hence, the proposed scheme can successfully resists the insider attack.

Man-in Middle Attack. The attacker intercepts the messages through which AS communicates C_5, C_6 to the user and C_7, C_8 to the target server 'S' on the public network. Now the attacker replace the value of C_5, C_6 by C'_5, C'_6 and C_7, C_8 by C'_7, C'_8. Now, the attacker computes the value K'_1, K'_2 for the intension to listen all messages. But, the session key actually depends on the following factors: $K_s=h(h(ID||X)||SID||K+2)||h(h(SID||Y)||K+2)||C_{13}+2||C_{12}+2)$. The adversary does not have the values of 'X' and 'Y'. Hence, he will not be able to set a common session key. Thus, this attack is not possible in this scheme.

Mutual Authentication. This scheme provides mutual authentication to the user and the target server. The user transmits $(UID||C_1||C_{12})$ to server S through the public network. The target server computes C_6 from $C_{12}=C_{11} \oplus C_6$ and compare the received value of C'_6 with the stored value C_6 which AS has sent previously. If it matches than the target server transmits $(SID||C_3||C_{13})$ to user through the public network. It also calculates secret key $K= (C_1)^b$ mod p. When a user receives C_{13}, it computes C_8 from $C_{13}=C_{11} \oplus C_8$ and compare the received value of C'_8 with the stored value C_8 which AS has sent previously. If it matches, then the user computes: $e_1 = h(C_{12} \oplus C_{13})$ and send the response message to target server S. In this way the scheme provides mutual authentication between the user and target server.

Table 3. The functionality comparison of our proposed protocol with previous existing protocols

Functionalities	Banerjee et al. [2]	Chuang et al. [6]	Xue et al. [17]	Li et al. [5]	Our Scheme
Man-in-the-middle attack	Yes	No	No	No	Yes
Impersonation attack	No	No	No	Yes	Yes
Mutual authentication	Yes	No	No	Yes	Yes
Replay attack	No	Yes	Yes	Yes	Yes
Perfect forward secrecy	yes	No	Yes	No	Yes
Insider attack	Yes	Yes	No	No	Yes
Password guessing attack	No	Yes	No	No	Yes
Computational cost for login and authentication	$17T_h + 17T_X$	$16T_h$	$27T_h$	$27T_h$	$16T_h + 10T_{exp}$

Server Spoofing Attack. In proposed protocol, the attacker not be able to provide authenticity of any user cause of servers do not keep any password table, To authenticate the user, server first needs to get authentication from authentication server and can then communicate with the user. The attacker can get the SID of the target server, but it is impossible to know the value of Y because it is randomly generated by the AS and kept secret. Therefore, this scheme resists server spoofing attack.

Perfect Forward Secrecy. The scheme is maintaining perfect forward secrecy. Even if the password of the past session is disclosed, then also the attacker cannot able to calculate the past session key. Assume that the attacker knows C_{12}, C_{13}. Now to generate the past session key, the attacker must know the values of h(SID||Y) and h(ID||X), which depend on two secret values X, Y. Now consider anyway the attacker knows these values. Then he has to calculate the value of K where $K = (g^{ab})$ mod p. Here, the attacker must know a and b to get the key. The attacker will not be able to guess them accurately and get the session key. Hence, it is proved that the scheme is maintaining perfect forward secrecy.

Performance Analysis. The functionality comparison in Table 3 shows that our scheme is more secure, robust, take less amount of time for authentication operations. The notation T_h, T_X and T_{exp} are shows as the time complexity for hashing function, time complexity for Ex-or operation and time complexity for exponential operation respectively.

5   Conclusions

This paper proposes an advanced and secure technique for remote users in distributed networks over an insecure channel. It resist all possible attacks in distributed networks. The scheme provides mutual authentication between target server and user and also generate different session key for different server. The weakness in Xie and Chen [9] scheme have been successfully removed by our scheme. The security analysis and comparison of the proposal proven that the proposed remote user authentication scheme is efficient, secure and takes less amount of time for essential authentication operation and can resist the major attacks.

References

1. Lamport, L.: Password authentication with insecure communication. Commun. ACM **24**(11), 770–772 (1981)
2. Banerjee, S., Dutta, M.P., Bhunia, C.T.: A perfect dynamic-id and biometric based remote user authentication scheme under multi-server environments using smart cards. In: Proceedings of the 8th International Conference on Security of Information and Networks, pp. 58–64. ACM, 8 September 2015
3. Li, L.H., Lin, I.C., Hwang, M.S.: A remote password authentication scheme for multiserver architecture using neural networks. IEEE Trans. Neural Netw. **12**(6), 1498–1504 (2001)
4. Yoon, E.J., Yoo, K.Y.: Robust multi-server authentication scheme. In: Sixth IFIP International Conference on Network and Parallel Computing, NPC 2009, pp. 197–203. IEEE, 19 October 2009
5. Li, X., Xiong, Y., Ma, J., Wang, W.: An efficient and security dynamic identity based authentication protocol for multi-server architecture using smart cards. J. Netw. Comput. Appl. **35**(2), 763–769 (2012)
6. Chuang, M.C., Chen, M.C.: An anonymous multi-server authenticated key agreement scheme based on trust computing using smart cards and biometrics. Expert Syst. Appl. **41**(4), 1411–1418 (2014)
7. Lee, J.H., Lee, D.H.: Efficient and secure remote authenticated key agreement scheme for multi-server using mobile equipment. In: International Conference on Consumer Electronics, ICCE 2008. Digest of Technical Papers, pp. 1–2. IEEE, 9 January 2008
8. Tsai, J.L.: Efficient multi-server authentication scheme based on one-way hash function without verification table. Comput. Secur. **27**(3), 115–121 (2008)
9. Xie, Q., Chen, D.: Hash function and smart card based multi-server authentication protocol. In: 2010 WASE International Conference on Information Engineering, vol. 4, pp. 17–19 (2010)
10. Zhu, H., Liu, T., Liu, J.: Robust and simple multi-server authentication protocol without verification table. In: 2009 Ninth International Conference on Hybrid Intelligent Systems, pp. 51–56. IEEE, 12 August 2009
11. Chen, T.Y., Hwang, M.S., Lee, C.C., Jan, J.K.: Cryptanalysis of a secure dynamic ID based remote user authentication scheme for multi-server environment. In: 2009 Fourth International Conference on Innovative Computing, Information and Control (ICICIC), pp. 725–728. IEEE, 7 December 2009

12. Shao, M.H., Chin, Y.C.: A novel dynamic ID-based remote user authentication and access control scheme for multi-server environment. In: 2010 IEEE 10th International Conference on Computer and Information Technology (CIT), pp. 1102–1107. IEEE, 29 June 2010
13. Chen, Y., Huang, C.H., Chou, J.S.: A novel multi-server authentication protocol. IACR Cryptol. ePrint Arch. **2009**, 176 (2009)
14. Das, M.L., Saxena, A., Gulati, V.P.: A dynamic ID-based remote user authentication scheme. IEEE Trans. Consum. Electron. **50**(2), 629–631 (2004)
15. Kalra, S., Sood, S.: Advanced remote user authentication protocol for multi-server architecture based on ECC. J. Inf. Secur. Appl. **18**(2), 98–107 (2013)
16. Hsiang, H.C., Shih, W.K.: Improvement of the secure dynamic ID based remote user authentication scheme for multi-server environment. Comput. Stand. Interfaces. **31**(6), 1118–1123 (2009)
17. Xue, K., Hong, P., Ma, C.: A lightweight dynamic pseudonym identity based authentication and key agreement protocol without verification tables for multi-server architecture. J. Comput. Syst. Sci. **80**(1), 195–206 (2014)

Miscellanous

Music Emotion Maps in Arousal-Valence Space

Jacek Grekow[✉]

Faculty of Computer Science, Bialystok University of Technology,
Wiejska 45A, 15-351 Bialystok, Poland
j.grekow@pb.edu.pl

Abstract. In this article we present the approach in which the detection of emotion is modeled by the pertinent regression problem. Conducting experiments required building a database, annotation of samples by music experts, construction of regressors, attribute selection, and analysis of selected musical compositions. We obtained a satisfactory correlation coefficient value for SVM for regression algorithm at 0.88 for arousal and 0.74 for valence. The result applying regressors are emotion maps of the musical compositions. They provide new knowledge about the distribution of emotions in musical compositions. They reveal new knowledge that had only been available to music experts until this point.

Keywords: Emotion detection · Emotion tracking · Audio feature extraction · Music information retrieval

1 Introduction

Emotions are a dominant element in music, and they are the reason people listen to music so often [12]. Systems searching musical compositions on Internet databases more and more often add an option of selecting emotions to the basic search parameters, such as title, composer, genre, etc. The emotional content of music is not always constant, and even in classical music or jazz changes often. Analysis of emotions contained in music over time is a very interesting aspect of studying the content of music. It can provide new knowledge on how the composer emotionally shaped the music or why we like some compositions more than others.

Music emotion recognition, taking into account the emotion model, can be divided into categorical or dimensional. In the categorical approach, a number of emotional categories (adjectives) are used for labeling music excerpts. It was presented in the following papers [5,6,11]. In the dimensional approach, emotion is described using dimensional space - 2D or 3D. Russell [13] proposed a 2D model, where the dimensions are represented by arousal and valence; used in [15,18]. The 3D model of Pleasure-Arousal-Dominance (PAD) was used in [3,10].

Music emotion recognition concentrates on static or dynamic changes over time. Static music emotion recognition uses excerpts from 15 to 30 s and omits changes in emotions over time. It assumes the emotion in a given segment does not change. Dynamic music emotion recognition analyzes changes in emotions

© IFIP International Federation for Information Processing 2016
Published by Springer International Publishing Switzerland 2016. All Rights Reserved
K. Saeed and W. Homenda (Eds.): CISIM 2016, LNCS 9842, pp. 697–706, 2016.
DOI: 10.1007/978-3-319-45378-1_60

over time. Methods for detecting emotion using a sliding window are presented in [9,11,15,18]. Deng and Leung [3] proposed multiple dynamic textures to model emotion dynamics over time. To find similar sequence pasterns of musical emotions, they used subsequence dynamic time warping for matching emotion dynamics. Aljanaki et al. [1] investigated how well structural segmentation explains emotion segmentation. They evaluated different unsupervised segmentation methods on the task of emotion segmentation. Imbrasaite et al. [7] and Schmidt et al. [14] used Continuous Conditional Random Fields for dimensional emotion tracking.

In our study, we used dynamic music emotion recognition with a sliding window. We experimentally selected a segment length of 6 s as the shortest period of time after which a music expert can recognize an emotion.

The rest of this paper is organized as follows. Section 2 describes the music annotated data set and the emotion model used. Section 3 presents features extracted by using tools for audio analysis. Section 4 describes regressor training and their evaluation. Section 5 presents the results of emotion tracking. Finally, Sect. 6 summarizes the main findings.

2   Music Data

The data set that was annotated consisted of 324 six-second fragments of different genres of music: classical, jazz, blues, country, disco, hip-hop, metal, pop, reggae, and rock. The tracks were all 22050 Hz mono 16-bit audio files in .wav format.

Data annotation was done by five music experts with a university musical education. During annotation of music samples, we used the two-dimensional valence-arousal (V-A) model to measure emotions in music [13]. The model consists of two independent dimensions (Fig. 1) of valence (horizontal axis) and arousal (vertical axis). Each person making annotations after listening to a music sample had to specify values on the arousal and valence axes in a range from −10 to 10 with step 1. On the arousal axis, a value of −10 meant low while 10 high arousal. On the valence axis, −10 meant negative while 10 positive valence.

Value determination on the A-V axes was unambiguous with a designation of a point on the A-V plane corresponding to the musical fragment. The data collected from the five music experts was averaged. Figure 2 presents the annotation results of a data set with A-V values. Each point on the plane, defined by values of arousal and valence, represents one of 324 musical fragments. As can be seen in the figure, the musical compositions fill the four quadrants formed by arousal and valence almost uniformly. The amount of examples in quarters on the A-V emotion plane is presented in Table 1.

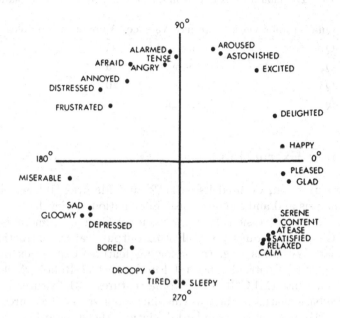

Fig. 1. Russell's circumplex model [13]

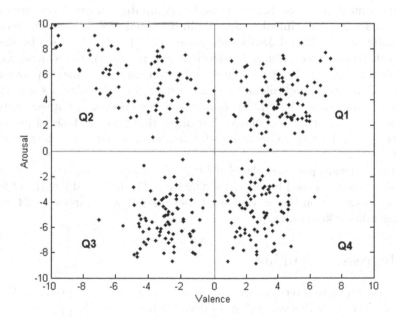

Fig. 2. Data set on A-V emotion plane

Table 1. Amount of examples in quarters on A-V emotion plane

Quarter abbreviation	Arousal-Valence	Amount of examples
Q1	High-high	93
Q2	High-low	70
Q3	Low-low	80
Q4	Low-high	81

3   Features Extraction

For feature extraction, we used Essentia [2] and Marsyas [16], which are tools for audio analysis and audio-based music information retrieval.

Marsyas software (version 0.5.0), written by George Tzanetakis, is implemented in C++ and retains the ability to output feature extraction data to ARFF format. With this tool, the following features can be extracted: Zero Crossings, Spectral Centroid, Spectral Flux, Spectral Rolloff, Mel-Frequency Cepstral Coefficients (MFCC), and chroma features - 31 features in total. For each of these basic features, Marsyas calculates four statistic features (the mean of the mean, the mean of the standard deviation, the standard deviation of the mean, and the standard deviation of the standard deviation).

Essentia is an open-source C++ library, which was created at Music Technology Group, Universitat Pompeu Fabra, Barcelona. Essentia (version 2.1 beta) contains a number of executable extractors computing music descriptors for an audio track: spectral, time-domain, rhythmic, tonal descriptors, and returning the results in YAML and JSON data formats. Extracted features by Essentia are divided into three groups: low-level, rhythm, and tonal features. Essentia also calculates many statistic features: the mean, geometric mean, power mean, median of an array, and all its moments up to the 5th-order, its energy, and the root mean square (RMS). To characterize the spectrum, flatness, crest and decrease of an array are calculated. Variance, skewness, kurtosis of probability distribution, and a single Gaussian estimate were calculated for the given list of arrays.

The previously prepared, labeled by A-V values, music data set served as input data for tools used for feature extraction. The obtained lengths of feature vectors, dependent on the package used, were as follows: Marsyas - 124 features and Essentia - 530 features.

4   Regressor Training

In this paper emotion recognition was treated as a regression problem. We built regressors for predicting arousal and valence using the WEKA package [17]. For training and testing, the following regression algorithms were used: SMOreg, REPTree, M5P.

We evaluated the performance of regression using the 10-fold cross validation technique (CV-10). The whole data set was randomly divided into ten parts, nine of them for training and the remaining one for testing. The learning procedure was executed a total of 10 times on different training sets. Finally, the 10 error estimates were averaged to yield an overall error estimate.

For measuring the performance of regression, we used correlation coefficient (CF). Correlation coefficient measures the statistical correlation between the actual values and the predicted values. The correlation coefficient ranges from 1 to −1. Value 1 means perfectly correlated results, 0 there is no correlation, and −1 means that the results are perfectly correlated negatively.

Table 2. Correlation coefficient obtained for SMOreg

	Essentia		Marsyas	
	Arousal	Valence	Arousal	Valence
Before attribute selection	0.69	0.51	0.79	0.39
After attribute selection	**0.88**	**0.74**	0.85	0.54

The highest values for correlation coefficient (CF) were obtained using SMOreg (implementation of the support vector machine for regression) and are presented in Table 2. CF improved to 0.88 for arousal and 0.74 for valence after applying attribute selection (attribute evaluator: WrapperSubsetEval [8], search method: BestFirst). Predicting arousal is a much easier task for regressors than valence in both cases of extracted features (Essentia, Marsays). CF for arousal were comparable (0.88 and 0.85), but features which describe valence were much better using Essentia for audio analysis. The obtained CF 0.74 was much higher than 0.54 using Marsyas features.

5   Results of Emotion Tracking

We used the best obtained models for predicting arousal and valence to analyze musical compositions. The compositions were divided into 6-s segments with a 3/4 overlap. For each segment, features were extracted and models for arousal and valence were used.

The predicted values are presented in the figures. For each musical composition, the obtained data was presented in 4 different ways:

1. Arousal-Valence over time;
2. Arousal-Valence map;
3. Arousal over time;
4. Valence over time.

Simultaneous observation of the same data in 4 different projections enabled us to accurately track changes in valence and arousal over time, such as tracking the location of a prediction on the A-V emotion plane.

5.1 Emotion Maps

Figures 3 and 4 show emotion maps of two compositions, one for the song Let It Be by Paul McCartney (The Beatles) and the second, Sonata Pathetique (2nd movement) by Ludwig van Beethoven.

Emotion maps present two different emotional aspects of these compositions. The first significant difference is distribution on the quarters of the Arousal-Valence map. In Let It Be (Fig. 3b), the emotions of quadrants Q4 and Q1 (high valence and low-high arousal) dominate. In Sonata Pathetique (Fig. 4b), the emotions of quarter Q4 (low arousal and low valence) dominate with an incidental emergence of emotions of quarter Q3 (low arousal and low valence).

Another noticeable difference is the distribution of arousal over time. Arousal in Let It Be (Fig. 3c) has a rising tendency over time of the entire song, and varies from low to high. In Sonata Pathetique (Fig. 4c), in the first half (s. 0–160) arousal has very low values, and in the second half (s. 160–310) arousal increases incidentally but remains in the low value range.

The third noticeable difference is the distribution of valence over time. Valence in Let It Be (Fig. 3d) remains in the high (positive) range with small fluctuations, but it is always positive. In Sonata Pathetique (Fig. 4d), valence, for the most part, remains in the high range but it also has several large declines in valence (s. 120, 210, 305), which makes valence more diverse.

Arousal and valence over time were dependent on the musical content. Even on a short fragment of music, these values varied significantly. From the course of arousal and valence, it appears that Let It Be is a song of a decisively positive nature with a clear increase in arousal over time. Sonata Pathetique (2nd movement) is mostly calm and predominantly positive.

5.2 Features Describing Arousal and Valence Values in Musical Compositions

To analyze and compare changes in arousal and valence over time (time series), we proposed the following parameters:

1. Mean value of Arousal;
2. Mean value of Valence;
3. Standard deviation of Arousal;
4. Standard deviation of Valence;
5. Mean of derivative of Arousal;
6. Mean of derivative of Valence;
7. Standard deviation of derivative of Arousal;
8. Standard deviation of derivative of Valence;
9. Quantity of changing sign of Arousal (QCA) – describes how often Arousal changes between top and bottom quarters of the A-V emotion model;
10. Quantity of changing sign of Valence (QCV) – describes how often Valence changes between left and right quarters of the A-V emotion model;
11. QCE – is the sum of QCA and QCV;
12. Percentage representation of emotion in 4 quarters of A-V emotion model (4 parameters).

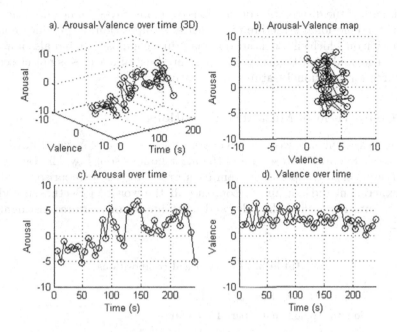

Fig. 3. A-V maps for the song let it be by Paul McCartney (The Beatles)

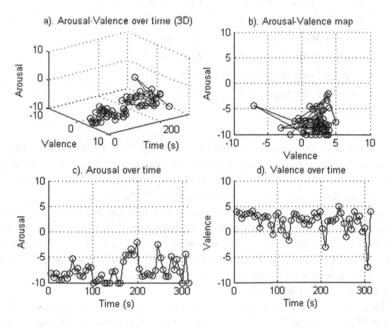

Fig. 4. A-V maps for Piano Sonata No. 8 in C minor, Op. 13 (Pathetique), part 2, by Ludwig van Beethoven

Analysis of the distribution of emotions over time gives a much more accurate view of the emotional structure of a musical composition. It provides not only information on which emotions are dominant in a composition, but also how often they change, and their tendency. The presented list of features is not closed. We will search for additional features in the future.

5.3   Comparison of Musical Compositions

Another experiment was to compare selected well-known Ludwig van Beethoven's Sonatas with several of the most famous songs by The Beatles. We used nine musical compositions from each group for the comparison (Table 3). This experiment did not aim to compare all the works of Beethoven and The Beatles, but only to find the rules and most important features distinguishing these 2 groups.

Table 3. List of musical compositions

L. v. Beethovens Sonatas	The Beatles
Sonata Appassionata, part 1	Hey Jude
Sonata Appassionata, part 2	P.S. I Love You
Sonata Appassionata, part 3	While My Guitar Gently Weeps
Sonata Waldstein, part 1	I'll Follow The Sun
Sonata Waldstein, part 2	It's Only Love
Sonata Waldstein, part 3	Yesterday
Sonata Pathetique, part 1	Michelle
Sonata Pathetique, part 2	Girl
Sonata Pathetique, part 3	Let It Be

Each sample was segmented and arousal and valence were detected. Then, 15 features, which were presented in the previous section, were calculated for each sample. We used the PART algorithm [4] from the WEKA package [17] to find the decision-making rules differentiating the two groups.

It turned out that the most distinguishing feature for these two groups of musical compositions was the *Standard deviation of Valence*. It was significantly smaller in The Beatles' songs than in Beethoven's compositions. *Standard deviation of Valence* reflects how big deviations were from the mean. The results show that in Beethoven's compositions valence values were much more varied than in the songs of The Beatles.

To find another significant feature in the next stage, we removed the characteristic that we found previously (Standard deviation of Valence) from the data set. Another significant feature was *Standard deviation of Arousal*. In Beethoven's compositions, the values of the *Standard deviation of Arousal* were much greater than in the Beatles' songs. This proves the compositions have a greater diversity of tempo and volume.

In the next analogous stage, the feature we found was *Standard deviation of derivative of Arousal*. It reflects the magnitude of changes in arousal between the studied segments. We found higher values of *Standard deviation of derivative of Arousal* in Beethoven's compositions.

The interesting thing is that in the group of the most important distinguishing features we did not find features describing emotion type (*Mean value of Arousal, Mean value of Valence* or *Percentage representation of emotion in 4 quarters*). This is confirmed by the fact that we cannot assign common emotions to the different sample groups (Beethoven, The Beatles); in all groups, we have emotions from the four quadrants of the emotion model. Features that better distinguish between the two groups of compositions were features pertaining to changes in emotions and their distribution in the musical compositions.

6   Conclusions

In this article we presented the approach in which the detection of emotion was modeled by the regression problem. Conducting experiments required building a database, annotation of samples by music experts, construction of regressors, attribute selection, and analysis of selected musical compositions. We obtained a satisfactory correlation coefficient value for SVM for regression algorithm at 0.88 for arousal and 0.74 for valence.

The result applying regressors are emotion maps of the musical compositions. They provide new knowledge about the distribution of emotions in musical compositions. They reveal new knowledge that had only been available to music experts until this point. The proposed parameters describing emotions can be used in the construction of a system that can search for songs with similar emotions. They describe in more detail the distribution of emotions, their evolution, frequency of changes, etc.

Acknowledgments. This research was realized as part of study no. S/WI/3/2013 and financed from Ministry of Science and Higher Education funds.

References

1. Aljanaki, A., Wiering, F., Veltkamp, R.C.: Emotion based segmentation of musical audio. In: Proceedings of the 16th International Society for Music Information Retrieval Conference, ISMIR 2015, Málaga, Spain, pp. 770–776 (2015)
2. Bogdanov, D., Wack, N., Gómez, E., Gulati, S., Herrera, P., Mayor, O., Roma, G., Salamon, J., Zapata, J., Serra, X.: ESSENTIA: an audio analysis library for music information retrieval. In: Proceedings of the 14th International Society for Music Information Retrieval Conference, Curitiba, Brazil, pp. 493–498 (2013)
3. Deng, J.J., Leung, C.H.: Dynamic time warping for music retrieval using time series modeling of musical emotions. IEEE Trans. Affect. Comput. **6**(2), 137–151 (2015)

4. Frank, E., Witten, I.H.: Generating accurate rule sets without global optimization. In: Proceedings of the Fifteenth International Conference on Machine Learning, pp. 144–151. Morgan Kaufmann Publishers Inc., San Francisco (1998)
5. Grekow, J.: Mood tracking of musical compositions. In: Chen, L., Felfernig, A., Liu, J., Raś, Z.W. (eds.) ISMIS 2012. LNCS, vol. 7661, pp. 228–233. Springer, Heidelberg (2012)
6. Grekow, J.: Mood tracking of radio station broadcasts. In: Andreasen, T., Christiansen, H., Cubero, J.-C., Raś, Z.W. (eds.) ISMIS 2014. LNCS, vol. 8502, pp. 184–193. Springer, Heidelberg (2014)
7. Imbrasaite, V., Baltrusaitis, T., Robinson, P.: Emotion tracking in music using continuous conditional random fields and relative feature representation. In: 2013 IEEE International Conference on Multimedia and Expo Workshops, San Jose, CA, USA, pp. 1–6 (2013)
8. Kohavi, R., John, G.H.: Wrappers for feature subset selection. Artif. Intell. **97** (1–2), 273–324 (1997)
9. Korhonen, M.D., Clausi, D.A., Jernigan, M.E.: Modeling emotional content of music using system identification. Trans. Sys. Man Cyber. Part B **36**(3), 588–599 (2005)
10. Lin, Y., Chen, X., Yang, D.: Exploration of music emotion recognition based on MIDI. In: Proceedings of the 14th International Society for Music Information Retrieval Conference (2013)
11. Lu, L., Liu, D., Zhang, H.J.: Automatic mood detection and tracking of music audio signals. Trans. Audio Speech Lang. Proc. **14**(1), 5–18 (2006)
12. Pratt, C.C.: Music as the Language of Emotion. The Library of Congress. U.S. Govt. Print. Off., Washington (1950)
13. Russell, J.A.: A circumplex model of affect. J. Pers. Soc. Psychol. **39**(6), 1161–1178 (1980)
14. Schmidt, E.M., Kim, Y.E.: Modeling musical emotion dynamics with conditional random fields. In: Proceedings of the 2011 International Society for Music Information Retrieval Conference, pp. 777–782 (2011)
15. Schmidt, E.M., Turnbull, D., Kim, Y.E.: Feature selection for content-based, time-varying musical emotion regression. In: Proceedings of the International Conference on Multimedia Information Retrieval, MIR 2010, pp. 267–274. ACM, New York (2010)
16. Tzanetakis, G., Cook, P.: Marsyas: a framework for audio analysis. Org. Sound **4**(3), 169–175 (2000)
17. Witten, I.H., Frank, E.: Data Mining: Practical Machine Learning Tools and Techniques. Morgan Kaufmann, San Francisco (2005)
18. Yang, Y.H., Lin, Y.C., Su, Y.F., Chen, H.H.: A regression approach to music emotion recognition. Trans. Audio Speech Lang. Proc. **16**(2), 448–457 (2008)

Attribute Grammars for Controlling House Layout Customization

Władysław Homenda[1,2] and Krystian Kwieciński[3(✉)]

[1] Faculty of Economics and Informatics in Vilnius, University of Białystok,
Kalvariju g. 135, 08221 Vilnius, Lithuania
[2] Faculty of Mathematics and Information Science,
Warsaw University of Technology, ul. Koszykowa 75, 00-662 Warsaw, Poland
[3] Faculty of Architecture, Warsaw University of Technology,
Koszykowa 55, 00-659 Warsaw, Poland
krystian.kwiecinski@arch.pw.edu.pl

Abstract. This paper introduces a new framework for design automation. The discussion is focused on syntactic processing nested in a selected architecture problem of house layout customization. House layout is interpreted as multi dimensional concepts structure of domain knowledge. Syntactic structuring is based on context-free methods. We propose constructions of context-free grammars driven by concepts of multidimensional knowledge space. The formalism affords consistent representation of an approximate grammatical correctness of house layout. Furnishing grammars with attributes allows for information flow between domain's concepts supporting features disclosing and constrains verification. The approach is validated on some simple house layout and the directions for the future development of the system are outlined. The paper focuses on conceptual framework only and, as such, is intended to stimulate further research into the various implementation considerations that are prerequisite of large-scale applications.

Keywords: Syntactic methods · Context-free grammars · Attribute grammars · Design automation · House layout

1 Introduction

One reason for which design automation is of significant research interest is that it provides a basic reference for comparing different processing technologies. However, a more fundamental reason is that it focuses on the essence of intelligent information processing, the formation of abstractions. This paper provides a valuable insight into the methodologies that lead to comprehensive and interpretable results and that ensure the transparency of final findings. In one way or another there arises an issue of casting the results as information structuring conceptual entities that capture the essence of the overall data set in a compact manner. It is worth stressing that information structures not only support conversion of detailed data into more tangible information entities but,

© IFIP International Federation for Information Processing 2016
Published by Springer International Publishing Switzerland 2016. All Rights Reserved
K. Saeed and W. Homenda (Eds.): CISIM 2016, LNCS 9842, pp. 707–719, 2016.
DOI: 10.1007/978-3-319-45378-1_61

very importantly, afford a vehicle of abstraction that allows to think of structures as different conceptual structures. A context-free grammars were chosen due to its simplicity and possibility of augmenting them with the mechanism of attributes propagation. Clearly the task of information structuring is not a trivial one and it is dependent to a large extent on the application domain.

Let us discuss the overall perspective on house layout design automation. Assuming that X is a set of basic design entities (living room, bedroom, kitchen etc.), we may express all possible arrangements of them as a power set (with repetitions of entities) $\mathcal{P}(X)$, as illustrated in Fig. 1. We build a context-free grammar to generate arrangements of entities of X. Of course, only a small proportion of elements of $\mathcal{P}(X)$ represent arrangements, which conform to the rules of such a grammar. These represent a subset of $\mathcal{P}(X)$, referred to as $\mathcal{G}(X)$. And the grammatically correct arrangements that are meaningful are represented by $\mathcal{S}(X)$ that is a subset of $\mathcal{G}(X)$. The entities (X) themselves have a dual nature; on one hand they have grammatical meaning (parts of arrangements) and on the other hand they have semantics defined by the concepts they represent (function, size, neighborhood etc.). The essence of syntactical analysis is to discriminate whether a given arrangement belongs to $\mathcal{G}(X)$ or $\mathcal{P}(X) - \mathcal{G}(X)$. Syntactical analysis dissects the arrangements into higher level parts of a house (bay, private zone, semipublic zone etc.) and checks for conformity with the rules of grammar until the bottom-most level of individual entities is reached. A standard approach to syntactical analysis involves application of parsing techniques to check the conformity of a given arrangements with the rules of grammar. As adverted above, not all syntactic correct arrangements $\mathcal{G}(X)$ are meaningful, i.e. many of them do not conform to semantic constrains. Elimination of incorrect arrangements is accomplished with attributes, which furnish the context-free grammar. Attributes provide mechanisms of information flow in a derivation (parsing) tree of given arrangement and in this way allow to encounter semantic information in terms of supplementary rules and constrains verification. This study is motivated by fundamental ideas of syntactic methods employed to knowledge processing [1,3] and their application in different domains, for example: intelligent man-machine communication [4,5], music information processing [6] and human behavior [9].

The paper is structured as follows. Next subsections introduce the subject (the domain of house layout design) and the tool used (context-free and attribute grammars). In Sect. 2 syntactic structuring of the target objects is outlined with

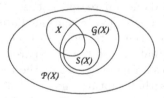

Fig. 1. Syntactic structuring and semantic analysis - an overall perspective.

context-free grammars employed. Section 3 attributes supplementing context-free grammars are pursued to accomplish semantic information.

1.1 The Subject: House Layout Customization

Automatic generation of house layouts has been previously studied both for historical architectural styles [10] as well as for the designs of contemporary living architects [2]. Previous researches utilized shape grammars in order to formalize architectural rules as a series of transformations of shapes.

An architectural design system proposed by Kwieciński [8], was intended to allow customers participation in the generation of customized houses. Proposed system, which consist of three modules: Site Planner, Home Planner and Facade Creator, was designed to produce single story or two story buildings, with a two bay house layouts and a gable roof. Home Planner, which is responsible for the generation and customization of house layout, collects architectural design principles responsible for the distribution of rooms into the bays on each floor. Spatial distribution of rooms takes place in relation to the external and internal context. For this purpose the orientation to the World coordinates (which affects indoor sunlight), orientation to the entrance to the plot and the privacy gradient (which suggests placing common areas, such as the living room, closer to the entrance, while private spaces, such as bedrooms farther away) are considered in the design system. Therefore the rooms are grouped into three zones: entrance zone, semipublic zone and private zone which constrain the freedom of layout configurations. Additionally some rooms are required to be placed next to each other like kitchen and dining room for example. Both of these rooms belong to semipublic zone together with living room, which is obligatory in every layout and home office which is optional and staircase which existence depends on the number of floors. If the house is not a single story building then localization of staircase is duplicated on the second floor and the generation of the first floor determines the generation of the second floor. When a planar layout of the spaces on each floor is completed it can be further customized by the user and further developed. Figure 2 presents exemplary two story building. Left side of the figure presents detailed floor plan with introduced walls and furniture and right side of the figure presents diagrammatic layout where rooms are represented by colored and named matrices of 60 by 60 cm modules. Building is having rectangular shape with only exception of garage which sticks out of the shape. Layout is divided in the middle into two part which represents different buildings bays. Bays are having same depth and equal length which is the same as the building length.

1.2 The Tool: Syntactic Structuring

Syntactic approach is a crucial stage and a crucial problem in the wide spectrum of tasks as, for instance, pattern recognition, translation of programming languages, processing of natural languages, music processing, etc., cf. [1,4,6]. By syntactic approach and syntactic methods we understand grammars, automata,

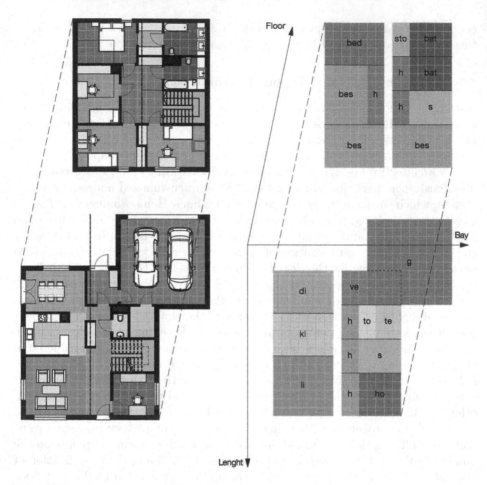

Fig. 2. Dimensionality of gablefront house layout: an example of two story two bay house layout and its decomposition in three dimensional space Floor-Length-Bay.

algorithms used in processing languages. In this paper we employ context-free grammars to controlling house layout customization.

Context-Free Syntactic Description. The discussion on describing and controlling house layout is based on common definitions of grammars, context-free grammars and attribute grammars. We assume that the reader is familiar with the basic notions of mathematical linguistic. Therefore, we only recall them.

Let us recall that a system $G = (V, T, P, S)$ is a grammar, where: (a) V is a finite set of *variables* (called also *nonterminals*), (b) T is a finite set of terminal symbols (simply called *terminals*), (c) a nonterminal S is the initial symbol of the grammar and (d) P is a finite set of productions. A pair (α, β) of strings of nonterminals and terminals is a production assuming that the first element α of the pair is a nonempty string. Productions are usually denoted

$\alpha \to \beta$. Grammars having all productions with α being a nonterminal symbols are context-free grammars.

A derivation in a grammar is a finite sequence of strings of nonterminals and terminals such that: (a) the first string in this sequence is just the initial symbol of the grammar and (b) for any two consecutive strings in the sequence, the later one is obtained from the former one applying a production in the usual way, i.e. by replacing a substring of the former string equal to the left hand side of the production with the right hand side of the production. We say that the last element of the string is *derivable* in the grammar.

For a context-free grammar a derivation can be outlined in a form of derivation tree, i.e. (a) the root of the tree is labelled with the initial symbol of the grammar and (b) for any internal vertex labelled by the left side of a production, its children are labelled by symbols of the right side of the production.

Attribute Grammars. An attribute grammar is a formal way to define attributes for the productions of a formal grammar, cf. [7]. The attributes are tied to symbols of productions (terminal and nonterminal symbols). The attributes are divided into two groups: synthesized attributes and inherited attributes. The attributes are assigned values at the derivation process. The values of the inherited attributes are passed down from parent nodes. The values of the synthesized attributes are the results of the attributes' evaluation rules applied to right hand side of the production or, for derivation tree, to children of a node. For simplification, the values of the synthesized attributes can be computed using inherited attributes and across from left neighbors.

In our approach, synthesized attributes are used to pass semantic information up the parse tree, while inherited attributes help pass semantic information down and across it. Attributes make it possible to validate semantic checks associated with a grammar, representing the rules of a language not explicitly imparted by the syntax definition. The strength of attribute grammars is that they can transport information from anywhere in the abstract syntax tree to anywhere else, in a controlled and formal way.

2   Syntactic Structuring - House Layout Customization

2.1   The Grammar

The initial productions of the grammar create the topmost level of hierarchy defining floors of the subjected house. Depending on the number of floors they are being placed in the Floor dimension. Floors of the house are having its length therefore they can also be placed in Length dimension. Building floors can be longitudinally divided into separate bays. If building is having rectangular shape then the floors are also rectangular and eventually bays are having equal length which is equal to the length of the building. Buildings might have various number of bays depending on its functional program, structural system and building typology. Therefore for the purpose of gable-front house presented grammar was simplified to the grammar generating just two bays of equal length on all the floors.

$<building> \rightarrow <floor> <buidling>$
$\quad\quad\quad \rightarrow <floor>$
$<floor> \rightarrow <bay1> <bay2>$

The fallowing part of the grammar divides Bays into zones. Zones allows to group rooms in order to prevent unallowable configurations of rooms. Rooms are grouped into three zones which correspond to degree of their privateness in the building. Lay out of zones create a sequence which begins with the entrance zone which is fallowed by semipublic zone and privet zone.

$<bay1> \rightarrow <zone\_entrance> <bay1>$
$\quad\quad\quad \rightarrow <zone\_semipublic> <bay1>$
$\quad\quad\quad \rightarrow <zone\_private> <bay1>$
$\quad\quad\quad \rightarrow <zone\_semipublic>$
$\quad\quad\quad \rightarrow <zone\_private>$
$<bay2> \rightarrow <zone\_entrance> <bay2>$
$\quad\quad\quad \rightarrow <zone\_semipublic> <bay2>$
$\quad\quad\quad \rightarrow <zone\_private> <bay2>$
$\quad\quad\quad \rightarrow <zone\_semipublic>$
$\quad\quad\quad \rightarrow <zone\_private>$

The next part of the grammar generate rooms in the Length dimension inside entrance zone. Entrance zone is divided into entrance slot and technical slot. Slots are introduced to allow placing collection of rooms across bays. They allow to generate rooms in the same bay and at the same localization along Length dimension but one after the other. The placed rooms have the width of the slot (exception is garage which protrude rectangular building shape) and the sum of rooms depth is equal to the depth of the slot. It is also used to introduce hall in front of the room.

$<zone\_entrance> \rightarrow <entrance\_slot> <technical\_slot>$
$<entrance\_slot> \rightarrow <vestibule> <garage>$
$<vestibule> \rightarrow vestibule$
$<garage> \rightarrow garage$
$<technical\_slot> \rightarrow <hall> <toilet> <tech\_room>$
$<hall> \rightarrow hall$
$<toilet> \rightarrow toilet$
$<tech\_room> \rightarrow tech\_room$

The fallowing part of the grammar presents method for generating sequence of rooms inside semipublic zone. For the purpose of constraining generation of rooms in relation to each other s_slot and s_set which stands for semipublic slot and set were introduced. As it was described in the previous paragraph slot allows to place collection of rooms across bay at the same Length dimension. Therefore it was utilized to introduce hall in front of the room. Contrary set allows to force generation of certain rooms next to each other. In the presented grammar kitchen is always being placed next to the dining room. Moreover both of this rooms can either have or not have a hall attached to it. Therefore the set in this case is combined of the slots allowing to introduce hall. Presented method could be easily adopted for the purpose of privet zone therefore presentation of this part of grammar was omitted in this article.

$<zone\_semipublic>$ → $<s\_slot>$ $<zone\_semipublic>$
                    → $<s\_set>$ $<zone\_semipublic>$
                    → $<s\_slot>$
                    → $<s\_sct>$
$<s\_slot>$ → $<hall>$ $<s\_slot\_room>$
            → $<s\_slot\_room>$
$<s\_slot\_room>$ → living room | home office | stairs
$<s\_set>$ → $<s\_set\_slot>$ $<s\_set\_slot>$
          → $<s\_set\_slot>$
$<s\_set\_slot>$ → $<hall>$ $<s\_set\_slot\_room>$
              → $<s\_set\_slot\_room>$
$<s\_set\_slot\_room>$ → kitchen | dining room

2.2   Derivation Trees

Derivation trees of language constructions in given grammar are best to identify syntactic structuring. Therefor, derivation tree of exemplary two story gablefront house, presented in Fig. 2, is considerd. Figure 3 presents a part of a derivation tree of the house layout from Fig. 2. The derivation tree covers second bay of the ground floor. The derivation is developed to the level of individual rooms area forming layout of the house.

3   Semantic Analysis - Design Control

To verify the design of the house layout the data regarding the total width of all the bays and the location, width, adjacency and accessibility of every room has to be verified. Therefore such data has to be provided in the grammar or - more precisely - in the derivation tree. To transfer needed data we can use attributive tools in the grammar, i.e. we use attributive grammars. Such grammar is obtained by furnishing productions with inherited and synthesized attributes.

Attributes are attached to the grammar considered in this paper. They are responsible for collecting and transferring important data between items of the information space. Complete grammar with all the attributes and rules of their evaluation is not being presented in this paper. Instead ideas of using attributes are being outlined.

3.1   Verification of Room Addition

In order to guarantee the completeness of building layout it has to be verified that all the required rooms were added. Figure 4 presents two methods for verifying

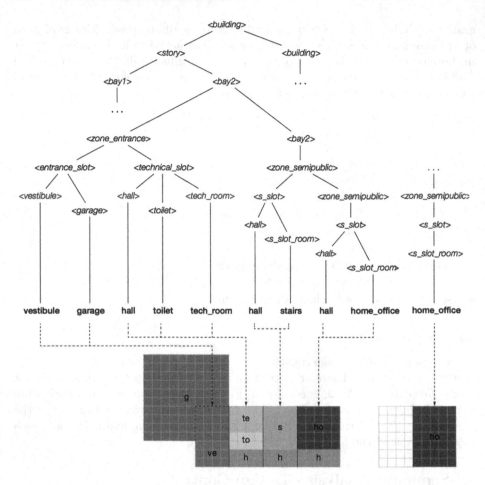

Fig. 3. Part of derivation tree in the grammar shown in Sect. 2.1. A second bay of the ground floor of the house from Fig. 2 (left part of the figure) and exemplary room without hall (right part of the figure).

this requirement. Left side of the figure presents an example of synthesizing the attributes of *count_s* which calculates the total number of stairs added to the building layout. The data collected by this attribute is being verified at the trunk of the derivation tree in order to check if the total amount of stairs meets the required amount. Right side of the figure presents an example of inheriting attributes of *count_s*. This attribute is also used to calculate the total number of stairs added to the building layout but the data collected by it is verified after any room is added to the layout. The second method allows to prevent invalid grammar productions before they are completed while the first one require to generate complete house layout which afterwards is being verified. Based on these methods the amount of all required rooms can be individually verified.

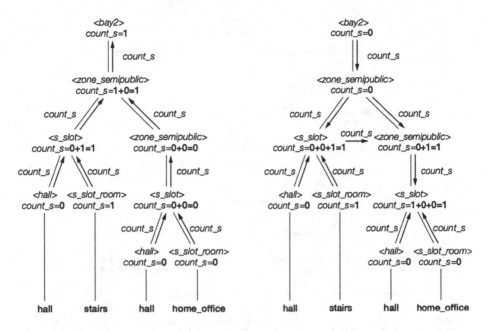

Fig. 4. Synthesized attributes (left part of the figure) and inherited attributes (right part of the figure).

3.2 Verification of Widths

Verification of room width in order to fit to the allowed range is a trivial task and is being checked at the level of individual rooms (leaves). Additionally verification of the length of all the bays on all the floors also has to be checked, in order to guarantee rectangular shape of the building. Figure 5 presents an example of inheriting attribute of the building width and synthesizing the attributes of rooms width. Attributes of given nonterminal and their values are listed below nonterminal's name. Arrows with attributes names show direction of flow of values of attributes. For instance, the nonterminal $< bay2 >$ has attribute: $free\_width$. This attribute get value from attributes of $< zone\_entrance >$: $free\_width$. Which in turn gets the value from synthesize attributes from generated elements of house layout $slot\_width$ and $slot\_width$ and inherit attribute from $< bay2 > free\_width$. The date collected at the nonterminal $< zone\_semipublic >$ of the derivation tree allows to further calculate total free bay's width which is left to allocate next room before it is being added. If attribute $free\_width$ is equal zero then no additional room can be added and the length of bays are equal and they are equal to the width of the building. If it is bigger then zero there is still left space to add another room. When it is lower then zero then the added room is too big and it's size has to be reduced or this room has to be removed. This verification allows to control that the house is in a rectangular shape.

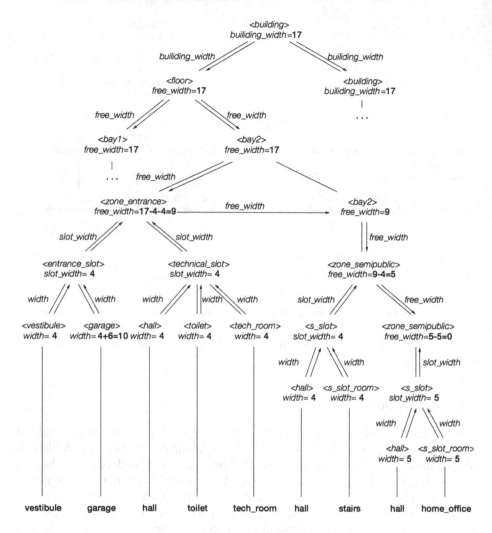

Fig. 5. Inherited attributes controlling equality of lengths of bays.

3.3 Verification of Zones Connectivity

As it was described in Sect. 2 bays are being divided into zones, which group rooms in order to place them next to each other. Therefore different bays could be differently divided into zones. In order to provide continuity of zones in the building layout the connectivity of this zones laying in different bays has to be verified. Figure 6 presents an example of information flow in the derivation tree of an attributive grammar which allows to control connectivity of semipublic zones on the ground floor. For instance, the nonterminal $< bay2 >$ has attributes: $bay2\_s\_start$ and $bay2\_s\_end$ which represents the beginning and the end localization of the semipublic zone placed in bay2. The attributes get the value of

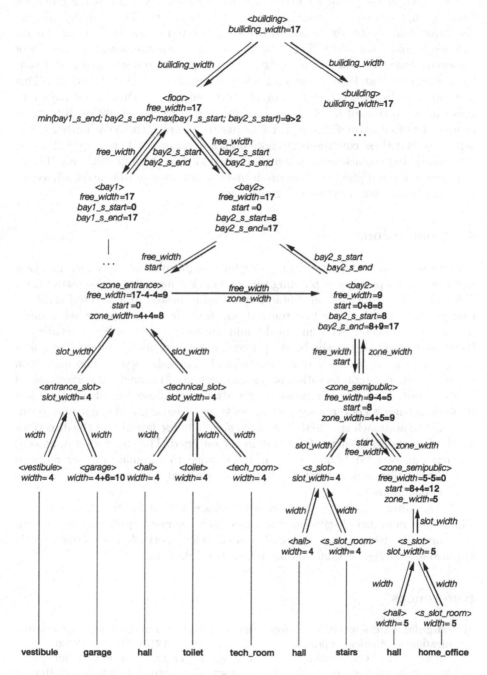

Fig. 6. Information flow in the derivation tree of an attributive grammar: control of bays length and zones connectivity.

$< zone\_semipublic >$: $start$ and $zone\_width$. The $start$ value is being inherited from the nonterminal $< zone\_entrance > zone\_width$. The $zone\_width$ gets the value from synthesize attributes from generated elements of house layout $slot\_width$ and $zone\_width$. The date collected at the nonterminal $< floor >$ of the derivation tree allows to calculate if the semiprivate zones placed in different bays overlap for at least 2 modules which guarantees their connectivity. This method can also be utilized to control rooms adjacency. Division of bays into zones allow to control if the rooms are grouped correctly. Additionally sets of rooms allow to control if the required rooms are placed next to each other in the same bay. But these conditions are not enough to ensure that the required rooms are placed next to each other when they are added to the different bays. Therefore presented in a previous paragraph method allows also to control adjacency of rooms being placed in two different bays.

4   Conclusions

This paper introduces a new framework for design automation, which is a case of more general problem of building tools for operating on knowledge structures. The discussion is focused on syntactic processing nested in a selected architecture problem of house layout customization. House layout is interpreted as multi dimensional concepts structure of domain knowledge. Syntactic structuring is based on context-free methods. We propose constructions of context-free grammars driven by concepts of multidimensional knowledge space. The formalism affords consistent representation of an approximate grammatical correctness of house layout. Furnishing grammars with attributes allows for information flow between domain's concepts supporting features disclosing and constrains verification. The approach is validated on some simple house layout and the directions for the future development of the system are outlined. The paper focuses on conceptual framework only and, as such, is intended to stimulate further research into the various implementation considerations that are prerequisite of large-scale applications.

Future directions for the introduced ideas are both theoretical and practical. The former ones include generalizing concepts to be more applicable in different domains. The later ones are intended to develop methods and tools directly applicable in design automation of architectural domain.

References

1. Bargiela, A., Homenda, W.: Information structuring in natural language communication: syntactical approach. J. Intell. Fuzzy Syst. **17**(6), 575–581 (2006)
2. Duarte, J.P.: Customizing mass housing: a discursive grammar for Siza's Malagueira houses. Disseration. Massachusetts Institute of Technology (2001)
3. Higuera, C.: A bibliographical study of grammatical inference. Pattern Recogn. **38**, 1332–1348 (2005)

4. Homenda, W.: Integrated syntactic and semantic data structuring as an abstraction of intelligent man-machine communication. In: Proceedings of the ICAART - International Conference on Agents and Artificial Intelligence, pp. 324–330 (2009)
5. Homenda, W.: Automatic data understanding: a necessity of intelligent communication. In: Rutkowski, L., Scherer, R., Tadeusiewicz, R., Zadeh, L.A., Zurada, J.M. (eds.) ICAISC 2010, Part II. LNCS, vol. 6114, pp. 476–483. Springer, Heidelberg (2010)
6. Homenda, W., Rybnik, M.: Querying in spaces of music information. In: Tang, Y., Huynh, V.-N., Lawry, J. (eds.) IUKM 2011. LNCS, vol. 7027, pp. 243–255. Springer, Heidelberg (2011)
7. Knuth, D.E.: The genesis of attribute grammars. In: Jourdan, M., Deransart, P. (eds.) Attribute Grammars and their Applications. LNCS, vol. 461, pp. 1–12. Springer, Heidelberg (1990)
8. Kwieciński, K., Słyk, J.: Interactive design system for provisioning of customized houses. In: eWork and eBusiness in Architecture, Engineering and Construction, pp. 649–655. CRC Press (2014)
9. Rosani, A., et al.: Human behavior recognition using a context-free grammar. J. Electron. Imaging **23**(3), 033016-1–033016-12 (2014)
10. Stiny, G., Mitchell, W.J.: The palladian grammar. Environ. Plan. B **5**(1), 5–18 (1978)

The Radio Direction Finding with Advantage of the Software Defined Radio

Josef Hrabal, David Seidl[✉], Michal Krumnikl, Pavel Moravec,
and Petr Olivka

Department of Computer Science, FEECS, VŠB – Technical University of Ostrava,
17. listopadu 15, Ostrava, Czech Republic
{josef.hrabal,david.seidl,michal.krumnikl,pavel.moravec,
petr.olivka}@vsb.cz
http://www.cs.vsb.cz

Abstract. The radio-frequency engineering recently has gone through extensive development. Software-Defined Radio (SDR) plays an important role in this development, bringing new possibilities to radio-frequency engineering and enables us to look at existing radio technologies in a new, innovative way. One such technology is a Doppler antenna, which allows us to find the direction from which the radio signal of given frequency is being transmitted. The SDR allows us to design and construct a highly-simplified system based on the Doppler antenna array. This paper deals with the design and implementation of such system used for the localization using the Doppler effect and the tests of the designed Doppler antenna system.

Keywords: Radio direction finding · Doppler antenna · Software-defined radio · SDR

1 Introduction

Radio Direction Finding (RDF) is the measurement of the direction from which a received signal was transmitted. This has many applications in different sectors. The RDF is used for example in the navigation of ships and aircrafts, for tracking wildlife, and to locate not only emergency transmitters but also illegal or interfering ones.

Nowadays, most of the radio frequency bands are occupied. Fast classification and location of the source of an illegal or interfering transmitters could be very helpful, especially when transmitters or networks are being built and maintained. The classification and locating can be simplified thanks to *software defined radio* (SDR).

2 Radio Direction Finding

The RDF is nearly as old as radio itself. Earliest experiments in the radio direction finding were carried out by Heinrich Hertz in 1888. Since then many types

© IFIP International Federation for Information Processing 2016
Published by Springer International Publishing Switzerland 2016. All Rights Reserved
K. Saeed and W. Homenda (Eds.): CISIM 2016, LNCS 9842, pp. 720–728, 2016.
DOI: 10.1007/978-3-319-45378-1_62

of radio direction finding techniques were discovered. The mostl frequently used ones are the Watson-Watt and the Doppler technique.

2.1 Watson-Watt Radio Direction Finding System

The first one from the mentioned techniques is older and was introduced by Robert Watson-Watt before the World War II. It utilises an antenna array consisting of four equidistant vertical elements (known as Adcock antenna [8]) and two separated precisely calibrated receivers. The *angle of arrival* (AoA) is then determined from the signals level difference. The presence of two receivers is the main disadvantage of this technique [1].

2.2 Doppler Radio Direction Finding System

The second technique uses the Doppler effect. This effect was described by Austrian physicist Christian Doppler in 1842 in Prague. Most people associate the Doppler effect with acoustic waves, but the theory is also applicable to radio waves as well. This well known effect describes a difference between the observed and emitted frequency of a wave for an observer which is moving relatively to the source of the waves.

The earliest Doppler direction finding systems used a single antenna placed on a fast rotating turntable. As the receiving antenna approaches the transmitter, the frequency increases and as the antenna recedes from the transmitter, the frequency decreases. The receiver then observes a frequency modulated signal at a rate equal to the frequency of the rotation (rotation tone). The received signal is then de-modulated by FM receiver, which then produces the demodulated rotation tone. The angle of arrival is then determined from the phase offset between the original and the demodulated rotation tone [2].

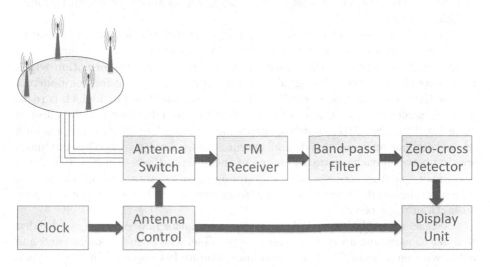

Fig. 1. Pseudo-Doppler block diagram

Spinning the turntable fast enough to produce high frequency signal efficiently is very difficult. Because of this, the physically rotated antenna could be replaced by an antenna array. This array can consist of three or more separate omnidirectional antennas placed evenly along the perimeter of a circle. Each of the antenna is switched successively to make an illusion of the physical rotation. This modified system is known as the Pseudo-Doppler direction finding system and is a result of combination of the Earp and Godfrey system [3] and the Whale system [2].

Block diagram of a simple Pseudo-Doppler direction finding system is shown in the Fig. 1. The Pseudo-Doppler antenna array is located in the top left corner of the image. In this case the array is assembled from four omnidirectional antennas. The antenna array is then connected to the antenna switch. This switch is driven by the antenna control unit and its purpose is to handle sequential switching of the antennas in the array. The radio signal then runs to a FM receiver, where is demodulated. In the next step, the audio output of the receiver is fed into a band-pass audio filter which passes frequencies within a range of rotation tone and rejects frequencies outside that range. To determine the angle of arrival, phase offset of this filtered audio signal is needed. This is carried out by the Zero-cross detector block. In the last step, phase offset of the signal is compared with the rotation tone and the angle of arrival is obtained.

2.3 Software Defined Radio

SDR is a radio communication system where components (such as demodulators, filters, amplifiers, etc.) that have been typically implemented in hardware are instead implemented as a software on a personal computer. The concept of SDR is not new, its origins can be tracked back to 1970's. For a long time computers were too slow to accomplish this task. As price of SDR hardware decreased in last years, SDR has gained a lot of popularity and its applications can be found in many sectors.

The main purpose of a SDR receiver is to transform desired frequency to an intermediate frequency and then convert it to digital data by a high speed A/D converter. Result of this process is a stream of digital information which represents the original radio signal by values of its sine and cosine component.

For the testing purposes, we decided to use the 860 MHz band which is regulated by general authorization VO-R/10/05.2014-3 and does not require a licence to use it. Band 860 MHz contains ultra short waves ($\lambda \sim 35$ cm) which allows us to combine antenna switch and antenna array base easily. The maximum spacing between each separate antenna of the array is limited to less than $\frac{\lambda}{2}$ [4]. Too small spacing increases mutual coupling between antennas, which in turn increases amplitude directivity of the antennas and reduces the Doppler tone strength in the receiver.

Because we wanted to include more usage scenarios in one design, we decided to make the antenna array as universal as possible. The Pseudo-Doppler antenna array with eight omnidirectional antennas mounted is depicted in Fig. 2. Each

Fig. 2. Pseudo-Doppler antenna array

antenna is connected through a SMA connector. This solution allows to mount any number of antennas or use this array only as antenna switch.

The classic antenna switch interconnection uses several passive components. The mechanism of antenna switching is described in [9]. Figure 3 shows the classic antenna switch circuit of Pseudo-Doppler antenna.

When we use antenna array with only four antennas, this circuit is sufficient. But for a larger number of antennas, the interconnection would become more complicated. Further, it is necessary to ensure that all used electrical components for antenna switching have the same electrical characteristics for each switched antenna. Should the characteristics of the components for individual antennas differ, the accuracy of the whole system would be negatively influenced and the performance of the whole Pseudo-Doppler system would suffer.

The switching element used according to Fig. 3 is a semiconductor diode D7 ... D14. The highest attainable frequency for antenna switching is dependent on the characteristics of the used diode. When we introduce signal to J1-1 ... J1-4 connectors, the corresponding antenna is disabled. To control the antenna switch, we need another integrated circuit – a shift register, which ensures the gradual antenna switching with specified frequency.

Our implementation of Doppler antenna array uses eight individual antennas. We have used HMC253 integrated circuit – which is suitable for high-frequency signal switching – to build high frequency electronic antenna switch. The HMC253 integrated circuit is able to process radio signal up to 3.5 GHz with maximum switching frequency of 10 MHz, which significantly exceeds the attainable switching frequency for classic antenna switch.

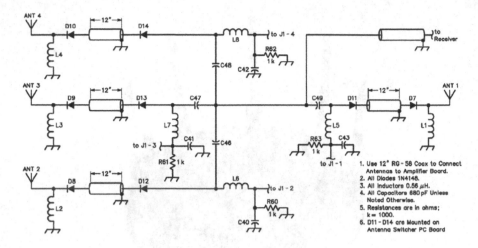

Fig. 3. Classic antenna switch for Pseudo-Doppler circuit [9]

The use of HMC253 circuit also significantly simplified the antenna switch circuitry. On the other hand, the disadvantage is that HMC253 circuit is presently available only with QFN socket, which is harder to mount on the PCB. The circuitry design is based on the HMC253 data sheet [5] and it is shown in Fig. 4. The HMC253 integrated circuit is placed in the center of the antenna array. The signal from individual antennas is sent to HMC253 integrated circuit through a coupling capacitor, each antenna is also loaded by a resistor.

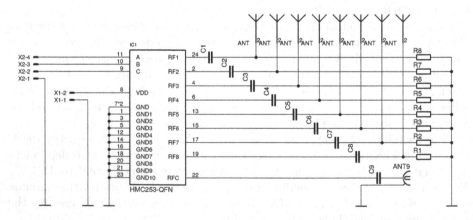

Fig. 4. New design antenna switch for Pseudo-Doppler circuit

Insertion loss is less than 1.7 dB in the entire bandwidth. The communication is done by a simple parallel interface consisting of three binary input pins which select the connected antenna based on the address derived from their logical values – each binary combination connects one of the eight inputs to the output [5].

On one hand, one of the greatest advantage of HMC253 integrated circuit is higher antenna switching frequency. On the other hand, the antenna switching in this case is discrete switching. However, to ensure the correct function of Pseudo-Doppler antenna, the switching should be smooth and the transition gradual, which means that the influence of an antenna should decrease and at the same time the influence of the following antenna should increase. In the classic antenna switch, this effect is attained by charging and discharging of the capacitors, which ensure that the antennas are turned on and off smoothly. This is not possible with the selected HMC253 integrated circuit, and the effect has to be achieved by high-frequency antenna switching, which imposes higher requirements on the further signal processing.

3   Signal Processing Using GNU Radio

Signal processing is based on the well known open source project GNU Radio [7]. This software development toolkit provides a signal processing runtime and processing modules with convenient tools for creating software radio implementations. As a software defined radio receiver we used the HackRF One from Great Scott Gadgets company [6] which is a very powerful and affordable open source hardware platform.

Part of the Pseudo-Doppler direction finding system which is implemented in the software is enclosed by an orange box in Fig. 5. To achieve a good synchronization between the data stream and the antenna rotation, the internal clock of the HackRF One is used. Other tasks like tuner settings, FM demodulation or band-pass filtering are implemented in a very simple way with the help of the GNU Radio modules. On the other hand, comparison of a phase offset is a much harder task.

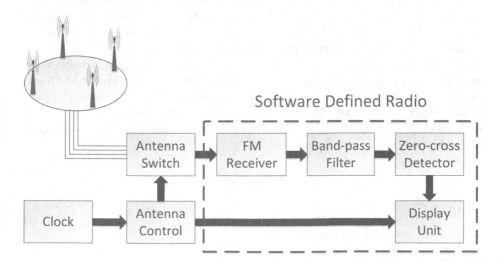

Fig. 5. Pseudo-Doppler block diagram with SDR

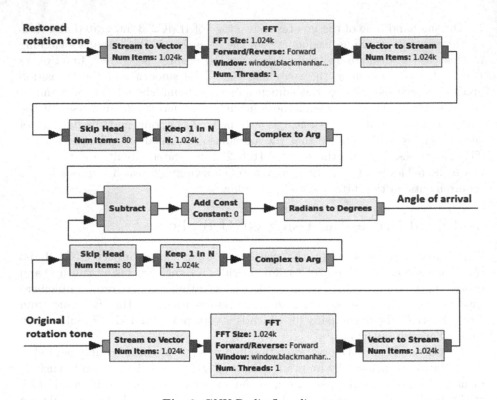

Fig. 6. GNU Radio flow diagram

The filtered signal cannot be compared directly because of the different power levels, interferences etc. The Fig. 6 depicts processing of both rotation tones and angle of arrival calculation. The output data stream must be converted from the time domain to the frequency domain. This is done by Fast Fourier Transformation (FFT). Part of the data, whose size is equal to the size of the FFT window, is captured by the *Stream to Vector* module and processed by the *FFT* module and converted back to a data stream by the *Vector to Stream* module. The data are in the frequency domain now and the data relevant to the rotation tone can be now separated. This is done by the *Skip Head* and *Keep 1 in N* modules. The Eq. (1) is used to determine the number of the data samples to be skipped.

$$N = \frac{f_s f_r}{N_{FFT}}, \tag{1}$$

where:

N Number of elements to skip
f_s Sample rate
f_r Rotation tone frequency
N_{FFT} Size of FFT

Since all digital samples of the signal are represented as complex numbers, the phase of the rotation tone is determined by their argument. The argument is obtained by the *Complex to Arg* module for each of the rotation tones. The phase offset, which is equal to the angle of arrival, is obtained after subtracting tones from each other.

Purpose of the *Add const* module is to calibrate angle of arrival with respect to the north. This calibration is needed after each start of the system. Automatic calibration with usage of the HackRF One is a subject of a future work.

4   Test in Real-Life Conditions

The final testing of the designed radio direction finding system was carried out in the open area with minimum of the obstacles. The AoA was measured from distance of 100 m in 10° increments. The result of this measurement is depicted in the Fig. 7. The Figure shows the expected AoA in degrees on x axis and the deviation between expected and measured AoA on y axis. As we can see, deviation angle of the system is less than 20°. The reasons for that low accuracy could be the ground slope of the area used for testing. The elevation level varied during the test and could be source of the low accuracy.

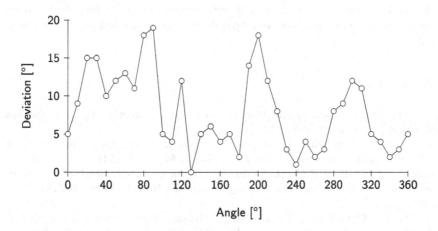

Fig. 7. AoA deviation

An interesting topic for future research will be the influence of the transmitter distance on Pseudo-Doppler antenna and the used antenna switching model. The use of specialized switching circuit instead of classic passive components brought both advantages and disadvantages. The influence of the new switching circuity on measurement precision has yet to be addressed.

We have tried to minimize the influence of the obstacles and the terrain profile on the measurements. The obstacles generally lead to reflections and the reflected signal negatively influences the measurement. Reflections generated step changes in measured values (angles), which complicates the use of Pseudo-Doppler antenna system inside in a closed environment or in a rugged area with many buildings. This was only the first test in real conditions and the development of the system continues.

5 Conclusion

The software defined radio brought new possibilities to many sectors and the implementation of the radio direction finding system is not an exception. The prototype of the Pseudo-Doppler direction finding system based on the software defined radio was presented in this article. The proposed Doppler antenna array was designed, constructed and tested. The original hardware based design of the Doppler system was reimplemented in the software. The paper has focused on the most complex parts of the proposed implementation.

The main advantage of the designed system is the possibility to analyse the entire bandwidth, which the software defined radio can provide at once. The number of the parallely analysed signals is limited only by the performance of the used computer. This is an enormous improvement against the traditional hardware implementation, where a separate receiver is needed for each individual signal.

References

1. RDF Products: Basics of the Watson-Watt Radio Direction Finding Technique. White Paper WN-004, Rev. B-01 (2007)
2. Whale, H.A.: A rotating interferometer for the measurement of the directions of arrival of short radio waves. Proc. Phys. Soc. B **67**, 553 (1954)
3. Earp, C.W., Godfrey, R.M.: Radio direction-finding by the cyclical differential measurement of phase. J. Inst. Electr. Eng. - Part IIIA Radiocommun. **94**(15), 705–721 (1947)
4. Peavey, D., Ogumfunmi, T.: The single channel interferometer using a pseudo-doppler direction finding system. In: 1997 IEEE International Conference on Acoustics, Speech, and Signal Processing, 1997, ICASSP-1997, vol. 5. IEEE (1997)
5. Analog Devices, Inc.: GaAs MMIC Sp. 8T Non-reflective switch, DC - 3.5 GHz. HMC253LC4 Datasheet v02.0414
6. Gadgets, G.S.: HackRF One (2015). http://greatscottgadgets.com/hackrf/. Accessed 3 Aug 2015
7. Radio, G.N.U.: The Free, Open Software Radio Ecosystem (2015). http://gnuradio.org/redmine/, Accessed 3 Aug 2015
8. Adcock, F.: Improvement in means for determining the direction of a distant source of electromagnetic radiation. British patent 130490 (1919)
9. Kossor, M.: A Doppler radio - direction finder part 2. QST 37–40 (1999)

A Quality Assessment Framework for Large Datasets of Container-Trips Information

Michail Makridis, Raúl Fidalgo-Merino$^{(\boxtimes)}$, José-Antonio Cotelo-Lema,
Aris Tsois, and Enrico Checchi

European Commission, Joint Research Centre (JRC), Ispra, Italy
{michail.makridis,raul.fidalgo-merino,antonio.cotelo,
aris.tsois}@jrc.ec.europa.eu, enrico.checchi@ec.europa.eu

Abstract. Customs worldwide are facing the challenge of supervising huge volumes of containerized trade arriving to their country with resources allowing them to inspect only a minimal fraction of it. Risk assessment procedures can support them on the selection of the containers to inspect. The Container-Trip information (CTI) is an important element for that evaluation, but is usually not available with the needed quality. Therefore, the quality of the computed CTI records from any data sources that may use (e.g. Container Status Messages), needs to be assessed. This paper presents a quality assessment framework that combines quantitative and qualitative domain specific metrics to evaluate the quality of large datasets of CTI records and to provide a more complete feedback on which aspects need to be revised to improve the quality of the output data. The experimental results show the robustness of the framework in highlighting the weak points on the datasets and in identifying efficiently cases of potentially wrong CTI records.

Keywords: Quality assessment · Knowledge validation · Qualitative indicators · Supply chain

1 Introduction

The vast majority of non-bulk cargo worldwide is transported in containers. The World Shipping Council, estimates that more than 18 million containers were active in 2011 [5], transporting in 2014 more than 171 million TEU (Twenty-foot Equivalent Unit) of goods [12]. Due to the high volumes of containerized trade, with big ports handling more than 80000 TEU a day [12], authorities can physically check only a small fraction of it, limiting their capacity to detect illegal activities and security threats. To mitigate the risks, authorities focus on obtaining high quality information on the transported cargo to conduct effective risk assessments.

The 2015 WCO Safe Framework of Standards [13], defines as high-risk the cargo for which either there is inadequate information or reason to deem it as low risk, or is indicated as such by tactical intelligence or a risk-scoring assessment

© The Author(s) 2016
K. Saeed and W. Homenda (Eds.): CISIM 2016, LNCS 9842, pp. 729–740, 2016.
DOI: 10.1007/978-3-319-45378-1_63

methodology based on security-related data elements. Customs administrations should ensure the interoperability of their IT systems by using the WCO Data Model. This data model identifies the key information elements for the Customs risk-scoring assessment methodologies and systems. Among them, WCO includes the container id, country of origin, place of loading, countries of routing, first port of arrival, place of discharge and date/time of arrival to the first port in Customs territory. The reason is that for goods shipped in containers, their route is equivalent to the container route since they are stuffed into the container (origin of the goods), until they are stripped out of the container (final destination of the goods). Unfortunately, poor quality information regarding the actual route followed by a container is quite common in Customs' declarations.

The logistics' industry and ocean carriers have been using for quite some time electronic records on the events and the whereabouts of the containers they handle. These records, called Container Status Messages (CSM) in WCO SAFE [13], are generated by different participants on the logistics chain (mainly container terminals) and are exchanged electronically to inform carriers, operators and final customers. Unfortunately, this information is often noisy, incomplete and non-standardized, requiring elaborated algorithms to remove the noise and improve the quality of the information. The works in [2–4, 18] focus on how CSM records can be processed in order to extract useful information on the routes of the goods and assist the Customs risk management processes. The key element proposed on them to describe the route of the goods is the Container-Trip Information (CTI) [4, 18]. In [4] an algorithm is presented for the computation of CTI records from CSMs based on Conditional Random Fields. Other algorithms, including decision trees, can also be applied to compute the CTI records.

The value of CTI records for Customs risk management is indisputable but it heavily depends on their quality. They are used to detect anomalies in the flow of millions of containers, so the quality of the CTI records extracted can impact severely the effectiveness of the risk analysis. Therefore, it is very important to be able to evaluate the quality of the models used to extract those CTI records. The final aim is to reduce the number of wrongly computed CTI records and their impact on the quality of the risk assessment, allowing a more efficient usage of the resources dedicated to container inspections by the authorities.

This paper proposes a CTI Quality Assessment Framework (CTI-QAF) that contributes to the improvement of the CTI record computation models and facilitates their evaluation. Based on quantitative and qualitative metrics, it provides both a way to evaluate the quality of the CTI computation model output and a way to identify the potentially wrong CTI records. Moreover, the output of the CTI-QAF facilitates the user to identify the CTI properties which are not correctly computed by the model.

The paper is organized as follows. Section 2 describes the related work. Section 3 formalizes the CTI representation to be used and describes the proposed CTI-QAF framework. Section 4 shows how this framework has been applied to assess the quality of four different case studies. Finally, Sect. 5 concludes the paper and highlights the main future lines.

2 Related Work

In this work we propose a quality assessment framework for automatically calculated CTI records (CTI-QAF). CTI-QAF provides useful information to improve the assessed CTI computation model and aims at facilitating risk assessment procedures by highlighting potentially wrong computed CTI records.

To be able to apply proposals like [6,19] to use CTI in Route-based Risk Indicators (RRIs), there is the need to develop algorithms to obtain this information from commonly existing data sources. In [2], CSMs were used to infer CTI records following a decision-tree like process. In [17] basic information on the container trip (origin, first port, last port and destination) is extracted from bill of lading documents [9]. In [4] a more sophisticated approach is proposed, extracting information on the different stages of a container trip from CSM data using Conditional Random Fields (see also [8] or [16]).

The assessment of the results in the above-mentioned techniques is based on traditional metrics of performance that focus on the generic accuracy of the proposed algorithm. They are not focused on the particularities of the domain and they cannot detect individual problematic cases. In other domains, like in the Part-of-the-speech tagging problem [11], one can find the usage of quality indicators. In this case, it is useful to know not only the precision of the algorithms when tagging words but also the *decision* (understood as the number of words non-ambiguously tagged [1]) or simply the sentence accuracy. Other examples of quality indicators can be also found in the Information Retrieval domain, as it is important to measure the document rank in web searches [7,10]. Such approaches are efficient in evaluating the overall quality of the information retrieval/extraction process, but they are not designed to evaluate the quality of the resulting data for outlier-detection environments.

In contrast, this paper proposes a new operational framework (CTI-QAF) that uses the CTI key element to formalize the goods route and proposes a set of quantitative (generic) and qualitative (domain specific) metrics to assess the overall quality of the model, the CTI properties and the individual CTI records.

3 CTI-Quality Assessment Framework

This section describes the proposed CTI-QAF, which is not only able to assess the quality of CTI datasets based on domain-specific metrics, but also capable to highlight potentially problematic CTI records. The outputs of the proposed CTI-QAF help the user to evaluate qualitatively the CTI computation model and to fine tune it by minimizing the number of wrongly computed CTI records.

3.1 CTI Formalization

A CTI record codifies the key route information regarding the transportation of goods in a container from an initial location where the goods were stuffed (inserted) into the container till the final destination where the goods were stripped (extracted) from the container. The CTI record splits the route in 5 phases:

- Stuffing phase, when and where got the goods stuffed in the container?
- First-load phase, when and where started its maritime transport?
- Transshipment phase, when and where was it transshipped (if any)?
- Final-discharge phase, when and where ended its maritime transport?
- Stripping phase, when and where got the goods stripped from it?

For each phase CTI encodes: (a) the main location(s) involved, (b) the time period covered by the phase and (c) the vessel(s) involved (if any).

Each CTI can be described using the following representation:

$$cti = (containerId, stuffing, loading, transship[], discharging, stripping)$$

identifying the container and collecting the relevant data of each phase:

- $containerID$ is the id that uniquely identifies a container box
- $stuffing$=(startDate, endDate, location)
- $loading$=(startDate, endDate, location, vessel)
- $transship[]$ is a (possibly empty) list of records in the form: $transship_i = (startDate, endDate, location, vesselIn, vesselOut)$, with $i \epsilon [1, n], n \geq 1$
- $discharging$=(startDate, endDate, location, vessel)
- $stripping$=(startDate, endDate, location)

We consider that a CTI record is wrongly calculated if a domain expert based on the same information would not conclude the exact same CTI record, even if the difference is in a single field of the CTI record.

Finding the potentially wrong CTI records out of a huge CTI set is not a trivial task when the computation model has a high precision. Random sampling and manual evaluation by domain experts (ground-truth) is not efficient as one would need to evaluate a very large number of CTI records before identifying enough wrong cases. The framework proposed addresses this problem by using qualitative metrics to identify the set of potentially wrong CTI records and using quantitative metrics to validate the quality of the selected dataset.

3.2   The CTI-QAF

The quality assessment upon a large result-set of any model is usually performed by defining one or more ground-truth subsets, which are then compared with the corresponding elements from the large results-set using quantitative metrics. The overall performance of the model can be then approximated by extrapolation. This type of quality assessment can be adequate in cases where an overview of the model's precision is enough for evaluation purposes. However, in cases such as the one discussed in this paper, we must be able to evaluate the expected impact that those wrongly computed CTI records will have on the risk assessment process.

The proposed CTI-QAF framework provides an overall quality assessment based on domain specific qualitative metrics, and additionally provides insight on which aspects need fine-tuning on CTI record computation models.

The workflow, depicted in Fig. 1, can be described as follows:

Input: A set of CTI records, *CTIset*, based on a specified computation model.

Stage A. Do a quantitative analysis on a small sample of *CTIset*.
  A.1 Select randomly a set of CTI records (we call that set *CTI-Xset*).
  A.2 Let experts create the ground-truth for *CTI-Xset* (*CTI-GT-Xset*).
  A.3 Perform quantitative analysis by computing *FDR* on the complete CTI records and *Precision*, *Recall* and *F1-Score* on CTI records' phases using *CTI-Xset* and *CTI-GT-Xset* (*QT-Xresults*).
  A.4 In case the *FDR* passes a predefined *FDRth* threshold, further improvement of the model is recommend.
Stage B. Perform the qualitative analysis on the entire CTIset.
  B.1 Apply the qualitative metrics *QLM* to the *CTIset* and extract a set of potentially wrong CTI records, *pwrongCTIset*.
  B.2 Order decreasingly the *pwrongCTIset* based on how many metrics signaled each CTI record, producing *RListpwrongCTIset*.
  B.3 For each metric, calculate the percentage (QLM_i) of the CTI records evaluated with it that have been detected as suspicious. If for any indicator the percentage is higher than a predefined *QLTh* threshold, the further improvement of the model is recommend.
Stage C. Do a quantitative analysis on a small sample of *RListpwrongCTIset*.
  C.1 Select the set of CTI records with highest risk according to the *RListpwrongCTIset* and call that set *CTI-RXset*.
  C.2 Let experts create the ground-truth for *CTI-RXset* (*CTI-GT-RXset*).
  C.3 Perform quantitative analysis by computing *FDR* on the complete CTI records and *Precision*, *Recall* and *F1-Score* on CTI records' phases using *CTI-RXset* and *CTI-GT-RXset* (*QT-RXresults*). The results can show: (1) if the qualitative metrics properly select the *RListpwrongCTIset* set and, (2) which are the weakness of the CTI computation model if any.

The next section describes the metrics used in the proposed CTI-QAF.

3.3   Quantitative and Qualitative Metrics

This section describes in detail the quantitative and qualitative metrics used in the framework in order to assess the input CTI dataset.

Quantitative Metrics. The metrics most commonly used to measure the performance of classification models are based on confusion tables by comparison of the classifiers' results with the ground-truth on a sample set [15]. In CTI-QAF we use *Precision*, *FDR*, *Recall* and *F1-Score*:

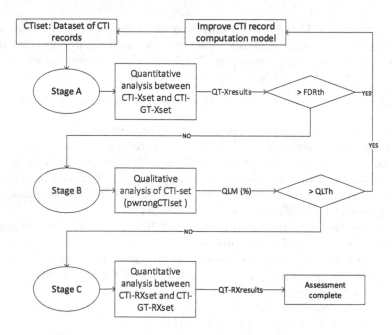

Fig. 1. Workflow of the CTI-QAF

- *Precision* is the success rate on those elements for which the model assigned a positive class and it is defined as: $Precision = \frac{TP}{TP+FP}$
- *False discovery rate* (FDR) is the opposite of precision: $FDR = 1 - Precision$
- *Recall* is the coverage of real positive elements achieved by the model and it is defined as: $Recall = \frac{TP}{TP+FN}$
- *F1-Score* provides combined information about the *precision* and *recall* of the results obtained from the model and it is defined as: $F1 = 2 \cdot \frac{Precision \cdot Recall}{Precision + Recall}$

where: *TP* is the number of True Positive (the classifiers resulted class coincides with the ground-truth), *FP* is the amount of False Positives (the classifier does not coincide with the ground-truth) and *FN* stands for False Negatives (classifier's results that are not included in the ground-truth result set).

Qualitative Metrics. We propose to use several domain-specific metrics aimed to assess the quality of the CTI record computation model.

We split the proposed metrics into heuristic metrics and semantic indicators. The first are based on a set of threshold functions that aim to detect CTI records outliers based on deviations from typical container trip characteristics. The second target semantically incomplete or potentially wrong CTI records, i.e., container trips or trip-phases having semantically incoherent properties.

The heuristic metrics defined below are based on the duration of the different parts of the trip and the number of transshipments.

– *Abnormally long trips*: Trips with duration equal or greater than 120 days.

$$TLong = (cti.stripping.endDate - cti.stuffing.startDate \geq 120)$$

– *Abnormally short trips*: Trips with duration equal or shorter than 5 days.

$$TShort = (cti.stripping.endDate - cti.stuffing.startDate \leq 5)$$

– *Trips with multiple transshipments*: Trips more than 3 transshipments.

$$TMulti = (|cti.transship| > 3)$$

– *Trips with prolonged initial phase*: Trips having cumulative duration of stuffing and first-load phases equal or greater than 20 days.

$$TSDLong = (cti.loading.endDate - cti.stuffing.startDate \geq 20)$$

– *Trips with prolonged final phase*: Trips having cumulative duration of final-discharge and stripping phase sequal or greater than 20 days.

$$TARLong = (cti.stripping.endDate - cti.discharging.startDate \geq 20)$$

The semantic indicators defined below assess the structure and quality of the CTI records through functions that highlight semantic inconsistencies.

– *Trips with same location for load and discharge*: Container trips having the same location as origin and destination.

$$TLocation = (cti.stuffing.location == cti.discharging.location)$$

– *Trips with at least one transshipment and having the same vessel at the loading and the discharging phases*: During the container trip several transshipments may take place, i.e. the containers are being discharged from the vessel and re-loaded to a different vessel.

$$TODVessel = ((cti.loading.vessel == cti.discharging.vessel) \wedge$$
$$(|cti.transship| \geq 1))$$

– *Trips joined with SAD declarations having different origin*: In the EU, the Single Administrative Document (SAD) [14] is used in the trade with third countries and for moving non-EU goods within the EU. The SAD declaration corresponding to the trip can be identified through the *containerID* and the acceptance date of the goods in the EU. Then, to calculate this indicator we are only interested in the field reporting the location of origin.

$$TSAD = (cti.stuffing.location \neq sad.location)$$

It is worth mentioning that the proposed framework is expandable and more metrics can be introduced according to the domain, the resources and the desired coverage that has to be achieved regarding the assessment of the model.

4 Experimental Results

This section presents four different studies derived by using two different CTI record computation models over two different data sources.

We have implemented two different CTI computation models: a rule-based logic deterministic model and a sequence-based probabilistic one. The rule-based model is defined by a complex set of deterministic rules manually induced by an expert (that we denoted as RULES). The second model is obtained by the application of the methodology described in [4] to construct a machine learning model based on Conditional Random Fields (that we denoted as CRF).

For the application of the proposed methodology two parameters of the CTI-QAF must be set up. For the cases presented in next subsections, we fix a maximum value of 20 % for the threshold of quantitative metrics (FDRTh), while for the qualitative indicators' threshold (QLTh) it is set up to 10 %.

4.1 CTI-QAF applied to RULES Models

In this section, CTI-QAF is applied to the CTI records obtained from two CSM data collections (Carriers 1 and 2) by the RULES models. These collections are part of the database of CSMs available within the ConTraffic project [6].

Case Study 1: Analysis of the performance of the RULES Model on Carrier 1. The input data to the CTI-QAF is the set *CTIset* computed by the RULES model. The number of containers processed for Carrier 1 by RULES was 692,233, corresponding to active containers during the period 2010–2015. The total amount of trips detected was 9,800,207.

The Stage A of the methodology measures quantitatively the performance of the *CTIset* using a random set of trips. With this aim, 72 CTI records (*CTI-Xset*) were randomly selected from *CTIset*. Then, an expert was asked to obtain the correct trips corresponding to those CTI records. A total of 70 ground-truth CTI records (*CTI-GT-Xset*) were extracted. Based on this, a False Discovery Rate (*FDR*) of 70.83 % was obtained for the *CTI-Xset* (i.e., 51 wrong trips). As the *FDR* exceed the threshold for quantitative metrics (*FDRth* = 20 %), the CTI-QAF recommends to reconsider the model before continue.

We compute then the *Precision*, the *Recall* and the *F1-Score* metrics for each CTI record's phase. Table 1 compiles the values of these quantitative metrics, showing problems in the proper identification of the discharging and stripping phases. Thus, the methodology provides hints in order to improve the model (e.g., creating new rules to better identify the final phases of the trips).

Case Study 2: Analysis of the performance of the RULES Model on Carrier 2. In this scenario, we give as input to CTI-QAF the set of CTI records generated by RULES (*CTIset*) from Carrier 2 data. 404,571 containers were processed (for the period 2010–2015) and a total of 4,631,965 trips were detected.

Table 1. Quantitative results for stage A of the RULES model for Carrier 1

RULES model	Precision (%)	Recall (%)	F1-Score (%)
Stuffing	100.00	88.24	93.75
First-load	98.49	91.55	94.89
Transshipment	94.12	94.12	94.12
Final-discharge	100.00	13.76	24.14
Stripping	61.11	28.21	28.60

In Stage A, the quantitative validation of *CTIset* was performed. With this aim, 90 records (*CTI-Xset*) were randomly selected from *CTIset* and an expert computed their ground-truth, obtaining 92 CTI records (*CTI-GT-Xset*).

The *FDR* for the RULES model was 14.29 % (12 wrong trips) and since it does not exceed the *FDRth* value we proceed to Stage B. The quantitative metrics computed for the different phases returned high values (all above 80 %).

In Stage B, the calculation of the qualitative indicators is carried out on the *CTIset*. Table 2 shows the results for each indicator. As they are all below the *QLTh* (10 % in our case), the assessment continues to the next Stage.

Table 2. Qualitative results on the trips obtained by the RULES model for Carrier 2

RULES model	Indicator value (%)
TLong	0.36
TShort	0.36
TMulti	0.05
TSDLong	0.73
TARLong	4.78
TLocation	0.21
TODVessel	0.09
TSAD	0.8

In Stage C, the ranked list of potentially wrong CTI records was obtained (*RListpwrongCTIset*), and its first 90 trips were selected for quantitative evaluation (*CTI-RXset*). According to the expert, 92 ground-truth CTI records were found (*CTI-GT-RXset*). The *FDR* obtained was 96.65 %, which means that the metrics for the selection of probably wrong trips have been effective.

Finally, the CTI-QAF can conclude that the model may have its most serious problems in the detection of the transshipment phase (based on the F1-Score obtained in the five phases, see Table 3).

4.2   CTI-QAF applied to CRF Models

The CTI-QAF was applied to the CTI records obtained by CRF models as well, something that demonstrates its versatility. These models were assessed using as input the same two different data sources than in previous case studies (see Sect. 4.1).

Table 3. Quantitative results for stage C of the RULES model for Carrier 2

RULES model	Precision (%)	Recall (%)	F1-Score (%)
Stuffing	50.59	94.44	65.89
First-load	65.41	65.41	65.41
Transshipment	22.22	3.95	6.70
Final-discharge	66.67	47.69	55.61
Stripping	50.00	42.86	46.15

Case Study 3: Analysis of the performance of the CRF Model on Carrier 1. In this case study, the CTIset was obtained after applying a CRF model to data from Carrier 1. 5,970,005 CTI records were computed by this model.

Stage A of the CTI-QAF measures quantitatively the performance of the *CTIset* using a random set of trips. Thus, 69 CTI records (*CTI-Xset*) were randomly selected from *CTIset* and an expert computed their ground-truth obtaining 70 CTI records (*CTI-GT-Xset*). The *FDR* was 13.18 % (i.e., 10 trips wrong), which is lower than the *FDRth* threshold (i.e., 20 %) and hence the assessment of the model can continue.

In Stage B, the qualitative indicators ranged from 0.03 % to 3.5 %, so they passed the QLth threshold which is set to 10 % for all metrics. The ranked list *RListpwrongCTIset* is then constructed, which can be analyzed by the user in order to further improve the CRF model.

Stage C allows the user to fine tuning the CTI construction model. To do this, the first 69 trips (*CTI-RXset*) from *RListpwrongCTIset* were selected and an expert calculated the ground-truth of this set, obtaining 70 CTI records (*CTI-GT-RXset*). Then, quantitative metrics for CTI records and phases are computed. The *FDR* was 95.92 %. The quantitative metrics obtained for each phase show that the stuffing phase is often wrongly computed (*F1-Score* = 34.88 %).

Case Study 4: Analysis of the performance of the CRF Model on Carrier 2. The data set (*CTIset*) contained 3,327,561 CTI records, which were computed by CRF on the data from Carrier 2 (described in previous sections).

In Stage A, we obtained the *CTI-Xset* extracting randomly 93 trips from the *CTIset*. These CTI records were given to an expert, obtaining a ground-truth set of 92 CTI records (*CTI-GT-Xset*). The *FDR* computed was 10.99 % (i.e., 12 wrong trips), which allows continuing with the Stage B.

Then, the calculation of the qualitative results was carried out, showing that in many cases the first two phases of the CTI records are not properly detected (*TSDLong* = 7.31 %). However, as all the indicators are below the qualitative threshold, the set *RListpwrongCTIset* is obtained.

In Stage C, the first 93 trips from *RListpwrongCTIset* were selected for expert annotation. The quantitative metrics show a *FDR* of 97.13 %. A deeper analysis revealed that the model had serious problems in the detection of the transshipment (F1-Score = 16.53 %) and stuffing phases (F1-score = 23.00 %).

5   Conclusions and Future Work

In this paper, a quality assessment framework for large datasets of Container-Trips Information (CTI) is proposed (CTI-QAF). The framework combines traditional quantitative metrics with domain specific qualitative indicators in order to achieve an overall assessment of the constructed CTI records dataset. The proposed CTI-QAF is able to assess the CTI records and also highlight the aspects of the CTI computation model with more improvement potential.

Incoherent CTI records can easily jeopardize the risk analysis on the goods route. The capacity of CTI-QAF to highlight potentially wrong records can be used to support the risk assessment procedure itself by providing information on the quality of each CTI record. Moreover, knowing the potentially wrong CTI records is useful for analyzing in deep the problems of the computation model.

Two different case studies were presented to demonstrate the application of the CTI-QAF. Two different CTI record computation models have been implemented; a sequence-based probabilistic model and a decision-tree based logic deterministic one. The experimental results involved data from more than 1.1 million containers for two operators (Carrier 1 and Carrier 2), which led to the assessment of more than 23 million trips constructed by the 2 models.

The experimental results shown the effectiveness of CTI-QAF to detect models with low performance at an early stage (see Case Study 1). It is also capable to identify problematic cases, helping to improve the model (see Case Study 4).

With regard to future research lines that would extend the result of this paper, a methodology should be defined to help the users to select the appropriate thresholds to be used in the framework. Moreover, the use of composite indicators could be useful to extend CTI-QAF in two directions. First, they could be used to provide a more effective measure of the quality of a CTI record, facilitating its integration on the risk assessment process. Second, a composite indicator could be developed to provide a quality measure that could be used to directly compare different computation models between them. Finally, it is worth mentioning that the proposed framework is expandable and more qualitative metrics can be introduced depending on the domain, the resources and the desired coverage that needs to be achieved regarding the model assessment.

References

1. Adda, G., Mariani, J., Lecomte, J., Paroubek, P., Rajman, M.: The grace french part-of-speech tagging evaluation task. In: Proceedings of the First International Conference on Language Resources and Evaluation (LREC), pp. 433–441 (1998)

2. Camossi, E., Dimitrova, T., Tsois, A.: Detecting anomalous maritime container itineraries for anti-fraud and supply chain security. In: Proceedings of the 2012 European Intelligence and Security Informatics Conference, EISIC 2012, pp. 76–83. IEEE Computer Society, Washington (2012)
3. Camossi, E., Villa, P., Mazzola, L.: Semantic-based anomalous pattern discovery in moving object trajectories. CoRR, abs/1305.1946 (2013)
4. Chahuara, P., Mazzola, L., Makridis, M., Schifanella, C., Tsois, A., Pedone, M.: Inferring itineraries of containerized cargo through the application of conditional random fields. In: Proceedings of the 2014 IEEE Joint Intelligence and Security Informatics Conference, pp. 137–144. IEEE Computer Society, Washington (2014)
5. World Shipping Council: Container supply review. World Shipping Council (2011)
6. Donati, A.V., Kotsakis, E., Tsois, A., Rios, F., Zanzi, M., Varfis, A., Barbas, T., Perdigao, J.: Overview of the contraffic system. Technical report, JRC. Joint Research Centre (2007)
7. Järvelin, K., Kekäläinen, J.: Cumulated gain-based evaluation of IR techniques. ACM Trans. Inf. Syst. **20**(4), 422–446 (2002)
8. Lafferty, J.D., McCallum, A., Pereira, F.C.N.: Conditional random fields: probabilistic models for segmenting and labeling sequence data. In: Proceedings of the Eighteenth International Conference on Machine Learning, ICML 2001, pp. 282–289. Morgan Kaufmann Publishers Inc., San Francisco (2001)
9. Levi, M.D.: International Finance, 4th edn. Routledge, New York (2005)
10. Liu, T.: Learning to Rank for Information Retrieval. Springer Science & Business Media, Heidelberg (2011)
11. Manning, C.D.: Part-of-speech tagging from 97% to 100%: is it time for some linguistics? In: Gelbukh, A.F. (ed.) CICLing 2011, Part I. LNCS, vol. 6608, pp. 171–189. Springer, Heidelberg (2011)
12. United Nations Conference on Trade and Development: Review of the Maritime Transport 2015. United Nations Publications (2015)
13. World Customs Organization: SAFE Framework of standards to secure and facilitate global trade. World Customs Organization (2015)
14. European Parliament and Council of the European Union: Comission Regulation (EC) 2286/2003 amending Regulation (EEC) No 2454/93 laying down provisions for the implementation of Council Regulation (EEC) No 2913/92 establishing the Community Customs Code5, vol. L343. Publications Office of the European Union, Luxembourg (2003)
15. Sokolova, M., Lapalme, G.: A systematic analysis of performance measures for classification tasks. Inf. Process. Manage. **45**(4), 427–437 (2009)
16. Sutton, C., McCallum, A.: An introduction to conditional random fields. Found. Trends Mach. Learn. **4**(4), 267–373 (2012)
17. Triepels, R., Feelders, A., Daniels, H.A.M.: Uncovering document fraud in maritime freight transport based on probabilistic classification. In: Saeed, K., Homenda, W. (eds.) CISIM 2015. LNCS, vol. 9339, pp. 282–293. Springer, Heidelberg (2015)
18. Tsois, A., Cotelo Lema, J.A., Makridis, M., Checchi, E.: Using container status messages to improve targeting of high-risk cargo containers. In: Research Track at the 5th World Customs Organization Technology and Innovation Forum, Rotterdam, Netherlands (2015)
19. Villa, P., Camossi, E.: A description logic approach to discover suspicious itineraries from maritime container trajectories. In: Claramunt, C., Levashkin, S., Bertolotto, M. (eds.) GeoS 2011. LNCS, vol. 6631, pp. 182–199. Springer, Heidelberg (2011)

Synthesis of High-Speed Finite State Machines in FPGAs by State Splitting

Valery Salauyou[⊠]

Faculty of Computer Science, Bialystok University of Technology,
Bialystok, Poland
valsol@mail.ru

Abstract. A synthesis method of high-speed finite state machines (FSMs) in field programmable gate arrays (FPGAs) based on LUT (Look Up Table) by internal state splitting is offered. The method can be easily included in designing the flow of digital systems in FPGA. Estimations of the number of LUT levels are presented for an implementation of FSM transition functions in the case of sequential and parallel decomposition. Split algorithms of FSM internal states for the synthesis of high-speed FSMs are described. The experimental results showed a high efficiency of the offered method. FSM performance increases by 1.52 times on occasion. In conclusion, the experimental results were considered, and prospective directions for designing high-speed FSMs are specified.

Keywords: Synthesis · Finite state machine · High-speed · High performance · State splitting · Field programmable gate array · Look up table

1 Introduction

Large-size functional blocks and nodes of a digital system and also the digital system itself, as a rule, include a control device or a controller. The speed of a digital system and functional blocks depends directly on the speed of their control devices. The mathematical model for the majority of control devices and controllers is a finite state machine (FSM). Because of this, the synthesis methods of high-speed FSMs are necessary for designing high-performance digital systems. Note that an implementation cost can be ignored in the synthesis of high-speed FSMs, because an FSM area takes a small part compared with other system components (for example, memory or transceivers).

Now, programmable logic devices (PLDs) are widely used for designing digital systems. Two types of PLD architectures are widely used: on the basis of two programmed matrixes (AND and OR), and on the basis of functional generators, an LUT (Look Up Table). The first PLD type is called Complex Programmable Logic Devices (CPLDs), and the second PLD type is called Field Programmable Gate Arrays (FPGAs). It is possible to represent an FPGA structure as a great quantity of LUTs united by interconnections. Every LUT allows realizing any Boolean function from a small number of arguments (as a rule, from 4 to 6). The methods of FSM synthesis on CPLD have been considered in [1].

K. Saeed and W. Homenda (Eds.): CISIM 2016, LNCS 9842, pp. 741–751, 2016.
DOI: 10.1007/978-3-319-45378-1_64

Many authors considered the synthesis problem of high-speed FSMs on PLD. Their methods were characterized by a large variety of approaches to deciding on a given task. In [2], a technique for improving the performance of a synchronous circuit configured as an FPGA-based look-up table without changing the initial circuit configuration is presented. Only the register location is altered. This improves clock speed and data throughput at the expense of latency. In [3], the methods and tools for state encoding and combinational synthesis of sequential circuits based on new criteria of information flow optimization are considered. In [4], the timing optimization technique for a complex FSM that consists of not only random logic but also data operators is proposed. The technique, based on the concept of a catalyst, adds a functionally redundant block (which includes a piece of combinational logic and several other registers) to the circuits under consideration so that the timing critical paths are divided into stages. In [5, 6], the styles of FSMs description in VHDL language and known methods of state assignment for the implementation of FSMs are researched. In [7], evolutionary methods are applied to the synthesis of FSMs. At the first stage, the task of state assignment by means of genetic algorithms is resolved. Then evolutionary algorithms are applied to the minimization of chip area and time delay of FSM output signals. In [8], the task of state assignment and optimization of the combinational circuit at implementation of high-speed FSMs in CPLD is considered. In [9], a novel architecture that is specifically optimized for implementing reconfigurable FSMs, Transition-based Reconfigurable FSM (TR-FSM), is presented. The architecture shows a considerable reduction in area, delay, and power consumption compared to FPGA architectures. In [10], a new model of the automatic machine named the virtual finite state machine (Finite Virtual State Machine - FVSM) is offered. For implementation of the FVSM, architecture based on storage and a technique of FVSM generation from traditional FSMs is offered. FVSM implemented on new architecture have an advantage on high-speed performance compared with traditional implementation of FSMs on storage RAM. In [11], an implementation of FSMs in FPGA with the use of integral units of storage ROM is considered. Two pieces of FSMs architecture with multiplexers on inputs of ROM blocks which allow reducing the area and increasing high-speed FSM performance are offered. In [12], the reduction task of arguments of transition functions by state splitting is considered; this allows reducing an area and time delay in the implementation of FSMs on FPGA.

This paper also uses splitting of FSM states, but the purpose of splitting is an increase of FSMs performance in LUT-based FPGA. Splitting of FSM states belongs to operations of equivalent conversions of an FSM and does not change the algorithm of its functioning. During splitting of FSM states, the machine type (Mealy or Moore) is saved, the general structure of the FSM does not change, and embedded memory blocks of FPGAs are not used. In the course of state splitting, the hierarchy of state names is saved, which simplifies the analysis and debugging of the project. Because of this, the offered synthesis method of high-speed FSMs in FPGA is aimed at practical usage and can be easily included in the general flow of digital system design.

This paper is organized as follows. Section 2 describes estimations of the number of LUT levels in the implementation of FSM transition functions in the case of sequential and parallel decomposition. Section 3 considers the synthesis method of high-speed FSMs, which includes two algorithms: a general algorithm and an algorithm for the decomposition of the concrete state. A detailed example shows the method. The experimental results are reported in Sect. 4. The paper concludes with a summary in Sect. 5.

2   Estimations for the Number of LUT Levels for Transition Functions

Let $A = \{a_1, ..., a_M\}$ be the set of internal states, $X = \{x_1, ..., x_L\}$ be the set of input variables, $Y = \{y_1, ..., y_N\}$ the set of output variables, and $D = \{d_1, ..., d_R\}$ the set of transition functions of an FSM.

A one-hot state assignment is traditionally used for the synthesis of high-speed FSMs in FPGAs. Thus, each internal state a_i ($a_i \in A$) corresponds to a separate flip-flop of FSM's memory. A setting of this flip-flop in 1 signifies that the FSM is in the given state. The data input of each flip-flop is controlled by the transition function d_i, $d_i \in D$, i.e. any internal state a_i ($a_i \in A$) of the FSM corresponds with its own transition function d_i, $i = \overline{1, M}$.

Let $X(a_m, a_i)$ be the set of FSM input variables, whose values initiate the transition from state a_m to state a_i ($a_m, a_i \in A$). To implement some transition from state a_m to state a_i, it is necessary to check the value of the flip-flop output for the active state a_m (one bit) and the input variable values of the $X(a_m, a_i)$ set, which initiates the given transition. To implement the transition function d_i, it is necessary to check the values of the flip-flop outputs for all states, such that transitions from which lead to state a_i, i.e. $|B(a_i)|$ values, where $B(a_i)$ is the set of states from which transitions terminate in state a_i, where $|A|$ is the cardinality of set A. Besides, it is necessary to check the values of all input variables, which initiate transitions to state a_i, i.e. $|X(a_i)|$ values, where $X(a_i)$ is the set of input variables, whose values initiate transitions to state a_i, $X(a_i) = \bigcup_{a_m \in B(a_i)} X(a_m, a_i)$.

Let r_i be a rank of the transition function d_i, where

$$r_i = |B(a_i)| + |X(a_i)|. \tag{1}$$

Let n be the number of inputs of LUTs. If the rank r_i for transition function $d_i (i = \overline{1, M})$ exceeds n, there is a necessity to decompose the transition function d_i and its implementation on several LUTs.

Note that by splitting internal states it is impossible to lower the rank of the transition functions below the value

$$r^* = \max(|X(a_m, a_s)|) + 1, m, s = \overline{1, M}. \tag{2}$$

In this method, the value r^* is used as an upper boundary of the ranks of the transition functions in splitting the FSM states.

It is well-known that there are two basic approaches to the decomposition of Boolean functions: sequential and parallel. In the case of sequential decomposition, all the LUTs are sequentially connected in a chain (Fig. 1).

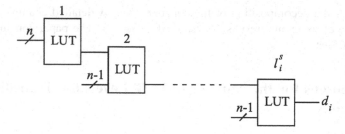

Fig. 1. Sequential decomposition of Boolean function

The n arguments of function d_i arrive on inputs of the first LUT, and the $(n-1)$ arguments arrive on inputs of all remaining LUTs. So the number l_i^s of the LUT's levels (in the case a sequential decomposition of the transition function d_i having the rank r_i) is defined by the expression:

$$l_i^s = \text{int}\left(\frac{r_i - n}{n - 1}\right) + 1, \tag{3}$$

where int(A) is the least integer number more or equal to A.

In the case of parallel decomposition, the LUTs incorporate in the form of a hierarchical tree structure (Fig. 2).

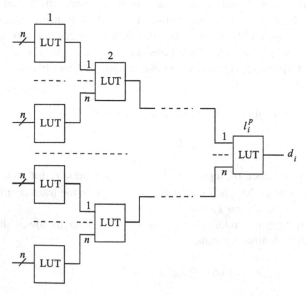

Fig. 2. Parallel decomposition of Boolean function

The values of the function arguments arrive on LUTs inputs of the first level, and the values of the intermediate functions arrive on LUTs inputs of all next levels. So the number of LUT's levels (in the case parallel decomposition the transition function d_i having the rank r_i) is defined by the following expression:

$$l_i^p = \text{int}(\log_n r_i). \tag{4}$$

It is difficult to predict what type of decomposition (sequential or parallel) is used by a concrete synthesizer. The preliminary research showed that, for example, the Quartus II design tool from Altera simultaneously uses both sequential and parallel decomposition. The number l_i levels of LUTs in the implementation on FPGA transition function d_i with the rank r_i can be between values l_i^s and l_i^p, $i = \overline{1, M}$.

Let k be an integer coefficient ($k \in [0,10]$) that allows adapting the offered algorithm in defining the number of LUT's levels for the specific synthesizer. In this case the number l_i of LUT's levels for the implementation of the transition function d_i having the rank r_i will be defined by following expression:

$$l_i = \text{int}\left(\frac{10 - k}{10} l_i^p + \frac{k}{10} l_i^s\right). \tag{5}$$

The specific value of coefficient k depends on the architecture of the FPGA and the used synthesizer.

The following problem is the answer to the question: when is it necessary to stop splitting the FSM states? The matter is that in splitting state $a_i(i = \overline{1, M})$, except for the increase of the number M of the FSM states, the number of transitions in the states of set $A(a_i)$ is also increased, where $A(a_i)$ is the set of states in which the transitions from state a_i terminate. When splitting state a_i, the cardinalities of sets $B(a_m)$ ($a_m \in A(a_i)$) are increased for the states of set $A(a_i)$. Therefore, according to (1) for the states of set $A(a_i)$ the ranks of the transition functions grow, which can lead to an increase of the values and l_i^s, l_i^p, and l_i.

In this algorithm, the process of state splitting is finished, when the following condition is met:

$$l_{max} \leq \text{int}(l_{mid}), \tag{6}$$

where l_{max} is the number of LUT levels, which is necessary for the implementation of the most "bad" function having the maximum rank; l_{mid} is the arithmetic mean value of the number of LUT levels for all transition functions. Note that in the process of splitting the FSM internal states, the value l_{mid} will increase and the value l_{max} will decrease, therefore the algorithm execution always comes to an end.

3 Method for High-Speed FSM Synthesis

According to the above discussion, the algorithm of state splitting for high-speed FSM synthesis is described as follows.

Algorithm 1.
1. The coefficient k ($k \in [0,10]$) is determined, which reflects the method used by the synthesis tool for the decomposition of Boolean functions.
2. According to (1) ranks r_i ($i=\overline{1,M}$) for all FSM transition functions are defined.
3. On the basis of (3), (4), and (5), for each transition function d_i the number l_i of LUT levels is defined.
4. The values l_{max} and l_{mid} are determined. If condition (6) is met, then go to step 7, otherwise go to step 5.
5. The state a_i, for which r_i = max, is selected. If there are several such states, from them the state for which $|A(a_i)|$ = min is selected.
6. The state a_i (which was selected in step 5) is split by means of algorithm 2 on the minimum number H of states $a_{i\_1},...,a_{i\_H}$ so that for each state a_{i_h} ($h=\overline{1,H}$) was fulfilled $r_{i\_h} \bullet r^*$, where r^* is defined according to (2); go to step 2.
7. End.

Further synthesis of the FSM is performed using traditional techniques, for example, automatically by means of using a design tool synthesizer. For this purpose, it is enough to describe the FSM received after splitting internal states in one of the design languages (Verilog or VHDL). The value of coefficient k (step 1 of Algorithm 1) is defined empirically by means of synthesis of the test examples in the used design tool.

For splitting some a_i state, $i = \overline{1,M}$, which is executed in step 6 of Algorithm 1, Boolean matrix W is constructed as follows. Let $C(a_i)$ be the set of transitions to state a_i. Rows of matrix W correspond to the elements of set $C(a_i)$. Columns of matrix W are divided on two parts according to types of arguments of transition function d_i. The first part of matrix W columns correspond to set $B(a_i)$ of FSM states, the transitions from which terminate in state a_i, and the second part of matrix W columns correspond to set $X(a_i)$ of input variables, whose values initiate the transitions in state a_i. A one is put at the intersection of row t ($t = \overline{1,T}$, $T = |C(a_i)|$) and column j of the first part of matrix W if the transition c_t ($c_t \in C(a_i)$) is executed from state a_j ($a_j \in B(a_i)$). A one is put at the intersection of row t and column j of the second part of matrix W if input variable x_j ($x_j \in X(a_i)$) accepts a significant value (0 or 1) on transition c_t ($c_t \in C(a_i)$). Now the task is reduced to a partition of matrix W on a minimum number H of row minors $W_1,...,W_H$ so that the number of columns, which contain ones in each minor W_h ($h = \overline{1,H}$), do not exceed value r^* defined according to (2). The rows of each minor W_h will define transitions in state a_{i_h} ($h = \overline{1,H}$).

Let w_t be some row of matrix W. For finding the row partition of matrix W on a minimum number H of row minors $W_1,...,W_H$, the following algorithm can be used.

Algorithm 2.
1. Put $h := 0$.
2. Put $h := h + 1$. A formation of minor W_h begins. The row w_j, which has the maximum number of ones, is selected in minor W_h as a reference row. The row w_i is included in minor W_H and the row w_i is eliminated from further reviewing, put $W_h := \{w_i\}$, $W := W\backslash\{w_i\}$.
3. The rows are added in minor W_h. For this purpose, among rows of matrix W, the row w_i is selected, for which the next inequality is satisfied $|W_h \cup \{w_t\}| \le r^*$, where $|W_h \cup \{w_t\}|$ is the total number of ones in the columns of minor W_h and the row w_t after their joining on OR. If such rows can be selected from several among them, row w_i is selected, which has the maximum number of common ones with minor W_h, i.e. $|W_h \cap \{w_t\}| = \max$. The row w_i is included in minor W_h and row w_i is eliminated from further reviewing, put $W_h := W_h \cup \{w_i\}$, $W := W\backslash\{w_i\}$.
   Step 3 repeats until at least a single row can be included in minor W_h.
4. If in matrix W all the rows are distributed between the minors, then go to step 5, otherwise go to step 2.
5. End.

We show the operation of the offered synthesis method in the example. It is necessary to synthesize the high-speed FSM whose state diagram is shown in Fig. 3.

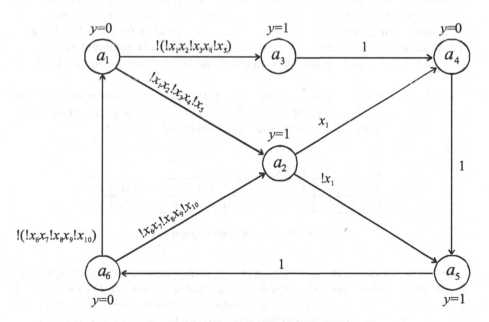

Fig. 3. State diagram of the initial FSM

This FSM represents the machine Moore, which has 6 states $a_1, \ldots, a_6$, 10 input variables $x_1, \ldots, x_{10}$, and one output variable y. The transitions from states a_3, a_4, and a_5 are unconditional, therefore the logical value 1 is written on these transitions as a transition condition. The values of sets $B(a_i)$ and $X(a_i)$, and also ranks r_i of the transition functions for the initial FSM are presented in Table 1, where $\emptyset$ is an empty set. Since for this example we have $\max(|X(a_m,a_s)|) = 5$, then (according to (2)) the value $r^* = 6$. It is necessary to construct the FSM on FPGA with 6-input LUT, i.e. we have $n = 6$.

Table 1. Values of $B(a_i)$, $X(a_i)$, r_i, l_i^s, and l_i^p for the initial FSM

State	$B(a_i)$	$X(a_i)$	r_i	l_i^s	l_i^p
a_1	$\{a_6\}$	$\{x_6,x_7,x_8,x_9,x_{10}\}$	6	1	1
a_2	$\{a_1,a_6\}$	$\{x_1,x_2,x_3,x_4,x_5,x_6,x_7,x_8,x_9,x_{10}\}$	12	3	2
a_3	$\{a_1\}$	$\{x_1,x_2,x_3,x_4,x_5\}$	6	1	1
a_4	$\{a_2,a_3\}$	$\{x_1\}$	3	1	1
a_5	$\{a_2,a_4\}$	$\{x_1\}$	3	1	1
a_6	$\{a_5\}$	$\emptyset$	1	1	1

According to (3) and (4), the values l_i^s and l_i^p are defined for each state (they are presented in the appropriate columns of Table 1). We do not know how the compiler performs a decomposition of Boolean functions, therefore we assume the sequential decomposition (a worst variant) and the value of coefficient k in expression (5) is equal to 10, i.e. we have $k = 10$. As a result, the number of LUT levels (which are necessary for the implementation of each transition function) is defined by the value $l_i = l_i^s$. Thus, for our example we have $\text{int}(l_{mid}) = \text{int}(8/6) = 2$. In other words, splitting FSM internal states stops as soon as each transition function can be implemented in two levels of LUTs.

For this example, we have $l_{max} = l_2^s = 3$, i.e. the condition (9) does not meet for state a_2, since $l_{max} = l_2^s = 3 > \text{int}(l_{mid}) = 2$. For this reason, state a_2 is split by means of Algorithm 2. Matrix W is constructed for splitting state a_2 (Fig. 4).

	a_1	a_6	x_1	x_2	x_3	x_4	x_5	x_6	x_7	x_8	x_9	x_{10}
w_1	1	0	1	1	1	1	1	0	0	0	0	0
w_2	0	1	0	0	0	0	0	1	1	1	1	1

Fig. 4. Matrix W for splitting state a_2

Matrix W has two rows. Row w_1 corresponds to the transition from state a_1 to state a_2, and row w_2 corresponds to the transition from state a_6 to state a_2. The execution of Algorithm 2 leads to a partition of rows of matrix W into two subsets: $W_1 = \{w_1\}$ and $W_2 = \{w_2\}$. So, state a_2 is split into two states a_{2_1} and a_{2_2}, as shown in Fig. 5.

The new values of $B(a_i)$, $X(a_i)$, r_i, l_i^s, and l_i^p are presented in Table 2. Now we have $l_{max} = l_{mid} = 1$ and (according to (6)) running of Algorithm 1 is completed.

Thus, for the given FSM by splitting state a_2 we reduced the number of LUT levels from 3 to 1, in the case of sequential decomposition, and from 2 to 1, in the case of parallel decomposition.

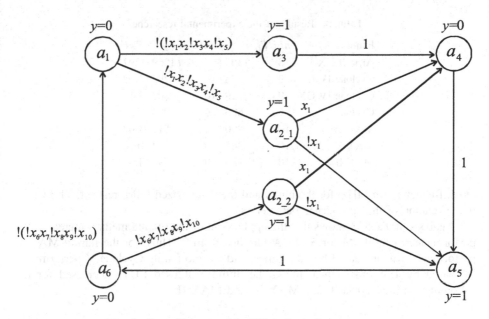

Fig. 5. State diagram of the FSM after splitting state a_2

Table 2. Values of $B(a_i)$, $X(a_i)$, r_i, l_i^s, and l_i^p after splitting state a_2

State	$B(a_i)$	$X(a_i)$	r_i	l_i^s	l_i^p
a_1	$\{a_6\}$	$\{x_6,x_7,x_8,x_9,x_{10}\}$	6	1	1
a_{2_1}	$\{a_1\}$	$\{x_1,x_2,x_3,x_4,x_5\}$	6	1	1
a_{2_2}	$\{a_6\}$	$\{x_6,x_7,x_8,x_9,x_{10}\}$	6	1	1
a_3	$\{a_1\}$	$\{x_1,x_2,x_3,x_4,x_5\}$	6	1	1
a_4	$\{a_{2\_1},a_3\}$	$\{x_1\}$	3	1	1
a_5	$\{a_{2\_2},a_4\}$	$\{x_1\}$	3	1	1
a_6	$\{a_5\}$	$\varnothing^1$	1	1	1

4 Experimental Results

The efficiency of the offered synthesis method was checked in the implementation of the initial FSM (Fig. 1) and the FSM after splitting state a_2 (Fig. 2) on FPGAs from Altera by means of the design tool Quartus II version 15.0. The main optimization criterion had been selected as the parameter «speed». The «one-hot» method of state assignment was selected for the initial FSM, and the «user» method of state assignment was selected for the FSM after synthesis (the state codes are defined from the FSM description).

Table 3 presents the results of the experimental research of the offered method for various FPGA families, where $nLUT_1$ and $nLUT_2$ are the number of LUTs used in the implementation of the initial and the synthesized FSM, respectively; F1 and F2 are the

Table 3. Results of the experimental researches

Family	$nLUT_1$	F_1	$nLUT_2$	F_2	F_2/F_1
Arria II GX	8	1307	7	1269	0.97
Cyclone IV E	9	778	10	793	1.02
Cyclone IV GX	9	729	10	802	1.10
Cyclone V	6	686	6	925	1.35
MAX 10	10	800	11	816	1.02
MAX V	10	343	9	314	0.92
MAX II	10	389	9	593	1.52

clock frequency (in MHz) for the initial and the synthesized FSM, respectively; F1/F2 is the relation of the appropriate parameters.

Analysis of Table 3 shows that the application of the offered method increased the performance of the FSM for 5 FPGA families from 7. Thus, for the family MAX II performance was increased by 1.52 times, and for the family Cyclone V performance increased by 1.35 times. In addition, the number of used LUTs decreased for the following families: Arria II GX, MAX V, and MAX II.

5 Conclusions

The presented results of the experimental research showed the following. Despite the fact that in the considered example the rank of transition function was reduced from 12 to 6, which allowed to reduce the number of LUT levels from 3 to 1 in the case of sequential decomposition, and from 2 to 1 in the case of parallel decomposition; however, the performance of the FSM did not increase for all FPGA families. This is a sign of the complexity of the synthesis task of high-speed FSMs. FSM performance depends not only on the results of logical synthesis, but also on the results of placing and routing. The reduction of the number of used LUTs for some FPGA families (as a result of the application of the offered method) can be accounted simply: with the reduction of the number of LUT levels, the LUT amount also decreases.

The present study was supported by a grant S/WI/1/2013 from Bialystok University of Technology and founded from the resources for research by Ministry of Science and Higher Education.

References

1. Salauyou, V.V., Klimowicz, A.S.: Logic Design of Digital Systems on Programmable Logic Devices. Hot Line – Telecom, Moscow (2008). (in Russian)
2. Miyazaki, N., Nakada, H., Tsutsui, A., Yamada, K., Ohta, N.: Performance improvement technique for synchronous circuits realized as LUT-based FPGA's. IEEE Trans. Very Large Scale Integr. (VLSI) Syst. **3**, 455–459 (1995)
3. Jozwiak, L., Slusarczyk, A., Chojnacki, A.: Fast and compact sequential circuits through the information-driven circuit synthesis. In: Euromicro Symposium on Digital Systems Design, pp. 46–53. IEEE Press, Warsaw (2001)

4. Huang, S.-Y.: On speeding up extended finite state machines using catalyst circuitry. In: Asia and South Pacific Design Automation Conference (ASAP-DAC), Yokohama, pp. 583–588, January 2001

5. Kuusilinna, K., Lahtinen, V., Hamalainen, T., Saarinen, J.: Finite state machine encoding for VHDL synthesis. IEEE Proc. Comput. Digit. Tech. 1, 23–30 (2001)

6. Rafla, N.I., Davis, B.: A study of finite state machine coding styles for implementation in FPGAs. In: 49th IEEE International Midwest Symposium on Circuits and Systems, San Juan, USA, pp. 337–341 (2006)

7. Nedjah, N., Mourelle, L.: Evolutionary synthesis of synchronous finite state machines. In: International Conference on Computer Engineering and Systems, Cairo, Egypt, pp. 19–24 (2006)

8. Czerwiński, R., Kania, D.: Synthesis method of high speed finite state machines. Bull. Pol. Acad. Sci. Tech. Sci. 4, 635–644 (2010)

9. Glaser, J., Damm, M., Haase, J., Grimm, C.: TR-FSM: Transition-based reconfigurable finite state machine. ACM Trans. Reconfig. Technol. Syst. (TRETS) 3, 23:1–23:14 (2011)

10. Senhadji-Navarro, R., Garcia-Vargas, I.: Finite virtual state machines. IEICE Trans. Inf. Syst. 10, 2544–2547 (2012)

11. Garcia-Vargas, I., Senhadji-Navarro, R.: Finite state machines with input multiplexing: a performance study. IEEE Trans. Comput. Aided Des. Integr. Circ. Syst. 5, 867–871 (2015)

12. Solov'ev, V.V.: Splitting the internal states in order to reduce the number of arguments in functions of finite automata. J. Comput. Syst. Sci. Int. 5, 777–783 (2005)

Correction to: Complex Adaptive Systems and Interactive Granular Computing

Andrzej Skowron

Correction to:
Chapter "Complex Adaptive Systems and Interactive
Granular Computing" in: K. Saeed and W. Homenda (Eds.):
Computer Information Systems and Industrial Management,
LNCS 9842, https://doi.org/10.1007/978-3-319-45378-1_2

The acknowledgement section of this paper originally referred to grant DEC-2013/09/B/ST6/01568. The reference to this grant has been removed from the acknowledgement section at the request of one of the authors.

The updated version of this chapter can be found at
https://doi.org/10.1007/978-3-319-45378-1_2

Author Index